BRANDEIS

Also by Lewis J. Paper:

John F. Kennedy: The Promise and the Performance

LEWIS J. PAPER

BRANDEIS

Prentice-Hall, Inc. • Englewood Cliffs, New Jersey 07632

Library of Congress Cataloging in Publication Data

Paper, Lewis J.
Brandeis.

1. Brandeis, Louis Dembitz, 1856–1941. 2. Judges—United States—Biography. I. Title.

KF8745.B67P36 1983 347.73'2634 [B] 83-3020
ISBN 0-13-081299-4 347.3073534 [B]

Printed in the United States of America.

10 9 8 7 6 5 4 3 2 1

This book is available at a special discount when ordered in bulk quantities. Contact Prentice-Hall, Inc., General Publishing Division, Special Sales, Englewood Cliffs, N.J. 07632.

Book design by Linda Huber
Jacket design by Hal Siegel
Manufacturing buyer: Pat Mahoney

Prentice-Hall International, Inc., *London*
Prentice-Hall of Australia Pty. Limited, *Sydney*
Prentice-Hall Canada Inc., *Toronto*
Prentice-Hall of India Private Limited, *New Delhi*
Prentice-Hall of Japan, Inc., *Tokyo*
Prentice-Hall of Southeast Asia Pte. Ltd., *Singapore*
Whitehall Books Limited, *Wellington, New Zealand*
Editora Prentice-Hall do Brasil Ltda., *Rio de Janeiro*

ISBN 0-13-081299-4

To my parents

CONTENTS

BRANDEIS

1

BEGINNINGS AND ENDINGS

The large black Pierce-Arrow wound its way down to the White House from California Street in the northwest section of Washington, D.C. The old man was dressed in a dark suit and sat stiffly in the back seat while the chauffeur maneuvered through traffic. The old man hated cars. They had a terrible impact on people. Transformed their personalities. The most placid person could become mean and aggressive behind the wheel of an automobile. Another sign of man's losing control of his environment. The old man could afford a fleet of Cadillacs, but he had vowed never to buy a car and had even resisted renting one for as long as he could. Washington was already becoming a motorized city when he came to live there in 1916, but he continued to use his horse and buggy until he was almost literally forced off the streets in the mid-1920s. No, the old man didn't like cars at all. In fact, he thought the world would be better off if Detroit were "blown off the face of the earth."

The car pulled up in front of the white mansion on Pennsylvania Avenue. The old man got out and stepped into the warm, almost balmy air. It was an unusual autumn day. But on this Saturday morning in November 1938, the old man had something more important than the weather on his mind.

He went into the mansion and was taken upstairs to the president's living quarters on the second floor. The president was getting ready to leave for Warm Springs, Georgia, for Thanksgiving and was receiving appointments in his personal residence instead of the Oval Office. At 11:20, the visitor was ushered into the room where the president was waiting.

Even though he was now eighty-two, the old man was still an imposing figure. He was beginning to stoop a little from age, but he carried his slim six-foot frame erect. His impressive shock of unkempt hair was white with a bluish tint; and his high cheek bones and other angular features made him look something like Abraham Lincoln (and for those who missed it, his wife was quick to point out the resemblance). Then there were the deep-set eyes with their bluish-gray coloring; they were so penetrating they seemed to look right through you. The old man had thousands of devoted admirers throughout the country. Some said he was the closest thing to a modern-day prophet. And Louis D. Brandeis, now a United States Supreme Court justice, looked the part.

Brandeis's relationship with Franklin D. Roosevelt went back more than twenty years. Roosevelt was an assistant secretary of the Navy and a devoted follower of President Wilson's when Brandeis was nominated to fill a seat on the Court in January 1916. Brandeis's confirmation fight in the United States Senate had been a bitter one, probably the most grueling in the country's history. Roosevelt kept in almost daily touch with the proceedings. It was primarily a matter of loyalty to Wilson. Brandeis was a nationally renowned social activist, "the people's attorney." His fate at the hands of the Senate would be a reflection of Progressive sentiment in the country, a crucial factor in Wilson's bid for reelection later that year.

Much had happened to Roosevelt since those early days. He still conveyed the same aristocratic, high-spirited air of confidence. He would still throw his head back and laugh at a joke. But he could no longer walk on his own. Polio had taken care of him there. And he was now president of the United States. He had taken the oath of office at the height of the Depression. One-quarter of the nation's workforce was unemployed. Production was only a pitiful fraction of what it had been only a few years before. Pessimism and despair abounded, and some people talked openly of a need for a new system of government.

Roosevelt did not have any well-defined program to meet the country's economic and social ills when he entered the White House. He was, first and foremost, a politician. He would listen to almost anyone and, if the politics were right, try almost anything that offered some promise. Brandeis had a lot of ideas on that score, and he had not been shy about getting his views to the president, either directly or indirectly through one of the many "disciples" who roamed Washington's halls of power. Brandeis's success with Roosevelt had been mixed; but through it all the president retained a high regard—almost reverence—for the old justice he affectionately called "Isaiah." Their relationship took a temporary turn for the worse in 1937 when Roosevelt proposed a law that would have "packed" the Supreme Court with justices sympathetic to his programs and policies. Brandeis played a key role in killing the plan, and Roosevelt was momentarily shocked and hurt by the old justice's behavior. You simply did not turn on your friends like that. And more than that, Roosevelt was convinced (at least for a time) that the Court-packing plan was a necessary step to fighting the Depression.

But on that balmy Saturday in November 1938, Brandeis did not come to talk about the Depression. He came to talk about the Jews.

The plight of Germany's 500,000 Jews had deteriorated rapidly after Adolph Hitler became chancellor in 1933. Matters reached a breaking point in early November 1938 when a seventeen-year old Polish Jew living in Germany killed Ernest Von Rath, a secretary in the German Embassy in Paris. Immediately after receiving the news, Germans all over the country erupted in "spontaneous" demonstrations against Germany's Jews. Temples were dynamited, Jewish shops were looted, and people were dragged into the street and beaten up by mobs. In the town of Düsseldorf—home of the young killer—mobs pulled a rabbi from his temple, stomped him to death, and then brought the mangled body to the rabbi's widow just to torment her.

Meanwhile, the German government waited twelve hours before Paul Joseph Goebbels, minister of propaganda, issued a statement requesting an end to the "demonstrations." Goebbels acknowledged that the German people were filled with "justifiable and understandable indignation" over Von Rath's murder. Goebbels promised, however, that the "final answer to Jewry will be given in the form of laws or decrees." Goebbels was not one to make false promises. At least not when it came to Jews. Within a week it was reported that between 40,000 and 60,000 Jews had been arrested. New decrees were announced prohibiting Jews from engaging in a retail business, directing an industrial or commercial enterprise, attending colleges or universities, or even attending public forums for entertainment. To add insult to injury, the government then placed a $400 million fine on Germany's affluent Jews to "pay" for all the damage inflicted by the mobs.

The series of events removed any hope Germany's Jews may have had of peaceful coexistence with Hitler. But for most it was too late. Hundreds of sobbing and desperate Jews filled the American consulate in Berlin, telling tales of husbands beaten or carried away, of homes that had been ransacked, and all asking for help to emigrate to America. It was, one observer reported, a "pathetic" sight. Hundreds of other Jews took matters into their own hands and tried to cross the border into France—only to be turned back by French guards who were on orders to admit only those with the necessary visas. After a few days, Great Britain's prime minister, Neville Chamberlain, issued a mild statement condemning the situation; but there was no outrage expressed to convey genuine concern. In the United States, Roosevelt made the unusual gesture of calling reporters into the Oval Office and, while seated behind a desk cluttered with souvenirs, he read a statement protesting Germany's actions. In responding to a reporter's inquiry, however, Roosevelt said he did not expect an increase in the annual quota of 27,370 German immigrants into the United States.

It was in this setting that Roosevelt called Brandeis. The old justice was the foremost Zionist leader in the United States, and, although age now limited his activities, his concern was beyond question. Adrian Fisher, Brandeis's law clerk, answered the telephone and heard a familiar voice identify himself as "the president." Fisher at first thought it was a practical joke, but much to his later relief, he did not challenge the caller's authenticity. Fisher told the president that Brandeis did not talk on the telephone anymore. "Well, Mr. Fisher," the president said, "can you have the justice set up an appointment with me to talk about Zionism?" The message was duly delivered, Brandeis nodded knowingly, and the appointment was arranged.

Brandeis had discussed the Jewish problem with Roosevelt a month earlier. Brandeis thought that the British should allow more Jews into Palestine. It was not only their obligation under the Balfour Declaration; it was the only way Jews could be saved from Hitler.

When Brandeis entered the White House on that Saturday in November, Roosevelt explained that he was about to go South and wanted to report to Brandeis about developments since their last talk in October. Shortly after that talk, Roosevelt said, he had called in Sir Ronald Lindsay, the British ambassador to the United States. Roosevelt wanted Britain to allow more Jews into Palestine. There was simply no merit to the Arab opposition, he told Lindsay. Palestine represented only 5 percent of the rab land area. The Arabs had more than enough land to meet their people's needs. Indeed, Roosevelt advised Lindsay, the Arab opposition probably reflected only the indecision and inconsistency of British policy. The ambassador countered that perhaps British Guiana could be opened to the Jews. Roosevelt did not think much of that idea, although Tanganyika and the Cameroons—two African colonies—might offer something. There the matter had been left.

After relating this conversation, the president told Brandeis that the events of the past week had disturbed him greatly. Perhaps they could use private and public sources to raise $300 million to move Germany's Jews, but for the time being he felt that he had done all he could do politically. He was going to Georgia for the next ten days, but if there was anything Isaiah felt he could do, the president said, he was prepared to return to Washington on short notice.

Brandeis was impressed with Roosevelt's efforts. He asked only one thing of the president before he left Washington. In the wake of the German uprising against Jews in the last week, more pressure had to be placed on the British to open Palestine. Reports of an increase in Jewish immigration quotas were already floating around Washington. Would the president issue a statement acknowledging the reports of increased immigration and express his hope that they were true? Roosevelt was agreeable to that. Their twenty-minute meeting over, Brandeis left the president for the ride back to his apartment on California Street.

Although Brandeis was pleased with the statement later issued by the president, he was not satisfied with the impact. For a variety of reasons, the British remained intransigent and did all they could to close the doors to Jewish immigration to Palestine. For Brandeis it proved to be too much. It would be better to rely on diplomacy. But if normal channels did not work, he was prepared to support other means. He had already provided thousands of dollars to David Ben-Gurion to buy arms for the Haganah, the Jewish defense force in Palestine. He continued to give Ben-Gurion money to use at his discretion, and he rejoiced in May 1939 when he learned that the Haganah had arranged to smuggle Jews into Palestine. Necessity sometimes had to be the mother of invention.[1]

There was a certain irony in Brandeis's interest in Jews and Zionism. He was not at all religious. In fact, he was puzzled by people who relied on God and religious institutions. So he did not join the Zionist Movement to push Judaism. He saw Zionism as a social experiment. Palestine offered the opportunity for people to mold their economic and political environment to meet their needs and still stay in control. The element of control was especially important. Man was weak and quite fallible, in Brandeis's view. Most people, however, did not understand that. They were always taking on far more than they could handle. Man, Brandeis thought, would find more fulfillment if he learned to live within his limits. That was what made Palestine so appealing to him. It promised a future that would be almost impossible to obtain in the United States. Everything was becoming too big in America—business, unions, even government. It was getting more and more difficult to be in charge of your own destiny. In Palestine, small and undeveloped, there was a better chance for a person to nurture his or her talents and interests. And, most important, a person could have more independence.

Brandeis's intense concern with Zionism was, in these respects, similar to the concerns that motivated him in other areas both before and after his appointment to the Court. It did not matter whether he was fighting the railroads, developing a new insurance system, attacking a president of the United States, or deciding cases as a justice of the United States Supreme Court. In every instance he was working for his vision of what society should be—a place where people could control their environments and maximize the chances of fulfilling their potential. It was, to be sure, a large task. But Brandeis was not one to be frightened by broad challenges. His intellectual skills were formidable. His ability to draw people to work with him was equally impressive. And perhaps of greatest importance, he had an extraordinary faith in his own ability to achieve. With tireless effort, patience, and a little luck, he believed, almost anything was possible.

All this makes the story of Brandeis's life a fascinating one. He was a complex figure of unusual talents who lived and worked at a time when America was experiencing many changes. He grew up in Kentucky during the Civil War, developed a large corporate law practice in Boston during the industrial revolution, embarked on a career of public activism during the height of the Progressive Movement, spearheaded the emergence of Zionism both in America and abroad, sat on the United States Supreme Court when it was almost the center of Washington society, and advised a president on how to cope with the Depression. When he died on the eve of Pearl Harbor, America looked a lot different from the country Brandeis had come to know as a boy in Louisville.

To understand Brandeis's development, then, is to understand something about the forces that shaped America's growth. For while we can debate the wisdom of his ideas and the value of his accomplishments, there can be no denying that Louis Brandeis had a profound influence on our nation's history. To fully appreciate all this, however, one must, as in all stories, begin at the beginning.

ONE

The Early Years

Life is what happens to you
While you're busy making other plans.

JOHN LENNON, "BEAUTIFUL BOY"

Like many American cities today, Louisville, Kentucky, shows some signs of deterioration from declining business. It used to be so different. One hundred and twenty-five years ago, Louisville was a principal commercial and shipping center of the United States. The Ohio River was, and is, a main tributary to the mighty Mississippi. Not surprisingly, it became a major link between the East and the South as well as what was then considered the West. At one point in the Ohio, however, the rock-strewn impediments interrupted the smooth flow of the water. People called it the Falls of Ohio, although in fact it is really little more than white water rapids.

It was here in 1778 that George Rogers Clark established an outpost from which to attack the British and the Indians. In 1780, Thomas Jefferson, the governor of Virginia (of which Kentucky was then part), signed the charter for Louisville—a town named for King Louis XVI of France, who had allied his country with the American revolutionaries against England. Within a short time, Louisville was bustling with business and new people. It had become a natural stopping point for those who had somewhere else to go. Barges and other boats coming down the Ohio had to unload their cargoes and passengers at Louisville in order to reduce the dangers when crossing the rapids.

Because it was both a link to the South and so near wheat and tobacco fields, Louisville also became a center for slave trade. "Jim Crow," in fact, was conceived here—a reference to a white man who played the part of Sambo in a Louisville theater in 1830 and did a rendition of a Negro song and dance that was attributed to "Jim Crow."[1] In a trip to Louisville in 1841, Abraham Lincoln, then a country lawyer, vividly described an event that was commonplace in Louisville and elsewhere in the South: "A gentleman had purchased twelve Negroes in different parts of Kentucky and was taking them to a farm in the South. They were chained six and six together . . . strung together precisely like so many fish upon a trout line. In this condition they were being separated forever from the scenes of their childhood . . . and going into perpetual slavery where the lash of the master is proverbially more ruthless and unrelenting then any other . . . and yet . . . they were the most cheerful . . . creatures on board."[2]

Not everyone in Louisville was in favor of slavery. Because of its easy access from the East and its proximity to rich farm land, the town had attracted thousands of foreign immigrants, especially Germans and Irish. Many of these immigrants had fled from religious persecution and governmental oppression in their homelands and, not surprisingly, took a dim view of a practice in which a human being could be treated like a piece of property. For these people there was no more courageous hero than Henry Clay, the Kentucky congressman and statesman who was willing to oppose local interests like slavery in order to preserve the Union. Someone who opposed slavery, then— and especially one who was a German immigrant—could find some like-minded souls in Louisville.

It was quite logical, therefore, for Adolph Brandeis to bring his growing family to Louisville in 1851. Brandeis had first come to America in 1848. He was then twenty-six, a slim young man with large, deep-set eyes and long black hair. His mission was to be a scout of sorts for the Brandeis, Wehle, and Dembitz families. They were all in Prague, then a part of Bohemia (and later Germany), and things were not going well for them there. As Jews they were subject to a growing array of government restrictions on their activities—permits that had to be acquired and prohibitions that had to be observed. Although those restrictions had not prevented the families from prospering—indeed, they were fairly well off—the future looked bleak. There had been an abortive revolution in 1848 (which Adolph had missed because he contracted typhoid fever at the time), and it seemed clear that the reactionary new government would now be more oppressive and certainly less tolerant of Jews than the previous regime. It was time to get out.

America seemed like the place to go, and farming seemed to be the right vocation. After all, stories of America's rich land were legion. Unfortunately, Adolph was the only one in the three families who knew the slightest thing about farming. He had graduated with honors from the Technical School of Prague, where he had taken some courses in agriculture. That was a good enough background for the other men, who were doctors and businessmen, so Adolph was the logical choice to find a farm for them in America.

For Adolph, there were some personal costs in going to America alone. He would have to leave behind his twenty-year-old fiancée, Frederika Dembitz. Though she had had only six months of formal school, Frederika was a well-educated and worldly young woman. She could speak several languages, was familiar with the significant writers of the day, had traveled widely, and was an accomplished pianist. No doubt it was these attributes—as well as her warm personality—that primarily attracted the attentions of Adolph. It was certainly not her appearance. She had a round face, was a little on the heavy side, and was a poor dresser—facts of which she was painfully aware. Adolph himself would candidly admit to outsiders that his betrothed was not the best in looks—but that she had other qualities which made her special.[3]

Before she met Adolph, Frederika had had an unsettling life. Her two-year-old brother fell off a merry-go-round and died when she was eleven, and the next year her mother died suddenly of a stroke. It was a severe blow to the young girl. "Was there ever a child of twelve who felt more deserted?" Frederika later recalled. "I hoped that I might die in a year as my mother had died one year after her own mother."[4] Her father, a doctor, was not very adept at filling young

Frederika's emotional void. In fact, he made it worse. He too was distraught by his wife's death. He became irritable and impractical, yelling at Frederika and her other brothers and traveling anywhere and everywhere at almost a moment's notice. Adolph offered Frederika the love and stability that had eluded her for so long.

Adolph sailed for America in the fall of 1848 and arrived in New York. To his great fortune he made contact with a gentleman identified only as his "friend D," a man commissioned by the French banking house of Rothschild to investigate the American condition. With D's credentials, Adolph gained access to people and places that might otherwise have been barred to him. Together the two adventurers traveled far and wide over the settled parts of America east of the Mississippi. Adolph had little trouble meeting people. He was an open and friendly person who found it easy to talk with just about anyone. He also had a spirit that was infectious.

All of these qualities were captured in the letters he sent to Frederika from America. "I already love our new country so much that I rejoice when I can sing its praises," he wrote in January 1849. ". . . When you look at people and see how they work and struggle to make a fortune, you might think you were living among merely greedy speculators. But this is not true. It is not the actual possession of things but the achievement of getting them that they care for. I have often thought that even the hard work of these people is a kind of patriotism. They wear themselves out to make their country bloom, as though each one of them were commissioned to show the despots of the old world what a free people can do."[5]

Adolph was equally impressed with the contrasts he found in America. On the one hand there were the rolling countrysides filled with trees and fresh streams; on the other hand were the dirt and grime of the crowded cities—especially in Pittsburgh, where the soot from the coal mines covered everything and made it so dark that you had to keep the gas lights on even in the middle of the day.

The people were similarly a study in contrasts. Adolph found them to be courteous and friendly. But he was also overwhelmed by their boorish behavior, especially while eating. "Imagine a very long room set for 200 persons," he wrote Frederika. "The corridors are full of people impatiently waiting for the dinner bell to ring. Finally the welcome sound is heard. Like raging lions they all rush in to get the best places. In a second they are all seated and are greedily pouring down the hot soup, which stands before them. All the rest of the food has already been placed on the table in shining metal dishes. . . . About thirty very tall Negroes dressed in white linen are standing about the table. At the sound of a small bell, they raise their right hands as to a solemn oath; at a second signal they put their hands on the covers; at a third, they swing the covers high over their heads and all march around the table and carry off the covers. Then everyone falls to and before you can recover from the extraordinary spectacle, the steaming roasts, the dainty pies, and the delicious fruit are gobbled up, and in a few minutes you find yourself deserted and only the unsavory remnants remain."[6] It was all quite an experience.

On the farming front, Adolph had some bad news for the group. It was simply not a good idea. True enough, the farmer could work the land and supply almost all of his own needs. But there was a price to pay for that. First of all, it was extremely hard manual labor—something unfamiliar to the Prague group. And more than that, it was boring, "and this tedium," Adolph wrote, "can become the most deadly poison in family life." A man could "sink to being a mere common beast of burden."[7] No, farming would not be a major plus for people used to more sedentary occupations.

Adolph had an alternative, however. It was something called a grocery. Instead of growing people's food, you would buy it from the farmer and sell it to those who did not have their own farms. Back in Prague, the group was skeptical of this course. Farming had seemed like such a good idea. How could Adolph give it up?

With their skepticism in tow, the group set sail from Hamburg on April 8, 1849. It was no small party. There were twenty people, twenty-seven large chests, two grand pianos, silk dresses, featherbeds, and an assortment of paraphernalia. Adolph met them in New York and took them all to Cincinnati, on the Ohio River, where he had rented a four-story house. There they could sort out everything and decide what they wanted to do.

In time, Adolph took most of them to Madison, Indiana, which was just down the river. Cincinnati already seemed overcrowded. Also, it was experiencing a cholera epidemic. Things seemed more promising and healthier in Madison. Moreover, there was a growing German community there that would ease the transition from the old world to the new. Within weeks, Adolph and other members of the group established a starch factory as well as a grocery and produce store under the name G. & M. Wehle, Brandeis & Company. The starch factory folded within a short time, but the grocery and produce store prospered.

Socially, the group found much to enjoy. Although many of them, especially the women, were still having trouble speaking English, there were no problems at night, when they all gathered around the piano and sang German songs. Drinking liquor added to the merriment, and, all in all, life seemed much improved over the last dark days in Prague.

On September 5, 1849, Adolph and Frederika were married. Within a year they had their first child, a girl whom they named Fanny, after Frederika's mother. But they did not remain content in Madison for long. The town did not grow, and Adolph, with his good business judgment, sensed that it was time to move on. In 1851 they went to Louisville, taking a little house on Center Street.

It was in Louisville that Louis David Brandeis was born on November 13, 1856. By that time his parents had already gone through many changes. To begin with, there were now four children in the family—his sister Amy had arrived in 1852, followed by brother Alfred in 1854. Adolph's new business had also prospered. After dabbling in the wheat-shipping business, Adolph had founded a partnership with Charles W. Crawford, and the firm of Brandeis and Crawford was off to a running start. Within a few years the firm was operating a flour mill, a tobacco factory, an 1100-acre farm, and a steam freighter called the *Fanny Brandeis*.

All was not peaceful for the Brandeis family, however. Before young Louis was five years old the nation was thrown into the Civil War. Kentucky was in a particularly precarious position. In some respects it was tied to the South; and in other respects it seemed to be a natural part of the North.

Kentucky was a slave state with more than 200,000 black people in bondage. Moreover, the state's economy—and especially business in Louisville—relied heavily on trade with the South. At the same time, Louisville was in the process of industrializing, and its need for slaves was not nearly as great as that of some other states. It was on this basis that the large contingent of abolitionists and other Union supporters argued that the future of the state lay with the North. There were also military factors to consider. The leaders in Kentucky were concerned that an alliance with the South would result almost immediately in an invasion of Union armies—an invasion that the new Confederate government would probably be powerless to stop. Primarily for these last reasons, the governor and legislators resisted pressures to join the Confederacy; but they also made it clear to the North that they would not fight against their brethren in the South.[8]

Lincoln watched developments in Kentucky closely. Because it was a border state that hugged the Ohio River, Kentucky's secession would be damaging to the Union. Indeed, at one point Lincoln is said to have remarked that "he hoped to have God on his side, but he must have Kentucky."[9] Fortunately for Lincoln, pressures were building up for Kentucky to abandon its policy of neutrality and cast its lot with the Union. By September 1861 the Union forces prevailed and the decision was reached to side with the North. Within weeks thousands of Union troops were camped in Louisville, and the city became a natural stopping point for Union armies preparing forays into the South.

Much of the Louisville population was cheered by the presence of Union soldiers. Not surprisingly, many gave whatever material comfort they could to the camping soldiers. Years later, Louis Brandeis would recall that his earliest memories were of his mother's bringing food and coffee to "the men from the North." Louis also remembered his father's moving the family across the river to Indiana when the armies of the Confederate General Braxton Bragg threatened to overrun Louisville in September 1862.[10]

The war had its compensations, though. Adolph suddenly found his fortunes enhanced considerably by lucrative government shipping contracts. The family moved from a house they had on First Street to a large limestone-front house in the exclusive Broadway section of town. Adolph also hired black servants and a black coachman. And then there were the trips. In 1864, while the battles raged on, Adolph took the family for a vacation to Niagara Falls and Newport, Rhode Island. The following summer Frederika and Adolph took the two boys to Canada, Niagara Falls, and Newport again. These trips were times of great activity—sailing, riding, eating with friends, and touring the sights.

In doing these and other things, the family remained extremely close. On the last vacation north, for example, Frederika, Adolph, or one of the brothers would write almost every day to tell the girls back home what was happening and to remind them of how much they were loved. And if a day or more went by without a letter from the girls, concern was expressed as to whether anything was wrong.[11] The lesson was not lost upon young Louis. Years later he would write almost every day to his daughters and his wife when he was away on business trips. The practice continued when his daughters grew up and left home. Their aging father, then a Supreme Court justice, continued to write to them almost every day. And if a day or more went by without word from his "girls," the void would be duly noted in his next letter.

The incessant letter writing was not an empty obligation. It was a way of staying in touch with loved ones, of retaining the warmth and security that Louis always treasured in family life. Even as a teenager he was extremely affectionate with his parents. When his mother was visiting friends in St. Louis with Alfred on her wedding anniversary, for instance, Louis felt impelled to write a note from Louisville:

> My dear darling Ma:
>
> As I can't write to you tomorrow morning, I use my time tonight to write a few lines and congratulate my dear Ma on her wedding day, the first one I have not been with you. I hope you are having a splendid time. I know Alfred is. We are all a little sick (home sick but not sick of home) today but otherwise are very well. . . . Hoping you will soon be back to your
>
> Loving son,
> Louis[12]

Meanwhile, Louis was growing up. He had a slim appearance that always made him seem younger than his years. He had his father's deep-set blue eyes and straight black hair. And perhaps of greatest importance, he seemed to have inherited his father's keen intellect. He excelled in his studies, a distinction clouded only by the poor reputation of Louisville's schools at the time. At the German and English Academy, Louis continually received the highest grades and ultimately a special commendation from the principal for conduct and industry. And in 1872, when he was sixteen, he received a gold medal from the Louisville University of the Public Schools for "pre-eminence in all his studies."

At home Louis was enjoying the protection and friendship of his family. Everyone looked out for everyone else. And family functions occupied a central place in his social life, especially dinners, where frequent guests and good conversation were often in evidence. Louis was also developing the special relationship he would maintain throughout life with his brother, Alfred. Louis had a great wit, but he always seemed a little more quiet and serious than other children—qualities his mother attributed to the experiences Louis had had during the Civil War. Alfred too was quiet. But in each other's company the two boys opened up and shared their innermost feelings, playing and talking on and on. Even separation could not dampen their enthusiasm for each other. Years later, when Alfred was in Louisville and Louis in Boston and Washington, the two brothers would exchange letters almost every day. Their affection for each other was obvious and a real source of pleasure for their parents. "My heart rejoices when I see you two happy together," Frederika wrote to Louis shortly after he became a Boston lawyer. "It seems to me that there never were two brothers who complemented one another so perfectly and were so completely one as you two."[13]

Long before Louis left Louisville, however, his father's fortunes began to slip. In the early 1870s many of the clients of Brandeis and Crawford were southerners who could not pay their bills. It was the first sign of an economic depression that would hit the country, and especially the South, in 1873. Adolph sensed that things were going to get a lot worse before they got better. He therefore decided to dissolve his business and take his family to Europe for fifteen months. Louis's sister Fanny became ill in Europe and, primarily for that reason, it was three years before the family returned to America.

They left Louisville in May 1872 and set sail from New York on the S.S. *Adriatic* on August 10, 1872, for the eight-day trip to Liverpool. After a few weeks traveling around Europe, Louis tried to enter the Gymnasium in Vienna to continue his education. Unfortunately, he could not pass the entrance exams. The Louisville School's gold medal simply did not carry much weight here. Undismayed, Louis decided to spend the academic year as a free agent traveling and attending selected university courses. The summer was spent hiking with his brother and father in Switzerland. For Louis, it was sometimes too much. Despite the many attentions of his parents, Louis was weak, almost frail, and very susceptible to illness. He did not have the physical strength of other boys, and it became evident when he traveled with Al and his father that summer in Switzerland. At one point the boys were resting under some trees when Alfred suggested that they find the source of the River Adder. Louis could take it no longer: "I don't see why I should have to find the source of every damned river in Europe!"[14] But all in all it was a time of great pleasure. In correspondence with Alfred years later Louis would continually refer to their European travel and the things they did on specific days.

In the autumn of 1873, Alfred, then nineteen, decided to return to Louisville to work. Louis decided to take another stab at formal education. He went to the Annen-Realschule in Dresden and inquired of the rector about the possibility of becoming enrolled. The rector responded stiffly that no one could be admitted without certificates providing proof of birth and the necessary vaccinations. Louis was not intimidated, retorting, "The fact that I'm here is proof of my birth, and you may look at my arm for evidence that I was vaccinated."[15] That was good enough for the startled rector, and Louis was admitted.

Louis did well in his studies and received a special award from the faculty in 1875. But for Louis the reward was far more than good grades. Years later he told his law clerk Paul Freund that it was at Dresden that he learned to think. "He said," Freund remembered, "that in preparing an essay on a subject about which he had known nothing, it dawned on him that ideas could be evolved by reflecting on your material. This was a new discovery for him."[16] After that discovery, "thinking" became a serious exercise for Louis. Even as a famous lawyer and Supreme Court justice, he often read and digested an abundance of material before reaching conclusions. "Thought for him was the product of brooding, not the windfall of inspiration," Felix Frankfurter, an intimate friend, later recalled. "He believed in taking pains, and the corollary of taking pains was taking time."[17]

But Dresden was not an entirely agreeable experience for Louis. He especially disliked the control that his elders tried to exercise over his activities. "I was a terrible little individualist in those days," he told an interviewer many years later, "and the German paternalism got on my nerves." One instance in particular stood out in his mind. "One night . . .," he recalled, "coming home late and finding I had forgotten my key, I whistled up to awaken my roommate; and for this I was reprimanded by the police. This made me homesick. In Kentucky you could whistle. . . . I wanted to go back to America, and I wanted to study law."[18]

The choice of law was no accident. His mother's brother, Lewis Dembitz, was a well-known lawyer in Louisville. He was also a writer, a Zionist (in later years), and a political leader who went as a delegate to the Republican convention in 1860 to nominate Abraham Lincoln for president. In many ways Uncle Lewis was the ideal to which Louis aspired. He was, Louis remembered later, "a living university. With him life was unending intellectual ferment. He grappled eagerly with the most difficult problems in mathematics and the sciences, in economics, government and politics. In the diversity of his intellectual interests, in his longing to discover truths, in his pleasure in argumentation and in the process of thinking, he reminded [me] of the Athenians. He loved books as a vehicle of knowledge and an inciter to thought; and he made his love contagious."[19] Louis's admiration for his uncle was so great that he eventually changed his middle name from David to Dembitz.

In any event, by this time Louis and the rest of the family were ready to leave Europe. They reached New York in May 1875 and, after a summer relaxing in Louisville, Louis set off for law school.

John Harvard was one of those people who happened to be in the right place at the right time. In 1636, the General Court of Massachusetts Bay decided to develop a college in Cambridge. Two years later, Harvard decided to give the school his library of 300 books and half of his fortune of 1500 pounds. The new Massachusetts school was duly appreciative and decided to rename the school after Harvard. In fact, they even went so far as to erect a statue on the school grounds identifying him as the founder. Historical accuracy could not stand in the way of a proper acknowledgment to an important donor.[20]

The school did not open a law department until 1817, and for its first fifty years or so the Harvard Law School plugged ahead—but just barely. There were rarely more than one or two professors in attendance—and they were rarely full time. The student body also was small. Until 1830 there were often no more than four or five students in attendance. At that point, the student population began to pick up, and by 1870 there were about 200. But even then the school operated on a shoestring budget. An 1861 visiting-committee report commented, for instance, on the practice of having the janitor act as the law school's chief executive officer in the absence of the librarian. This was symbolic of the disarray that generally reigned at the school. As early as 1847, for example, the Board of Governors required all law degree candidates to take exams; for more than twenty years, however, the law faculty stubbornly refused to comply.[21]

Fundamental changes were introduced beginning in 1870. In 1869, Charles Eliot, a thirty-five-year-old chemistry professor at MIT, was appointed to Harvard's presidency. The following year he brought in Christopher Columbus Langdell as the new law school dean. Langdell had been a practicing lawyer in New York City, and he had a new approach to teaching law that became known as the case method. In the old days, the teachers had simply rambled on about the law, advising the students about key principles and offering anecdotes to illustrate points. Langdell thought that that style left something to be desired. It did not teach students to think as lawyers. Langdell liked the socratic approach instead. He asked his students to read a particular case and then, with his probing questions as a lead, had them dissect and analyze the elements of the decision. In this way, students could appreciate, theoretically at least, the intellectual blocks on which the decision was built.

Langdell's case method was nothing short of revolutionary at the time. Many traditionalists were aghast at the heresy. Boston University's law school was created just to offer an alternative to the "crazy" ideas governing law curriculum on the other side of the Charles River. But Langdell also had his followers. And few proved to be as devoted as Louis D. Brandeis.

When he entered Harvard Law School in the fall of 1875, Brandeis was nineteen and had no college training. None of that proved to be a problem. He passed some entrance exams and soon became a leading member of the student body. His fellow students took note of the slender, bright-eyed youth who spoke often in class with precision and confidence. Rumors circulated that there might even be "some Jew blood in him." But no matter. He was clearly an intellectual force to be reckoned with. "The professors listen to his opinions with the greatest deference," one fellow student explained to his mother. "And it is generally correct. There are traditions of his omniscience floating through the school. One I heard yesterday. A man last year lost his notebook of Agency lectures. He hunted long and found nothing. His friends said: 'Go and ask Brandeis—he knows everything—perhaps he will know where your book is.' He went and asked. Said Brandeis, 'Yes, go into the auditors' room and look on the west side of the room, on the sill of the second window, and you will find your book.' And it was so." Another student remembered years later that Brandeis had "the keenest and most subtle mind of all. . . . Nearly forty years have passed since I was present at those scenes in the Harvard class room, and yet I can recall as clearly as if it were yesterday the pleasant voice of the youthful student, his exact and choice language, his keen intellectual face, his lithe figure, his dark yet handsome aspect, and finally the unaffected suavity of his manner, that had in it something of the Old World. Intellect, refinement, an alert and receptive spirit, were written all over his attractive personality."[22]

For his part, Louis was in love with Harvard Law School. He attended classes, read the cases, and participated in the moot court as a member of the Pow Wow Club. It was all so new and so stimulating. "You have undoubtedly heard from other[s] of my work here, how well I am pleased with everything that pertains to the law . . .," he wrote his friend Otto Wehle, who married his sister Amy. "My thoughts are almost entirely occupied by the law. . . ." Louis also waxed eloquent on the benefits of Langdell's case method. "Law schools are splendid institutions," he told Otto. ". . . I remember a few Sundays before I left [Louisville]—you, Al and I were up in your room comfortably reclining on the bed, and talking about lectures. You thought they were of no earthly use—and I almost agree with you now. A lecture alone is little better than the reading of textbooks, but such lectures as we have here in connection with our other work are quite different things. . . ." Later he wrote to his sister Amy, "Law seems so interesting in all its aspects—it is difficult for me to understand that any of the initiated should not burn with enthusiasm."[23]

Louis was also spending a good part of his time running around and trying to meet Henry Adams, Ralph Waldo Emerson, and other intellectual celebrities who populated Boston at the time. No doubt he recognized the benefits of being accepted by high society. For a long time he diligently maintained an address book of all the seemingly important people he had met. But Louis was no fool. He could often see through the veneer of respectability that society arbitrarily placed on people. On one occasion he told Amy about some art lectures he had attended that featured a well-known figure. "How wise one becomes?" he satirically asked his sister. "Two weeks ago I should not have had any idea what all this means, and now I can write so learnedly on the subject!" He also advised his sister that Cambridge women were "not necessarily omniscient," referring as a case in point to the two girls who believed that Egypt was in Asia. ". . . [A]ll Cambridge people are not intellectual giants," he later confessed. No, he found he enjoyed himself better when he did not have to deal with the Boston aristocracy. "Very much of society would surely bore me," he observed.[24]

Not surprisingly, Louis's parents took a great deal of delight in their son's happiness. "The account of your schedule is charming," his father wrote at one point, "and if you were not my son and dearer to me than I myself, I would envy you. Enjoy this beautiful time to its fullest and with full knowledge; for it will not stay as beautiful as now . . . no matter how favorable good fortune may be." His mother was equally supportive. "How pleasant your life in Cambridge is!" she later wrote to Louis. "How refreshing and wholesome this gay, intellectual atmosphere!" But she wanted her son to know that he could always turn to her if things should not be entirely perfect: "I hope that you continue to write me about *yourself;* but everything, the disagreeable too, if it should come."[25]

In fact, all was not well for Louis in Cambridge. For starters, he remained physically weak. The doctor at the newly opened Hemenway Gymnasium at the law school was almost startled by Louis's frail appearance. He instructed the young student to maintain a regular schedule of exercise. It was advice Louis took to heart and followed all his life. Until his last days he always reserved time for some kind of physical activity. The difficulties with his eyes were not so easily resolved, however.

The problem first surfaced in the spring of 1877 when he was doing some legal work for Otto in Louisville. He had great trouble in being able to focus well enough to read. No doubt the problem reflected, to some extent at least, the great amount of reading Louis did under the dim and flickering gas lights in his room at Cambridge. The eye doctor he visited in Cincinnati was not reassuring. Another doctor in Boston advised Louis to give up law and undertake a profession in which he would not have to use his eyes. Louis was not so easily discouraged. At the urging of his father, he went to see a well-known eye doctor in New York, who told him his eyes were organically healthy and would ultimately come back to full strength with regulated use. But it would be a slow road to recovery. So when Louis returned to Cambridge, he enlisted several friends to read to him. It sharpened his memory and eventually enabled his eyes to regain their full strength.

With friends, Louis treated the whole episode philosophically. "My eyes have been troublesome ever since last spring," he explained to his former classmate and roommate Walter Douglas. "The oculists agree that they are perfectly healthy, that their present useless condition is merely a freak of the near-sighted eye which will pass over. I am able to use them hardly three or four hours with most careful use but my oculists promise me a brilliant future."[26] But the experience was not one to be forgotten, and Louis would rarely—even as a lawyer or Supreme Court justice—work at night.

Fortunately for Louis, the eye trouble did not really begin until after he had received his law degree in 1877. By the time he explained his problems to Douglas, he was halfway through an extra year of graduate study at Harvard—a program that did not require a lot of work or concern with grades. Getting his law degree in 1877 was no easy matter, however. Louis had completed the necessary four terms of law school with a brilliant academic record—his two-year average of 97 included three marks of 100 and two of 99. Under normal circumstances that record would have entitled Louis to be valedictorian. But Harvard had certain rules, and one of them was that a person had to be twenty-one before he could get a law degree. Louis would not reach the magic age until the following November. Initially the bureaucratic forces suggested that he simply wait. But a hurried conference with President Eliot in June led to a waiver of the rule, and Louis received his degree with the rest of the class.[27]

Louis could not stand the thought of leaving Cambridge, though. "Those years," he later recalled, "were among the happiest of my life. I worked! For me the world's center was Cambridge."[28] It did not take much to convince himself to stay a year for post-graduate study in law. Even the financial difficulties were erased. Adolph had lost his fortune before he took the family to Europe in 1872, and, although he now had a new shipping business, he could not provide his son with financial assistance during his years at Harvard. The first two years Louis had relied on loans from his brother and the funds he earned as a private tutor. To help tide him over in the third year he secured a job as a proctor at Harvard College.

Nothing that happened to him in Louisville in the summer of 1877 deterred Louis from returning to Harvard. A riot by striking railroad employees led to vandalism—and a broken bay window in the Brandeis home on First and Walnut Streets. Louis and Al were drafted into patrolling the streets with rifles—a situation that made Louis rather nervous. With his inexperience in the use of a gun, he was more likely to injure himself than any striking worker. The intellectual ferment of Harvard seemed much more to his liking. And so he returned to Cambridge, weak eyes and all, to enjoy the atmosphere and decide on his future.

There was a great deal of pressure for Louis to return to Louisville to practice law after his final year at Harvard. He loved his family. They had given him so much. And they wanted him to come back. There was the practical side of it as well. Adolph's business was not faring well. In response to his son's inquiries from Harvard, Adolph assured Louis that he was in good humor and "reconciled" to his position. Adolph generally was an optimist, but in truth the change in fortunes depressed him greatly. And Louis was enough of a realist to recognize that the family business could use some young blood to get it going again.[29]

Then there was the tug of St. Louis. St. Louis was the gateway to the West, and many lawyers and other professionals were flocking to the city to share in the profits from its expected growth. There was also family in St. Louis. His oldest sister, Fanny, had married Charles Nagel, a St. Louis lawyer destined to become a member of President Taft's cabinet. Many years later Louis, then a crusading activist, would be the leading attorney in the investigation of one of Nagel's fellow Cabinet members, Richard A. Ballinger. In the course of the investigation, Louis not only made Ballinger look foolish by his close cross-examination; Louis also publicly trapped Taft in a lie. The episode would add greatly to his reputation as "the people's attorney," but it would also mean the end of his relationship with Charlie Nagel. Because of loyalties to Taft and Ballinger, Nagel could not forgive Louis for his role in the whole affair. The two men never became reconciled after that.[30] But back in 1878 it was a different story. Nagel had good feelings about his brother-in-law, and he did everything possible to lure him to St. Louis. He offered Louis a job in his law firm and the opportunity to live with him and Fanny as a means of cutting costs. Fanny even visited her brother in Cambridge to talk to him about the benefits of life in St. Louis.

There was another factor to be considered in addition to the emotional one. Louis wanted the satisfaction of being independent. He did not want to feel that his future was set for him because of his family relationships. He therefore rejected the idea of going back to Louisville. He also rejected Nagel's job offer. Instead he accepted a position as an attorney in the St. Louis office of James Taussig, an offer that Nagel had engineered. Louis was not so independent as to reject all of Nagel's help. Nor was Louis entirely free from doubt in his choice. Shortly after his decision he sent his mother a letter with the attached note:

> Dearest Mama:
>
> Since writing this letter I have doubted somewhat whether I was right in the course I pursued in this matter. If after reading the letter you think I was *wrong*, I most humbly beg your pardon.
>
> Lovingly,
> Louis[31]

Frederika graciously accepted her son's decision, and the warmth they shared never diminished. Always Frederika would continue to speak of the glow that Louis added to her life. "It is such happiness to be your mother," she wrote him many years later, "to be able to say to myself that I contributed at least a little to what you are; to feel that in you, my youngest child, everything is present that should make a mother proud and happy, that all my dreams of high ideals and of purity are united in you." Adolph was similarly supportive of his son's decision to go to St. Louis. "I had given up hope a long time ago that you would settle here," he wrote his son, "and therefore the news that you had decided for St. Louis was not a very big disappointment. The reasons for this which you mention in your last letter are entirely convincing to me, especially your wanting to try your skill tilting with the world, before you decide to settle down to a purely scientific career [in law]. With your energy and with your persevering diligence you cannot, with the help of God, miss altogether in any career, and it is only a question of which gives you the best opportunity to express your talents."[32]

Louis welcomed and appreciated his parents' encouragement. But there was always a residue of guilt in his decision not to return to Louisville. It was aggravated by the fact that, coincidentally, his brother, Al, was also considering a job in a place other than Louisville at the same time. Ultimately Al decided to stay in Louisville, and it proved to be a boon to the family. Under Al's stewardship, the family shipping business began to flourish again. Louis never forgot the contribution his brother made at that point, and years later he decided that it would only be fair if he were to assume the financial responsibility for members of the family, cousins and all, who needed help. If he could not be in Louisville, at least he would make his presence felt.[33]

It took Louis several months to reach St. Louis. He decided to accept an offer from one of his professors, Charles S. Bradley, to spend the summer tutoring Bradley's son at their home in Rhode Island. There was more play than work, however. He spent a good part of the time riding horseback, playing ball, and generally enjoying normal summer activities. It was, all in all, a good time. His scheduled arrival in St. Louis was postponed, however, when he became ill and had to gain back his strength.

Louis finally arrived in St. Louis in November 1878, took up residence with Fanny and Charlie Nagel at 2044 Lafayette Street, and was admitted to the St. Louis bar on November 21, 1878. His arrangement with James Taussig was quite flexible. He could do work for Taussig or his younger cousin, George W. Taussig. Louis was also given the freedom to develop his own clients. The flexibility was appealing, but it did not compensate for the boredom Louis found in his practice. He was writing petitions and briefs (few were printed, and typewriters were not in use); he was also getting into court to argue some cases. But most of the matters were small collection cases that did not stir the imagination or get the juices flowing. "Litigation and legal business is very much depressed here," he wrote Otto Wehle in April 1879. "Even in our office business is poor. A hash of *old* cases, dating from better times, alone serves to keep us occupied."[34]

The only matter of any real interest to Louis was a legal issue he stumbled over in one of his cases: whether a creditor could sue an estate in certain circumstances on a contract made by the trustee of the estate. In his mind, Louis resolved that the creditor could sue. Unfortunately, the firm was representing the trustee, so Louis kept his true feelings in check—at least until the case ended. He then did some additional research, wrote a paper supporting the creditor's right to sue, and sent it to Oliver Wendell Holmes, Jr., then a Boston lawyer and editor of the prestigious *American Law Review*. Holmes was impressed with the article, and in due course it was published—and Louis D. Brandeis, for the first time, became an author.[35] The article did not create any kind of sensation; in fact there was hardly a ripple in the legal community. But it was a start.

Socially, Louis found St. Louis rather tiresome. He almost never worked at night and spent most of his evenings going to parties and dances. He even took a stab at acting, playing Romeo in a local rendition of the Shakespeare play. But he had no misconception about his theatrical ability. "Absurdly ridiculous!" he advised his sister Amy, "most terrible inconsistency—most palpable incongruity. I! a devoted—an inanely devoted lover! Dead gone in a girl of fourteen!—forty would be nearer the mark. Truly the extreme touch here—making me [a] lover. . . . Have been hoping that I should be called off to Washington to argue a case before the Supreme Court—merely for the purpose of escaping this trial." Despite these protests, he later admitted that the play had gone off well. But it was not enough to keep him going. He found the St. Louis crowd boring, and at one point he told Amy that he was "disposed to become melancholy and to moralize on the total depravity of man and woman."[36]

It all made him long for the activity and intellectual stimulation he found in Cambridge. True, people could be snobbish and artificial there. But at least there were some real minds in Cambridge, people who were interested in important things and interesting to listen to. Louis was like an overripe fruit, waiting to be plucked and brought back to Boston. Fate then intervened, and Samuel Dennis Warren came to the rescue.

TWO

The Boston Practice

It is more important to know where you are going than to get there quickly. Do not mistake activity for achievement.

MABEL NEWCOMBER

Poor Gilbert Stuart. It was a sad way to end up. He had achieved so much fame as the man who painted portraits of George Washington and as one of America's preeminent artists. When he died it was only fitting that they lay his body to rest in the Boston Common. He had lived in Boston for the last twenty years of his life, and now, it was believed, he would be a permanent part of the city. But then the people in Narragansett, Rhode Island—where Stuart had been born—decided that his remains should be returned there. All the arrangements were made. And then, much to everyone's surprise, they could not remember exactly where on the Common Stuart was buried. It was just one of those things. There was not much the Boston authorities could do except to put a plaque right outside the Common stating that Stuart was in there—somewhere.

The Boston Common, though, was much more than a place to bury honored figures of the past. It was, in many respects, the center of Boston's life. Commercial activity in colonial times had grown up around the Common. Later, important people gave speeches there denouncing England's colonial rule. English soldiers trained there, and skirmishes sometimes erupted on its grassy knolls after the Revolution was started. Years later people sometimes tended their cows on the Common's rolling slopes. And on occasion it was used for public executions of convicted criminals.

While the uses of it varied, the Common remained almost unchanged in appearance over the years. The same could not be said about the rest of the city. Until 1845 or so, Boston survived as a small, quiet town with little industry and a fairly homogeneous population of white Anglo-Saxon protestants. It was in the middle of the nineteenth century that the great waves of Irish immigrants descended on Boston. There were so many of them, and they were so poor. Most of them stayed. By 1880 more than half of Boston's population consisted of immigrants, and most of those were Irish. Boston would never be the same again.

To begin with, the Irish immigrants needed someplace to live. Warehouses and old mansions were converted into tenement apartments. Families, and even groups of families, were squeezed into small apartments. And then they all needed work. Their wants were small, and they were willing to put in long hours at low wages. It was a natural invitation for industries to come to Boston. And come they did. Industrialization was so rapid and so far-reaching that Boston became one of the country's largest manufacturing cities by 1880. Textiles, shoes, ready-made clothing, and other items became well-known Boston products.

Established members of Boston society—themselves the descendants of earlier immigrants—resented the invasion by the Irish. They were poor and dirty, they had a funny accent, and, worst of all, they were making Boston into a city different from the one earlier generations had come to love. Not surprisingly, people became very conscious of class and ethnic background. It was difficult to be accepted by the blue-chip Brahmin group unless you had the right credentials and were the product of a family that had lived in Boston for four or five generations. Neighborhoods also became divided according to social and economic status. The Brahmin society began to move to the suburbs of Newton and Brookline. The Irish kept to their separate ghettos. No one wanted to associate with them. Even the newly freed blacks did not want any Irish to move into their neighborhoods—it could mean reduced status and urban blight.

Boston's growth and changed complexion did have its compensations, though. Many people found that new business and industry meant access to greater wealth. Lawyers were among the groups that profited. In earlier times most of Boston's lawyers were solo practitioners who handled small personal matters and on occasion did some trial work. Things were different now. By 1880 there were opportunities for lawyers to advise emerging business and industry on a whole range of problems—contracts, labor conditions, government regulations, and other questions that arise in the conduct of a large organization. It was an exciting time. An enterprising lawyer with some social contacts could do well—at least that's what Sam Warren thought.

Samuel Dennis Warren, Jr., was a member of the Boston aristocracy. His father ran a very successful paper mill in Boston, and the family enjoyed the pleasures that wealth could bring. They lived on Mt. Vernon Street in fashionable Beacon Hill, a street that Henry James identified as one of the best in America. They had homes elsewhere, and they traveled a great deal. Sometimes, though, the family's use of wealth was counterproductive. Sam, for example, was sent to the best boarding schools. Because of his many prolonged absences, however, he was not able to take full advantage of the relationships with his parents or his sister and three brothers. "Sam . . . was much away at boarding school," his sister later recalled, ". . . [and] was not usually counted as one of the children."[1] This was probably most unfortunate for Sam. He was a shy and very sensitive person, and he might well have benefited greatly from more interaction with his family.

In any event, after a tedious two-year apprenticeship with his father's paper mill, Sam went off to Harvard Law School. He did not make friends easily. Quite the contrary. The other students generally considered him to be aloof and almost haughty. But no one could deny that Sam was smart, very smart. He had an excellent record at the law school. In fact, there was only one person in his class who had better grades—Louis D. Brandeis.

Like Louis, Sam loved the law. And like Louis, Sam longed for the independence that a lawyer's life could bring. Immediately after law school Sam went to clerk for the Boston firm of Shattuck, Holmes & Monroe. It was a natural choice for Sam, given his close relationship with Oliver Wendell Holmes, Jr., who was one of the firm's partners. But Sam did not expect his stay at the law firm to be an extended one. He was anxious to strike out on his own. And he could think of no one better to do it with than Louis Brandeis.

Sam and Louis had been friends at the law school. Indeed, Louis was one of the few friends Sam had there. And when Louis needed people to read to him because of his eye trouble, Sam was more than happy to help out.

Sam was disappointed when Louis decided to move to St. Louis after law school. He felt that the opportunities for advancement were better in Boston. Even before Louis had settled into his new job, Sam was asking him to return. "Your determination to settle in St. Louis is of course absurd and indefensible in every point of view," he wrote Louis on November 9, 1878, "Boston being the only locality in which a civilized man can exist. . . . I wish you would put up your shingle with me. I am confident enough money can be made to keep alive with and together we could make a more gallant fight against the whole army of heresies and fallacies of which the law must be purged before it can be reduced to an orderly system."[2]

Louis was skeptical at first. After all, he was hoping the practice with James Taussig and the proximity to his sister Fanny would make St. Louis attractive. Sam was not one to give up so easily, though. He kept pounding away at Louis, writing him periodically in the hopes of enticing him back to Boston. And on that score he appealed to his friend's ego. "The only satisfactory thing for me would be to start a firm which would be sure not only to make money and have moderate success, but to take a leading position in the profession," Sam wrote in May 1879. "There are plenty of fellows who could help you do the former, but there is only one who can help me do the latter and that is yourself." Sam was smart enough to realize, moreover, that Louis was looking for something more than money. "As far as money goes," he continued, "I suppose you would make more in New York or St. Louis, but this I do not regard as the whole or even an important part of success and I do not think you do. . . . The bench and the bar of Massachusetts are the most civilized bodies of the kind in the country. . . . Life in this old city has a background, a perspective and a dignity which no other city on this continent possesses."[3] As insurance against financial problems, Sam suggested they could become editors of a law review. And if that did not work out, he would be willing to advance Louis part of his office and living expenses.

Louis was beginning to soften. St. Louis was not what he had hoped it would be, and he was almost pining to be back in Boston. On May 10, 1879, he wired Sam that his offer seemed like "a good thing." On that same day he wrote a letter explaining his feelings in greater detail. The law review editorship sounded like a good idea, so long as it remained only an incidental part of their business. "For, although I am very desirous of devoting some of my time to the literary part of the law," Louis explained, "I wish to become known as a practicing lawyer." But before making a final commitment, he told Sam he wanted a better idea "of the prospects of a young law firm and more particularly your social and financial position."[4]

On paper it sounded as though Louis were being the careful lawyer, checking out the situation fully before making a decision. As a practical matter, however, the decision had already been made. He was going back to Boston. The law review editorship did not materialize, and, aside from his father's paper mill business, there was not much more Sam could be sure of in the way of clients. But none of those was a fatal flaw. Sam and his family certainly knew a lot of people. Boston was a thriving city. Somehow, some way, things would work out.

Once again, though, Louis had to grapple with some emotional drawbacks. For one thing, Louis hated to leave Charlie Nagel and his sister Fanny. He loved them both, and they had been good to him. After Louis had left St. Louis, Charlie wrote him a note about the move. Charlie was opposed to the partnership with Sam for various reasons, but he recognized that it was an exciting opportunity and wished Louis the best. "We rejoice with you, Louis," Charlie said; "but you cannot blame us for feeling the one regret, that you are to a great extent lost to the family, and to Fanny and me and [our son] particularly."[5] Louis was very moved by Charlie's warm sentiments. "Your long letter was read with much attention and not a little heart-beating," he wrote back. Although Charlie's letter left him "blue and doubting for a day or two," Louis felt that he had made the right decision: "Although the loss of the advice, support and assistance of the family is very great, I find much comfort and consolation in the feeling that whatever I have achieved, or may achieve here, is my own—pure and simple—unassisted by the fortuitous circumstances of family influence or social position. There is indeed small comfort in this thought if nothing is achieved, but if anything is accomplished that thought would give me much satisfaction."[6]

Louis explained to Charlie that already things seemed to be going smoothly. He had secured a clerkship with Horace Gray, then chief justice of the Massachusetts Supreme Court, later an associate justice of the United States Supreme Court. However, that was only a part-time job. For the rest, he and Sam had rented a room on the third floor of an office building on 60 Devonshire Street in downtown Boston. Not coincidentally, the offices of the Warren family business were located nearby. Louis was also pleased by his former classmate's approach to the law business. Sam, Louis told Charlie, was showing "the same bulldog perseverance and obstinacy" which brought Louis to Boston. And then there was the possibility of getting a teaching position. "The law as a logical science has very great attractions for me," he told Charlie. "I see it now again by the almost ridiculous pleasure which the discovery or invention of a legal theory gives me; and I know that such a study of the law cannot be pursued by a successful practitioner nor by a judge. . . ."[7] So, all in all, there was much to look forward to.

Louis conveyed similar feelings to his mother, who was again disappointed that her son had chosen another city over Louisville. Louis understood her feelings. He wrote his mother from Boston that "it seems to me as if I were a fool to have settled here instead of staying with you and enjoying you and your love." Other more powerful forces were at work, though. "[M]an is strange, at least this one is," he explained to his mother; "he does not enjoy what he has—and he always wants what he does not yet have. That probably is called ambition—the delusion, for which one is always ready to offer a sacrifice. And so," he concluded, "I think that I shall be happier here, in spite of being alone, and if I can write you about success, it will counterbalance all the privations. And, I believe," he added, with a shrewd understanding of his mother, "that you too will enjoy me more from a distance if you know that I am happy."[8] On that basis his mother would have much to enjoy in the years to come.

Organizing the firm was not terribly difficult. Louis was admitted to the Massachusetts Bar in July 1879 without taking an examination—an event, Louis explained to his brother, that was "contrary to all principles and precedent."[9] He and Sam decided that, in naming the firm, they would follow established practice and give the first position to Sam since he had been admitted to the Massachusetts Bar first. The firm of Warren & Brandeis celebrated on the evening of Louis's admission to the Bar by drinking a mixture of champagne and beer in Warren's room with Oliver Wendell Holmes, Jr., who was fast becoming a renowned figure in Boston legal circles.

The practice did not have the best beginning. The firm's first litigation case was for the Warren paper mill business. They wanted to sue one Martha E. Berry, but she could not be found. The two young attorneys, however, were not discouraged. They kept plugging along, asking friends and relatives for someone, anyone, who needed some legal services. Among other people Louis turned to Jacob Hecht, a prosperous merchant in Boston whom Louis had met in law school. The Hechts used to hold open house on Saturdays at their home on Commonwealth Avenue. When he was at Harvard, Louis had often gone there to mingle with the artists and intellectuals who frequently attended. In time, he became quite close to Jacob Hecht, and Hecht was more than happy to have the young attorney represent him. In fact, Louis's first argument before the Massachusetts Supreme Court was on behalf of the United Hebrew Benevolent Association, an organization that Hecht headed. It was not a very complicated matter—only the collection of $25 in back dues from a delinquent member. But it was a start.

Louis also benefited from his association with Professor Charles Bradley, whose son he had tutored the summer before he went to St. Louis. Through Bradley's contacts Louis was asked to argue a case before the Rhode Island Supreme Court. Louis was so impressive that he soon found himself beset by numerous requests for assistance. Sam was especially appreciative. "My dear Old Man," he wrote his partner, ". . . I knew you would come out strong, and the faint praise you allow yourself is, I know, to what you deserve, as dawn to sunrise." Warren also had some news of his own: some new cases, including one matter involving an estate worth more than half a million dollars. "The success of W & B is assured," Sam crowed.[10]

Before long the practice was indeed thriving. The first year saw a gross intake of $3,000 in fees, which produced almost $2,500 in profits for the partners to share. But the two lawyers were not satisfied. They kept thinking of ways to generate business. They joined a host of social clubs—the Boston Art Club, the Union Boat Club, the Turnverein athletic club, and several others. Louis kept lists of people he met and how he met them. And they were always on the outlook for new acquaintances or old friends who needed help. In November 1880 Adolph Brandeis advised his son that at least Chief Justice Gray was impressed. "I consider Brandeis the most ingenious and most original lawyer I ever met," Gray had said, "and he and his partner are among the most promising law firms we have got."[11]

Things were hopping on the social front as well. Louis took a room at 21 Joy Street near the State House and the Beacon Hill area. His schedule gave him plenty of time to enjoy himself. He usually arose at seven o'clock in the morning and had breakfast and a long walk, arriving at Gray's offices around nine o'clock. He would stay there until two o'clock in the afternoon, discussing cases with the chief justice and then taking dictation from him. After lunch he would wander over to the firm's offices on Devonshire Street and review cases with Sam and take care of whatever business he could. He would leave at six in the evening for some exercise—boating, tennis, swimming, or even a horseback ride. The exercise did not entirely correct his frail health, but it apparently gave him enough stamina to float around town going to various dinners and parties.

Women were then, as they always would be, a major part of Brandeis's life. Even as an elderly justice on the United States Supreme Court, he never lost his appreciation for women. Those who knew him well recognized that trait of his. "The Justice was a sucker for beautiful women," Felix Frankfurter later recalled. But as a young attorney in Boston, Louis was not at all ready to settle down with anyone. No, he was convinced, as he explained to Charlie Nagel, "that there are more fish in the sea than ever were caught." On one occasion he described to his sister Amy a twenty-eight-year-old woman he met at a dinner party. She was tall, had "a finely chiseled, half Southern face with black hair and sparkling jet eyes. . . ." She was also an "excellent talker," and before long Louis found himself deeply engrossed in conversation with her. After reciting all this, Louis realized that his sister might think he was smitten with the young woman. "But Alas! it is not so," he told Amy. "One mistress only claims me. The 'law' has her grip on me—and I suppose I can't escape her clutches without going on a ranch cattle raising."[12]

Louis never really gave any thought to going anywhere to escape the clutches of the law. But he did seriously consider exchanging his shingle for a lectern. The whole thing started with Holmes in the winter of 1880–81. Holmes had given the Lowell Institute lectures at Harvard, and there was an enthusiastic reaction to his view that the law should be more concerned with the realities of experience than with the logic of theories. The lectures were published as a book, *The Common Law,* which was extremely popular. But publishing Holmes's lectures was not enough. His friends wanted to bring him to Harvard on a permanent basis as a law professor. Unfortunately, the school did not have adequate funds to provide Holmes with an office and salary. It was at this point that Professor James Bradley Thayer turned to Brandeis.

Thayer, like all Harvard law professors up to that time, was a product of both Harvard College and Harvard Law School. He had practiced law for a number of years and then, in 1874, had accepted Langdell's request to teach at the law school. Thayer's thinking would be a major influence on Brandeis. Thayer believed that a judge had no right, except in certain clear-cut circumstances, to interfere with the majority will as expressed in written laws. As he became older, Louis became more and more convinced of the wisdom that lay behind Thayer's principle of judicial restraint. After all, if people were to develop themselves and have control over their lives, they had to have the responsibility for making judgments. There really was no other way.

But when he got in touch with Brandeis in the winter of 1881, Thayer was not interested in judicial restraint. He was interested in money. As a star performer at the law school and a rising young attorney in Boston, Brandeis might have some ideas on how to raise support funds for Holmes. Thayer was in luck. Louis was thinking about the matter when he happened to run into William Weld on the Common. Weld had been one of the students Louis tutored at Harvard, and now he was the proud beneficiary of a $16 million estate left to him by his grandfather. Louis discussed the Holmes matter with Weld, and he agreed to give $90,000 for a professor's chair so long as the donor remained anonymous.

It was one of those circumstances that brought Holmes and Brandeis even closer together. As Louis was developing his Boston practice, he would see more and more of Holmes. They might have a beer after work, or Louis might meet Holmes and his wife for dinner at the Parker House near Beacon Hill, or Holmes might simply ask the young lawyer to come over so that Louis could review an article Holmes was working on. Then, as later, Holmes—who had a tendency to brood—would always be impressed by the buoyancy and optimism that Brandeis conveyed. He never seemed to get down. And Holmes was not reluctant to tell Brandeis how much he appreciated the lift. "For many years you have, from time to time, at critical moments, said things that have given me courage," Holmes wrote at one point, "which probably I remember better than you do. You do it again now, with the same effect and always with the same peculiar pleasure to me. I thank you. . . ."[13]

Louis's offer to help Thayer reflected more than his personal feelings for Holmes, however. He was still in love—as he always would be—with Harvard Law School. He had a special affection for the place that had taught him so much and made possible his financial and social success. Not surprisingly, he gave a great deal of thought to joining Holmes as a member of the faculty. Thayer expected to take a short leave in the winter of 1881 and asked Louis if he would take over Thayer's course on evidence. He was of course agreeable to that, but money again got in the way. There were not enough funds to allow Thayer to take his leave. The next year things worked out better, and Louis Brandeis, at the age of twenty-five, taught the evidence course on a part-time basis for $1,000.

Louis knew that his parents would be excited about the teaching appointment, and he sent them President Eliot's letter announcing the appointment. The response was predictable. "My dearest child," his mother wrote, "how happy you make me feel! My heart is a prayer of thanksgiving, and at the same time it is filled with the deepest wish that heaven may protect you." Adolph Brandeis also thought it was "the greatest honor that can be given to a young man of your age." But Adolph was concerned about the impact of the new job on his son's health. Despite his regular exercise, Louis did not always feel well, and he tired easily. His father hoped his son would not sacrifice health for career advancement. "If something must be sacrificed," Adolph advised, "then sacrifice rather a part of your practice than the smallest bit of your health. For the former sacrifice will be in any case only temporary, while your health must last your whole life, please God." Uncle Lewis Dembitz was equally proud of Louis. "It's the first time that I felt glad at your changing your middle name from 'David' to 'Dembitz,'" he wrote.[14]

The course went well, and the law school invited Brandeis to come back the following year as a full-time professor. He gave it some thought, and some friends advised him to take the position. One who did was Nathaniel S. Shaler, a Kentuckian and geology professor with whom Brandeis had become close during his student days. Shaler felt that Louis was more suited to teaching law than to practicing it. "You're too sensitive," he told the young attorney. "A lawyer should be made of sterner stuff. You won't be able to stand the gaff of opposition." Brandeis felt differently. He sensed that law practice, especially trial law work, would give him more satisfaction than teaching. He therefore rejected the law school invitation. As he explained to his father, "What I should prefer is some position that would give me practice in trying cases. I feel I am weak in this experience and think that with practice I could do well at it."[15]

It was, in retrospect, a gross understatement. Within a short time Brandeis would obtain the desired experience trying cases, and few would doubt his extraordinary talent in the arena. He would learn first to master the facts of the particular case because, as he later told an interviewer, "It has been one of the rules of my life that no one shall ever trip me on a question of fact." He would also learn to retain his composure at all times, even during the heat of argument. It was a characteristic that was obvious to most and especially disconcerting to his adversaries. Even noted attorneys like George Wharton Pepper were impressed. Pepper participated with Brandeis in the "prosecution" of the Ballinger case before a congressional committee in 1910. At one point during the hearing John J. Vertress, an experienced Southern lawyer who represented Ballinger, jumped up and repeatedly accused Brandeis of being a liar. Brandeis stood silently with his arms folded and a small smile on his lips. When Vertrees's tirade had ended, he asked Vertrees if he were finished and then, without a word of response, returned to his cross-examination. Brandeis, Pepper later remembered, was in total control of the situation. No wonder, then, that Brandeis learned to love the struggle and exhilaration of a trial. At one point in the early Boston years he told his brother of his frustration with his light case load. ". . . I really long for the excitement of the contest," he wrote, "that is a good and prolonged one covering days or weeks. There is a certain joy in the draining exhaustion and backache of a long trial, which shorter skirmishes cannot afford."[16]

Not surprisingly, Sam and Louis's practice continued to grow quickly. By 1881 they had their first associate attorney, D. Blakeley Hoar, and by 1884 they had added a second, Charles Frederick Chamberlayne. Both men were Harvard Law graduates and added to the prestige of Warren & Brandeis. Louis was in fact becoming quite well known in legal circles, and soon the firm had no need to search for clients. They came from all over. Even Mark Twain wanted to use Brandeis. One day he came to talk to the young attorney about a possible libel suit. Years later the memory of the encounter remained fresh in Brandeis's mind—Twain dressed shabbily in a long overcoat buttoned up to his neck, pacing back and forth as he discussed the matter with the young attorney (who advised against bringing the action).[17] The early fame that came to Brandeis also led to another relationship that would dramatically change his life.

Elizabeth Gardiner was born in New Rochelle, New York, in 1856 to Edward Gardiner, a wealthy man who later became one of Boston's most famous patrons of the arts. It was not an entirely happy childhood. Elizabeth's mother died when she was quite young, and her father, although attentive, could not completely fill the void. Elizabeth, or Bessie, as she was called by friends, was very much a product of her environment. Although full of vigor and intelligence, she was not allowed to go to college and grew up feeling very insecure about herself. It was the Victorian age, and while there might be a woman behind every successful man, Bessie was taught to believe that the woman could not expect to be in charge of her own destiny. That was a man's job.

In the summer of 1877, Bessie, then a very attractive woman of twenty-one, met Glendower Evans. He was a sensitive, bright young man a few months younger than Bessie. They spent the summer swimming and sailing, and before long they were deeply in love. Bessie adored Glen, and she was ecstatic when they were married in 1882.

Glen was a graduate of Harvard Law School and eventually landed a job in Holmes's law firm. Even then Holmes was a delight to be with. "Now, Evans," Holmes would say, "if you will advance any proposition I will refute it for you." But the person Glen was more interested in meeting was Louis Brandeis. He had been something of a legend at the law school, and Glen used to tell Bessie how much he regretted the fact that Louis had already graduated by the time Glen had arrived. One Sunday Glen and Bessie went to call on Barrett Wendell, an English professor at Harvard. Coincidentally, Louis was walking out the door as Bessie and Glen were walking in. Because of his youthful appearance, Bessie at first thought that Louis was one of Wendell's students. Glen quickly corrected her and informed her that that was the Louis Brandeis he was so anxious to meet. "Well," she replied, "why don't we ask him to dinner?"[18]

Thus began a lifelong relationship for the three of them. Louis would come to dinner frequently, and, while Bessie sat in the background, he and Glen would engage in animated conversation about any number of diverse topics. On Sundays the three of them would either go walking or canoeing and, as at dinner, Glen and Louis would do most of the talking. After a while Bessie and Glen learned that Louis was Jewish—a fairly unusual phenomenon in those days in Boston, and, as Bessie later recalled, "it gave an aroma to his personality" to know that Louis was descended from the Hebrew prophets.[19]

Unfortunately, the relationship was a short one for Glen. He, like Louis, was frail, and in 1886, at the age of thirty, he died suddenly. It was a catastrophic event from which Bessie would never fully recover. She had loved Glen so much and depended upon him to such an extent. She felt very much lost without him. Her memory of and love for him would never fade. For more than twenty years after Glen died she insisted on wearing black to reflect her state of mourning. She would constantly refer to him in conversation with intimates, trying to determine how Glen would have reacted to specific situations. In this frame of mind she could of course never contemplate marrying anyone else. In fact, she would do anything to keep the memories of Glen fresh. As a matronly woman in her sixties and seventies, Bessie would even resort to seances with a mystic and a ouija board in an effort to establish contact with her deceased husband (although she was skeptical enough to recognize that the voice she heard was not Glen's, since it would not use the nicknames Glen had used for her).

Louis tried to fill the void that Glen's death created. In a very real sense, he became, and always remained, the man in Bessie's life. There was a certain irony in the attention Louis showered on Bessie almost immediately after Glen's death. Shortly before Glen became sick, he and Louis had had a heated argument about the possibilities of life after death. Glen felt there might be something to it. Louis disagreed vehemently. Man's mind could not know what lies beyond the present life, Louis said. Religion was of no practical use. Glen felt otherwise and challenged his friend. Bessie, sitting quietly in the background, thought that Glen was getting the better of their guest. But Louis would have none of it. He was not used to losing arguments. In the middle of the discussion he picked up his hat and abruptly left. He returned only when he heard that Glen was seriously ill.

Louis's willingness to help was not entirely surprising. He was then a carefree bachelor, Bessie was still an attractive young woman, and they were friends. They began to see each other regularly. As Bessie later remembered, Louis just took "charge of my life." It was a friendship that would take them through many good times and many sad times. Louis was always there to encourage her to step out of mourning and use her vital mind in productive ways. Once, when she took his advice and ran into controversy, he sent her off to England to learn about socialism. "I can never tell you, dear Louis," Bessie later wrote, "how it touches me that in all the pressures of your big affairs you have taken the time to grapple with this ruckus of mine. You are the only person, except Glen, who had ever taken care, as it were, of me. And I know that you do it for his sake. You are a loyal friend. . . ."[20]

The relationship was a reciprocal one, though. Louis felt he could confide in Bessie and reveal to her intimate feelings one did not usually express in those Victorian days in Boston. Once, while he was still a bachelor and in England on business, Louis wrote to Bessie how much he appreciated English women. "Man delights me," he wrote. "Ah!—and women too. There is danger that Anglophobia will be succeeded by Anglomania."[21] And Bessie was there to help when needed. When Alice Brandeis, Louis's wife, suffered a nervous breakdown, Bessie spent the summer with both of them at Cape Cod.

It was, from both sides, a true and strong friendship. Many years later, as Bessie was approaching her eightieth birthday and lay dying in Boston, she would use her secretary, Anna, to dictate a letter to her companion, then an elderly and famous Supreme Court justice, and pay homage to their relationship. "Louis, dear," she began, "I did not say yesterday what was in my heart to say—that no one knows but you and I the devotion and the protecting power that you have had toward me ever since Glen died; the way you have always kept near enough to jump in when the occasion called [for it]. . . . Anna was touched to the quick last summer by what you told her of Glen—what only you and I know. You have made a new thing of friendship and loyalty—all your own—I never forget."[22]

The relationship with Bessie, however, did more than give Louis a friend for life. It gave him the impetus to take on public causes and ultimately become "the people's attorney."

THREE

The Public Advocate Emerges

No man is an island entire of itself. Every man is a piece of the continent, a part of the main. . . . Any man's death diminishes me, because I am involved in mankind. Therefore never send to know for whom the bell tolls. It tolls for thee.

JOHN DONNE

Almost from the beginning, Brandeis was quick to recognize man's faults. But he almost never abandoned his efforts to seek perfection in whatever he was doing—or in those with whom he was doing it. As his thirty-second birthday approached, Louis tried to explain this perspective to his mother. "I must send you another birthday greeting," he wrote, "and tell you how much I love you; that with each day I learn to extoll your love and your worth more—and that when I look back over my life, I can find nothing in your treatment of me that I would alter. You often said, dearest mother, that I find fault—but I always told you candidly what I felt and sought to change only that little which appeared to me possible of improvement." In this context, the answer to the world's problems was obvious. "I believe, most beloved mother," Louis added, "that the improvement of the world, reform, can only arise when mothers like you are increased thousands of times and have more children."[1]

There is no evidence that Brandeis pursued this "interest" in genetics. By the time he wrote that letter, though, he had already made some efforts to correct the faults in Boston society. Until 1884 he had been a Republican. He had supported James A. Garfield's campaign for the presidency in 1880 and told his brother he could not "quite reconcile myself with the idea of a Democratic rule yet." Things were different in the next presidential election. Brandeis did not feel comfortable with James Blaine, the Republican candidate. He agreed to join the local group of Mugwumps and support Grover Cleveland, the Democratic candidate. The Mugwumps were not rank and file types, however; their members generally came from the social and economic elite of Boston society. Sam Warren's father, for example, was a part of the Mugwump crowd. Not surprisingly, the Mugwumps did not regard every one as being entirely equal. Because of their backgrounds, most Mugwumps felt they had a certain intellectual and moral superiority that entitled them to provide a guiding hand in community affairs. It was all done with the best of intentions, though.[2]

By this time Brandeis himself had decided to take a hand in community affairs. He was elected to the executive committee of the Civil Service Reform Association in the fifth congressional district and later joined the Boston American Citizenship Committee. But it was Bess Evans who first began to awaken him to the deeper problems of democratic politics.

It all started out simply enough. Bess was riding the train one day in 1887 to visit a state reform school. She was on the board of trustees, and, as in all her civic activities, Bess took this one very seriously. Lizzie Putnam, another trustee, was also on the train. It was terrible, said Lizzie. The Irish were getting more than their fair share of things. She had read in the paper that the state legislature was about to give the Good Shepherd School and Church $10,000. That was a Catholic institution, Lizzie observed, and before you knew it other Catholic institutions would also be getting public money. It was not right. Public money should be only for public institutions.

Bess was impressed. She was prepared to help Lizzie write letters to the editors of the Boston papers protesting the proposed appropriation. But Bess was willing to do more than that. Her "dear brother" Louis Brandeis happened to be the lawyer for the Good Shepherd in the legislative proceeding. She would talk to him about it.

Louis listened to Bess intently. There seemed to be a small smile on his lips. But he said nothing in response, and Bess had no idea what Louis thought of her argument—until the Legislature resumed consideration of the money bill. Brandeis was not there, and a new lawyer tried—unsuccessfully—to get final approval of the appropriation for the Good Shepherd. Later Louis explained to Bess that her presentation had had a tremendous impact on his thinking. "You argued your case very ably, but not ably enough," he said. "Your case is stronger than you know. It is not just private religious institutions which should be denied the expenditure of public money, it is private interests, now defended by the ablest lawyers in the land and who ask for public money with no one on the committee who knows enough to understand the other side."[3] The public advocate was off and running.

But first there had to be an intermediate stop on the way. Harvard Law School needed help, and not only money. The school needed a continuous infusion of ideas to ensure that it could retain its high standards and produce good lawyers. For Brandeis, little more had to be said. There was almost nothing he would not do for his school. In August 1886 he and six other Harvard graduates sent a circular to the Harvard alumni explaining the purpose of the soon-to-be-created Harvard Law School Association. On September 23, 1886, the group was formally organized and Brandeis became its secretary. He remained an officer until his appointment to the Supreme Court in 1916.[4]

Brandeis's relationship with Harvard was not confined to the Association, however. He maintained a regular correspondence with the dean and faculty members, proposing courses and offering advice on the management of the school. He was also instrumental in the establishment of the *Harvard Law Review.* Many of the faculty members and students thought it would be a good idea to establish a magazine at the school that could periodically publish articles on timely legal topics. It would provide good experience for the students and might contribute to the development of the law. Brandeis was enthusiastic about the idea. He gave his time and money to the project, and in 1889 he, James Barr Ames, and George Nutter (then an associate at Warren & Brandeis) became the *Harvard Law Review*'s first trustees and took charge of the $250 in its bank account.

As with the Association, the *Review* remained a lifelong preoccupation of Brandeis's. As both a lawyer and a justice of the Supreme Court he was very interested in the articles it was publishing. He and Sam contributed some of the first pieces on the basis of cases they had had.[5] He was also quick on later occasions to advise the students and the faculty on how to make their product more relevant. Thus, Brandeis did not hesitate to speak his mind in 1912 when the *Review* asked his advice about an unusual project concerning legal developments during the time of Richard II of England. "There has been no time in the history of our nation," Brandeis told them, "when there is greater need for the progressive lawyer than there is today. The reputation of the profession has suffered mightily from its failure to grapple with twentieth century problems. It is undoubtedly true that we need legal scholars, but the more pressing demand of today is for the enlightened lawyer. His absence is the real cause of the lack of confidence in the Bench and Bar." In this setting, pure historical research seemed to be of little value. "If the *Law Review* is to make any departure from the courses hitherto pursued," Brandeis concluded, "it ought to be in the line rather of prospect than of retrospect; to constructive work rather than archeological research."[6] So much for the era of Richard II. And when he later felt frustrated by the votes of his brethren on the Supreme Court, Brandeis often proposed to Felix Frankfurter and other faculty members that they crank out articles that might lead to a different result in the future. But none of these comments or suggestions was as important—or as celebrated—as the article Sam and Louis wrote for the *Review* in 1890.

In December 1890 the *Harvard Law Review* published an article by Louis D. Brandeis and Samuel D. Warren, Jr., entitled "The Right to Privacy." In essence, the article argued that, except in limited situations, people should be given legal protection against invasions of privacy by other citizens. It was no small matter in the authors' view. Of course, idle gossip had probably been a problem from the first days of civilized society. But now there were new inventions and practices to enlarge the capacity of prying eyes. "Instantaneous photographs and newspaper enterprise have invaded the sacred precincts of private and domestic life," Louis and Sam wrote; "and numerous mechanical devices threaten to make good the prediction that 'what is whispered in the closet shall be proclaimed from the house-tops.' " The authors were especially concerned with the gossip trade that had recently mushroomed in the newspaper industry. "Gossip is no longer the resource of the idle and of the vicious," they observed, "but has become a trade, which is pursued with industry as well as effrontery. To satisfy a prurient taste the details of sexual relations are broadcast in the columns of the daily papers. To occupy the indolent, column upon column is filled with idle gossip, which can only be procured by intrusion upon the domestic circle." The columns were not the worst of it, however. Photographs were being taken of people and circulated in the press. It was simply not right. It was time to provide some legal remedy for those whose privacy had been invaded. After all, people had, as Judge Thomas Cooley, the eminent scholar, had observed, a right "to be let alone."[7]

Sam and Louis thought that the common law provided an answer to the problem. They noted that the law already offered some protection against mental distress. For instance, a person's private letters could not be made available to the public under normal circumstances. Why not extend that principle to cover situations when the matter at hand involved "idle gossip" or photographs that exposed a person's private actions to public scrutiny? "The principle which protects personal writings and any other productions of the intellect or of the emotions is the right to privacy," the authors concluded, "and the law has no new principle to formulate when it extends this protection to the personal appearance, sayings, acts, and to personal relations, domestic or otherwise."[8]

The article had certain shortcomings. Although they vehemently protested the excesses of a scandalous press, Sam and Louis offered virtually no evidence to support their claim; and later scholars found in fact that the press of that day, and particularly the Boston press, was quite respectable. Moreover, although the authors acknowledged that the press should be able to print items of public interest, they did not explore the inevitable conflict between the right to privacy and the right to a free press. They did not speculate on what would happen, for example, if a newspaper printed information about a person that it believed to be of public interest but that the person felt was of only private interest.[9]

None of these defects seemed to matter much to readers. The reaction to the article was nothing short of incredible. Lawyers read it, magazines reviewed it, and courts relied on it—all to the seeming end of creating a new right to privacy. Twenty-six years after its publication, Dean Roscoe Pound of the Harvard Law School observed that the article "did nothing less than add a chapter to our law."[10] Subsequent scholars were just as impressed. One commentator referred to it as "the outstanding example of the influence of legal periodicals upon the American law."[11] Another writer said that the article was "perhaps the most influential law journal piece ever published."[12] In some sense all of this praise was justified. After all, concerns for privacy in part motivated the American Revolution; and there could be no doubt that protection of privacy was a central concern of the populace.

Amid all the fanfare produced by the privacy article, there was a natural curiosity as to what motivated Brandeis and Warren to write the piece. Most scholars agreed that it was Warren's displeasure at seeing the Boston press report on his family's activities. One Brandeis biographer called particular attention to the *Saturday Evening Gazette,* which, it was said, described the Warren family activities in "lurid detail."[13] Other scholars accepted this description and added that the breaking point came when the press covered the wedding of Sam Warren's daughter.[14] One eminent legal scholar was particularly touched by the irony of the situation. "All this is a most marvelous tree to grow from the wedding of the daughter of Mr. Samuel D. Warren," Dean William Prosser wrote. "One is tempted to surmise that she must have been a very beautiful girl. Resembling, perhaps, that fabulous creature, the daughter of a Mr. Very, a confectioner in Regent Street, who was so wondrous fair that her presence in the shop caused three or four hundred people to assemble every day in the street before the window to look at her, so that her father was forced to send her out of town, and counsel was led to inquire whether she might not be indicted as a public nuisance." Yes, it was a wonderful image for the woman who inspired a new legal right of privacy. "This was the face that launched a thousand lawsuits," Prosser concluded.[15]

Actually, it is very doubtful that Warren's daughter launched any lawsuits. Warren was not married until 1883, and in 1890—when the privacy article was published—his daughter was only six years old. Nor were there any newspaper articles discussing the Warrens' social life in "lurid detail." Even by standards prevailing then, the coverage of the Warrens' social life was minimal and quite tame. The *Saturday Evening Gazette*—the periodical most often cited by historians of the Brandeis and Warren privacy article—was anything but a scandal sheet. Most of that weekly paper was devoted to news, political analysis, and art and literary reviews. Even its competitors recognized the *Gazette* as a first-class operation. The *Boston Herald* called the *Gazette* "the queen of society newspapers. It is printed for a special class of patrons, and it is admirably edited." The *Boston Post* said the paper was "almost indispensable to every household."[16]

The *Gazette* did report on social events. But its columns were not exactly sensational. One social column, for example, reported that "in some of the finest houses in Newport, there is a great deal of misery." Another column reported that "Miss Grant . . . popped corn and ate baked apples with the second Comptroller and Congressman Ned Burnett the other afternoon in their bachelor quarters." As for Sam Warren, he received virtually no attention from the *Gazette.* Between 1883 and 1890 his name appeared in the *Gazette* only twice—once because he, along with Brandeis and others, wanted to announce publicly that they were joining the Mugwumps; the other time in June 1890, when Katherine H. Clarke was married and it was reported that "Mr. and Mrs. Samuel D. Warren, the former a cousin of the bride, gave a breakfast for the bridal party. . . ."[17] Not quite the drama that historians seek.

Nevertheless, it does seem clear that Warren was upset with the Boston press and that he did ask Brandeis to help him write the article.[18] Given his very sensitive nature, there are any number of matters that could have disturbed Warren. For one thing, the *Gazette* was not very fond of his father-in-law. Sam had married Mabel Bayard, the daughter of Senator Thomas Francis Bayard. He had been a presidential candidate in 1884, and, after Grover Cleveland's election, Bayard was appointed secretary of state. The *Gazette* did not think much of Bayard's performance in that position. As he was about to leave office, the *Gazette* was especially colorful in its criticisms. "Happily he has but a few days more in which to strut about like a pompous turkey-cock with wings drooping in defiance at the smaller denizens of the political farmyard while his angry gobble-gobble strikes terror into their private souls," the *Gazette* observed. "Secretary Bayard will go into private life unwept, unhonored, and unsung, and it is to be sincerely hoped that he may be kept there for good and all."[19]

Criticism like that might have been enough to rile Sam Warren. If so, there would have been a certain irony in Brandeis's coming to the rescue of Mabel Warren's father. For Mabel did not really care for Louis.[20] It was one of those quirks of fate that Brandeis would run into periodically. He was not terribly popular with the wives of some men to whom he was extremely close. In later years, for instance, Oliver Wendell Holmes and Felix Frankfurter were among Brandeis's closest associates; and yet neither Fanny Holmes nor Marion Frankfurter was very fond of him.[21] But Brandeis apparently took the matter in stride, and it does not seem to have affected his relationships with the men. And it obviously did not deter him from helping Sam develop a new right to privacy.

Brandeis had a certain ambivalence toward the piece, however. Like Warren, he hoped "to make people see that invasions of privacy are not necessarily borne—and then make them ashamed of the pleasure they take in subjecting themelves to such invasions." But he was not convinced that the article was well done. When he first got back the page proofs he did not feel that the article was "as good as I thought it was." And more than that, there were other subjects of greater interest to him. "Lots of things which are worth doing have occurred to me as I sit calmly here," he wrote his fiancée shortly after the privacy article was published. "And among others to write an article on 'The Duty of Publicity'—a sort of companion piece to the last one that would really interest me more." It all reflected Brandeis's growing belief that corruption in government could be minimized if the public knew more about the activities of public officials. "If the broad light of day could be let in upon men's actions," he observed, "it would purify them as the sun disinfects."[22] In time Congress would pass laws incorporating that philosophy.[23] Long before then—indeed, even as he suggested the "publicity" article—Brandeis was trying to practice what he hoped to preach.

It all happened quite by accident. In 1890 a group of men were trying to obtain the public charter for the subway in Boston. It was believed that they were not relying solely on the merits of their case. There was talk that they were instead relying on their power to grease the pockets of the State legislators. As a Mugwump and a member of the Citizens Association, Brandeis was, to say the least, offended by this corruption—if indeed it existed. He therefore offered to help George Fred Williams, who was fighting the takeover of the subway charter. Williams was more than happy to accept the offer of assistance. He asked Brandeis to find out which legislators could be bribed.

Brandeis turned to his client and friend William D. Ellis. He was a member of the Liquor Dealers Association, and Brandeis had heard that the Association had a great deal of contact with the legislature; and, more importantly, Brandeis had heard that they were not above doing a little bribing of their own. When Ellis came to his office, Brandeis pulled out the list of legislators from his roll-top desk. Which of these men can be bought, he asked Ellis. In a calm, deliberate manner, Ellis began checking off names. Brandeis was aghast. "Ellis, do you realize what you are doing?" he asked.[24] Ellis told him it was a necessary way of life, but Brandeis would accept none of that. What kind of example is that to set for your fourteen-year-old son, the young lawyer demanded. And not only that, he continued, but the corruption was not paying off. The legislature was still adopting laws that were intolerable to the Liquor Dealers Association.

Ellis was moved by his attorney's talk. Later he brought in some of his colleagues to hear the sermon. After discussing it among themselves, they came back to Brandeis in the fall of 1890 and asked him to represent them in forthcoming legislative proceedings. The men were especially concerned because the legislature was to consider two important matters: the anti-bar law, which prohibited the sale of a drink except with a meal, and the twenty-five-foot law, which allowed any property owner within twenty-five feet of a proposed saloon to object to its right to sell liquor.

Brandeis accepted the Liquor Dealers as a client on two conditions. First, he wanted it understood that the Association was not to spend any money without his prior approval. Second, he wanted Ellis appointed as chairman of their executive committee. The men agreed, and Brandeis began preparations for the hearing.

For Brandeis, it was not only a question of ending corruption. By this time he had begun to appreciate the importance of the community's controlling its own affairs. To be sure, men had weaknesses and could succumb to temptation. By the same token, one could not assume the worst and strip people of the right to control their lives. Yet that was precisely the posture taken by the legislature with respect to liquor dealers. The legislators had created a licensing board to determine who could or could not become a liquor dealer; and then they removed virtually all discretion in the matter by imposing incredibly stringent rules on the sale of liquor. It was no wonder that the law was openly defied, or that the liquor dealers felt compelled to resort to sordid means of persuasion with legislators. It was time to face up to reality and give the community more power over its own affairs.

On February 27, 1890, Brandeis appeared before the Joint Committee on Liquor Law. He decided to be blunt with the committee. "If the drinking of liquor were a wrong, there would be nothing for you to do, Mr. Chairman, but to report to the Legislature a bill for the prevention by punishment of that wrong, as you punish embezzlement, or crimes of any other nature," Brandeis said; "but the use of liquor is not a wrong. It is the abuse and not the use which is wrong, and, consequently, you must not allow yourself to be carried away by your emotions; you must not be misled by your indignation at the misery which liquor has produced. Remember the weaknesses of men and endeavor to protect them, but do not forget that even the weak are strong enough to resist too severe restrictions." But above all, he added, the legislators had to adapt the law to the realities of human experience. "Take the community in which you live," he advised them; "do not imagine one very different from your own where men will not drink because you say they shall not." Considerable damage had already resulted because the legislators had imposed laws that almost invited defiance and corruption. It seemed inevitable to Brandeis. "You can make politicians of shoemakers or of farmers," he observed; "you can make politicians of any class of people or of those in any occupation if you harass them, if you make it impossible for them to live unless they control, unless they have secured power to determine when, and how, and where they may live. You can remove liquor dealers from politics by a very simple device—*make the liquor laws reasonable.*"[25] The legislators were impressed, and in due course the laws were relaxed to give the liquor dealers some of the control they desired.

Brandeis took a considerable amount of satisfaction in the experience. There was a certain sense of accomplishment and power that flowed from these kinds of public excursions. For that reason he decided to charge the Liquor Dealers only $2,000—far less than what his services would normally cost. It was a step in the direction of a practice he would later adopt of charging nothing for services rendered in public causes.

In the meantime, other matters were demanding his attention. The Massachusetts Institute of Technology wanted Brandeis to teach a course in business law, and he had quickly agreed. He asked William H. Dunbar, an associate in his firm, to collect cases and prepare memos on various subjects. Brandeis decided to use the course as a vehicle to criticize the mass of social legislation that Massachusetts and other states had adopted recently to help the working man and, incidentally, the growing union movement.

It was not that Brandeis opposed the creation of labor unions. In fact, he thought they were a necessary economic force to counterbalance the growing power of industry. He accepted the views of Henry Demarest Lloyd and other writers who argued for some limits on the reach of large corporations. But after all, that did not mean that the government had to tilt the scales so that the unions and their friends would be *more* powerful than industry. In Brandeis's view "the law [already] accorded to the laborer full power to protect himself by means of combination. . . ." Although he viewed this power as "ample," many state legislatures believed otherwise. At least they were willing to yield to the pressures of labor and produce "a mass of legislation more or less crude, designed to improve the condition of the laborer."[26]

One area that especially disturbed the young attorney was legislation that restricted the hours people could work. Fifteen years later Brandeis would gain national recognition for his fight in the United States Supreme Court on behalf of such legislation. But in preparing his MIT lectures, he felt differently—no doubt in part because his circle of friends and clients then were not very sympathetic to the labor movement. If someone wanted to work long hours, Brandeis thought, why should the state command otherwise? "Working long hours in the day," he noted, "would probably be no more injurious to the health than not taking exercise, or than the eating of mince pies by people with weak digestion. . . ." The legislature could certainly step in to protect the public health, but not if it were a question of only private health. Otherwise there would be "no such thing as a guaranty to individual liberty." Brandeis took some comfort, however, in "the belief that the courts will declare such broad legislation void."[27]

Brandeis's views here also reflected his perspective on large corporations. In later years he would become known as a figure who lashed out at "the curse of bigness." He would argue then that most major commercial and industrial developments evolved from the daring of single individuals like Alexander Graham Bell and Samuel Morse and that large corporations were generally oppressive. But now he saw much merit in the large business enterprise. Without corporate combinations, Brandeis observed, "it is difficult to conceive how the great industrial development of the present century would have been possible. The wealth, or at least the courage of single individuals would not have been equal to the task of constructing our railroads, [or] of extending the systems of telegraph over the continent. . . ."[28]

All of these views went through radical revision in the autumn of 1893 after Brandeis read about the strike of steel workers at the Carnegie plant in Homestead, Pennsylvania. In an effort to curb the union, Carnegie had employed Pinkerton guards, who had opened fire on striking workers. Many people were killed, many more injured. Brandeis was shocked. He could not reconcile his course notes with the violence that had erupted at Homestead. He wrote letters to the attorneys in Homestead, trying to determine what legal proceedings had been initiated and whether any new law had developed. But these were legal niceties. In his heart, Brandeis now realized that the social struggle between labor and management was weighted heavily on management's side. "I saw at once," he told a reporter years later, "that the common law, built up under simpler conditions of living, gave an inadequate basis for the adjustment of the complex relations of the modern factory system. I threw away my [MIT] notes and approached my theme from new angles. Those talks at Tech marked an epoch in my own career."[29]

The plight of the striking workers in Homestead, however, was nothing compared to the hell endured by the paupers on Long Island in Boston Harbor. The state-run home for poor people was abominable. The superintendent resided in comfortable quarters, ate porterhouse steaks almost every night, and was waited on by innumerable servants. The paupers within his charge did not fare as well. The food was minimal and watered down; the sanitary facilities were so limited that people urinated in the sinks where puddings were made and dishes were washed; the clothing was ragged and in such short supply that many women stayed in bed all day because they had nothing to put on; there was only one doctor to handle a hospital with 144 beds, and even at that he was often not available; and when people died—as they did with increasing frequency—they were "stored" in a back room until they could be placed in a mass grave.

Alice Lincoln, the philanthropist and social activist, was disturbed by this state of affairs. She wrote a blistering letter to the editor of the *Boston Transcript* and people began to take notice. A visiting board was established, and Alice Lincoln's friend Bess Evans was put on it. But the bureaucratic forces resisted any thorough housecleaning. A good, aggressive lawyer was needed to make things happen. Once again Bess turned to Louis.

After a considerable hassle, the city finally agreed to formal hearings before the Board of Aldermen. They began in 1894 and in nine months covered fifty-seven days of hearings. Brandeis was magnetic—a tenacious and eloquent spokesman for people who had languished without defense. Witness after witness testified to the sordid conditions at the Long Island Home. And at every opportunity Brandeis hammered on the point that these paupers were fellow human beings who needed help—not animals to be discarded. He also made it clear that the city had the opportunity—and the obligation—to make the paupers self-reliant so that they could realize their potential and contribute to the community.

"Men are not bad and men are not degraded because they desire to be so,"

Brandeis told the board. "They are degraded largely through circumstances, and it is the duty of every man—and the main duty of those who are dealing with these unfortunates—to help them up and to let them feel in one way or another that there is some hope for them in life." In this context, he argued, it was particularly important to provide training so that the paupers could get jobs and gain self-respect. It was not, moreover, an issue of concern only to the paupers, Brandeis informed the aldermen, "because what you do to those there is an example to others. It does not merely affect those in the institutions—it affects a great deal more those who are out."[30]

In the end, Brandeis wanted the aldermen to be guided by compassion. "You must remember, and remember every moment of the day," he told them, "that these are human beings, that they have emotions, that they have feelings, that they have interests, and that these emotions, feelings and interests which they have may carry them to the good or may carry them to bad.... and that it is for you, you who have charge of them, to undertake to help them, to point the needle in one direction or the other." And if there should be any doubt of the need for that commitment, Brandeis reminded them of the environment the residents had to endure. "They call this a Home for Paupers," said the young attorney. "Home! With that name is associated every tender memory and feeling that one has, every attention, every kindness, and every little thing that may make one feel a little better, a little kinder towards his fellow men. You pass through those long wards, bed next to bed—everything alike, nothing to enliven, nothing to cheer. If there is any one thing that is depressing in life it is to go through that institution. Every one of you must have felt it," Brandeis suggested to the committee. "Did you think for a moment when you were down there that that place is called by the city of Boston a 'home'?"[31]

It was a powerful performance, and it created a bond between Louis Brandeis and Alice Lincoln that would last many years. She would remember his help, and she would call on him periodically when things started to slip again. Even in later years, when pressed by matters of national importance, he would still be responsive to her, because for Brandeis those hearings on the Long Island matter were an especially moving experience. And it gave him an opportunity to implement his practice of providing public work for free. Of the $3,000 in fees that Mrs. Lincoln gave him in 1894, he gave some to his partners at the firm and the rest to charities.

This work in the public sector was beginning to have a dramatic impact on Brandeis's law practice. He was spending less and less of his time practicing law and more and more of his time testifying at legislative hearings or performing some other public work. In 1897 he even arranged to testify before a congressional committee on a bill proposing an increase in tariffs. Although he was supposed to appear on behalf of the New England Free Trade League, Brandeis felt that he was also representing the general consuming public. It was an attitude that would cause him problems in later years. Most lawyers and legislators did not understand how an attorney could claim to represent a specific client and simultaneously represent the general public. Aside from the unusual nature of the representation, it contained the seeds of conflict. For the interests of the specific client could and probably would be inconsistent with at least some of the interests of the public (assuming, of course, that one really knew what the "interests" of the public—as opposed to those of private parties—were).

None of these questions troubled Brandeis when he appeared before the Ways and Means Committee of the House of Representatives on January 11, 1897. He was there because he felt that higher tariffs would not only discourage competition; they would also undercut the individual initiative that Louis was beginning to regard as indispensable to progress and to a healthy community. "I desire to speak," he told the committee, "on behalf of those who form, I believe, a far larger part of the people of the United States than any who have found representation here. I appear for those who want to be left alone, those who do not come to Congress and seek the aid of the sovereign powers of the government to bring them prosperity." One congressman pointedly asked Brandeis whom he represented. There was jeering and laughter in the committee room when Brandeis identified his clients as The Free Trade League and "the business men and laboring men and the consumers. . . ." Such notions of representation seemed ludicrous on their face. But the "public" lawyer stuck to his guns, and later some newspapers gave him credit at least for courage. Brandeis himself remained disturbed by the notion that industrialists needed a protective tariff. "This asking for help from the government for everything should be deprecated," he told the Free Trade League afterwards. "It destroys the old and worthy, sturdy principle of American life which existed in the beginning when men succeeded by their own efforts."[32] The curse of bigness was beginning to evolve.

FOUR

The Private Life

Public business ought to be conducted in private because what we do here isn't important enough to be made public, and private business should be made public because if it were kept private the public wouldn't know about it.

WHITE RABBIT TO ALICE

Brandeis loved the outdoors. He especially liked camping. And he was pretty good at it, too. He could handle an axe like a regular Paul Bunyan. He was also extremely good with canoes. His balance was almost perfect. It was so good that one time, it was said, he fell out the back of a canoe and his partner in the front did not even realize it. Brandeis could also sail, although he felt more comfortable with a canoe. In fact, people on Cape Cod—where Brandeis spent many summer vacations—remembered that, if it got very windy, he would put away the sailboat and take out his canoe.

But Louis did enjoy sailing with his millionaire friend Herbert White. Herb was a friendly sort who moved in and out of various positions in publishing and other businesses. He was not at all involved in politics or civic reform, but he was great company. He and Louis spent many weekends and vacations sailing and trout fishing. As much as he liked that, the Boston lawyer could not always take his mind off the public work back home. One night Louis and Herb were sitting around a campfire in Maine after a good day of fishing. "I wanted to plan for tomorrow," Herb recalled. "But he started off on the damnedest belly ache you ever heard. The tie-up between government and money; the way banks used other people's money against their interest; the way big corporations skinned the public and pushed the laboring man around; insurance companies fought savings bank insurance, and railroad management didn't know its own business or interest. On and on it went. Finally," Herb remembered, "I'd had enough. 'Louis Brandeis,' I said, 'you've had the best day ever on the river, a wonderful dinner, and your pants are dry. What the hell's the matter with you?' "[1]

That was all after Brandeis was married and had become a national figure. In the early days, when he was just a young Boston lawyer, Brandeis took most of his vacations with his family. On a big holiday like Thanksgiving or Christmas, and often during the summer, he would travel back to Louisville, where he would spend hours talking with his mother, riding horseback with his father, or taking walks with his brother, Al. He would also take time to visit with his sisters, Fanny and Amy, who were not far away. And on other occasions his parents would go to Boston or meet him at Newport, Rhode Island, and spend a few weeks with him.

Almost always these were times of smiles and warmth and good feelings. "Your visit, dear Louis, was like a flaming meteor's flight," his mother wrote after one stay in Louisville. "You brought me joy and happiness and before I could really believe that you were with me, you disappeared again."[2]

Then tragedy struck. It was Brandeis's sister Fanny. She was extremely bright, but she was also very sensitive and prone to depression. In 1888 her infant son, Alfred, died of typhoid fever. The family was afraid how she would react and did not tell her—a concealment that was possible since Fanny herself was sick at the time. When she finally learned of Alfred's death, Fanny took it extremely hard. For a while she refused to eat anything. The family was naturally happy when Fanny gave birth within a year or so to a new baby, a girl named Hildegard. Perhaps now Fanny would find contentment. But it was not to be. Fanny fell into a deep postpartum depression, and in March 1890 she killed herself.[3]

Brandeis rushed home to Louisville. There were, however, some definite silver linings in this cloud. For he ran into his second cousin, Alice Goldmark, who was visiting relatives in Louisville. Alice was a very attractive woman of twenty-four with long dark hair pulled back, beautiful eyes, and a slim build. Louis was captivated almost at once. The relationship quickened the following summer when their two families took vacations together in the Adirondacks in New York. By September they were engaged.

Louis was ecstatic. Alice was the embodiment of his dreams. "I thought, Alice," he wrote a few weeks after they became engaged, "how much you will love the canoe—and how well it expresses you; the silent dignity, strong but tender, sensitive to the slightest touch, responsive to every mood." Sam and Bess shared their friend's excitement over the forthcoming marriage. Sam wrote Alice to congratulate her and to wax eloquent on his friend's virtues. "What you do not know about him," he wrote of Louis, "you may trust to the future to develop with absolute confidence in the joy it will bring you. . . . I know that his courage is high, his fidelity perfect, and his sense of honor delicate. For weapons he has an acute and highly trained intellect, and for motive power a high enthusiasm for the right." Bess was equally happy for Louis and Alice. She took note of their passion for each other and was especially pleased that Louis had decided to buy a small row house at 114 Mt. Vernon Street on Beacon Hill, which was near her home on Back Bay.[4]

The wedding was set for the following March. Until then Alice was to stay with her family on Park Avenue in New York City while Louis remained in Boston. Almost every weekend he would travel down to New York to visit his fiancée. Even with that, the separations were agonizing to the young lovers. "Louis," Alice wrote one weekday in December 1890, "Saturday seems very long in coming—I do wish you were here to-night, for I want you very much." Louis was equally frustrated by the long absences. "I long for the time when you will be with me always," he wrote Alice at one point. "You have become so large a part of my life that I rattle about sorely when you are absent. Is it not strange?" he asked. "For seventeen years I have stood alone—rarely asking—still less frequently caring, for the advice of others. I have walked my way all these years but little influenced by any other individual. And now, Alice, all is changed. I find myself mentally turning to you for advice and approval—indeed, also for support, and I feel my incompleteness more each day. I feel myself each day growing more into your soul, and I am very happy." He became even more anxious as the wedding day approached. "Occasionally I am oppressed by the multitudinousness of things, and I sigh for the rest and peace which can only come in the thought of your continuous presence," he wrote eight days before the wedding. "If the twenty-third were not fixed immutably, I should feel like anticipating it, and like the Barons of old, break away and carry you off."[5]

In the meantime Louis wanted Alice to "exercise the prerogative of a partner" to help him set up the house. He had made the decision to buy the home on Mt. Vernon Street, and he began to feel a little out of his element in trying to fix it up. He got estimates for household furnishings, checked the wallpaper for arsenic (which was then often used in the manufacture of wallpaper), and trained a horse to pull the new buggy he had purchased. Some things were beyond his control, however. "Alice," Louis wrote in January, "we shall not be able to escape one of those tall clocks. That client-bringing client of mine, Mr. Ellis, insists upon presenting us one—of fabulous cost and wants me to select the kind of wood. I settled for him yesterday a much litigated case—which had cost him much money—and I refused to receive any more pay. So this is his revenge."[6]

Louis and Alice were married in a civil ceremony by Alice's brother-in-law, Felix Adler, on March 23, 1891, in Alice's apartment. It was a small gathering of just the family. Immediately afterwards the couple went off to a resort in Massachusetts for a honeymoon. For a woman raised in the "purity" of the Victorian Age, Alice found the intimacy with Louis overwhelming. After a few days she wrote to Bess Evans, with whom she had grown close in the preceding months. "I never dreamed that such happiness was possible as has been mine in these days," Alice confessed. "I cannot speak of it even to you—it is so sacred—but you understand, I know."[7] Bess, in the meantime, was given the key to the home on Mt. Vernon Street and was unpacking Alice's things so that life would be that much less hectic when she returned from her honeymoon.

Alice and Louis agreed to live simply. From his earliest student days Brandeis had learned to live on little money. And while finances were no longer a problem, he remained convinced that material possessions were more trouble than they were worth. The more things you had, the more responsibilities you had. Something was always going wrong, and it took time and energy to straighten things out—time and energy that could be spent on more fruitful endeavors. In fact, this thinking in part led them to sell their house by the end of the decade and move into a rented house at 6 Otis Place, right down the street from Bess.

In the view of Alice and Louis, money was really good for only one thing. It gave you freedom. Almost from the beginning Brandeis was ready to start building his financial security. When he graduated from law school he bought a railroad bond with some extra cash he had. It was part of his philosophy—one he followed all through life—of reducing consumption and saving for the future. Money was a necessary evil, but the ultimate reward—especially if one were patient—was worth it.

Louis and Alice were not only thinking of themselves, however; they wanted to have children. The problem was Alice's health. She was very frail, and she tired easily. The doctors could do nothing except prescribe rest. Long vacation trips had to be canceled because they were too tiring, and Louis and Alice had to content themselves with more limited excursions. They could accept all that. The real concern was whether Alice could have children. In the middle of 1892, Alice became pregnant, and both she and Louis were joyous. Alice was suffering from headaches, and she could do little more than take ten-minute walks around the block. But friends visited her, and she was sustained by the hope that the childbirth would go smoothly.

On February 27, 1893, Susan Brandeis entered the world. Within a week, Louis wrote about the event to Bess, who was then abroad. With tongue in cheek, he explained to Bess that "Susan is pronounced a very fine child. She is certainly exemplary in her behavior." As for Alice, she "caused us some alarm the first day but has improved so steadily since, that we may well hope for much better health than she has had in the past years." Louis added, however, that "Alice has been lovelier than before. There has been much of the time a calm madonna-like serenity and strength which seemed to lift her above things worldly." Although Alice continued to be troubled by headaches and indigestion, she still had the energy to nurse the baby—a fact that gave her immense pleasure. "I never dreamed I should be able to," she wrote to Bess.[8]

Three years later—on April 25, 1896—Alice gave birth to a second girl, and this one, Alice and Louis decided, should be named after their intimate friend Bess. She was touched by the compliment, and always after that Bess referred to Elizabeth Brandeis as her "twin."

Although from the same heritage, Elizabeth was very different from her real sister. Susan was bright and extroverted, even aggressive at times. Elizabeth was extremely quiet and shy, although possessed of an equally keen intelligence. The slightest suggestion of a reproach from her parents was enough to evoke tears. But both daughters had at least one thing in common—love for their parents.

Mornings would begin with a breakfast with Father, or "Papsy," as he was called in those early years. Brandeis would generally get up around 5:30, do some work, and sit down for breakfast around 7:15. He would almost always have oatmeal, hot chocolate or coffee, and some kind of meat—a pork chop or steak or something similar. The girls would have shredded wheat. Because she continually suffered from headaches, Alice needed her rest and almost always had breakfast in bed—a service made possible since there were generally three servants in the house. At breakfast the girls would read aloud to their father or just chatter away about their busy lives. After breakfast Susan would walk her father across the Boston Common to his office or, if they were staying at their summer house in Dedham, she would go with him to the train station. Later, after Susan became older, it was Elizabeth who accompanied Father to the train or across the Common.[9]

Brandeis generally got to work between 8:00 and 8:30. He took care of clients and other matters, ate lunch at one of the many clubs in downtown Boston, and left work promptly at 5 P.M. He would then go back to the house, change his clothes, and, depending on the weather and his mood, go horseback riding, play tennis, or take out a canoe. But even while he was getting ready for his daily exercise, Brandeis would keep the girls amused. Usually he would tell them a chapter in a story like Robert Louis Stevenson's *Kidnapped* or Charles Dickens's *Great Expectations.* The girls would listen with great intensity and anxiously await the next "installment."[10]

Dinners were also fun for the girls. Louis would almost always wear a jacket and tie, and Alice dressed accordingly. The food usually consisted of vegetables and meats—veal or roast beef, or some kind of fowl, or even fish. They also might have ale or sherry with dinner. Desserts were a favorite, though. Both Louis and Alice had a sweet tooth. He loved ice cream and had it regularly. For her part, Alice enjoyed imported chocolates and candied fruits that she got regularly from S.S. Pierce.[11]

There were often guests for dinner—usually people involved in one of Brandeis's many public activities. But regardless of who attended, you could expect animated conversation about history, public affairs, and even local gossip. There would also be humor. Like almost anyone, Brandeis enjoyed a good joke—although he himself was not very good at telling them. He could never hold his laughter until after he delivered the punch line. Everyone in the family recognized his deficiencies on that score. "I can still hear him chortling far too soon," his niece Jean Tachau recalled, "and one often missed the point [of the story as a result]."[12]

Despite his shortcomings as a story teller, Brandeis was then, as he always would be, a superb host. He had a great deal of charm and a natural ability for getting people to talk about themselves. He would lower his head a little, and with his penetrating blue-gray eyes, look directly at his guest and ask some pointed question about his guest's interests or activities. Few could resist the open invitation to discuss some matter of concern to themselves. Years later, when he was a Supreme Court justice, people took note of Brandeis's uncanny talent to make his guests feel comfortable. "You could be doing some esoteric study on aborigines in Australia," one law clerk later observed, "and he would make you think it was the most important thing to him too."[13]

If there were no guests for dinner, Louis would lie down afterwards and Alice would read to him. That was a pastime they both enjoyed from the beginning—reading aloud to each other. And the selection of books would vary widely—from art to history to public affairs. Louis would in due course fall asleep from Alice's reading. After a short nap, he would get up, read the *Boston Evening Transcript,* the leading evening paper in the city, and go to bed about 10 o'clock.[14]

Vacations were also important to Brandeis. It was not only a question of enjoyment. He was concerned about overtaxing his strength. Daily exercise had helped a great deal, but he was never in robust health. Sickness was not an uncommon occurrence for him. He similarly felt that his work would suffer if he did not take regular vacations. He once watched a fellow attorney make a drastic mistake because of fatigue, and he vowed to himself that he would never run that risk. In 1893 he explained his philosophy to William Dunbar, then an associate attorney in his firm. "A bookkeeper can work eight or ten hours a day, and perhaps twelve—year in–year out—and possibly his work may be always good (tho' I doubt it)," Brandeis observed. "But a man who practices law—who aspires to the higher places of his profession—must keep his mind fresh. It must be alert and he must be capable of meeting emergencies—must be capable of the tour de force. This is not possible to one who works alone—not only during the day but much of the night—without change, without turning the mind into new channels, with the mind always at the same tension. The bow must be strung and unstrung," he explained; "work must be measured not merely by time but also by its intensity; there must be time also for the unconscious thinking which comes to the busy man in his play. . . ."[15]

Brandeis tried to follow his own advice. "I soon learned," he later said, "that I could do twelve months' work in eleven months, but not in twelve."[16] Consequently, he usually took the whole month of August off from work. Until his father died in 1906 he and the family would spend a good part of the vacation in Louisville. After that he would take the family to New Hampshire or Cape Cod. But he did not wait for August to change scenery. Soon after he and Alice were married he began renting a house for the summer in Dedham, which was located southwest of Boston. Before long he purchased a large two-story colonial on Village Avenue in Dedham. It was against his grain to have to buy the house. But he and the family liked it, and the owner threatened to sell it to someone else who would probably not rent it out. It was too much of a risk, so they took the plunge.

It proved to be a wise move. In the summers the whole family would stay there and Brandeis would commute to Boston by train. He liked Dedham. He had been going out there with Sam even when he was a young bachelor. He and Sam, in fact, were charter members of the Dedham Polo Club. And although Brandeis did not play polo, he used the club frequently to go horseback riding, a sport at which he ultimately developed considerable skill. When he became a permanent member of the Dedham community, he also joined the prestigious Norfolk Country Club. He did not make much use of the club, however, primarily because of his other activities and because Alice's frail health restricted her social life.[17]

The family also used the Dedham house in the winter. In the early days the whole family would drive out to the house in a wagon on late Saturday afternoons after Brandeis came home from work. As the children grew older, they would go out to the house on Saturday mornings with Sadie Nicholson or one of the other servants, and Alice and Louis would meet them in the afternoon. Saturday nights would be spent entertaining guests or dining alone. Sundays would be reserved for the family, with skating or boating or some other activity.

Despite the many attractions of home life, Brandeis spent a good deal of time away from his family. In part, it was because business required him to travel a fair amount. On other occasions he could not leave the city when Alice felt it necessary to visit her mother and relatives in New York City. But whatever the reason, the two of them would exchange letters almost every day, reporting on the day's events and expressing the deep feelings they felt toward each other. "Dear heart," Alice wrote one day in 1896 when Brandeis was in Wisconsin on a case, "take good care of yourself & take a great, great deal of love from Alice." When the children got older, Brandeis also made sure to write to them as well. He did not bore them with the law, however. They had other things on their mind. "How do you like New York," Brandeis wrote to seven-year-old Elizabeth from Boston one Christmas. "And how does your doll like to be with Grandma and all the Aunts and Uncles? I hope she has not cried much. The Christmas tree and Santa Claus are very anxious to see you and Susan again and want to know whether they shall wait until you come back from New York. Santa Claus would like to come down from the tree and rest in Susan's bed. Do you think I should let him?"[18]

All in all, then, it was a good time, a time when the family felt close and free of the social pressures that would later arise when Brandeis challenged powerful establishment interests. It was also a time when Brandeis could enjoy the economic independence he craved so much. It had not been achieved without some struggle, though. Indeed, there had been some bumps in the road to success.

For a long time things had been moving smoothly in the law firm. Sam's predictions of prosperity had been realized. The firm's reputation was secure, and there was no lack of clients. And then Sam's father died. Sam, being the oldest child, felt compelled to take over the family paper business. No one else seemed capable of handling it. It was, a friend later recalled, "a great sacrifice, for he loved and was peculiarly fitted for law." Sam hoped the departure from the firm would be only temporary. He and Louis therefore agreed that the name of the firm would remain unchanged and that there would always be an office available for Sam when he eventually returned. It proved to be a false hope.[19]

In the meantime, Brandeis took charge of the growing practice. In 1889 he made his first argument before the United States Supreme Court—an opportunity that came about only because the attorney who was supposed to argue did not make it to Washington in time and, as the junior counsel on the case, Brandeis was the logical substitute. It was symbolic of the rapid growth the firm was experiencing. New lawyers—all top graduates from Harvard Law School—were being hired to help carry the load. Soon the cramped offices at 60 Devonshire Street were overflowing with people and files. It was time to move. Louis and Sam agreed to relocate the firm in a larger suite on Devonshire Street—the location of the Warren paper business offices—so that Louis could "see something of Sam." The offices were sparsely furnished and the heat was kept low in the winter—devices, it was said, to make sure that clients did not loiter around any longer than they had to and waste the attorneys' time. Brandeis wanted to take advantage of technical progress, however, and the firm became one of the first in Boston to have a telephone.[20]

Brandeis's practice by this time was quite varied. He handled complex litigation of all sorts—much of it involving the kinds of balance sheets and financial transactions that he would later encounter when fighting the large insurance companies or J.P. Morgan's railroads.[21] Although he was not known as the most eloquent of advocates, Brandeis's skill as a trial lawyer was regarded highly by attorneys inside and outside the office. He immersed himself in the record and usually knew more about the problem at hand than the client. And he could be tenacious in defense of his clients' interests, pushing witnesses to the extreme and making sure the record was as complete as it could be. He could also handle jury cases with ease, and once he confessed to his sister Amy that he was "becoming quite enamored of the common sense of the people—and somewhat doubtful of the uncommon sense of the judges."[22]

Despite his considerable talents in the courtroom, Brandeis did everything he could to keep his clients away from litigation. He had always been impressed with the way Sam's father developed his paper business. He tried to accommodate people, did not take advantage of their weaknesses, and believed in conciliation rather than conflict in settling disputes. It seemed like a good approach to the law business as well. By the end of the nineteenth century, lawyers were becoming more and more involved in the planning of business and commercial enterprise. Brandeis enjoyed that role, and he also took pride in advising his clients to be fair with their competitors and customers, even when such tactics might be more costly in the short run. Brandeis tended to think that he had an obligation to be fair to all sides, a responsibility that transcended his duty to his client. It was a perspective that would cause him trouble during the fight over his Supreme Court nomination. But years later, when Brandeis was nearing the end of his career on the Court, Edward Filene, one of his friends and early clients, paid tribute to Louis's philosophy of law practice. "I recall . . . how mystified I was at first at a great lawyer's efforts to keep his clients out of court," Filene wrote. " 'Agree with thine adversary quickly' was of course a familiar doctrine, but I did not know it was such good, efficient legal practice; and when it seemed to me that you were making unnecessary concessions to your opponents, I could not comprehend the strategy. But you taught me the wisdom of conciliation," Filene admitted; "and if I haven't been a pupil to be proud of, I have at least done much better than would ever have been possible without your demonstrations."[23]

Brandeis followed his own advice when billing clients. He was extremely careful not to overcharge, and if a client suggested that the bill was too high, he told the client to pay whatever he thought was fair. Brandeis's reputation was so good, however, that clients felt satisfied just knowing he had reviewed and approved the bill before it was sent out.[24]

As the firm grew and as Brandeis became more active in public affairs, the dynamics of the firm began to shift. He trained the young associates and as soon as he felt they were sufficiently experienced, gave them major responsibility for the cases. He was always there to give advice to the attorney or to appear in court if the client thought it necessary to have the senior attorney present. But otherwise Brandeis felt content to let the younger attorneys handle things. After all, that was how he developed his own legal skills.

Although he relied on the younger attorneys to do the work that he brought into the firm, Brandeis was also anxious to have them acquire their own clients and achieve a sense of independence for themselves. He encouraged the younger attorneys in this way not only because it was good for the firm; he was also genuinely interested in the associates' development as lawyers. This concern was particularly evident in the case of William Dunbar, who had joined the firm in 1888. Dunbar had had a distinguished academic career, graduating near the top of his class at Harvard and then clerking for Horace Gray, who was then an associate justice on the United States Supreme Court. Despite all these academic achievements, Dunbar's advancement in the firm was slow. He was very shy, almost retiring, a manner that probably resulted in part from the fact that he had difficulty hearing. Dunbar himself was aware of his slow advancement. He knew, for example, that the gregarious George Nutter, a Harvard graduate three years behind him, was Brandeis's "first lieutenant" in the firm—a position that Dunbar should have held, at least in terms of seniority.[25]

Dunbar poured out his frustrations in a letter to Brandeis, who was then in Washington. The senior attorney understood at once and wrote back immediately, offering his young associate some advice as to how he could improve his situation. "Cultivate the society of men," Brandeis advised, "particularly men of affairs. This is essential to your professional success. Pursue that study as heretofore you have devoted yourself to books. Lose no opportunity of becoming acquainted with men, of learning to feel their personal and business habits. . . ." In Brandeis's eyes this acquaintance with influential people was essential because law practice involved far more than an understanding of legal principles. "You are prone in legal investigation," Brandeis told his associate, "to be controlled by logic and to underestimate the logic of facts. Knowledge of the decided cases and of the rules of logic cannot alone make a great lawyer. He must know, must feel 'in his bones' the facts to which they apply—must know, too, that if they do not stand the test of such application the logical result will somehow or other be avoided." This was especially important because of the changing role of the lawyer in industrial America. "The duty of the lawyer today," he explained, "is not that of a solver of legal conundrums; he is indeed a counsellor at law. Knowledge of the law is of course essential to his efficiency, but the law bears to his profession a relation very similar to that which medicine does to that of the physicians. . . . It requires but a mediocre physician to administer the proper drug for the patient who correctly and fully describes his ailment. The great physicians are those who in addition to that knowledge . . . know not merely the human body but the human mind and emotions, so as to make themselves the proper diagnosis—to know the truth which their patients fail to disclose and who add to this an influence over the patient which is apt to spring from a real understanding of him."

The key to ultimate success, however, was responsibility. The good lawyer had to know his client's affairs and be prepared to perform the necessary tasks—and all this had to be done with a certain amount of independence. It was on this last point that Brandeis thought Dunbar particularly weak. "You are prone to defer to others," he wrote, "or rather to ask the advice of others in the office for the solution of trifling matters which you ought to decide yourself and which if you were knocked about a little among men you would readily so decide—in the office this is a matter of internal economy and it is very expensive; but as to clients the willingness to assume responsibility and the ability to carry out responsibility so assumed is indispensable. Clients want support—if they did not they would rarely be clients." In this context, it was equally important that Dunbar make an effort to get his own clients instead of relying on those brought in by others. "You have, I think, been led to underestimate the importance of having clients of your own," Dunbar was told. "The fact that plenty of work has always been supplied to you has no doubt let you imagine that you need give yourself no concern about getting personal clients. If so, you have overlooked the important educating influence of clients. If you had more clients of your own, you would be led to feel their dependence on you—the necessity of your help and with it would come willingness to assume responsibility, ability to carry responsibility and that confidence in your own powers which begets confidence in others."[26]

Dunbar wrote back to Brandeis quickly to let him know that he was very grateful for the advice and the sentiments that lay behind them. He said he was "fully and painfully aware" of his shortcomings, but that every effort would be made to act on the senior attorney's suggestions.[27]

It was this kind of interchange that created a strong bond between Brandeis and the younger attorneys. They respected his legal skills and admired greatly his ability to handle people, especially in delicate situations. But none of the junior attorneys was on intimate terms with Brandeis. As was the custom in those days, the men (there were no women attorneys in the office) called one another by their last names. Only the closest of friends called each other by their first names. Edward McClennen, for example, worked with Brandeis for more than twenty years before he began addressing him as "Louis"—and that was only because of the intimacy they shared in fighting to get the Senate to confirm Brandeis's nomination to the Supreme Court. Brandeis, in turn, began calling McClennan "Ned" during that Court fight. Aside from unusual situations like the Court fight, Brandeis was a little more formal with his associates, calling them by their last names and signing his notes and letters to them "LDB."

The attorneys were prepared to accept social customs concerning names. After a while, however, they were not prepared to accept the way the firm was organized. By the mid-1890s it became apparent that Sam Warren was not going to return to the firm. And some of the associates decided that the working arrangement was no longer satisfactory. Although they had gladly toiled under Brandeis's tutelage for years, and although Brandeis was quick to give responsibility when the young attorneys were capable of handling it, the firm was still Brandeis's. It was his name and his reputation alone that sustained it. That was frustrating to the younger attorneys. They wanted the stature and responsibility that would come by being partners instead of associates.

Ironically, it was Dunbar who first informed Brandeis of these frustrations among the younger attorneys. In a letter dated August 17, 1896, Dunbar advised Brandeis that he, George Nutter, and Ezra Thayer had decided to leave the firm. "I suppose that every professional man of ordinary ambition hopes to make for himself some reputation, to have his work, if in any degree successful, count not only as a source of income but as giving his name some individual value," Dunbar explained. "This result it seems to me he can reach only by having his name known and by working as a principal. Our present arrangement I think does not permit of this. My work yields to me almost literally no return except a pecuniary compensation. . . . The results seem to me the necessary consequence of an organization like ours in which there is not in fact any real partnership between the different persons associated together."[28]

Brandeis, of course, wanted his associates to assume responsibility, but not *that* much responsibility. He simply was not yet prepared to make his associates partners. He therefore wrote a letter to Dunbar in response that explained the virtues of a large law firm like his but avoided the thrust of Dunbar's concern. In a large law firm, Brandeis said, every man could find and develop the work most suited to his individual personality and talents. Such firms were also likely to enjoy great financial success—a fact evidenced by the prosperity of the large Wall Street firms in New York. There was a certain irony in this observation. For Brandeis believed that an individual had to control his environment in order to realize his potential and that such control was unlikely to be found in large organizations. He himself had formed a partnership with Sam Warren to achieve independence. Nonetheless, Brandeis told Dunbar that he would do better to stick with his firm than to be "standing alone."[29]

Dunbar was not convinced. He made it clear again that he and the others were still prepared to leave if there were no change in the working arrangement. Brandeis finally succumbed to pressure, and, in a letter to Dunbar dated November 2, 1896, confirmed that, as of January 1, 1897, the name of the firm would be changed to Brandeis, Dunbar & Nutter. Thayer and D. Blakeley Hoar would also become partners. Instead of getting fixed salaries, they would each take a share in the firm's profits. Together the four new partners would split (in varying percentages according to seniority) one third of the firm's profits; Brandeis would keep the rest. Later, when the firm got much larger, Brandeis alone decided how much each partner would get by using a personal formula. And although there were no complaints about the division of partnership profits, no one knew how Brandeis calculated each partner's share. Even after he left the firm to join the Supreme Court, Brandeis's profit-sharing formula remained a mystery to his partners.[30]

The new arrangement did not change matters all that much. The firm was still known as Brandeis's. But at least the introduction of additional partners made his colleagues more secure. And it also facilitated the respect and even affection that the attorneys felt for Brandeis. But few people in the firm were as devoted—or as important—to him as his two secretaries, Alice Grady and E. Louise Malloch.

Alice Grady was a large woman with a driving personality. She was smart, and she had ambition as well. She was born in Toronto and moved with her family to Melrose, Massachusetts, when she was ten. In 1894, at the age of twenty-one, she joined the firm of Warren & Brandeis as a stenographer. Her advancement was rapid, and not without good reason. She knew how to make herself needed. She bought her own typewriter and made it clear that she was prepared to accept any assignment, no matter what the hours or pressures. It was not unusual for her to work as many as sixteen hours a day, racing around town to take dictation or transcribe a proceeding. Brandeis came to depend on her and confide in her. As a result, she eventually felt free to make suggestions to him concerning his speaking schedule or even matters relating to legal work.[31] In later years, when travel kept him away from Boston for weeks at a time, Brandeis expected her to handle routine correspondence on her own, arrange for the publication of articles and books of his, and perform other substantive tasks that he could not do himself.

There was a personal side to the relationship as well. Brandeis came to genuinely like and respect Alice Grady. She was one of the very few office workers who would be invited to the Brandeis home for dinner. Alice Brandeis liked her, and so did the children. In some respects she became like a member of the family. No doubt this helped explain why she was given the responsibility for supervising almost all of the family's financial accounts; the only major exception was Brandeis's investment portfolio, which was handled by Louise Malloch. It was Alice Grady, though, who made sure that the bills were paid and the accounts kept current. If Alice Brandeis needed her monthly allowance of $250 early, or if she needed more money than that, she would write a postcard to Grady or, on other occasions, telephone her to make the request. Grady would also assist on other family chores. If the plumbing in the Cape Cod vacation home went haywire, Susan Brandeis might call her father, but he would almost immediately turn the matter over to his secretary. If arrangements had to be made to paint the house or fix the carriage, she would handle those tasks as well.

Brandeis was not one to wear his heart on his sleeve. But when the occasion arose he would let Grady know of his feelings for her. When her mother became seriously ill one Christmas, for example, Brandeis took time from a very hectic schedule to write a note expressing his deep concern. Grady was moved by the gesture. "As you know," she wrote to him, "words are poor tools on the tongue of an awkward user of them like myself. But there are some things that demand to be said even though they have to wriggle out at the end of a pen. I was deeply touched that you should have been taking thought for me when you were pressed on all sides by important and troublesome matters claiming your time and attention. This new evidence of your kind appreciation was the best of all the gifts that Santa Claus brought me."[32]

Although no other secretary could match Alice Grady's stature in the office, Louise Malloch ran a close second. She came to Warren & Brandeis as a young girl shortly after Grady arrived. Her skills and diligence were so impressive, and the demands of Brandeis were so great, that soon she became his assistant secretary and the trusted custodian of his ever-expanding investments.

The investments generally consisted of mortgages and bonds. Brandeis did not think it wise to invest in common stocks. They were too dependent on the vagaries of the economy and required more time and attention than he was prepared to devote to financial matters. He was, however, willing to loan money to friends and acquaintances so that they could purchase homes; even some of the young attorneys in the office borrowed money from him for that purpose. In other cases Brandeis simply took a mortgage as a straight investment or in the settlement of a case he was handling. By the time he took his place on the Court in 1916, he held dozens of mortgages. Malloch often visited a home before the loan was made and offered an assessment as to whether it was worthwhile. She also kept track of the payment schedules and advised Brandeis when refinancing might be prudent.

It was in the bond market that Louise Malloch's special skills became clearly evident. She studied the figures, traced developments, and kept current on impending changes in the field. Brandeis did not make a move without consulting her. In fact, he generally followed her recommendations. None of this was taken lightly. Brandeis's bond investments were essential to his philosophy that a man should invest conservatively and try to make large profits from his business.[33] And he would never be too busy to discuss bond questions with Malloch. It did not matter if he was in Washington advising the president and Congress on antitrust legislation or prosecuting complicated cases before the Interstate Commerce Commission; even then he would take time to exchange postcards and telegrams with Malloch on a regular basis to discuss bond sales and purchases. Perhaps the highest compliment came when Brandeis was a Supreme Court justice and recommended that his brother consult with Malloch about the bond market.

All these investments provided Brandeis with a growing net worth that was approaching a million dollars by the turn of the century. At bottom, however, his ability to makc all these investments flowed from the considerable sums he was making in the practice of law. In 1897, for instance, his share of the partnership profits amounted to almost $40,000.[34] The magnitude of this sum can be appreciated when it is remembered that the average lawyer at the time was making less than $5,000, and a nice three-story home on Back Bay (where Brandeis began living in 1899) could be rented for $100 a month.

None of this left Brandeis entirely satisfied, however. Material comforts were not an end in themselves to him; they were but a means to becoming independent to do other things. And foremost among those "other" things was service to the public. "Some men buy diamonds and rare works of art," he later told an interviewer; "others delight in automobiles and yachts. My luxury is to invest my surplus effort, beyond that required for the proper support of my family, to the pleasure of taking up a problem and solving, or helping to solve, it for the people without receiving any compensation." The notion that he performed this service for free—without obligation—was of immense importance to him. "Your yachtsman or automobilist would lose much of his enjoyment if he were obliged to do for pay what he is doing for the love of the thing itself," he explained. "So I should lose much of my satisfaction if I were paid in connection with public services of this kind. I have only one life, and it is short enough. Why waste it on things I don't want most? I don't want money or property most. I want to be free." For Brandeis, then, "the great happiness in life [was] not to donate but to serve." To fulfill this goal ultimately required that he not only restrict his own practice; it also meant that some clients had to be turned away because he could not personlly serve them. Years later, when Brandeis had all but given up the commercial practice of law in favor of public activities, Edward Filene suggested to him that he reorganize his firm so that he would not have to turn away so many paying clients. But Brandeis would have none of that. "Don't you think there is such a thing as having too much business?" he responded. "Don't you think there is such a thing as having so much business that a man would no longer be free, that a man might tie himself up against his best possibilities by being too engrossed in his profession or business?"[35]

Filene understood his friend's perspective. In fact, Filene not only shared much of Brandeis's view of work and public service; Filene was also instrumental in getting Brandeis involved in the first major public controversy of his career.

FIVE

The Transit Fights and Their Aftermath

All law is a dead letter without public opinion behind it. But law and public opinion interact—and they are both capable of being made. Most of the world is in more or less a hypnotic state—and it is comparatively easy to make people believe anything, particularly the right.

LOUIS D. BRANDEIS TO ALICE GOLDMARK, DECEMBER, 28, 1890

There is generally not much social significance attached to rags, but for Brandeis they became a vehicle to learn about the dangers of monopoly. It all happened because the firm of Warren & Brandeis represented the Warren family business and other paper manufacturers in the 1880s. The rags were needed for their production process, and, because of the great volume involved, tons of them were imported from abroad. Not surprisingly, Boston had a health law which required that all imported rags be disinfected. There was no problem with that. But the paper companies wanted to have the rags disinfected right before they were shipped from the foreign port. The reason was simple. The foreign disinfectant process was cheaper than the domestic variety. But the Boston City Council was not impressed. Even if the rags were disinfected before they were shipped, they had to be processed again by the Boston Disinfecting Company—the only firm licensed for such work in the city. Brandeis tried to get the city council to change the ordinance so that the cheaper foreign disinfectant would be accepted. He soon found, however, that logic would not carry the day. The Boston Disinfectant Company was a local monopoly that had a *very* close relationship with the council members. And it did not take much to "persuade" the council that Brandeis's position had no merit.

For Brandeis it was a real eye-opener. He was only about thirty when he experienced this defeat, and it made him realize that there was more to law practice than books and briefs. Monopoly power—even when exercised in support of a good cause like public health—could involve fraud and waste. But monopolies were not invincible. Brandeis recognized that there was a higher authority: public opinion. The pressure of popular sentiment could almost always turn things around. As he explained to his brother during the rag fight, "It is only ignorance and dark dealing that we must fear."[1]

Edward Filene should not have been surprised, then, when Brandeis later agreed to help him fight what appeared to be a local subway monopoly. The young lawyer saw it as an opportunity to correct a basic social flaw. If monopolies were bad—and he was already convinced of that—no effort should be spared to restrain them. In retrospect, though, it is not clear whether Brandeis had the better argument in the subway battle.

Henry Whitney thought he was bringing progress to Massachusetts. He had purchased seven of the Boston area's railways by 1889 and consolidated them to create the country's first electrical railway system. That seemed much more efficient than the horse-drawn trolleys that crowded Boston's streets. But it was not enough for Whitney and his West End Company. They wanted to give Boston a metropolitan system that would relieve the incredible traffic congestion that clogged the narrow streets of downtown Boston. The legislature was agreeable to that. In 1894 it authorized the construction of a subway under Tremont Street, one of the main corridors of the business district. Although the subway would be owned by the city, the law authorized the lease of it to Whitney's West End Company for fifty years.

This was a novel approach for the Bay State. Most Massachusetts railway systems operated under a limited franchise that the local authority could revoke after a year or two. In this way the public could control the railway in case it adopted fares or services that were considered unsatisfactory. From the perspective of the West End Company the unusually long lease for the Tremont Street subway made perfect sense—how else could it attract the large amounts of money needed to rebuild the Boston railways? Few people, it was asserted, would be willing to invest in the new system if the company's right of access to the streets could be revoked by the state after a short time.

There was some merit to that view. But it did represent a break with tradition, and in some circles that factor was more important. Filene, for one, was disturbed. He was a conservative man who now headed his family's clothing business. And while he was willing to accept innovative management techniques, he did not like the idea of a single company's having so much control over the city's transportation system. So when the subway bill came up again in 1896, he searched about for a lawyer to help him make his case to the legislature. No one was interested—until he raised the question with Brandeis. Filene never imagined that this corporate lawyer, who represented the family business on numerous matters, would be interested in the transit controversy. But Brandeis was very interested. He had been in the rag fight. He appreciated the problems with a monopoly. And now he was willing, even anxious, to give his time and effort to help the community retain control over its own affairs.

Brandeis, Filene, and others made their argument to the legislative committees in the fall of 1896. Popular opinion—tradition—was with them. The legislature yielded and reduced the Tremont subway lease to twenty years. The West End Company was to pay the government an annual rental fee that equaled 4⅞ percent of the $7 million construction cost. It was not a total victory for Filene and Brandeis—but it was only the beginning.[2]

Even before this matter was settled, Whitney and his crew were moving on to bigger and better things. A good transit system—especially in a crowded city like Boston—required tracks that would run above the ground. In 1894 Whitney joined forces with J.P. Morgan, the millionaire railroad magnate, to form the Boston Elevated Railway Company. They then secured a charter from the state legislature that would enable the company to build some elevated tracks in the city. In 1897 the Elevated was using its muscle to push through the legislature some amendments to its charter. The amendments had two basic purposes. First, they would enable the Elevated to maintain a five-cent fare for thirty years; and second, the amendments would limit the Elevated's annual payments to the city for thirty years. These annual payments would equal half of 1 percent of the Elevated's yearly gross earnings and would constitute the total rental fees for the Elevated's use of the city streets.

Brandeis became aware of the amendments shortly before they were adopted by the legislature. He was not, to say the least, pleased with them. The amendments gave too much away. Control, again, was the key element. For the amendments, if adopted, would severely restrict the city and state from regulating the most basic features of transportation service—fares and rentals.

Brandeis was not one to let fate take its own course. He wrote a letter to the editor of the *Boston Evening Transcript* and asked that it be published. Public education was critical, and he would do what he could. The letter laid out the arguments against the Elevated amendments. "The right of the Legislature to regulate fares or charges of quasi-public corporations is carefully reserved in the charter of every such corporation now doing business in Massachusetts," Brandeis observed. ". . . No good reason can be alleged why the corporation which now has a substantial monopoly of the street railway traffic of Boston and its suburbs should be free from practically all public control in this most important respect."[3] Within a couple of weeks, Brandeis made a similar argument before the legislature as the representative of the Transportation Committee of the Municipal League, an umbrella civic group representing several metropolitan organizations.[4]

The arguments of the Boston lawyer were to no avail. The amendments were adopted by the legislature. Brandeis did succeed, however, in creating an impression of deception with his adversaries. Albert Pillsbury, the Elevated's lawyer, understandably did not recognize the possibility of a busy lawyer like Brandeis taking time to argue a case solely as a matter of principle. Surely someone was paying him. Rumors of these imagined clients reached Brandeis. He was angry, and he shot off an indignant letter to Pillsbury. "I am not retained by . . . any . . . person or corporation or association," he advised the Elevated attorney, "and have opposed this measure merely as a matter of duty, believing it to be absolutely prejudicial to the interests of the Commonwealth."[5] Pillsbury no doubt remained skeptical. After all, Brandeis had spoken (and would speak again) on behalf of the Municipal League—a group that included many powerful businessmen. Brandeis could not really be so financially disinterested. When Brandeis's nomination for the Supreme Court was before the United States Senate years later, Pillsbury would testify that Brandeis was a man "of duplicity . . . who works under cover, so that nobody ever knows where he really is or what he is really about."[6]

Brandeis was not deterred by Pillsbury's views. There was no time to worry about idle gossip. The subway monopoly was moving forward to expand its control of the city transportation system. To the railroad managers, there was nothing insidious about that course. Would it not be better for both the stockholders *and* the public, they reasoned, if the Elevated and West End Companies were consolidated into one organization? Would there not be a more efficient use of resources and better service if there was a single company to operate the lines leading to Boston as well as the lines in the city? Perhaps. But when the Elevated tried to secure government approval of its plan, it underestimated the forces of tradition and the lawyer representing them.

The vehicle for this contest was the Elevated's proposal to lease the West End's facilities for ninety-nine years. The proposal was ratified by the companies' stockholders. Many of Boston's citizens—including prominent businessmen—were not so convinced of the plan's merits. To some extent this view reflected ties with a simpler past. Massachusetts was used to granting short-term franchises to tiny railroad systems that operated independently in local communities. There was no precedent for the creation of this large metropolitan system that would operate in so many communities.

These arguments would find sympathetic ears in the Board of Railroad Commissioners—the governmental body that had to review the Elevated's proposal. This time Filene and Brandeis were ready. They carefully dissected the Elevated's financial statements and showed that the company's proposal was far more advantageous for the private interests than the public interests. To begin with, the Elevated's proposed rental fees to the West End Company were excessive. This was important, because, under the plan, the Elevated—which would be running the new system—could not be forced to reduce passenger rates until it earned a certain amount more than its costs. If its costs were unduly high, it decreased the possibility of fare reductions.

To Brandeis and Filene, the Elevated and West End combination plan was a fraud upon the public. Since the two companies were owned by many of the same people, it was readily apparent what was happening. By paying the West End an excessive rental, the Elevated would keep the money in the "family," so to speak, and simultaneously create a device—the allegedly high fixed costs—to avoid reductions in fares. The Elevated proposed to use the same tactics to keep to a minimum its rental payments to the city (for use of the streets), because the plan also provided that the city could not increase that rent until the Elevated made a certain amount above its costs.

Brandeis, Filene, and others exposed the scheme to the Railroad Commissioners. Those defects, coupled with the inordinate length of the lease, led the commissioners to reject the Elevated's proposal. The company yielded, reduced both the rental fees to the West End and the length of the lease, and then secured the commissioners' approval.[7]

To many conservative elements in the city, the Elevated's compromise was not very satisfying. Despite changes in the lease, the Elevated had been able to consolidate forces with the West End into a single metropolitan system. This concern was expressed by Charles Warren, who reminded the Massachusetts Reform Club that there was still "a demand from the conservative voices of the people for government interference with quasi-public corporations to the extent of more rigid restrictions and control in giving of franchises and privileges to such corporations."[8] So when Filene and Brandeis decided to organize a civic group to fight these quasi-public corporations, they had no trouble securing members. By 1900—when the Elevated decided to make another attempt to improve its system—the Public Franchise League was ready and waiting.

It was really not that bad a deal. The Elevated wanted to build a subway under Washington Street, another crowded thoroughfare in downtown Boston. The company would pay the entire cost and own the subway outright—although the city would have the right to buy the subway in 1937 (presumably after the Elevated had been able to get a good return on its investment through passenger fares collected before 1937).

The proposal did have its advantages. The city would have a new subway without laying out a cent of public money. Brandeis and his group, however, were horrified. And they were prepared to fight. In their view there was no acceptable alternative except public ownership. That was how the Tremont Street subway was built. Any other course would weaken the public's control of this transportation monopoly.

In addition to the Public Franchise League, other forces were prepared to join battle against the Elevated. The Associated Board of Trade, a group of Boston merchants, wanted to become involved. At the recommendation of Richard Carter, who headed the Boston-based Carter Ink Company, the Board retained Brandeis to represent them. The Board wanted the Washington Street subway built on the same terms as the Tremont Street subway, and Brandeis was to dc he could to achieve that goal. But he was not to be paid for his services. He was now enjoying the "luxury" of working for free in public causes.[9]

By April 1900, the matter was before the legislature. The Elevated said that it would build the Washington Street subway only on its terms, and it doubted that anyone else would step in to finance the operation if the legislature chose another course. As a concession, company representatives did promise certain services and fees to the city, including extensions to Boston's growing suburbs and adequate rental for use of the city streets.

Brandeis lost no time in trying to punch holes in the Elevated's case. For starters, no confidence could be placed in the Elevated's promises. Even if the company executives were acting in good faith, said Brandeis, it was not enough. "You might be willing to rely upon the representations of the distinguished individuals who have appeared before the [House] Committee on behalf of the Boston Elevated Railroad Company," he advised the legislators, "but these men may not be in office, and may not represent the Company next year or the year after, indeed might be dismissed from office for the very reason that they desired to carry out the promises and representations which they made before the Committee here."[10] For that reason, the Boston attorney suggested that all of the Elevated's promises should be incorporated into the written law. He was also prepared to rebut the Elevated's suggestion that no one else would operate the proposed Washington Street subway. He organized a group of leading financiers in Boston to take over the project if the Elevated should balk.

Brandeis recognized, however, that he had to have more than truth and justice on his side. He also needed public opinion. He therefore kept in close touch with editors of some of Boston's newspapers, sending them drafts of his bills and urging the publication of editorials. He also kept peppering his colleagues with suggestions as to how they could assist the public relations effort. Many editors were quite responsive to these requests. Indeed, some of them, like Edward Clement of the *Boston Evening Transcript* and John H. Fahey of the *Boston Traveler,* worked with the Public Franchise League and regularly attended its meetings at the Bellevue Hotel in Boston or the working sessions at the homes of Brandeis and other members.[11] The press was not quite as "independent" as it sometimes seemed.

In any case, the Elevated was not at all prepared for this onslaught by the Board and the League. It requested and got a postponement of the legislature's consideration of its plan. It regrouped its forces, and in 1901 it got the Citizens Association—another group of prominent businessmen and the sponsor of its earlier proposal—to get a second bill introduced. The new bill included some significant changes. To begin with, the bill proposed that the Washington Street subway, like the Tremont Street subway, would be owned by the city. As before, the Elevated would bear all construction costs—up to $6 million, at the least. In return, the Elevated asked that it be allowed to use the subway rent-free for fifty years.

None of Brandeis's ingenuity could stop legislative approval of the Elevated's new proposal, although they did reduce the lease to forty years. It had the support of both Republican and Democratic leaders as well as the Boston Central Labor union, the city's principal labor group. The state House and Senate passed the measure by overwhelming margins. The only hope now was a veto by the governor. And that was a real possibility.

Brandeis had gotten to know Governor Winthrop Murray Crane a few months earlier when the wealthy Ayer family built an apartment house in Copley Square that exceeded established height limitations. Under the guidance of Albert Pillsbury, the legislature adopted a private bill that would allow that exception. His sense of propriety offended, Brandeis went to the governor and persuaded him that it would be a drastic mistake to permit one wealthy family to do what was denied to everyone else. "My only interest in this matter was as a citizen," Brandeis later recalled. "I induced Governor Crane to veto the bill on the ground that it was condoning a deliberate violation of the law. Crane practically embodied my view in his veto message and that was the beginning of my relations with him as Governor."[12]

The relationship with the governor proved immensely helpful to Brandeis while Crane was considering the Elevated argument. The charm was turned on, the soft, melodious voice explained in clear terms why the Elevated bill was a mistake, and on June 18, 1901, Crane vetoed the legislation. Brandeis was duly appreciative. And in an interview with the *Transcript* the next day, he reminded his readers that the community should never relinquish control of its affairs to large private corporations—even if urged to do so by the kind of prominent people who constituted the Citizens Association.[13]

The fight was far from over, though. Although the governor's veto was sustained by the legislature, the Elevated was back again the following year with yet another proposal. This one was indeed creative. The idea of a Washington Street subway was abandoned. Instead, the Elevated proposed to build a "deep tunnel" that would connect its elevated tracks. The tunnel would be constructed entirely at the Elevated's own expense but would be and always remain the Elevated's property. Wringing its hands in despair, the Elevated claimed that it could not afford to proceed in any other manner.

At a legislative hearing on the proposal, Brandeis bore through a "cloud of figures" offered by Pillsbury to show that in fact the Elevated could afford to operate the Washington Street subway and pay rent to the city. With statistics from the public record, Brandeis pointed out in his deliberate, self-assured way that the Elevated was a prosperous company and that it was growing more and more prosperous every year. It had paid out 6 percent dividends on $10 million worth of stock, and the price of a share had recently jumped from 105 to 170. A plea of poverty by the company was hardly justified.

To Brandeis the main issue remained one of control. The notion of short-term rentals for major metropolitan rail systems was soon to become an antiquated one. But for the Boston lawyer no other course seemed appropriate. "It is your business, gentlemen," he told the House Metropolitan Affairs Committee, "and it is our business, who are not officers and managers of the company, to see that the interests of the community are protected, and to look not merely to the interest of the community today, but to look out for conditions a generation to come. We are to see that the control rests with the community, that the Elevated Railway Company, or any other company that serves us as transporters of passengers, is the servant and not the master of the public. . . ." Pillsbury inquired whether a lease that lasted more than a generation could really be called offensive. Brandeis's answer was quick. "I think it is an offensive provision," he told the Elevated lawyer. "Your company tried to get that which would give it absolute control of the situation, while the control ought to rest with the people, with the community and not with any corporation, whether domestic or foreign."[14]

Pillsbury was not at all persuaded. When Brandeis later sent the Elevated attorney a written statement incorporating his argument, Pillsbury immediately came back with a curt note. "I acknowledge with thanks the receipt of a copy of your statement (which I understand has already been torn to pieces by our auditor)," he wrote. "In exchange for your sophistries, I hereby return you the Truth."[15] But Pillsbury's "truth" could not overcome the tremendous publicity generated by Brandeis's group—or the public support it inspired for the League's position. The legislature passed a bill providing for city construction of the Washington Street subway with a twenty-five-year rental to the Elevated. The annual rental fee was to be 4½ percent of the construction cost. The Elevated submitted, and Brandeis secured his first major victory as a lawyer for the people.

The experience in the Elevated fight brought many changes to Brandeis's thinking and way of life. From the personal side, it increased his dependence on his wife, Alice. She had fully agreed with his decision to involve himself in public causes like this. But there was a price to pay for that involvement. Although he was supported by some established figures in Boston society, many of those on the other side were offended by his approach. Few denied that his skills as an attorney were impressive. But he seemed to be so secretive. Doubts persisted that he was really acting as a matter of public duty. And he seemed so self-assured, so independent, so, well, aloof. He was not "one of the boys." Some people stopped socializing with him. He was hurt by that—but it did not break his resolve to stay in the fight. Friends could come and go, but he still had the love and support of Alice. She remained in frail health, but she was always there with a word of encouragement for his work. "I could not have lived my life without Alice," he later told Bess Evans. "If my wife had been hurt, how could I have had the strength to go on?" He shared his sentiments with Alice. "You have had many hard days these years," he wrote at one point during the Elevated controversy, "and one shall hope that this may become otherwise—but we shall be indeed fortunate if another ten years of happiness is granted us."[16]

The support of Alice was especially important because Louis no longer enjoyed the comfort and support of his mother. It happened in August 1901 while he was with his parents in Petersham, Massachusetts. Frederika was now in her seventy-fifth year and suffering from serious illness. The doctor prescribed morphine to ease her pain, but it could not hold back the inevitable. It was a wrenching experience for all, particularly when Frederika became delirious. Louis was at least happy that he could be with his mother in her final moments. "Even in her delirious condition Mother seemed to know me," he wrote to Alice, "and smiled at the thought of my being with her." She died the next day.[17]

Dislocations in Brandeis's family life were accompanied by some shifts in his political views. Even more than the rag fight several years earlier, the Elevated matter illustrated the dangers of monopoly power. By this time the Elevated was a very large company that employed thousands of people in the Boston area. And jobs meant political power. Legislators who wanted to stay in office had to be ready to help out a needy constituent looking for work. This was particularly critical in Boston since every year brought thousands of immigrants looking for assistance.

It did not take long for Brandeis to recognize the problem. In June 1901, shortly before the final legislative vote on the Elevated's proposal to build and own the Washington Street subway, he advised Filene that the state legislators from Boston represented the "greatest danger" to their position. Brandeis's warning was to no avail—almost all of the Boston legislators sided with the Elevated in that vote. Later he explained the problem to William McElwain, one of his clients. "In our subway fight," Brandeis wrote, "we found the great evil that we had to deal with was the influence of the corporation, due largely to the patronage which it exerts; that is, the Civil Service Laws have not done away with most of the evils of the spoils system in municipal and state affairs. The legislators, councilmen and others in position rely upon the public service corporations who are getting favors from them to furnish places to the men who work for the nomination and election of the respective candidates, some aldermen and senators having from one to two hundred men in this way on the pay-roll of companies. This," he said, "we find to be the most serious and widespread form of corruption."[18]

As before, Brandeis was not prepared to accept this social problem quietly. The Elevated fight had made him a well-known figure in Boston circles. His name and picture appeared regularly in the press, and now he was frequently invited to give speeches. And there was no theme closer to his heart at this time than government corruption. It was not only the improper influence of monopolies; it was also the bribery, the payoffs with meaningless jobs for constituents, and the needless expenditure of public funds. It was a terrible situation all around, and the public had to be alerted.

It was a good cause—so good, in fact, that on occasion Brandeis got carried away with his own rhetoric. On March 18, 1903, for example, he gave a dinner address at the Boot and Shoe Club on the corruption he claimed was rampant in government. "The question is," he asked, "can you afford to be represented in the State and City of Boston by the class of men that represent us." To Brandeis the answer was obvious. There was no more glaring instance than the tremendous increase in public expenditures in recent years. "Why, the painting of a ward room in Boston took three men 38 days and cost the city $549," Brandeis exclaimed. In this setting there was no better cure than an educated public. "It is needed that public opinion be aroused," said the attorney, "and that good, honest, honorable men be drafted into service as our office holders. . . . It is necessary to force the people to think of this corruption, and the great need of action for the public good."[19]

The speech was widely covered in the press the next day. The reaction was not entirely favorable, especially from people who happened to be in the government. Many of them took issue with the speech. Brandeis had promised never to be tripped up on a question of fact, but it was not long before he found himself flat on his face in trying to defend the accuracy of his speech. Benjamin Wells of the city public works department was one person who let Brandeis know where he stood. "[V]iolent and exaggerated criticism, while it may arouse temporarily public feeling," Wells wrote, "certainly does not accomplish good results in the end." Wells had a specific bone to pick with Brandeis. As evidence of corruption, the speech cited the fact that the Street Department's expenditures increased 82 percent, as compared with only 2 percent for the Fire Department. Well, Brandeis was told, if the facts had been checked, you would have understood that the Street Department had to undertake a great deal of new construction, whereas the Fire Department did not assume any new responsibilities.[20]

George Crocker, the Boston city treasurer, also took issue with the facts in Brandeis's speech. Yes, Brandeis admitted to Crocker, he had said that government workers were only one-half to one-third as efficient as private employees—"but I do not think I could have used any expression referring specifically to the 'financial department' " under Crocker's control. Indeed, Brandeis told Crocker, "I know of no one . . . more competent than yourself to judge as to how the amount of work done by the clerks in your department compares with the work done in well organized commercial business. . . ." And if Crocker had statistics on that score, Brandeis would be happy to review them.[21]

Although perhaps embarrassed by these corrections to his comments, Brandeis was not in the least deterred from his crusade against government corruption. In fact, he intensified his efforts. He and others formed the Good Government Association—a civic group designed to fight public waste. The Good Government Association began to oppose pension plans for city workers, reductions in the minimum hours of firemen, and other measures that would increase taxes. The Association's tenacity in these political matters soon inspired adversaries to refer to them as the "goo goo" group, and even those with no axe to grind believed that Association members consisted of "tax-dodging, holier-than-thou Pharisees, without political experience or judgment."[22]

It was not, of course, the highest compliment. But Brandeis had been personally attacked before, and he was getting used to it. And he would not shirk from his duties as a public-spirited citizen simply because someone hurled some labels at him. His skin was thicker than that.

Brandeis did recognize, however, that public education and new civic groups were not the total answer to the problem of corruption and waste. In fact, the Elevated fight convinced him even more that one necessary weapon was the development of strong labor unions. It was perhaps one of the best ways to cut the strong bond between the legislators and large corporations that gave jobs to constituents.

Long before the transit controversies, Brandeis had come to appreciate the importance of unions. Through Bess Evans he had become friendly with John O'Sullivan, a labor reporter for the *Boston Globe,* and his wife, Mary Kenney, a labor organizer who had previously worked for the American Federation of Labor in Chicago. In the early 1890s, Louis spent many evenings with Jack and Mary in their home in Boston's Irish quarter, listening to them explain the plight of the workingman and exploring possible solutions to labor problems. Louis was captivated and once told Bess that he looked to the workingman "for our general political salvation."[23]

Experience with his corporate clients further sensitized him to labor's problems. Many of the firms he represented operated on a seasonal basis. Employees might work for several weeks or months and then find themselves laid off for several weeks or months. For anyone trying to make ends meet in providing for a family, this irregular employment was intolerable. The off-and-on workers never knew whether they would be getting a paycheck and, if they did, how much it would be for. When clients complained about labor problems, one of the first things Brandeis asked about was the regularity of employment. "You say your factory cannot continue to pay the wages the employees now earn," he almost shouted at one client. "But you don't tell me what those earnings are. How much do they lose through irregularities in their work? You don't know? Do you undertake to manage this business and to say what wages it can afford to pay while you are ignorant of facts such as these? Are not these the very things you should know, and should have seen that your men know too, before you went into this fight?"[24] And when McElwain, who was a leading shoe manufacturer, asked for Brandeis's help on a labor matter, he found his lawyer having more sympathy for the employees than for management. McElwain wanted to cut employee wages because he felt they were already too high. To prove his point, McElwain showed payroll figures to his lawyer. "Are you giving me the average pay they receive for fifty-two weeks a year," Brandeis inquired, "or are you giving me the pay they earn while they are working?"[25] McElwain confessed that it was the latter. Well, offered Brandeis, both you and your employees would benefit if you regularized your operations so that you were producing and they were working all year round. Much to his later satisfaction, McElwain took the advice and reorganized his plant.

These and other actions made Brandeis the corporate attorney widely known as a friend of labor. He even attracted national attention. As the Elevated controversy was winding down, another labor fight was flaring up in Pennsylvania. But this one, unlike the transit fight, had national implications.

In May 1902, coal miners in Pennsylvania went on strike, demanding union recognition, higher wages, and a shorter day. Because of coal's importance to both industrial and residential users, the strike threatened to cause severe disruption to the economy, not to mention people's comfort. As the midterm congressional elections approached, Senator Henry Cabot Lodge of Massachusetts was deeply concerned that the strike and anticipated rise in coal prices would be devastating to his Republican Party. Lodge addressed his concern to President Theodore Roosevelt. "Trusts, thanks to you, we can manage. . . . Tariff revisions we can discuss. . . . But the rise in the price of coal," Lodge warned, "we cannot argue with."[26] Roosevelt was no political novice. He knew something had to be done. He called all the parties to the White House, treated them royally, and persuaded them to support the creation of an independent commission that would review the miners' grievances.

No sooner was that done than Brandeis was contacted by Henry Demarest Lloyd, the writer whose earlier study of corporate oppression had received wide acclaim. Brandeis toured the coal mines with Lloyd and agreed to assist Clarence Darrow, the famed Chicago labor lawyer, in presenting the miners' case to the commission. In letters to both Darrow and Lloyd, Brandeis emphasized his concern with irregular employment by the miners. Too often, he found, miners were laid off for extended periods, a fact that overshadowed the problem with low wages. "I feel very strongly that one of the great evils from which the employees suffer," he told Darrow at one point, "is the lack of continuous occupation."[27] Unfortunately, the commission decided to limit its inquiry and Brandeis never got an opportunity to make his argument.

In pushing for regularity of employment here, Brandeis did not in any sense feel that management's control of labor was malicious. Some of the best-intentioned employers—like McElwain—just did not appreciate the necessity of workers' standing up for themselves. "We must avoid industrial despotism, even though it be benevolent despotism," Brandeis later remarked. ". . . Some way must be worked out by which employer and employee, each recognizing the proper sphere of the other, will each be free to work for his own and for the common good, and that the powers of the individual employee may be developed to the utmost. To attain this end," he added, "it is essential that neither should feel that he stands in the power—at the mercy—of the other. The sense of unrestricted power is just as demoralizing for the employer as it is for the employee. Neither our intelligence nor our characters can long stand the strain of unrestricted power."[28] That in turn meant that workers had to have the right to unionize and engage in collective bargaining. There was no other way they could match the employer's power.

Brandeis recognized, though, that labor would not obtain the right to organize and protect itself without a struggle. "In the last resort," he once told an interviewer, "labor will fight for its rights. It is a law of life. Must we not fight, all of us, even for the peace that we most crave?" In fact, from his perspective there was a certain self-confidence and sense of accomplishment that required at least some conflict. "There is something better than peace," said the Boston attorney, "and that is the peace that is won by struggle. We shall have lost something vital and beyond price on the day when the State denies us the right to resort to force in defense of a just cause."[29] It was all part of his view that people needed responsibility over their lives—and the drive to take control when things were not going right.

But if people were to be responsible for themselves, Brandeis thought, they also had to be accountable. That was true for labor as well. And it was no small matter. Violence was not uncommon when workers and management found themselves in disagreement. People often got hurt, and much time was spent trying to decide who was at fault. Brandeis was not, of course, prepared to say that labor was always in the wrong. In fact, he was more likely to think the contrary. But if labor was the wrongdoer, then labor had to pay the consequences.

The problem was that unions were not incorporated and there was a great deal of controversy over whether they could be sued for damages caused by their membership. Brandeis thought it would be in everyone's interest if the uncertainty were eliminated by requiring unions to be incorporated. The union leadership was not convinced that Brandeis's view was in fact the best one.

As the controversy was heating up, Brandeis—by now a leading community figure—agreed to debate the issue with Samuel Gompers, the president of the American Federation of Labor. The two men appeared before a packed audience in the Tremont Temple in Boston on the evening of December 4, 1902. Brandeis opened the debate. He put his right hand in his pants pocket, leaned on the lectern, and spoke in a soft, deliberate, almost conversational voice. The unions' "practical immunity" from litigation did not serve labor's interest, said Brandeis. "It tends to make officers and members reckless and lawless," he observed, "and thereby to alienate public sympathy and bring failure. It creates on the part of the employers, on the other hand, a bitter antagonism, not so much on account of lawless acts as from a deep-rooted sense of justice arising from the feeling that the union holds a position of legal irresponsibility."

Gompers was quick to respond. "Well, heavens, that may be true," said the union leader, "but that is not our fault, but the fault of you employers of labor who have given us such low wages that we cannot put funds in our trade unions. You can't take much from those who have so little; and we protest against you putting your hand upon that little." Brandeis was not moved. Gompers's "eloquent address," he said, ". . . has not wholly removed from my mind the fear that the action of labor unions may sometimes be governed by emotion." That statement brought prolonged applause from the audience.

Gompers was not ready to concede. "I take second place to no man in this country in my respect for the law and in my respect for judges, too," he retorted, "if I as an individual and as an American citizen should be brought before them. But the whole history of jurisprudence and the practice has been to look upon the laborer as the property of the employer and it is the trade union's effort to emerge out of that." He then turned to Brandeis, and with sarcasm dripping from his voice, said, "This may sound emotional, but it is simply emphatic." Gales of laughter and applause filled the temple.[30]

Brandeis had the last laugh. Two decades later he was a United States Supreme Court justice when the Court had to decide whether an employer could sue a union for damages. The case involved a sad tale of a bitter struggle between the Coronado Coal Company and miners in the fields of Arkansas. The company wanted to cut costs. The union that operated its mines was considered expendable. So the company broke its contract with the union, fired all the miners, and hired non-union men at lower wages to take their place.

The company knew that these actions would not go down well with the union. It prepared for armed combat. And it was not disappointed. Enraged by the company's cavalier treatment of them, the union men armed themselves. Speeches were made and a band played. And then they attacked the mines. The company people surrendered, and a banner was hoisted: THIS IS A UNION MAN'S COUNTRY. But the fight was not over. The company brought in more armed guards, and, after a bloody struggle, these too beat a hasty retreat. The union men then destroyed the mines. The company felt it had no alternative but to go to court to make the union pay for the damages.

The company based its court action on the Sherman Act, a federal antitrust law which prohibits activities that unreasonably restrain interstate commerce. There was no secret behind the company's choice here, for the Sherman Act also provides that violators can be fined an amount equal to three times the damages caused. So if the company could prevail in court, it could make a nice profit.

The question before the Supreme Court was whether the company could rely on the Sherman Act in its suit against the union. Section 6 of the Clayton Antitrust Act of 1914 seemed to answer the question in the negative. The Sherman Act applies only to actions affecting interstate commerce; section 6, however, stated plainly that "the labor of a human being is not a commodity or article of commerce" and that nothing in the Sherman Act could "restrain individual members of [unions] from lawfully carrying out the legitimate objects of their organization." Labor was jubilant over the Clayton Act because it seemed to give them the protection they had sought for so long. Gompers, in fact, hailed the new law as "the industrial magna charta" because the measure "removes all possibility of interpreting trust legislation to apply to [unions]."[31]

When the Supreme Court first considered the *Coronado* case, a majority took a different view. True, the Sherman Act applies only to interstate commerce, but that was really no problem. After all, by destroying the mines the union had prevented the Coronado Coal Company from shipping coal in interstate commerce. No one could argue with that. And with the triple damages penalty, the union would have to pay dearly for all the destruction it caused.

Brandeis was not with the majority the first time around. To begin with, he did not see how the court could punish the union under the Sherman Act. In an earlier case, the Court had explicitly stated that coal mining was not interstate commerce. But more than that, Brandeis did not think courts could settle problems of industrial combat. In another case decided about this time he had included in an opinion some relevant language largely drafted by his law clerk Dean Acheson. "All rights are derived from the purposes of the society in which they exist," the opinion said; "above all rights rises duty to the community. The conditions developed in industry may be such that those engaged in it cannot continue their struggle without danger to the community. But it is not for judges to determine whether such conditions exist, nor is it their function to set the limits of permissible contest and to declare the duties which the new situation demands. This is the function of the legislature. . . ."[32]

Although the legislature could define the rules of combat, Brandeis adhered to the views expressed in his debate with Gompers. The unions had to be liable for the consequences of their actions. There could be no industrial peace unless the labor men recognized that.

It was an appealing thought to William Howard Taft, the man who became chief justice of the Supreme Court in the spring of 1921. Unlike Brandeis, he was not known as a radical. No, the Republican ex-president was someone who understood legal tradition and appreciated the importance of conservative principles. He was someone the Court majority could follow. So when he realized that the majority had made a mistake the first time around in the *Coronado* case, he told them so. And they listened. The case was held over for re-argument, and the majority became convinced that Brandeis was right—unions could not be punished under the Sherman Act because coal mining was not interstate commerce. At the same time, Taft agreed with Brandeis that the unions had to be made liable for the damages they caused. The majority was certainly in accord with Taft on that point. So he wrote an opinion supported by all his brethren, including Brandeis, that said the Coronado Coal Company could sue the union for damages under state law.[33]

The unions considered the decision a defeat—not realizing how close they had come to losing a larger battle with the triple damages of the Sherman Act. For Brandeis it was a bittersweet victory. Without Taft, his views would not have carried a majority, let alone a unanimous Court. Referring to his conservative colleagues, Brandeis later said to Felix Frankfurter, "They will take it from Taft but [won't] take it from me."[34] But being on the Court often involved compromise—and Brandeis was no stranger to that art. In fact, he had used it with some success many years earlier when, as a much younger attorney, he attacked the gas problem in Boston.

SIX

The Gas Fight

The pessimist sees the difficulty in every opportunity; the optimist, the opportunity in every difficulty.

L.P. JACKS

The men at the stockyards didn't catch on at first. To be sure, the cattle coming in to be slaughtered weighed more than they usually did. But there was certainly no limit to what a steer could eat or how much it could weigh. These heavy cattle were probably just better fed.

It did not take too long before the scheme was exposed. The heavier steers were not, in fact, better fed. Ranchers simply took their stock to a watering hole a couple of days before the end of the cattle drive. The steer filled up on water and their weight skyrocketed. No one discovered that the increased weight was illusory until long after the cattle were sold to the stockyard. But the increased weight meant more dollars in the ranchers' pockets—and who could argue with some "ingenuity" in the drive for higher profits?

In time people began to worry about another kind of watered stock—securities representing the assets of a business. People acting in good faith assumed that a business security, or stock certificate, represented something of value in the company (at least when the stocks were first issued). Sometimes, however, the assumption proved to be too much. Promoters looking for a quick profit might offer far more stock in the business than was justified. Selling stock equal to twice the value of the company, for example, might give the company some undeserved money; but it did nothing for public confidence in business ethics. By the end of the nineteenth century, many states, including Massachusetts, had adopted laws prohibiting what became known as "watered" stock.

The problem was especially troublesome in the case of public utilities. These companies provided an important public service and in most states were guaranteed a certain return on their investments. If a company could convince the regulatory authority that its stock was not watered, the owners could usually obtain a return on all the funds that had been invested in the company. It all came down to a question of the company's capitalization—or how much money had actually been put into the business.

Edward Warren (not related to Sam Warren) understood all these basic concepts of utility regulation; and that was what bothered him about the Boston gas situation in the early 1900s. The public, he explained to friends and colleagues, was about to be cheated.

The situation had changed dramatically since 1823, when the Boston Gas

Light Company became the first firm to offer natural gas to the public in Massachusetts. It appeared to be a good business, and by 1855 there were thirty-eight companies. Competition was keen, and there seemed to be no ethical limit to the devices firms used to beat their rivals. The environment was not entirely pleasant—predatory pricing, public deception, and other sordid practices became commonplace. And more than that, there was an unnecessary duplication of facilities. Government regulation seemed to be the only satisfactory answer, and in 1885 the legislature created the Board of Gas Commissioners, which, when the agency assumed supervisory authority for electricity, became the Board of Gas and Light Commissioners. The Board was given broad responsibility for the regulation of gas companies and their rates. In 1894 the legislature added an anti–stock-watering provision that empowered the board to control the price of new stock offered by the gas companies.

But all these regulatory measures were not enough. There was still too much competition—and with it too much duplication and waste. In 1903 the eight gas companies serving Boston and Brookline, a suburb of the city, decided to consolidate themselves into a single company. The legislature approved the consolidation and directed the Board of Gas and Light Commissioners to determine the "capitalization" of the new company—the amount of money that could be used as a basis for calculating the prices of the new stock; that figure would in turn determine the amount of money the new company could collect in gas rates from the consumer (since the rates would enable the company to earn a certain return on its capital, or investment).

Brandeis and Filene's Public Franchise League opposed the consolidation bill. As in the earlier transit fight, the League was convinced that the creation of a single large public service company would create monopoly power that could dominate the regulatory authorities and escape public control. The law also offered a chance for mischief when it directed the Gas Commissioners to give "fair value" in assessing the amount of capital in the company. There was too much room in that loose phrase for shady deals. Who could really say what was "fair"?

Brandeis had not taken much interest in the 1903 consolidation bill. He was too preoccupied with his private practice and his other civic activities. Instead, Edward Warren had carried the ball for the League—and he felt that his lack of success in the legislature could be attributed to the lack of support from Brandeis and some other League members. So when the matter of capitalization was scheduled to come before the Board of Gas and Light Commissioners, Warren became concerned. He was afraid that the gas company would get approval for a capitalization higher than it deserved.

Warren's fears were not academic. The gas company wanted to capitalize at about $20 million. The company claimed that the value of the stock of the eight consolidated companies was more than $24 million, and the proposed $20 million valuation was the minimum it would accept from the Board. Warren took a different view. Only about $9 million had been invested by stockholders in the companies, and the companies had borrowed another $6 million. Therefore, the company could not be valued at any more than $15 million—and even that might be high because all of the money might not have been used for capital investments. As for the $24 million claimed by the company, Warren thought that that was clearly excessive. The $9 million difference between his value figure and the companies' represented surplus earnings the companies had obtained from the public. Warren concluded that the companies were able to acquire that surplus only because they had charged the consumer too much for gas. And it would be the height of irony if those overcharges could be used by the consolidated company to increase its valuation to $20 million, because then the company could use that valuation to justify charging the public even higher rates. In short, if the company's plan were adopted, the public would be exploited not once but twice. And for Warren, once was too much.

He knew, however, that logic and statistics might not be enough to carry the Board. He needed the support of public figures like Brandeis. They alone could counter the pressure that would certainly be exerted by the gas company. Warren's analysis was sound in theory; he just didn't know whether the League would give him the support he needed. Warren was not shy about expressing his apprehension. "I cannot help feeling that the Public Franchise League is not concerning itself as it should with the Gas situation," he wrote to Brandeis on April 30, 1904. Mayor Patrick Collins was very upset and was prepared to use his office to prevent the Board's approval of an excessive capitalization for the consolidated gas company. The League had to be prepared to fight with the mayor, Warren said. In fact, it might even be wise to get the legislature to repeal the 1903 law and avoid the whole issue of capitalization. But Warren was adamant that the League had to take a firm stand. "If the League is not disposed to take this course," he added, "I feel disposed to interest a new set of men, for I think it is of too great importance to be neglected. I sometimes fear the League has outlived its usefulness but I hope it is not so."[1]

Brandeis did not take the challenge lightly. He too recognized the dangers of a powerful monopoly in the provision of important public services. A community could not control its own destiny if the government were more responsive to the pleas of special interests. So there was no doubt that the situation was indeed serious. But Warren, Brandeis thought, was getting a little carried away.

In a letter to his colleague, the Boston attorney explained that an effort to repeal the 1903 law would be "quixotic." Better to deal with the existing situation than to waste energy arguing about something that had already been decided. But in resolving the capitalization issue, Brandeis agreed with Warren that it would be necessary to enlist the "moral support and assistance" of outside groups. And the League remained a leading member of those outside groups. "I do not share your fear," Brandeis wrote Warren, "that the League has outlived its usefulness, but I am of the opinion, which I think I have expressed to you from time to time, that its membership should be strengthened by the introduction to it of new men, preferably younger men. I think it would be a great mistake," the lawyer cautioned Warren, "to form a separate organization and thus lose the influence which the Public Franchise League has justly earned for itself."[2] And as a measure of his own good faith to become more actively involved, Brandeis sent another letter to Warren within a few days that discussed some of the legal principles involved in the capitalization issue.[3]

Warren was satisfied with this response, and he made no effort to bolt the League—at least not yet. Brandeis carried through on his promise and took charge of the campaign. He kept close tabs on developments. He continued to work with the press in maintaining the League's public relations effort—as in the transit fight, he knew that public opinion could ultimately prove to be critical. He also conferred with Thomas Babson, the city's attorney, and the mayor, whom he addressed as "General Collins." But that was not enough. Although the mayor and Babson indicated that they shared the League's perspective, Brandeis maintained a certain skepticism that they would come through in the pinch. So he secured the services of an aggressive and independent attorney to "assist" Babson. George W. Anderson, then forty-three, entered the scene. He not only initiated a relationship with the city attorney; he also began a friendship with Brandeis that was to endure many conflicts and last the rest of their lives.

Before long Anderson was doing most of the legal work for the League in the gas fight. Brandeis was more interested in getting other "outside" groups into the act. In early March 1905, he approached the Massachusetts State Board of Trade and offered to represent them for free on the gas question. As an association of merchants, the Board was of course concerned with utility rates. It was too good a deal to turn down, so Brandeis became the Board's attorney. And none too soon. Governor William Lewis Douglas was considering legislation on the whole question, and the Board wanted to get its views registered before the governor reached any conclusion. And more than that, the Joint Legislative Committee on Public Lighting was about to convene its hearings on the capitalization of the Boston gas company. More and more people were criticizing the 1903 law's command to give the gas company "fair value" in assessing its capital. It was hoped that the law could be made more precise. The legislature was also being pressed to consider a new law that would govern *all* utility consolidations and not just the one for gas companies.

On March 9, 1905, Brandeis appeared before the Committee on behalf of the State Board of Trade. At the outset he made it clear that the Board's only goal was to ensure that the gas consolidation "be in accordance with the wise and established policy of the Commonwealth prohibiting stock-watering of quasi-public corporations. . . ." Of course, said Brandeis, the company was entitled to rates that would give it a fair return on its investment. But "in order to determine what a reasonable compensation is and to limit the return on capital to a reasonable compensation, it is essential that there should be before the public a knowledge of the capital originally invested in the enterprise."

Because anti–stock-watering laws placed a limit on profits, some people viewed them as "communistic or socialistic." Brandeis did not give much credence to those concerns. "To my mind," he told the legislators, "nothing can be farther from the fact. When Massachusetts passed the anti–stock-watering laws, it adopted a measure of a most conservative character—a measure more potent for the protection of individual property than any other which could have been devised. The greatest factors making for communism, socialism, or anarchy among a free people are the excesses of capital. . . . It is certain," Brandeis observed, "that among a free people every excess of capital must in time be repaid by the excessive demands of those who have not capital. Every act of injustice on the part of the rich will be met by another act or many acts of injustice on the part of the people."

It was vital, said the Boston attorney, that no special exception be made for the Boston gas company. "The moment you make an exception and grant special privileges to one set of men," he noted, "you create a score of evils. You create a feeling of unrest. You lay the basis for a charge of favoritism and of injustice." It was therefore important for the gas consolidation to be implemented under general laws and policies. And if the gas companies get less than what they sought, so be it. "They will lose nothing more," said Brandeis, "than the improper hope which was entertained at one time."

Here again, the basic issue was the right of the people to control their own affairs. "We have a system [in Massachusetts]," Brandeis explained, "by which the public service company is sure of its rights as long as it deals justly with the community; and the knowledge that this continued existence is dependent upon the good will of the people protects the companies from committing arbitrary or unjust acts which would incite public indignation and lead to curtailment or destruction of their rights."[4]

That was all well and good, but the Committee had a specific case before it. Could the gas company declare its normal 8 percent dividend on its $9 million surplus and then use those dividends to impose higher rates on the public? Brandeis's response was not as tough as his rhetoric. Yes, he replied, there could be some dividends on the surplus—but no higher than the 4 or 5 percent interest that could be charged on a loan. Apparently, Brandeis did not want to totally alienate the company. Compromise was probably a necessity.

Dr. Morton Prince, a member of the Public Franchise League, immediately rose to say that Brandeis did not represent the League and that the League was strongly opposed to any dividends on surplus. Brandeis was not moved. "There is in the community," he said, "such a thing as vested wrongs as well as vested rights. The community was wrong in allowing the surplus to pile up. There should be some return on the surplus; that fund is one in which the community has an equitable interest, but it has no right to confiscate it."[5]

Brandeis knew that the gas company would still find his position objectionable. He was willing to allow dividends on surplus at a reduced rate; company representatives wanted the standard 8 percent dividend applied to surplus—and they thought they had enough influence with the legislature to get it.

Edwin Sprague, an official of the State Board of Trade, was still pleased with Brandeis's performance. "I want to say," Sprague wrote, "that your argument before the Committee on Public Lighting today was a most excellent and forceful presentation. . . ."[6] Edward Warren did not share Sprague's enthusiasm. After all, Brandeis's views did not coincide with the League's, and wasn't Brandeis the League's attorney? "There seems to have been an unfortunate misunderstanding in regard to your position at the hearing before the Public Lighting Committee, as far as the Public Franchise League is concerned," Warren wrote to Brandeis on March 10, 1905. "In the first place our Executive Committee certainly understood that you had volunteered to represent the League, as well as the State Board of

Trade, on behalf of the general bill. Secondly, you advocated to the Committee the desirability of dividends being paid on the surplus earnings of a public service corporation, though I believe at a lower rate than on the paid-in capital. So far as I know this doctrine is not held by the members of the League. . . . Don't you think," Warren concluded, "we should have a clearer understanding in the future?"

Brandeis could certainly appreciate someone who vigorously fought for what he thought was right. He had done it—and would do it again—many times himself. But he was losing patience with Warren. The man was so obsessed with the policy against stock watering that it blinded him to political realities. The surplus may have been a wrong to begin with, but now the money legally belonged to the gas company. It would be unfair to prevent any dividends on it—or so Brandeis thought at the time.

Brandeis tried to set Warren straight. He was certainly right, Brandeis wrote, that an attorney representing the League "should represent fully the views of the League," regardless of "whether he is paid counsel or not. . . ." But Brandeis was not acting for the League. Moreover, Prince had fully explained the position held by Warren, so no damage was done. Finally, Brandeis said that, to his knowledge, the League members had never voted on the matter—but maybe now they should. The critical questions would involve the value of the new stock and the dividend to be allowed on it. Brandeis accepted the view that the amount of capital could determine the value of the stock; but, said Brandeis, the dividend rate should "have nothing whatever to do with fixing the amount of the capitalization. . . ." Instead, the dividend should be tied directly to the rates. If the company charged the public $1 for a unit of gas, it should get a lower dividend than if it charged seventy-five cents. This was a "sliding scale" designed to give the company an incentive to lower rates. The lower the rates, the higher the dividends.[7]

Warren was not at all persuaded. So when the League executive committee and the State Board of Trade representatives met in a joint meeting at the Hotel Bellevue on May 3, 1905, Warren argued strenuously for his position. Both the dividend and the rates should be fixed, he asserted; otherwise the monopoly would—somehow, some way—take advantage of the situation. Brandeis disagreed just as vehemently. It was important to give the company an incentive to lower rates. Regulation by statute was inefficient and likely to be ineffective in the end. "Brandeis made a wonderful speech," Warren recalled years later. "I have always felt personally that it was his forceful personality, his determination to carry the point, which carried the committee. . . . Brandeis has a wonderful magnetism when he speaks, and he has a wonderful way of carrying his points, and he carried those men right off their feet."[8] The vote was overwhelmingly in support of Brandeis.

However much he admired Brandeis's rhetorical skills, Warren was not about to give up. At a luncheon meeting of the League the following day, the matter came up again. If the legislature hadn't reported the bill yet, Warren said, couldn't the subject be discussed one more time? Morton Prince quickly supported Warren. He pointedly asked Brandeis whether the issue could be reopened. Brandeis had had enough. He turned to Prince and Warren and sarcastically said,

"Don't cry, baby!" That reaction hit Warren like a bulldozer, and years later he would cite the episode to justify his opposition to Brandeis's appointment as a Supreme Court justice.[9]

In part, Brandeis's impatience with Warren and Prince no doubt reflected the fact that he had already worked out a compromise with the Boston gas company. It had not been entirely his doing. In fact, he found some unexpected allies in the gas company itself.

The publicity agents for the company had come upon an ingenious scheme. They began sending out "news" stories to the daily papers; and if the papers agreed to run them without indicating the source, the company would pay the paper's normal advertising rates. Some papers could not resist the temptation. "I'm a merchant just like you," Charles H. Taylor, owner of the *Boston Globe,* told an inquiring Edward Filene. "I sell my merchandise at a dollar a line."[10] Other papers had a little more integrity. The *Springfield Republican* exposed the scheme in bold headlines, and soon the gas company felt public support ebbing away. It was time to cut a deal.

The new president of the gas company, James L. Richards, decided to call on Brandeis. Richards was a tall, dark, handsome man with pointed features. He had made his fortune in the tobacco business and then quit. Because his reputation as a businessman was so good, and since he was available, the gas company got him to take over. Richards explained to Brandeis that he had nothing to do with the ads and agreed that they should be condemned. He also had some ideas on a bill to allow the consolidation of the gas companies. Both he and Brandeis now knew that the legislature would not adopt a general bill concerning all consolidations by utility companies. The question, then, was how much stock and dividend the gas company would be allowed. Richards proposed a capitalization of $15 million and a sliding scale system along the lines proposed by Brandeis.

Brandeis was having second thoughts about pushing for the sliding scale system now. He had already received some indication of political resistance to the concept.[11] He did not want to undercut Richards's offer by fighting for a provision that was probably doomed to failure. Politics was the art of the possible, and Brandeis was willing to settle for a fixed amount of capitalization. The sliding scale proposal, he told Richards, could wait until next year.

Over the next few days Brandeis and company representatives conferred at length on a compromise bill. Upon inspection it turned out that Richards's $15 million proposal did involve a small amount of stock watering. This was so because the value of some of the stock now exceeded its original cost; hence, the consolidated company was paying more for the stock than it represented in investment. Brandeis was no purist, however. He could compromise for the sake of resolution.

Not so other people. Edwin Sprague and the State Board of Trade, for instance, were very disappointed with the compromise gas bill. None of that seemed to matter much to Brandeis. Although he had agreed to represent them in the gas fight, it was now clear that their views were largely irrelevant. Brandeis had the chance to accomplish something; and although he would try to persuade the State Board of the bill's merits, he did not feel duty bound to advocate the board's viewpoint.[12] Nor was he deterred by criticism from other members of the Public Franchise League. George Anderson, for one, wrote to Brandeis that he opposed the bill and wanted none of the credit—or responsibility—for it.[13]

With Brandeis now on the "other" side, the opposition lost much of its influence. Before the summer arrived the law was adopted. In addition to the capitalization issue, the law did include one measure of relief for the public: Gas rates would be reduced from $1 to ninety cents per 1,000 cubic feet. But the job was hardly completed. Brandeis was now fixated on the sliding scale principle. And he was prepared to labor again to see it enacted into law.

Adolph Brandeis was getting old. He was now past eighty, and he was beginning to slow down. But his mind was as alert as ever. Frederika and Fanny were no longer with him, but he had Alfred and the rest of his family nearby. And he still had Louis.

His youngest child took vacations in Louisville. And he continued to correspond regularly with Adolph about a whole assortment of things—city planning in Europe, trade with the Far East, Secretary of State John Hay, immigration policy, and the "trick" of New York bankers who got rich on "other people's money." And when Louis had lunch with the chief negotiator for the Japanese in settling the Russo-Japanese War, he made sure that Al told their father all about it. Adolph and Louis even discussed football—and here Louis agreed with his father that the financial aspects of the game had changed it from a sport to an obsession in which any tactic was employed to win.[14]

Louis also kept his father advised of his political activities, and there was plenty to report on that score. In addition to his numerous civic causes, Louis was now heavily involved in Boston's mayoral election. It was an annual event, and in the autumn of 1905, Brandeis had a special reason for becoming interested: Louis Frothingham was seeking the position at City Hall.

Frothingham was descended from a long line of distinguished forebears, including the legendary Puritan governor John Winthrop. He was in every sense a blueblood. He had attended the prestigious Boston Latin School and then Harvard College. In 1901 he was a Republican serving the first of four consecutive one-year terms in the Massachusetts House of Representatives. He then became one of only four representatives from Boston to vote against the Washington Street subway bill being pushed by the Elevated Railway Company. Brandeis took note of the young man's courage. And that admiration was enhanced considerably when Frothingham became Speaker of the House and helped push the compromise gas bill through the legislature. Brandeis knew a good leader when he saw one, and being a public figure of sorts himself now, he wanted to do what he could to help his political ally.

For Brandeis it was an easy choice. The other candidate for the Republican nomination was a political hack named Henry Dewey, and Frothingham ultimately defeated him in the November primary. The Democratic opposition was another story. John F. Fitzgerald—"Honey Fitz" to friends and admirers—was a young Irish politician with a lot of clout. Decades later he would achieve fame posthumously as the grandfather of a United States president named John F. Kennedy.

But in 1905 Fitzgerald's reputation was not one of an eloquent idealist. Quite the contrary. Many people thought he was just another corrupt politician who traded patronage for votes. Edmund Billings, a member of the Good Government Association, wrote to Brandeis in late November that, according to reliable sources, Fitzgerald "is an out and out 'grafter' and . . . no kind of 'graft' is too small for him to stoop to."[15] Brandeis asked Billings to substantiate the charges, and in a few days the Boston attorney wrote letters to the editors of Boston newspapers explaining his support for Frothingham. I may be a Democrat, Brandeis said, but the Republican nominee was clearly the better candidate.

It was all to no avail. Fitzgerald easily defeated Frothingham and remained mayor. Even without the help of Frothingham, though, Brandeis was still ready to push for adoption of the sliding scale system in gas regulation. If they couldn't have the help of old friends like Frothingham, they would make new ones. And that they did.

The governor had already appointed a special committee of five to review the operation of the sliding scale system in London. The three Gas Commissioners on the panel found much to criticize. The system could lead to higher corporate dividends; and although those increases would be accompanied by lower rates, they probably would include a deterioration in service as well. One of the other two members on the panel was Charles Hall, a close friend of Brandeis's. Hall and the other member saw much merit in the plan, and they were willing to let Brandeis help them write their minority report.[16]

Brandeis recommended that the gas company be allowed an initial 7 percent dividend—a 1 percent reduction of the current dividend. However, Brandeis offered the company a carrot—for every five-cent reduction in unit rates, the company could get another percent added to the dividend. So if the company reduced its rate from ninety cents to eighty-five cents, it could distribute 8 percent dividends to its stockholders.

There was a great deal of dissension in the Public Franchise League over this proposal. Edward Warren and some others resigned from the League and publicly voiced their criticisms. But there was one man who still sided with Brandeis in the controversy: James L. Richards. The gas company president believed in the wisdom of the sliding scale system. On April 20, 1906, he wrote to Brandeis that he was willing to go along with the plan—as long as he remained free in public to disavow it if it should fail in the legislature. The company was asserting a right to an 8 percent dividend from the start, and they did not want to be undercut by agreeing to accept the 7 percent dividend advocated by the League.

Brandeis smelled success. He began to crank up his public relations efforts. He checked his elaborate filing-card system, determined which newspapers had supported him in the earlier gas fight, and then sent letters asking for continued support.[17] The articles and letters were duly published, and it helped pave the way through the legislature. "We have won so far, triumphantly in the House, and the prospects are good in the Senate," Louis reported to Al on May 20, 1906. "But we have many opponents—the most active being some of our own former associates who are in my opinion fanatics, and as ready to do injustice to capital as the capitalists have been ready to do injustice to the people."[18]

Within a few days the bill was passed by the Senate and sent to Governor Curtis Guild for signature. He ultimately signed it. But it was no simple matter. "The Governor signed our Sliding Scale Gas Bill, after much heartrending wrestling yesterday," Louis wrote to Al on May 27. "The poor man was sorely distressed and made me lots of work." As for his own role in the affair, Louis was rather matter-of-fact about it. "I succeeded in running this campaign mainly by putting others on the firing line," he told Al; "as your [daughters] would say, 'the man behind.' "[19]

For Brandeis there was much reason to feel satisfied with the result. There would now be no need for government ownership of the gas company—a prospect that carried the risk of corruption. Nor would there be a need for detailed regulation by government—a prospect that carried the risk of inefficiency. Instead, the gas company itself would have an economic incentive to be both efficient and fair. It was perhaps the ideal way for the community to retain control over its affairs. The only question was whether the system would remain viable.[20]

Ten years later Brandeis had more important matters on his mind. He was fighting for confirmation as a justice of the United States Supreme Court. But James L. Richards, still president of the Boston Consolidated Gas Company, was in constant touch with him on the gas legislation. Things had not fared as well as they had hoped under the new law. By 1907 the gas rate had been reduced to eighty cents and the dividends increased to 9 percent. And there things stood. In nine more years there were no more changes. Meanwhile, in cities that did not have the sliding scale system, like Lynn and Worcester, the rate was already down to seventy-five cents. The Gas Commissioners, who never liked the system to begin with, complained that the gas company was using "unorthodox" accounting methods and hiding extra profits. People were clamoring for a change in the law, and in a short time they got it. The sliding scale system was dead.

In retrospect, it was easy to see the law's principal defects. The idea was sound as long as there was a close relationship between management and ownership. But as companies grew large and the stockholders became more dispersed, the system broke down. It was not enough of an incentive for managers to be told that their efficiency would be rewarded by increased dividends to stockholders—people who probably didn't even know the names of company officials. The managers needed a piece of the pie too—something that would be more tangible for them. Maybe that's why they used "unorthodox" accounting methods.

Aside from that problem, there were others down the road. To begin with, technological innovation would enable the company to reduce costs—but it was not the kind of development that warranted a reward for the stockholders. And then there was the prospect of inflation. With increasing costs there would be little likelihood—even with increased efficiencies—of reducing gas rates substantially. If anything, the price pressure would be upward.

The real significance of the gas fight, then, was not in any long-term control of gas rates. Rather, the effort was more noteworthy for what it revealed about Brandeis's goals and methods in working for reform. First and foremost, the gas fight reflected his keen desire to find attractive alternatives to government regulation of business. To him, such regulation was usually inefficient, sometimes corrupt, and almost always less desirable than a system built on the natural incentives of the entrepreneur. In this context the sliding scale was almost an ideal solution.

Brandeis, however, did not entertain false hopes for the future. He recognized that changing circumstances sometimes made today's solutions inapplicable to tomorrow's problems. Indeed, it was for this reason that he himself drafted the provisions enabling the legislature to review and, if warranted, repeal the sliding scale system. So he could not have been entirely surprised when the legislature used that opportunity to try something else after ten years' experience.

Lastly, the gas fight exposed the persistent drive that was to be a Brandeis hallmark in later activities, even on the Supreme Court. Achievement required careful work and patience, he believed. So he would not push for results unless the foundation for success had been laid; but once it was, he would strike as soon as the iron was hot—even, sometimes, if it required that he compromise personal and professional obligations. The compromise could mean, as in the gas fight, the abandonment of clients or organizations to which he had earlier been committed; or, as in later years, it could mean a willingness to retreat, if only temporarily, from otherwise cherished principles.

These occasional compromises did not indicate any indifference to moral precepts. Quite the contrary. Brandeis was very sensitive to doing the right thing. His scale for measurement, though, did not always coincide with others'. But whatever could be said of his standards for evaluation, he was a tenacious fighter, a man who believed that almost any obstacle could eventually be overcome. And if there was any doubt on that score, it surely was laid to rest when he tried to rectify the inequities in the insurance system.

SEVEN

The Struggle for Savings Bank Life Insurance

He has the right to criticize who has the heart to help.

ABRAHAM LINCOLN

James Hazen Hyde really enjoyed the insurance business. It was not that he knew more than other people. In fact, he spent very little time in the study of insurance matters. But he did know how to spend money. And the insurance business was good for that.

He owed it all to his father. In the late nineteenth century Henry B. Hyde was the president and controlling stockholder of the Equitable Assurance Society, one of the nation's more profitable insurance companies. In 1888 the elder Hyde and his senior vice president, James W. Alexander, decided that they needed a little extra cash and some protection for the future. They decided that Hyde would get a salary of $75,000 and that, if he died, Alexander would take over the company and Hyde's widow would get $25,000 a year for life. At a time when there were no income taxes and an elegant dinner could be had for less than one dollar, Hyde had a good deal. It did not take much to justify the new arrangement to the Equitable Board of Directors. In fact, it didn't take anything because they weren't told. Directors asked too many questions.

In 1899 Henry B. died and Alexander became president. James Hazen Hyde was only twenty-three at the time. And although he inherited his father's controlling interest in the company, the terms of the will placed the stock in a trust until James reached the age of thirty. That was fine with James. He would not suffer. The company made him a vice president, and by the time he was twenty-six in 1902 he had a salary of $75,000.

The problem was that younger Hyde did not fit in with the other corporate magnates. Paris and fine wines interested him more than New York and stock deals. So he maintained a close-cropped beard and a French-style haircut, bought a French chateau, became a patron of the arts, ordered flowers out of season, acquired a special car, gave elaborate dinners for the French ambassador, and entertained other high society friends with a masked ball—all at company expense.

The other officers were a little disturbed by James's tastes. There was of course nothing wrong with an exorbitant salary and the purchase of material things. But the other officers were more into railroads and banks. Those kinds of acquisitions were more American. And they were more discreet. That was no small advantage. Hyde's activities were attracting a great deal of attention both inside and outside the company. People were beginning to ask questions—difficult questions that did not have good answers.

As Hyde approached the magic age of thirty, the Equitable Board of Directors decided it was time to do something. They could not strip him of the stocks left by his father, but they could dilute the voting strength of those stocks. So the Board resolved to give all policyholders the right to vote. That could eliminate Hyde's anticipated control and, since the policyholders would probably bow to the company's expertise, it would also leave the existing management in place.

However sound the plan may have been in theory, it did not go over well in practice. For one thing, Hyde did not like it. Nor did he like the charges that the Board leveled against him to justify the new voting policy. Hyde was no shrinking violet. He had some interesting knowledge of his own about the other members of the Equitable team, and he decided to make his own accusations. Before long the controversy was dominating the pages of the trade press. "We believe that the best interests of the business demand that this matter shall not be hushed up, but shall be thoroughly opened to the public," observed the *Life Insurance Independent* in April 1905. The Equitable Society "today is like a patient whose tissues are threatened by some dread disease. The only proper course of treatment is to open the wound, to cleanse it thoroughly of poisonous matter, and after excising the rotten tissues, permit the normal vitality of the body to effect a cure."[1] The governor and legislature of New York—where the Equitable had its headquarters—responded with investigations that exposed rampant fraud and inefficiencies throughout the entire company.[2]

Meanwhile, the Equitable scandals were having a ripple effect in New England. Equitable policyholders, many of whom were prominent businessmen, felt that their policies and investments were endangered. They needed help. And they turned to Louis Brandeis.

At this point Brandeis was putting the final touches on the bill that would allow the consolidation of the eight gas companies. But he was more than happy when William Whitman, a major woollens manufacturer, asked if he would be interested in representing some Equitable policyholders. To Brandeis, the insurance scandals were another example of the community's being exploited by large corporations. The matter of insurance, moreover, was an especially important one. Life insurance was often essential to a family's financial security, and if that security depended on the whims of corporate managers, people could never hope to be independent.

There was one small hitch in dealing with Whitman's group of policyholders: Brandeis already represented the Equitable management. It was nothing terribly important. The New York law firm of Alexander & Greene, which handled most of the Equitable account, often sent the Brandeis firm cases requiring attendance in courts and other forums in New England.

Brandeis saw no ethical problem at all in taking on the policyholders as clients. After all, his goal—and presumably theirs as well—was to take actions that in the long run would benefit the company. His only real concern was that representation of the policyholders might hurt Alexander & Greene, since the firm had acted for the old management. Brandeis discussed the issue with his partner George Nutter, and finally, as Brandeis later recalled, "we agreed that I should go ahead and take our chances."[3]

Whitman and Edwin Abbott, another member of the newly formed committee of policyholders, came to see Brandeis. He was prepared to become their attorney, but with one major qualification. He would not be paid for his services. More was at stake than the interests of individual policyholders, he said; this was a matter that could also have a tremendous impact on the public, and he wanted the freedom to do what he thought best. Brandeis had apparently learned from his experience with the State Board of Trade in the gas fight. He did not want to be chained to the directions of a specific client when the public welfare was at stake.

It was a strange theory of legal representation, and it invited a storm of protest from Whitman and Abbott. They wanted an attorney to defend their group, not a public crusader bent on social reform. The attorney in their presence would not yield. Those were his conditions. Whitman and Abbott were faced with a difficult choice. They had not expected this. But they knew Brandeis, and they knew he was good, indeed, unusually good. So they submitted to his terms, and Brandeis quickly took charge.

Within a short time, he met with the company's new trustees to present the views of the Protective Committee of Policy Holders of the Equitable Assurance Society, a group that claimed to speak for almost all of Equitable's domestic and foreign policyholders. The committee's first priorities were to end the excessive spending and to transform Equitable into a company that provided insurance policies at the lowest cost. To that end, the policyholders wanted Equitable "conducted as a benevolent institution. No one should be induced to take out a policy unless it is advisable to do so in the interests of those whom he desires to protect by it." And to protect individual investments the committee proposed that the Society be fortified with legal safeguards similar to those applied to savings banks.[4]

While the committee and the trustees grappled with the specific problems of the Equitable, Brandeis decided that he had to learn more about the insurance business in general. He was in great demand as a public speaker, but he did not want to comment on the subject until he had a better fix on the situation. And he was convinced that no harm would be done by letting the matter drag out. As he explained to his father, "It is extremely fortunate that the Equitable disclosures came out so gradually. If all the 'exposures' had come at one time the country would have been shocked and then have quickly forgotten the matter as it is apt to do with abuses."[5]

So almost every night Brandeis took the train to Dedham weighted down with books and pamphlets on the insurance business. After Labor Day he was besieged with other work on both private and public causes, including the sliding scale issue in gas regulation. But Brandeis had decided to take on this problem of insurance, and he would not ease up until he had mastered it. On October 26, 1905, he delivered a speech on the abuses of life insurance before the Commercial Club of Boston. It was a long and often dry speech, full of statistics and heavy thoughts. But it demonstrated that this man knew what he was talking about—and that others would do well to listen to him.

Brandeis focused on the top five insurance companies, which included the Equitable. There was no mystery to these choices. Those five companies dominated the field. As of January 1, 1905, the ninety major companies received annual premiums of almost $500 million; the top five companies held almost 70 percent of the 21 million policies covered by these premiums. The top five also possessed more than 60 percent of the total $2.5 billion worth of assets controlled by the ninety major insurance companies.

Not surprisingly, Brandeis found much to criticize in those top five companies. He generally concluded that the management of those companies was handled "selfishly, dishonestly, and in the long run, inefficiently."[6] The inefficiencies were especially galling to him. Most of the policies were held by "the people," he observed—the lower- and middle-income groups whose average policy benefit ranged from $178 to $2,648. The problem was the expenses incurred to provide those policies. Between twenty-two and thirty-eight cents of every premium dollar went to cover the companies' costs. This fared poorly when compared with Massachusetts savings banks' handling of personal savings accounts. Brandeis thought this was an appropriate comparison since, to him, insurance was a form of savings for the future. Measured by total assets, the insurance companies' expenses were seventeen times as great as the banks'.

Brandeis rejected federal regulation as the answer to the insurance company mess. Senator John F. Dryden had introduced a bill proposing that course of action, and it was supported by President Theodore Roosevelt. Brandeis placed no confidence in the proposal. Dryden happened to be the president of the Prudential Insurance Company—one of the top five. The bill might have produced uniformity in insurance regulation by centralizing control in the federal government, but there was a cost for that assumed benefit. As Brandeis explained it, the bill would "free the companies from the careful scrutiny of the commissioners of some of the States. It seeks to rob the State even of the right to protect its own citizens from the legalized robbery to which present insurance measures subject the citizens. . . ."[7]

Instead of federal controls, Brandeis thought that individual states could adopt various measures to reform the insurance business. As he had earlier told the Equitable trustees, insurance investments could be protected by safeguards similar to those applied to savings banks. Uniform accounting systems and other standard forms could also be prescribed. Of perhaps greatest significance, however, was the proposal to limit the size of individual insurance companies. Brandeis said companies should not be allowed "to expand beyond the point of greatest efficiency." He did not know what that point was, but he knew that it was there. To him there was a "danger arising from concentration of quick capital in the hands of a few individuals." And although he offered no specifics in support, he concluded that "many of the abuses in the life insurance business . . . result directly from the size of the company."[8] For this reason, Brandeis thought that true capitalists had more to fear from corporate giants than from those who advocated socialism. "The talk of the agitator alone," he asserted, "does not advance socialism a step; but the formation of great trusts . . . and their frequent corruption of councils and legislatures is hastening us almost irresistibly into socialistic measures. The great captains of industry and of finance, who profess the greatest horror at the extension of governmental functions, are the chief makers of socialism."[9]

The speech attracted a great deal of publicity. Brandeis contacted the editors of the major papers. He printed 25,000 copies of the speech and distributed them to people far and wide, both in and out of Boston. And he continually talked to civic and business leaders about the issue, asking them if they had read his speech and if they had considered possible solutions. It was not enough to identify a problem. In the end, people cared more about results.

Insurance was not the most absorbing problem Brandeis had to confront. It was Alice. Despite their hopes for improved health for her, things seemed to go from bad to worse. In the summer of 1905 her doctor prescribed care away from home, and Louis found the long absence frustrating. "I wish you would tell your esteemed doctor," he wrote his wife at one point, "that he must do a hurry-up job as we aren't prepared to leave you with him much longer. Indeed I felt quite like carrying you off with us in his absence."[10]

Louis's exhortations might have lifted Alice's spirits, but they did little for her health. The next summer Alice's doctor sent her to St. Hubert's, a facility in upstate New York. Her condition remained serious—in fact, for a while she could not even sit up. Letter writing was obviously difficult, and the dearth of mail pained Louis. "The heart has not yet brought me anything from Saint Hubert's today," he wrote in mid-September 1906, "and I feel quite lost." By the fall Alice was back home, but the impact of her headaches and general condition remained with her. As always, her husband was full of encouragement. "The sun shines here," he wrote in November from New York City, "and I trust it shines also with you. And that you will be as joyous when this reaches you. . . . You have had all the burdens of our fifteen years and you have borne them with a patience and courage which are of the noblest." Alice's response was full of despair, and Louis again tried to pick her up. "Don't lose your courage, dear, which has been so fine," he implored her. "The good times are coming."

Sadly, Louis's optimism was premature. Alice continued to suffer from headaches and poor health. In the summer of 1907 he went with her to Petersham for a quiet rest. He talked to her, he read to her, and he tried to give her hope. It was not easy. In early August he explained Alice's condition to their daughters. "Mother is not especially uncomfortable," he reported to Susan and Elizabeth, "but is very tired of the whole business. She talks much of wanting to die but also of wanting to get well. She evidently enjoys my being here and is eager to see you, which I tell her shall be later. She is really enjoying the reading aloud—listens quite a little and remembers less—but concentrates her thoughts I should think rather more than last year."[11]

Louis's care and patience would, in time, reap enormous benefits for both him and Alice. The wage earner would similarly benefit from Brandeis's persistence. The difficulties with Alice did not divert him from his study of insurance matters. And the more he studied, the more he realized that there was one practice that was especially troublesome: industrial insurance. This was a form of life insurance made available to low-income workers who toiled in the factories and warehouses of the inner city. Unlike regular life insurance, the policies were solicited by agents who climbed the tenement steps and went door to door in hopes of signing up clients. Often agents would check the hospitals' recent lists of births and advise the new parents of all the horrible contingencies that could befall them and leave their new child penniless in the cold, cruel world. For only fifty cents or so a week, the agent would explain, you could have a life insurance policy with a benefit of about $140—enough to cover the costs of a serious illness and a burial if the unfortunate should happen to the breadwinner. What made this insurance technique even more insidious was the agent's usual failure to inform the worker of the policy's limitations. For instance, in most cases there was no coverage until a few months of premiums had been paid, and strict forfeiture clauses left the worker little leeway if he missed a weekly payment. Lapsed policies were very common.

Not surprisingly, industrial insurance was very profitable for the companies that handled it. But from Brandeis's perspective that was not the worst of it. As always, he felt that people could not control their lives and fulfill their potential until they were financially secure. And that security should not depend on the good faith of companies interested only in the bottom line of a balance sheet. "In order that our working people may attain and preserve what we call the American standard of living," he told a journalist, "it is essential that every working man should make adequate provision for the future. The 'living wage' is not satisfied by a sum sufficient to supply the immediate demand for food, shelter, clothing, education and recreation; to be a 'living wage' it is necessary that there should be a surplus to provide for the contingencies of the future, the contingency of unemployment or sickness or accident to the wage earner, or his superannuation or his premature death." Life insurance, then, was not to be merely a bet against untimely death; it was also to be a means to provide security in retirement. To Brandeis, few things were more demoralizing than a tax that would be levied against wages and charge the government with the financial responsibility of caring for senior citizens. "The American spirit demands," he said, "that provision for the workingman's future be made through his own efforts to secure a wage sufficiently large to leave a surplus applicable to such purpose and to the development on his part of strength of character and self control which shall induce him voluntarily so to apply it."[12]

Brandeis came to believe that savings banks might be the answer to the problem. In many ways they performed many of the same functions as insurance companies. Both collected the worker's money, invested it, and paid it back when the worker or his family needed it—although of course the insurance company had more limitations on the return of the investment. There were some tasks that insurance companies alone performed—the medical exam, verification of the insured's death, and the actuarial calculations. But Brandeis was convinced that the worker and the savings banks could take on those added responsibilities with minimum cost. If so, savings bank insurance would have several advantages over that offered by the insurance companies. To begin with, it could eliminate the cost of agents soliciting insurance; the worker could pick up the insurance where he saved his money. It could also introduce other features that would help the worker plan for old age—such as investment standards that would guarantee a certain return after retirement.

Although he sensed that his idea was workable, Brandeis knew enough to know that he was no actuary or statistician. In November 1905 he wrote to Walter Channing Wright, an actuarial consultant who had already advised Brandeis that the plan was practical. The tenacious lawyer was not satisfied with that observation, however; he wanted to popularize the idea with the public and then present it to the legislature. In order to succeed he needed more than general conclusions; he needed specific facts and analyses. Would Wright, he asked, be willing to help? He certainly would. He was a strong advocate of efficiencies in insurance regulation, and Brandeis's proposal held a lot of promise in that area.[13] Thus began an extended correspondence that would eventually give Brandeis the information he needed.

By June 1905 Brandeis had completed a draft of an article explaining the abuses of industrial insurance and his proposal to use savings banks as a solution to the problem. It was no easy task. Writing was—and always would be, even when he was a Supreme Court justice—a chore for him. It took him much thought and many drafts before he could settle on the right words to convey his exact meaning. And being a perfectionist did not speed things along.

Brandeis was nonetheless satisfied that his article was at least at the point where he could solicit comment from Wright and a host of other friends and insurance experts. To Charles Hall, the friend who had helped him on the gas question, the Boston attorney explained his intentions. "If you agree with the [article's] conclusions," said Brandeis, "I want you to join with me in the effort to have our Legislature at its next session pass a law authorizing savings banks to take over this business. Any bill introduced to that end," he continued, "will meet with strenuous opposition from the insurance companies with their multitudinous ramifications throughout the community, and will also meet a serious obstacle in the conservatism of savings banks' trustees. The campaign must, therefore, be very carefully planned, and we must secure for the work all possible support."[14]

Brandeis knew how to maximize that support. He contacted Norman Hapgood, the editor of the much-respected *Collier's* magazine. Hapgood, a wiry young man, had reached his position with the magazine through unusual channels. He had graduated from Harvard College and Harvard Law School, found the practice of law boring, and then turned to writing. Within a short time he produced popular biographies of George Washington and Abraham Lincoln. And then he began a career in journalism, ultimately getting together in 1903 with Robert Collier, the twenty-seven-year-old owner of the magazine bearing his name. Brandeis was convinced that there would soon be great public demand for insurance reform, and he inquired whether Hapgood "might deem it wise to have *Collier's* lead in the movement."[15] Within a short time Hapgood responded affirmatively. It was the beginning of a lifelong and intimate friendship that would lead them to take on the leaders of big business, a hostile Congress, and even a naïve president.

As Hapgood prepared Brandeis's article for publication, the attorney suddenly found himself placed in a ticklish situation. In August 1906, George Peters, an Equitable stockholder, filed a lawsuit in a Massachusetts court asking for an accounting of the company's expenses. Although Peters's complaint did not mention Brandeis's widely distributed speech to the Commercial Club, the complaint looked as if it could have been written by Brandeis himself. The complaint recited all the abuses described in the Brandeis speech and asked the court to require the company to open its books so that people like Peters, who had a direct interest in the company's affairs, could find out whether their money had been misused. It seemed like the very relief sought by Brandeis on behalf of the Equitable policyholders.

Since the lawsuit had been filed in Massachusetts, the Alexander & Greene law firm asked Brandeis to defend the company. And he agreed. Once again, Brandeis saw no inconsistency in representing Equitable. To be sure, he thought that Equitable had made mistakes and owed the public an accounting, but he did not think it should be pried from the company through a court case. Brandeis later explained to his partner Ned McClennen that "the Peters action was directly inimical to the Company; that if he obtained that accounting, it would have opened the door to liability to accounting in every State and Country, and would have subjected the Company to very heavy liability—all for the benefit of an individual. . . ."[16] It was a technical explanation that would satisfy some impartial observers.[17] But for a social reformer who ardently subscribed to the cleansing power of public exposure, it was a strange position. After all, the company would have faced a "very heavy liability" only if it had done something wrong and someone was entitled to relief.

While he argued for the Equitable against Peters, Brandeis busied himself with his savings bank proposal. The *Collier's* article came out in September 1906.[18] The article had virtually no passion to it. But the cold statistics laid bare the sad situation. If a wage earner saved fifty cents a week from the time he was twenty-one until the age of sixty-one—then the average life span of an American male—he would have almost $2,300 in the bank in principal and interest. If the same man took the same fifty cents a week and bought industrial insurance, his heirs would receive only $820 if he died at the age of sixty-one. The plain and simple fact, the article argued, was that industrial insurance was inefficient and inadequate. Proportionately, it cost the policyholder twice as much as a normal life insurance policy; and because of the conditions applied to it, about two-thirds of the policies were forfeited within three years. Savings banks, the article said—with their existing staffs and their goodwill in the community—could offer life insurance in low amounts for low premiums. And a new law could establish a guaranty fund that would protect both the bank and the policyholder in case of an unforeseen drain on the bank's resources.

Brandeis had carefully laid the groundwork with newspaper editors, and press reaction to the article was generally widespread and favorable. The trade press was not quite as charitable. The *Insurance Press* characterized Brandeis's savings bank proposal as "positively grotesque in its absurdity." The *Insurance Post* had similar disdain for the scheme. "Getting life insurance, like 'getting religion,' has never been achieved to any appreciable extent by hanging out a sign or [by] distribution of printed exhortations. . . ." The magazine therefore saw nothing to worry about in Brandeis's proposal: "Nobody need lose any sleep over the dream of the Boston theorist, for the dream has about one chance in a million of ever coming true."[19] Which shows how little the trade press knew about the "Boston theorist."

Brandeis had already begun to prepare for the legislature's consideration of his savings bank proposal. In August 1905, he had contacted Norman White, the younger brother of his good friend Herbert White. Since White faced no opposition in his campaign to become a state representative, Brandeis assumed that he was "beginning to think of what you are to do to make your first term in the Legislature most useful and effective." Brandeis had a suggestion. "It seems to me," he told White, "that you could do nothing better for the community and yourself than to make a thorough study of the life insurance situation, and possible legislation."[20] White agreed, and in a short time he became Brandeis's first lieutenant in pushing the savings bank insurance bill through the legislature.

Brandeis had also talked to John Cole, the Speaker of the House, about his appointment to the Joint Recess Committee, which was to study the insurance question in the autumn of 1906. These initial efforts with Cole and other legislators, however, did not produce immediate results. When the committee met, there seemed little enthusiasm for the savings bank proposal. After one stormy session, Representative George Barnes, who was sympathetic to the proposal, met Brandeis in the State House corridor. "Perhaps you would like to know how the committee voted on your plan," Barnes said. "Yes," said the attorney eagerly, "how did it go?" "Fourteen to one against you," Barnes replied.[21]

Brandeis could not have been terribly surprised. He knew the power of the insurance industry. And he also recognized that the savings banks themselves would be against the proposal. They just didn't like to fiddle around with new ideas. "We have trouble enough as it is now from depositors who are hardly able to write their names," one bank president lamented, "and if an insurance department were to be added here I don't see how we could find time or floor space to handle it."[22]

None of these obstacles discouraged Brandeis. He had faced tough hurdles before. And that experience proved useful here. As in other legislative fights, public opinion was the key. "What we need primarily," he told a friend, "is publicity, which shall make clear to the community the enormity of the present system." And the educational effort was especially important with respect to savings bank trustees and wage earners. "If we should get tomorrow the necessary legislation, without having achieved that process of education," he added, "we could not make a practical working success of the plan."[23]

Organization was an essential element to any sustained educational effort. So on November 26, 1906, a group of prominent citizens met for lunch and established the Savings Bank Insurance League—a group that would, as in earlier Brandeis struggles, maintain a barrage of publicity to persuade people of the merits of their cause. Although he was not an officer of the League, Brandeis remained the principal moving force behind it. He would arrange to speak as many as six times a week—even to the point of keeping a dinner suit in his office so that he could change and go directly from his office to the speaking engagement. And as before, he always made sure to notify the editors of the various newspapers, advise them of the new disclosures in his speech, and suggest that they might want to have a reporter present. It worked like a charm, and Brandeis's name and picture became regular features in the city press.

The insurance people began to see the handwriting on the wall, and they did not like the message. Something had to be done. On December 5, 1906, a businessman advised Brandeis that a new insurance company was being formed, that he had been selected as one of those to be invited to become a stockholder, and that, because of his significance, the company was prepared to make him a "special proposition."[24] Brandeis knew a bribe when he saw one and quickly rejected the offer. "My interest in life insurance is wholly with the view to aiding and correcting what I deem to be great evils in the present system which cause heavy burdens upon those least able to bear them . . .," he responded. "I should, therefore, under no circumstances become connected with any enterprise with the view to investment or personal profit."[25]

The insurance company proposal was clearly an act of desperation by the industry. But their concerns were more than justified. Brandeis conferred several times with Governor Curtis Guild, and in his message to the legislature on January 3, 1907, the governor endorsed the savings bank plan. Within a few days the Joint Recess Committee issued its report and, in a complete reversal of its earlier stance, approved the plan in principle. The smell of success was in the air.

Brandeis was finding similar encouragement in his battles to demonstrate the merits of his plan to savings banks. He directed League officials to concentrate on bank trustees, since collectively they would decide the matter for their respective banks. To help make his case more persuasive, Brandeis knew it would help to secure the endorsements of prominent (and conservative) businessmen. He got a real boost in that area when William L. Douglas, a former governor and a well-known shoe manufacturer, endorsed the savings bank plan. "It is intolerable," Douglas told the Savings Bank League, that the workingman "should be obliged to give up so much of his earnings to obtain a few hundred dollars of insurance. I believe your plan . . . [to be] not only sound and feasible, but the best way of furnishing to workingmen life insurance at cost. . . ."[26] And more than that—as president of the People's Bank of Brockton, Douglas said he would personally provide a $25,000 guaranty fund to help his bank start an insurance department as soon as the law permitted it.

Douglas's statement was given wide publicity, and League members invoked it often with other bank men. By March hundreds of bank trustees were members of the League, and two banks explicitly stated that they would establish an insurance department as soon as it was authorized.

Even before the Douglas endorsement was clinched, Brandeis was starting to feel positive about the effort. "We are having quite a resistance from the ultraconservatives, particularly among the savings bank officials," he told his brother on January 3, "but the movement has acquired such a momentum that it will be very hard for them to stop us now. They began too late."[27] But the opposition, as Brandeis well knew, had hardly given up.

March 23, 1907, was Al's fifty-third birthday. Louis, of course, remembered it, and he could not let the day go by without a note to his most intimate friend. "Only a hasty line that this birthday greeting may reach you," he wrote on March 21. "...[R]emember our arrival at Venice 34 years ago."[28] With the note went Louis's deep concern for his brother's health. In recent months, Al had been dragging and found the supervision of farm and business operations very trying. Louis knew all about those kinds of problems, and at one point he suggested that Al quit work daily at 2 P.M. Al no doubt appreciated his brother's advice and the good wishes on his birthday. The separation of distance had not at all weakened the bond between them.

Birthday wishes were not the only matters on Brandeis's mind on March 21, 1907. In fact, for those interested in savings bank insurance it was a big day. Hundreds of people crowded into Room 204 of the State House, with the overflow spilling out into the corridors. Louis D. Brandeis was about to testify on his proposal before the Joint Legislative Committee. For three hours, he treated the committee to a careful dissection of the problems of industrial insurance. As the lunch hour approached, the chairman asked if he could finish by one o'clock. "Most certainly not," Brandeis replied. "Even if a small part of the people who favor this measure appeared before the committee each speaking the words—'I favor this bill'—the committee would be unable to hear them in the entire month of April."[29] The comment evoked laughter, and Brandeis joined in. He never could deliver a humorous line without being among the first to laugh himself. The chairman accepted the comment graciously and adjourned the hearing until April 2.

During the break, Brandeis consulted with Warren A. Reed, a municipal judge with extensive experience in Massachusetts politics. Reed had some advice for Brandeis to help assure his success. "At our hearing," said Reed, "we need to make the committee feel that [ours] is a public demand, rather than a private hobby of a few well-meaning gentlemen. We must remember that laws are passed in answer to a public demand, rather than because they are good, and our first object should be to start such a demand."[30] It was especially important, Reed added, that committee members feel pressure from the labor unions—because they would probably be the only ones to counter the strong influence of the bankers. Brandeis took Reed's advice to heart, and when the hearings resumed on April 2, the room was filled with labor men.

Brandeis did not let the matter rest there. He continued to talk to the legislators themselves and urged others to do so as well. A slight hitch in these legislative maneuvers arose when William S. Kyle, an important representative, complained to Brandeis about Norman White's "asinine" behavior and "exaggerated ego." Things would go more smoothly, Kyle counseled, if the legislative leadership were left to others. Brandeis was not about to let the ship sink because of one man, and White, in a spirit of accommodation, agreed to take a back seat in the final stages.[31]

Brandeis nonetheless continued to rely on White to keep him abreast of developments. Almost daily White would provide him with a list of the legislators and an indication of their inclinations. Brandeis then used the lists to determine whom to talk to and where to apply pressure. The legislature, used to intense lobbying campaigns, was nonetheless impressed with Brandeis's organization. One senator, in fact, observed that no bill in his memory had been lobbied for as heavily. "Paid representatives have time and time again asked us to vote for the bill," Senator Guy W. Cox commented; "great piles of literature have been forced upon the members and a great amount of money, legitimately spent, has been used to push this bill through."[32]

All the work paid off. By the middle of May 1907, the Joint Legislative Committee approved the bill by a vote of 10–4. On June 5, the bill passed the House with a vote of 146–26, and the Senate shortly followed suit by a vote of 23–3. Confident of the Senate vote and the governor's willingness to sign the bill, Brandeis began to make plans for its implementation. As the legislation neared its completion, Louis told his brother what lay ahead. "A respite in work would follow this much desired consummation," he wrote Al, "but a respite only, as it will take much more work to make the bill a practical success than it has to march it along this far."[33]

It was a fair prediction. Although two banks began insurance departments by 1908, it took many years and long hours of hard work before the new law was functioning smoothly. In later years, though, it would provide much satisfaction to Brandeis. In fact, he would call savings bank life insurance—with its contributions to the all-important independence of the workingman—his greatest achievement.[34]

He would feel almost as good about his battle with J.P. Morgan and the New Haven Railroad—a battle that was starting to heat up when the savings bank plan became law.

EIGHT

The Rise and Fall of the New Haven Railroad

Even the woodpecker owes his success to the fact that he uses his head and keeps pecking away until he finishes the job he starts.

COLEMAN COX

In his well-read treatise on America of the early nineteenth century, Alexis de Tocqueville had identified the Bench and the Bar as the only real aristocracy in the United States. By the end of the century, however, few people retained that view. The legal profession was under attack. And like most industries in America at the time, it too became subject to the spirit of reform that seemed to pervade the country.

The diminished status of the lawyer reflected the change in his role. Early in America's history, lawyers had been valued counselors who invoked lofty principles to defend their clients in court. That kind of practice was now largely a relic of the past. The lawyer's responsibilities had changed as the industrial face of America had changed. Large corporations could not always afford to resolve their problems through the costly and time-consuming process of litigation. More and more lawyers were asked to counsel their clients on legal problems *before* they got to court—and sometimes how to sidestep the law entirely. People began to take notice. Lawyers no longer seemed to be independent advisors. They now appeared to be "kept" men—mere appendages of the clients they represented. "Many of the most influential and most highly remunerated members of the bar in every centre of wealth," President Theodore Roosevelt observed in 1905, "make it their special task to work out bold and ingenious schemes by which their very wealthy clients, individual and corporate, can evade the laws which are made to regulate in the interest of the public the use of great wealth."[1]

Brandeis was, of course, aware of the lawyer's new role as a corporate advisor. In fact, he and Warren had capitalized on it in building their practice. But with more experience (and more money in his pocket) Brandeis felt it was time for change. So when the Harvard Ethical Society asked him to discuss the opportunities for a law career in the spring of 1905, he decided to talk about the shortcomings—and potential—of the legal profession.

Brandeis candidly advised his audience at the Phillips Brooks House of the lawyer's diminished status. To him the explanation was clear. "Instead of holding a position of independence, between the wealthy and the people, prepared to curb the excesses of either," he said, "able lawyers have, to a large extent, allowed themselves to become adjuncts of great corporations and have neglected the obligation to use their powers for the protection of the people. We hear much of the 'corporation attorney,' " he noted, "and far too little of the 'people's attorney.' The great opportunity of the American Bar is and will be to stand again as it did in the past, ready to protect also the interests of the people."

The problem was particularly acute in legislative affairs, Brandeis said. Lawyers frequently confused that situation with the defense of a client in a purely private controversy. As a result, he observed, lawyers representing private clients "often advocated . . . legislative measures which as citizens they could not approve. . . ." In Brandeis's view, this was unacceptable, because the professional ethics involved in legislative matters were entirely different from the ethics applied in private controversies. "In the first place," he said, "the counsel selected to represent important private interests possesses usually ability of a high order, while the public is often inadequately represented or wholly unrepresented. Great unfairness to the public is apt to result from this fact." Brandeis also observed that lawyers would tolerate practices in legislative affairs that they would condemn in private litigation. Bribing legislators, for example, was openly accepted, even though it would be considered highly immoral to bribe a judge.

Brandeis warned of dire consequences if the legal profession did not revise its ethical standards. "The next generation," he predicted, "must witness a continuing and ever-increasing contest between those who have and those who have not." It was therefore necessary for both new and old lawyers to take heed, lest quiet doubts explode into "a revolt of the people against the capitalists. . . ."[2]

Even as he issued this warning, Brandeis was becoming involved in a new controversy—one that would soon lead citizens far and wide to identify him as "the people's attorney."

J.P. Morgan was used to getting what he wanted. As the head of a vast corporate and financial empire, he had the money and the power to satisfy almost any whim. Even the slightest frustrations could infuriate him. Forgetful servants often found food and clothing being thrown at them when a certain act or omission caused discomfort to their boss. No one was immune from these incessant demands—not even his lawyers. When one company counselor advised Morgan that a proposal of his was illegal, the tycoon showed nothing but contempt. "Well," said Morgan, "I don't know as I want a lawyer to tell me what I cannot do. I hire him to tell me how to do what I want to do."[3]

One thing Morgan wanted to do was to make a success out of the New York, New Haven & Hartford Railroad, a company he had purchased around the turn of the century. Morgan had grown up in Connecticut and had a soft spot for New England, the principal location of the railroad's lines. So he was prepared to do whatever he could to make the New Haven the best railroad in the Northeast.

The only real problem with Morgan's dream was the competition. There was too much of it. How could the New Haven prosper when people could just as easily use one of New England's many other rail or steamship lines? Morgan was not intimidated by that. He had faced competition before. So he did what he usually did—he bought the competition out.

Railroad consolidations were nothing new in Massachusetts. The Board of Railroad Commissioners had approved several around the turn of the century, and the public benefited from decreased rates and more efficient service. In fact, the Railroad Commissioners openly encouraged the many small rail lines in their state—especially those with financial problems—to consider consolidation. So Morgan's desire for a larger New Haven Railroad was certainly consistent with the established policies of Massachusetts.[4]

Morgan, however, was not interested in following the procedures required by law. He therefore selected a perfect agent to carry out his wishes: Charles S. Mellen. With a round face, white hair, and a full white moustache, Mellen looked like a corporate magnate. He had the experience to act like one as well. He had started out as a clerk for the New Hampshire Railroad in 1869 at the age of eighteen. By the time Morgan picked him to become president of the New Haven in 1903, Mellen was president of the Northern Pacific Railroad and had achieved fame in railroad circles as one of the most aggressive and dynamic managers in the business. The only thing Mellen lacked, really, was a good moral code. And that, in the end, was to prove his undoing.

For starters, Mellen decided to buy some inter-urban railway systems in western Massachusetts. An 1874 state law stated clearly that a railroad could not acquire the stock of any other railway without the prior approval of the Railroad Commissioners. Mellen had a way around that. He used the cloak of the Consolidated Railroad Company, a firm chartered in Connecticut and designed to act as a holding company for the New Haven. The scam fooled no one, and in 1905 the Boston and Maine Railroad petitioned the legislature for authority to avoid the 1874 law so that it could do what the New Haven was doing.

The matter generated a lot of publicity, and before long the Joint Special Committee on Railroads decided to hold a hearing to consider, among other things, the propriety of the New Haven's acquisitions. Brandeis appeared on behalf of the Public Franchise League. The obligation to obtain the approval of the Railroad Commissioners was not, in his view, debatable. As to whether the commissioners should approve the New Haven acquisitions, Brandeis was open minded. "It is perfectly possible," he told the legislators, that the New Haven's arguments "may remove any doubts in my mind or another's, and I only wanted that opportunity for light which I think the community should have before being quite competent to express an opinion."[5]

After almost a year of discussion, Governor Curtis Guild entered the fray. Guild, a Progressive who did not enjoy the political support of corporate magnates like Morgan, resented the fact that this corporation—a "foreign" one chartered in Connecticut—was so cavalier in its disregard of Massachusetts law. On June 23, 1906, Guild issued a special message to the legislature that bore the Brandeis imprint. "The present railroad situation," Guild said, ". . . is most unjust and inequitable." It was not only the decrease of rail competition in western Massachusetts; as Brandeis himself would argue later, Guild stated that the primary issue was the domination of rail transportation by a corporation chartered in Connecticut instead of Massachusetts. "Slowly, surely," Guild observed, "the control of our railroads, the control of passage to market of every Massachusetts product, the control of the transportation to and from his work of every Massachusetts citizen is passing from our hands to those of aliens."[6]

Guild asked the legislature to require the New Haven to give up its illegal purchases. But Guild's influence could not match the New Haven's—especially when Mellen publicly advised the legislature that the New Haven would acquire no more rail interests until the state's attorney general could get a ruling from the state courts whether such acquisitions were illegal. That satisfied the legislature, and the 1906 session adjourned without any action being taken.

Unfortunately, the legislators underestimated Mellen's imagination—and his willingness to ignore his own promises. Within a short time he established the New England Security & Investment Company, an association that was technically beyond the reach of the 1874 law and other measures governing Massachusetts corporations. Mellen transferred New Haven's street railway stock to the New England company and resumed the purchase of Massachusetts rail companies as well as steamship lines that could compete with rail service. Mellen then used the New England Navigation Company, a New Haven subsidiary, to negotiate the purchase of more than one-third of the stock of the Boston & Maine Railroad, a purchase designed to presage a merger of the two rail systems. The only thing Mellen did not bargain for in this transaction was the opposition of the Lawrence family—or the tenacity of Louis Brandeis.

When rumors circulated around Boston in the spring of 1907 that the New Haven had purchased the B&M Railroad, Governor Guild wrote to Mellen to inquire whether there was any truth to the stories. Mellen had hoped to complete the sale without public scrutiny, but that was an idle dream now. He told the governor that interests affiliated with the New Haven had indeed purchased some B&M stock. The newspapers trumpeted the information to the public, and before long everyone was discussing it.

There were many people who thought the merger of the New Haven and B&M railroads a wise move. Many businessmen and civic leaders were convinced that this merger, like others approved by the Railroad Commissioners, would lead to increased efficiencies and lower rates. This seemed especially probable since the B&M seemed to be having some financial difficulties. Moreover, the merger would not produce many duplicated lines, since the B&M lines were located primarily to the north of Boston, areas not served by the New Haven. For these reasons, even some members of the Public Franchise League, like Edward Filene, endorsed the merger in principle.

Brandeis took a different view. To him, it was not really a question of competition. As he confided to his colleague William Dunbar, the merger would have only a "slight" impact on the availability of competing lines. Instead, Brandeis was bothered by a single company chartered in Connecticut having so much power over the Massachusetts transportation system. As a Connecticut corporation, the New Haven, he feared, would be less susceptible to regulation by the Massachusetts government. "The question . . . before us," he told Filene, "is whether the whole transportation system of Massachusetts shall be turned over to a single monopoly, and that one controlled by aliens. . . ." He knew it would be difficult to educate the community on the dangers involved. "Our businessmen fail to grasp

. . . the evils of monopoly," he wrote to Al, "and are cowards besides." But he had faced tough obstacles before, and so he was not about to give up.[7]

Brandeis drafted a bill that would require the New Haven to give up its B&M stock by April 1, 1908, would prohibit any future purchases of B&M stock, and would impose criminal penalties on those who defied the law. After the bill was introduced by state Representative Robert Luce, Samuel and William Lawrence asked Brandeis to represent them in the matter. They owned 1,000 shares of B&M stock and, like Brandeis, resented a Connecticut corporation's taking over the venerable B&M. Brandeis accepted the Lawrences as clients, and at the hearing before the Legislative Committee on Railroads on June 10, 1907, he appeared on their behalf.

Brandeis told the legislators that the merger issue was "probably the most important economic question which has come before this Legislature in a generation." In part, this was because this issue involved the efficiency of the Massachusetts transportation system. Brandeis explained that there existed "a certain limit of greatest efficiency. . . ." Although he could not identify that limit, he was confident that the New Haven's proposed transportation monopoly exceeded it. Brandeis told the committee that "no man wants to put all his eggs in one basket, and I think that the community is in danger of being in a trust, all those eggs being in one basket."[8]

Later that same day Mellen testified. He was in rare form—sharp, witty, and sarcastic. Before long he had the legislators and the packed audience in stitches. If people were concerned about localism, said Mellen, he could accommodate that. He would paint the word *Boston* on the top, bottom, and sides of all the railroad cars. When asked if he had read Brandeis's extremely tough bill, Mellen replied that he had and that he had "but one objection to it: it was not quite strong enough." Mellen said he would amend the bill by requiring the New Haven to sell its B&M stock and prohibit its purchase by anyone else. "And," the New Haven president added, "I would put anybody in prison that discussed the subject."

Brandeis rose to inquire whether he could ask Mellen a few questions. The committee chairman said it was permissible, but Mellen was under no obligation to answer. Mellen knew an opening when he saw one. As Brandeis turned to him, the railroad man was already packing up his things and making his exit. When Brandeis tried to explain the basis for his questions, Mellen cut him off, saying, "I will read them in the newspapers in the morning, if you please." And that was that. Or so Mellen hoped.[9]

Under the backdoor guidance of Senator Lodge—who was primarily concerned about the national political ramifications of the merger question—the legislature adopted a bill that would prohibit the New Haven from voting its B&M stock until June 1, 1908. It was basically a holding action, and it did not at all please Brandeis. But he was not about to idle away his time. The fight was only just beginning.

Asa French, the United States Attorney for the Boston district, asked Brandeis in June 1907 for his assistance in preparing an antitrust lawsuit against the New Haven. Brandeis did not think that French had much of a case, but he asked Dunbar to do some legal research. For his part, Brandeis decided to make a thorough review of the company's financial situation. It was a painstaking task, but in the end it was a real eye opener.

Mellen's schemes involved a tangled web of corporate relationships. In addition to the Connecticut and Rhode Island rail systems it owned, the New Haven used the New England Security & Investment Company and other subsidiaries to disguise its true interests. Brandeis found, however, that few of these corporate interests had been disclosed to the Railroad Commissioners, even though the law required the New Haven to file a complete financial statement. "One might study the report filed with your Board from end to end," Brandeis informed the Railroad Commissioners in October 1907, "and never know that the New Haven held any interest in the Boston and Maine Railroad stock, or in the Rhode Island Street Railway System, or in any of the Massachusetts Street Railways controlled by the New England Security & Investment Co."[10] He asked the Board to get additional information from the New Haven. In the meantime, he wrote to the Interstate Commerce Commission and requested the New Haven reports on file with that agency.

Brandeis recognized that it would take a mountain of work to get the facts and make them available to the public. It was a challenge he treasured. He was already telling Al that "there ought to be some fun ahead bringing out the facts." He was also confident that the public would eventually see the light. "I think before we get through," he advised his brother, "the estimable gentlemen who scrambled for the chance of exchanging their B&M stock for New Haven will feel that they have been [fooled]."[11]

The State Commission on Commerce and Industry gave Brandeis his first opportunity to discuss some of his new discoveries about the New Haven. There was some mystery as to the exact function of the commission and why Governor Guild had asked them to investigate the merger issue. But Brandeis would talk to almost anyone. He dutifully came to Room 440 of the State House on the morning of November 22, 1907. He brought some friends and some newspaper reporters with him, but the commission members would have none of that. They were conducting a *private* investigation, it was explained, and journalists were not welcome. After a brief huddle in the hall, Brandeis decided to testify before the commission anyway. There was probably nothing to lose.

He carefully explained to the commission the difficulties he had had in obtaining accurate information about the New Haven. He had communicated with the various government departments, and he had even corresponded with Mellen himself—all to no avail. They were keeping close wraps on the situation. No one from New Haven would even debate him in public on the issue. "I therefore say that your Commission is just as incompetent to pass a final judgment that there shall be no merger as to pass a judgment that there shall be a merger," Brandeis asserted, "because you have not, and cannot get together, the data. And if you could get together the data, the conclusions which you would reach in regard to facts would not be entitled to the confidence of the community, because they would not be reached after that opportunity of testing and of cross-examination and of criticism, to which conclusions on any important subject of public interest should be subjected."

The situation was especially important because New Haven stock had been the premier blue chip investment. Widows and orphans, it was often said, bought New Haven stock with their inheritance money. Savings banks also kept a large portfolio of the stock. "I have noticed," Brandeis commented, "that in all these great financial transactions, even the richest men have extremely little money. It is other people's money they are doing business with. In the case of the New Haven, they are doing it with the money of that corporation, which is the money of some fourteen to twenty thousand different people. . . ."

In concluding his remarks, Brandeis warned the commission not to rely on Mellen. "I not only do not believe in him as a man," the attorney said; "I believe he has proved himself a man who ought not to be trusted, and my own belief is that he will prove a Napoleon of finance and fall." It would, in time, be seen as a fair prediction. But Brandeis indicated that he would object to the merger of the New Haven and B&M lines even if Mellen were a saint. "I should object strenuously," he said, "to turning over to a foreign hand the instruments by which the welfare of Massachusetts is so largely governed."[12]

In view of the growing interdependence of the states' transportation systems and economies, Brandeis's position on the merger was subject to valid criticism. After all, the creation of a consolidated rail system in New England was probably the only way the area could compete for shipping business with the large rail conglomerates in New York. It was also unlikely that small, intrastate lines could satisfy the growing transportation needs of Massachusetts' citizens—needs that reflected an increase in interstate business. But Brandeis's view was based more on political and moral considerations than on economic analyses. Big corporations were bad for the community and the individual, he felt—even if they did secure some additional material benefits.

Brandeis pushed ahead in his attack. But by this juncture he was no longer acting as counsel for the Lawrences. He had too much of a personal interest in the matter, and, as in the insurance fight, he wanted the freedom to do as he pleased. At the same time, he was beginning to feel guilty about all the time these public causes were taking. The firm was prospering, but there was no reason why his partners should suffer financially because he wanted to enjoy the luxury of working for free. He therefore decided to substitute himself as the client and to pay the firm for his services.[13] In time, he would give the firm $25,000 in legal fees to cover his involvement in the New Haven controversy.

The arrangement was unusual, but it did distinguish Brandeis from the crowd—although he did not lack for publicity after he issued his pamphlet on the New Haven in December 1907.

The seventy-seven-page document reflected the factual research he initiated after United States Attorney French requested his assistance. French was no doubt glad to see that Brandeis's initiative was fruitful. But no one was prepared for the public sensation created by the pamphlet.

Almost everyone had assumed that the New Haven was in sound financial shape and that the B&M was the line in need of help. Brandeis challenged those assumptions with an avalanche of statistics. "The New Haven Company," the document warned, "instead of being strong, is financially weak. The Boston & Maine, instead of being hopelessly weak, has been growing steadily in financial strength." To support his conclusion, Brandeis cited the New Haven's own financial statements. With great precision he demonstrated that the New Haven did not have the money to continue its annual 8 percent dividends to stockholders—in fact, they had fallen short by $1.7 million the previous year and had had to rely on some accounting tricks to justify the 8 percent dividend.

Then there was the problem of management. With ownership of so many railroads and steamship lines, Brandeis believed that the time and abilities of New Haven officials were already taxed to the "uttermost." It was inconceivable to him that they could take on the additional responsibilities of managing the Boston & Maine. After all, there was a limit to what a person could do.

There was no need for New Haven officers to assume more responsibilities anyway, Brandeis asserted. The B&M line had had some financial difficulties, but it was now showing a "steady, conservative growth." It had more miles of track than the New Haven (2,232 to 2,006) and would do just fine by itself.[14]

It was all too much for the public to believe. The newspapers wasted no time in taking Brandeis to task for being so audacious. How could an attorney like himself claim to know more about railroad finance than respected managers like Charles S. Mellen? The *Boston News Bureau* characterized the Brandeis pamphlet as an "almost continuous and unbroken strain of errors, misstatements and fabrications." The *Boston Herald* rippled with sarcasm. "Brandeis speaks," the paper observed, "and the gaunt world should, but does not, hang quivering in space, suspending its customary functions.... The merger has got into Mr. Brandeis' head again, and rouses his stern soul. He sees the State destroyed, the republic gasping its last breath, and humankind swept from the starry watches of the night, all humankind save Brandeis, who, bestriding New England like a colossus, exudes righteousness and brave texts over a desert world." Even papers that had supported Brandeis's public campaigns in the past could not accept the pamphlet's conclusions. Thus, the *Springfield Republican,* a paper that had vigorously supported Brandeis in the gas controversy and other causes, almost apologized for the "grave injustice" Brandeis had done to the New Haven.[15]

Brandeis was not deterred by all this criticism. He remained convinced that his position was sound. He forged ahead. "The pamphlet has created quite a stir," he wrote to Al in January 1908. "The New Haven people have supported the stock and I am told their bankers advise them not to answer it. If they don't Mellen is doomed—and I don't believe they can. Nothing but a miracle of good times could make their way smooth." For all this progress, though, Brandeis recognized there was a social cost. "I have made a larger camp of enemies than in all my previous fights together . . .," he wrote to Al. Indeed, it was primarily for this reason that he declined an invitation from the Republican Committee to run against Mayor Fitzgerald. "[T]he chances of a really good fight were not the best," he told his brother. "My course in knocking heads right and left is not exactly such as to create an 'available' candidate." But the personal sacrifices were worth it. It was only a matter of time, he believed, until victory would be his.[16]

Although Brandeis may have been impressed with his financial analysis, Morgan was not. He casually inquired of Mellen whether there was anything to the Brandeis pamphlet. Mellen replied in the negative. Morgan was satisfied with that and dropped the subject.[17]

Despite his assurances to Morgan, Mellen recognized that the New Haven might have to change its strategy. Up until now Mellen had insisted that the New Haven was not really interested in a merger with the B&M. The New Haven had purchased the B&M stock, it was said, only as an investment—although New Haven officials said it was prepared to merge if the public wanted that. Mellen must have realized that this argument would not be taken seriously under close examination. Consequently, he and other New Haven officials steadfastly and repeatedly refused Brandeis's invitations to debate the issue in public. That posture could not be retained for long, however. Too much pressure was being exerted on both sides.

In December 1907 Brandeis organized the Massachusetts Anti-Merger League, a coalition of people similar to the group he had organized in fighting for savings bank insurance. Another group, the Businessmen's Merger League, was established to counter the efforts of the Brandeis league. With all this citizen activity, the governor felt obligated to speak out. Brandeis was not pleased with what he heard. In contrast to his earlier strong statement against "alien" control of the Massachusetts transportation system, Governor Guild issued a message in January 1908 approving the concept of a merger if it included "adequate safeguards" to protect the public interest. The New Haven, it appeared, was gaining ground.

Brandeis did not let up. He continued to spend the major portions of his days and nights talking to citizens about the issues, urging editorials by newspapers, and giving speeches to various groups. As in his other controversies, he continued to believe that public education was the key. In virtually every forum he would highlight the merger issue as the most important one to face Massachusetts in a generation. The New Haven, he would invariably explain, was acquiring all the rail, trolley, and steamship lines in Massachusetts and neighboring states in an effort to establish a transportation monopoly in New England. This raised the specter of "alien" control, which Brandeis found intolerable. "We must not," he told the New England Dry Goods Association on February 11, 1908, "entrust the determination as to what our welfare demands to the decisions of persons who may be influenced by considerations other than the interests of Massachusetts."

Aside from the control issue, Brandeis explored the dangers of an organization's taking on more than it could handle. As before, he would discuss the "unit of greatest efficiency." He never could identify that point of maximum efficiency, but he was always confident that the New Haven had exceeded it. "Man's works have outgrown the capacity of the individual man," he told the Dry Goods Association. "No matter what the organization, the capacity of the individual must determine the success of the particular enterprise, not only financially to the owners, but in service to the community. Organization can do much to make possible larger efficient concerns; but organization can never be a substitute for initiative and for judgment. These must be supplied by the chief executive officers, and nature sets a limit to their possible accomplishment."

Human nature also explained the inherent dangers of giving people any form of monopoly power. For this reason Brandeis placed little faith in Governor

Guild's hope that the New Haven transportation monopoly could be controlled with "adequate safeguards." "This would be like surrendering liberty and substituting despotism with safeguards," the Boston attorney observed. "There is no way in which to safeguard people from despotism except to prevent despotism. There is no way to safeguard the people from the evils of a private transportation monopoly except to prevent the monopoly. The objections to despotism and to monopoly," he continued, "are fundamental in human nature. They rest upon the innate and ineradicable selfishness of man. They rest upon the fact that absolute power inevitably leads to abuse. They rest upon the fact that progress flows only from struggle."[18]

It was, as could be expected from Brandeis, an eloquent and forceful statement. Nevertheless, there were many people—including prominent businessmen and civic leaders who had previously supported Brandeis's public campaigns—who continued to feel differently. However meritorious the objections to despotism and uncontrolled monopolies, these people believed it unrealistic to expect that a transportation system in the modern age could meet the needs of a state's economy without being an interstate operation. The idea of competition in rail transportation seemed to be the hope of a bygone age. And if human nature made it unwise to confer unlimited power, Massachusetts could adopt laws to regulate rates and other conditions of the New Haven service.

The heat of the contest only energized Brandeis. "The fight goes merrily on," he wrote Al at one point.[19] He was especially pleased when the New Haven came out of the closet and finally agreed to debate him in public. Their chosen representative was Timothy E. Byrnes, one of the company vice presidents. He was, as Brandeis himself acknowledged, "quite a spell-binder, who combines the capacity of endless lying and unbounded promising with a charming personality and facility of speech."[20] Those qualities were clearly in evidence when Byrnes met Brandeis on the evening of March 25 to debate the merger issue before the Cambridge Citizens Trade Association.

Byrnes opened by saying that he had a "high regard" for Brandeis, but the attorney just did not understand the problem involved. According to Byrnes, the New Haven had bought the B&M stock because it was up for sale anyway and, but for the New Haven, would have been sold to interests—rumored to be E.H. Harriman's group—located outside New England. The purchase was therefore made, said Byrnes, to improve the B&M's service and retain it as a New England institution.

Byrnes received considerable applause from the large audience. Brandeis was up to the challenge, however, and drew laughter when he began by saying, "Some corporations are born monopolies, some achieve monopoly, and some have monopoly thrust upon them." Brandeis recited his well-known objections to the New Haven's proposed monopoly. He also warned the audience not to be taken in by Byrnes's charm. "Men may come and men may go," he observed, "and this very delightful personality that we have with us tonight, representing the New Haven, Mr. Byrnes, may go as he has come, but the monopoly goes on forever if once it is started."

In a later exchange, Byrnes casually said that the New Haven would gladly relinquish its B&M stock if "the State of Massachusetts would take it and agree to keep it and never let it go to anybody else. . . ." Brandeis jumped up at once and asked Byrnes if he were authorized to make that offer because, if so, he thought "it may lead to a solution of this problem." Brynes was taken aback and, after fumbling around, said he did not think "there will be any difficulty in our getting together on that proposition." It turned out to be fluff. In a subsequent letter to Brandeis, Brynes explained that his offer was not authorized but had only expressed his personal opinion of an option that the New Haven should consider.[21]

Byrnes's hijinks were not at all surprising. At that point the New Haven had no need to compromise. The Commission on Commerce and Industry had just released its report endorsing the merger, and there was every expectation that the legislature would approve the New Haven's proposed bill to make it official. Then disaster struck.

In early May the state Supreme Court ruled that the New Haven's acquisition of trolley lines in western Massachusetts had violated the 1874 statute and was therefore illegal. It was recognized at once that the decision applied with equal force to New Haven's proposed merger with the B&M line. The next blow to the New Haven concerned the favorable report of the Commission on Commerce and Industry. The commission's credibility had already been undermined to some extent by disclosures that it had used an accountant from an investment house selling the B&M stock to New Haven and that the three commissioners in the majority all had some New Haven stock. But then in early May Brandeis, with the able assistance of Norman White, exposed a letter written to the commission from the New Haven attorney, Charles F. Choate, Jr., in February 1908. The letter included recommendations that had been adopted almost verbatim by the commission.[22] The "independence" of the commission could no longer be asserted.

This disclosure was in turn capped by an announcement that the federal government would institute an antitrust lawsuit against New Haven for unreasonably restraining interstate commerce. Brandeis played an integral role in that decision. He had met with President Roosevelt in February and April and on each occasion explained the problems caused by the New Haven. Whatever doubts Brandeis may have had earlier about an antitrust lawsuit were washed away, and he urged Roosevelt to take action. Mellen had also been visiting the "Little Father," as Roosevelt was affectionately called by corporate insiders. At a dramatic Cabinet meeting, Roosevelt finally decided against the lawsuit. His attorney general, Charles Bonaparte, was insistent, however, and said he would resign if the matter were dropped. Roosevelt yielded, and the complaint was filed on May 22, 1908.[23]

All of these developments gave Brandeis hope. He was moving at full steam now, making speeches, consulting with the legislators, and even writing editorials to be published by the *Boston Post.* As the legislature moved closer to a decision, he was optimistic. "The New Haven put up a fair array of witnesses," he told his brother after one hearing; "but I still think we shall whip them."[24]

There was a momentary setback when the Senate passed a bill allowing the New Haven to retain B&M stock until 1910 (unless the courts ruled otherwise in the federal suit). But Brandeis regrouped and, with his lieutenants roaming the halls of the State House, secured an amendment in the House of Representatives that would force the New Haven to sell the stock by 1910. By June 14 Brandeis gleefully told his brother that the merger was dead and that "nothing remains now but to bury the corpse."[25]

In July, Brandeis's prognosis seemed confirmed when the New Haven sold its B&M stock to John Billard, a Connecticut citizen. As Brandeis told an interviewer from the *Boston Herald,* he thought the sale was "excellent," that it had been made in good faith, and that the New Haven had "put this situation just where we wanted it fourteen months ago. . . ." To his brother, Brandeis expressed similar satisfaction with the Billard transaction. "That suits me entirely," he wrote. "If it is genuine it is what we want. If it is not genuine, the New Haven must be even more kinds of a fool than I have found the present management."[26] Within a short time, though, it became clear that Brandeis was the one who had been fooled.

Over the course of the summer and autumn the controversy lay smoldering. Brandeis periodically checked the New Haven's financial reports and remained convinced that they could not stay afloat long. But he was surprised in April 1909 when Eben Draper, the new governor of Massachusetts, recommended after a meeting with Mellen and Brynes that the legislature act to bring Billard's stock back to Massachusetts. That would be wise, said the governor, so that the state could retain full control over all B&M holdings. Within a short time the state attorney general followed up on the governor's recommendation and drafted a bill that would create a new holding company to house all of B&M's stocks and bonds. The New Haven, in turn, would be permitted to own the holding company. The underlying assumption of the bill was that the New Haven could persuade Billard to return his B&M shares to Massachusetts if the New Haven would benefit. It turned out to be a fair assumption.

Although he previously had made much of "alien" control, Brandeis now thought that the "importance of having the Billard stock brought back into Massachusetts has been greatly exaggerated." At the same time he was prepared to go along with a holding company bill—but not one like Draper's. That bill, he thought, was designed to leave the New Haven uncontrolled. The bill did not in any way punish the New Haven for its past violations of the law; nor did the bill include any provisions that would give the state the right to supervise rates, expenses, or exchanges of stock.[27] In short, the governor's bill put the New Haven exactly where it wanted to be.

Brandeis drafted amendments to the governor's bill that would limit the holding company's acquisition to the Billard stock. The amendments would also limit the use of the stock and direct the Board of Railroad Commissioners to investigate the matter and recommend action concerning the future operations of the B&M. With these amendments, Brandeis believed that the Billard stock could be returned and the legislature could then proceed in an orderly fashion to resolve the controversy.

Brandeis laid out all his arguments before the Legislative Committee on Railroads, which met to consider the bills on May 19, 1909. At the outset he made clear his view that the legislation was entirely unnecessary if its sole purpose was to "recapture" the Billard stock. "The Legislature has power to take by right of eminent domain any stock in any Massachusetts corporation . . .," he explained. "The Governor's message and all this talk proceeds upon an absolute forgetfulness of the law in this respect." Brandeis also expressed his deep concern that the New Haven would not be sanctioned for its unlawful behavior. "The New Haven has been declared by a unanimous court [in the 1908 trolley case] to be a violator of law," he told the committee. "The violations of that corporation have been called definitely to your attention. They are today as flagrant and as unatoned for as they were then. . . . [T]he whole of our civilization and all of our hope rest upon respect for the law, and the belief in the community that that law will be dealt out with equal justice to the rich and to the poor . . .; and now this bill undertakes in an extraordinary way . . . not only to authorize . . . the holding in violation of law, but to reward it. . . ."[28]

It was another persuasive appeal. The legislators, however, were not impressed. Other more powerful forces were at work. Brandeis could see the handwriting on the wall, but he would not give up. Shortly after his testimony he conveyed hope to his brother. "It looks now as if we should still be able to beat the enemy," he wrote Al; "and if we do it will be extraordinary; for the press, reptile and otherwise, is also agin us. But I know that our enemies are badly scared. They look it; and we are of good cheer."[29]

He and Norman White continued to talk to journalists, write letters, and generally ask citizens to urge their respective representatives in the legislature to defeat Governor Draper's bill. Alice Grady was an integral part of the operation, receiving information from her boss's numerous contacts and passing notes to him describing the latest developments. By the beginning of June, however, even Brandeis was getting down, and he reported to his brother that the situation was "desperate" and that "only a miracle can land us safely." Nine days later the governor's bill passed the legislature, and Brandeis advised his brother that "we got unmercifully licked." But even in defeat there was something for Brandeis to feel good about, and something even to hope for. "[I]t took all the power of the Republican machine and of the Bankers' money to do it," he said, "and I am well content with the fight made. The aftermath of fighting continues."[30] His faith in the cause would soon be rewarded.

Alice Brandeis had not yet fully regained her strength, despite the attentions and hopes of doctors and nurses. She required a considerable amount of rest and depended greatly on the assistance of Sadie Nicholson and other servants to take care of the children and maintain the house. During the days she did become involved in school matters and other civic activities. She also loved the long canoe rides with Louis on the Charles River or at Cape Cod, where they began to spend their vacations after Louis's father died in 1906. She would often take a pair of field glasses with her and chatter away when she saw some interesting birds—a habit that sometimes annoyed Bess Evans, who often joined Louis and Alice on the canoe rides.

Although she much preferred to spend her evenings with just Louis and the children, there was almost always a steady stream of visitors for dinner—Norman Hapgood, the writer Lincoln Steffens, Lincoln Filene, Herbert White, and others whom Louis had become close to in his many travels and fights. On occasion, however, the activity became too much for Alice, and Louis was forced to modify his social calendar. It seemed to happen especially in the summer. Louis liked the heat and did not at all mind the humid weather that could sometimes hit Massachusetts. It apparently drained Alice, though. One summer Louis had to suggest to Al that his children come to visit them at the Cape one at a time because Alice was too weak to handle them all at once.

Louis's attentions were reciprocated. People had begun to say nasty things about him during the New Haven fight, and the Brandeises were not as welcome socially as they had once been. Alice accepted the turn of events as a necessary cost of living with her husband. She never deviated from her support for him.

For his part, Brandeis was largely unconcerned with the enemies he made. When the New Haven controversy first heated up he told his brother that "labor men are the most congenial company. The intense materialism and luxuriousness of our other people make their company quite irksome." Consequently, his later exclusion from some of society's fashionable homes was a small cost for the pleasure of his public campaigns. And he took a great deal of satisfaction from knowing that the press was beginning to call him "the attorney for the people." He earned the compliment and remained ever vigilant on matters affecting the community's control of its own affairs. That applied most especially to the New Haven, because, as he later remarked in a speech about the controversy, "nothing is settled until it is settled right."[31]

It did not take long before New Haven matters again required his efforts. The railroad had ultimately secured everything it wanted from government. Even the federal antitrust suit was no longer. It had been dropped when William Howard Taft became president; Attorney General George Wickersham said there was no sense in attacking a merger favored by the state. But Mellen began to realize in 1910 and 1911 that the company could not pay off all the debts it had piled up to purchase railways and steamships and still maintain an 8 percent dividend to stockholders. Something had to be cut, and Mellen decided it should be service rather than dividends. Freight service became particularly unreliable and slow. Accidents became much more frequent.

From his vantage point, Brandeis saw that the fall of the New Haven was in sight. In September 1911 he anticipated that the inevitable reduction of the New Haven dividend would mean Mellen's departure from the scene, and he suggested to Norman Hapgood that *Collier's* use something Brandeis wrote as a fitting "obituary notice" when the time came. "Mellen was a masterful man," the attorney playfully wrote, "resourceful, courageous, broad of view. He fired the imagination of New England; but, being oblique of vision, merely distorted its judgment and silenced its conscience. For a while he trampled with impunity on laws human and divine; but as he was obsessed with the delusion that two and two make five, he fell at last the victim to the relentless rules of arithmetic. . . ."[32]

In March 1912 the new governor, Eugene Foss, summoned Brandeis to the State House to discuss the railroad situation. Foss was a wealthy manufacturer who had campaigned as a Progressive and had secured his first election to the governorship in 1910. He was very disturbed about the deterioration of rail service and, after consulting with the New Haven representative, was disposed to accept their proposal, which was, in essence, to disband the holding company and formally merge with the Boston & Maine. The company also wanted to electrify rail service in Boston and build a tunnel to accommodate passenger service between the North and South Stations in Boston. Brandeis thought the proposal was crazy. Spending more money was hardly the way to cure the state's transportation ills, he felt. "The patient is sick," he told Foss, "and we have no knowledge what the nature or extent of the disease is, nor its cause. Let us have a diagnosis."[33]

Foss, however, could not decide on the best course to take. He wrestled with the problem through the summer, continually seeking the counsel of the "people's attorney." Finally Brandeis laid down the law. At a luncheon meeting in September the lawyer advised the governor "that it was up to him to determine definitely whether he wanted monopoly or competition. . . . I told him he must make up his mind, and when he did make up his mind, it must be irrevocable and not wobbly."[34] Foss apparently took the advice to heart, for the proposal was abandoned. And none too soon.

At the end of September the Interstate Commerce Commission resumed hearings in Boston to investigate the deterioration in New Haven service. The hearings had commenced on July 1, and Brandeis appeared on behalf of the Boston Fruit and Produce Exchange, a local association whose members required good shipping services for their produce. As in his other campaigns, Brandeis refused any compensation for his services.

Public attention remained focused on the New Haven even after the initial hearings were adjourned. But now people were beginning to think that Brandeis may have been right all along. The joint operation of the New Haven and the Boston & Maine was not producing great benefits; it was creating problems. Newspapers were very interested in Brandeis's reaction to developments, and in December 1912 a stream of articles—most adorned with headlines and large pictures of Brandeis—featured his views on the New Haven situation. After reciting his position, Brandeis made it clear that Mellen was really not to blame for the mess in which the New Haven found itself. "It seems to me that it is a great mistake," he said, "to assume that Mr. Mellen is personally responsible for the deplorable condition of the railroads. . . . The real cause of this condition is the policy of monopoly."[35]

Mellen was not as charitable in response to Brandeis, blaming him for all of the New Haven's troubles. "Mr. Brandeis poses as a public disclaimer of all personalities in the controversy which he has started against the New England railroad system," Mellen observed. "Yet he maintains an organization that has been preparing for very many weeks to inflame the public by volleys of attacks of the most personal, vicious, cruel and unrighteous character upon me personally and upon my management of the New England lines, assailing my integrity, denouncing the financial management with false and distorted figures, and defaming New England in every newspaper avenue. . . . Every one of these attacks defaming New England and its railroad system, so far as I have learned, traces back to Brandeis, his associates or organization."[36]

All the rhetoric in the world, however, could not save Mellen now. The newspapers—once a bastion of New Haven support—turned on the company with a vengeance, citing the poor service and the many accidents as evidence of poor management. The most vigorous attacks were made by William Randolph Hearst's *Boston American,* and Hearst himself signed an editorial at the end of December condemning the New Haven's monopoly. The resumption of the ICC hearings in April only added fuel to the fire.

Before he got too deeply into the hearings, Brandeis suddenly found himself without a client. Alton E. Briggs, president of the Boston Fruit and Produce Exchange, wrote him that the Exchange was concerned only with the New Haven service and not company finances, the subject of the new hearings. The loss of the client was irrelevant to Brandeis. He showed up the next day at the hearings and informed the presiding officer that he was now representing himself as a citizen. It was too much for Charles F. Choate, the New Haven's attorney. He rose to say that he too would "represent the people, the same as my dear brother, Mr. Brandeis."[37] Although he had previously expressed the opinion that an attorney working for free owed the same duty to his client as an attorney earning a fee, Brandeis now made much of the fact that Choate had in fact been paid by the New Haven. The clear implication of Brandeis's comment was that Choate could not assume the mantle of "people's attorney" because he had received fees; Brandeis apparently felt that he *could* assume that mantle since he had not received any money from the Fruit Exchange—although there was no doubt that, as an organization of shippers, the Exchange's interest in the New Haven proceeding was solely a financial one. In any case, Choate backed down, and the hearings moved forward.

The testimony did not help the New Haven's cause. Brandeis had, as usual, prepared well for his examination of New Haven witnesses. His task was eased by the assistance of Joseph Eastman, the secretary of the Public Franchise League. Eastman had spent weeks at the ICC in Washington reviewing thousands of pages of financial reports and other documents. Eastman was not happy with the chore ("This is the worst job I ever was on," he told Brandeis), but the labors paid off. At the hearings Brandeis clearly had the edge. The deciding blows came when Mellen testified. When asked about the company's complex financial structure, Mellen candidly stated, "I know very little about the New Haven's accounts." He did know, however, about the floating slush fund that was used to make substantial "donations" to legislators and other politicians. As for the company's extravagant expenditures, Mellen again maintained that he was not in charge. He stated, for example, that he had been against spending $36 million for the eighteen-mile long Westchester railroad. With an allusion to J.P. Morgan, the New Haven president said that "a higher authority than mine determined otherwise and the deal was put through."[38]

On July 9, 1913, the ICC issued a report finding serious fault with the New Haven's management. The company's stock began to fall rapidly and it looked as though the company would crumble, especially because the driving force behind the New Haven was gone—Morgan had died the previous March, and the new leaders were not as tolerant of extravagant expenditures and duplicitous policies. Mellen's power quickly eroded. He resigned from the presidency of the Boston &

Maine on the same day the ICC report was released and shortly afterwards resigned from the New Haven presidency as well. The company press release explained Mellen's resignation by saying that it was "impossible for one man to handle" the joint operations of all the railroads under the New Haven's control. It was a tacit admission that, after all was said and done, Brandeis knew more about human limitations than the railroad company.

Meanwhile, Brandeis had been making considerable efforts to have the federal government file another antitrust suit against the New Haven. With President Woodrow Wilson's inauguration on Marrch 4, 1913, Brandeis had a friend in the White House. And he took full advantage of the relationship. Before his administration was a week old, Wilson found himself listening to Brandeis urge the need for federal action. Wilson was sympathetic, but the new attorney general, James McReynolds, was a different story.

McReynolds and Brandeis already knew each other, and they were to learn a lot more about each other in the years to come. McReynolds had little interest in the case. Brandeis would not accept no for an answer. Over the next month he met repeatedly with McReynolds at various places and various times. At one point McReynolds suggested that Brandeis become special counsel for the government in the investigation, but Brandeis rejected that suggestion because of his previous involvement in the case. The government's actions would not seem impartial to the public if Brandeis were leading the charge. Despite all this talk, McReynolds never gave Brandeis a final answer. That came from another source.[39]

On the evening of May 15, 1913, Brandeis was taking a carriage ride with Colonel Edward House, the diminutive Texan who was Wilson's most intimate advisor, although he held no official position with the government. House found Brandeis quite engaging, and the two men talked often about affairs of state. On this particular evening House informed the Boston attorney that the decision had been made to move against the New Haven. Thomas Gregory, a friend of House's, was to be the special counsel for the government, and House hoped that Brandeis would assist Gregory.

Although McReynolds was the country's chief law enforcement officer and nominally in charge of the New Haven prosecution, he was obviously not making all the decisions here. In fact, Brandeis appeared to have more control over the situation than McReynolds. He conferred with House and the treasury secretary, William McAdoo, about the New Haven case at Beverly, Massachusetts, over the summer. And in September, Gregory met Brandeis at his house in Dedham to discuss the particulars.

Back in Washington, McReynolds was complaining to House that he did not like the handling of the New Haven case. McReynolds also told House bluntly that he resented the fact that the president did not talk to him more often and that people outside the Department of Justice seemed to know more about its activities than he did. House was beginning to appreciate McReynolds's strange manner and did not want to antagonize the attorney general needlessly. He told McReynolds to work the problem out with Gregory and hoped that that would be the end of it. In time McReynolds came around, and the indictment was prepared.

It was held in abeyance, however, while the government engaged in discussions with the new management at the New Haven to try to settle the matter.

McReynolds was no doubt beginning to feel hostile toward Brandeis. The "people's attorney" was making life very unpleasant for the attorney general. Newspapers were repeatedly and roundly criticizing McReynolds's delay in moving against the New Haven—*La Follette's Weekly,* which often took its lead from Brandeis, condemned McReynolds for not uncovering information discovered by the ICC; and the *Boston American,* another Brandeis supporter, called for the attorney general's dismissal. Senator George Norris, another Progressive, said that McReynolds should take action instead of negotiating with the New Haven. Finally McReynolds made a proposal to the New Haven which would require that the B&M be turned over to a new board of trustees. It was hoped and expected that Brandeis would be one of the trustees, but he declined because he was too busy with other matters. The refusal embarrassed McReynolds and George Anderson, a Brandeis friend working on the matter. They had counted on his help. Brandeis was, after all, the one who had pushed for action all those years. McReynolds, then, had many reasons for feeling bitter toward Brandeis—and in later years it would be a bitterness that would make Brandeis's life on the Supreme Court somewhat difficult.[40]

In the meantime, other governmental agencies were moving forward with separate investigations of the New Haven. The Massachusetts Public Service Commission conducted a wide-ranging inquiry that produced some very interesting facts. Over the years of the Mellen presidency the New Haven had handed out money to just about anybody who could help them. Reporters for the Associated Press received between $500 and $1,400 for every legislative session; a Harvard law professor, Bruce Wyman, received $10,000 for "scholarly" lectures on transportation problems; and Clarence W. Barron, publisher of the *Boston News Bureau* and the *Wall Street Journal*—both persistent critics of Brandeis in the New Haven matter—received $133,000 from the railroad during one eighteen-month period (with the implication that there had been payments at other times as well).

None of these disclosures outwardly intimidated the New Haven and its supporters. The magazine *Truth*—one of those subsidized by the New Haven—had some unkind words about Brandeis's religion. "His job," the magazine said, "was to carry on an agitation which would undermine public confidence in the New Haven system and cause a depreciation in the price of its securities. . . . We do not say this, remember, in order to criticize, but simply in the interest of truth. The New England railroad fight is simply part of a world movement. It is the age-long struggle for supremacy between Jew and Gentile." Brandeis was used to these kinds of attacks, however. Even before the Public Service Commission's disclosures he had written to his brother that the company and "its backers are fighting hard—the inevitable and me—with increasing bitterness. But," Louis informed Al, "arithmetic must ultimately prevail, even over false accounting."[41]

If there was any doubt about that, it was removed when the ICC released its second report on the New Haven in July 1914. "The result of our research into the financial workings of the . . . management of the New Haven system," the report began, "has been to disclose one of the most glaring instances of maladministration revealed in all the history of railroading." The report made it pathetically clear that Mellen was not entirely responsible for the mess because he had not been in charge. When Morgan had decided to buy the Westchester railroad for an exorbitant fee, Mellen complained to the corporate tycoon that it was a bad deal and that more information was needed to justify the expenditure. In response Morgan quickly cited a favorable report prepared by his attorney, Francis Lynde Stetson. "Well," Morgan rhetorically asked Mellen, "doesn't Stetson know more about how it should be drawn than you do?" Mellen meekly retired and expressed his frustration on the back of Stetson's report. ". . . I don't like the looks of it," Mellen wrote, "and I don't see why the matter should not be made plain. . . . I have never known the first thing about who originally held the securities, what they were sold for; and no one has thought I was entitled to know. Perhaps I am not. I would feel better if there were at least a disposition to let me know something more than [what] appears in the record."

As for the New Haven's acquisition of the Boston & Maine, the ICC report called it "impolitic, unwise, illegal, and disastrous." The B&M, as Brandeis had originally observed, was really in good financial shape and, without New Haven control, "would have continued to pay dividends and serve its constituency of passengers and shippers with responsible rates and adequate facilities."

The sale of B&M stock to Billard, it turned out, had been a complete fraud. The ICC said its investigation had been hampered because Billard had burned his books and papers. However, the evidence before the agency made it clear that Billard had used the New Haven's money to purchase the stock and still made a profit of $2.7 million when he later returned it. The ICC said that New Haven stockholders should consider a lawsuit against the company management to recover the waste.

The report reserved some of its harshest language for the individuals who were supposed to be running the New Haven's 336 corporations. The use of dummy directors and managers was so flagrant that a twenty-one-year-old secretary was made president of one of the companies. "The practice of one man serving on many boards of directors cannot be too strongly condemned," the Commission stated. ". . . There are too many ornamental directors and too many who have such childlike faith in the man at the head that they are ready to endorse or approve anything he may do." None of the mismanagement and political corruption practiced by the company would have been possible, the report observed, if the directors had done their jobs.[42]

To Brandeis the report only confirmed what he had maintained all along. "The decline of the New Haven," he had written, "was due to a disregard of inexorable laws. First, the fundamental law of business which has recognized the need of competition as an incentive to efficient action; second, that fundamental law of human nature which recognizes the limitations of man, namely, that there is a limit to the amount or number of things which any man or body of men can accomplish or do well; and third, the inexorable law of arithmetic by which two and two will always make four, despite reports of presidents and financial advisers who insist on stretching it into five."[43] These were three principles that Brandeis would invoke again and again as he moved into new spheres and new controversies.

Unfortunately, the lessons did little for the New Haven. It had already ceased issuing dividends, and in July 1914 the Justice Department finally filed its antitrust action. The company knew it was over and entered a consent decree in August that required the company to sell its Boston & Maine stock as well as its interests in the steamship and trolley lines. By 1935 the company was bankrupt.

For Brandeis, the nine-year fight had been a tedious, tense, and time-consuming process. But it remained one of the great experiences of his public life. To him it was a dramatic illustration of monopoly failure. "We owe Mr. Mellen our gratitude," he told a group of businessmen at one point, "because his restless, resourceful spirit has made it possible for every man to know what a monopoly does when it grips the transportation facilities of a people as the New Haven has gripped those of New England. Ordinarily such enterprises have their beginning in one generation and their development in the next, but we have seen the beginning of an error and its results."[44] Almost always in later years Brandeis cited the case of the New Haven if the subject of monopoly came up. And when William O. Douglas came to Washington in 1934 to head the Securities and Exchange Commission, Brandeis, then a Supreme Court justice, summoned him to his apartment on California Street. Douglas reminded Brandeis of himself in his days as a fighting public lawyer in Boston. Douglas understood the treachery of large corporations. And during one of their many talks, Brandeis made Douglas promise that he would write a book someday about the New Haven affair—a promise that Douglas made but never fulfilled.

When Brandeis's name was before the United States Senate for confirmation as a Supreme Court justice, his adversaries contacted Mellen. Surely, they thought, the former New Haven president would have a lot to say about Brandeis's professional ethics and tactics. Mellen surprised them. He wired the Senate subcommittee that he had no information of any value concerning Brandeis's fitness to sit on the Court. It was apparent that, whatever their past differences in public, Mellen did not bear any bitterness toward Brandeis. The same could not be said about Richard A. Ballinger.

NINE

The Ballinger–Pinchot Controversy and Its Aftermath

The elephants are kindly but they're dumb.

PAUL SIMON AND ART GARFUNKEL, "AT THE ZOO"

All Clarence Cunningham wanted to do was to make some money. And as a businessman and a speculator, he found nothing more promising in the early 1900s than the rich and virgin coal fields in Alaska. The coal fields were located on federal property, but that would be no problem. Clarence would form a company with a few friends from the Pacific Coast; they would stake claims and invoke applicable law to get the government to deed the property to the group. It was such a good idea it was already like money in the bank.

Unfortunately, Cunningham was not terribly bright. Nor did he have much foresight. But then again, it would have been difficult for anyone to anticipate in the early 1900s that Clarence Cunningham's financial dreams would eventually lead to the downfall of a president and the disgrace of one of his Cabinet officers. It would have been equally difficult to foresee that the whole controversy would be the springboard by which an experienced Boston lawyer named Louis D. Brandeis would become a national figure.

Brandeis himself never expected to become involved in the affair. In January 1910 he received a telephone call without warning from Norman Hapgood, who was still an editor with *Collier's* magazine. Hapgood asked his friend Louis if he could come to New York City at once for a meeting. *Collier's* was in danger of being sued for libel, and Hapgood could think of no one better able to protect the periodical's legal interests.

The source of *Collier's* problems was an article it had published the previous November, "The Whitewashing of Ballinger." The piece had been written by Louis Glavis, who had been fired in September 1909 from his position in the Department of the Interior. Glavis had tried to blow the whistle on his superiors, claiming that they had all conspired to push Clarence Cunningham's Alaska coal claims through to approval even though, according to Glavis, everyone knew that the claims were illegal. Glavis saved some of his choicest accusations for Richard A. Ballinger, then the secretary of the interior.

Needless to say, Ballinger did not take kindly to Glavis's charges. The secretary was a self-made man. He had worked his way through Williams College and then, after an apprenticeship, become a lawyer in Seattle. He had written two books on Washington state law. He was a respected member of the community. People thought so much of him, in fact, that they elected him Seattle's mayor. His college friend James Garfield, secretary of the interior under Theodore Roosevelt, also thought highly of Ballinger and asked his former classmate to leave his Seattle law firm to become commissioner of the Department of the Interior's Land Office. Ballinger yielded and served as a commissioner for one year, from 1907 to 1908. When William Howard Taft succeeded Roosevelt as president in 1909, he implored Ballinger to return to the capital—this time as a replacement for Garfield. Ballinger again accepted—presuming all along no doubt that the Cabinet position would be a glorious cap to his government career. The experience, however, was not to be so glorious.

There were many things about Glavis and his accusations that troubled Ballinger. Perhaps nothing bothered him more than Glavis's decision to take them up with the president himself. But after listening to Glavis and consulting with Ballinger and some others, Taft publicly issued a letter in the middle of September 1909 exonerating Ballinger of any wrongdoing on the Cunningham claims and other areas raised by Glavis. "I have examined the whole record most carefully," the president's letter stated, "and have reached a very definite conclusion. . . . It is sufficient to say that the case attempted to be made by Mr. Glavis embraces only shreds of suspicions without any substantial evidence to sustain his attack." The letter went on to praise Ballinger for his "sympathy with the attitude of this administration in favor of natural resources." As for Glavis, the president authorized Ballinger to dismiss him "for filing a disingenuous statement, unjustly impeaching the official integrity of his superior officers."[1]

Ballinger was only too happy to exercise that authority, and within a day or so Glavis found himself unemployed. He did advise the president by letter, though, that he felt obligated to bring his information to the attention of the public. "Since there may be now even greater danger that the title to these coal lands will be fraudulently secured . . .," Glavis wrote, "it is no less my duty to my country to make public the facts in my possession, concerning which I firmly believe you have been misled. This I shall do in the near future. . . ."[2]

Glavis made good on his promise. One publisher offered him $3,000 for his article, but he turned that down. For what he claimed to be public-spirited reasons, he decided instead to give it to Hapgood and have *Collier's* publish it without receiving any compensation. *Collier's* was one of the country's most highly respected journals, and Glavis probably hoped that the magazine's prestige would facilitate the circulation of his charges. If that was his purpose, he made the right choice. *Collier's* cover for the issue of November 13, 1909, trumpeted the publication of the article, and within a short time major newspapers across the country were discussing the issue on their front pages.

There was no mystery behind the attention received by Glavis's article. Theodore Roosevelt had made much of the need to conserve the nation's natural resources. Gifford Pinchot, who was chief of the Forestry Bureau in the Department of Agriculture and had been Roosevelt's principal advisor on conservation issues, was a flamboyant figure who helped keep the "cause" in the public eye. Therefore, when Glavis attacked Ballinger for pushing Cunningham's fraudulent claims to virgin territory in Alaska, it was bound to generate considerable interest.

Robert Collier, the young owner of the magazine, was delighted with the publicity created by the article. He became concerned, however, when he was in Washington and heard rumors that Ballinger was considering suing him for libel. Ballinger, it was said, would await the outcome of a congressional committee's inquiry into the matter slated to begin at the end of January 1910; if the results of the inquiry were favorable—which was likely, given the committee's domination by supporters of the Republican administration—Ballinger would reportedly use the committee's findings to attack *Collier's*.

In this light, Hapgood and Collier were very much interested in attending the strategy session scheduled at the home of Henry Stimson, a Republican stalwart and a leading member of the New York City Bar. Stimson had agreed to consider representing Gifford Pinchot in the forthcoming congressional proceedings. Even though Taft had initially retained Pinchot as head of the Forestry Bureau, Pinchot was an outspoken critic of Ballinger during this episode. The matter reached the breaking point when Senator Jonathan P. Dolliver read a letter from Pinchot on the Senate floor in which the chief forester explained why members of his Bureau had assisted Glavis in the preparation of his article. It was too much for Taft, and he fired the conservation advocate at the beginning of January 1910.[3]

Even before his dismissal, Pinchot knew that he would need an attorney for the congressional proceedings. They had been expanded to cover his management of the Forestry Bureau, and he would undoubtedly be facing some hostile questioning. Stimson was his first choice, but the Wall Street attorney eventually bowed out, primarily under pressure from Republican Senator Elihu Root, his former partner. Stimson, Root said, would find the atmosphere in the congressional hearing politically unpalatable. Stimson did not want to leave his potential client without an attorney, though, so he got George Wharton Pepper, a distinguished lawyer from Philadelphia, to represent Pinchot.

That left *Collier's* and Glavis needing representation. Hapgood argued strongly that Brandeis was the man for the job. And while *Collier's* probably did not have the right to participate in the congressional hearing, Glavis certainly did. Unfortunately, the ex-federal employee was only twenty-six, was going through a costly divorce proceeding, and did not have enough money to hire an attorney. Consequently, it was agreed that Brandeis would be hired by *Collier's* to represent Glavis at the congressional hearing. He would be paid $5,000 a month for his services and be asked to lead the defense.[4]

Brandeis liked the Harvard Club in midtown Manhattan. When he went to New York without Alice—which he did with increasing frequency as the years progressed—he would generally use the club. It offered good service and quiet rooms. And that was exactly what Brandeis needed as he began his preparation for the congressional inquiry into the Ballinger–Pinchot controversy. If he were to be effective, it was necessary that he understand the inner workings of the Interior Department and every detail related to Glavis's charges. That, in turn, would require him to study a voluminous collection of files, letters, and memoranda.

Brandeis arrived at the Harvard Club on January 12, 1910, took a room, and wired his brother to meet him there over the weekend. In the meantime he began to examine the record. He would generally get up around four o'clock in the morning to do some work. After a while he would have a breakfast of hot chocolate, hot oatmeal, a small rare steak, and rolls, and then return to his room for further study or for conversations with Glavis and Hapgood. His only breaks in the day were for lunch and dinner.

For Brandeis the Ballinger–Pinchot controversy was more than an opportunity to help Hapgood. It was another example of single individuals' trying to defend against the encroachment of large organizations, of men trying to retain control of their lives and to help preserve the chance for individual achievement. The laws and policies that governed development of the Alaskan frontier were specifically designed to prevent exploitation and domination by corporate conglomerates. If there were any truth to Glavis's charges, it not only meant that Ballinger had flouted his responsibilities as a public servant; it also meant that Ballinger was trying to compromise the protection that law and policy afforded to individual landowners, because part of Glavis's claim was that Clarence Cunningham and his friends had joined forces with the powerful Morgan–Guggenheim syndicate. To Brandeis, this kind of combination was extremely troublesome. "[T]he whole purpose of our land law," he later explained to the congressional committee, "is to secure an opportunity of individual ownership in small parcels. . . . Now, when an agreement is made with parties to cooperate . . . when they have no right to consider that, they have then done an act contrary to the spirit and purpose of our land law. . . ."[5]

Long before he made that argument Brandeis had begun to appreciate the incredible amount of bumbling involved in the controversy—starting with Clarence Cunningham and ending with the president himself. As he studied the record in the Harvard Club in January, Brandeis learned that Cunningham had initially filed a claim for Alaskan coal land in 1903. The first major problem for Cunningham was that the law did not allow such a claim. The statute that then governed the disposition of applications for federal coal lands had a provision that specifically excluded Alaska.

Fortunately for Cunningham, Congress adopted a law in 1904 that in effect extended the provisions of the existing statute to cover Alaska. Under the law, an individual could obtain a government deed for only 160 acres. An association of individuals could, prior to the "entry" of the claim, apply for 640 acres—the "entry" being the last of several steps before the deed was issued. Here, Brandeis discovered, Cunningham encountered another problem: it was virtually impossible, as a practical matter, to establish a working coal mine in Alaska with even 640 acres. The capital investment required for extracting and transporting coal—particularly in the hazardous terrain and climate of Alaska—was so great that thousands of acres were needed to make the venture worthwhile.

Cunningham had an answer to that problem. However, as Brandeis discovered, it was not one that was permitted under the law. Cunningham invited his friends and associates to file claims to contiguous 160-acre plots with the understanding that they would all form a single operating company after the deeds were issued. With the thirty-three claims arranged by the Cunningham group, their company would have more than enough acreage to justify the large capital investment required for coal operations.

Cunningham's ruse was not particularly imaginative. Of the 900 or so Alaska claims filed under the 1904 law, most or perhaps even all of them were fraudulent. Anyone familiar with the coal business knew that the law's acreage limitations were impractical, and people felt that they had no choice but to get "dummy" applicants who could then be joined into a larger group after the 160-acre deeds were issued. Here again, though, Brandeis found that Cunningham was able to distinguish himself from the crowd. He had made a record of his group's illegal agreement in his 1903 journal; and when the government was later investigating the legality of Cummingham's claims, Clarence saw no problem in making that journal entry available to the inquiring government agents.

In fairness to Cunningham, it must be said that his desire to cooperate was not really naïve. He thought he had "friends" in Washington who would watch out for his interests. And as Brandeis soon learned from his examination of the record, Cunningham was not entirely wrong in that belief. From the numerous reports he read and from the comments of investigators he had working on the West Coast, Brandeis also came to the conclusion that Cunningham's ability to find influential friends in Washington was not a coincidence.

Under Brandeis's theory, Ballinger—a significant political figure in the state of Washington—had joined forces with others to have Samuel H. Piles elected as a United States senator in 1905. Some of these other individuals were claimants in the Cunningham group, and they wanted a helping hand in the Department of Interior. According to Brandeis, these individuals, including Piles, then secured Ballinger's appointments as commissioner of the Land Office, which administered the coal laws, and then, with Taft's election, secretary of the interior. Ballinger was naturally grateful for the assistance and was therefore willing to do what he could for his friends.

The congressional committee was rather skeptical of Brandeis's theory, and Ballinger himself maintained under cross-examination that his arm had had to be twisted in order to get him to leave his Seattle law practice.[6] All that may have been so. But it was indeed peculiar how a person with Cunningham's ineptitude could get so many breaks as he tried to work his claims through the bureaucratic maze in Washington.

Perhaps the most important break came in the summer of 1907. Horace T. Jones had just been assigned to conduct the government's investigation of the Alaskan claims, and Ballinger had personally directed him to make it a thorough one. Initially, Jones thought that would require affidavits from almost 500 people, and he energetically plunged ahead with the task. He had been at it for only a few weeks when Ballinger suddenly developed a change of heart. He had been thinking about it, he told Jones, and maybe they could get by with affidavits from only a representative sample. Ballinger explained that the process could take too long otherwise, and he was already thinking of recommending remedial legislation to

Congress. Like almost everyone else familiar with the situation, Ballinger knew that the law's acreage limitation was unrealistic, and he wanted to suggest to Congress that it be lifted and that past violations be excused.[7]

Jones, of course, was willing to abide by his supervisor's instructions to limit the scope of the investigation. But that did not mean, at least to Jones, that the inquiry was to be abandoned altogether. So later he reported to Ballinger that the local papers in Seattle kept referring to the Guggenheims' secret interest in the Alaskan claims and that the matter should be investigated by "an experienced and fearless agent."[8] Within a short time Jones was transferred to Salt Lake City.

As Brandeis discovered from reading the record, these events coincided with a new development in Cunningham's schemes. Cunningham's group had indeed just given the Morgan–Guggenheim syndicate an option to buy one-half of the anticipated coal company. To Brandeis, the limitations on Jones's investigation and his later transfer to Salt Lake City were designed to clear the road ahead for Cunningham.

It was at this juncture that Glavis appeared. Although only twenty-four, he had had considerable experience in land claim investigations. He was appointed chief of the Portland Field Division in the autumn of 1907. Under examination by Brandeis, Glavis related to the congressional committee how Ballinger initially ordered a complete investigation of the Cunningham claims. "I told him," Glavis said of his conversation with Ballinger, "that the people at Seattle were saying that there was not going to be any further investigation, and that they were saying they were going to get the [deeds]. . . ." Ballinger, according to Glavis, said that the new division chief should push ahead—even though many of the Cunningham claimants were personal friends and business associates of his. "Now, Glavis," Ballinger reportedly said, ". . . I want you to understand that no matter whom it hurts you are to go right after them, whether they are friends of mine or not."[9]

Glavis was already keyed up by possibilities of conspiracy involving some of America's largest corporate magnates. When he left Washington, D.C., for the Pacific Coast on December 19, 1907, he was prepared to leave no stone unturned in the pursuit of justice. Ballinger, it turned out, had other plans.

On December 26, 1907, ex-Governor Miles C. Moore, a member of the Cunningham group, met with Ballinger for a few minutes in the commissioner's office in Washington, D.C. No doubt Moore informed Ballinger that the Morgan–Guggenheim syndicate had just exercised its option to buy one-half of the coal company at a considerable price. It was essential that the coal applications be expedited.

Although he had just ordered Glavis to conduct a full-scale investigation into the Cunningham claims, Ballinger took a quick look at a report prepared by a government agent named Harry K. Love, concluded that the report recommended approval of the Cunningham claims, and then ordered that the necessary deeds be prepared. It was all very efficient.[10]

Brandeis later challenged Ballinger's reliance on the Love report, but Ballinger responded under cross-examination that it was "absurd" to suggest, as Brandeis did, that there was any reason to question the validity of Love's judgments. There was simply no basis, Ballinger assured his questioner, "which would warrant me in holding Mr. Love in suspicion as to the truth of the character of reports which he might make."[11]

That, however, was a little difficult to accept. First of all, Love himself had stated that his report—which had been prepared before Horace Jones had entered the case—was intended to raise questions about the Cunningham claims, not resolve them. There was another reason to question the validity of Love's so-called favorable report. During this time he was lobbying hard to be appointed a federal marshal in Alaska. Part of those efforts required him to get the support of the very people he was investigating. Even Love realized the ethical problem there; he told Jones that he was anxious to get off the case because he felt very uncomfortable. Jones then reported the conversation to Ballinger, Jones adding that Love's investigation had only been "half hearted." According to Jones, Ballinger agreed that Love's removal from the case was necessary.[12]

When he approved the Cunningham claims in December 1907, Ballinger said he could recall none of this. None of it mattered anyway. While Ballinger was having the deeds prepared, one of his assistants wrote a letter to inform Glavis of the decision. Glavis did not stand on ceremony. He immediately wired Ballinger, urging him to reverse the decision because serious questions remained unanswered. Ballinger was no doubt taken aback by his subordinate's challenge—but there was little he could do without openly flouting the law. At the same time, Ballinger apparently felt that Glavis could not stand in the way of the Cunningham claims forever. He therefore wired Moore that there would be a "temporary" delay in issuing the deeds. The delay did not turn out to be so temporary.

When Hapgood first called him down to New York in January 1910, Brandeis knew that there would not be much time for preparation. In fact, he had less than two weeks to study the voluminous record on the Ballinger–Pinchot controversy before the congressional hearings convened. Within that short period, however, he came to master it all. Even long-time members of the bureaucracy—who prided themselves on their knowledge of arcane procedures—were impressed with this out-of-state lawyer's knowledge of the Interior Department. Edward Finney, an experienced Interior employee, saw it firsthand when Brandeis interrogated him closely on the witness stand. Afterwards Finney approached the man responsible for Brandeis's selection. "Mr. Hapgood," Finney addressed the journalist, "I have no respect for you. I think you are doing this to make circulation for your paper. But I want to say you have a wonderful lawyer. He knows the business of the department today as well as I do."[13]

There was a personal sacrifice in all this for Brandeis. Although exhilarated by the excitement of the hearing and the unfolding drama, it did mean long absences from home. He tried to get away from Washington by Saturday so that he could spend at least some of the weekend with his family. But he would have to leave after a short visit in order to make a Sunday-night meeting at Hapgood's apartment on East 73rd Street in Manhattan. There he would meet with Hapgood, attorney George Rublee, and others to review strategy and plan the week's testimony. Then the Boston attorney would return to his room at the New Willard Hotel in Washington near the White House and steel himself for another week of combat. It was a grueling schedule, and for the first time in a long while he could find virtually no time for exercise.

There was another personal cost for Brandeis in all this—one he could never recover. Sam Warren, his old law partner, had been under tremendous pressure in the last few months. A big legal battle was being waged by Sam's brother over the terms and implementation of their father's estate. It was alleged that Sam had cheated his brother out of some money from the inheritance. Brandeis and his firm were representing Sam and the estate. The legal ethics and issues of the matter were probably secondary to Sam. No doubt he was more disturbed by the publicity generated by the trial. Every day the local papers reported on the day's events in court. Sam wanted Louis there, but his friend had bigger fish to fry in Washington. Besides, Ned McClennen, Brandeis's law partner, was an able trial attorney and would do an excellent job. Toward the end of February, Brandeis was summoned back to Boston. Sam Warren had shot himself to death.

Brandeis must have had regrets that he could not have been with his friend. He and Sam had had a long and trusting friendship. But Brandeis had other clients and other responsibilities to which he was also committed.

Ballinger no doubt understood a lawyer's loyalty to his client. But when Brandeis questioned him on the witness stand about his services for Cunningham in 1908, Ballinger was rather nonchalant about it. The whole thing had arisen quite unexpectedly, he said. Cunningham became distressed when he learned that Glavis planned to use the 1903 journal entry to show that Cunningham had always intended to violate the law. Cunningham's troubles were compounded because he had also given Glavis an affidavit in which he swore—falsely—that his group had not joined forces with anyone, not even the Morgan–Guggenheim syndicate.

When he appreciated the nature of his predicament, Cunningham ran to Ballinger. The former Seattle mayor had resigned from the Land Commission in March 1908 and had returned to his hometown to practice law. There was a conflict-of-interest law that arguably could have prevented him from working on matters, like the Cunningham claims, that were in his office while he was commissioner. But Ballinger read the law narrowly and agreed to help his old friend.

It was really not much, Ballinger later told Brandeis under cross-examination. The same service, he said, "might have been performed by a dentist, or a doctor, or anybody else. . . ."[14] All he did was advise Cunningham on the intricacies of a new land law that had been adopted in May 1908, prepare an affidavit (which also proved to be false) to explain away the earlier one, and then personally carry the affidavit to Interior Secretary Garfield (on vacation at his Ohio home) and then to the new land commissioner in Washington, D.C. All of Ballinger's efforts were to no avail, however, because Garfield was convinced by now that the Cunningham claims were indeed fraudulent.

Luck then seemed to appear again on Cunningham's behalf. Taft was elected president in 1908, and Ballinger replaced Garfield as interior secretary on March 4, 1909. Ballinger's ethical sensibilities went through a metamorphosis—

on the surface, at least. While he downplayed the nature of his legal services to Cunningham in 1908, he now claimed that his representation of Cunningham prevented him from participating in any action as secretary of the interior that might affect Cunningham. He therefore issued "strict instructions" to his staff not to involve him in any question affecting that group's coal claims. It certainly sounded good. But somehow Ballinger managed to stay in the thick of things. In his closing argument to the congressional committee, Brandeis likened Ballinger's instruction to "clubs where they expect to do a lot of gambling, [and] the first rule of the club [is] that 'card playing for money is not permitted in this club.' "[15]

The initial question that Ballinger's Interior Department had to resolve was the scope of the new land law adopted on May 28, 1908. The law stated that persons who had filed claims in good faith under the 1904 law could now consolidate claims of up to 2,560 acres. That was clearly a more practical approach to coal mining in Alaska. The issue was whether the Cunningham group had acted in good faith previously. Glavis thought that the new law's definition of "good faith" could not include schemes like Cunningham's. Others in the Interior Department disagreed. In May 1909 Ballinger stated that an opinion should be secured from the attorney general.

The letter was duly drafted. For some reason, the attorney general never got it. Instead, an Interior subordinate gave it to First Assistant Secretary of the Interior Frank Pierce. On May 19 Pierce reached his opinion that the new law should be "liberally construed" and should not exclude claimants, like Cunningham, against whom a "technical objection" could be raised. Pierce then telephoned Moore and gave him the good news.

Meanwhile, Glavis became greatly distressed to learn that an opinion had not been requested from the attorney general and that Pierce had given what Glavis viewed as an indefensible interpretation of the new law. Through the intervention of a friend, Glavis was invited to visit George Wickersham, the attorney general, in his office on May 25, 1909. Wickersham agreed with Glavis that Pierce's analysis of the new law was wrong. The attorney general said he would ask Ballinger about the matter at a Cabinet meeting later that morning.

Under cross-examination by Brandeis, Ballinger disputed those facts. The secretary obviously did not want it to appear that he had gone to the attorney general—which he had originally asked his staff to do—only because of Glavis's intervention. Ballinger said that on the morning of May 25 he had received another letter from Moore, dated May 24 and mailed from Chicago, complaining about the department's failure to process the Cunningham claims. Ballinger said he had then realized that the attorney general had not issued an opinion. Initially, Ballinger went to Senator Wesley Jones of Washington and then President Taft on the morning of May 25. After discussing the matter with them, Ballinger testified, he went—on his own initiative—to see Wickersham. As for Glavis, Ballinger regarded his visit with the attorney general as an act of "insubordination" and part of a plot to "ruin" the secretary's reputation.

Brandeis found Ballinger's testimony incredible. In his view, it was a complete lie. In cross-examining the secretary, Brandeis wanted to expose the perjury. It was not easy; Ballinger was a tough witness. And most members of the congressional committee—already hostile to Brandeis's aggressive questioning over a three-month period—had no patience for his effort to trap Ballinger:

MR. BRANDEIS. Now I will ask you [Mr. Secretary] how could the letter of Miles C. Moore of the 24th written at Chicago have been here and been on your desk and opened early enough on the morning of the 25th, which was the date of the Cabinet meeting, for you to have considered it, . . . taken it up with Senator Jones and taken it up to the President?

SECRETARY BALLINGER: Are you through with your question?

MR. BRANDEIS: Yes, sir.

SECRETARY BALLINGER: I do not see that it is an impossibility.

MR. BRANDEIS: Will you have the goodness to ascertain?

SENATOR ROOT: I shall be very glad to be informed as to the slightest importance of it.

MR. BRANDEIS: The importance of the question is this: The Secretary has stated . . . that Mr. Glavis had nothing whatever to do with the taking of this matter up with the Attorney General.

SENATOR ROOT: Well, what of it? It all seems to me to be chicken feed.

MR. BRANDEIS: I think, in view of all the circumstances and the Attorney General raising this quesion, I was at least justified in cross-examining with regard to it.

SENATOR ROOT: I do not mean, Mr. Brandeis, to say that you are not justified in it, but we have been here forty days, and it is time the children of Israel should get out of the wilderness.[16]

In due course, Wickersham did issue an opinion reversing Pierce's interpretation of the new law. The Cunningham group then pressed for a final disposition of their claims under the old law. At the end of June 1909 Glavis was directed by his supervisor, H.H. Schwartz, to submit his final report and to prepare for an immediate hearing. Glavis wired back from Seattle that new evidence was being developed and that the hearing should be postponed sixty days. Schwartz would have none of that. He repeated the instructions to move forward at once.

Glavis was not one to take all this lying down. In the middle of July 1909 he went to Ballinger, who was then in Seattle. Ballinger was not sympathetic to Glavis's request for delay. As for Schwartz, he became furious when he learned that Glavis had appealed the hearing order to the secretary without advising him of it. Schwartz immediately removed Glavis from the case and appointed another government agent to take his place.

Glavis was becoming more and more suspicious. He had heard the rumors in Seattle that the Cunningham claimants had "friends" in government; he had seen Ballinger as Land Commissioner attempt to approve the claims almost immediately after directing Glavis to conduct a thorough investigation; and now he had witnessed Ballinger's efforts as secretary to help the group by avoiding the attorney general and resisting a relatively short delay in the hearing. Images of conspiracy danced in Glavis's head. He felt surrounded by the enemy. He needed help. So he went to the one man he knew would understand—Gifford Pinchot.

The nation's chief forester already had ample grounds to distrust Ballinger. In large part, it reflected a difference in styles. Pinchot, the tall, suave aristocrat, was willing to read the laws liberally to realize his dreams of conservation. Ballinger, in contrast, felt that the government could not do anything for conservation unless it was expressly authorized by the law. These differing approaches had led to numerous clashes between the two when Ballinger was land commissioner under Roosevelt.

The future of their relationship did not look bright when Taft appointed Ballinger secretary of the interior in March 1909. Aside from their different professional approaches, there was now a personal side to it also. Pinchot had expected his good friend James Garfield to stay on as head of the Interior Department. Taft had reportedly given Roosevelt that assurance, and Garfield had relied on it in renewing the lease on his Washington home. Pinchot was greatly disappointed when he learned of Garfield's departure. Privately, he told intimates that he expected trouble with Ballinger. "I couldn't work with him as I have with Jim [Garfield]," he told a journalist. "Jim and I think alike. . . . Ballinger and I might clash."[17]

Not surprisingly, the prediction came to pass, and there were numerous squabbles about national forests, water power sites, and other matters of conservation. In each instance Pinchot was convinced that Ballinger was doing his utmost to reverse the policies that Pinchot had developed under Roosevelt.

In this setting, Pinchot's aides were most receptive when Glavis suggested that Ballinger might be involved in a conspiracy to help the Morgan–Guggenheim syndicate gain control of the Alaskan coal fields. Pinchot stepped in immediately. Since the Cunningham claims arguably involved some national forests, he asked Interior to postpone the hearings until the Forestry Bureau could study the matter.

All hell broke loose when the Interior people learned about Pinchot's intervention. They knew it meant trouble. Fred Dennett, the new land commissioner, told Schwartz that it looked "treacherous."[18] Not surprisingly, they had a tough time deciding whether to postpone the hearing on the Cunningham claims. And worst of all they felt it necessary to have guidance from Ballinger—even though the secretary had long ago told his aides that he was not to be involved in the Cunningham matter. In his closing argument to the congressional committee, Brandeis caught the flavor of Interior's frantic reaction to Pinchot's involvement.

"Now just think of this," the Boston lawyer told the committee. "A real crisis came in this matter when Glavis sought to protect the people by getting a delay in the hearing and others attempted to thwart him. . . . Then it began to appear that, doubtless for political reasons, it would be unwise, in view of the forestry intervention, to insist upon that hearing taking place immediately." To Brandeis the whole episode reeked with favoritism for Cunningham. "Gentlemen," he addressed the committee, "just think how unimportant ordinarily consenting to a delay in the hearing of a case is. Why should there have been this terrible difficulty about consenting to a delay of two or three months, most of which is the vacation period?" To Brandeis the answer was clear. "[I]t was because the Secretary had his hands, his grip, on these cases," Brandeis observed. "This control is not evidenced by documents. He did not need writings. He was surrounded by men of the category of those who, 'at the winking of authority . . . understand a law.' "[19]

While Ballinger and his cohorts were wrestling with the question of postponement, Pinchot was advising Glavis to take his case to the president personally. The young government agent prepared a short summary of his view of the facts. Pinchot gave Glavis two letters to facilitate his meeting with the president. In one Pinchot told Taft that he had known Glavis for years and could vouch for his integrity; on the witness stand Pinchot was later forced to admit that that was a lie since he had really met Glavis only recently. In the other letter Pinchot briefly outlined the controversy, concluding that the Forestry Bureau had stopped the issuance of the Cunningham deeds; that too was a lie or, as Pinchot preferred to call it on the witness stand, "a mistake."[20]

William Howard Taft was a congenial president who did not like being chief executive. In fact, he hated the whole political process. "Politics makes me sick," he once wrote his wife.[21] His wife, Nellie, however, had plans for her husband. Prodded from behind, the Ohio lawyer enjoyed an unusually illustrious career: solicitor general of the United States, judge on the United States Court of Appeals, secretary of war, governor-general of the Philippines. In 1908 Roosevelt picked Taft to succeed him, convinced that the former judge would remain loyal to Roosevelt's policies. In many respects Taft fulfilled and even exceeded those expectations. But he did not enjoy the headaches that came with the job. When he was asked by a reporter during the Ballinger–Pinchot hearings whether he liked being president, Taft replied, "I would rather be Chief Justice of the United States, and a quieter life than that which comes at the White House is more in keeping with my temperament."[22]

In addition to his distaste for politics, Taft had one other feature that distinguished him among American leaders: his weight. At 332 pounds, Taft weighed more than any president in history. His rotund figure was a constant source of humor in Washington circles. One story had it that Taft was the perfect gentleman who one day got up in a streetcar and gave his seat to three women.

Glavis probably had no way of knowing that Taft would not be very receptive to the young agent's report or his letters from Pinchot. Not that Taft was against conservation; in many ways he was better at it than Roosevelt. But Pinchot's abrasive style clashed with Taft's more placid view of life. As Taft told his brother in June 1909, Pinchot—for all his virtues as a government servant—was "a good deal of a radical and a good deal of a crank. . . ."[23]

So when Glavis went to the summer White House in Beverly, Massachusetts, on August 18, 1909, the conscientious and polite president listened intently to the charges. He took Glavis's report and asked him to await further word. After four days Glavis was told to go home to Seattle. On that same day Taft forwarded

Glavis's report to Ballinger in Seattle and asked him to advise the president of his comments by letter or telegram. Ballinger did better than that. He collected a mass of material, which later constituted 661 pages in the printed record, and brought it to Beverly personally on September 6, 1909. Even on a small matter like that, though, Ballinger could not truthfully answer Brandeis's questions before the committee:

MR. BRANDEIS: Now having brought together all the material, why did you personally go to Beverly with them instead of sending those documents for the consideration of the President?

SECRETARY BALLINGER: I had an invitation, practically, in the President's letter for me to come East [from Seattle], or communicate with him by letter, and I concluded I would do both.

MR. BRANDEIS: Will you point out in the letter of the President what you call an invitation to come East, which I suppose you mean to visit him at Beverly?

SECRETARY BALLINGER: The President says—reading the second paragraph of his letter of August 22, 1909:

"I start west on the 14th of September. If after reading these papers you think you ought to come to Washington for the purpose of writing your comment on the same, you could probably do so and send me your comment before I leave for the West. If, on the other hand, you are able to write what you wish . . . without reference to the Washington records, will you be good enough to advise me by telegram that you are about to do so and when I may expect your written comment?"

I took that to be an invitation for me to come East, or use my own judgment as to what course I would pursue in preparing my answer.

MR. BRANDEIS: Now, is there a word there, Mr. Secretary, which could be construed by any man properly as being an invitation to come to Beverly and to personally present to the President your views on the matter?

SECRETARY BALLINGER: Strictly speaking, no sir.

MR. BRANDEIS: Well, then, why did you go to Beverly?

SECRETARY BALLINGER: Because I wanted to.[24]

Taft did not attribute much importance to the matter anyway; he was spending his time planning speeches and playing golf. Ballinger and the assistant attorney general assigned to interior, Oscar Lawler, had to wait until evening to see the president. They then spent a few hours with him. Taft obviously did not have time to review all the documents that Ballinger and Lawler brought with them. Nonetheless, he was convinced that Glavis was on a witch hunt. The day after the meeting, Taft instructed Lawler to prepare a letter—"as if he were President"—exonerating Ballinger.

Buoyed by Taft's support, Ballinger and Lawler rushed back to Washington to prepare the president's letter. Ballinger was especially hopeful that the letter would be the end of Glavis. Even before they made the trip to Beverly, Ballinger had told his associates that he proposed "to kill some snakes."[25] Glavis, no doubt, headed the list.

Lawler, Ballinger, and other top Interior aides worked into the night feverishly preparing the document for the president's signature. When the letter was finalized, copies were distributed to the main participants, the drafts were burned in the fireplace in the secretary's office, and Lawler left to return to Beverly.

The president was not entirely pleased with Lawler's thirty-page memorandum. Not surprisingly, it was very critical of Pinchot. Taft was sufficiently astute politically to know that there was nothing to be gained in gratuitously challenging the chief forester. Pinchot had a large and loyal following in the country, and an attack on him would only compound a controversy that was already overblown. So Taft deleted the references to Pinchot, toned the letter down, dated it September 13, 1909, and released it to the public on September 16. In a separate letter to Ballinger, Taft—anticipating a congressional inquiry—told Ballinger that he would be glad to submit all the material to Congress but "to leave out of your answers any references to Pinchot or the part he took in bringing Glavis' report to my attention."[26]

In retrospect, that turned out to be Taft's first fundamental error. The second concerned the written summary that Taft asked Attorney General Wickersham to prepare after the decision had been made. Neither mistake affected the substance of the controversy between Ballinger and Pinchot. And Taft had every reason to believe that the inner workings of the presidential process here would remain known only to his intimates and pass into history without public notice. But then Taft did not know about Louis Brandeis and his obsession with factual detail.

Brandeis had voted for Taft in the 1908 presidential elections. "Taft is admirably qualified for the position and doubtless will . . . prove a fine President . . .," Brandeis wrote his brother at the time. But he was concerned that special interests might wield more influence under Taft than they had under his predecessor. As he told Al, ". . . I fear the Republican Party will be less manageable than under Roosevelt and that we shall see much of the moneybags we abhor. . . ."[27]

When he first accepted the assignment to defend Glavis fourteen months later, Brandeis had no intention of attacking Taft himself. In fact, he was hopeful that the matter could be pursued without involving the president. From the outset Brandeis and his colleagues tried to paint a picture of a leader who had been led astray by misguided subordinates.

The strategy failed to account for Taft's personal qualities. He was a man who stuck by his friends. More important, he was also a leader who was not afraid to do what he considered the right thing, no matter what the political pressures. Even at the conclusion of the congressional proceedings—when Ballinger had been exposed as an evasive and often untruthful witness—Taft refused to join the chorus of criticism because he still believed that the interior secretary had been unfairly maligned. "If I were to turn Ballinger out," he wrote a complaining citizen in May 1910, "in view of his innocence and in view of the conspiracy against him, I should be a white-livered skunk. I don't care how it affects my administration and how it affects the administration before the people; if the people are so unjust as this I don't propose to be one of them. . . . [L]ife is not worth living and office is not worth having if, for the purpose of acquiring public support, we have to either do a cruel injustice or acquiesce in it."[28]

Brandeis regarded Taft's willingness to stand by Ballinger as "foolish." "We had left him the loop-hole by pointing out how he had been misled," he told his mother-in-law, "but he insists that he knew and knows it all."[29]

This, as it turned out, would be Taft's undoing. For Ballinger's misdeeds, when all was said and done, had really not amounted to much. True, his assistance to the Cunningham group was, both in reality and appearance, ethically inappropriate. But he had never completely shut Glavis off from the case, and he had enough integrity to know that there was a limit to what he could do for his friends. Even Brandeis recognized that the charges against Ballinger were not all that serious. Under repeated and close questioning by committee members, the Boston attorney made it clear that he did not accuse the interior secretary of "corruption" or of violating any particular law (except the one concerning an ex-government employee's involvement in cases that he had handled while on the federal payroll). Nor did Brandeis recommend that Ballinger be impeached. The most he could say was, in effect, that the president had made a bad appointment and that Ballinger was not a trustworthy custodian of the nation's natural resources.

None of that prevented Brandeis from pursuing the case with the zeal and tenacity that had brought him success in so many other matters. He not only mastered the inner workings of the Interior Department; he also used newspaper reports and eyewitness accounts to determine the precise movements of Taft, Ballinger, and other key players at different stages. The committee was so overwhelmed by Brandeis's knowledge of everyone's activities that Senator Root asked the lawyer at one point whether he had had a detective following Ballinger; and later Oscar Lawler complained from the witness stand that he had been constantly followed by "gum-shoe men" and that Brandeis was "the flower of this foul flock."[30]

The committee did not always appreciate Brandeis's style. He was repeatedly asking for documents, and the committee—made up of six Senators and six members of the House of Representatives—was just as repeatedly denying them, usually by a vote of 7–5. At an early stage in the proceedings Brandeis had a heated argument with Senator Knute Nelson of Minnesota, the committee chairman, over the production of documents. At another point during the cross-examination of Ballinger, Brandeis was trying to get Ballinger to identify the land cases he had handled as a private attorney; when the secretary avoided a direct answer, Nelson suggested that the attorney simply identify the specific cases on which he wanted the secretary's comment. "I do not think it is a proper way of cross-examining the witness," Brandeis replied. Nelson did not like the nature or tone of Brandeis's response. "You need not snap at the committee, either," the chairman retorted. "I want you to act in a gentlemanly manner when here before this committee. . . . You insulted the witnesses, but you can not insult this committee." At that point a woman in the packed audience in Room 207 of the Senate Office Building yelled out, "The committee has no right to insult him either."[31]

In part, Brandeis's aggressive style was necessary because the government witnesses were so uncooperative. And none proved more recalcitrant than Ballinger. The interior secretary was guarded and always prepared to exchange verbal lashes with his tormentor. He simply did not like to give direct answers. His responses were frequently surrounded with qualifications such as "I can't recall" or "I don't remember."

Brandeis, however, could not be turned aside. He used his vast knowledge to bore holes in Ballinger's testimony and to force out admissions. At one point the secretary appealed to the committee "for protection against the insolence of this man who is attempting to cross-examine me."[32] And at another juncture Ballinger told Brandeis testily, "The record is full of your attempts at illumination which do not illumine anything, but cast aspersions on my character."[33]

Brandeis's associates no doubt admired the skill he exhibited at these times. His secretary Alice Grady, for instance, was present for part of Ballinger's cross-examination. "Needless to say," she wrote Alfred Brandeis, "I thoroughly enjoyed the occasion. Feeling ran high. Mrs. Ballinger and Mrs. Vertrees [the wife of Ballinger's lawyer] occupied front seats at every performance; and if looks could kill, Mr. Brandeis would have experienced a thousand deaths during the two days in question, but he was . . . as Daniel in the lions' den. The occasion appeared to be a joyous one for him. Having attended the hearings yourself, you can understand how keen was my pleasure in observing the masterful way in which Mr. Brandeis had stacked and shuffled his facts and presented them sweetly one by one to the consternation of his wriggling victim."[34]

Alfred Brandeis had also observed the hearings. But he was not as favorably impressed as Alice Grady. In fact, he had already written his brother to criticize his zeal in attacking Ballinger and the Taft administration. Brandeis remained intransigent. "Your remarks are entirely pertinent," he replied to his brother, "but I think not sound. There is nothing for us to do but to follow the trail of evil wherever it extends. . . . In the fight against special interest we shall receive no quarter and may as well make up our minds to give none. It is a hard fight," he added. "The man with the hatchet is the only one who has a chance of winning in the end. . . . [E]very attempt to deal mercifully with the special interests during the fight simply results in their taking advantage of the merciful."[35]

The trail of "evil" that Brandeis was pursuing, moreover, was leading him closer and closer to the president. The first matter that caught his attention was the summary of events that had been prepared by Attorney General Wickersham. The summary was dated September 11, 1909, and Taft had forwarded the document to the congressional committee when it had requested all materials that Taft had relied on in preparing his September 13 letter exonerating Ballinger. Brandeis was suspicious of the Wickersham document. On September 6 Ballinger and Lawler had given Taft a mass of material that occupied 661 printed pages in the record. It was inconceivable that Wickersham had digested and analyzed all that material within five days—especially since Brandeis knew from his study of newspapers that Wickersham was heavily involved at the same time in drafting amendments to legislation then pending in Congress.

Something else bothered Brandeis about the Wickersham summary. It contained a refutation of some charges that Glavis did not include in his report to the president; those particular charges had not been made public until *Collier's* published Glavis's article two months later. To Brandeis it was overwhelming proof that the Wickersham summary had been prepared long after Taft wrote his letter of exoneration. The document had apparently been pre-dated, however, to create the impression that Taft had relied on it—an impression that would bolster the foundations of Taft's conclusion.

Late one night Brandeis took a long walk with Norman Hapgood. The editor had never seen his friend so excited. Louis poured out his theory to Norman, telling him that the whole thing was beginning to look like a set-up. The attorney wanted some additional proof, though. The next day he intended to cross-examine Edward Finney, a long-time Interior employee who had been close to the main events. Louis would ask him probing questions that suggested a knowledge of the true nature of the Wickersham summary; Norman would watch Finney's face and try to determine whether the intonations of Brandeis's inside knowledge were causing discomfort.

It worked like a charm—and both friends were convinced that their theory was accurate. Brandeis quickly requested the committee to direct the attorney general to furnish all materials related to the preparation of his September 11 summary. Despite Brandeis's anticipation of success here, he did not feel entirely comfortable with his actions. He sensed that Wickersham had not been responsible for the pre-dating. He wrote home to Alice, saying that he felt like "an executioner," that it would be "an awful thing" for Wickersham to recognize Taft's guilt in the matter, and that he was glad Norman was with him to share responsibility for the disclosure.[36]

None of it mattered, however—at least at first. The committee majority was convinced that Brandeis was only trying to prolong the circus atmosphere of the hearing. After a heated debate, Brandeis's request for documents was denied by a vote of 7–5. The silence of the White House and the Department of Justice, however, convinced Brandeis that his suspicions were well founded.

In the meantime, another document began to assume importance: the memorandum that Lawler had drafted at Taft's direction and that the president had used in preparing his letter of September 13. Taft had not forwarded the Lawler memorandum to the committee in January even though the committee had requested all the materials on which he had relied and he had in fact used it. Taft had told Ballinger he did not want to disclose the Lawler memorandum because it was too critical of Pinchot, and the president was a man of his word. It was an unusual brand of loyalty. Taft's refusal to disclose the document was especially incredible because by the time the committee requested it, Pinchot had already been fired for insubordination.

Unfortunately for Taft, his sense of personal honor could not hold back the floodgates. By the time Brandeis began his cross-examination of Ballinger, the

Boston attorney already knew of the existence of the Lawler memorandum.

It happened quite by accident. Frederick Kerby was a young stenographer who worked for Ballinger. His services had been needed when the secretary and Lawler returned from Beverly in September to prepare the letter for the president's signature. Kerby therefore knew all about the document's preparation and related the story in confidence to Hugh Brown, a friend who had worked for Garfield when the latter was secretary of interior. Garfield was scheduled to testify at the congressional hearings and, through Brown, knew of the Lawler memorandum. The memorandum was significant for two reasons. First, it showed that Ballinger and his aides had really exonerated themselves and that Taft's letter was a whitewash; second, the existence of the document would demonstrate that Taft had lied when he told the committee he had given them all relevant documents. Brown posed the question to Kerby. Could Garfield mention the Lawler memorandum during his appearance?

One evening in the middle of February 1910 Kerby went to Pinchot's home on Rhode Island Avenue in Washington. There he conferred with Garfield and then Brandeis. If the memorandum's existence were to become known, Kerby said it would have to be through his testimony. He was the one who had firsthand knowledge of it. But Kerby had no great desire to testify. He knew that his testimony would result in his immediate dismissal from government. Consequently, he asked Brandeis to have the document disclosed without his testimony, if possible. The attorney said that he would do what he could.[37]

In the beginning of May, Brandeis tried to maneuver Ballinger into admitting the existence of the Lawler memorandum. It was not easy:

MR. BRANDEIS: And Mr. Lawler was there [in Beverly] on the 13th [of September], the day of the date of the letter—you recall that fact, do you not?

SECRETARY BALLINGER: I think he was there; yes.

MR. BRANDEIS: Now, why did Mr. Lawler go to Beverly?

SECRETARY BALLINGER: At the request of the President.

MR. BRANDEIS: Why did he go?

SECRETARY BALLINGER: I decline to state any conversation with the President in connection with the matter.

MR. BRANDEIS: I did not ask you to state any conversation. . . . What did Mr. Lawler take with him when he went to Beverly . . . ?

SECRETARY BALLINGER: A grip with some clothes in it. I do not know what else he took.

MR. BRANDEIS: You know that he did have something else?

SECRETARY BALLINGER: And some records. I know he had other things; yes.

MR. BRANDEIS: What were they, bearing particularly upon the Glavis–Pinchot controversy?

SECRETARY BALLINGER: He had some of the records of the case or memoranda.

MR. BRANDEIS: What?

SECRETARY BALLINGER: I could not definitely define just what he had in his portfolio or what he took with him.

MR. BRANDEIS: What were the memoranda that you know of?

SECRETARY BALLINGER: He had a memorandum covering a sort of resume of the facts as set out in the records.

MR. BRANDEIS: And you say made by himself? . . .

SECRETARY BALLINGER: I think he prepared it himself, and I think he consulted with other persons in connection with it.

MR. BRANDEIS: Did he consult with you?

SECRETARY BALLINGER: I would not say that he consulted with me, but I went over his memoranda.

MR. BRANDEIS: Well, will you state to the committee what you know as to the contents of [those] memoranda?

SECRETARY BALLINGER: I have stated about all I know or can recall as to the contents of it. It was a resume of the facts as to the Glavis charges, and whether it related to the papers that were delivered to the President regarding the [Cunningham] cooperative certificate matter or withdrawals I do not remember.[38]

It was, of course, all a lie. The interior secretary was intimately familiar with the background, preparation, and contents of the Lawler memorandum. Ballinger knew it. Brandeis knew it. And Kerby, sitting in the audience, also knew it. The government stenographer sensed that his testimony would be necessary. Later Brandeis came to confer with him in private. He explained that Kerby's testimony now appeared to be the only way to disclose the existence of the Lawler memorandum. It was a tough decision. Brandeis understood that Kerby would be fired if he told what he knew. Brandeis could not tell him what to do. He would have to make his own decision.

Kerby talked it over with his wife that evening and then told Brandeis he would testify. His decision had been made easier when he learned that a newspaper syndicate would give him a job after his expected dismissal from government.

Kerby wrote an article describing the true state of affairs, and it was published in the newspapers in the middle of May 1910. It created a tremendous stir, and people began talking of the hidden secrets in the Ballinger–Pinchot affair. Brandeis was troubled by the whole sequence of events. It indicates, he wrote his wife, "the extent to which men are driven when the path of deceit is entered upon." It certainly did not reflect well of the president. "I think as ill" of Taft's morals now, he added, "as of his intellect."[39]

The beleaguered interior secretary was not about to give up, however. As soon as he saw the news, Ballinger rushed over to the White House. The president, he learned, was on a golf course in Chevy Chase, Maryland. Through the intervention of a harried aide, Ballinger had a long telephone conversation with Taft. It was agreed that Ballinger would draft a statement for release by the White House asserting that there was "absolutely no foundation" to Kerby's story.

Unhappily, it was another case of poor planning for Taft. Ballinger forgot to consult Wickersham before he released the White House statement. It was a costly oversight, because the attorney general was simultaneously sending the Lawler memorandum over to the congressional committee and explaining in a cover letter that, after another diligent search of his files, he had suddenly discovered it.

The truth was out, and the president knew it. The next day he wrote a long letter describing the true background of the Lawler memorandum and the September 13 letter of exoneration. The president also admitted that the Wickersham summary had been pre-dated—a course that Taft tried to justify by claiming that the summary was nothing more than a written record of the conclusions that Wickersham had given him orally.

After some further testimony, the hearings were adjourned. In due course the committee, by a divided vote, gave its expected endorsement of Ballinger. The committee's approval, though, could not preserve the political future of Taft or Ballinger. The interior secretary's health was broken by the long ordeal, and in March 1911 Taft finally accepted Ballinger's resignation, Taft stating in a letter of regret that he would not have accepted the resignation if it had been based on the "unjust" attacks Ballinger had endured.

As for Taft, he received the Republican nomination in 1912 but faced stiff competition from the Democratic nominee, Woodrow Wilson, and from Theodore Roosevelt, who was trying to recapture the White House through the independent Bull Moose Party. Pinchot had been instrumental in Roosevelt's decision to run. While Roosevelt apparently had some sympathy with Taft's predicament in the episode, he was also persuaded that Taft was not completely loyal to his predecessor's policies. Given this and other disagreements, Roosevelt felt compelled—so he said—to make the run for the presidency to revive the old Progressive programs and policies. With the popular Rough Rider in the race, Taft did not have a chance, and he finished a poor third.

It did not have to be that way. Even Brandeis recognized that. "It was the lying that did it," he later told Norman Hapgood. "If they had brazenly admitted everything, and justified it on the ground that Ballinger was at least doing what he thought best, we should not have had a chance. Refusal to speak the truth is the history of many a downfall."[40]

There were other lessons in it for Brandeis. He learned to appreciate the importance of independent thinking in government. "The danger in America is not of insubordination," he forcefully told the committee in his closing argument, "but it is of too complacent obedience to the will of superiors. With this great Government building up, ever creating new functions, getting an ever increasing number of employees who are attending to the people's business, the one thing we need is men in subordinate places who will think for themselves and who will think and act in full recognition of their obligations as part of the governing body."

In Brandeis's view, there were no better examples of good public servants than Glavis and Kerby. Both had followed their instincts to do what they thought right—even if it meant the loss of a job. To Brandeis they had done the "manly" thing. In his mind there could be no higher compliment. "We are not dealing here with a question of the conservation of natural resources merely," he advised the committee; "it is the conservation and development of the individual; it is the conservation of democracy; it is the conservation of manhood." Glavis and Kerby, he added, prove "that America has among its young men, happily, men of courage and men in whom even the heavy burden of official life has not been able to suppress manliness."[41]

Brandeis also realized that financial necessity could just as easily have precluded Glavis or Kerby from doing what they thought right. If either had really needed the government job, they might have been forced to keep their silence. Reflecting on the experience in later years, he told his law clerk Dean Acheson that a person should not go into government service unless he were financially independent. Otherwise, the justice said, the individual would not be free to speak his mind, and the government would then lose its most valuable resource.[42]

The experience exemplified one of Brandeis's most unusual traits. Where most people saw concrete problems, he saw fundamental moral issues. A publisher's concern with a libel suit had been transformed into an examination of the ethics of whistle-blowing by government officials. It was an important lesson, one that remained with Brandeis. And so, when a government official approached him in the mid-1930s with a delicate problem, Brandeis—then a Supreme Court justice—had an answer. The official was concerned that contemplated action by his agency—the Agricultural Adjustment Administration, a New Deal relief organization—would adversely affect the public. Should he disclose the information to a journalist? "Well," Brandeis responded, "this is a decision you have to make, but if I were in your place, I would consider my obligation to . . . the people you're supposed to be protecting, the consuming public. If you think it will protect them, and if you don't care about keeping your job, I think there's no question. I think you ought to give it to him."[43]

Brandeis returned to Boston in June 1910. He was glad to see his family and to resume canoeing and other activities he had missed during his long stay in the capital. But he longed for the excitement of the congressional hearings, and he had difficulty adjusting to the quiet atmosphere of his law office. He reported to his brother the surprise people registered when they saw how well he looked after months of hard work. "[B]ut for a man who would rather fight than eat," he observed, "the surprise is unwarranted."[44]

His involvement in the Ballinger–Pinchot controversy did, however, spark his interest in the development of Alaska—truly the last frontier. In long letters he detailed for friends and associates his view of how that development should proceed. The key was to ensure that the opportunities for individual development were not eliminated through the domination of large corporations. To that end, he was convinced that the government, and not private enterprise, should provide the capital needed to build transportation systems and other key facilities.[45]

The involvement in the Ballinger matter also led Congress to seek Brandeis's services in another controversy that threatened to be even more explosive than the earlier one. Once again the Morgan–Guggenheim syndicate was reported to be involved. And once again Brandeis could not resist the temptation to enter the fray.

In the autumn of 1910 it was reported that Taft had signed an order removing 12,800 acres from the Chugach Forest in Alaska. The acreage was frontage on the Controller Bay and, according to reports, was to be given to a company that secretly represented the Morgan–Guggenheim interests. Senator Robert M. La Follette introduced a resolution in April 1911 calling for another congressional inquiry. Newspapers said it would "open up the most sensational chapter yet written in connection with the operation of the Guggenheims in Alaska."[46]

Matters heated up when Myrtle Abbott, a young reporter, released her article in the summer of 1911. Abbott had given the article to Hapgood to be used in *Collier's,* but the editor had begged off. His friend Walter Fisher had just succeeded Ballinger as interior secretary, the Cunningham claims had just been canceled, and Hapgood was not interested in causing the new secretary any headaches just yet. Abbott was forced to take her piece elsewhere, and after the wire services picked it up, things began to jump.

Abbott claimed to have found a letter in the Interior Department files that conclusively proved the presence of the Morgan–Guggenheim syndicate in the matter. The communication, dated July 13, 1910, was from Richard S. Ryan, president of the Controller Railway & Navigation Company, to Richard A. Ballinger, then secretary of the interior. Ryan's company had secured the Controller Bay land to build railways and to provide a shipping outlet for Alaskan coal. The letter to Ballinger, however, indicated that Ryan really represented someone else:

> Dear Dick:
>
> I went to see the President the other day about this Controller Bay affair. The President asked me whom I represented. I told him, according to our agreement, that I represented myself. But that didn't seem to satisfy him. So I sent for Charlie Taft and asked him to tell his brother who it was I really represented. The President made no further objection to my claim.
>
> Yours,
> Dick[47]

The White House said that the "Dick to Dick" letter was a forgery and bore no relation to the truth. It would have been hard to believe otherwise. Coming right after the administration's miserable showing in the Glavis episode—which had just concluded—it would have taken an incredible amount of stupidity and gall to make the same mistakes again.

Nonetheless, congressmen and senators, always eager for publicity, assumed a more frantic pace and played the item for all it was worth. Representative James Graham, chairman of the investigative committee, knew the man to handle the matter. But when he got in touch with Brandeis, the Boston attorney put him off, saying he wanted to talk to Hapgood first. No doubt Brandeis wanted to know why his friend had declined to publish Abbott's article. When he could not reach Hapgood, Brandeis decided to take the plunge and accept the assignment. If Abbott's allegations were true, it was a most disturbing development, especially to Brandeis. For if a private company—any private company—could control Controller Bay, it would undercut his plans for Alaska's development. And whatever the outcome of the congressional inquiry, it would surely beat the boredom of law practice.

Brandeis immediately turned to the same techniques he had found so successful in preparing for the Ballinger hearings. He used investigators, friends, and newspaper reports to determine the movements of key characters. He also conducted an extensive interrogation of Abbott. None of this revealed evidence of wrongdoing. Brandeis could not establish the authenticity of the "Dick to Dick" letter. And he could not find any hard facts to demonstrate that Taft or Ballinger had acted illegally or unethically. Moreover, Ryan himself took the air out of the balloon by withdrawing his request for the Controller Bay territory. In the autumn of 1911 Brandeis advised Graham that a mistaken policy had been corrected and that the investigation should be dropped.

William A. Sutherland was a diminutive youth of twenty-two when he became a law clerk to Justice Brandeis in 1917. There was no separate Supreme Court building at the time, so Sutherland spent his time poring over law books in a small rented apartment in Washington, D.C. The apartment had two rooms—one for the clerk, and one that Brandeis used as an office.

Alice was very strict with her husband. She would not let him stay in the office too long. Exercise was important for Louis. So every two hours or so he would leave the apartment, go down the stairs, take a walk around the block, and then return for more work. The schedule ran like clockwork.

One day Sutherland heard voices and a great deal of noise as the justice returned from one of his walks. It was obvious that Brandeis had brought someone back with him. There was animated conversation and a good deal of laughter. Even though he could not see the visitor through the half-opened door, Sutherland knew who it was. The laugh was unmistakable.

After a while the visitor left and Brandeis opened wide the connecting door to his clerk's office. "Do you know who that was?" the justice inquired. There was a very broad smile on his face. "Why, yes," Sutherland replied. "That was ex-President Taft. I'd know that laugh anywhere." "That's right," said Brandeis, the smile as wide as ever. "I haven't talked to him in years, since the Ballinger–Pinchot controversy."[48] It was perhaps a forecast of the smooth working relationship he would establish with Taft after the latter became chief justice of the United States Supreme Court in 1921. It was, in a way, a testament to Brandeis's ability to sustain relationships with people. At least in most cases. Unfortunately, he would not find a similar durability in his relationship with the garment workers in New York City.

TEN

A New Labor–Management Partnership

He who will not apply new remedies must expect new evils;
for time is the greatest innovator.

FRANCIS BACON

Alice was looking older. It was not only her age—in the summer of 1910 she was forty-four. Her frequent illnesses were also taking their toll. Although she had more than enough help to avoid unnecessary exertion, she would often succumb to sickness that would sap her energy. She was heavier now and her hair was almost completely white.

To Louis, his wife was a constant source of concern. His hopes of improved health for her had never been fully realized. And he had to be careful lest the demands of family and friends unduly tax her strength. But Louis never seemed to mind these concerns and limitations. His marriage was as good as ever, and he still took considerable comfort from Alice—even during long absences.

After the extended stay in Washington for the Ballinger–Pinchot hearings, Louis decided to spend some extra time relaxing with his family. In early July he, Alice, daughter Elizabeth, and Alice's sister Pauline went to the Bretton Woods resort hotel in New Hampshire. They found the opulence of the place too much, however, and soon decided to move to more modest quarters elsewhere in New Hampshire. After that, Louis was planning to take the family back to the Bray Cottage in South Yarmouth for the entire month of August. The cottage was located in Cape Cod and was so appealing that Louis broke his cardinal rule against material acquisitions and tried—without success—to buy it.

For a while, though, it seemed that he might never make it to Bray Cottage for the summer. It was Lincoln Filene's fault. Lincoln was the younger brother of Edward and along with his brother helped to manage the family's growing clothing business in Boston. And like Edward, Lincoln was very close to Louis. The Boston attorney handled corporate and personal legal matters for both of them. Lincoln too was very civic minded, and he and Louis often took long walks home together engaged in animated conversation about politics and social reform. No doubt those talks helped convince Lincoln that Louis was the right person to consult about his problem.

In early July, Filene came to Brandeis to tell him about the garment workers' strike in New York City. The situation was desperate. For many years the garment industry in New York had involved cutthroat competition. It was a lucrative business and one that was easy to enter. And there was no shortage of firms. To reduce costs they took advantage of the garment workers, most of whom were Jewish immigrants from Eastern Europe. The result was incredibly poor working conditions—low wages, long hours, poor lighting, chairs with no backs, toilets that didn't flush, and fire escapes that didn't work.

The International Ladies' Garment Workers Union had been created in 1900, but its success in organizing the workers and protecting their interests was mixed. There were approximately 60,000 employees, many of whom did not speak the same language and most of whom had differing opinions on how to improve working conditions. The local unions often criticized the union leadership as too conservative. Many of the locals wanted to be aggressive, and they were not afraid to take action. At least once a year, if not more frequently, there was a strike at one of the garment companies, usually a faltering one. The ploy did help the union's tough image, but the resulting instability did little for the workers' financial security. With so many companies and continued dissension among union leaders, the employers generally had an easy time keeping the workers at bay.

Things began to change in the summer of 1910. The working conditions had become intolerable, and an unusual unity developed among the workers. By the beginning of July a broad-based strike was emerging, and the employers suddenly found themselves on the defensive. For the first time they felt the need to organize a common defense organization, which they called the Cloak, Suit and Skirt Manufacturers' Protective Association.

The slowdown in the garment industry was of obvious concern to retail clothing merchants like the Filenes. Soon after the strike began, Lincoln Filene journeyed down to New York City to assess the situation firsthand. It did not take long for him to appreciate the hostility between the two camps. Things were at a stalemate. Some kind of mediating force was needed—and fast. "I am going over with the idea of seeing some of the leaders among the employers' organizations," Lincoln wrote his brother on July 18, "and try to get them to secure Brandeis to represent them. If I fail in impressing them of the value of this, it is my intention to get [Samuel] Gompers [of the American Federation of Labor] to secure Brandeis. It does not seem to me to make very much difference which side has him so long as one side gets him. I think he will succeed in bringing about an adjustment much better than is at present possible."[1]

Filene's faith in his lawyer's mediating ability was based in part on experience. Ever since the 1890s Brandeis had been involved in labor disputes. And while he generally represented management, he had demonstrated his willingness to recognize the other side's perspective.

This balanced attitude was evident in a speech that the Boston attorney delivered in April 1904 to the Boston Typothetae, an association of printers. Brandeis had just concluded the successful representation of the organization in a fight with the Typographical Union, the labor group representing the pressmen. The result of the legal battle was that the printers could maintain an "open shop" in which union and non-union men could be hired freely. Despite the joys of victory, Brandeis warned his audience of employers that they could not expect to run a prosperous business unilaterally. Continuing cooperation with labor was essential. And that cooperation in turn required the employers to understand their employees' perspective. "Nine-tenths of the serious controversies which arise in life," Brandeis observed, "result from misunderstanding, result from one man not knowing the facts which to the other man seem important, or otherwise failing to appreciate his point of view. A properly conducted conference involves a frank disclosure of such facts—patient, careful argument, willingness to listen and to consider." To Brandeis's mind such a conference was "impossible where the employer clings to the archaic belief commonly expressed in the words 'This is my business, and I will run it as I please.' . . . Such conferences will succeed only if employer and employee recognize that, even if there be no so-called system of profit-sharing, they are in a most important sense partners. . . ."[2]

There was no better application of these principles than the formation of the Filene Cooperative Society, which Brandeis had helped to establish in 1905. Through this organization, the employees of the Filenes' clothing store were given the opportunity to share in both the management and profits of the company. It was an unusual experiment, and it had special appeal for the Filenes' lawyer. To Brandeis it meant that workers would have more control over their working conditions and their financial security. There was a cost for this benefit, though. As Brandeis explained to the Filene workers when the cooperative association was formed, industrial democracy could succeed only "among people who think; among people who are above the average intelligence. And that thinking," he added, "is not a heaven-born thing, that intelligence is not a gift that merely comes. It is a gift men make and women make for themselves. It is earned, and it is earned by effort. . . . The brain is like the hand. It grows with using."[3]

With this kind of open-minded and enlightened approach, Lincoln Filene was sure that his friend could be helpful in settling the garment strike. After discussing the matter with both sides of the dispute, Filene went back to Boston and asked Brandeis to return to New York with him.

At an earlier stage—before Filene's first trip to New York—Brandeis had rejected any possibility of his involvement. The major impediment was the union's insistence at that point on a closed shop—a system whereby only union members could be employed. "Then and there," Brandeis later said of his first conversation with Filene, "I told him that I would have nothing to do with any settlement of the strike involving the closed shop. That I did not believe in it, and that I thought it was un-American and unfair to both sides."[4] To Brandeis it was again a question of control. The employer had to have the right to hire the most efficient workers—even if they did not belong to the union. Proper management, in his view, ultimately depended on that right.

When Filene returned from New York, he carried with him a commitment from the union leadership that the demand for a closed shop would be dropped. He also brought back with him the invitation of both the union and the manufacturers for Brandeis to preside at a settlement conference. In this capacity Brandeis would not represent either side but would instead play the role of mediator.

Brandeis was now willing to change his tune, especially since this offered an opportunity to mold a relationship where both sides would have more control of their working environment. On July 24, 1910, he signed an agreement with both parties agreeing to mediate the controversy—but with the understanding that "the closed shop is not a subject which can be discussed at the conference."[5]

The whole matter almost collapsed before it even got started. Although the employers had written to Brandeis asking his participation, their trade publication, *New York Call,* issued a statement identifying Brandeis as the representative of only the strikers. The paper congratulated the employers on their "victory," since Brandeis's opposition to the closed shop—a principal stumbling block for the employers—was well known. The press announcement did not add to the spirit of cooperation. The union denied that Brandeis was its attorney or that the union had abandoned its demand for a closed shop. It looked as though it might be a long and fruitless conference.

On Thursday morning, July 28, 1910, Brandeis convened the conference of delegates for labor and management at the Metropolitan Life Insurance Building in New York City. "Gentlemen," he said to the twenty delegates and their respective attorneys, "we have come together in a matter which we must all recognize is very serious, and an important business, not only to settle this strike, but to create a [relationship] which will prevent similar strikes in the future."[6] Speaking for the labor delegates, J.B. Lennon explained at the outset that the garment workers were largely "untrained and undisciplined," that it was "not an easy matter to reach a consensus of opinion . . .," and that it might take a while before any settlement agreement could be approved by the unions. For the manufacturers' part, their attorney, Julius Cohen, remarked that it was his "hope and prayer, personally, that out of this conference, approached in a sincere and genuine spirit, we shall find that we shall agree upon something. . . . It is not a time for any hatchets or any pistols or any knives; our[s] are on the table; we hope yours are too." Cohen then added that he was especially pleased that "we have been able to secure as the presiding officer over our deliberations a man who enjoys the confidence of the labor men and of the country, as he enjoys the confidence of the business men of the country, and with his legal training, with his knowledge of what is the best and most expeditious way of disposing of such matters, I am sure that Mr. Brandeis's presence in the chair is the best assurance you can all have that this conference will proceed expeditiously. . . ."[7] It was a generous sentiment, but it would not stand the test of time.

Brandeis arranged to take up the union's grievances one at a time. The emphasis was to be on finding areas of agreement and isolating points of disagreement. Through patient but persistent questioning, Brandeis moved the conference along. If a delegate for either side digressed in a statement, Brandeis brought him back on track. If a matter seemed especially troublesome, he proposed that the delegates confer among themselves and return with some constructive suggestions. It did not take long, however, for one labor representative to state that the key issue was whether all employees should be unionized in what would be a closed shop. Brandeis quickly interrupted to say that they had all agreed that that was not a topic for discussion.

As the conference moved forward, Brandeis began to sense that this settlement conference was different from any other he had attended. Although in bitter disagreement on many points, the labor and management representatives were generally polite to one another and almost always willing to listen to one another. He also could not help but notice that the bonds of religion and culture seemed to reach across economic bridges. Virtually all the representatives for both labor and management were Jewish, or "Hebrews," as they were often called. And in the course of debate they often fell back upon their heritage to make a point. At times the Boston attorney heard the men yell at each other in Yiddish, "Shame: Is this worthy of a Jew?" In other instances the delegates would support their arguments with quotes from the Old Testament. It was, to say the least, an unusual and at times moving experience. "What struck me most," he later said, "was that each side had a great capacity for placing themselves in the other fellow's shoes."[8]

All that fellowship could not prevent the settlement conference from foundering on the issue of the closed shop. By the morning of Saturday, July 30, substantial progress appeared to have been made on a number of issues. There was agreement on numerous new facilities and procedures that would be used in the shops. Brandeis felt compelled to congratulate the conferees. "I want to say," he remarked, "that I have never had the opportunity of participating in a conference on labor matters which has been conducted, on the whole, with such intelligence and fairness and consideration as this one. I have never had the opportunity of attending . . . any conference where I felt that the progress made in the interests of a . . . better condition of the working people has advanced so rapidly as here."[9] The congratulations were a bit premature. And Brandeis probably knew it.

Shortly before he applauded the efforts of the conferees, the union representatives again brought up the issue of the closed shop. Brandeis again reminded them that that was not for discussion. He could sense, though, that a mere recital of the earlier agreement on his participation would not be enough. More innovative measures were needed. After a short recess, Brandeis returned with a new suggestion: the creation of the "preferential union shop."

Brandeis acknowledged at the start that the existence of an open shop would undercut the union. But he had an alternative, one that was not as drastic as a closed shop. "It seems to me," he said, ". . . that aid could be effectively and properly given by providing that the manufacturers should, in the employment of labor hereafter, give the preference to union men, where the union men are equal in efficiency to any non-union applicants." In other words, the employer would be obligated to hire union men unless a particular non-union applicant was more qualified than the union applicant. Brandeis recognized that his plan was not as simple as it might sound. To begin with, he thought that the employer should be the one to assess the applicants' capabilities—otherwise the employer would lose substantial control over his operations. That, of course, could prove to be a giant loophole for the manufacturers to hire non-union workers, but Brandeis said that an arbitration board could decide whether there had been any unreasonable discrimination.[10]

The manufacturers agreed to the idea, but the union delegates were not impressed. To them it was just a subtle attempt to break the union. Later Brandeis tried to make the proposal more palatable by labeling it a "union shop" instead of a "preferential shop." The union delegates remained adamant in their opposition. "For the sake of self-preservation," one delegate told his colleagues, "you would be committing suicide to go into an agreement where such a condition prevailed." He turned to Brandeis and said, "Give us a chance for half a year [with a closed shop], and let us see if we can make good." "That is what we say," Brandeis replied. "But I have no faith in it," the labor delegate protested. "I have no faith in yours," was the response. The labor delegate was not to be moved. "It is something too new," he said of Brandeis's preferential shop. "It cannot be done at this crisis." There seemed no way to break the stalemate, and Brandeis laid the blame at the union's doorstep. "The outcome is still in doubt with probabilities against settlement, . . ." he wrote to Alice on July 31. "The union leaders are afraid of the hordes behind them and obsessed with the closed shop idea. I have brought the manufacturers to a most advanced position—as far as I should go on general lines." He added that they were trying to enlist the help of Gompers but that the union leader was "trying to evade responsibility."[11] It seemed hopeless, and Brandeis finally decided to return to Boston and a vacation on the Cape.

Lincoln Filene, however, was not about to give up. He enlisted the aid of two well-known Jewish leaders, Jacob Schiff and Louis Marshall. The three of them conferred with Cohen and Meyer London, the union's attorney. Others were brought into the picture. On September 2, 1910, the manufacturers and the union signed a protocol that accepted Brandeis's plan for a preferential shop—although the system was to be known as a "union shop"—where union conditions would prevail and employers could give preference only to non-union applicants who were more qualified than union applicants. When Filene informed Brandeis of the good news, the attorney was surprised and happy—but, as he said later, "I was most of all surprised."[12]

In addition to the "union shop," the protocol set forth practices to be followed in the shops and procedures for resolving grievances by either side. Thus, workers were to be furnished electric machines, pay scales were to be fair and uniform, wages were to be paid regularly, and work was to be fairly distributed. To correct the defects in the health and safety area, the protocol established a Joint Board of Sanitary Control to be made up of union and management representatives. The board was empowered to establish standards and to enforce them. The most important mechanism created by the protocol—in theory, at least—was the Board of Arbitration. This board was composed of a labor representative, a management representative, and Brandeis as chairman. The board was authorized to settle any controversy arising between the parties.[13]

The initial reaction to the protocol was euphoric on all sides. The union publication, *Ladies Garment Workers,* proclaimed that the protocol "has become a permanent instrument in adjusting labor conditions in the cloak trade in this city." The employers' periodical, *The Cloak and Suit Review,* was equally pleased. "It is as epoch-making as the invention of the steam engine by Watt or of the loom by Arkwright," said the magazine. "The last two inventions ushered in the new way by which man was to control nature; the protocol introduced a new way by which man was to deal with man in his conflict with nature for a higher civilization."[14]

Backed by this kind of praise, the protocol became attractive to many other industries. Within a short time the preferential union shop was accepted by several other warring labor and management factions. The source of the idea was widely known, and before long newspapers—especially those on the East Coast—were giving front-page coverage to the scheme and to interviews with Brandeis. The Boston attorney did not harbor any illusions about the plan's potential impact. "No," he responded when asked by one interviewer whether his proposal was the "final solution" to the labor problem. "I hardly think," he said, "one would be justified in making such a claim for any man-made plan."[15] Brandeis frankly admitted that the plan had not eliminated all of the problems. "Perfection is unattainable," he told another interviewer. But he hoped that the proposal would bring out the "manly" quality in labor and management representatives. "What is wanted is men," he observed. "And there are such, no doubt, in most of these places where the present troubles are, or some men doing business with either side who have an accommodating temperament and a happy way of making men agree."[16]

No doubt that was the way Brandeis liked to view his role. But for all his optimism and skill, things were not going as smoothly in the garment industry as he would have liked. Even before the protocol was four months old, Julius Cohen wrote Brandeis, saying he was "very blue" because many of the union leaders' actions were "foolhardy" and seemed to violate the spirit of the protocol. Union men were not always ready to settle their grievances peacefully, and many would walk off the job without giving discussions a fair chance. From other sources Brandeis learned that the manufacturers were not purists either. Because the protocol added to their overhead and their labor costs, many companies were subcontracting work to be done out of state, where the strictures of the protocol would not apply.

Despite these problems, Brandeis was reluctant to convene the Board of Arbitration. If the protocol was to work, each side would have to learn to deal with the other directly rather than through the intervention of an arbitrator. To this end the protocol had in fact established a Committee on Grievances that consisted of only union and management representatives. All complaints, no matter how major, were to be filtered through the committee before the arbitration board would act. Brandeis did everything he could to force the parties to settle their problems at that level, and despite the pleas of the parties, he resisted a meeting of the arbitration board for as long as he could.

Things began to take a real tailspin in the spring of 1913. To begin with, a decline in the general economy led to decreased business in the garment industry. That, in turn, increased the pressure on both sides to gain every possible advantage in resolving disputes. And it also accelerated the tensions and hostilities that were building up on both sides. All this became quite evident when Isaac Hourwich, a member of the Committee on Grievances, requested a meeting with the employers' association in May to discuss a new contract. The manufacturers requested that the meeting be postponed until June because many of their key representatives were away and would not be back until then. Hourwich was ready to jump to conclusions, though. In his view the employers' delay reflected nothing but bad faith. In an angry letter to Brandeis, Hourwich said that the relationship was deteriorating fast, that they might soon have a strike similar to the one in the summer of 1910, and that Hourwich did "not want to foretell the consequences" if the employers persisted in their "dilatory" tactics.[17]

Brandeis was taken aback by Hourwich's wild charges. "The attitude of ominous threats disclosed by Hourwich is rather disconcerting," he wrote to Henry Moskowitz, the clerk for the arbitration board. "I think you and some of our other friends ought to get in touch with him at once."[18]

The conference with the employers so ardently sought by Hourwich was held in July 1913. The problem of wages remained unresolved, and that was referred to the arbitration board. But a more fundamental concern was also raised. Hourwich, with substantial support among his labor colleagues, demanded an increase in the membership of the arbitration board, from three to six. Hourwich regarded Brandeis as paternalistic and "dictatorial." And he also did not like Brandeis's aversion to convening the board. "With all due respect to you gentlemen," Hourwich told the board members in August 1913, "our Board of Arbitration is something like the Council of the Dalai Lama of Tibet; it is too invisible. We have all the respect in the world for your gentlemen, but we have got to have a Justice of the Peace a great deal more often than a session of the Supreme Court, and unless we have it, I do not see how this protocol can live."[19] Hourwich continued on in fiery tones, and people were beginning to feel uncomfortable.

Afterwards the manufacturers decided that they could not tolerate Hourwich's caustic and disruptive attacks. They requested and got another meeting of the arbitration board to consider the matter. In October, Hourwich was censured for "insurrection and rebellion" inconsistent with the spirit of the protocol. Privately, Brandeis warned another member of the board that Hourwich was "an inveterate troublemaker" and that they would "have no peace with him in position."[20]

The situation grew more serious by the day. The possibility of a general strike was becoming more real, and Brandeis remained convinced that the source of the trouble was Hourwich. In January 1914 he convened another meeting of the board to consider Hourwich's position. Brandeis acknowledged that each side had a right to choose its own representatives for the protocol's machinery. But he left no doubt that Hourwich could perform a magnanimous service by his own choice. "While the manufacturers have no right to compel his withdrawal," the Boston lawyer remarked, "he himself has the right to withdraw, and if in his loyalty to the union and to the protocol he should voluntarily decide to do so, a continuance of the protocol would in our opinion be assured, and a dangerous and anomalous crisis, involving the certainty of great suffering for tens of thousands of men, women, and children, would be averted."[21] Hourwich yielded to the pressure—but not before he could release one more denunciation of Brandeis and the whole protocol process.

Within a short time changes were made in the protocol machinery. Brandeis still did not want the arbitration board to be convened frequently. But he did go along with the creation of an intermediary panel that would be chaired by an "impartial" person and decide matters that the grievance committee could not.

None of that, however, could forestall the slide downward. By early 1915 even the labor representatives were complaining to Brandeis about the lack of discipline among union men and women. Brandeis refused to accept defeat. "Of course discipline is essential to continuing democratic success," he wrote to one labor leader, "but I am confident that the Jewish workers, with their many good qualities, intellectual and moral, will in time learn discipline also." Brandeis also tried to instill in others the same optimism he almost always conveyed. "I am convinced," he told the same labor man, "that this is not a time when criticism is useful. What we need particularly is encouragement and tact. Criticism, however well founded, if allowed at this time, will do harm, and may prove fatal. The protocol needs nursing. . . ."[22]

Through all this Brandeis refused to acknowledge that his distance from the battlefield or the particulars of the protocol were responsible for the deterioration of labor–management relations. "The protocol is being subjected to a most severe test at present," he told another labor leader at this time; "a test due not to inherent weakness, but to the extraordinary strain which bad business places on employer and employee alike. The protocol is as little to be blamed for most of the troubles, as is President Wilson for the unemployment common in the country at the present time."[23]

Others who were closer to the action took a different view. They were not only dissatisfied with the particulars of the protocol; they were equally unhappy with Brandeis and his moralizing from a distance. In May 1915, one of the attorneys for the employers wrote an article criticizing the protocol as being founded on "sophistry" foisted on the industry by "certain settlement workers, social uplifters, and reformers." The writer was especially disturbed because labor–management relations under the protocol were governed "not by economics and business principles, but by theoretical precepts which were often communicated over the long distance telephone."[24]

The article was, to be sure, overblown in its criticisms. From the outset everyone knew that the unions were not a cohesive group that would accept directions from the arbitration board or even their own leaders. Nor could there be any doubt that the decline in business increased the temptations for manufacturers to avoid some of the costly procedures and wages mandated by the protocol.

In this volatile atmosphere, though, Brandeis's hope for "manly" leaders was really too much to expect. While there was, as he well knew, no guarantee of success, there could be no doubt that the guidance of a respected and neutral hand could have reduced the conflicts considerably. Without that guidance, it was almost inevitable that the old tensions and hostilities would rise to the surface and undercut cooperation. This conflict was especially likely given the nature of the "preferential shop." It was, in the end, a halfway measure that left too many loopholes for employers who wanted to avoid the spirit of the protocol. And that possibility—which materialized with increasing frequency—frustrated the unions. The employers, however, were the first ones to expressly repudiate the protocol.

As the protocol moved toward dissolution, Brandeis accepted its fate with an unusual sense of resignation. In the early summer of 1915 the mayor of New York City established a Council of Conciliation to fill the void left by the arbitration board's failure. Brandeis attended the initial sessions of the Council but did not speak. When he was notified later of another meeting of the Council in August, he informed a colleague that he was not really interested. ". . . I had been planning to go off with Mrs. Brandeis on her and my vacation," he wrote to George Kirchwey, "and . . . after my many transgressions of the past year, I did not want to postpone Mrs. Brandeis's trip unless it was absolutely necessary." And he did think that was the case here. "I judge that the trouble is wholly from the manufacturers' end," he added, "and in view of that, my absence would be quite as helpful as my presence."[25]

Brandeis's defeatist attitude was a forecast of the future. Within a year some manufacturers locked out their union employees because of the deadlock. The union retaliated with a general strike, and the protocol was dead.

The protocol was Brandeis's last involvement as a mediator in labor–management disputes. The experience was a profitable one for him nonetheless. It reinforced views he had long held concerning the importance of regularity in employment. At arbitration meetings he continually implored both sides to eliminate the gaps in employment for individual workers. To his mind, they only aggravated existing tensions. But he was not content to rest on exhortation to good will. He had a proposal.

After years of observation and study, the "people's attorney" was convinced that the worker needed insurance to protect him against unemployment and to help sustain him in retirement. It all related to the individual's control over his life. In earlier days, he observed, "every American boy could look forward to becoming independent as a farmer or mechanic, in business or in professional life. . . ." Now it was all changing. America was becoming "largely a nation of employees. . . ."[26] In short, people no longer worked for themselves; they worked for somebody else—someone, usually, who was more interested in a balance sheet than the fate of his workers. And that made all the difference.

"Can any man be really free," Brandeis asked in a June 1911 speech, "who is constantly in danger of becoming dependent for mere subsistence upon somebody and something else than his own exertion and conduct? . . . Financial dependence is consistent with freedom only where claim to support rests upon right, and not upon favor." It was therefore important that every worker be insured against unemployment—whether it be through layoff or retirement. To Brandeis the cost of this unemployment and old-age insurance should be nothing more than another cost to the employer for doing business. "The manufacturer who fails to recognize fire insurance, depreciation, interest and taxes as current charges of the business," he observed, "treads the path to bankruptcy. And that nation does the like which fails to recognize and provide against the economic, social and political conditions which impose upon the workingman so large a degree of financial dependence."[27]

In this context he had little respect for plans, like those developed by United States Steel Corporation, where the company paid all the bills but had complete discretion to terminate the plan at any time. "No pension system," Brandeis told a congressional committee in 1912, "can be satisfactory which makes the granting—or the continuance of a pension after it has been granted—a matter of discretion."[28] He believed that both the employer and the employee should contribute to the cost of the insurance. He also believed that insurance rights should remain intact even if the worker changed jobs. Otherwise the worker would lose the freedom that the insurance was designed to secure. A company could use the insurance as a means of discouraging employee complaints and unionization; and, if the company was unscrupulous, it could fire the employee shortly before his scheduled retirement.

Brandeis did not confine his observations to general principles. During the height of the protocol's success he gave Lincoln Filene a detailed scheme to provide for unemployment insurance. "Irregularity of employment," he told the clothing retailer, "is to my mind the greatest of industrial wastes, and one of the main causes of social demoralization."[29] Under Brandeis's proposal, the evils of irregular employment would be reduced by a relatively simple device. The employer would place a percentage of the employee's wages in a trust account; if the employer provided the employee with more than a normally full year's work, the employer would get back a portion of the amount deposited; if the employer provided less than full employment, the employee would receive funds from the trust account as compensation. In no event, however, would the employee's right to the funds depend on his remaining with a particular company.

There were certain problems with Brandeis's plan. For example, he was not entirely clear how the proposal would work when an individual changed jobs. How could the employee take funds from one employer's trust account if a subsequent employer was the one who failed to provide regular employment?

But these were only details. Brandeis remained wedded to the essence of his proposal for the rest of his life, and he continually urged editors, labor leaders, manufacturers, congressmen, and even presidents to consider it. In time, his persistence would be rewarded. He could not say the same about his efforts to prevent an increase in railroad shipping rates.

ELEVEN

Grappling with the Railroads

The prosperity of the railroads and the prosperity of the country are inseparably connected and those connected with the actual management and operation of the roads have spoken very plainly and very earnestly with a purpose we ought to be quick to accept.

WOODROW WILSON, ADDRESS TO CONGRESS, JANUARY 20, 1914

Supreme Court Justice Oliver Wendell Holmes had a high regard for the railroad magnates who were known as the "robber barons" of the nineteenth century. "Oh, he thought some of those 'buccaneers' were great statesmen," Alger Hiss, one of Holmes's clerks, later recalled. "Thought they should have statues erected for them."[1] Despite their affinity on many matters of law and policy, Brandeis did not entirely share Holmes's view of the robber barons. To be sure, they had built up America's railroad systems rapidly as the country moved into the twentieth century. But they had indulged in some questionable practices. Secret rebates to favored customers. Predatory pricing to drive out small competitors. Bribes for influential legislators. And, of course, misuse of corporate funds for personal luxuries. All of this was not only unethical; it was also bad social policy. Individual entrepreneurs, especially small ones, could not survive in that atmosphere.

Brandeis's perspective on railroad issues here was shaped, in part, by his long "association" with the New Haven railroad. There were other influences as well. Many of his law firm's clients were merchants and manufacturers who used the railroads to ship their goods all around the country. And then there was his brother. Alfred Brandeis was a grain merchant who also relied on the railroad's shipping services. In his almost daily correspondence with Louis, Al often talked about business problems, including the discriminatory rates and practices of the railroads.

So when David Ives, the manager of the transportation department of the Boston Chamber of Commerce, approached Brandeis in the summer of 1910 about a railroad matter before the Interstate Commerce Commission, the Boston attorney was most interested. The railroads wanted to increase their shipping rates, and they thought they were entitled to it. After all, they had not received an increase in rates since the Interstate Commerce Commission was created in 1887. During that time they had invested literally millions of dollars in new equipment and facilities to make their services more efficient; and to a large extent they had succeeded in that effort.

Although the number of railroad employees had almost doubled between 1898 and 1910, productivity—services per employee—had increased even more. The statistics showed that railroads were now 20 percent more efficient in their use of labor. Similar gains were evident when comparing equipment changes. Trains in 1910 were carrying more goods and doing it more quickly than in 1898. In fact, revenues per train-mile were up 33 percent. The only problem was that operating expenses—especially labor costs—had risen 42 percent during the same period.[2]

The railroad men felt proud of their accomplishments. Sadly, they were victims of their own success—at least that's what they thought at first. As it turned out, the shippers and much of the public had little sympathy for a rate increase. Railroads were now so efficient, they said, that a rate increase was not needed to offset increased operating expenses. Increased productivity would surely give the railroads enough money to meet rising costs.

This kind of argument was bound to find a sympathetic ear at the Interstate Commerce Commission. The agency was originally established to review the "reasonableness" of railroad charges and rates and to order the discontinuance of those it found unreasonable. In 1906 and again in June 1910, laws were passed that gave the agency rate-making power. Of greater concern to the railroads, however, was another new provision that required them to demonstrate that proposed rates were reasonable; and if the ICC was not satisfied with the railroads' rationale, it could prevent the rates from going into effect. In many quarters—particularly in Congress—it was expected that the agency would use these new powers to limit the robber barons' ability to exploit their customers unfairly. In short, the railroads could not expect smooth sailing if they sought a rate increase.[3]

The railroad managers apparently did not appreciate these legal and political problems when they applied for ICC approval of rate increases in 1910. Their sensitivity, however, was heightened shortly after they encountered Louis Brandeis.

At the request of Ives, Brandeis agreed to represent the Committee of Commercial Organizations, an association of shippers. His task was to advance the group's position in the ICC hearings on the Eastern railroads' request (while other advocates handled the Western railroad hearings simultaneously taking place in Chicago). It was a task Brandeis would come to relish.

His first "meeting" with the railroad managers occurred in the ballroom of the Waldorf-Astoria Hotel in New York City in September 1910. After the opening pleasantries, the railroads put on their witnesses to present their case. Charles F. Daly of the New York Central thought the railroads' need for more money was self-evident. Brandeis took a different position in cross-examining him:

MR. DALY: The lake and rail rate was so sufficiently low, in our opinion, that the service justified that [proposed] advance [in the rates].

MR. BRANDEIS: Why do you say it was low?

MR. DALY: Because it was.

MR. BRANDEIS: Well, that mere statement, to say that a thing is low or that it isn't low, is nothing that carries conviction, I submit.

MR. DALY: Possibly not.

MR. BRANDEIS: One must have a reason why he says it is low, and I want to get, so far as you are able to furnish it, the reason why you say that that is low.

MR. DALY: Well, I am afraid I couldn't give you any more definite reason than that, in my judgment, based on experience, that it is true. Now, if that isn't satisfactory—

MR. BRANDEIS: Will you tell us what elements—I mean what facts—you say your experience . . .

MR. DALY: The best of my judgment, sir.

MR. BRANDEIS: I know—the best of your judgment, Mr. Daly. That may satisfy you, but I think others would want to know on what you base your judgment.

MR. DALY: I am afraid you will have to accept that.

MR. BRANDEIS: Yes; but if you have a judgment on which the commission, or at least others who are endeavoring to learn from you, are expected to rely, I think they might reasonably ask that the basis of your judgment, if you are able to express it in words, should be stated.

MR. DALY: The basis of my judgment is exactly the same as the basis of a man who knows how to play a good game of golf. It comes from practice, contact and experience with the particular subject at issue.[4]

Brandeis was incredulous at Daly's responses. The man simply did not understand that facts—not opinions—would be needed to satisfy the railroads' burden under the new law. Brandeis decided to give Daly another chance—not so much to help him but to make it clear that the railroad managers really had no facts to support their judgments. Daly claimed that his company had carefully considered the need for rate increases in shipping steel and cement. Brandeis saw his opening:

MR. BRANDEIS: . . . Where can you show that you have exercised, in regard to each individual rate, I mean each individual article—

MR. DALY: We have not professed to.

MR. BRANDEIS: That same judgment . . . that you exercised when you dealt with the makers of steel or the makers of cement.

MR. DALY: Impossible, Mr. Brandeis. There are hundreds of articles in each class [of goods shipped].

MR. BRANDEIS: If it has been impossible to consider the effect upon existing industries, would it not be more reasonable to leave unchanged the burden on those industries and deal with those other articles of commerce as to which it is possible to make an investigation, and in connection with which you can exercise a trained and experienced judgment?

MR. DALY: Well, from the best of our knowledge the belief, based on, as I repeat again, great experience, and others who have had a great deal more than myself, we do not feel that the rate which it is proposed to inaugurate in the classes is unduly high, or that it will have any serious effect on any of the manufacturers.

MR. BRANDEIS: Well, now, Mr. Daly, we have absolute respect for the integrity of your feelings.

MR. DALY: Sure.

MR. BRANDEIS: But what we need is not feelings but thoughts in dealing with the affairs of business, and when the shippers of the [Atlantic] seaboard come here and protest against a raise of rates, . . . they say that the act is an arbitrary act, however well intentional it may have been.

MR. DALY: We have stated why and what we did. Now, you say that this will have a terrible effect on the business of your clients. We haven't anything from you or your clients, except your statement, which is not in our judgment worth any more than mine, and in this particular instance I don't think it is worth as much.

MR. BRANDEIS: What I want, of course, is an understanding on this question. You understand, of course, that under this new law the burden—

MR. DALY: I understand it thoroughly.

MR. BRANDEIS: Rests upon you.

MR. DALY: Yes, sir.

MR. BRANDEIS: To show that the change you propose making is reasonable.[5]

After a while Brandeis tried to summarize Daly's testimony. "So far as the rates you do make are concerned," he observed, "all you know about it is that inner feeling that comes in the experienced man as to what is high enough and what is not." The statement was not well received. "It comes from that same experience that teaches you to be such a learned lawyer," the witness retorted.[6]

It was not the railroads' finest hour. And it did not get better. They simply could not explain with any detail why shipping rates for hundreds of goods had to be increased. They did not even seem to understand their precise financial status. When he cross-examined James McCrae, president of the Pennsylvania Railroad, Brandeis showed that the railroads had accumulated a considerable surplus, had issued dividends and other benefits to stockholders that amounted to a more than 12 percent annual return on investment, and that the railroads' credit was not as shaky as they portrayed it. This all appeared to be news to McCrea. He continually gave vague and unresponsive answers. "Let me see whether you have not misunderstood my question," Brandeis said at one point. "I think I likely have," McCrea confessed. "I do not follow the drift of a good deal of what you are saying."[7]

To Brandeis the performance of the railroad managers not only revealed poor accounting practices; it also confirmed his long-held view that people—especially executives in corporate conglomerates—were assuming too many responsibilities. There was virtually no way, in his mind, that a single individual could absorb all the facts and make all the judgments required in the supervision of a large railroad.

In his closing argument to the commission, Brandeis referred to this problem as "the curse of bigness." He was particularly impressed by the fact that the big railroads earned so little on gross revenues that were so large. "I ask the commission," he said, "to consider whether there is not a causal connection between the fact of bigness, the fact of this extraordinary gross [income], and the fact of the reduced net [income]." To him it was clear that the railroads had exceeded "what may be called the limit of greatest efficiency. . . . These railroads are run by men; and, preeminently, they are determined by one or two men. Everybody in his experience knows his own limitations; knows how much less well he can do many things than a few things."

If the commissioners had any doubt about the limitation of human judgment, Brandeis pointed to the fact that the smaller railroads seemed to be in better financial shape than the larger lines. Is it not probable, he explained to the commissioners, that the managers of the larger companies, "regardless of what their ability may be, have undertaken to perform tasks greater than it is possible for the individual man to perform well? Because," he continued, ". . . however much you may subdivide the work . . . the railroad president [who] is called upon to exercise the judgment and make the decision in the important matters should do what?" Brandeis did not wait for a reply from his listeners. "He should have before him the data upon which to form a correct judgment," the attorney observed. "And I submit that it is impossible for these presidents to have in mind, for the exercise of a sound judgment, the facts necessary to enable them to reach it." Brandeis emphasized that he did not mean to engage in personal criticism of the railroad presidents who had testified. "We are engaged in questions too large and too important to have them degraded or obliterated by a discussion of individuals; but you can not fail to recall," he told the commissioners, "from what has taken place in this room, instances of a failure of knowledge on the part of executives that would indicate that there was not present in their minds the facts necessary to a comprehensive and consequently a correct judgment of what occurred."[8]

The railroad presidents' judgments were also tainted by another fundamental problem that troubled the Boston attorney: conflicts of interest. Many individuals sat on the boards of directors of both the railroads and other companies that did business with the railroads as shippers or suppliers. Of the sixty-five directors for the four major steel companies, for example, Brandeis found that forty were also directors for railroad companies. Since steel companies sold goods to the railroads and used them to ship material, the conflict of interest was clear.

Through much of his legal career, Brandeis felt that he could, in effect, act as counsel for both sides of a controversy—even if only one of the parties had actually retained him. As he once explained to an inquiring adversary, he viewed himself as attorney "for the situation." He had great faith in his own ability to see both sides of a situation and to act fairly. But Brandeis did not feel that other individuals could act as dispassionately and as fairly when they sat on the boards of corporations doing business with one another. "You cannot serve two masters," he told the commission in his closing argument, "and the same men cannot be in the corporations, each dealing with the other, and carry out any of the ordinary principles of trade."[9] To prove his point, Brandeis noted that the railroads proposed very few increases in rates for shipping steel—an omission that seemed too coincidental to have been made in good faith.

The issue of interlocking directorates was one that would occupy Brandeis's thoughts and efforts for many years. And in time he would see many of his ideas enacted into law. The same could not be said about his preoccupation with "scientific management."

The term was one coined by Brandeis himself as he prepared his case for the ICC. He was aware of works by Frederick W. Taylor, James M. Dodge, and others who advocated a new approach to business. While the particulars varied with each proponent, the thrust of the proposals was identical. In essence, the schemes required each business manager to make a precise determination of how quickly a task could be completed. Employee efforts would then be measured against that standard. If the employee did not match it, the manager would know that his operations were not as efficient as they could be. If the employee surpassed the standard, he would be entitled to a bonus of some kind. The whole system was designed to measure and, it was hoped, improve business efficiency.

There were some obvious shortcomings to this approach. To begin with, in any large organization—like an interstate railroad system—the number of tasks was enormous, and the circumstances of each situation were quite varied. In this context it would be virtually impossible to expect that any meaningful standard of efficiency could be determined for every job.

Brandeis surely recognized the difficulty here. Despite his many pronouncements on the subject, there is virtually no instance in which he could articulate a standard for any task. He also recognized the substantial risk that employees and their unions would face under this kind of program—it would enable employers, even those acting in good faith, to "speed up" work and demand more from employees than they had a right to expect. In addition, the bonus system would increase the worker's financial dependence on the employer and simultaneously decrease his dependence on the union. It was, in a word, a system geared toward individual bargaining rather than collective bargaining.

Brandeis nonetheless found the idea very appealing. It coincided with his deep concern with individual responsibility. He was convinced that the idea, if it worked, would give the employer more control over his business and the employee more control over his productivity. And to Brandeis's mind, the railroads needed that kind of improvement.

The railroad managers' testimony had exposed an unacceptable ignorance of their own operations. Why, when Brandeis asked one president how much it *should* cost to repair a locomotive, the witness could identify only the *actual average* cost. "Just see how uncertain that factor is," Brandeis replied. ". . . You are taking the average. The only way you could tell whether the work on any one of those cars was efficiently done, is it not, would be for you to know the particular thing that was done on that particular car?"[10]

With the system proposed by Taylor and others, Brandeis felt that this kind of uncertainty could be eliminated. For ease of comprehension, though, they needed a single label for the basic concept. In a meeting with some of his expert witnesses in October 1910, he discussed the idea at great length. Brandeis suggested "scientific management," and everyone agreed it was an appropriate term.[11]

By November 21, 1910, the hearings had been moved to Washington, D.C. On that day Brandeis asked for permission to address the commission. Everyone, including the newspapermen in attendance, waited with great anticipation. It was widely expected that the "people's attorney"—a skillful fighter—had another dramatic trick up his sleeve. He had done it in the Ballinger–Pinchot hearings the previous spring. Could he do it again?

Brandeis did not disappoint the crowd. He did not dispute the fact that the railroads needed money. Their net income was indeed too low. However, he did not think that increased rates were the answer. The problem, he explained, was that the railroads were not very efficient. "Now there, precisely, is the point at which we take issue most largely with the railroads," he told the commissioners. "We say that this situation, this practical declaration of hopelessness which comes from the railroads, this incompetence to deal with the great problem of labor and the great problem of costs, is due to a failure [to consider what] . . . most progressive manufacturers in competitive lines of business have been led to adopt, namely, the science of management." Then he dropped his bombshell. If the railroads were prepared to use scientific management, he was convinced that they could collectively save one million dollars a day in costs—an estimate which he later told the commission was "moderate."[12]

Brandeis then produced a parade of witnesses—ten in all—to testify to the virtues of scientific management. All waxed eloquent on the system's benefits. The most important was Harrington Emerson. A consulting engineer for the Santa Fe Railroad, Emerson explained that he had used scientific management in the Santa Fe's maintenance operations and had found tremendous savings. It was he, in fact, who had boasted that scientific management could save the railroads at least $300 million a year—or almost one million dollars a day. With this kind of "expert" testimony, Brandeis seemed to have made his case, and the news was carried in major newspapers across the country.

There was a certain inconsistency in Brandeis's new-found fondness for scientific management. Initially, advocates for the shippers claimed that the railroads' efficiency had improved to such an extent that they did not need a rate increase to cover rising costs. Now, Brandeis, their powerful lawyer, was stating that the railroads could not meet rising costs because they were too inefficient. The railroad managers felt they were getting squeezed from both ends. And they didn't like it.

As for the $300 million savings that scientific management might accord, the railroad managers thought that that was merely a clever public relations ploy. Some Western railroad presidents decided to respond with a ploy of their own. On November 23—even before Emerson had testified—the group of railroad managers sent Brandeis a telegram, telling him that they would gladly employ him if he could tell them how to save a million dollars a day. The railroad presidents said that the Boston attorney could even set his own salary. Then, with sarcastic reference to Brandeis's argument, the telegram concluded, "This proposition is made to you in the same spirit of sincerity in which you rendered your statement to the Commission."

The railroad managers had underestimated their adversary. He took their bait and made them eat crow. In a reply telegram—which was given considerable publicity—Brandeis said that he would be more than happy "to arrange for conferences with these Western presidents at an early date and point out how scientific management will accomplish these results." He also suggested that the Eastern presidents be invited as well. As for setting his own salary for this service, Brandeis was not interested in money. "I must decline to accept any salary or other compensation from the railroads," he said, "for the same reason that I have declined compensation from the shipping organizations I represent—namely, that the burden of increased rates, while primarily affecting the Eastern manufacturers and merchants, will ultimately be borne in large part by the consumer through increasing the cost of living, mainly of those least able to bear added burdens. I desire that any aid I can render in preventing such added burdens should be unpaid services." He then asked the railroad presidents to suggest a time and place for the first conference.[13]

The railroad presidents did not respond. That was, from their perspective, probably unfortunate, because it is highly doubtful that Brandeis could have ever succeeded in saving the railroads $300 million a year. His claims for scientific management probably were, as one trade paper observed, "the merest moonshine."[14]

Emerson had based his savings estimates on the assumption that labor was usually 5 percent inefficient. That, of course, was not much more concrete than the railroads' "feeling" that rates were too low. In any event, the railroads' cumulative labor bill for the year ending June 30, 1910, was only $1.1 billion; 5 percent of that was $50 million—or a little more than the $34 million in wage increases that labor wanted for the next year. As for Emerson's experience at the Santa Fe, that too was not reliable. He had taken over maintenance operations at a time when the company was fighting a strike. The company had also refused to use high-speed drills until Emerson took over—even though such drills were in common use elsewhere in the industry. By resolving the strike and introducing new tools, Emerson saw productivity skyrocket. But it was hardly a basis for saying that the railroads could save $300 million a year.[15]

The labor unions were equally disturbed by Brandeis's invocation of scientific management at the ICC hearings. "I do not believe that the workmen employed by the railroads should do any more work than they are now doing," said John M. Mitchell, the former United Mine Workers president who was now a member of the National Civic Federation. ". . . If there is a waste of $300 million a year it lies outside the sphere of cost occupied by the workmen."[16] Other labor leaders echoed Mitchell's criticism, but Brandeis never tired—even after the ICC proceedings were over—of trying to persuade them otherwise. "We who have had occasion to consider the hostility of labor leaders to the introduction of scientific management," he observed at one point, "know that the hostility has in large measure been due to misunderstanding."[17] When properly analyzed, Brandeis argued, scientific management meant only more productivity with less effort. He therefore believed that scientific management would benefit the worker by giving him regular work at higher wages—and what union could be against that?

In theory, it did sound impressive. But when all was said and done, there were few specifics to back it up. Even the ICC commissioners remained skeptical. They were, of course, prepared to deny the railroads' request for rate increases—that was almost a forgone conclusion. But they were not prepared to embrace scientific management. At most they would only cast an approving glance in its direction. "We cannot escape the impression," Commissioner Charles Prouty said in his opinion for the agency, "that the railroad operators have not given to this important subject [of scientific management] the attention it deserves."[18] Brandeis was pleased nonetheless and called the commission's decision "an event making strongly for conservatism."[19] And while the ICC did not flatly endorse scientific management, he was still convinced that the railroads would eventually learn to rely on it. "The [ICC] decision compels them to look within, instead of without, for relief," he told an interviewer. "The able railroad managers will soon learn to increase greatly their net incomes by scientific management."[20] On this occasion at least, the optimism was not warranted.

Brandeis's face was now a familiar one in Washington, especially at the Interstate Commerce Commission. He was taking the midnight train to Washington with increasing regularity. On some occasions Alice joined him. If she did, they often stopped off to see Alice's mother, who lived on the upper West Side of Manhattan on the edge of Harlem. Louis was very close to her and called her "Mother." He was even closer to Alice's sisters, Pauline and Josephine Goldmark—the latter known affectionately to almost everyone as "Do." Like Louis, both sisters were active in social reform. And both—especially Do—were instrumental in many of his public causes.

Neither sister, however, had any real interest in railroads or the ICC. Brandeis himself was not eager to pursue any and all problems dealing with railroads. They had to be connected in some way with the vision he had for America and for which he was struggling with great enthusiasm. So when May Childs Nerney, the secretary of the National Association for the Advancement of Colored People, wrote to him about filing a complaint with the ICC concerning racial discrimination in rail passenger service, Brandeis was not interested. He would be happy to see her, he responded, but he very modestly added that "it does not seem to me possible that I should be able to give you any advice of value in regard to the Jim Crow car situation, and the work which I have on hand would prevent my entering upon an investigation of the matter."[21]

His reaction had been quite different when Commissioner James Harlan of the ICC had earlier asked Brandeis to act as special counsel in a reopening of the rate case. The railroads complained that their efficiency was picking up (without the use of scientific management), but that they were still losing the battle against rising costs. In May 1913 they filed a formal petition with the commission asking for rate increases that averaged about 5 percent. It was not really much, and certainly not nearly what the railroads thought they deserved. But if they could just break the ice with even a small rate increase, perhaps the ICC would be more open-minded in the future.

Even before he had time to study the new figures, Brandeis was fighting the increase. "No increase in freight rates ought to be allowed at the present moment," he wrote to the journalist Livy S. Richard, "so long as the vicious system of interlocking directorates makes it impossible to know how much of the money is honestly and efficiently spent."[22] He urged his friends in the press to speak out against the rate proposal. "I don't know whether I shall actively take part in Rate Advance matters," he wrote to Al about two weeks later, "but I have inspired some editorials the country over, demanding efficiency and abolishing interlocking directorates first."[23]

If Brandeis had had to wait on the shippers, he might never have participated in the case. Some of the more vigorous opponents of the 1910 rate increase now agreed that the railroads were entitled to more money. That meant nothing to Brandeis. Important questions were involved, and he took the initiative. In June he had a conference with Morris L. Cooke, a scientific management advocate, and John Marble, one of the new ICC commissioners. They discussed the impending rate case and the approach the agency should take.

In August, Harlan wrote to Brandeis. "We are of course aware of the fact that the carriers will not fail fully to present their side of the case," the commissioner said, "and the Commission has felt that every effort should be made in the public interest adequately to present the other side. Would you care to undertake that burden?" At first blush it appeared that Harlan wanted Brandeis only to present the case *against* the rate increase. But that was not so. Harlan really wanted Brandeis to view the matter objectively and to see that "all sides and angles of the case are presented of record, without advocating any particular theory for its disposition."[24]

Brandeis apparently understood Harlan correctly. He agreed to accept the assignment at a compensation to be determined by the agency.

While Brandeis may have been clear about his role, others were not. When his appointment as special counsel to the ICC was announced in the papers, it seemed that Brandeis would be leading the opposition. Al wrote to give him some advice on the presentation of evidence. And Clifford Thorne, one of the shippers' leading attorneys in the 1910 case, wrote to offer "hearty congratulations" to their new ally. ". . . I understand from press dispatches that you are in general charge of the case on behalf of the public," Thorne wrote. "I think this method is wise." He then proposed some ideas on the presentation of the case.[25]

Harlan did not help matters. Amidst public speculation concerning Brandeis's role, the commissioner was quoted as saying, "Doubtless certain protestants will have their own attorneys, but Mr. Brandeis will be the general channel through whom the views of others opposing the proposed advance may be presented of record." Finally, E.E. Clark, the ICC chairman, issued a statement which stated flatly that Brandeis would not represent a particular side. His only role would be to help the commission make an objective evaluation of the record.

Brandeis went to Washington and immersed himself in the record. He also dispatched seventy-eight questions to each of the railroads, asking them to detail the costs and revenues for various services. When the hearings opened at the Willard Hotel in Washington in the autumn of 1913, everyone was there in full force. As the appointed hour approached, Brandeis nervously kept running his hands through his hair, a habit that gave it a tousled look.

No one seemed more nervous than the railroad representatives, however. It had been agreed that they could initially put their case on before the ICC without submitting their witnesses to cross-examination by the Boston attorney. Brandeis nonetheless felt free during the course of the hearing to make suggestions designed to help witnesses explain themselves more clearly. The railroad men were wary of their old adversary, though, and they became quite agitated whenever Brandeis offered assistance. Nonetheless, Brandeis was impressed—at least to some extent. The railroads "are well prepared this time," he wrote Alice, "and made a good *prima facie* case and are doubtless telling largely the truth, but not the whole truth."[26]

As the hearings progressed, Brandeis questioned the railroad managers closely about their operations. He was convinced that they had not learned as much as they should have from the 1910 proceeding. He was, for example, still appalled at the special treatment given to favored customers—such as moving private cars to sidings on a customer's premises without charge. He similarly criticized the persistence of interlocking directorates. "You have no assurance and can have no assurance," he later told the commissioners, "that these railroads have done all that could be done to stop the leeches as long as these conflicting relations continue."[27] And of course, he was still of the view that most—but not all—of the railroads had failed to provide the specific kind of information that would justify rate increases. "Leading American manufacturers know accurately today the cost of every one of the numerous articles made and sold by them," he explained at one point. "Railroads which make and sell a most varied transportation service do not know the cost of any of the services which they furnish."[28]

To the railroads, this was all nitpicking. There could be no doubt, they argued, that their efficiency had improved; and yet cost increases were still outstripping revenue increases. "Now, what is the conclusion of all this," one railroad president rhetorically asked the commissioners toward the end of the hearing. "I am worn out with figures . . . and hope this marks the end of an intimate relationship that I have had with the accounting department for the last six months. [Laughter.] But in these last three years . . . the parties have expended $666 million and at the end find themselves $16 million worse off."[29] Brandeis remained unmoved. "If these gentlemen will cooperate to the same extent in conserving revenue as they cooperate in their efforts to get a greater gross revenue out of the community through an increase in rates," he said, "they will be able to secure that additional revenue."[30]

Brandeis made one exception to his criticism: the railroads in the Central Freight Association, which included lines located in the Midwest. Unlike the carriers in the East—the Official Freight Association—the Central railroads had "extraordinarily" low revenues that could not be cured by better efficiencies. Most observers agreed with Brandeis that the only answer was to allow a rate increase in the Central territory. There was one dissenting voice, however.

Despite the ICC's earlier clarification, Clifford Thorne remained under the impression that Brandeis was on the shippers' side. He sat at the counsel table with the shippers. And shortly before the testimony was concluded, Brandeis came up to Thorne and told him that his work had been "wonderful" and that his exhibits should be published quickly so that "the public could see the other side of the case."[31]

Thorne took heart from these compliments. As a lawyer from Iowa, he was steeped in Progressive politics and was convinced, no matter what the railroads said, that they could meet rising costs without a rate increase. He assumed that Brandeis would take that position too. After all, that had been his view in the 1910 case—in which Thorne had also participated—and Brandeis had said nothing to indicate that his views had changed.

To be sure of his evaluation, Thorne approached the ICC special counsel shortly before the oral arguments and asked what his position would be. "Well, now, Mr. Thorne," Brandeis responded, "I believe that some of these railroads are not earning enough money, and I think the situation is bad in [the] Central Freight Association territory."[32] For some reason Thorne did not pursue the matter further. He simply assumed that Brandeis would argue—as he had in the 1910 case—that the railroads could get additional revenues through scientific management and other efficiencies.

At the outset of his argument—which followed everyone else's—Brandeis explained that he thought the rates should be increased in the Central territory. Thorne was "dumbfounded." "This was not an ordinary case," he recalled years later. "The railroads had been fighting for four years to get that fact established. . . . And in the closing argument, after every other party on behalf of the public had concluded, the special counsel for the commission appointed to see that all phases of the case were developed—in the final closing argument on behalf of the public, without any notice or warning to other counsel taking place in the argument, he concedes the very point at issue. . . ."[33]

Thorne's outrage was not shared by anyone else. All the other counsel—even those for the shippers—concluded that Brandeis had done only what the commission had asked him to do: give his objective assessment of the record. Thorne nonetheless remained very bitter about the episode, and years later he would cite it to justify his opposition to Brandeis's appointment to the Supreme Court.

Thorne's disgust with Brandeis was aggravated by a second incident at the closing argument. Brandeis felt that railroads—like any business—needed some surplus of money as insurance against bad times. He said that he felt compelled to disagree with Thorne on that score, but he thought it "essential" to the health of the railroads. Thorne interrupted. "Did you understand me to deny any surplus?" he asked the special counsel. "I thought you were rather niggardly as to surplus," Brandeis replied. Thorne was taken aback. "I allowed the same surplus that the Commission did in 1910," he said. Now, Thorne reasoned, Brandeis could not attack him without also criticizing the ICC's 1910 decision—a decision that Brandeis had supported.[34]

It was, in all, a minor squabble. But Thorne was obsessed with every detail of the rate case. He filed a supplemental brief with the ICC denouncing Brandeis's "vicious" attack on him. And, as in the case of the closing argument, he later tried to persuade the Senate that the whole episode reflected poorly on Brandeis's judicial temperament.

None of this had any impact on the ICC's decision. In July 1914 the agency issued an order that embraced virtually every position advocated by its special counsel. The agency conceded that the railroad managers could be very proud of their achievements. "Many improvements have been made in railroad facilities," the opinion said, "many economies in transportation have been effected, and a general expansion and improvement in transportation conditions have taken place."[35] Nonetheless, it was not enough to justify a general rate increase for everyone. In fact, said the agency, all the improvements should have led to a rate reduction. They would make one exception, however, and allow a small rate increase in the Central territory.

Brandeis had to have been pleased with the decision. Any satisfaction, however, was to be short-lived. Within a month the "guns of August" were firing in Europe, and people sensed the imminence of a world war. A good transportation system was necessary to a good defense. In America, though, the railroads were going under.

Part of the problem was the ICC's lack of courage to face up to the realities of the railroad business. To begin with, it really made no sense—despite the agency's insistence—to look at the railroads' average rate of return. More important was the marginal rate of return—the money they were getting back on recently invested dollars. The commission, however, saw no significance in the fact that the railroads' marginal rate was declining rapidly and had already become a negative figure. Revenues also continued to decline after the commission's July decision. The surplus was disappearing, and railroad men stated openly that bankruptcy was inevitable without a meaningful rate increase.

At the end of August they asked the ICC to reopen the case. Few people doubted the railroads' need for more money. Harrington Emerson—Brandeis's scientific management expert in the 1910 case—supported the railroads' request. Alfred Brandeis similarly accepted the validity of the railroads' request for a rate increase, at least as it applied to grain shipments. "I have not objected to an advance in grain rates per se," he wrote his brother in October. His only concern, said Al, was discrimination.[36] Louis agreed. "I have no doubt," he replied, "that the grain rates ought to be advanced. . . . Of course I do not know to what extent discrimination [among favored shippers] exists, or may be aggravated by the proposed increases. . . ."[37]

Despite these admissions in private, Brandeis's public posture remained virtually unchanged. The railroads had still not provided enough specific information to justify their proposed rate increases. That posture, however, did not enjoy much support. "Mr. Brandeis is wrapped up in the ideal railroad," the *New York Times* said in an editorial; "he has hitherto carried the Commission into the clouds with him, but the time has come for the Commission, at least, to come down to earth."[38]

The ICC heeded the advice, and in November 1914 the agency granted the other railroads the same small rate increase that had been granted to the Central lines. Even before the decision was announced, Brandeis saw the handwriting on the wall. The railroads and bankers "did not do themselves much credit," he wrote to Al in October. "If they have their way they will utterly break down the Commission and even if they are beaten they will have succeeded in greatly impairing its standing and their own defense against lawlessness and public ownership."[39] And in Brandeis's view, there was nothing worse than public ownership. A man could not control his business or his life if the government was in charge.

By December 1917 there had been many changes. Louis Brandeis was no longer special counsel to the ICC. He was now a United States Supreme Court justice. America was at war, and the railroads were under the control of the federal government. In March 1917 they had come back to the ICC once more—this time for a 15 percent rate increase. Virtually no one opposed the rate hike. The agency acknowledged the railroads' desperate financial plight. The commissioners wrung their hands in despair and lamented that there was nothing they could do. It was a national problem for Congress to handle. Within months the railroads were no longer in private hands.

Unfortunately, the federal government did not have much experience in running railroads. Advice was needed. President Wilson could think of no one better to turn to than Brandeis. Joseph Tumulty, the president's secretary, telephoned ICC Commissioner Robert Woolley, and the two of them visited with the justice in his apartment on Stoneleigh Court on Friday afternoon, December 7th. What did the former "people's attorney" think of William McAdoo as the director general of the railroads? Excellent choice, said Brandeis, but there was one problem. McAdoo, the president's son-in-law, was already secretary of the treasury, and he could not handle both jobs simultaneously. Men—even talented and energetic men like McAdoo—had their limitations. Tumulty asked if the justice would call upon Wilson at the White House and pass this advice along to the president. Judicial propriety prevented Brandeis from taking the initiative, but if the president requested his attendance, he said, he would go.

Brandeis waited anxiously for the president's call. By Sunday afternoon it had not come. He was getting nervous. He telephoned Woolley. What should I do? Before he could take any action, there was a knock at the door. Alice opened it and found the president, with two Secret Service men, standing there. Wilson said he needed to talk with the justice. When Brandeis appeared, Wilson explained his presence. "I could not request you to come to me," he said, "and I have therefore come to you to ask your advice."[40]

The two men retired to Brandeis's study. There, amid numerous law books strewn about the floor, they discussed the management of the railroads. Wilson was glad to hear of Brandeis's endorsement of McAdoo. The president did not share the justice's views on man's limitations, however. McAdoo wanted to retain the Treasury post, and Wilson could see no reason why he shouldn't.

In time, Wilson's faith in McAdoo was vindicated. He proved to be an extremely able administrator in both jobs. One of his first actions as Director General was to give the railroads a 28 percent rate increase. And before the lines were returned to private control in 1920, they were given another 32 percent rate increase. Almost everyone seemed to agree that the rate increases were necessary for the railroads' survival. From his apartment on Stoneleigh Court, Brandeis said nothing about McAdoo's actions.

If Brandeis was disappointed with the decisions of Wilson and McAdoo, he probably took it in stride. He had given advice before, and he was no stranger to disappointment. But he also had had his share of victories. And few proved to be as rewarding as—or of greater significance than—his argument on behalf of Oregon's women.

TWELVE

A New Window on Social Legislation

The life of the law has not been logic; it has been experience.

OLIVER WENDELL HOLMES

By 1910 Louis D. Brandeis was a household name. People far and wide throughout the country knew of "the people's attorney," of his many exploits to save the individual citizen from the oppression of large corporations and corrupt governments. Of equal note was his ability to organize groups and enlist the dedicated efforts of others to fight with him. It was not only his choice of issues that accounted for this success; Brandeis also had an uncanny talent for bringing out the best in people. His own enthusiasm, and the eloquence with which he expressed it, could generate fire in others as well. He could make people feel part of a cause. And he could do it without the drama of a major speech and a large crowd. In the privacy of a small meeting at his home or office or an eating club, he would lean over, touch his companion's arm, and whisper something in a way that conveyed intimacy and importance. For many people these appeals could not be resisted.

Almost everyone, even his adversaries, recognized him as a major political force. Not surprisingly, his presence and opinion were eagerly pursued. Civic organizations wanted him to speak at their meetings; trade associations wanted him to testify on their behalf in legislative proceedings; and newspapers tried to report his every move and word. His activities and views were considered so important and so newsworthy that many editors would do almost anything to keep tabs on him. William Anderson of William Randolph Hearst's *Boston American*, for example, passed the word to Brandeis that his newspaper was "willing and eager" at any time to give him as much space as he wanted "on any public question"—even if the paper differed with Brandeis in its editorial pages.[1]

Politicians naturally courted his support. An endorsement from Brandeis could be critical. In the 1911 gubernatorial campaign in Massachusetts, Brandeis endorsed Eugene Foss, and it was said that the endorsement was worth at least 10,000 votes. As one newspaper explained it, "Progressives of both parties . . . take their cue from the leading progressive in Massachusetts."[2] Foss won the election by only 8,500 votes, but his gratitude to Brandeis was short-lived—as the Boston attorney would soon find out.

In the meantime, citizens of virtually every stripe looked to Brandeis for help in dealing with the government—even if it involved only an individual problem. On one occasion a widow came to see the famous attorney with her little boy. The Street Department, she said, was not treating her fairly. They had torn up the sidewalk outside her modest home for some reason and, try as she might, she could not get them to repair it. The "people's attorney" said he would see what he could do. The woman and her son left, no doubt filled with hope.

She was not disappointed. A phone call was made, the sidewalk was fixed, and the appreciative woman returned to Brandeis's office with her son to find out how much the legal services would cost. Would a dollar be fair, Brandeis inquired. Oh, said the woman, I think that would be very fair. At that she reached into her purse, took out a dollar bill, and handed it to Brandeis. He then looked at the little boy and asked if he liked candy. The answer was predictable. Brandeis then gave the dollar to the boy, and both he and his mother left feeling very satisfied with the whole experience.[3]

Others had found Brandeis equally successful in arguing their case—and few could have been more pleased than Florence Kelley. Brandeis too must have found the relationship with Kelley rewarding. It not only had enabled him to further his desire to protect individual employees from domineering employers; the relationship had also added immeasurably to his professional stature.

Kelley was the head of the National Consumers League, and in 1907 she needed an attorney to take on an important case. It concerned a state law in Oregon that prohibited women from working in factories and laundries more than ten hours a day. Curt Muller operated a laundry in Oregon, and he did not like the law. His women employees worked for more than ten hours, and so he was arrested. He challenged the law on constitutional grounds and lost in the state Supreme Court. The last stop was the United States Supreme Court, and Muller had good reason to believe he would find salvation there.

Most courts at this time—but especially the United States Supreme Court—had a very eclectic record when it came to social legislation affecting the hours and wages of employees. In 1898 the Supreme Court had sustained a Utah statute that limited the hours of mine workers to eight hours a day. "These employments, when too long pursued," the Court said, "the legislature has judged to be detrimental to the health of the employees, and so long as there are reasonable grounds for believing so, its decision upon the subject cannot be reviewed by the Federal courts."[4] It appeared, then, that individual states were free to adopt legislation concerning hours and perhaps other conditions of employment as well. At least until the Supreme Court decided the *Lochner* case seven years later.

New York, perhaps taking the lead from the Utah decision, enacted a law that prohibited men and women from working as bakers for more than ten hours a day. The record contained statistics and reports indicating the health dangers if individuals worked in baking factories for longer periods. A majority of the Court ignored those facts and held that the New York law was unconstitutional because it violated the employers' and employees' freedom to make their own contracts—a freedom, said the Court, that was protected by the due process clause of the Fourteenth Amendment. "There is no contention," the Court majority said this time around, "that bakers as a class are not equal in intelligence and capacity to men in other trades or manual occupations, or that they are not able to assert their rights and care for themselves without the protecting arm of the State, interfering with their independence of judgment and of action."[5]

Kelley was disturbed by the Court's decision. Before joining the National Consumers League she had worked as the chief factory inspector for Illinois. She was very familiar with the unsanitary conditions of most factories—poor lighting, inadequate ventilation, crowded tables and machines, and unbearably long hours. She also knew that individual employees had little leverage to change those conditions. The "liberty of contract" that the Court so proudly hailed as a constitutional right was, to her mind, merely a cloud to justify employers' exploitation of working men and women.

Inequality of bargaining power was only part of the problem. Kelley saw poor legal representation as another. In a 1907 New York case—this one involving a law that prohibited employment of women after 10 P.M.—the state attorney general did not even bother to send someone to argue the case. Kelley, who went to the court hearing with high hopes, was appalled. She learned her lesson. "Never again would we be caught napping," a colleague later recalled. "Never again would we leave the defense of a labor law to an indifferent third assistant attorney general. Somehow we would see that a better lawyer handled the case, one who believed in the law and was better prepared to show the court why it was needed to protect women's health."[6]

So when the Oregon Consumers League contacted Kelley in the autumn of 1907 about the *Muller* case, Kelley knew whom she wanted: Louis Brandeis. A complex assortment of interrelationships made her very familiar with his work and opinions on labor matters. He had spent many evenings discussing labor issues with Jack O'Sullivan and his wife, Mary Kenney, who had worked with Kelley in Illinois. Kelley also knew Bess Evans, since Kelley's daughter had lived with Bess for two years in her house, which was down the street from the Brandeis home. And last, but certainly not least, Kelley's most trusted adviser at this time was Josephine Goldmark—Alice Brandeis's sister.

Brandeis almost never made it into the case, however. When the call came in from Oregon, Kelley was out of town on a speaking engagement. When she returned to the Consumers League's headquarters in New York City, she found that an enterprising member of her staff had made an appointment for her with Joseph H. Choate, a leading corporate attorney in New York who on occasion gave his services to public causes. Although she had no interest in retaining Choate, Kelley felt duty-bound to honor the appointment.

Luck was on her side. After listening to Kelley's explanation of the situation, Choate failed to grasp the problem. "A law *prohibiting* more than ten hours a day in laundry work," he boomed. "Big, strong laundry women. Why shouldn't they work longer?" Kelley saw her chance for escape. "Why not, indeed," she replied. "There is much to be said for that view. But I realize that we should not have intruded on your valuable time, Mr. Choate, in this small matter. Pray forgive me. . . ." And with that she was gone.[7]

On the next day, November 14, 1907, Kelley and Goldmark were sitting with Brandeis in the library of his home on Otis Place overlooking the Charles River. He listened intently as the two of them explained the situation. Years before, when he prepared his MIT course, he had taken a dim view of legislation limiting the hours of workers. But all that had changed with the Homestead strike and subsequent experience. If individuals were to be free of corporate domination, if workers were to attain control over their lives, the state would sometimes have to lend a helping hand.

"Yes," he said thoughtfully. "I will take part in the defense."[8] He had two conditions, though. First, he wanted an invitation from the state attorney general to be identified as counsel for Oregon; he did not want to appear only as an *amicus curiae,* "friend of the court," because the Supreme Court justices would not pay much attention to him in that capacity. Second, he wanted Kelley and Goldmark to research the facts for the brief. In the *Lochner* case, the Court majority said that the hour-limitation for bakers could not stand because there was no demonstration that the law was necessary to protect the health of the workers. Apparently the Court wanted more information than it got then. Brandeis would not make that mistake here. He would overwhelm the Court with facts—reflecting the experience and observation of people in Oregon and elsewhere—that long manual labor for women was not healthy.

Kelley and Goldmark rushed back to New York, elated by the prospect of having Brandeis on their side. Kelley secured an invitation for the Boston attorney to be co-counsel for Oregon. His sister-in-law began a frantic search for facts in the New York Public Library and the Columbia University Library. She obtained reports and quotations from government agencies, social workers, doctors, and others concerning the impact of long hours on a woman's health. In three weeks she was back in Boston to present the package to Louis. He was impressed. In the next two weeks he and Do put the brief together. The state attorney general was already filing a brief discussing the legal arguments, so Brandeis decided to devote his brief almost exclusively to the facts. He wrote a two-page summary of applicable legal principles and worked with his sister-in-law in organizing the factual material. Do prepared short summaries for each section of the brief to introduce the various reports and quotations. By the time they were done, the brief contained 113 pages.

In great detail, the brief's factual material catalogued the ill effects of hard work on women. "Long hours of labor are dangerous for women," the brief asserted, "primarily because of their special physical organization. In structure and function women are differentiated from men. Besides these anatomical and physiological differences, physicians are agreed that women are fundamentally weaker than men in all that makes for endurance: in muscular strength, in nervous energy, in the powers of persistent attention and application. Overwork, therefore, which strains endurance to the utmost, is more disastrous to the health of women than of men, and entails upon them more lasting injury."

It was not only a question of physical damage, however. The brief said that long hours prevented women from doing necessary housework. "[A]s we have seen," the brief observed, "85+ per cent of the working girls in Boston do their own housework and sewing either wholly or in part, and this housework must be done in addition to that performed for their employers." And if the women were not occupied with housework in off-hours, then there was a great likelihood that the strain of long hours led them to other, less virtuous activities. To this end the brief quoted a mule skinner who had testified before a United States Senate committee. "I have noticed," he said, "that the hard, slavish overwork is driving those girls into the saloons."

For these and other reasons, the brief concluded, "it cannot be said that the Legislature of Oregon had no reasonable ground for believing that the public health, safety, or welfare did not require a legal limitation on women's work in manufacturing and mechanical establishments and laundries to ten hours in one day."[9]

Presenting the brief was an audacious move. In preceding cases lawyers usually referred only to facts that were a formal part of the record. Here, Brandeis asked the Court to accept the truth of factual material that was outside the record. That was no small request. Neither Curt Muller's attorney nor any other lawyer had had an opportunity to test the accuracy of that factual material through cross-examination or other court procedures. Brandeis claimed, however, that the facts were so plainly correct that nothing could be said to dispute them.

At oral argument Brandeis dwelt almost entirely on the facts. "The distinguishing mark" of his argument, Josephine Goldmark later remembered, "was his complete mastery of the details of his subject and the marshaling of the evidence. Slowly, deliberately, without seeming to refer to a note, he built up his case from the particular to the general, describing conditions authoritatively reported, turning the pages of history, country by country, state by state, weaving in with artistic skill the human facts—all to prove the evil of long hours and the benefit that accrued when these were abolished by law."[10]

Brandeis's arguments were effective. In February 1908 the Court handed down its decision upholding the Oregon statute. The Court also took the opportunity to acknowledge the contribution of the Brandeis brief. "It may not be amiss," Justice David J. Brewer observed, ". . . to notice the course of legislation as well as expressions of opinion from other judicial sources. In the brief filed by Mr. Louis D. Brandeis . . . is a very copious collection of all of these matters." Brewer found the material instructive. "The legislation and opinions . . . may not be, technically speaking, authorities and in them is little or no discussion of the constitutional question presented to us for determination, yet they are significant of a wide-spread belief that woman's physical structure, and the functions she performs in consequence thereof, [justifies] special legislation restricting or qualifying the conditions under which she should be permitted to toil."[11]

Kelley and Goldmark were delighted with the result. They were also quick to recognize that the technique could be used in other cases as well. Over the next few years Goldmark and her brother-in-law prepared similar briefs—some as long as 600 pages—in support of hours and wage legislation in Illinois, Ohio, California, and other states. In most cases they were successful. The word spread, and other attorneys in other cases used the "Brandeis brief." It truly was, as Felix Frankfurter observed, an "epoch-making" technique.[12]

When he later became an associate justice of the Supreme Court, Brandeis would discover that the technique would not always work and on some occasions might even be counterproductive. But his basic faith in the approach never faded. And there would be no shortage of attorneys and judges who shared that faith.

Amidst all this praise and glory, Brandeis was once asked what title he would put on the Oregon brief—a collection of diverse factual material to show that women are different from men and would suffer great harm if they spent too many hours at hard labor. Brandeis's answer was succinct and to the point. "What Any Fool Knows," he replied.[13]

THIRTEEN

Finding a New President

We lived many lives in those swirling campaigns, never sparing ourselves any good or evil; yet when we had achieved, and the new world dawned, the old men came out again, and took from us our victory, and remade it in the likeness of the former world they knew. . . . We stammered that we had worked for a new heaven, and a new earth, and they thanked us kindly, and made their peace.

T.E. LAWRENCE

Robert and Belle La Follette liked their new friend. He was not only an unusually talented lawyer; he was also a wonderful social guest. Dinners with him were always animated affairs, with the topics of discussion ranging far and wide. It was always good to see him when he made his frequent trips to Washington, D.C., from Boston, and he had a standing invitation to join the family for dinner or breakfast at their large home on 16th Street whenever he was in town. Even the La Follette children liked their new acquaintance, and before long they were referring to him affectionately as "Uncle Louis."

Once again, it was Bess's doing. She was traveling widely and taking a leading role in many significant matters of social reform. In the winter of 1909 she journeyed to Madison, Wisconsin, to meet the La Follettes. "Fighting Bob" La Follette had been a popular Republican governor of the Badger State, and he was now representing it in the United States Senate. Bess found the La Follettes to be engaging people. The senator was a hard-driving man with wide interests; above all, he was a man who cared deeply for the working man and his plight in industrial America. Belle La Follette was an intellectual and political force in her own right, having been one of the first women to graduate from the University of Wisconsin Law School and having played crucial advisory roles in her husband's many campaigns.

Bess knew that the La Follettes and her friend from Boston would like each other. The La Follettes certainly knew of Brandeis—his success in the *Muller* case was widely reported and no doubt attracted them to Brandeis even before they met him. Like Brandeis, the La Follettes were dedicated to correcting social and economic inequities. And more than that, Senator La Follette was gearing up to run for the presidency, and one of the central issues of his campaign would be the need for legislation to protect the individual citizen and the small businessman from the oppression of the giant corporations. The campaign could use a man like Brandeis.

So when "the people's attorney" was called to Washington to participate in the Ballinger–Pinchot hearings in 1910, Bess urged him to contact the La Follettes. Brandeis took her up on the suggestion. By the time the hearings concluded in May, the relationship was a close one. As he prepared to leave Washington, Louis sent them roses to express his appreciation for their warmth and hospitality. Belle was touched. "Every day since you left Washington," she wrote to him, "I have thought I would write you—not just to thank you for the roses—which were indeed lovely and lasted a long, long time—but to tell you how much we thought of you, how much we missed you, and how glad we were that this year had brought you to us."[1]

After that the La Follettes corresponded regularly with Brandeis on a whole assortment of matters both private and public. When Alfred Brandeis became very ill at one point, Senator La Follette dashed off a telegram of support. "My dear friend," he said, "no trouble can come near to you or any of your loved ones that will not cast its shadow over this house too. When you feel you can write me about it, please do."[2] But no subject received as much time and discussion as the growth—and danger—of giant corporations.

Even while he was wrestling with the problems of Louis Glavis, Brandeis was almost preaching to La Follette about the problems of the New Haven railroad. The Boston attorney even took time from the congressional hearings to help prepare a very detailed speech for the senator on the subject. This collaboration on matters affecting large trusts intensified after the United States Supreme Court issued its decision in the Standard Oil case in May 1911.

The Standard Oil Company of Ohio had been formed by John D. Rockefeller in 1870. The company refined and shipped oil, and Rockefeller had big dreams for his fledgling enterprise. Within a year he embarked on a scheme to eliminate the competition. He would combine operations with other companies, secure discriminatory rebates from the railroads, and drive other firms out of the market. As Rockefeller explained it, he wanted only big companies in his organization. "As for the others," he said, "unfortunately they will have to die."[3]

The plan achieved rapid success—although at times company agents had to resort to dynamite and other sordid means to convince a competitor that pastures were greener elsewhere. By 1882 the Rockefeller group was large and unwieldy. There were simply too many companies with too many different executives. Centralization was needed. Rockefeller therefore created a trust to control his diverse corporations. The thirty-seven stockholders in all the companies signed an agreement that placed all their holdings in a single trust to be directed by Rockefeller and eight other men. The trustees ran the show efficiently, forming new companies like Standard Oil of New Jersey and earning enormous profits for their investors. In one year alone they made more than $3 million in dividends on a $3.5 million investment.

Standard Oil's history was symptomatic of combinations taking place in other industries. Food producers, railroads, steel manufacturers, machine companies—in virtually every area trusts and other mergers were being formed to beat the competition. Many people became upset with the unethical and often violent tactics of the large companies. Congress took note and in 1890 adopted a law—named after its sponsor, Senator John Sherman of Ohio—designed to preserve competition. The first section of the statute prohibited "[e]very contract, combination in the form of trust or otherwise, or conspiracy, in restraint of trade or commerce. . . ." Senator Sherman observed that the law was intended "to prevent and control combinations made with a view to prevent competition, or for the restraint of trade, or to increase the profits of the producer at the cost of the consumer."[4]

By the beginning of the twentieth century the growth of the trusts had nonetheless intensified. Theodore Roosevelt, the young and bullish new president, promised to enforce the Sherman Antitrust Law; and in 1907 his administration filed a suit to dissolve Standard Oil of New Jersey, now the principal holding company of the Rockefeller empire. On May 15, 1911, the Supreme Court ruled that Standard Oil must divest itself of thirty-seven companies. In the course of its opinion, though, the Court gave what then appeared to be a strange twist to the Sherman Act. The law explicitly prohibited "every" contract or combination that restrained commerce; the Court, however, said it would apply "the rule of reason" to this provision and overturn only contracts that "unreasonably" restrained commerce.[5]

Businesmen were elated by this interpretation. It signified that at least some combinations—those that "reasonably" restrained trade—would be lawful. Other observers were not happy with the Court's opinion. Senator La Follette, for one, saw the Court's new language as a giant loophole that would in effect sanction the presence and growth of oppressive trusts. He wanted to fight back. He quickly organized a meeting to draft a bill that would reverse the Court's interpretation and restore what he saw as the original intent of the Sherman Law. And no one would be more helpful in that effort than Brandeis. A telegram was sent and the Boston attorney responded that he was taking the next train to Washington.

Brandeis met with La Follette, Congressman Irvine Lenroot, and others in the offices of Senator Jonathan Bourne. They debated the problem and eventually it was agreed that Brandeis, Lenroot, and another reform lawyer named Francis Heney would draft some amendments to the Sherman Antitrust Act. But it was Brandeis who took the lead, and over the next couple of months he worked closely with La Follette in drafting the legislation. It was introduced by the Wisconsin senator in August 1911, and Lenroot introduced a similar bill in the House of Representatives.

The bill proposed three principal changes in the law. First, the bill tried to catalogue the kinds of activities that were an unreasonable restraint of trade; prohibited activities included low prices designed to drive out a competitor and a refusal to deal with customers who purchased a competitor's goods. Second, the law placed the burden on the company to demonstrate that any restraint of trade was reasonable and therefore lawful. Third, the bill allowed damaged competitors to obtain relief from the offending company if the government proved that the company had violated the Sherman law; no longer would the offended competitor have to endure the cost and delay of establishing legal violations already proved by the government.

Senator Moses Clapp of Minnesota was anxious to push the bill to adoption.

As chairman of the Senate's Committee on Interstate Commerce, he had some leverage along those lines. In December 1911 he convened some hearings to consider the La Follette proposal and other measures. Brandeis, an acknowledged author of the La Follette–Lenroot bill, was asked to testify.

Brandeis began by pinpointing the evil social effects of large corporations and trusts that unfairly exploited their workers. Of particular concern to him were the crowded, poorly lit, and generally unsafe factories of the United States Steel Corporation. The company used unscrupulous methods to block unions; and at the same time, it required its employees to work in miserable conditions for long hours and with low wages. "I ask you gentlemen," Brandeis addressed the committee, "how can any man—is it not amazing that the human body should stand, even for a short period of years, working 7 days, 12 hours a day, and occasionally 18 or 24 hours a day, under the conditions prevailing in the steel industry? . . . Such conditions in a rich industry could not possibly have continued in America unless management had succeeded in driving out or silencing every human being in its employ who could raise his head, and establishing repression as bad as any conditions of peonage found in the United States." Brandeis then referred to a recent incident in which some union men had bombed the offices of the *Los Angeles Times* in retaliation for the paper's anti-union editorials. "[T]hese horrible crimes are . . . the unintelligent protest against the conditions of hopelessness and despair in which these working people find themselves," he observed, "and is not that condition of helplessness and hopelessness a byproduct of this trust and other trusts?"

The real problem with the trusts, then, was that they generated social unrest. "And this social unrest among the American people," Brandeis asserted, "is due to the industrial injustice of which such flagrant examples are afforded by the promotion of the United States Steel Trust, the conduct of the Tobacco Trust and the Standard Oil Trust, and the sense of helplessness which confronts our people opposed to such forces. . . . You cannot have true American citizenship," he added, "you cannot preserve political liberty, you cannot secure American standards of living unless some degree of industrial liberty accompanies it. And the United States Steel Corporation and these other trusts have stabbed industrial liberty in the back."

To Brandeis there was no mystery as to why oppressive trusts had prospered in America. The companies simply offered stock to the public with high dividends. As long as those dividends remained high, the stockholders were prepared to back management. So management had the best of both worlds: someone else's money and the freedom to do as they pleased with it. "Large dividends," Brandeis commented, "are the bribes which the managers tender the small investor for the power to use other people's money."

This was an unfortunate development. "The trust problem can never be settled right for the American people," Brandeis concluded in his opening statement, "by looking at it through the spectacles of bonds and stocks. You must study it through the spectacles of people's rights and people's interests; must consider the effect upon the development of the American democracy. When you do that you will realize the perils to our institutions which attend the trusts. . . ." The depth of the problem could not be overestimated. "The situation is a very serious one," he observed; "unless wise legislation is enacted we shall have as a result of that social unrest a condition which will be more serious than that produced by the fall of a few points in stock-exchange quotations."

It was a passionate and powerful performance. But not all of the senators in attendance entirely understood or agreed with Brandeis's position. They detained him for three days to ask questions and explore his views.

One of the first inquiries was from Senator Albert Cummins, who wanted to know if Brandeis would be offended by a big corporation even if it did not engage in anticompetitive practices. Brandeis replied that he did not know of any such company, but, in any event, his opposition to bigness was based more on morality and politics than on economics. "I have considered and do consider that the proposition that mere bigness cannot be an offense against society is false," Brandeis told Cummins, "because I believe our society, which rests upon democracy, cannot endure under such conditions. Something approaching equality is essential. You may have an organization in the community which is so powerful that in a particular branch of the trade it may dominate by mere size. Although its individual practices may be according to rules, it may be, nevertheless, a menace to the community." Upon further questioning, however, Brandeis could not suggest any way of determining exactly when a company became too big. "I feel very clear about the proposition," he explained, "but I do not feel equally clear as to what machinery should be invoked or the specific provision by which that proposition could be enforced."

He was much more specific when he discussed the federal government's antitrust suit against the Tobacco Trust. The case had been decided by the Supreme Court on the same day as the Standard Oil case. As in that case, the Court directed that the Tobacco Trust be dissolved into smaller companies. The Tobacco executives came up with a dissolution plan that divided most of the market among four companies. Brandeis thought the arrangement was still unacceptable because the resulting companies would be too large and able to stifle competition. He therefore filed a brief on behalf of some small independent companies opposing the plan. His efforts were in vain. The lower court felt that the dissolution plan, however flawed, was still a dissolution plan, and the court felt powerless to propose changes.

Brandeis thought that that problem too should be corrected by a change in the law. And while he praised the performance of James McReynolds, the assistant attorney general in charge of the case, he had some harsh things to say about the government's support of the dissolution plan. He was especially disturbed by the government's willingness to meet with the Tobacco Trust's officials in devising the plan without the participation of the public or the small independent companies.

In all of this Brandeis tried to make it clear that he was not interested in criticizing individuals; his only goal was to change the system. But he was not afraid to make personal references if he thought them appropriate. And when the committee members started asking him about the proper level of profits for the United States Steel Corporation, Brandeis could not help making another one. He referred to reports of the $500,000 pearl necklace that Judge Elbert Gary, the chairman of the company's board, was going to give his wife for Christmas. "See what that means to the social unrest," Brandeis declared. "Is it not just the same sort of thing which brought on the French Revolution. . . ." The observation was not appreciated by most of the press. It was called a "demagogic appeal" to popular prejudice, and Judge Gary himself issued a statement that he had thought Brandeis a "bigger man" than that.[6] The point was well taken nonetheless, and Brandeis apparently felt no remorse at having made it. In fact, he was quite satisfied with his performance. ". . .I think most of the Committee's faith in Bigness has been jarred," he reported to Alice.[7]

Brandeis returned to Washington the following month to testify about the Lenroot bill before the House Judiciary Committee. To him the danger of trusts was readily apparent. "Now, it seems to me perfectly clear, as a general proposition, that what we must do in dealing with business, with the liberty of business, is precisely the same as what we must do in liberty of the individual," he commented. "Any one of us might be knocked down when we go through the streets by somebody who is a good deal stronger than we are. I am certain that I might be so knocked down." But the law, he said, does not permit that kind of freedom. "The law undertakes to restrain the liberty of that physically strong individual," Brandeis explained, "by not allowing him to exercise his right to do as he pleases and [preventing] his knocking me down, unless it should be in self-defense or in some other justification or infringement of his rights. What is done there? That is the regulation, the restriction of the liberty of one which is absolutely essential to the preservation of the liberty of the other. Now, that same principle applies, of course, in business. . . . The Standard Oil did not compete with those individual companies when it went and destroyed them," he observed. "They committed industrial murder just as much as the man who physically [uses] his strength to put an end to persons about him."[8]

For all these analogies and arguments, Brandeis was not able to push his bill—or any bill—through Congress. It was not a reflection of the bill's weaknesses or of Brandeis's shortcomings as an advocate. The drafting of major legislation had to take back seat to the 1912 presidential campaign.

Brandeis had mixed feelings about his involvement in La Follette's presidential campaign. At one point he confessed to his brother that he would prefer "to have no political obligations."[9] But that did not stop him from campaigning for La Follette. Or enjoying it.

Even before he went to Washington to testify on the antitrust bills, Brandeis was approached by two key La Follette supporters who wanted to know if the Boston attorney would direct the La Follette campaign in Massachusetts. Brandeis declined, stating modestly that "I am not a political man. . . ."[10] He added, however, that he would do what he could to help. As he explained to one fellow Progressive, Senator La Follette "seems to me just the man whom the country needs at this critical time, possessing great courage, indomitable will, high constructive ability, and that deep sympathy with the working man which is essential to an understanding and solution of our present problems."[11] For that reason Brandeis felt comfortable issuing an endorsement of La Follette in September 1911.

The endorsement caused a stir among Democrats. True, La Follette was a Progressive, but he was still a Republican. Massachusetts Democrats had hoped to use Brandeis in their campaigns, but now all that was in doubt. "The Democrats want a Democratic platform," one newspaper explained, "and they want a Democrat to write it; and one, no matter how well written, when prepared by a La Follette Republican insurgent, is not to their taste."[12] To Brandeis it did not matter. He viewed La Follette as the man for the job, and he was not going to let party labels stand in the way.

Brandeis made trips to the Midwest to speak on La Follette's behalf. He told the campaign managers that he had no experience in making political speeches, but they were not deterred. They knew a good thing when they had it. Posters were hung at each stop announcing the forthcoming speech of "The People's Attorney." The crowds were good and Brandeis found the whole adventure exhilarating.

Unfortunately, the rest of the campaign was not going smoothly. For a variety of reasons, former President Theodore Roosevelt had entered the race for the Republican nomination. The famous Rough Rider was still a popular figure. Even Brandeis found Roosevelt "pretty near irresistible."[13] So did other Progressives, and many, like Gifford Pinchot, were instrumental in persuading him to make the run.

The problem was that many of those same Progressives had urged La Follette to pursue the presidency. By January 1912 Pinchot, Edward Filene, and others were trying to persuade Brandeis to abandon La Follette and join the Roosevelt effort—a campaign, they said, that was destined for victory.

Brandeis held firm for La Follette. He was a friend, he was capable of handling the job, and Brandeis was not prepared to leave the ship—even if it was sinking.

No doubt Brandeis's decision to stand by La Follette reflected, in part at least, his view of Roosevelt's policies, especially on the trust issue. Unlike Brandeis, the former president saw nothing inherently wrong with large corporations. In fact, he thought their size enabled them to undertake research and introduce innovations that smaller companies might find too costly. Roosevelt therefore proposed that the government accept large corporations but adopt rules and procedures to prevent abuse.

Brandeis scoffed at Roosevelt's theory. In his mind regulation of trusts could never be successful. The government would almost always lack the resources and the will to do it properly.

Whatever the merit of Brandeis's analysis, it did little to revive La Follette's sagging campaign. Roosevelt appeared to be the man of the hour. It was all too much for the Wisconsin senator. Beset by illness in his own family, bitter at colleagues like Pinchot who had deserted him, and tired from endless hours of politicking, La Follette seemed to crack under the strain. It happened when he was in Philadelphia to address a group of newspaper publishers on February 2, 1912. He felt nauseated before the speech but decided to go forward anyway. Before long he launched into a long, rambling denunciation of the press and its treatment of him, repeating himself and casting aspersions that were not, to say the least, well received by his audience.

He went into seclusion immediately afterwards, and the press reported that the La Follette campaign was all but over. Brandeis, on his way back from a campaign speech in St. Louis, sent a note of sympathy to Belle La Follette. "My thoughts have been much with you and Bob and the children . . .," he wrote. "Only make Bob take the rest he needs and make a pleasure trip out of this necessity. When he comes back we will take up the good fight again together." He signed it "with much love."[14]

Despite the words of encouragement, Brandeis did not have much hope of La Follette's return to the campaign trail. Nor did others. Amos Pinchot, Gifford's brother, wrote to his friend in Boston for help with Roosevelt's campaign. California was critical to the former president's hopes, and that state's governor, Hiram Johnson, could help. But Johnson was a La Follette man and would not change allegiance until La Follette personally released him. Amos Pinchot had tried to reach La Follette himself, but those efforts, not surprisingly, were unsuccessful. "I think that you have more influence over the Senator than anyone else at this juncture," Pinchot wrote to Brandeis. "He has lost confidence and is unwilling to talk to most of the crowd." Would Brandeis approach La Follette about Hiram Johnson?[15] Brandeis refused to cooperate, telling Pinchot in response only that the situation was "an unfortunate one."[16]

Later, George Rublee—an attorney who had worked closely with Brandeis in the Ballinger case—wrote his colleague about the possibility of joining the Roosevelt team. Rublee said that he had spent some time with Roosevelt at his home on Oyster Bay, Long Island, and that the former president had spoken of Brandeis "in the friendliest way" and was anxious to meet with him. Would Louis be interested in making the trip out to Long Island? "My dear George," Brandeis replied, "I should be glad indeed to go down to Oyster Bay with you to spend the evening talking social and industrial questions with Colonel Roosevelt." However, Brandeis did not think it was an appropriate time for such a meeting. "At present I am nearly the only one of the original Progressive group which surrounded La Follette, in whom he has confidence," he explained. ". . . I may be able to aid in restoring cooperation between the discordant factions, if La Follette retains his confidence in my loyalty. I fear that if I should hold a conference with Roosevelt, under the existing circumstances, La Follette might construe my so doing as a defection, and I want to avoid that possibility."[17]

Brandeis was hardly committed to Roosevelt at that point. In fact, he probably remained skeptical that the Rough Rider's approach to large corporations would ever be satisfactory. Brandeis remained aloof from the campaign in the following months—although at the end of April he confided to his brother that there was "a fine fight" between President Taft and Roosevelt in the Massachusetts Republican primary and that he was "sad" not to be involved.[18] All that was to change shortly.

Woodrow Wilson was picking up steam in Democratic ranks. New Jersey's governor was tall, lean, and austere-looking, and he had impressed people in his home state and around the country with his eloquence in defense of Progressive causes. And his record as governor demonstrated that he was prepared to stand behind spoken commitments. Although he had been brought into office on the coattails of political bosses, he lost no time in establishing his independence. Others took note of his presidential qualities, and, led by George Harvey, a prominent New York publisher, his supporters finally engineered his nomination at a badly divided Democratic Convention in the early summer of 1912.

No sooner had Wilson become the Democratic nominee than Brandeis expressed an inclination to support him. "I have never met or seen Wilson," he wrote to Norman Hapgood on July 3, 1912, "but all that I have heard of him and particularly his discussion of economic problems makes me believe that he possesses certain qualities indispensable to the solution of our problems."[19] Within a week Brandeis issued a statement to the press endorsing Wilson. "Progressives should support Wilson," he said, "not only in order to secure his election, but in order to enable him after election to carry out those progressive policies which he has so much at heart.... Without loyal support from the progressives of the country Wilson's war upon unjust privilege must be futile."[20]

Brandeis felt especially good about his choice when it was reported in the press that Wilson favored a reduction in tariffs to foster competition from exports. Fifteen years earlier Brandeis had testified before a congressional committee—without much success—in urging a similar tariff reduction. He wrote a letter of praise to Wilson, saying that his tariff position "is further evidence that the Country may expect from you a wisely progressive administration."[21] The Democratic nominee responded within a few days. "Your letter of August first has given me a great deal of pleasure," he wrote. "I have been very much cheered and reassured by the knowledge of your approval and support. I sincerely hope that the months to come will draw us together and give me the benefit of many conferences with you."[22] Brandeis did not have long to wait.

By the end of the month an invitation came for him to meet the governor for lunch at his summer home on the New Jersey shore at Sea Girt. Brandeis took the train to New York and then a boat to the Wilson residence. The meeting, which took place on August 28, 1912, was to prove a momentous occasion for both men.

Up to that point Wilson thought that tariff reform would be the key campaign issue. Brandeis convinced him otherwise. It was the power of monopolies, he said, that should receive your greatest attention. Wilson, of course, understood the general problem, but his insight into the issue was not very sophisticated. He thought monopolies could be curbed if meetings of the board of directors were opened to the public and if individual corporate officers were held personally liable for corporate misdeeds.

Brandeis thought both ideas were impractical. There could be legitimate reasons for closing some board meetings. And criminal punishment of individuals would have little impact. The pressures to evade the law were often considerable, and, as Brandeis later recalled, "it was demanding too much of human nature that a man had to be a martyr or a hero to stand up against the evils inherent in the system." He also thought judges would be reluctant to punish corporate officers, and by now Brandeis had learned that "no rule of law is so clear and no array of evidence so conclusive" that the court could not "escape from a conclusion which it is disinclined to reach. . . ."[23]

Roosevelt had talked about allowing monopolies to prosper and then regulating them. Brandeis told Wilson it was much better to regulate competition than to regulate monopolies. The size of corporations should be limited somehow, and the government should establish certain procedures to ensure that competition did not become cutthroat. A completely free enterprise, Brandeis thought, also had its dangers.

It is not entirely clear if Wilson fully understood everything that Brandeis said to him. But he knew it must be sound. Everyone—including Brandeis's critics—said he was brilliant. "I found him in accord with my views on the trust question," Brandeis told reporters at Sea Girt after his three-hour luncheon meeting with Wilson. The Democratic nominee issued a similar statement of agreement. "Both of us," said Wilson, "have as an object to prevent monopoly. Monopoly is created by unregulated competition, by competition that overwhelms all other competitors and destroys them, and the only way to enjoy industrial freedom is to destroy that condition."[24] Wilson used the right words, and later Brandeis wrote to his brother that he was "very favorably impressed with Wilson. He is strong, simple, openminded, eager to learn and deliberate."[25]

Homer S. Cummings was in charge of the Democratic Party's speakers bureau, and he wanted Brandeis's help. The Boston attorney was becoming more experienced as a political spokesman, and he gladly accepted Cummings's invitation to speak for Wilson in New England and the Midwest. At each stop he would deride Roosevelt—who had lost the Republican nomination to Taft but was running anyway as the candidate of his own independent Bull Moose Party. Roosevelt said things that sounded good, but when you looked at them closely his promises did not amount to much, especially for the workingman. "The superstructure is beautiful," Brandeis observed; "but the foundations are fatally defective."[26] The Bull Moose platform did not even include an unqualified endorsement of labor's right to organize unions.

Meanwhile, Brandeis had prepared some articles for Norman Hapgood to use in *Collier's.* He also gave Norman some editorials. All of the material was extremely critical of Roosevelt and very supportive of Wilson. "I am glad you and the family like the *Collier's* articles," Louis wrote his brother in mid-September. "I think they are creating some trouble for the enemy."[27]

On September 27, Wilson spoke before a cheering and tumultuous crowd at the Tremont Temple in Boston. He took the occasion to spend some additional time with Brandeis discussing the problems of monopoly—a topic that had become central to Wilson's campaign speeches. The next day Wilson wired Brandeis: "Please set forth as explicitly as possible the actual measures by which competition can be effectively regulated. The more explicit we are on this point the more completely will the enemy's guns be spiked."[28]

Brandeis was tied up at the moment with ICC hearings on the New Haven railroad. Nonetheless, that same day he sent Wilson his *Collier's* articles. And within a couple of days he sent a detailed memorandum on the subject.

The memo stated that the differences between the Bull Moose Party and the Democrats on the monopoly issue were "fundamental and irreconcilable." Relying on the legislation he had drafted for La Follette, Brandeis then outlined a specific program to control monopolies. First, he said, the Sherman Act should specify the kinds of activities that unreasonably restrained trade. Second, the law should be changed to make it easier for parties to collect damages against corporations that had engaged in anticompetitive behavior. Third, the federal government should create a commission to investigate and help prosecute violations of the antitrust laws. "I have no doubt that your definite declaration on the lines indicated in this letter will make some enemies, as well as some friends," Brandeis told Wilson, "but I assume that you have considered that matter adequately."[29]

Actually, Wilson had not considered that problem adequately. In his rush to master a new subject, Wilson—a former college professor—had neglected some hard political realities. Being too specific was almost always a mistake in political campaigns. It provided too much ammunition to the opposition. William McAdoo, Wilson's campaign manager, recognized the risks. He telephoned Brandeis in Providence, Rhode Island, on October 2. While he thought Brandeis's work was "admirable," he questioned the wisdom of Wilson's using it. Much better, said McAdoo, if the memorandum were published under Brandeis's name, and then Wilson could say he agreed with most of it. McAdoo suggested that Brandeis discuss it with Wilson himself. Brandeis made an immediate phone call to the Democratic nominee, and Wilson said he would think it over. Within two weeks the material was used in an unsigned article in *La Follette's Weekly Magazine.*[30]

The campaign had its compensations. The constant travel made it difficult for Brandeis to go horseback riding or to undertake one of the many other activities he pursued for exercise. So he started walking, and he found it a good substitute. "Blessed is the walk," he wrote to Alice from a campaign stop in New York City, "& the liberation from the old heresy that a horse was a necessary element of exercise."[31] He also used the travel to spend a quiet day alone with Al, who was recovering from an operation. And last but not least, he found that he was enjoying the speech making, and he was getting better at it all the time.

Norman Hapgood did not find the campaign as rewarding. In fact, it cost him his job. Robert Collier was an intimate friend of Roosevelt's, and he did not like Hapgood's ardent support of Wilson. He became especially disturbed when he learned that Brandeis—a known Wilson supporter—was supplying Hapgood with editorials in support of the Democratic nominee. Hapgood was fired on the spot. Collier then wrote an editorial endorsing Roosevelt.

Collier did not hold Brandeis personally responsible. After all, it was Hapgood who had extended the invitation for him to write the editorials. Collier wrote Brandeis that "I trust the recent rumpus in this office will not deprive our readers of the benefit of an occasional contribution from yourself."[32] Hapgood did not receive the same magnanimity. Collier felt that he had been betrayed, and he contemplated publishing a broadside attack against his former editor. Brandeis counseled conciliation. "I hope you will . . . conclude," he wrote Collier on November 9, "that the character of *Collier's* can be sustained without an attack on Norman personally. Such an attack would, of course, be answered; and from controversies of this nature both parties usually emerge as losers."[33] Collier had already decided that there would be no personal attack on Hapgood. He did, however, publish an article revealing that Brandeis had written the editorials in support of Wilson and apologizing for using one candidate's partisan to write the magazine's editorials.

None of this had any bearing on the outcome of the election. Wilson polled a clear plurality of the popular vote and more than 80 percent of the electoral vote. Brandeis wrote a note of congratulations to the president-elect, and Wilson responded with a warm note from his vacation retreat in Bermuda. "You were yourself a great part of the victory . . .," he wrote to Brandeis. "It now remains for us to devote all our strength to making good."[34]

Brandeis too was looking to the future. While he privately told people that he was not interested in public office, he surely must have contemplated the things he could accomplish in an official role. Even if he did not harbor dreams of high position, his friends had great hopes for him. And they were prepared to do something about it.

People began to talk to Wilson about naming Brandeis to the Cabinet as attorney general. The possibility was widely reported in the press, and by early December some newspapers claimed that Brandeis's selection was "conclusive." After all, his reputation as "the people's attorney" was known throughout the country, and few people had been as influential as he in shaping the substance of Wilson's campaign positions.

That was now history, however. The president-elect had immense respect for Brandeis, but other people were writing to him as well, and they had some very unkind things to say about Brandeis. To be sure, he was a skillful lawyer. But he had his shortcomings. He seemed secretive, untrustworthy, and one never knew for whom he was really working. "I know of no reputable lawyer here who has a good word for him," wrote one prominent State Street banker from Boston, ". . . [and] what I say to you in this letter is from one comrade who wishes another well."[35] As much as he liked and respected Brandeis, Wilson could see the political problem. He did not want to initiate his presidency with a fight over a Cabinet officer. Within a couple of weeks after the election—even before he wrote his warm note of thanks to Brandeis from Bermuda—Wilson conferred with Colonel Edward House, his close advisor, about the possibility of Brandeis as attorney general. "We practically eliminated Brandeis for this position," House observed shortly afterwards, "because he was not thought to be entirely above suspicion and it would not do to put him in such a place."[36]

House had never met Brandeis, though, and a few days later a luncheon was arranged for him, Brandeis, and Hapgood. Wilson's unofficial advisor was favorably impressed. "He has less of nervous force and imagination than I had thought," said House, "and I found that he was not 'a know it all' but seemed open to suggestions."[37] Other meetings were arranged, and House was becoming very fond of the Boston attorney.

Still, the letters of opposition poured in. "The best men here," one prominent citizen wrote to Wilson, "men of affairs as well as lawyers, all of whom voted for you or President Taft, will regard the appointment of Mr. Brandeis as a member of your Cabinet, should it be made, with profound regret." Edward Warren, who had locked horns with Brandeis over the gas controversy, wrote Wilson that Brandeis's appointment would cause "serious apprehension" in Boston. Even Brandeis's friend George Anderson advised against the appointment. "It would stir up a good many animosities," Anderson observed, ". . . [and] alienate the affections of a great many who now think very well of you and of the Democratic Party under your leadership." Several newspapers added to the opposition. One periodical sarcastically said it hoped Brandeis would be appointed to the Cabinet "since then he will have to come out in the open and be where his actions and not his explanations will be the basis of his reputation. . . ."[38]

Wilson could not believe all the derogatory comments about Brandeis. His manner was mild, his intelligence obvious, his dedication to Progressive causes deep. How could so many people—and established figures at that—dislike him so intensely? In mid-December he again raised the matter with House. The Colonel remained opposed to Brandeis's appointment. He regretted his opposition because he liked Brandeis personally, but he felt that his placement in the Cabinet would cause too many problems.

The president-elect would not let the matter rest. He wrote letters to friends in Boston, asking them about Brandeis's reputation. He also dispatched Hapgood to Boston to do some investigating on his own. Norman and Louis were close friends, but Wilson trusted the former editor to report the facts accurately. By the end of January 1913 Hapgood completed his inquiry. Many people were vehement in their criticism of Brandeis. Some said that his appointment to the Cabinet would cause a financial panic on State Street. Hapgood did not take all this talk at face value. "It is true," he wrote to Wilson, "that lawyers who have been on the opposite side of cases have criticized him for lack of professional courtesy. . . . Mainly I think the men who are making up the feeling against Brandeis are the men who will oppose you anyway. . . ."[39] In a supplemental report, Hapgood added that there might be some legitimacy to Brandeis's fighting unfairly. But that was minor, he said, when compared with his many admirable qualities and achievements.

Hapgood's report confirmed Wilson's feelings about Brandeis. But none of it really mattered. Even before Wilson received Hapgood's conclusion, House told the president-elect that it was all irrelevant. Whether justified or not, the criticism of Brandeis existed, and it would make his appointment as attorney general extremely controversial. Wilson reluctantly agreed, and on January 26 they agreed to name A. Mitchell Palmer attorney general.

Wilson had an alternative, however. Why not appoint Brandeis to be secretary of commerce? That was a less sensitive post than the Justice Department, Brandeis's knowledge of commercial matters was extensive, and the opposition would probably be minimal. House respected Brandeis's expertise on commercial issues, but he could not accept the suggestion. Even at Commerce he was bound to generate controversy, and that would minimize his value to the administration. Wilson pressed the point, and House finally acquiesced to the appointment on February 13, 1913.

The news was leaked to the press, and within a few days the papers were reporting that the anti-Brandeis movement had run out of steam and that the Boston attorney would get the Commerce position. The reports did not help Brandeis. The opposition emerged again, stronger than ever. A group of Democratic Massachusetts politicians—including Governor Eugene Foss—came to visit Wilson in New Jersey. Brandeis was a Republican, they said. He was not only registered as a Republican voter, but he had also worked for Republican candidates. He had supported Louis Frothingham for mayor in 1905, he had campaigned for La Follette in the presidential race, and even in announcing his support for Wilson he had told the press that he was neither a Republican nor a Democrat but only a "Progressive" working for the best candidate. To some, of course, that might be called intelligent selection; to the Democratic Party stalwarts, it was pure heresy and totally unacceptable. Wilson was angry. He just did not want to believe that a man of Brandeis's talents and dedication could generate so much heated opposition. But facts were facts. On February 28, 1913, House and Wilson agreed that Brandeis could not be in the Cabinet. William Redfield, who was slated to become an assistant secretary of commerce, was given the top slot. As for the post of attorney general, that went to James McReynolds. He had distinguished himself in the prosecution of the Tobacco Trust case, and Wilson had decided that Palmer would also be controversial, because his law practice included the representation of some large railroads.

The Cabinet list was given to the press on March 2, 1913. The absence of Brandeis's name caused excitement—both favorable and unfavorable. But almost everyone was surprised, because his appointment at Commerce had been reported as a sure thing. Brandeis had never discussed the matter with Wilson, and he took the news philosophically. "Today's papers will have removed the mystery as to the Cabinet," he wrote his brother. "As you know I had great doubts as for its being desirable for me; so I concluded to literally let nature take its course and do nothing either to get called or to stop the talk, although some of my friends were quite active." Brandeis understood why his friends' efforts were not successful. "State Street, Wall Street and the local Democratic bosses did six months' unremitting work," he told his brother; "but [they] seem not to have prevailed until the last moment. The local Democratic bosses were swayed partly by their connections in the financial district, partly by the fear of being opposed in job-seeking. It is almost, indeed quite, amusing how much they fear me, attributing to me power and influence which I in no respect possess." Shortly later, during a trip to Washington, he told Alice that seeing "the crowd of office seekers & the like besieging the Secretaries" only confirmed his "contentment with existing things as to myself. . . ."[40]

As the state elections approached in the autumn of 1913, the Democratic leaders cast about for someone to run for attorney general of Massachusetts—someone with stature, a person committed to the Democratic Party. Yes, there was an individual who could meet those standards. The local bosses sent a two-man delegation on their behalf. Would he run on the Democratic slate for attorney general? Louis Brandeis declined. "It is rather amusing," he later told La Follette, "in view of the fact that I was not a good enough Democrat for them a few months ago."[41]

Despite his willingness to turn away the local Democrats, Brandeis would not reject President Wilson's pleas for help. In fact, even as an unofficial advisor, the Boston attorney soon became the "chief architect" of Wilson's "New Freedom" legislative program.[42]

FOURTEEN

The Nation's Advisor

This business of general guide, counsellor and friend grows a bit wearisome. . . .

LOUIS D. BRANDEIS TO ALICE G. BRANDEIS, FEBRUARY 5, 1914

Brandeis wanted businessmen to compete like gentlemen. If people could take a broad perspective, surely they would see that there was far more to business than making money. It was an opportunity to structure social and economic relationships—relationships that would largely determine the individual's ability to develop his talents and become independent. The robber barons of the past need not be the models for the future.

So when Brown University asked Brandeis to deliver its commencement address in June 1912, he had some advice to pass on to the graduating students. Business was not a lowly endeavor, he told them. Business was a profession like medicine and law. After all, he observed, business, like other professions, was "pursued largely for others and not merely for one's self." And as with other professions, "success in business" meant "something very different from mere money-making." Here he cited the experience of two of his clients, William H. McElwain and the Filene family. Both operated multi-million-dollar firms. But their real achievements, said Brandeis, lay in their decisions to create working environments that assured employees of regular work and a share in the management of the company. If their example were followed, Brandeis was confident that "big business" would lose its "sinister meaning." Instead, he said, " 'Big business' will then mean business big not in bulk or power, but great in service and grand in manner."[1]

Like almost all commencement speeches, this one had its share of inflated rhetoric. It was, to be sure, a fair reflection of Brandeis's hopes for the future, a goal toward which students could aspire. But he did not live in a dream world. He knew that greed still played a larger role than social conscience in the conduct of most business. And he realized that the economic system itself made it difficult for businessmen to do otherwise.

Fortunately, as of March 4, 1913, there was a new man in the White House, a leader prepared to introduce fundamental changes in the economic system. And when he faced his first major decision, Woodrow Wilson felt that he could not choose until he received the counsel of Louis Brandeis.

The issue involved the nation's banking system. By 1913 virtually everyone—even the bankers—agreed that the system was in trouble. Correcting the problem, though, was no easy matter. To begin with, the subject was a very complicated one, and few of the nation's political leaders understood it very well. The need for reform was evident by the early twentieth century, but President Theodore Roosevelt refused to attack the issue aggressively. "I do not intend to speak, save generally, on the financial question," he wrote to a friend in 1903, "because I am not clear what to say. . . ." Five years later he had not progressed very far. "This financial business is very puzzling," he confessed in 1908.[2]

Wilson's knowledge of banking was not very extensive either. The new president publicly called the concentration of financial power in Wall Street "the most pernicious of all trusts," and even before his inauguration he urged Congressman Carter Glass, chairman of the Banking and Currency Committee, to develop remedial legislation. Privately, however, Wilson conceded that he "knew nothing" about banking theory or practice.[3]

The matter was a constant topic of discussion, though, in both banking and government circles. The nation had endured several financial "panics" that were attributed to the deficiencies of the banking system. The most recent panic had occurred in New York City in 1907, and it dramatically exposed those deficiencies.

The nation's money supply was at the heart of the problem. There was no centralized control over that supply, and, consequently, no easy way to expand or contract the amount of money available to banks. This was a critical void. If people had too much money to spend in inflationary times, it was extremely difficult to reduce available funds and, with it, the excessive demands that were sending prices upward. Conversely, the nation was equally powerless if people had too little money and a recession became imminent. So when stock prices began to fall rapidly in October 1907, there was a rash of selling, and some banks could not muster the necessary cash to stay afloat. Even the giant financiers of Wall Street felt helpless. J.P. Morgan went to see President Roosevelt, and the federal government agreed to move some of its deposits to help the banks. But even that assistance could not prevent two New York banks from going under.

The experience was especially unsettling to the larger national banks. Their charters from the federal government limited their ability to make loans, extend credit, or open savings accounts. Most smaller state banks did not operate under those limitations. As a result, they were expanding their control over the nation's business—a development of some concern to the large national banks. The state banks' growth not only threatened the power of the national banks; because that growth proceeded with few safeguards, it was creating an instability that affected the entire economic system. "We love the country bankers," one national banker commented, "but they are masters of the situation. We dance at their music and pay the piper."[4]

Not surprisingly, the larger banks and their trade associations were at the forefront of reform efforts at the turn of the century. By 1913 they felt they had a sympathetic friend in the White House. In public statements Wilson seemed to promise federal control of the entire situation. But the legislation prepared at his direction by Congressman Glass was another story. The bill proposed a new Federal Reserve Commission that would include six members appointed by the president and three by private bankers. The commission would enforce some new restrictions on banks. On critical issues, however, the bankers would be in charge. Thus, control of the money supply—a primary concern of the bankers—would be placed in private hands. To this end the Glass bill proposed the establishment of private regional banks that would regulate the money supply within their respective regions. Important members of the banking community passed the word to Glass that they liked his bill.

In initial meetings, Wilson likewise indicated his satisfaction with the Glass bill. The satisfaction was short-lived, however. Secretary of State William Jennings Bryan—the Nebraskan populist who decried the bankers' exploitation of the common man—angrily told Wilson that the Glass bill was unacceptable. The Democratic Party's platform—the one on which Wilson had campaigned—had promised that *the government* would control the nation's currency. Moreover, Bryan found it unacceptable to allow private bankers to sit on the Federal Reserve Commission. That body would oversee matters of paramount importance to the public. It was inappropriate, Bryan asserted, to allow participation by men motivated by private interests.

Bryan's arguments had a certain political appeal to them. Wilson felt confused. He wanted some independent advice, the views of someone who had no political interests to further. He needed Brandeis.

Despite the Cabinet debacle, Brandeis remained an important figure in Wilson's administration. Within a couple of months of his inauguration, Wilson asked Brandeis to become chairman of the United States Commission on Industrial Relations, a government body investigating America's changing management–labor relations. Although the subject matter was close to Brandeis's heart, he turned down the offer. He saw it for what it was—a consolation prize that did not have nearly the power or prestige of a Cabinet post. Nonetheless, Brandeis was a frequent visitor at the White House. Other members of Wilson's political "family"—but especially Treasury Secretary McAdoo, Attorney General McReynolds, and Edward House—also turned to him repeatedly for advice on matters of patronage and policy. So on a critical issue like the Federal Reserve bill, it was quite natural for the president to want "the people's attorney."

Coincidentally, in the beginning of June 1913 Brandeis was in Washington to deliver some speeches and attend to some ICC business. Wilson summoned him to the White House and explained the situation surrounding the Glass bill. How should the matter be resolved?

To Brandeis, the answer was clear. "The power to issue currency should be vested exclusively in Government officials, even when the currency is issued against commercial paper," he told the president. "The American people will not be content to have the discretion necessarily involved vested in a Board composed wholly or in part of bankers; for their judgment may be biased by private interest or affiliation." Brandeis recognized that this posture would not be received well by big business. In his view, there was no way to avoid that opposition. "The conflict between the policies of the Administration and the desires of the financiers and of big business is an irreconcilable one," he advised Wilson. "Concessions to the big business interests must in the end prove futile. The administration can at best have only their seeming or temporary cooperation. In essentials they must be hostile."[5] It sounded glib, but Brandeis recognized the difficulty of the choice confronting Wilson. "The administration is having pretty hard nuts to crack . . .," he wrote to his brother.[6]

Wilson was up to the task, though. Within a week of his meeting with Brandeis, he informed all the major participants that he now agreed with Bryan. In due course the presidential recommendation was conveyed to Congress, and by December 1913 the Federal Reserve Act—in substantial compliance with Brandeis's recommendation—was enacted. The Boston attorney was not involved in the congressional bargaining that preceded the bill's adoption. But there is no doubt that his intervention had turned the tide at a critical moment.

The Federal Reserve Act of 1913 was a major accomplishment. By allowing the new Federal Reserve Board to increase and decrease the supply of money, the law gave the nation's currency a much-needed elasticity. The creation of new standards and a regional banking system also helped to bring stability to the nation's economy. For all its virtues, however, the bill did very little to assist small business or further Brandeis's goals of a more honorable competition. That did not discourage him. He knew there would be other opportunities for remedial legislation. The foundation had to be laid, however. First and foremost was public education. He had learned from his many battles in Boston that reform could not succeed without public support. He therefore decided to help the cause along with some articles explaining his many views on how banking affected competition and individual development.

Brandeis's ideas on these subjects had been germinating for a long time. In early 1911 he wrote to Norman Hapgood about the conflicts and dangers when bankers used "other people's money" to engage in business. "They do not realize . . .," he told Norman, "that the power which the control of other people's money gives them to grant or to withdraw credit is a trust for the public—a power to be exercised impartially. . . ." Louis explained that, unfortunately, banks were anything but fair in making loans and extending credit. Indeed, many banks used the funds to buy other businesses—a practice that he found insidious. "By controlling the money of other people at the same time that they are engaged in industrial and other occupations," he observed, "they suppress competition and get other advantages by means that are illegal."[7]

The situation had not changed much during the first months of the Wilson administration. But at least the new people in power were willing to listen. Brandeis decided to speak out, and he had a perfect vehicle: *Harper's* weekly magazine. He had engineered the sale of the periodical to Norman Hapgood in 1913 so that he could stay in the publishing business after Collier fired him. Hapgood became the chief editor of *Harper's,* and his friend in Boston was anxious to help get things rolling. In the summer of 1913 Louis told Norman that he would prepare a series of articles on the "money trust," that loose amalgamation of individuals and companies that had a stranglehold on banking and investment houses. The hope was that the pieces would add to the circulation of *Harper's* and simultaneously generate public support for remedial legislation.

The initial focus of Brandeis's efforts was the report in 1912 of a congressional committee headed by Representative Arsene Pujo. Guided by the tough questioning of its counsel, Samuel Untermeyer, the Pujo Committee exposed the tremendous power wielded by J.P. Morgan and other investment bankers. One table showed that five banking firms held 341 directorships in 112 corporations that in turn controlled $22 billion in assets. These and other statistics dominated the front pages of the nation's newspapers for months and seemed to whet the public's appetite for more information about Wall Street bankers.

Brandeis spent the summer toiling away at his articles. He wanted to dramatize the Pujo Committee's findings and explain the remedies that were warranted. Most of the articles were written in his rented vacation bungalow in South Yarmouth, a quiet area in Cape Cod where he took the family in August. His recommendations for action were much more stringent than those advocated by the Pujo Committee; Brandeis felt that political considerations prevented the committee from requesting all the changes justified by the facts it found.

By the beginning of September 1913 he reported to Al that the articles were nearing completion. "There will be some cries of 'Holy Murder' if the legislation I propose ever gets passed," he told his brother; "but less than that will do little good."[8] By the end of the month he informed Norman that seven of the nine anticipated articles were either finished or in the final stages of being edited.[9]

The first article was published on November 22, 1913, and it was not until January 1914 that the last was released. Building upon the findings of the Pujo Committee, Brandeis hammered away at investment bankers who used the public's deposits to buy control of other business firms. "The goose that lays golden eggs has been considered a most valuable possession," he remarked. "But even more profitable is the privilege of taking the golden eggs laid by somebody else's goose. The investment bankers and their associates now enjoy that privilege. They control the people through the people's own money." To Brandeis, the irony of the situation was obvious. "The fetters which bind the people," he observed, "are forged from the people's own gold."[10]

To Brandeis, the problem was not measured in dollars alone. Investment bankers were surrounded by conflicts of interest. Perhaps the most pervasive conflict concerned interlocking directorships. Investment bankers would regularly make business deals with firms even though they sat on the other firm's board of directors. "The practice of interlocking directorates is the root of many evils," Brandeis commented. "It offends laws human and divine. . . . It tends to disloyalty and to violation of the fundamental law that no man can serve two masters."

To illustrate the problem, he cited a hypothetical example involving J.P. Morgan. "J.P. Morgan (or a partner), a director of the New York, New Haven & Hartford Railroad," Brandeis wrote, "causes that company to sell to J.P. Morgan & Co. an issue of bonds. J.P. Morgan & Co. borrow the money with which to pay for the bonds from the Guaranty Trust Company, of which Mr. Morgan (or a partner) is a director. J.P. Morgan & Co. sell the bonds to the Penn Mutual Life Insurance Company, of which Mr. Morgan (or a partner) is a director. The New Haven spends the proceeds of the bonds in purchasing steel rails from the United States Steel Corporation, of which Mr. Morgan (or a partner) is a director. The United States Steel Corporation spends the proceeds of the rails in purchasing electrical supplies from the General Electric Company, of which Mr. Morgan (or a partner) is a director. The General Electric sells supplies to the Western Union Telegraph Company, a subsidiary of the American Telephone and Telegraph Company; and in both Mr. Morgan (or a partner) is a director. . . . Each and every one of the companies . . . markets its securities through J.P. Morgan & Co.; and with these funds of each, the firm enters upon further operations."[11]

Interlocking directorships were not only morally offensive to Brandeis; they were also an obstacle to innovation. In his early days as a lawyer he had viewed corporate combinations as the spur to industrial development; now he claimed that innovation was usually initiated "by some common business man" who received no aid from investment bankers. He cited some examples to prove his point, but in doing so he avoided an obvious—and very difficult—question. Why should a banker risk "other people's money" on new ventures when many, if not most, showed little promise at first?

Instead of grappling with that question, Brandeis moved on to other criticisms. In his view the conservatism and conflicts among investment bankers led to large corporate conglomerates—enterprises that stifled individual development and independence. The experience with the New Haven railroad remained fixed in his mind, and he referred to it in his articles. Benefits would begin to flow, he said, if the law required the New Haven and other railroads to sell their non-railroad interests. Financial concentration would be terminated and smaller, more efficient railroads could flourish.[12]

From the beginning there was interest in collecting the *Harper's* articles in a book. Norman White, Brandeis's former colleague from the gas fight, was now with Small, Maynard & Co., a small publisher. He approached Alice Grady in November 1913 about publishing the pieces. She communicated the offer to Brandeis, who was then in Washington, and he told Grady to work it out with Hapgood. Eventually Hapgood decided to have the articles published with Frederick A. Stokes Company under the title *Other People's Money and How the Bankers Use It.* The book came out in early 1914 with all nine *Harper's* articles and another one that had been published in the summer of 1913.

The book enjoyed only modest sales, and the reviews were mixed. But the articles were simply written and clear. And they adequately conveyed the distrust that Brandeis harbored toward big business. However adequate on that score, the articles probably raised more questions than they answered. It was relatively easy to demonstrate that large corporations had diverse and in some cases conflicting interests. And one could—in theory at least—understand why these large corporations might, as Brandeis said, suppress competition and "arrest development."[13] But he rarely cited specific facts to demonstrate that this was indeed the case. Nor did his facts or statistics show convincingly that small corporations were almost always more efficient and generally more beneficial to consumers than large corporations. In fact, many authorities claimed that large corporations used their enormous resources to sponsor innovation and introduce new efficiencies.[14] And last—but certainly not least—the articles generally avoided complex issues that had to be resolved before Brandeis's views could be implemented. At what point, for example, did a company become too large? How much risk should bankers take when investing other people's money? And how did you know whether bankers were in fact suppressing competition?

Brandeis no doubt recognized the shortcomings of his articles. In the winter of 1914 he testified before various congressional committees and was grilled about the details of his proposals. He did not deviate from his basic conclusions; but he was forced to admit that there were some difficulties in reducing his ideas to written laws that others could enforce. At one point after an especially tiring congressional appearance, he wrote to Alice back in Boston. She was still his most trusted friend and advisor. He could reveal to her his innermost feelings. As in the case of the privacy article he wrote with Sam Warren, he could be candid with her about his own work. And he had some doubts about the *Harper's* articles. "*Other People's Money* seems pretty stupid now," he confessed.[15]

Brandeis was disappointed with Norman's decision to have Stokes publish *Other People's Money.* He would have preferred Norman White's company, Small, Maynard. After all, Norman was a colleague from earlier reform fights and the brother of his good friend Herbert. It seemed like a natural fit.

On January 10, 1914, Ralph Hale, an editor with Small, Maynard, came to see Brandeis in Washington. Would the Boston lawyer be interested in putting together another collection of his published articles, this one to be published by Small, Maynard? Brandeis was indeed interested. He wrote to Alice Grady from the Hotel Gordon in Washington, where he was staying, asking that she get together his previously published articles and send them over to his wife. He wanted her to review the pieces and select the ones to be included in the new book. Speed was important. Congress was actively considering antitrust legislation and he wanted the book to come out as soon as possible.

Alice Grady moved with dispatch. She sent the articles over to Mrs. Brandeis and then contacted Ernest Poole, a writer who had published a long interview with Brandeis in 1911. The interview included extensive discussions of Brandeis's many achievements, and, if the article could be updated, it would provide a good introduction to the new book. The problem was Poole. He was very ill and did not have the energy to do the necessary research on Brandeis's latest exploits. Grady would not let that stand in the way. She contacted her boss's colleagues—Norman Hapgood, Joseph Eastman, Josephine Goldmark, and others—and asked them to prepare memos on Brandeis's most recent activities. She then sent the memos to Poole so that he could revise his article.

By the end of February 1914 Grady had worked everything out. The book would come out shortly under the title *Business—A Profession,* a choice based on the theme of Brandeis's 1912 commencement address at Brown. Grady's only concern now was Brandeis. Between his work as special counsel for the ICC on the 5 percent rate case and the work he was doing for the Wilson administration, he was feeling himself pulled in every direction. The strain was beginning to show. Although he continued to eat regularly and take long walks, he was approaching his fifty-eighth birthday and finding it more and more difficult to endure the tensions and long hours. Grady reported her observations to Joe Eastman, Brandeis's colleague at the Public Franchise League. The dedicated secretary told Eastman that she had arranged for Poole to send his article to Brandeis in Washington so that he could contribute "a finishing touch here and there if it is ... needed. That is, if he's living," she added. "When I saw him on Sunday, he looked so wretchedly far from well that I felt as if I wanted to chloroform the Interstate Commerce Commission and every member of the Cabinet and send L.D.B. South for the balance of the winter."[16]

Actually, Brandeis would not have agreed to his exclusion from ICC work. He was enjoying his role as special counsel in the 5 percent rate case, and, if anything, he would have much preferred to avoid the many demands that Wilson and his administration were placing on him. "The ICC matters are so interesting," he wrote to Al, "that I greatly begrudge the time which trust & kindred legislation are taking. . . . I long for the days of Ballinger isolation."[17]

He was now a victim of his own success. His credentials as a clear thinker and a tenacious fighter were well known. And as the president and Congress prepared to amend the Sherman Antitrust Act, there were few people who were needed more. At the end of January 1914, William C. Adamson, chairman of the House Committee on Interstate and Foreign Commerce, was at the White House and learned from Wilson that Brandeis was in Washington doing some work for the ICC. Adamson immediately wrote to ask him to testify the next day at some hearings his committee was holding on antitrust legislation.

Brandeis agreed. There was really no way he could avoid it. Nor was there any problem with the short notice from Adamson. Brandeis's thoughts on antitrust matters—especially after his collaboration with La Follette—were well developed. He was also abreast of developments in Congress. Ever since the autumn he had employed George Rublee, a colleague from the Ballinger case, to assist in the formulation of antitrust legislation. Rublee had left his law firm the preceding summer and approached Brandeis in Boston about the possibility of working with him on antitrust matters. Brandeis thought highly of Rublee and was delighted to have his assistance. Rublee stayed with the Brandeis family for a few weeks in the early autumn of 1913, spending many hours with Louis discussing legal points and legislative strategies. He then moved to Washington to apply his skills in the drafting of legislation and to keep Louis informed of any progress.

Ironically, Wilson did not share Brandeis's sense of urgency in developing new antitrust legislation. It was not only his failure to appreciate the problems of "bigness" that Brandeis saw. Wilson had also come to feel that big business could be harnessed without a frontal assault on its assets. After all, the business community had been most helpful in securing passage of the Federal Reserve Act. Would they not similarly support "reasonable" measures to eliminate anticompetitive practices?

Attorney General McReynolds, for one, shared this perspective, and he had every reason to believe that the president would remain firm in his opposition. As head of the government's antitrust program, he presumably had the greatest institutional stake in any amendments to the Sherman Act. He was opposed to any change, however, because he thought it was unnecessary. "I gain the impression more and more from week to week that the businessmen of the country are sincerely desirous of conforming with the law," Wilson wrote to him in December 1913, "and it is very gratifying indeed to be able to deal with them in complete frankness and to be able to show them that all we desire is an opportunity to cooperate with them."[18]

McReynolds was not at all happy with subsequent developments. Within a month of that letter the president stood before the Congress and recommended some fundamental changes in the law: prohibitions against interlocking directorates, elimination of price discrimination that would "substantially lessen competition," prohibition against "tying" arrangements where a company made it a condition of the sale of goods that the buyer agree not to buy from a competitor, and a provision that would enable a private party to use the findings in a government antitrust suit to prove that the private party had been damaged by anticompetitive conduct. The sweep of the proposals was broad, but Wilson shrewdly packaged it in a spirit of cooperation with business. "What we are purposing to do . . .," he told Congress and the nation, "is, happily, not to hamper or interfere with business as enlightened businessmen prefer to do it. . . . The antagonism between business and government is over. . . . The Government and businessmen are ready to meet each other half way in a common effort to square business methods with both public opinion and the law."[19]

It was an unusually warm, balmy day in Washington after Wilson delivered his recommendations to Congress, and Brandeis was happy to be able to take a long walk without his overcoat. But he was thinking about more than the weather. He had good reason to be pleased with the president's message. "He has paved the way for about all I have asked for," he wrote to Al, "& some of the provisions specifically are what I got into his mind at my first interview." He did, however, think that the president "overdid the Era of good feeling" with business. But Brandeis knew the game of politics, and he recognized that Wilson was trying to minimize business opposition to his proposals. "Doubtless the President is playing his game a little as well as they," he told Al, "& he is a fine player."[20]

A few weeks later Brandeis was given an opportunity to expound on his general theories in amending the antitrust laws. The occasion was an appearance before the House Judiciary Committee. The committee chairman, Henry Clayton, had introduced bills incorporating the president's proposals, and Clayton was using the hearings to refine those measures.

The principal problem, in Brandeis's view, was the failure of Congress to provide for the enforcement of the Sherman Act. All it did was state general principles. "We have not made the machinery, we have not been whole-hearted in the way we ought to have gone about it," he told the committee. "If we want the Sherman law, and apparently all of the people of the United States do want it, let us be honest with ourselves and make the machinery that will produce the results. If we do not want that thing, do not let us have the law at all." It was equally important, he said, to focus on the system rather than on the individual corporate official. "I think the improper things are far more largely the result than the cause—the result of our system," he observed. "I do not believe these men enter upon this proposition with the intention of wrongdoing other people; but they do."[21]

Of particular concern here was interlocking directorates. Brandeis spent considerable time wrangling with the committee about the details of the provision prohibiting such directorates. In his mind Clayton's proposal was too broad. It prohibited virtually all interlocking directorates regardless of the size of the company and regardless of the impact on competition. Brandeis thought that the provision should center on large banks. He could not get a fix on exactly how that would be defined, though. At first he suggested banks that had more than $2.5 million in resources, had $500,000 in capital, and were located in cities of more than 100,000 population. Later he changed his mind and suggested banks with more than $5 million in capital and resources. Ultimately the committee—and later Congress—accepted this latter definition. The prohibition against interlocking directorates was also revised to include other competing corporations with more than $1 million in capital, surplus, and profit.

In some respects Brandeis found it easier to talk with Congress than to deal with the administration. Despite the president's endorsement of strong antitrust legislation, McReynolds stubbornly refused to be cooperative. After frequent meetings with him, Brandeis complained to Alice that the attorney general was "very conservative" and "a great time waster" and that "he ought to be off in some vast wilderness."[22] Brandeis was not to be turned aside, though. He kept coming back to McReynolds, talking to him and seeking his help. In the end, virtually all of Wilson's antitrust proposals were adopted by Congress, and the Clayton Antitrust Act became law in October 1914. By then Brandeis had made another major contribution to help breathe life into the antitrust laws, one that involved the creation of a new governmental agency.

Congress created the Bureau of Corporations in 1903 to be a clearinghouse of information on business in America. The bureau had performed some useful studies, but it had no powers to remedy the problems it exposed. As public sentiment moved toward greater specificity in the antitrust laws, business clamored for some guidance as to what it could or could not do. In his message to Congress in January 1914, Wilson picked up on some earlier bills and proposed the establishment of a Federal Trade Commission to replace the Bureau of Corporations. The commission would investigate problems and cooperate with the Justice Department in the prosecution of antitrust violations.

Brandeis was the principal draftsman of the bill introduced in Congress to further Wilson's commission proposal. It was an idea that Brandeis fully supported. He had serious doubts that government regulation was the answer to any problem, but he saw much merit in the idea of an agency that would collect and analyze information to determine whether there were antitrust violations. Antitrust matters were often so complex that a concentrated government effort was often necessary. And, of course, ever since the Supreme Court had announced its "rule of reason" test in the 1911 *Standard Oil* case, Brandeis was convinced of the need for a specific catalogue of anticompetitive activities that could be the focus of the new agency's agenda.

As the Brandeis proposal moved toward adoption in the House of Representatives, it encountered opposition from an unexpected quarter. George Rublee did not like it. Rublee, a seasoned lawyer with considerable Washington experience, thought Brandeis's bill was too narrow and would ultimately prove inadequate. George never bothered to explain these doubts to his friend. Louis was too busy with ICC and other matters, and George himself was apparently too sensitive to challenge his friend—at least at that point. Instead, Rublee went to a friend of his, Congressman Ray Stevens of New Hampshire. Together they drafted a substitute bill. It proposed to have five trade commissioners instead of the three proposed by Brandeis; it proposed to expand the commission's power so that it could prosecute complaints on its own initiative without waiting on the Justice Department; and it proposed to eliminate the specific catalogue of abuses and instead generally prohibit "unfair methods of competition."

This last change, in Rublee's view, was critical. The circumstances of business conditions were too dynamic and the facts of specific controversies too varied to compile a meaningful list of abuses. Who could say what would be anticompetitive five, ten, or twenty years from now? He therefore decided to use a phrase that some courts had employed in antitrust cases under the Sherman law. It lacked the specificity that many thought so helpful; but the general phrase would state the purpose of the law and give the commission the flexibility to deal with unanticipated facts and circumstances. After all, if the commission was to be a responsible body, some trust had to be placed in its discretion.

Stevens introduced the new bill, but it received virtually no support in the House committee. Brandeis's bill, in contrast, seeemed destined for passage. Rublee realized that administration support was critical, and he could think of no one more important on that score than the attorney general. McReynolds offered no encouragement. "Why, my dear man," he told Rublee, "this is all settled. Everything is decided about this. There is nothing you can do about it. Why don't you give this up?" As on other occasions, however, McReynolds underestimated the flexibility—and influence—of Brandeis.

Rublee was completely disheartened after his talk with McReynolds. There seemed no hope for his proposal. His wife felt differently. Why had he not discussed the matter with his friend Louis? And what about the president—didn't he have the final word on administration policy?

Rublee was willling to give it one more try. He contacted Stevens and an appointment was made with the president at the White House for May 21, 1914. Rublee told Brandeis of the meeting and asked if he would attend. Louis said that he would go, but he stipulated that he would not commit himself to anything.

Rublee, Stevens, and Brandeis arrived at the appointed hour and were ushered out to the garden on the South Lawn of the White House. It was a beautiful spring day. The president, dressed impeccably, came out to greet them. Stevens briefly explained the background of his proposal and then turned the floor over to Rublee. The young attorney argued vigorously for his proposal. Suddenly

Brandeis broke in and explained why Rublee's idea represented an improvement over the administration's bill. He was clear, logical, and persuasive. Wilson listened intently. In due course he agreed that Rublee's approach was indeed better. As the three guests left the White House, Brandeis was exhilarated. "That's the most remarkable interview that I've ever been present at," he told Rublee. "I've never seen anything like this before." The turnaround in Congress was equally dramatic. By September 1914 Rublee's vision of the Federal Trade Commission was a reality.[23]

McReynolds got his revenge. Six years later he and Brandeis were sitting on the United States Supreme Court when the justices were asked to decide a case involving the scope of the FTC's powers. In one of its first cases, the commission issued a complaint against one Benjamin Gratz and his partners for engaging in "unfair methods of competition." It seemed that Gratz and his partners were agents for the Carnegie Steel Company in the sale of steel ties to bag cotton. The problem, according to the FTC, was that Gratz sometimes would not sell the ties unless the customer also purchased the bagging material from his company. Because Gratz had a substantial part of the cotton tie market, and since "tying" arrangements were among the abuses cited by Brandeis and others in drafting the FTC Act, the commission held hearings and issued an order prohibiting further use of Gratz's tying arrangement.

Gratz and his partners appealed to the courts and wound up with more than they bargained for. McReynolds saw his chance to limit the FTC's power, and he took advantage of it. Writing for a majority of the Court, he held that the FTC had had no right to issue the complaint against Gratz in the first place—a point that no one, not even Gratz, had argued. "The words 'unfair method of competition' are not defined by statute," McReynolds observed, "and their exact meaning is in dispute." He then proceeded to strip the commission of the discretion that Rublee had envisioned for the agency in deciding what those words meant. "It is for the courts," McReynolds said, "not the commission, ultimately to determine as a matter of law what they include." And in the Court's view, the complaint failed to cite facts to show that Gratz's tying arrangement, even if true, was anticompetitive.[24]

Brandeis dissented. In a lengthy opinion he pointed out that the FTC was modeled after the ICC and that the commerce agency was not required to cite facts in its complaints. Indeed, that's what hearings were for—to find the facts. Moreover, said Brandeis, it was intended that the FTC—not the courts—would determine what was an unfair method of competition. Recalling Rublee's analysis, the Justice asserted that "an enumeration, however comprehensive, of existing methods of unfair competition must necessarily soon prove incomplete, as with new conditions constantly arising novel unfair methods would be devised and developed."[25] The courts' basic role was to decide whether the evidence supported the FTC's conclusion, and in the case of Gratz, he stated, there could be no doubt about that.

Despite his defense of the FTC's powers, Brandeis was disappointed with the agency's performance. In April 1915 the members of the new commission made the unusual gesture of asking him to attend a meeting and advise them on the nature of their role. For all this deference to Brandeis, the commission was anything but an aggressive defender of the public interest. Most of Wilson's first appointments went to men from the business world who were all too eager to accommodate their former associates. Years later Brandeis called the FTC a "stupid administration" and specifically blamed the president's appointments.[26]

Susan and Elizabeth were growing up. Like many of the women in her mother's family, Susan went to Bryn Mawr College in Pennsylvania and then, eager to emulate her famous father, to the law school at the University of Chicago. Elizabeth took a different course. She did not want to go to Bryn Mawr. Her sister would still be there, and she was tired of the competition. So she went to Radcliffe College in Cambridge, Massachusetts. Also in contrast to her sister, she did not want to become a lawyer. As time went on she became more and more interested in economics, an interest that eventually took her to a teaching position at the University of Wisconsin in Madison.

Despite their divergent paths, the girls remained close to their parents. It was getting difficult, however, to keep up with their father. He was always busy, always on the go, and often away from Boston. It was getting rare for him to spend more than a couple of weeks in the city in one stretch. But then he was doing important things. People all over the country—but especially in Washington—were clamoring for his time and help.

Brandeis could not always guarantee success to those who needed him—although he wished he could in the case of resale price maintenance. This issue concerned a manufacturer's right to determine the price at which his product would be sold. Large department stores often disregarded a producer's wishes and discounted items. This troubled Brandeis. Manufacturers rightfully became concerned because the discount might imply to the consumer that the product was not of a high quality. Brandeis thought that small retail operations would also suffer because they often could not offer the same discounts found in larger stores.

The Supreme Court did not share Brandeis's perspective. In 1911 it ruled that a manufacturer of a trademark item could not dictate the resale price.[27] This decision did not cause Brandeis to reassess his position. "It seems to me," he told one inquiring reporter, "that . . . the case was due to a [judicial] failure to understand the trade facts. . . . The suppression of this system of price maintenance of individual trademarked articles must result to a large extent in the substitution of capitalistic chains or stores, mail order houses, or actual monopolistic concerns for the numerous independent manufacturers and dealers."[28]

By June 1913, Brandeis had prepared an article on the subject. He gave the piece to Norman Hapgood and it was published in *Harper's* in November under the title "Cut-Throat Prices." In Brandeis's view, a manufacturer should be able to negotiate a contract with a retailer that would establish the resale price of a trademark item—that is, an article sold individually and clearly identified with the producer. According to Brandeis, "abundant experience establishes that the one-price system . . . has . . . greatly increased the efficiency of merchandising, not only for the producer, but for the dealer and the consumer as well."[29]

Substantial costs would ensue, Brandeis claimed, unless the manufacturer could fix the prices of his products. Large stores would advertise specific items—"leaders"—at a substantial discount. The discount would not only undercut the reputation of the particular item; it would also mislead consumers into believing that other items in the store were similarly discounted.

In Brandeis's view, the price fixing he advocated was not anticompetitive. "The independent producer is engaged in a business open to competition," he observed. "He establishes his price at his peril—the peril that, if he sets it too high, either the consumer will not buy, or, if the article is nevertheless popular, the high profits will invite more competition." This was the American way. Any other course would perpetuate monopolies. "Americans should be under no illusions as to the value or effect of price-cutting," Brandeis concluded. "It has been the most potent weapon of monopoly—a means of killing the small rival. . . ."[30]

The most remarkable feature of Brandeis's article was the total absence of facts. Not one statistic or example was cited to indicate that his views rested on experience. For a man who prided himself on an intimate knowledge of the record before reaching conclusions, it was especially surprising. Brandeis was not oblivious to the problem here. Long before the article was published, he pestered William Ingersol, a member of the Fair Trade League, for data concerning the need for resale price maintenance. The efforts were not very productive. But no matter. Brandeis knew the causes and effects of bigness. He no longer needed facts.

Brandeis and Rublee persuaded Congressman Stevens to introduce a bill on resale price maintenance. In essence, the measure would have reversed the Supreme Court decision and allowed producers to determine the prices at which their items would be sold. When the bill was considered at hearings, Brandeis was the most prominent witness.[31]

The Stevens bill did not pass, but Brandeis did not give up hope. Patience was the key. The issue would come up again, and he would renew his efforts. He did not have long to wait.

In 1921 Brandeis and the rest of his colleagues on the Supreme Court were asked to decide a case involving the American Hardwood Manufacturers Association. The business of producing hardwood was an extremely competitive one. Fluctuations in prices were frequent and dramatic. Many companies prospered with excessive profits; others found the going tough, and some did not survive the market test. Several hundred manufacturers—who collectively controlled about 30 percent of the market—decided to form an association to exchange information and stabilize competition. Of primary significance was a competitor's prices. By providing access to those data, the association hoped to develop a certain "uniformity" in prices and other trade practices. "There is no agreement to follow the practice of others," the association's manual explained, "although members do naturally follow their most intelligent competitors. . . ."[32]

By any reasonable account the association had indeed restricted "free" competition. The Department of Justice concluded that the association was a conspiracy to restrain trade unreasonably, and a lawsuit was filed alleging that the group had violated the Sherman Antitrust Law.

Justice Brandeis thought that the Justice Department had made a mistake. Some restrictions on competition were inevitable if small firms were to survive. He prepared a short memorandum for his colleagues. "The evidence in this case," he observed, "far from establishing an illegal restraint of trade, presents, in my opinion, an instance of commendable effort by concerns engaged in a chaotic industry to make possible the intelligent conduct of it." To be sure, the association's plan might mean higher prices for the consumer and larger profits for the hardwood producers. But other, more important questions were at stake. The association's plan promoted "true competition. For by distributing knowledge of trade facts to all, the plan tends to create for rival producers—and for buyers as well as sellers—equality of opportunity." Brandeis then invoked the same arguments he had advanced in support of the Stevens bill. "Low prices," he said, "may restrain trade. Ignorant price-cutting has been one of the most potent causes leading to the development of trusts; . . . [and] their most effective instruments."[33]

No facts or statistics were cited to support that last conclusion. Additional facts probably would not have helped Brandeis anyway. Most of the justices thought the case fairly simple. The association wanted to establish uniform prices and trade practices, and to that end it was rather successful. How could anyone doubt that such a plan restrained trade? The Court majority supported the Department of Justice. Brandeis dissented.

But Brandeis would not remain disappointed. Within a few years a change in the Court membership led to a softening of its position on the issue. And by the mid-1930s additional pressures emerged in support of a resale price maintenance bill. In 1937 the goal was achieved with the adoption of the Miller–Tydings Act. Many years later, though, people began to question the utility of the new law. It seemed to do little for the consumer or the competitive ideal. It was repealed in 1975.[34]

The face of America was changing, and Brandeis did not entirely like it. People were becoming too concerned with material things and high living. "You see men on small salaries," he told an interviewer in 1912, "dining in fashionable cafés side by side with men who do not have to give a thought to the money they are spending. Yet the little struggling clerk must bedeck his wife with bizarre clothes so that he can take her out and impress upon those who behold her in all her magnificence that he is making big money, that this excursion is nothing out of the ordinary in his life, and that he is a 'big spender.' " It was not only morally offensive to him; Brandeis considered it disruptive to stable family life. "That's the rock on which domesticity often founders," he concluded.[35]

Brandeis was not opposed to all social change, however. He had once vigorously opposed the right of women to vote; but by the second decade of the twentieth century he was supporting it just as vigorously. His experience with Bess Evans and other women convinced him that, in matters of political judgment, they were equal to men. He was also beginning to appreciate the importance of diverse cultures in America. It was so important to him, in fact, that he decided to stress the significance of cultural diversity in the speech he was to give at Faneuil Hall in Boston on July 4, 1915.

The July 4th oration at Faneuil Hall was a local tradition. The original building had been donated to the city in 1742 by Peter Faneuil, who had directed that it be used for public meetings to discuss community affairs. The people took advantage of the gift, and Faneuil Hall became a popular and frequently used forum for meetings and speakers of all kinds. Few events, however, were as important as the July 4th oration. Each year a prominent figure was selected, and the speech was usually well attended.

In 1915 the speech was to be given on July 5th since July 4th fell on a Sunday. At 9:45 in the morning a mayoral aide picked up Alice and Louis Brandeis at their Dedham home. The trip back to Faneuil Hall was considerably delayed when the car experienced a tire puncture in the driving rain. The packed crowd at the Hall waited patiently. When Brandeis finally walked to the speaker's rostrum they gave no sign of displeasure at the delay. They stood and cheered for several minutes, giving the Boston attorney the kind of rousing welcome that most leaders seek but rarely find.

The topic of his address was "true Americanism." The country was now flooded with immigrants from Europe and other foreign lands. It was vital that they become "Americanized," Brandeis said. "To become Americanized," he explained, "the change wrought must be fundamental. However great his outward conformity, the immigrant is not Americanized unless his interests and affections have become deeply rooted here." To that end the immigrant must learn to share the American ideals—the foremost of which was "the development of the individual for his own and the common good." They must therefore work for an America in which there was industrial liberty, fair wages, and leisure "to work at something besides breadwinning."

Although conformity to these ideals was vital to America, Brandeis did not want them imposed on the peoples of other countries. "The new nationalism adopted by America," he said, "proclaims that each race or people, like each individual, has the right and duty to develop, and that only through such differentiated development will high civilization be attained."[36] He did not specifically mention the development of a Jewish homeland in Palestine. It could not have been far from his mind, though. In the summer of 1915 it was his major preoccupation.

FIFTEEN

The Emergence of a Zionist Leader

The secret of success is consistency of purpose.

BENJAMIN DISRAELI

Leo Frank learned about anti-Semitism the hard way—and he paid dearly for his knowledge. On April 26, 1913, Mary Phagan's body was found in a pencil plant in Atlanta, Georgia, clearly the victim of foul play. People said—wrongly—that Frank, a factory superintendent in the plant, had been the last one to see Mary alive and that he was guilty of murder. For some people, though, it was not enough to merely arrest Frank. He was Jewish, and that did not go over well with people in Atlanta. The crowds outside the courthouse kept chanting "Hang the Jew," and the defense counsel forgot to pay attention to what was going on inside the courthouse. Frank was convicted and sentenced to death. The governor, however, recognized the gross irregularities in the trial and commuted Frank's sentence to life. Unfortunately, there was a "higher authority" than the governor. On August 16, 1915, an angry mob snatched Frank from the prison hospital (where he was recuperating from an attack by another prisoner) and lynched him.

Frank's murder created a sensation throughout the country. Lynching blacks was almost commonplace in the South, but Frank was white and the member of a religion whose members controlled newspapers and occupied important positions in business circles. The Anti-Defamation League of the B'nai Brith was organized, and citizens of all religions expressed concern about mob rule.

The Frank case was indeed a national tragedy. But it was almost nothing compared with the experiences of Jews in foreign lands, especially Russia. Jews there were often herded into ghettos on the poor side of town, restricted as to what schools their children could attend, limited in the jobs they could hold, and, perhaps worst of all, subjected to periodic attacks by mobs that often included the government's own soldiers and police. These pogroms kept most Jews in a constant state of terror. Things reached a new peak in 1903 when a Gentile youth was murdered near the Russian town of Kishineff. Although it later turned out that the murderer was a relative, rumors quickly spread that the culprits were Jews who needed Christian blood for their Passover services in the spring. Newspapers fanned the flames of prejudice, anti-Semitic organizations were formed, and in April 1903 pogroms erupted in Kishineff and spread across Russia. After three days of rioting, at least forty-seven Jews were dead, hundreds more injured, and thousands made homeless.

Jews in America wanted to help their brethren across the ocean. They formed a relief committee and presented petitions of protest to President Theodore Roosevelt. They also decided to establish a permanent organization dedicated to the protection of the Jewish people's civil rights, and in 1906 the American Jewish Committee, supported by the country's most prominent Jews, came into being.

Louis Brandeis was not touched by this experience. Although he was Jewish by birth, he had had little contact with organized religion. His mother's family had belonged to a mystical sect in Europe that believed the Messiah's coming was imminent and that observation of dietary laws and traditional services were unnecessary for the spiritually pure. As a little girl Frederika Dembitz enjoyed the pleasures of a Christmas tree, and she continued the practice when she and her family celebrated Christmas in America.

Although both Frederika and Adolph Brandeis continued to believe in God, they had little use for the strictures and discipline of organized religion. "I do not believe that sins can be expiated by going to divine service and observing this or that formula," Frederika once explained to Louis; "I believe that only goodness and truth and conduct that is humane and self-sacrificing towards those who need us can bring God nearer to us, and that our errors can only be atoned for by our acting in a more kindly spirit. Love, virtue and truth are the foundation upon which the education of the child must be based. They endure forever."[1]

Louis was a reflection of his mother's teachings. Initially he believed in God. But he also had little contact with the traditions of the Jewish religion. He did not attend temple services, did not have a bar mitzvah as induction into manhood at the age of thirteen, and had little exposure to the rituals that often bind a culture.

Few of his attitudes changed when he was a lawyer in Boston. People often suspected him of being "oriental"—the prevalent code word for Jewish—and he would readily admit to his religious heritage if the situation called for it. And while Alice joined the Unitarian Church, he remained uninterested in formal religious exercises. He was not completely indifferent to the problems of the Jewish people, however. Many of his first clients were Jewish, and he was a charter member of the Federation of Jewish Charities in Boston, an amalgamation of charitable organizations. (In fact, at one point he offered a $175 donation to the Federation in exchange for a promise "of not being called upon to pass upon all requests which would naturally come in from the numerous organizations, most of which are no doubt very deserving."[2])

Brandeis's sensitivity to religion increased dramatically during his battles with Charles Mellen and the New Haven railroad. People were not content to dissect the crusading attorney's arguments. They resorted to personal attacks of the vilest kind. Brandeis was hurt by that, especially when they criticized him for being Jewish.

Another experience had alerted Brandeis to the ties that bind Jews everywhere. During the New York garment strike in 1910, he saw Jewish workers and Jewish employers—economic adversaries—treat each other with uncommon respect. And he could not forget how comfortable *he* had felt on those hot August evenings drinking beer and talking with the Jewish men after a day of negotiations. It was something to think about.

Prior to 1910 Brandeis had made only one public reference to Jews and Judaism. The occasion was a speech on November 28, 1905, before the Century Club, a local Jewish group, to commemorate the 250th anniversary of the Jews' landing in America. His focus was not on the struggles that Jews had faced in foreign lands, struggles that had led them to their new country. Instead, he concentrated on the duties that American citizenship involved. The first and most important need was to discard all distinction of race and religion, for people to become assimilated completely into their new environment. "This country demands," he said, "that its sons and daughters whatever their race—however intense or diverse their religious connections—be politically merely American citizens. Habits of living or of thought which tend to keep alive difference of origin or to classify men according to their religious beliefs are inconsistent with the American ideal of brotherhood, and are disloyal." Citizenship also required active participation in government. "Of him who has most in ability and intelligence," Brandeis asserted, "most is required, as the rich should contribute most in money to the expense of government."

Brandeis had no doubt that Jews could satisfy these demands. "Through energy, perseverance, self-restraint, and devotion," he said, ". . . men of Jewish blood have, wherever opportunity permitted, taken rank among the foremost in almost every branch of human activity." Their greatest achievements, though, were in spiritual matters. " 'To the Hebrews,' " he said, quoting a noted scholar, " 'it was committed to proclaim to mankind the One and Supreme God—to keep alive His pure worship, to assert the inexorable moral law in a corrupt and heathen world.' "[3]

The reference to God was unusual for Brandeis. While he would give literally hundreds of speeches on Jewish affairs in the years to come, it would be extremely rare for him to even mention supernatural forces. The absence of divine references was not at all coincidental. "I do not understand what you mean by experiencing God's presence," he told a visitor in later years. "I have faced many trials, had to make grave decisions, tasted of the sweet and bitter, was depressed and elated, worked and studied, and thought and meditated. I have lived through many a moment in which, according to the faithful, God should have spoken and helped." But he found no evidence of divine intervention. "I sensed no power outside of myself working along with me," he commented. "Nor would I describe what was going on in me as supernatural, irrational, or mysterious. I believe that I was reasoning through by concentrating and recalling what good men had said and done before me."[4]

Brandeis also had little use for resurrection or any mystical belief in a life after death. "I know how we love our precious little body," he once observed, "how much attention some bestow on it, and how loath we are to part from it, if part we do. I am not unacquainted with the weakness of man and his conceitedness," he continued, "and I can understand that in the infancy of the race he was impelled to mistake death for a long sleep. But that human beings should be under the illusion to this day attests [to] both the deep darkness in the human mind and the failure of education and science."[5] He was not, to say the least, enamored of organized religion.

Other Jews took note of Brandeis's distance from religious circles. When Woodrow Wilson was considering him for a Cabinet post in early 1913, he asked Max Mitchell, a local banker, to find out whether the Jewish community would favor the Brandeis appointment. The response was not enthusiastic. "I have been asked from time to time recently whether Mr. Brandeis may be considered a representative Jew," financier Jacob Schiff told Mitchell, "and to this I was able to give a qualified reply only, but he is, without doubt, a representative American."[6] It was a courteous but clear rebuff to Brandeis, and it was one that Mitchell heard frequently when he posed the question to other Jewish leaders.

There was a certain irony in this lack of support from the Jewish community. For Brandeis was already becoming deeply involved in Jewish affairs, and, within two years of Schiff's comment, he would be considered one of the most respected Jewish leaders in the world.

Jacob deHaas needed an idol. It was probably a matter of personality. He never seemed to belong, and he required the anchor of a leader to keep him afloat in society. He had been born to Dutch Sephardic Jews in 1872, and as he entered adulthood, he found himself on the outside looking in. As a member of London's Fabian Society, for example, he spent most of his Sundays heckling the speakers who frequented London's Hyde Park.

Things changed quickly for Jack deHaas after he encountered Theodore Herzl, who was twelve years his senior. Herzl was a Hungarian Jew who had a dream that had come to him after he witnessed the anti-Semitism in the trial of the French captain Alfred Dreyfus. In 1896 Herzl explained his dream in a book called *The Jewish State*. As the title implied, Herzl argued that the Jewish people needed a nation they could call their own. Without it, there was no hope for them.

Although others had expressed similar ideas before, Herzl's book created a sensation. It fired the imagination of Jews eager to escape persecution in foreign lands. And more than that, Herzl was a magnetic figure who seemed almost capable of performing miracles. In his hands the dream of a Jewish nation might very well become a reality.

Herzl's book did not specify a particular location for this Jewish state, but most people assumed it would be in Palestine, the land of Zion, the birthplace of Jewish heritage. One thing was clear, however. Despite his personal magnetism, Herzl could not create a nation by himself. He needed help. So in 1897 he called a meeting of interested Jews to discuss the particulars. At the end of August more than 200 men and women convened a meeting in Basle, Switzerland, and the Zionist movement took its first faltering steps toward the creation of a Jewish homeland.

From the beginning, deHaas was attracted to Herzl and became his secretary. The problem was Jack's personality. Many of Herzl's colleagues found the young Dutch Jew abrasive. Partly for this reason, and partly because the Federation of American Zionists needed assistance, Herzl sent deHaas to the United States in 1901, where he soon became the chief administrative officer of the American organization.

Things fell apart when Herzl died of heart failure in 1904. Without his direction the Zionist movement became stalled, and deHaas felt obliged to move on to other activities. In time he became an editor of the *Jewish Advocate,* a Boston periodical that covered civic affairs of primary interest to the Jewish community. It was in this capacity that deHaas met his new idol.

It happened in December 1910 when he went to interview Brandeis about savings bank life insurance. Toward the end of a rather dry discussion, deHaas asked Brandeis what he thought of Zionism. "I have a great deal of sympathy for the movement and am deeply interested in the outcome of the propaganda," the attorney replied. "These so-called dreamers are entitled to the respect and appreciation of the entire Jewish people." But he had little personal interest in the development of a Jewish homeland in some foreign place. "I believe that the opportunities for members of my race are greater here than in any other country," he observed.[7]

Then deHaas referred to Lewis Dembitz as "a noble Jew." At first there was no reaction, but when deHaas repeated the observation, Brandeis asked for an explanation. After all, until his death in 1907, Uncle Lewis had been an important figure in his life. He had always admired him, had even changed his middle name because of that admiration. And he knew that Uncle Lewis, in contrast to his mother, followed the traditions of the Jewish religion. He could remember the joy and awe with which Uncle Lewis welcomed the Sabbath and how he seemed so pious in his observation of religious rituals. No doubt deHaas's comment triggered these warm memories in Brandeis's mind.

The *Advocate*'s editor proceeded to speak of Lewis Dembitz's considerable talents and many achievements in helping to establish the Zionist organization in America. It piqued Brandeis's curiosity. He wanted to know more about this cause to which his uncle had been so devoted. Over the course of the next few months deHaas spent many hours with Brandeis, telling him the story of Herzl and his dedicated efforts to find a homeland for the Jewish people.

In time Zionism took on a new dimension for Brandeis. He saw it as an extension of the goals for which he had been fighting in his earlier reform activities. With a new country, the individual Jew could shape his own environment in a small community and find a satisfaction that was becoming more and more difficult to find in the United States. By February 1911 he was committed to the cause. "My sympathy with the Zionist movement," he told one Jewish journalist at the time, "rests primarily upon the noble idealism which underlies it, and the conviction that a great people, stirred by enthusiasm for such an ideal, must bear an important part in the betterment of the world."[8]

It was an emotional as well as an intellectual commitment for Brandeis. And he would never forget that deHaas had been the one to introduce him to Zionism. He would refer to his bearded companion as "my teacher," would rely on him with increasing frequency as the commitment to Zionism expanded, and would defend him when colleagues criticized deHaas for being dictatorial and disagreeable. Even in deHaas's last years, when he had managed to offend almost everyone of influence in the Zionist organization, Brandeis—then a member of the United States Supreme Court—repeatedly urged friends in the movement to find some place, any place, for Jack.

Whatever his personal faults, deHaas made a singular contribution to the Zionist cause when he enlisted Brandeis's services. The "people's attorney" was a national figure, one who moved easily in high government circles in Boston and Washington. His name could give the Zionist cause a legitimacy and respectability it had never attained in the United States. It was not only that the American organization lacked leadership; that was perhaps the least of it. The principal problem was that many American Jews—especially German Jews who had acquired established positions in business and other professions—were against Zionism. Throughout history, world leaders had constantly wondered whether Jews—separated from their Biblical heritage in Palestine—could be true citizens in a foreign country. Napoleon, for instance, was reported to have asked France's chief rabbi in 1807 whether the Jews, once emancipated, would be "unreservedly loyal to the state."[9]

The same questions were asked in America. Jews trying to assimilate were often in fear that their loyalty was being questioned. For these people—particularly those who found American life rewarding—there could be nothing worse than to join a cause interested in developing a Jewish homeland somewhere else. Jacob Schiff commented that Zionist membership "places a lien upon citizenship" and would create "a separateness which is fatal." Louis Marshall, a prominent lawyer and leader of the American Jewish Committee, considered Zionism impractical and a blot on the Jewish community's desire to be an accepted part of America. Adolph Ochs, the publisher of the *New York Times,* held similar views and directed that his paper should give no support and little space to Zionism. Even rabbis opposed the cause. Rabbi Isaac Mayer Wise, a member of the Central Conference of American Rabbis, referred to Zionism as "that crazy scheme" and urged others to reject "that new messianic movement over the ocean."[10]

None of this deterred Brandeis's interest and immersion in Zionism. He was not at all concerned about his place in society. He was secure about that. Zionism offered something special, something exciting, and he wanted to be part of it. People talked about building a new life in Palestine, one they could control, and that was worthy of his efforts. Even the seemingly small accomplishments exhilarated him. When Aaron Aaronsohn, a Jewish pioneer, described a new wheat that he had developed, one that would prosper in Palestine's arid climate, Brandeis wrote to his brother that the exposition "was the most thrillingly interesting I have ever heard. . . ."[11] And when Aaronsohn explained that there was virtually no crime among the Jewish settlements in Palestine, Brandeis saw in it a lesson of universal application to Jews everywhere. "[T]he ages of sacrifice have left us with the sense of brotherhood," he told a meeting of a local Young Men's Hebrew Association in May 1913. "That brotherhood has given us the feeling of solidarity which makes each one of us press forward with loyalty to fulfill the obligations of the brotherhood; for we know, by the many sacrifices of our people, that the traditions of the race, the traditions that are sacred to the race, depend for their life upon the conduct of every single one of us."[12]

The outbreak of war in Europe in the summer of 1914 raised new problems for Zionism. Up to that point the world Zionist headquarters had been in Berlin. Coordination with other Zionist offices now became difficult and in some cases impossible. Communications were limited or cut off completely. The future looked bleak. It would be unwise to expect much organizational or financial support from capitals more concerned with survival than with the fulfillment of Herzl's dream. A new Zionist headquarters was needed. America—which was still neutral and would remain officially out of the war until 1917—was the most logical place.

Ironically, Shmaryahu Levin, a member of the Actions Comité—the Zionist executive council—found himself stranded in America when the European hostilities erupted. He recognized the problem of his organization, and he decided to do something about it. He called for an emergency meeting of Zionist representatives at the Hotel Marseilles in New York City, and deHaas asked Brandeis if he could nominate him to chair the new Zionist committee that would be formed. To his delight, deHaas received an affirmative response.

The rest was easy. The 150 delegates at the meeting recognized the value of a leader with national stature. On August 30, 1914, Brandeis was elected chairman of the newly created Provisional Emergency Committee, an organization that was to assume the central authority previously exercised from Berlin. In accepting the assignment, Brandeis was candid about his road to Zionism. "I feel my disqualification for this task," he told the assembled delegates. "Throughout long years which represent my own life, I have been to a great extent separated from Jews. I am very ignorant in things Jewish. But," he added, "recent experiences, public and professional, have taught me this: I find Jews possessed of those very qualities which we of the twentieth century seek to develop in our struggle for justice and democracy; a deep moral feeling which makes them capable of noble acts; a deep sense of the brotherhood of man; and a high intelligence, the fruit of three thousand years of civilization."[13]

The delegates no doubt congratulated themselves on the wisdom of their choice for chairman. But it did not take long for them to discover that they had acquired a lot more than they had bargained for. Most of the delegates expected Brandeis to play a largely ceremonial role. After all, he was busy advising the president and the Congress about antitrust matters and other national issues. He would certainly have no time for the details of running a world Zionist organization.

The delegates underestimated their new chairman. He called a business meeting for the day after his election to review the entire situation. What really surprised the other committee members was that he meant it. He took off his jacket, loosened his tie, tousled his hair, and sat quietly while others described the organization's past structure and present needs. Occasionally he would interject a question or two, and at times he would lightly tap the table with a pencil, but for the most part he just listened. Few could believe this demonstration of patience and determination.

It was not to be an unusual occurrence. Brandeis assumed the reins of leadership with a vigor and decisiveness that left many speechless. Not that his help was unwelcome. Zionism was in bad shape. There were only about 12,000 members of the Federation of American Zionists, a budget of only a few thousand dollars, and no direction.

Brandeis changed all that. He explained that the first priorities of the Provisional Executive Committee were to increase the membership rolls and the organization's operating funds. Their brethren in Europe and elsewhere needed help, and they could not provide it unless the organization were strengthened. To move things along, Brandeis began to make frequent trips to New York City, where the PEC's offices were located. There he would hold continual meetings, probing, questioning, and deciding. But meetings were not enough. He wanted written reports from everyone on a regular basis—weekly in some cases but always at least monthly. He wanted to centralize control of the organization, and he needed to keep in close touch with its activities.

He supplemented this oversight with letters and speeches to people all over the country. People appointed to committees received short notes from the chairman urging action; people offering assistance received requests for funds and new members; and people who failed to perform their tasks expeditiously received pointed inquiries about the delay. Similar energies were devoted to the scheduling and preparation of speeches. The chairman emphasized that his appearances were to be made in small halls to increase the appearance of an "overflowing" audience.

Of all the Zionist speeches made by Brandeis, few were as important or as widely distributed as his address to the Eastern Council of the Central Conference of Reform Rabbis in June 1915 entitled "The Jewish Problem and How to Solve It." The problem, of course, was anti-Semitism and the Jews' inability to enjoy the same rights accorded to others. The development of Palestine would be a partial answer to the problem. "The Zionist Movement is idealistic," he observed, "but it is also essentially practical. It seeks to realize that hope; to make the dream of a Jewish life in a Jewish land come true as other great dreams of the world have been realized—by men working with devotion, intelligence, and self-sacrifice." At the same time, he recognized that Palestine could not accommodate all the world's Jews and, moreover, that not all of them would want to go there anyway. But now he saw no inconsistency between Zionism and loyalty to the United States. "Indeed," he said, "loyalty to America demands rather that each Jew become a Zionist. For only through the ennobling effect of its strivings can we develop the best that is in us and give to this country the full benefit of our great inheritance." Mere membership in the organization would not be enough, however. Brandeis exhorted his audience: "Organize, Organize, Organize—until every Jew in America must stand up and be counted—counted with us—or prove himself, wittingly or unwittingly, of the few who are against their own people."[14]

The speech, an articulate exposition of the Jewish community's problems and hopes for the future, received ample coverage in the press. But not everyone agreed with the analysis. One Jewish paper was especially outraged. "No one will deny . . . that Mr. Brandeis is entitled to his opinion that Zionism is the panacea for all Israel's ills," the *American Israelite* commented. "But when he says that all those who do not agree with him 'are against their own people,' he is guilty of uttering that which is not true and of being grossly impertinent at the same time. Who is Mr. Brandeis to judge his brethren?"[15]

Brandeis could not have been surprised by this kind of criticism. He knew that many elements of the Jewish community opposed his views. In fact, as he was speaking on how to solve the Jewish problem, his conflict with the American Jewish Committee was reaching a critical stage.

As Al approached and passed his sixtieth birthday, he was not in the best of health. He tired easily and his weight kept dropping—at one point going to as low as 124 pounds. Louis was concerned. No one, except Alice and his daughters, was more important to him than his brother. Advice was freely given from Boston, including an admonition to see a doctor frequently. "Man ought at least to treat himself as well as a machine," Louis remarked.[16]

In the meantime Louis kept Al abreast of his numerous trips and speeches "Zionizing." Al was impressed with his brother's energies and devotions. He was moved when he heard his brother speak about the plight of Jews. And he would even help Louis raise money for Zionism in Louisville. But Al really had no interest in the cause. He had no first hand experience with the "Jewish problem." He had married a Gentile, and while he belonged to the Jewish country club as well as the Gentile country club in Louisville, few of his friends and business associates were Jewish. He was an accepted and respected member of local society. So he saw no need to develop Palestine, and he could not see how the establishment of small communities there would be the answer to problems in America or anywhere else.

Members of the American Jewish Committee shared Al's sentiments. Since many of them were successful and established figures in American society, they had little enthusiasm for the development of Palestine. They were, however, concerned about Jews in Europe and Russia who faced the ravages of war. So when Brandeis asked for the AJC's cooperation in planning a conference of "representative" Jewish organizations to discuss measures to help their brethren overseas, Louis Marshall, the AJC president, was initially responsive. At the time he had little idea that that "conference" would prove to be a divisive force among Jewish groups.

In part, the tension reflected a certain annoyance on the part of the AJC leaders that the new PEC had seized the initiative from the more established group. Another and more critical factor was the difference in the membership of the two organizations. The Provisional Executive Committee was supported primarily by Jewish immigrants from Eastern Europe, people with deep emotional ties to Judaism and the Land of their Fathers in Palestine. Few of these people had attained the stature enjoyed by AJC's members. And they knew that the AJC had a certain disdain for them, fearful that their emotionalism and ties to Zionism would breed anti-Semitism and make life difficult for assimilated Jews.

When Brandeis suggested a conference, the AJC therefore thought it best to select representatives of "appropriate" Jewish organizations and hold a meeting with a set agenda. Elements in the PEC convinced Brandeis that this was the wrong approach. Better, they said, to have an open meeting at which delegates could be selected and the agenda established by popular vote. It would be a true congress of American Jews and be entitled to speak on their behalf.

After much haggling, Brandeis agreed to discuss the issue with Cyrus Adler, the AJC representative, at the Hotel Astor in New York City on the afternoon of July 12, 1915. Felix Frankfurter, then a Harvard law professor, was also there. As the years progressed Frankfurter would come to play a vital role in Brandeis's political and Zionist activities. On this occasion both sides thought that the law professor's presence would be helpful since he was a member of both the AJC and the PEC.

The meeting did not go well. Adler wanted a small, controlled conference. Brandeis wanted an open and popularly directed congress. There was talk of preliminary conferences and even pre-preliminary conferences. Both men eventually agreed to go back to their respective executive councils to explore possible solutions. On July 21, 1915, Adler wrote to Brandeis that the AJC was willing to make some concessions. The AJC and the PEC, he said, could jointly select the groups to attend the "conference," and the call for the meeting could be issued under the name of the eight major Jewish organizations. The AJC, however, remained committed to a limited agenda that would consider only questions relating to the treatment of Jews in "belligerent lands."[17]

Brandeis found the AJC's concessions inadequate. "Your Committee's Conference plan is undemocratic," he told Adler. "Democracy demands that those representatives of the Jews of America who are to assemble in Conference to take action concerning the problems of the Jewish People shall have some voice in determining the conditions under which the conference shall convene and the scope of its deliberations. Your Committee," he admonished Adler, "has assumed to determine these matters for itself; to determine in advance not only when and where the Conference shall be held; what the aggregate number of delegates shall be; which organizations shall be permitted to send delegates; and what number of representatives of each such organization shall have; but also what its plan and scope shall be." The PEC chairman said that neither the AJC nor the PEC had the right to "arrogate" such power to itself.[18]

Adler did not take kindly to this response. To begin with, he did not view the AJC as just another Jewish organization with a limited purpose. It was, Adler told Brandeis in response, created in 1906 as an umbrella group designed generally to protect the civil rights of Jews everywhere. In this context, Adler added, Brandeis was "very wide of the mark" in suggesting that the AJC was "arrogating" power to itself. Adler said he would be happy to review with Brandeis the details of the conference—including the participating organizations and the delegates assigned to each. But he doubted that any criticisms of the AJC could be made in those areas—and Brandeis had in fact made no specific criticisms. As for the size of the meeting, Adler could not see how a meeting of 150 delegates representing three million American Jews could be "undemocratic" when the United States

Congress—which represented all 100 million Americans—had only about 500 members.

Adler also had some views on the agenda for the conference. "A meeting, whether it be a conference or a congress, . . . without any restriction as to the questions to be discussed, would, I am certain, be futile and dangerous . . .," Adler said. Since Jewish workers had many concerns that had nothing to do with Jews in foreign lands, an open meeting could easily lead to discussions of hours and wage legislation and other irrelevant issues.

Finally, Adler was convinced of the need for secrecy. The conference should be held in "executive session" with only the results announced to the public. "The inflamed condition of public opinion in Europe and in America," he explained, "the large number of Jews in belligerent lands . . . make the possibility of intemperate and even ill-considered speech so great, that we feel that we in this country have no right to risk injury to our unhappy brethren abroad in these times."[19]

Brandeis was not moved. He was especially distressed by the AJC's desire to hold a closed meeting. "Secrecy necessarily breeds suspicion and creates misunderstanding," he wrote Adler. ". . . It is only through a frank and open discussion of the conditions, the sufferings, and hopes of our people, that we may expect to secure the co-operation of non-Jews in our effort to obtain justice and rights."[20] He wanted an opportunity to speak directly to the AJC committee about the whole matter—he had great faith in his powers of persuasion when dealing with people face to face. But the AJC would not agree to hear him.

There seemed to be no way to end the stalemate. And then the Jewish congress movement received an unexpected boost from a most unlikely source: President Wilson.

SIXTEEN

Fighting for Confirmation

Character is what you are in the dark.

DWIGHT L. MOODY

As Alice and Louis approached their twenty-fifth wedding anniversary, they were still dedicated to each other, still confident of each other's judgment, and still very much dependent on each other for support and comfort. However, the years were beginning to take their toll. Both had to be more careful to husband their energy for the many demands on them. Alice, as always, preferred a quiet social life, hours alone with Louis to have dinner, talk, and read to each other. There had of course always been interruptions because of Louis's many activities and the many friends and colleagues who came to dine with them. But now the interruptions were constant. Louis's absences from home were becoming longer and more frequent. Alice could not keep up with it all.

Zionism had become a principal occupation of her husband's. But much thought and time were also devoted to the law and the legal profession. Louis now spent very little time in the commercial practice of law. But that isolation from commercial practice did not keep him out of court. In fact, between 1910 and 1915 he appeared frequently on behalf of public and civic groups before the United States Supreme Court and in the supreme courts of various states to argue on behalf of social legislation of one kind or another. His signature on a brief drew public attention to a case, and his presence in court was usually anticipated with an excitement reserved for few national figures. One matter of particular note was *Stettler* v. *O'Hara,* a proceeding that involved Oregon's new statute establishing minimum wages for women.

The case was argued before the United States Supreme Court in December 1914. As in many matters like this, Brandeis appeared as counsel for the state. His audience behind the bench was clearly ready to listen. "In view of the function of women as the bearers of children, and in view of the fact that women may become in any community an instrument of immorality," he explained, "the legislature found that in Oregon, if women did not have wages sufficient to maintain them in health and in morals, detriment would result to the state. . . ." Brandeis recognized that the law could be flawed. But that would not justify any judicial limitation on the state's right to adopt the measure. "Nothing could be more revolutionary," he told the justices, "than to close the door to social experimentation. The whole subject of woman's entry into industry is an experiment. And surely the federal constitution—itself perhaps the greatest of human experiments—does not prohibit such modest attempts as the woman's minimum wage act to reconcile the existing industrial system with our striving for social justice. . . ."[1]

It was another powerful performance. One lawyer who witnessed it wrote to Felix Frankfurter at Harvard that it was "one of the greatest arguments" he had ever heard.[2] Not all of the justices were impressed, though. The matter was scheduled for reargument, and by the time the case finally came up for decision, Brandeis was a member of the Court. He abstained from voting, and the other eight justices were evenly split. As a result, the Oregon state court decision—upholding the law—was allowed to stand.[3]

It was not the best way to win, but it was a victory nonetheless. And victories on issues affecting social legislation were not common. Judges of all kinds frequently invoked "liberty of contract"—which they said was protected by the due process clauses of the Constitution—to strike down all kinds of social legislation. To those interested in moving with the times, it was disheartening. America was industrializing and the courts were all too often found defending an economic simplicity that no longer existed.

Brandeis was among those who expressed concern. He was all for the simple economic life of an earlier America. He was prepared to fight to preserve some of that heritage. But facts were facts. The country was changing, and the legal system had to change with it. "Political as well as economic and social science noted these revolutionary changes," he told a meeting of the Chicago Bar Association on one occasion. "But legal science—the unwritten or judge-made laws as distinguished from legislation—was largely deaf and blind to them. Courts continued to ignore newly arisen social needs." Not surprisingly, judges became an obstacle to social progress. "Where statutes giving expression to the new social spirit were clearly constitutional," he observed, "judges, imbued with the relentless spirit of individualism, often construed them away." In other contexts Brandeis could appreciate the value of individualism. But judicial intransigence here was becoming "dangerous" and explained the desire of many Progressives to limit the courts' powers. And that would be unfortunate, he said. The courts were the last check against arbitrary governments, and any dilution of that check could have unintended—and ominous—consequences for the country.[4]

Those observations were made on January 3, 1916. Brandeis knew, of course, that it was easier to criticize the system than to change it. But he could not know at the time that forces were already at work that would give him an opportunity to become a member of the judiciary and to practice what he preached.

Joseph Lamar's family had already had one United States Supreme Court justice—Lucius Q.C. Lamar, who had served from 1888 to 1893. So the family no doubt felt especially proud when Joseph received the nod from President Taft in 1910. Lamar had served his native Georgia as a member of the state legislature and then as a member of the state Supreme Court. He was not on close personal terms with the president. In one basic area, however, there was a bond. Taft liked Lamar's politics. The president often had occasion to play golf in Augusta, Georgia, and on these visits he usually spent some time with Lamar. The round-faced corporate attorney was much respected in local circles, and Taft too felt comfortable with Lamar's conservative view of social and economic issues. In December 1910 the fifty-three-year old Georgian was confirmed by the Senate to sit on the Supreme Court.

Lamar's five years on the Court were uneventful. No opinions were issued or decisions made to bring him national attention. Even his death was a quiet affair. He became sick in the autumn of 1915 and, after developing a severe chest cold, died at his New Hampshire Avenue home on January 2, 1916.

President Wilson was about to leave for a weekend of rest at the Homestead, the fashionable resort in the Appalachian Mountains in Virginia. The president had married Edith Bolling several weeks earlier and had spent his honeymoon there. He apparently liked the place enough to seek an early return. But now he had a new matter to ponder. While he sent the expected telegram of condolence to the Lamar family, his thoughts were probably more concerned with Lamar's replacement.

Up to that point Wilson had made only one other Court appointment: James McReynolds. While the former attorney general had won much praise from Progressives for his role in the Tobacco Trust case, his decisions as a Supreme Court justice were anything but progressive. Maybe Wilson should have expected no better. McReynolds had a strange personality, and his political views had shifted to some extent even before he was elevated to the Court.

In any event, Wilson did not want to make the same mistake twice. He wanted someone whose political views were acceptable and would remain acceptable. Someone who had thought things through and was comfortable with progressive ideas, someone who would be tough enough to withstand the pressure of colleagues who felt differently. One lawyer clearly fit the bill: Brandeis.

Wilson could not have forgotten his disappointment about being unable to put Brandeis in his Cabinet. Wilson was a new president then, and he had succumbed to the intense opposition to the Boston lawyer. Things were different now. Wilson was more secure in his position. He had accomplished things and was generally less willing to consult others before making decisions. Even Colonel House had taken note of it. "The President is a peculiar man," House confided to his diary, "in as much as he does not care for many people. He never seems to want to discuss things with anyone, as far as I know, excepting me."[5]

People, however, were talking to the president, urging him to appoint Brandeis. William McAdoo, the treasury secretary and Wilson's son-in-law, suggested it. So did Tom Gregory, McReynolds's replacement at the Department of Justice. Congressman William Kent of California also chimed in. Kent told the president that "there is no man in the country more free from suspicion of sordid motives, although the enemies of progress and the friends of special privilege have made it their end and object to discredit him."[6]

By the time Kent's letter was received at the end of January 1916, the decision had already been made. Aside from other factors, the politics of the situation could not be avoided. Wilson had secured only about 40 percent of the popular vote in 1912, and he wanted to enhance his chances for reelection in 1916. Theodore Roosevelt seemed to be the main threat, and Wilson had to persuade progressives that he—not the famous Rough Rider—was their real champion. What better way to demonstrate that than to appoint "the people's attorney" to the High Court? On all counts, then, Wilson saw Brandeis as the logical choice.

The choice was not so obvious to others. Many people hoped, and some even expected, that the nomination would go to ex-President Taft. "President Wilson would give new strength and dignity to the court," the *New York Times* editorialized; "he would recognize proved and distinguished judicial capacity by appointing ex-President Taft." The *Washington Herald* agreed. "The whole country would commend the selection of Mr. Taft," the paper observed. ". . . His profound legal knowledge, fortified by a broad experience in statecraft, would add greatly to the strength of the highest court in the land."[7]

Taft himself wanted the appointment desperately. He loved the Supreme Court and there was nothing that he wanted more than to sit there. But he knew it would take an act of high statesmanship for Wilson to appoint a former political adversary, and Taft did not think the president had it in him. "While I may do him an injustice," Taft wrote to a friend, "I feel certain that he could not recognize a generous impulse if he met it on the street."[8] Still, even Taft would be surprised when he learned of Wilson's choice.

Shortly after noon on Friday, January 28, 1916, the clerk rose in the half-empty United States Senate chamber to read a message from the president. Louis D. Brandeis of Boston had been nominated to fill the vacancy on the Supreme Court. The immediate reaction was one of shock. Wilson had not consulted with any senators on the appointment except La Follette, and even there the president had not fully disclosed his hand. He only asked the Wisconsin senator whether the Republican progressives would stand with him if the court nominee were someone close to La Follette. Although La Follette gave Wilson an affirmative answer and probably guessed Wilson's choice, the rest of the Senate remained completely in the dark.

Wilson may have used secrecy to avoid the kind of speculation—and opposition—that had arisen when rumors spread that he planned to name Brandeis to his Cabinet. Whatever the reason, the reaction was predictable. "President Wilson sent a bomb to the United States Senate yesterday," the United Press dispatch read. ". . . The bomb exploded. With the reading of the nomination Senators started for the cloakrooms. To them it was the biggest sensation of the season." Gus Karger, a journalist who was present, shared this view. "When Brandeis' nomination came in yesterday," he wrote to Taft, "the Senate simply gasped. Today some of the Senators are coming up for air and trying to take stock. There wasn't any more excitement at the Capitol when Congress passed the Spanish War resolution." At first, Karger noted, it seemed that the nomination was doomed to defeat. But within twenty-four hours the situation had begun to change a little. "Many Senators who might base their opposition to him on sound and logical grounds, if he were a Presbyterian," Karger added, "are reluctant to take a stand, lest their opposition be misconstrued."[9]

The senators' concern was easy to understand. Brandeis was only the second Jew ever nominated to the Court, and he had a chance of becoming the first actually to serve on it. (The first Jewish nominee, Judah Benjamin, had declined

President Millard Fillmore's offer in 1853 in order to take a seat in the Senate.) The Leo Frank case had sensitized people to anti-Semitism, and senators did not want their opposition to Brandeis—however soundly based—to be interpreted as prejudice.

Many of the nation's leading publishers were not inhibited by that possibility. "In all the anti-corporation agitation of the past years one name stands out conspicuous above all others," the *Wall Street Journal* commented. "Where others were radical he was rabid; where others were extreme he was super-extreme; where others would trim he would lay the ax to the root of the tree." The *Detroit Free Press* was equally bitter about the nomination. "Of all the Americans who have passed before the public view in the last ten years," the paper remarked, "Louis D. Brandeis is in temperament and in training perhaps the least fit for the calm, cold, dispassionate work of the Supreme Court of the United States." Some periodicals, like the *New York Sun,* called particular attention to the nominee's religious background and its potential impact on the Senate. "It is clearly apparent," the *Sun* declared, "that if he were obliged to go before the Senate purely on his merits he would be defeated. There is, however, danger that the racial issue will become involved in the struggle, and in that event it would be difficult to predict how members of the Senate would vote."

Coincidentally, Brandeis and his wife were in Washington when the nomination was announced. He and Alice were occupying two large rooms in the Hotel Gordon on 16th Street, and the two of them were besieged by reporters as they left the hotel that evening to go the McAdoos' for dinner. "I have nothing whatever to say," he told the reporters; "I have not said anything and will not." Later a *Sun* reporter asked about specific charges that might be raised at the Senate hearing. "I have nothing to say about anything," Brandeis replied, "and that goes for all time and to all newspapers, including both the *Sun* and the moon."[10]

Privately Brandeis had mixed feelings about the whole matter. Before the announcement Wilson had dispatched George Anderson, the United States Attorney in Boston, to find out whether Brandeis would accept the nomination, and Anderson had, to Wilson's delight, returned with an affirmative answer. But Brandeis's response was not without some reservation. As a Supreme Court justice, he would have to give up some of the independence and political activity that he had treasured for so many years. At the same time, he was pleased that the president wanted to make the appointment. It was a show of commitment to the progressive viewpoint; and, of course, if he were confirmed, Brandeis would—for the first time in his life—have some official power to make decisions. He could, after all those years of arguing and advising, have a vote in resolving social, economic, and political issues that meant so much to him. It was not something to be lightly turned aside.

It was left to Alice to convey the kaleidoscope of emotions the two of them were experiencing. "I had some misgivings [about the appointment]," she wrote to Al from Boston, "for Louis has been such a 'free man' all these years, but as you suggested, his days of 'knight erranting' must have, in the nature of things, been over before long. It is of course a great opportunity for service," she added, "and all our friends here feel that he is the one man to bring to the Court what it greatly needs in the way of strengthening." She knew that some would say the nomination was designed only to advance Wilson's chances for reelection. But Alice scoffed at such speculation. "The President himself told Louis," she reported to Al, "that he wanted him on the Court because of his high respect for and confidence in him." As for the avalanche of newspaper reports, Alice found them "amusing." "We never expected that!" she remarked to Al: "I tell Louis, if he is going to retire, he is certainly doing it with a burst of fireworks!" Alice knew there might be some rough times ahead; but she assured Al that Louis "would be confirmed—in time."[11]

For all this optimism, the storm clouds were gathering over the Brandeis nomination. It was a constant topic of discussion in Washington. Aside from Alice, few were prepared to predict the outcome. But there was little doubt about the principal issue. "Of course no one questions Brandeis' ability," Senator Henry Cabot Lodge of Massachusetts wrote to a constituent. "Everyone recognizes that the question is solely one of character."[12]

Jacob Schiff and other members of the German–Jewish community had a dilemma. Of course they wanted a Jew on the United States Supreme Court. It would give their community a stature and legitimacy it needed. They did not, however, want Brandeis. It was not only their disagreement with him over the Jewish Congress proposal. They could perhaps handle a difference of viewpoint on a specific issue. No, their principal concern was that Brandeis—for all his Zionist activity—was not one of them. He had no real background in the Jewish religion, he did not practice it, and, until his recent involvement with the PEC, he had not shown any real concern for the plight of Jews in America or anywhere else. If Wilson wanted to appoint a Jew to the Court, there were plenty of qualified candidates. Louis Marshall was certainly one.

Despite these deep reservations, the Jewish community was caught. Brandeis was Jewish and he had been nominated. It was still a milestone and an opportunity that might not come again to the Jewish community. They had to go along.

Taft appreciated the dilemma of the Jewish community. They had tried, without success, to have him appoint Marshall to the Court in 1910. "The humor of the situation over Brandeis grows as I think of it," Taft wrote to his brother. "Speyer, Schiff, Kahn, Louis Marshall all have to praise the appointment and all hate Wilson for making it. As I think the appointment over," the ex-president continued, "of course I am deeply concerned to have such an insidious devil on the Court, but it is interesting to study the Machiavellian traits of our President."[13]

Brandeis knew what lay ahead. They had always tried to attack his character; he was used to it. Now he would have a public forum to be vindicated. To be sure, it would be a fight, perhaps a bitter one. But he always liked a good fight—and he was pretty good at it. Let them lay out all their charges. The facts would come out and the truth—he hoped and believed—would prevail.

There was a certain serenity about him as the Senate hearings approached. To friends and colleagues who offered congratulations he was calm and even coy about what lay ahead. One associate, Charles Russell, could not avoid commenting on the irony of the situation. As an editorial writer and participant in public causes, he knew Brandeis as a compassionate and dedicated advocate for the people. And now all these people were saying nasty things about the Boston attorney, impugning his motives and casting aspersions on his character. "Ah ha! I see you are unmasked at last," Russell wrote to Brandeis shortly after the nomination was announced. "You have deceived us all, but you could not fool the eagle eye of the editorial writer. I had always fondly believed that if there was a man in this country absolutely calm and cool of temperament, reasonable, just and tenacious of righteousness under all conditions, you were the man. I learn now," Russell said, "that you are 'passionate,' 'prejudiced,' 'unreasonable,' 'unfair,' and 'wholly destitute of the judicial temperament.' Deceiver that you are, how could you hide all these things from your closest friends?" Brandeis took the challenge. "What a rumpus the President has started up!" he told Russell. "And all over a peace-loving individual."[14]

For all his serenity, Brandeis was not about to let nature take its own course. Life was mastered by those who took the initiative, and this was no time to change habits. In early February he had breakfast at the Cosmos Club in Washington with Edward McClennen, who was still his law partner, and George Anderson. They also consulted with Attorney General Gregory. The opposition would be formidable, and a defense strategy would be needed. It was agreed, first of all, that the nominee would return to Boston. According to custom (which would prevail until 1939), Supreme Court nominees were not called to testify, and no one saw any reason to break with tradition. The Senate hearings, they agreed, should not be viewed by the senators or the public as a trial in which adversaries were pitted against one another. Brandeis should therefore say nothing unless specifically asked by the Senate. Despite the attacks in the press, he was not being charged with having done anything wrong. Let the opposition make its case. Anderson and McClennen, the firm's senior trial attorney, would make sure that the senators had access to all the facts, not just those advanced by opponents. Brandeis was chomping at the bit and anxious to do battle in person with his detractors. But he had the highest respect for Anderson and McClennen, and he yielded to their advice.

The first subcommittee meeting of the Senate Judiciary Committee was called to order at 10:30 in the morning on February 9, 1916. The committee room in the Capitol was packed with spectators, and many more waited outside in the hope that seats would become available as the hearings progressed. Behind the dais were the five members of the subcommittee: Senator William Chilton of West Virginia, an energetic progressive and a Democrat who was serving as subcommittee chairman; Senator Duncan Fletcher of Florida, another Democrat who had only passing interest in progressive causes; Senator Thomas J. Walsh of Montana, an articulate Democrat who would prove to be Brandeis's most vigorous champion; Senator Clarence Clark of Wyoming, a senior and colorless Republican; and Senator Albert Cummins of Iowa, a Republican progressive who, in his heart, was closer to La Follette than to Taft.

The first witness was Clifford Thorne, Brandeis's colleague and sometime adversary from the ICC railroad hearings. Thorne was a major political force in his native Iowa, and Cummins wanted his constituent to come across well. Thorne did not understate the significance of his allegation against Brandeis. "In the first place," he told the subcommittee, "the gentleman whom you have under consideration, I believe, was guilty of infidelity, breach of faith, and unprofessional conduct in connection with one of the greatest cases of this generation."[15] Not surprisingly, that great case also happened to involve Thorne—the 5 percent railroad rate case in which Brandeis had acted as special counsel for the ICC. Thorne was still upset by what he regarded as Brandeis's betrayal. The complaint boiled down to two specific propositions: first, that Brandeis had told the ICC that the railroads' surplus was "niggardly" even though it reflected a 7½ percent return on investment; and, second, that Brandeis told the ICC at the last moment—without any warning to Thorne or other attorneys for the shippers—that some of the railroads deserved a rate increase.

Despite the vehemence of his protest, Thorne's testimony did not have much of an impact on the subcommittee. On the surplus issue, the senators simply could not understand how that tainted Brandeis's character. "If he honestly thought it was niggardly," Chilton asked Thorne, "ought he to have said so or told you an untruth?" Thorne of course said the truth should be told; but Brandeis was an impartial special counsel, and Thorne felt—for some reason—that he should not have reached a conclusion on the issue and made a recommendation to the commission.[16]

The senators had similar difficulty in following Thorne's basis for complaint on the revenue issue. As they saw it, Brandeis had been asked to develop all sides of the issue and, after considering all the facts, had decided that some of the companies needed more income. Thorne did not challenge the preparation that lay behind the special counsel's recommendation; he just did not like the timing of it. "Do you think," Chilton asked Thorne, "if he had intended to take the other position—for instance, agree with you in that case—he should have notified the railroads that he was going to do that, and let them have an opportunity to defend against him?"[17] Thorne avoided the inquiry and, despite some leading questions from Cummins, could not quite demonstrate the validity of his concerns. Within an hour or so the subcommittee thanked him for his testimony and sent him on his way.

The opposition was looking weak. "Thorne peaked out to less than nothing," McClennen advised the office in Boston. Neutral observers agreed. "The first round in the fight on Brandeis was a scream," Karger wrote to Taft. "Clifford Thorne, the Iowa reformer, charged 'perfidy' and bad faith in the railroad rate case—failing, however, to make much of an impression on the committee."[18] The Brandeis forces took hope, but it was, after all, only the first round.

The second day of hearings cast further doubt on the opposition's strength. Clarence Barron slid his 300-pound bulk into the witness chair and dryly told the subcommittee that he was a farmer from Cohasset, Massachusetts—indeed, he had the largest farm in that small community. The subcommittee was not interested in farm issues, however. Barron had some other business interests on the side. He published the *Wall Street Journal,* the *Boston News Bureau,* and the *Philadelphia News Bureau.* And he had been an ardent foe of Brandeis's for many years. That had been reflected in the editorials of his papers, and now the subcommittee wanted to know if Barron had any facts to support his opinion.

The Massachusetts farmer assured the senators that he had a whole dossier of facts. "About ten years ago Mr. Brandeis warned me that I must be particular concerning what I said about him in the financial field . . .," Barron explained; "and ever since then I have endeavored to comply with his request and have been very careful, and therefore I have had the court records of Massachusetts examined and have always kept on file in my safe memoranda in relation to what was of record as to Mr. Brandeis. . . ."[19] Barron quickly added that he and the nominee were not enemies and that he had not even spoken to him for thirty years.

Actually, the source of Barron's differences with Brandeis stemmed primarily from the New Haven railroad battles. Barron's papers had received "contributions" from the New Haven to help them report the facts, and now Barron was prepared to give the subcommittee the fruits of his research. He told the subcommittee it could have a letter which described a report on Brandeis that his attorneys had prepared in 1913. Senator Walsh would have none of it. "If Mr. Barron knows anything outside of the investigation he has told us about, which was made by investigators in his employ, of what the public records disclose, I shall be very glad to hear it," Walsh said, "but I shall refuse to sit here and listen to or even to read a letter written by Mr. Barron, giving his interpretation of a report made to him by certain investigators employed by him to examine into certain public records in the city of Boston. I insist upon getting the public records."[20]

This became Walsh's standard line throughout the hearings. He repeatedly expressed opposition to consideration of hearsay statements or other information that was not based on the witness's own observation and experience. Otherwise, he said, the subcommittee would have a difficult time ascertaining the true facts. In Barron's case the other senators were willing to agree. As a result, Barron appeared as ineffectual as Thorne. Although he could refer the senators to particular controversies in Brandeis's career, he knew virtually nothing about the details.

In other quarters the opposition seemed to be making more progress. Charles F. Choate, Jr., Brandeis's legal adversary in the New Haven fight, had been organizing a petition to be signed by members of the Boston bar. As Barron was leaving the witness chair, the petition was already on its way to Senator Lodge in Washington. "We the undersigned citizens of Massachusetts," the petition read, "are opposed to the appointment of Louis D. Brandeis to the vacancy in the Supreme Court of the United States. . . . We do not believe that Mr. Brandeis has the judicial temperament and capacity which should be required in a judge of the Supreme Court. His reputation as a lawyer is such that he has not the confidence of the people." The petition was signed by fifty-five lawyers. Choate was not among them—he apparently thought his name would make the petition appear as a vendetta for past legal encounters. The most prominent of the signers was A. Lawrence Lowell, Harvard's president. In later years Lowell would achieve notoriety as the man who tried to impose a Jewish quota on Harvard admissions and who would, as the head of an official inquiry, conclude that Sacco and Vanzetti had been given a fair trial despite some obvious irregularities. At the present moment, though, Lowell was more interested in keeping Brandeis off the Court. As soon as the nomination had been announced he had dashed off a letter of protest to Lodge, claiming that the nominee was "unscrupulous." The Massachusetts senator wanted to be responsive; but when he asked Lowell for ammunition to make the charges stick, the Harvard president confessed that he had nothing specific to offer.

The other signers of the petition, it turned out, were lawyers who had had some connection with Brandeis's past fights. J. Butler Studley, a young attorney in the Brandeis firm, did an elaborate study that identified all thc adversarial relationships. No one in the office was surprised. Nor did they attach much significance to the petition. Even before it was sent to Lodge, the firm advised McClennen not to worry. "The men . . . concerned in it outside of Choate were chiefly laughable," George Nutter wrote, "and I am inclined to think the matter will fall by its own weight."[21]

For his part, Brandeis took the whole matter in stride. These kinds of personal attacks were to be expected. But it did confirm his feeling that he could not have declined the nomination. As he explained to Al, it "would have been, in effect, deserting the progressive forces." Nonetheless, he was not about to take the matter lying down. He had just received a letter from Walter Lippmann, an editor of *The New Republic.* The nomination was a fundamental issue to all progressives, Lippmann told him, and his magazine stood ready to do anything it could to help. Brandeis decided to take advantage of the offer. He sent Studley's analysis to Lippmann in the hope that an appropriate analysis could be given to the public. Lippmann did not disappoint Brandeis. "Why has so much suspicion fastened [on] him?" Lippmann's article rhetorically asked. "The answer is plain. Mr. Brandeis has been a rebellious and troublesome member of the most homogeneous, self-centered and self-complacent community in the United States." And if there was any doubt about that, one had only to read the names of the Boston lawyers who were opposing Brandeis's nomination. "Among the petitioners there were few 'outsiders,'" Lippmann observed, "but the overwhelming majority were men more closely connected with one another by economic, social and family ties than existed in the case of any other similar community in the country. For the most part they transact the same kind of business in the same neighborhood; they belong to the same clubs; they are bound together by a most complicated system of relationships by blood and marriage."[22]

When the hearings resumed on Tuesday, February 15th, the subcommittee began to focus on some of the specific matters cited by Barron. The first case involved Sam Warren's family. When Sam's father died in 1888, he left behind an extremely profitable business, one that had been making an annual profit of between $300,000 and $460,000. He also left behind a wife, four sons, and a daughter who had never operated a paper mill. Brandeis had acted as the attorney for the entire family, and ultimately a complicated arrangement was made to keep the business going. The trustees of the Warren estate were Sam's mother, Sam, and Mortimer Mason, one of the stockholders. The trustees agreed that they would lease the business to an entirely new company owned by Sam, Mason, and

Fiske Warren, one of Sam's younger brothers. The three lessees would then receive a compensation based in part on the company's profits.

Everyone seemed happy with the new arrangement. The money continued to roll in and no complaints were heard. Then Mrs. Warren died in 1901 and a new trustee was needed. Sam and Mason wanted Sam's sister, Cornelia, but Edward Warren, another brother, wanted the appointment. The problem, as Sam and Mason saw it, was that Ned, as he was called, was living in Europe and did not have much business sense. Ned, in fact, spent virtually no time in the United States. He used his father's lavish inheritance—just as he had used the family's money before his father's death—to travel around the continent buying antiques. Ned became miffed at not being chosen as a trustee, and his annoyance grew when the annual checks from the paper business—which he received as a beneficiary under his father's will—began to get smaller. In 1902 he hired attorneys to look into the family business. By 1909 he filed a formal lawsuit charging that Sam and the others had cheated him out of some of his inheritance. The legal action generated considerable publicity and was ultimately settled shortly after Sam's suicide.

The nub of Ned's complaint was that he never got all the information he should have from Brandeis; that the Boston attorney could not have ethically represented the trustees, the lessees, and the beneficiaries since their respective interests were at least in potential conflict; and that Brandeis's new arrangement was nothing but a scheme to secure unconscionable profits for his former law partner. Brandeis of course took a different view of the matter. True, Sam had made between $100,000 and $200,000 a year from running the paper business. But the family knew what Brandeis was doing and there were no objections until, more than ten years after the senior Warren's death, Ned expressed concern about the size of his inheritance checks.

Hollis Bailey, one of Ned's attorneys, was the first to discuss the details of the case with the subcommittee. Senator Walsh was not impressed. "Really, Mr. Bailey," he demanded, "is it not a fact that the arrangement by which the Brandeis firm [was] to act as counsel in the matter, the affairs apparently being entirely amicable, was known to all the parties?"[23] Bailey insisted that it was not known because Ned never got the full accounting about the lease arrangement or the estate's assets; and as for Brandeis, said Bailey, he should have recognized the potentially conflicting interests and at least advised Ned of the merits of obtaining independent counsel.

Later, William S. Youngman, Ned's principal attorney, testified in support of Bailey's conclusions. Sam, Youngman testified, had been very troubled about the conflicts in the situation and had sought out his former law partner for advice. Youngman was not particularly impressed with the response Sam received. "Mr. Brandeis is on record," he told the subcommittee, "as producing a sort of chloroform in the form of a legal opinion that put Mr. Warren's brains and conscience to sleep. . . ."[24]

McClennen took issue with that conclusion. He later testified and reminded the subcommittee that Sam Warren was probably as good an attorney as Brandeis and that Sam had been the principal draftsman of the contract that offended Ned. Moreover, said McClennen, Ned had signed a trust agreement relating to the lease of the business, and he had also been furnished the full details of the lease itself. His later lawsuit was nothing more than sour grapes, said McClennen, at not becoming a trustee and at seeing his inheritance checks become smaller.

There was certainly some merit to McClennen's comments, but the matter was not as cut and dried as he claimed. Brandeis had constantly railed against people who served as directors of companies that were doing business with one another. No man could serve two masters, he always said, and even someone acting in good faith would have a tough time being fair to both parties. Interlocking directorships among companies that competed or traded with one another, he concluded, were inherently unethical.

None of that seemed to apply to him when it came to representing the Warren family's potentially conflicting interests. He could be fair to all sides. Moorfield Storey, an attorney who represented Fiske Warren in the matter, told the subcommittee that Brandeis's actions reflected a "bad practice" that was nonetheless common in Boston legal circles and one that he too might have followed in handling the Warren estate. Sherman Whipple, another of Ned's attorneys, agreed with Storey. Unlike Youngman, Whipple was convinced that Brandeis had acted with the purest motives and had not intentionally tried to defraud the younger Warren. But the family attorney was not entirely blameless either. "I had the feeling with Mr. Brandeis," Whipple explained to the senators, "somewhat like Mr. Storey has expressed, that he was possibly careless in not making very, very clear to Mr. Edward Warren just the whole transaction and its possible effect upon his rights, but I felt at the time and I feel now that Mr. Brandeis, who has been the family counselor and been trusted for many years, thought that there was a perfect understanding and accord among all members of the family. . . ."[25]

Cornelia Warren viewed the proceedings with dismay. She knew how much her brother had cared for Louis and how much the family had depended on him all those years. She wrote a letter to Brandeis expressing her regret that the issue was coming up in the confirmation hearings. "I hope most sincerely that your nomination will be confirmed," she added, "and that the whole country will have the benefit of your ability, and of your unselfish devotion to the public good." Brandeis appreciated Cornelia's sentiments. He let her know that the personal attacks did not bother him. "Nine years of persistent abuse had so inured me to personal attack," he wrote, "that the renewal of charges in public, under conditions which would compel their being inquired into, brought no regrets, and indeed was most welcome." Nor was he concerned with criticism that he had represented conflicting interests. "My position was that of being on neither side," he told Cornelia, "but of holding throughout the period of trust, as I had during your father's lifetime, the position of advisor of the family. . . ." He was disturbed, however, by anything that tarnished Sam's memory, especially since Sam was so "indifferent to money." It might be helpful, he suggested, for Cornelia to write to the subcommittee directly. Perhaps that would show them that Ned's complaint was not well founded.[26]

Brandeis could not dispose of his problems with the United Shoe Company as easily as the Warren case. The nominee could not have been surprised when the matter was raised during the Senate hearings. After all, it was one that had occupied his thoughts for many years and had already generated considerable publicity in Boston and Washington.

The issue developed from Brandeis's early relationship with the shoe company. United was formed in 1899 when several smaller shoe companies joined together to form a business they hoped would prove to be more efficient and, as a result, more profitable. Brandeis represented a family that had large holdings in one of the smaller companies, and they asked him to participate in the new company as a director. He agreed, and his firm wound up representing the new company in various commercial and litigation matters.

The new company prospered. Sidney Winslow, United's president, was also pleased to have access to Brandeis's services. He was an effective advocate, one who appreciated the nuances of business and legislative affairs. And those talents were in great demand when United found itself under attack in 1906.

The attack focused on United's leases for equipment. The company manufactured machines that were in turn used by other companies to produce shoes. The most important machines were covered by patents and generally were leased to shoe manufacturers. There was no objection to that. In fact, the availability of a lease benefited small shoe companies because they could enter the market without investing the huge sums that would be necessary if they had to buy the heavy equipment. The problem lay in the conditions United imposed on its lessees.

The production of shoes was a complicated process that could involve the use of more than fifty separate machines. United told the shoe manufacturers that, if they leased certain important machines, they could not use them in conjunction with other machines unless those other machines were also leased from United. In short, United used the leverage of its patented machines to require shoe manufacturers to lease other United machinery.

Some shoe producers objected to these "tying" provisions in the United leases, because they restricted the producers' freedom to select the best and most inexpensive machinery. By 1906 the problem attracted the attention of some state legislators, and a bill was introduced in the Massachusetts legislature that would prohibit the tying clauses.

Winslow viewed the legislation with great concern. It would undermine the control that United exercised over the market. If the shoe producers were completely free to select machinery, they might not use all of United's equipment. Something had to be done. The legislators had to be persuaded that the bill was ill considered. Brandeis, Winslow thought, was the man for the job.

The Boston attorney appeared on United's behalf at a legislative committee hearing in April 1906. He was forceful, articulate, and persuasive. He told the committee that the law did not allow a state to restrict the conditions which a company like United put on the use of patented machinery. But even if the state could impose restrictions, Brandeis said, they would be unwise. He represented some shoe manufacturers as well as United, and he advised the committee that those manufacturers had not supported and would not support the bill against

United. "Why?" he asked. "Because while this company does control shoe manufacturing machines, it is the greatest promoter of competition that there is."[27] This was so, he explained, because the small manufacturer was placed on the same footing as the large producer. There were no quantity discounts and no need to expend large sums of money to buy equipment.

Contrary to Brandeis's arguments, the shoe manufacturers did have some concern with United's tying clauses. They agreed to let the bill die, however, if United would consider their objections. That was easy. Winslow was a patient man and one who would be only too happy to consider complaints. Doing something about them, though, was another story.

The more Brandeis listened to the shoe manufacturers, the more convinced he became that United's tying clauses were indeed anticompetitive. A recent court decision also persuaded him that his testimony was wrong and that the state could restrict United's use of patented machines. He went to Winslow and asked if the president would consider some alterations in the leases. Winslow, who liked and respected Brandeis, would consider anything his attorney suggested. At one point he listened to Brandeis for five hours without interruption. But none of it convinced him that United should change its ways. Too much was at stake.

Brandeis could not abide by the decision and resigned as a director. "I suppose," McClennen said to him at the time, "that means we lose that client." "I suppose that is so," Brandeis replied.[28] But it was an acceptable loss. Being successful allowed Brandeis the freedom to discard clients whose practices offended him.

Had the matter ended there, the senators considering Brandeis's Court nomination probably never would have heard of United's tying clauses. But Brandeis did not simply walk away from the client. He ultimately joined forces with its adversaries.

It did not happen right away. After a few years a man named Thomas G. Plant began to develop machinery to compete with United. Many shoe manufacturers—some of whom were still Brandeis's clients—thought that Plant was offering a better deal. The promise of competition, however, never materialized. For some reason Plant could not get credit to finance his operation. Rumors circulated that United had used its contacts to stop Plant. Confronted with financial strangulation, Plant sold out to United.

Brandeis was appalled by this development. It was, he told La Follette at the time, "the most flagrant instance of violating the antitrust law that I have known. . . ."[29] He therefore decided to speak out. He agreed to represent an alliance of shoe manufacturers that wanted to put an end to United's monopoly. They were fighting on numerous fronts, and Brandeis decided to advance their cause wherever he could, including in the United States Congress.

In December 1911 Brandeis appeared before a Senate committee to discuss the La Follette antitrust bill that he had drafted. "He gave a great performance when he talked," Senator Cummins recalled during the confirmation hearings, "the most comprehensive review of the subject which I have ever known. . . ."[30] Part of the discussion focused on United. The company's creation was an unreasonable restraint of trade, Brandeis observed, because it brought together companies that had been competitors. He also objected to the company's reliance on tying clauses in its leases. He now found them unlawful and inconsistent with good business practice. The Sherman Act should be amended, he told the committee, to remove any possible doubt about their legality.

Not surprisingly, Winslow did not take kindly to Brandeis's criticism of United. Brandeis had been the company's attorney for many years, he had defended them, he had sat across from Winslow in his office and discussed the conduct of business; theirs had been a relationship of mutual trust and confidence, Winslow thought, and now this. The United president wrote a letter to Senator Moses E. Clapp, chairman of the committee before whom Brandeis had testified. "Up till the day of his resignation and his acceptance of employment by clients who have interests hostile to ours," Winslow said of Brandeis, "he never gave any intimation that in his opinion there was any legal or moral wrong either in the organization of the company or its methods of doing business.[31] To support his points Winslow attached copies of Brandeis's 1906 testimony and a legal memorandum that his firm had prepared in defending the tying clauses before the Massachusetts legislature.

Brandeis countered with a letter of his own to Clapp. It was true, he said, that until 1906 he had not objected to United's business operations. But things had changed since then. For one thing he now had a different view of tying clauses and their impact on competition. Among other things, he cited United's refusal to let its customers use Plant's equipment. And then there were the rumors that Plant's credit had been denied because of pressure from United.

However correct Brandeis was on the merits, his later attack on United was a grave error in judgment. An attorney is obligated to avoid actions that could create even the appearance of impropriety. As Brandeis well knew, a public impression of wrongdoing by attorneys breeds disrespect for the legal profession and undermines confidence that the legal system is fair. Yet Brandeis almost invited public criticism by attacking United. He had advised the company on the legality of its creation and its leases; he had defended them in public forums; and he had had numerous conversations with Winslow about the possibility of changing the leases. United had a right to expect that Brandeis would never use or divulge confidential information against it. The confidentiality of attorney–client communications is protected even after the attorney–client relationship is terminated. By criticizing leases almost identical to those he had earlier defended, Brandeis generated a reasonable concern that he might use confidential information to further his new cause.

So when Brandeis's Court nomination was announced, Winslow was anxious to go to Washington to tell them about the nominee's ethics. "I believe," the United president told the subcommittee, "that Mr. Brandeis, since he left our company, has been guilty of unprofessional conduct and of conduct not becoming an honorable man. . . .[32] Winslow recited the history of the matter and offered various documents to prove his point, including a circular that the company had distributed to the public attacking the "reversible mind" of "the people's attorney." None of the testimony or documents stirred the senators. There was no indication that Brandeis had actually misused confidential information, and most of the senators viewed the whole affair as much ado about nothing.

By the time Winslow completed his testimony, two new actors were on the scene: Austen G. Fox and George Anderson. The Boston attorneys who had organized the protest petition were concerned that their case might not be presented effectively to the subcommittee. They therefore arranged to have Fox, a prominent New York lawyer, present their side of the case. The subcommittee was only too happy to have Fox's assistance. The Brandeis nomination occupied center stage in the news media, and the senators wanted all the help they could get in developing a record. Unhappily for them, Fox did not prove to be very effective. Despite his reputation as a skilled trial lawyer, he ignored some basic principles of litigation. He did not read all the transcripts of the proceedings and was sometimes ignorant of what had occurred earlier; he did not always interview witnesses before they appeared and sometimes found them making statements that conflicted with his representations to the subcommittee; he often failed to read documents before they were offered in evidence and was sometimes unable to explain their relevance to the subcommittee.

All this stood in contrast to Anderson, who was also asked to assist the subcommittee in the development of the record. Although he was officially designated a Senate staff member, Anderson was to make sure that the case for Brandeis was presented. McClennen was concerned that the use of Anderson and Fox would create the impression that Brandeis was a wrongdoer on trial, but Anderson was an extraordinary asset for the Brandeis forces. He was well informed, sharp in his questioning, and able to sense when the senators did or did not have enough from a particular witness. All of Anderson's talents, however, could not obscure Brandeis's questionable conduct in the Lennox case.

Patrick Lennox and his son James ran a tanning company in Massachusetts, and, like many companies during the financial panic in the summer of 1907, they were facing serious financial difficulties. In fact, bankruptcy looked imminent. Abe Stein did not want to see that happen. He ran a leather business in New York City and he liked the Lennoxes. He had done business with them. They were his friends. And besides, they owed him more than $200,000.

In early September, Stein and his lawyer, Moses J. Stroock, took a train to Boston to see Lennox and resolve the situation. They discussed their need to get a Boston lawyer and, on the basis of a recommendation from a traveling companion, decided to approach Brandeis. It was a recommendation that Stein would later recall with sorrow.

Stroock and Stein met with James Lennox, the son, shortly after they arrived in Boston. Did Lennox have an attorney to help him, they inquired. When Lennox said no, various possibilities were discussed. Lennox rejected one attorney because he represented a bank that was a creditor of his company and would therefore have a conflict of interest. Stroock suggested Brandeis, and Lennox seemed agreeable to that.

The three of them went to see Brandeis. He listened to their description of the Lennox firm's plight. During the course of the discussion it was revealed that the Brandeis firm represented Weil, Farrell & Co., a banking house that was also one of Lennox's creditors. Stroock asked Brandeis if he could represent Lennox in light of that possible, if not actual, conflict. Brandeis said he would like to discuss the question with his partner, George Nutter, and asked his visitors to return after lunch.

When Stroock, Stein, and Lennox came back, Brandeis informed them that he would take the case and act for Lennox. Stroock again inquired whether Brandeis could remain in the case in light of his firm's relationship with Weil, Farrell & Co. "Yes, I think I could," Brandeis responded. "The position that I should take if I remained in the case for Mr. Lennox would be to give to everybody, to the very best of my ability, a square deal." In fact, said Brandeis, his representation of Weil, Farrell & Co. would serve that goal "because they would at once say, 'Well, those people will see that creditors are properly protected.' "[33] Of course, the fact that the creditors would be pleased to see Brandeis act for Lennox should have alerted Brandeis to the potential conflict of interest, but he didn't see it. After all, he would consider everyone's interests and give them only what they deserved.

The first thing Brandeis said he would do for Lennox would be to prepare an assignment of the Lennox firm's assets to Brandeis; the attorney would then do what he could to pay off all the creditors. That would serve Lennox's interests too, Brandeis told his visitors, since Lennox said he wanted to be fair with everyone and preserve his reputation. At this point Stroock chimed in to urge Lennox to accept Brandeis's advice. "Without in any way being a flatterer," Stein's attorney said, "I think Mr. Brandeis' reputation in the community would best work this out." "You are speaking now of Mr. Brandeis acting as my counsel?" Lennox asked. "Not altogether as your counsel," Brandeis explained, "but as trustee of your property."[34]

Brandeis felt that this explanation satisfactorily described his role. Lennox, however, did not. While he was a fairly sophisticated businessman, Lennox apparently missed the point of Brandeis's legal jargon. He said he would trust in Brandeis and do whatever he suggested.

Unfortunately, the relationship was not a long or harmonious one. To begin with, Lennox and his father tried to withhold some of the firm's assets for themselves instead of allowing them to be used to pay off the creditors. The creditors then became very nervous and demanded that a formal bankruptcy petition be filed in court. That was easy because the assignment of the firm's assets to Brandeis constituted an act of bankruptcy—a small detail that Brandeis forgot to explain to Lennon. Brandeis then told Lennox that, as trustee for the property, he could no longer represent the Lennoxes on a personal basis. The Lennoxes were rather surprised—and annoyed—at that development. They immediately secured another attorney, and, after a long and complicated process, the creditors received their payments.

Each of the principals—except Brandeis—told his side of the story to the Senate subcommittee. Senator John D. Works, a sixty-eight-year-old Republican from California, had replaced Clark on the subcommittee, and Works was very disturbed by what he heard. He was especially troubled by the fact that Brandeis and Stroock—who represented creditors—told Lennox how to resolve his problem. "What do you think," Works rhetorically asked Stroock, "about the propriety of two attorneys, who are representing half a million dollars of claims against an estate, advising with him and suggesting to him even that it was better for him to assign his property for the benefit of creditors?"[35]

Sherman Whipple, the attorney who ultimately represented the Lennoxes, tried to explain to the subcommittee the flaw in Brandeis's approach. As soon as he got into the case, Whipple asked Brandeis about his suggestion to Lennox to make an assignment for the benefit of creditors. Brandeis insisted that he never agreed to act for the Lennoxes personally and that his actions did not reflect a conflict of interest. "For whom were you counsel when you advised him to do that, if not for the Lennoxes?" Whipple demanded. "I should say," Brandeis responded, "that I was counsel for the situation."

Whipple was taken aback by Brandeis's remark. Lawyers do not represent situations; they represent specific clients. Any other manner of proceeding is bound to lead to conflicts of interest. At first Whipple thought Brandeis was motivated by money, since his firm's fees as a trustee of the Lennox property would be much greater than if he just represented the Lennoxes personally. But later Whipple came to a different view. "My belief was at the time, and is now," Whipple told the senators, "that Mr. Brandeis was misunderstood. . . . I think Mr. Brandeis was so much absorbed in the question of caring for the situation, and so much interested in the development of his ideas as to how this estate should be administered, that he unconsciously overlooked the more human aspect of it, which would perhaps have appeared to another; but here was a man confronted with perplexities and charges and troubles, who wanted his personal and individual care and attention. But I think Mr. Brandeis looked upon it as a problem of distribution. He did not view Mr. Lennox," the witness concluded, "with his difficulties and troubles and desires, in quite the human way that certainly some lawyers would."[36]

Back in Boston, Brandeis fumed as he read the testimony concerning the Lennox affair. "The important thing as to our attitude," he wrote to McClennen, "is the fact that Lennox was untrue to the terms and conditions upon which we agreed to take over the matter." Lennox was supposed to be honest and disclose all the firm's assets—something he and his father later resisted. "Almost at the outset," Brandeis observed, "he was dishonest. . . ."[37] All of which may have been true, but not once did Brandeis seem to grasp the ethical difficulties of his approach.

Concern for the equities of the situation did serve Brandeis well on other occasions, though. Waddell Catchings told the subcommittee about one such incident. He was an attorney with the New York firm of Sullivan & Cromwell in 1907 when they represented E.H. Harriman in a fight to retain control of the Illinois Central Railroad. Catchings had to travel around the country asking other attorneys to help secure proxy votes to back the railroad's management. Since the Illinois Central paid these local attorneys for the efforts, Catchings had no trouble finding assistance. That is, until he went to Brandeis, Dunbar & Nutter. Catchings explained the situation to Nutter and, since the Brandeis firm normally handled

Sullivan & Cromwell's Boston business, he expected no problem. But Nutter said that they could not take the matter until Brandeis himself was persuaded that the railroad's position was just.

As he related the incident to the subcommittee, a smile appeared on Catching's face. "I do not know why you smile," said Austen Fox, who was questioning the attorney, "but I see that you do." Catchings could not resist responding. "I accordingly had to lay the situation before Mr. Brandeis," he said, "and I may say that the hardest interview I had during the whole campaign was with Mr. Brandeis in convincing him of the justness of our cause, so to speak."[38]

None of the other specific controversies discussed in the initial hearings amounted to much. There was testimony concerning Brandeis's representation of the Equitable Assurance Society at the same time that he was urging reforms in the insurance system. Testimony was also taken in an effort—which proved largely fruitless—to show that Brandeis concealed the fact that he was being paid by *Collier's* magazine to represent Louis Glavis in the Ballinger–Pinchot hearings. Fox then made a weak attempt to criticize Brandeis's ethics in representing various parties in a fight for control of the Gillette Safety Razor Company. A Temperance Union man reminded the committee that, twenty-five years earlier, Brandeis had represented a liquor trade group in urging the enactment of laws to facilitate drinking. And lastly, there was some discussion of Brandeis's representation of some nominal stockholders in lawsuits against the New England Railroad in 1893. When Moorfield Storey described this particular episode, it seemed that it would prove very damaging to the nomination. It turned out that the New Haven railroad—an aggressive rival of the New England railroad—eventually began to finance a continuation of the litigation; if true, this would have involved Brandeis in a deception to the courts and an abuse of their processes. But the effort to implicate Brandeis as a front man for the New Haven evaporated since there was no evidence that he knew of the New Haven's participation (and probably withdrew from the cases even before the Morgan line became involved).

As Senator Lodge had earlier predicted, the senators did not concentrate on the merits of particular cases because they wanted to decide them all over again. Rather, the main issue remained Brandeis's character. How did the specific cases reflect on Brandeis's ethics, on his temperament, on his ability to be a fair and honest judge? At almost every turn the senators asked witnesses—no matter what their background, no matter what their relationship to Brandeis—to tell what they knew of the nominee's reputation. The responses revealed as much about the Boston bar as they did about Brandeis.

McClennen, perhaps to a better degree than his partner, understood the dynamics of the bar's view of Brandeis. One incident in particular stood out in his mind.

It all began innocently enough. A client in the 1890s asked Brandeis to correct what he thought was an injustice in the legal system. Under the law, a successful plaintiff was entitled to get from the defendant a fixed sum of costs (in addition to whatever other moneys were due the plaintiff). As a general practice, these "costs" were retained by the successful attorney as part of his compensation. On one occasion, however, a single plaintiff brought a host of identical cases against many defendants. The plaintiff was successful and, as a result, his attorney became entitled to the fixed costs for *every* case—even though success in the first lawsuit virtually guaranteed success in all the other cases. Brandeis represented one of the losing defendants; and the client convinced Brandeis that, although the system might be fair in individual cases, it resulted in a windfall to the attorney when all the lawsuits were identical and, for all practical purposes, tied together.

Most attorneys would have probably dismissed the matter rather than attack a custom of fellow attorneys. Not so Brandeis. Having been persuaded that justice and right were on his side, he proceeded to prosecute an action to reduce the cost allowances to which the successful attorney was entitled. Older members of the bar—men who lived and died by tradition—were shocked and offended by Brandeis's behavior. To them there was no excuse for this attack on a well-settled practice.

Sherman Whipple, a prominent member of the Boston Bar, may have had this incident in mind when he told the senators about his colleagues' view of Brandeis. He acknowledged that some lawyers admired Brandeis and found him beyond reproach. Other, usually more conservative, members of the bar felt differently, and it all came back to Brandeis's approach to law practice. "He is a deep thinker," Whipple observed. "He is a man of original ideas, [but] after he has worked out the problem, so far as I can ascertain, he never consults anybody; he gives very little thought as to how it is going to affect the mind or minds of other men, and sometimes," Whipple added, "I have thought he took a delight in smashing a bit the traditions of the bar which most of us revere but many of which I think ought to be smashed."[39] Under questioning by the subcommittee, Whipple freely admitted that Brandeis's detractors were generally men who opposed the social reforms advocated by "the people's attorney." Still, said Whipple, these men were high-minded attorneys, men who would not oppose Brandeis solely because of some past adversarial relationship. They just did not understand him.

It was hard for the senators to accept Whipple's explanation at face value after they heard Albert Pillsbury's testimony. Under Fox's examination, Pillsbury, like Moorfield Storey and Hollis Bailey before him, bluntly told the subcommittee that Brandeis was an able attorney but a deceitful person whom other lawyers found untrustworthy. Fox, no doubt pleased with the testimony, turned the witness over to Anderson. Have you ever had any dealings with Brandeis, the United States Attorney inquired. "I do not remember that I ever had any personal or professional connection with him," Pillsbury replied. "I have taken some pains to avoid it." Well, said Anderson, weren't you and Brandeis adversaries in the fight concerning the Boston Elevated Railway at the turn of the century? Oh, came the response, I had completely forgotten about that. And wasn't it widely reported, Anderson inquired, that Brandeis had personally persuaded Governor Winthrop Crane to veto a bill in 1901 that would have enabled Pillsbury's client to construct a building in Boston exceeding the city's height limitations? Pillsbury said that he had no recollection of Brandeis's involvement in that matter. And finally, asked

Anderson, hadn't Brandeis and Pillsbury been on opposing sides in the gas controversy ten years earlier?

Backed against the wall, Pillsbury explained that he was not giving his own view of Brandeis; he was describing only "his reputation as it has come to me, as a fact." When pressed to give the substance of whom he had talked to and what they had said, however, Pillsbury suddenly ran out of steam:

SENATOR WORKS: . . . On what do you found your opinion that he has such a reputation?

MR. PILLSBURY: On what I have heard said of him during the past 25 or 30 years probably.

SENATOR WORKS: By whom?

MR. PILLSBURY: I can not undertake to say by whom.

SENATOR WORKS: Can you state any of them?

MR. PILLSBURY: I can tell you the names of two or three lawyers with whom I have talked recently. I have talked with Charles S. Rackerman.

SENATOR WORKS: What did he say about it?

MR. PILLSBURY: I don't remember; I can not quote his words.

SENATOR WORKS: Give the substance of what he said.

MR. PILLSBURY: I do not think I can give the substance of it.[40]

Anderson was getting tired of witnesses like Pillsbury who condemned Brandeis's reputation and then sat speechless when the senators asked for specifics. Edward Hutchins, a member of Boston's Bar for more than forty years, told the subcommittee that Brandeis was known for not being straightforward. But after decades of observation, Hutchins said he "had no experience which would lead me to suppose that Mr. Brandeis . . . was untrustworthy."[41] Nor could Hutchins explain why so many lawyers had such a low opinion of the nominee. Arthur Hill, however, had no such difficulty.

Hill was a forty-six-year-old Boston attorney. His conservative credentials were impeccable. Among other attributes, he could cite his representation of and friendship with Henry Cabot Lodge. In fact, shortly after the Brandeis nomination was announced, Hill and Lodge exchanged a series of letters discussing the nomination. To Lodge's charge that Brandeis was not qualified, Hill demanded proof. When Lodge could not cite any, Hill expressed what he already knew. The establishment would not, could not, support Brandeis—because he was not one of them. He said things in public they disagreed with, he proposed things they did not like, and, sadly for them, he was often successful. And, to cap it all, Brandeis was Jewish. It was an intolerable combination.

Hill summarized his feelings in a letter that Anderson read to the subcommittee on the eleventh day of hearings, February 29, 1916. Hill acknowledged at the outset that many lawyers, including his friends, regarded the nominee as unscrupulous. But the view was not based on Brandeis's seemingly unethical conduct; there were other forces at work. "He is a radical," Hill commented, "and has spent a large part, not only of his public, but of his professional career, in attacking established institutions, and this alone would, in my judgment, account for a very large part of his unpopularity. It would be difficult, if not impossible, for a radical to be generally popular with Boston lawyers, or to escape severe adverse criticism of his motives and conduct. . . . When you add to this," Hill continued, "that Mr. Brandeis is an outsider, successful, and a Jew, you have, I think, sufficiently explained most of the feeling against him." Hill noted that Brandeis was a "merciless antagonist" who would use every advantage the law accorded him. But he had also rendered important service to the community, and Hill had no doubt that, once Brandeis was on the Bench, the criticisms would be forgotten and he would prove to be an honest and insightful jurist.[42]

Other character witnesses supported Hill's analysis. Asa French, the former United States Attorney in Boston, told the subcommittee that "we have what I may call an aristocracy of the Boston bar. I do not use the word at all offensively," he advised the senators; "on the contrary, they are high-minded, able, distinguished men. But they can not, I think, consider with equanimity the selection of anybody for a position on the great court of the country from that community who is not a typical, hereditary Bostonian."[43]

People were running out of things to say about Brandeis, and the hearings were finally adjourned on March 8. The nomination appeared to be in good shape. "The Brandeis hearings are going on," Gus Karger informed Taft a few days before the adjournment, "but nobody pays much attention to them. The subcommittee, it seems, will vote three to two in favor of his confirmation." Tom Gregory, the attorney general, agreed. "Brandeis will undoubtedly be confirmed," he wrote to a friend in early March. ". . . He is a radical, but one radical in nine is not a bad thing on the Supreme Bench." Even McClennen was optimistic. He informed Nutter back in Boston that "things look well. The general impression is that a vigorous and mean attempt has been made to discredit LDB and that it has been a miserable failure."[44] For all these good feelings, Brandeis supporters would soon find that they still had a rough road to travel before they achieved success.

Brandeis tried to maintain a semblance of normal life while his career and reputation were being hotly debated in Washington. He reduced his travel, turned down most invitations to speak at public forums, and tried to content himself with office activities. He continued to spend considerable time on Zionist affairs, writing letters, talking on the telephone, and taking occasional trips to New York City to review the progress on the American Jewish Congress proposal. But his attention could not stray far from the Senate proceedings. They were examining his career, his beliefs, his personal relationships. Everything he ever did—or didn't do—was a potential subject of discussion. Anderson and McClennen could say he was not on trial, that they should avoid the impression that the subcommittee was presiding over an adversarial contest. But he knew better. He was on trial. And he wanted to be where the action was.

So when McClennen advised him that the subcommittee was thinking of reopening the hearings at Fox's request (so that he could present more evidence against the nominee), Brandeis could hardly contain himself. "It looks to me as if the Committee were beginning either to perpetuate an outrage or to make themselves and me ridiculous by these continued hearings," he angrily told his junior partner. He was also feeling frustrated about the low-key approach adopted by Anderson and McClennen, saying that "our position is not one of apology; but on the contrary in regard to nearly every one of these transactions, we have taken a very much higher standard than ordinarily prevails, and I feel very strongly that that point of view should be emphasized. . . ." And, if need be, he was prepared—even eager—to go to Washington and personally make his own defense. "I have accepted the opinion that it would be unwise for me to go down to Washington and appear," he told McClennen, "but if the proceedings continue on the lines which have been taken, making it appear that we are defending ourselves or excusing our conduct, I think I would rather go down and testify."

McClennen tried to soothe Brandeis's hurt feelings. "Do not let anything permit you to harbor the thought for a moment of responding to any suggestion that you testify," McClennen wrote from Washington. ". . . You would dignify the adverse claims by coming here. And your presence would surely be misconstrued to mean that you were seeking the position." McClennen understood Brandeis's frustration at seeing the hearings re-opened. But he was confident that the subcommittee would report favorably. However, given the national attention focused on the nomination, the senators did not want to give anyone a chance to say that there was evidence they had overlooked.[45]

Brandeis yielded to the sound advice offered from Washington. And if he had any reservations about his choice, they were undoubtedly removed as he read about the second set of hearings.

They commenced at 10:30 A.M. on March 14, 1916. Fox proudly told the subcommittee that he had a communication to present to the senators before they began hearing testimony. It was a letter expressing the "painful duty" of the writers to oppose the nomination because of the nominee's "reputation, character and professional career. . . ." The document was signed by seven lawyers—all of whom were former presidents of the American Bar Association. The most prominent of the signers was former President Taft, who explained to his journalist friend Gus Karger that he did it as matter of conscience. "I think it is a blow at the Supreme Court," Taft explained, "which I cherish as a kind of sacred shrine, to have a man whose reputation is shady in respect to the ethics of his professional practice, to be put on the Bench."[46]

Brandeis, of course, saw it differently. The ex-president, he reasoned, was no doubt influenced by the Ballinger affair. "I think Taft's injecting himself into this controversy is a fact which, if properly used, will compensate somewhat for the annoyances of the last six weeks," he told Norman Hapgood. ". . . It gives an opportunity for making clear what we omitted to make clear nearly six years ago—the gravity of Taft's and Wickersham's act in connection with the antedating." And Brandeis had resources of his own to make the case against Taft. He discussed the Taft matter with Felix Frankfurter one evening and later gave him some materials to pass along to Lippmann. In due course an editorial appeared in *The New Republic.* "One would have supposed," Lippmann wrote, "that ex-President Taft was the last man qualified to express a judgment on Mr. Louis Brandeis. For if Mr. Taft will search his memory he will remember that it was Mr. Brandeis who caught him in what is perhaps the most discreditable episode in which a president of the United States has been involved."[47]

Other periodicals did not share this perspective. Many saw the ABA presidents' protest as the crowning denunciation of a slippery nominee. No one, however, seemed to recognize that nine other former ABA presidents—a clear majority of that esteemed group—had refused to sign the letter of protest. None of it seemed to matter much anyway. Despite the headlines, Karger informed Taft that the protest would probably change few votes, that a majority of fifty-eight senators appeared ready to vote for Brandeis, and that the only way to stop the nomination was to prevent it from coming to a vote on the Senate floor. And that could only happen if the full Judiciary Committee did not report the nomination out.

The testimony at the second set of hearings proved to be even more innocuous than the ABA presidents' letter. William F. Fitzgerald was the first witness. He was a Boston stockbroker and one of the contingent that had gone to see President Wilson in February 1913 to prevent Brandeis from being appointed to the Cabinet. Fox anticipated that Fitzgerald's testimony would be extremely damaging to the nominee. It was to be a false expectation.

On the basis of an earlier interview with Fitzgerald, Fox had submitted a summary of proof to the subcommittee. The summary explained that the issue revolved around the reorganization of the Old Dominion Copper and Smelting Company in 1903. Brandeis, as counsel for the company, had tried to develop a new financing plan when the company encountered serious economic difficulties. Ultimately a proposal was made to merge with Phelps, Dodge & Company, a large corporation with various mining interests.

As a major stockholder in the company, Fitzgerald was vitally interested in these developments. For various reasons, however, he felt that he would be better off if the company went bankrupt. In that event he could, with a minimum of investment, take control of the entire operation. The proposed merger with Phelps, Dodge would completely undermine those hopes. Fitzgerald became more optimistic, though, when he learned that the Old Dominion board of directors had a consulting report that cast doubt on the fairness of the Phelps, Dodge merger. When he asked Brandeis about it, the Boston attorney told him that he was only the attorney for the corporation and that the board of directors decided what information to make available to the stockholders. But, according to this summary, Brandeis apparently had been compromised by the prospect of some quick profits from the merger. He was reported to have told Fitzgerald, "Fitz, you had better come over on the other side. That's where the big money is. I have got on the bandwagon, and you had better do the same."[48]

It did indeed sound ominous. But when Fox asked Fitzgerald to explain it all to the senators, it came out quite differently. Brandeis was, actually, providing Fitzgerald with sound advice. The company was not going bankrupt; the merger with Phelps, Dodge would benefit all the stockholders, and Fitzgerald would be foolish to push for any other result. Try as he might, Fox could not get Fitzgerald to give the testimony that would revive the opposition. In fact, the witness turned around on his interrogator. "Perhaps," Fitzgerald said, "I have given the wrong impression of it. I would say Mr. Brandeis was conserving my interests in telling me to get on the bandwagon. . . ." And certainly, Fitzgerald added, he did not mean to imply that Brandeis was working secretly for the Phelps, Dodge Company. By the time he concluded his testimony after two hours, the senators were prepared to evaluate it. "I hope it is not improper," Cummins observed, "for me to say that Mr. Fitzgerald's testimony did not make the slightest impression on me." None of Cummins's colleagues took issue with that assessment.[49]

Fox did not fare any better with the rest of his witnesses. William Youngman returned to respond to some testimony given by McClennen on the Warren case in the first set of hearings. The subcommittee quickly became impatient with him, though, since he introduced few new facts and seemed intent only on rehashing arguments the senators had already heard. Edward Warren, Brandeis's colleague and sometime adversary in the gas controversy, was the last to testify in the second round. He recited the facts of his dispute with Brandeis, but no one seemed very interested. McClennen offered to provide the subcommittee with some bills and other information, but Senator Walsh cut him off. "I should not think," he said, "that it could by any possibility be of consequence."[50]

It was a joyous ending for the Brandeis forces. "The smile will not come off my face," McClennen wrote to the nominee afterwards. After the subcommittee had heard the facts about the gas controversy, McClennen said, "Fox looked like after a shampoo before the hair is fully dry." It was indeed encouraging. "No general staff could have planned so good a finish as our friends the enemy provided," McClennen observed.[51]

President Wilson had mixed feelings about the nomination proceedings. He knew that Brandeis had enemies and that many of them would be relentless in their opposition. He had seen it firsthand when he tried to appoint the Boston lawyer to his Cabinet. Still, he could not quite get over the effort they were making to keep Brandeis off the Court. Unspecified charges about misconduct. Complaints that he was somehow unscrupulous. After the hearings were adjourned, rumors circulated in the Senate cloakroom that Brandeis did not believe in a written constitution. Attorney General Gregory felt obligated to ask Brandeis about it, and the nominee exploded. It was not fair play—especially after two months of seeing his enemies parade their complaints before the Senate and the public. Wilson understood Brandeis's frustration. "There is more lying about the Brandeis case," the president told the Zionist leader Stephen Wise at one point, "than any matter of which I know."[52]

Despite all this, Wilson remained satisfied that he had made the right appointment. Brandeis was certainly qualified. He was brilliant; he was dedicated to serving the public interest; and the nomination was proving to be a political plus for the president personally. He had discussed the nomination with Samuel Gompers before he sent it to the Senate, and the labor leader readily endorsed Wilson's choice. Now the president was receiving an avalanche of mail from labor men hailing the nomination. There were resolutions, telegrams, and other documents. The spirit of these communications was perhaps captured best by a letter from a local union in West Virginia's mining country. "Mr. Presedint," the letter began, "at the lat regular meeting of Trades Council, a resolution was passed approving your nomenatition of attorney Brandies for Supreme Court judge. Labor is Hartiley in favor of Mr. Brandies and wont forget any favors when the opperunity presents itself. . . ."[53]

Meanwhile, McClennen and Anderson waited impatiently for the subcommittee to vote. It had been an especially trying experience for Anderson. He had had to play a delicate balance between giving the senators enough information to undercut the accusations but not so much information that they would get lost in legal complexities. He had performed well, and now he could relax a little. "Only my sense of humor enables me to get along at all in this vale of tears," he wrote to Brandeis at the end of March. "Cultivate yours. You need it. Your philosophy is admirable. If you can only mix a little more humor into your career, the balance of your life will be a perfectly rendered character."[54]

Fox and his assistant, Kenneth Spence, were not relaxing. They prepared an elaborate brief summarizing the charges against the nominee. Their chief complaint concerned Brandeis's character. How could a man be confirmed for the Supreme Court, they asked, when so many upstanding members of the Bar opposed him? The brief was widely distributed in the Senate and throughout the country. Almost every law office of any size got a copy. Even Brandeis's firm received one.

It was all to no avail. On April 3 the subcommittee issued a report recommending, by a 3–2 vote, that Brandeis be confirmed. It was a straight party line vote, with the Democrats for the nomination and the Republicans against it. Chairman Chilton dutifully ran through the charges and the evidence collected with respect to each. Senator Walsh issued a separate report that touched on the fundamental question. "The real crime of which this man is guilty," said Walsh, "is that he has exposed the inequities of men in high places in our financial system. He has not stood in awe of the majesty of wealth." For the minority, Senator Works had no real quarrel with Walsh on most of the facts. But a Supreme Court justice, he concluded, "should be free from suspicion and above reproach." And whatever else you could say about the nominee, Works said, there was no denying the suspicion he had generated among distinguished members of the bar. Whether the suspicion was justified or not was irrelevant. "He is of material that makes good advocates, reformers, and crusaders," Works said of Brandeis, "but not good or safe judges."[55]

Ironically, some of Brandeis's supporters shared Works's conclusion. Henry Morgenthau, in fact, had met with the nominee in New London, Connecticut, a couple of days before the subcommittee issued its report to discuss an unusual proposition that would, he said, do justice to the situation. Morgenthau advised Brandeis that he had arranged for him to be confirmed by the Senate within a few days. As soon as that was accomplished, Morgenthau suggested that Brandeis resign and announce his candidacy to run against Henry Cabot Lodge for the United States Senate. That way, Morgenthau reasoned, Wilson's faith in progressivism would be vindicated; Brandeis, if he won the election, would have a forum where he could accomplish more for the public than he could on the Court. It was, to say the least, a wild scheme built on Morgenthau's fantasies. Brandeis listened to the proposal and then politely rejected it.

Brandeis knew even then that confirmation by the full Senate would not be achieved so easily. A favorable report from the full Judiciary Committee was the chief obstacle. There were eighteen members of the committee. The Democrats held a 10–8 edge, but more was at stake here than partisan politics. Although the Democrats would not casually alienate a president of their own party in an election year, other pressures were operating. Numerous committee meetings were held in April to discuss the nomination. The only thing that was clear was that the nominee did not yet command a majority. McClennen was excellent at counting noses, and in early April he informed Brandeis that the committee vote would be 9–9—and thus deadlocked—unless they could secure the vote of either William E. Borah of Idaho or Senator John Knight Shields of Tennessee.

At the outset it appeared that the Brandeis forces would have a better chance with Borah. Although a Republican, the large, granite-faced senator was known for his independence and his progressive views. Surely, the Brandeis people thought, he could be persuaded to vote for confirmation.

Stephen Wise was dispatched to Washington to talk to the senator. To his surprise, he found that Borah was leaning toward a negative vote. He had been following the hearings closely, he told Wise, and several issues disturbed him. For one thing, he agreed with Thorne that Brandeis had turned his back on the public in recommending a rate increase for some of the railroads in the 1914 ICC case. For another thing, Borah felt that Brandeis's conduct in the Equitable matter was unethical. How could he attack the company management in one breath, then turn around and defend the management against complaints almost identical to his? Borah told Wise that his mind was not completely made up on the nomination. He had in fact thought of inviting Brandeis to testify himself before the full committee, but that Brandeis supporters had rejected that proposal. As a result, Borah said, he would just study the subcommittee materials.

Wise reported back to Boston that Borah could not be counted on. The situation looked even bleaker when it came to Shields. The Tennessee senator was almost a caricature of a politician from another age. Tall, thin, with dark hair, dark eyes, and a walrus-sized mustache cutting across his face, Shields was an imposing figure. Formal cutaways were his usual dress, but the constant wad of tobacco in his mouth gave some indication that this gentleman might be a little tougher than most. And Shields was indeed tough. He had climbed to success in the rough-and-tumble world of Knoxville politics, and before entering the United States Senate he had served on his state's supreme court.

A constant watch was kept on Shields. Wilson invited him to the White House for a friendly chat. McAdoo contacted friends who knew the senator. None of this courting seemed to affect Shields, and there was no indication of what he would do. By the beginning of May, McClennen told Brandeis that he now had two inside reports on Shields—one saying that he would vote for confirmation, the other saying that he wouldn't. Brandeis in turn passed the information on to Al. Not that he expected his brother to do anything about it. It was just part of his almost daily correspondence with Al. Still, it turned out to be a crucial move.

Anderson was getting itchy. Things seemed to be stalemated in the Judiciary Committee. Charles Culberson, the distinguished chairman from Texas, did not have control. Not that Culberson was disloyal to Wilson. He would back his president all the way. But Culberson, now nearing the end of eighteen years of service in the Senate, was sick, suffering from paralysis agitans, a muscular disease that made it impossible for him to speak more than a few sentences without stuttering. In this state he was finding it difficult to impose his will on his fellow committee members.

Matters had already gotten out of hand. Senator George Sutherland of Utah, a Republican committee member, had gone to the Senate floor to criticize a Democratic colleague, Senator Henry Ashurst of Arizona, for telling the press that the Republicans were holding the nomination up in committee. Not true, said Sutherland. There was no vote because the Democrats didn't have the votes. Advised that Sutherland was attacking him on the floor, Ashurst burst through the cloakroom doors to make his own accusations. "If the nominee had been a man who all his life had been steering giant corporations around the law," Ashurst said, "there would have been a yell of approval from the Republican side."[56]

Some leadership was needed. Anderson asked Attorney General Gregory to arrange for the president to speak out. Although Wilson's motivation for appointing Brandeis was well known, he had not said one word in public to explain the basis for his choice. The time was now. It was arranged that Culberson would ask for the president's views, and Wilson would respond with a letter that could be made available to the public.

Brandeis was not surprised by this development. McClennen had already reported to him that the president was talking to senators and that he was "ready to go to the mat for this appointment." ("If you do not know what that means," McClennen told his partner, "Herbert White or some other of your sporting friends will tell you."[57])

The president's letter was given to the committee on May 8, 1916. It had been group effort, with Gregory doing most of the writing. It was, nonetheless, an eloquent testimonial to Brandeis's virtues. And it spoke volumes about the trust that the president had placed in him.

Wilson told Culberson that he was aware of the charges against Brandeis and the subcommittee's report on them. "I perceived from the first," the letter stated, "that the charges were intrinsically incredible by anyone who had really known Mr. Brandeis. I have known him. I have tested him by seeking his advice upon some of the most difficult and perplexing questions about which it was necessary for me to form judgment. I have dealt with him in matters where nice questions of honor and fair play, as well as large questions of justice and the public benefit, were involved. In every matter in which I have made tests of his judgment and point of view I have received from him counsel singularly enlightening, singularly clear-sighted and judicial, and above all, full of moral stimulation. He is a friend of all just men and a lover of the right; and he knows more than how to talk about the right; he knows how to set it forward in the face of his enemies. I knew from direct and personal knowledge of the man what I was doing when I named him [to] the highest and most responsible tribunal of the United States."[58]

The reaction to the letter was mixed. Ashurst said the communication made a "profound impression" on the committee. Shields, for one, did not share that view. To him the letter smacked of presidential pressure, an effort by the chief executive to impose his will on the Senate. But he kept his counsel and said nothing about how he would vote on the nomination.

The opposition, however, was afraid that the tide was running against them. At Senator Sutherland's request, another day of hearings was scheduled to consider Brandeis's advice favoring a merger involving the United Drug Company. It was alleged that the Boston attorney would sidestep his antitrust concern if he were paid enough money. The matter was explored in subcommittee on May 12 and fizzled quickly. There seemed to be nothing inconsistent with Brandeis's advice there and his support of strong antitrust legislation. His opponents resorted to other tactics. New rumors were circulated in the Senate cloakroom. Brandeis, it was said, would use his position on the Court to overturn racial segregation laws in the South. After all, as a man from Louisville, Brandeis was intimately familiar with those laws. And now that he was living in the North, as he had been all his adult life, he was prepared to attack his heritage.

McClennen saw the rumors for what they were, but he was not sure what to say in Brandeis's defense. He wrote to Nutter, explained the problem, and asked if their senior colleague had ever said anything about racial segregation. Nutter wrote back immediately, saying that Brandeis "has never expressed an opinion one way or the other on this subject, and as a matter of fact"—if McClennen needed further ammunition—"would approach it with an entirely open mind."[59] That was not enough. McClennen wrote Nutter again, asking if Brandeis had ever done anything for Negroes.

The firm did not respond to that specific question. They were busy discussing the merits of a mass meeting in Boston to demonstrate Brandeis's popular support. McClennen objected to the proposal. The vast majority of participants, he said, would be Jews and labor men, and that would only confirm the opposition's characterization of him as a radical. The Brandeis group understood McClennen's objections. But there was more to the proposed meeting than a large crowd. They hoped to secure Charles Eliot, the retired Harvard president, to preside at the meeting. Eliot was a much respected and beloved figure in establishment circles. He knew Brandeis well—indeed, he had waived the school's rules so that young Louis could get his law degree with the rest of his class. A favorable word from Eliot could be important.

Eventually, it was agreed that a letter from Eliot would be equally effective, and in May he wrote to Culberson. "I have known Mr. Louis D. Brandeis for forty years," Eliot observed, "and believe that I understand his capacities and his character. He was a distinguished student. . . . He possessed by nature a keen intelligence, quick and generous sympathies, a remarkable capacity for labor, and a character in which gentleness, courage and joy in combat were intimately blended." Eliot recognized that Brandeis had created many enemies by his advocacy of numerous reforms—many of which Eliot said he opposed. But there was no question of Brandeis's honesty and sincerity. "Under present circumstances," Eliot concluded, "I believe that the rejection by the Senate of his nomination to the Supreme Court would be a grave misfortune for the whole legal profession, the court, all American business, and the country." The letter was well received by the press and seemed to have the desired impact. It was, said Nutter, "a thunderbolt to the other side." "Next to a letter from God," McClennen told Senator La Follette, "we have got the best."[60]

No one, however, knew how Shields would vote. On May 24, the Judiciary Committee finally gathered together to resolve the nomination issue. Wilson and his administration had been lobbying hard to keep the Democratic senators in line. Nothing more could be done. The time for decision had arrived. Shields had reached Washington's Union Station only that day on an early-morning train from Tennessee. His first stop was a call at the offices of Senator Hoke Smith, another Democrat. Smith and Senator James Reed had met the nominee at a party arranged by Norman Hapgood. Both senators were now solidly in the Brandeis camp. (Smith would vote for him, he told McClennen, "if for no other reason—because of the enemies he has made."[61]) Shields entered the committee room just as Culberson was beginning to call the roll. Everyone was quiet. The tension was clearly evident.

"Mr. Shields?" the chairman inquired.

"Aye," replied the senator from Tennessee.

It was over. The nomination was approved by the committee by a straight party-line vote, 10–8. (Borah voted against confirmation.) Within a week the full Senate, as predicted by McClennen, voted to confirm the nominee by a twenty-five-vote margin, 47–22.

Back in Boston, Brandeis was not completely surprised by Shields's committee vote. Alfred Brandeis knew the new senator-elect from Tennessee, Kenneth McKellar. Al used his friendship to have McKellar talk to Shields. Brandeis had no better defender than his brother. And McKellar apparently had the inside track to Shields. It was an unbeatable combination.[62]

Alice Brandeis had several nicknames for her husband. "Demby" was one. "Bitz" was another. And one she used with increasing frequency as they moved into their later years was "Lerps." But when Louis arrived from work at their Dedham home on June 1, 1916, she greeted him glowingly as "Mr. Justice." It was indeed a happy occasion. All the charges, all the attacks, all the recriminations—it was now behind them. He had been vindicated. Now he would join his new colleagues in Washington and undertake a new role.

The people at the office were ecstatic. It had been a long, grueling campaign for them as well. Nothing so dominated the conversation and work at the office as developments in the confirmation fight. But even before the final vote had been taken, they had been optimistic. Although he was never sure how Senator Shields would vote in committee, McClennen kept feeding the office favorable reports. They had taken him at his word, and in May Alice Grady had taken a trip to Louisville to gather some biographical facts about her boss that could be used in a major article that would be released as soon as he was confirmed. Grady also planned a surprise greeting for the new Supreme Court justice on the day of his confirmation. While he and Alice took a buggy ride around Dedham, Grady and the other members of the office gathered at the house. When he and Alice returned at 8 o'clock in the evening, they found a dozen red roses and their most cherished supporters.

After many months of waiting, everything now seemed to be happening quickly. Brandeis had hoped to spend the summer in Massachusetts and to be sworn in when the Court's session began in October. But McClennen had discussed the matter with the chief justice, Edward White, as well as Justice Oliver Wendell Holmes and Senator La Follette. All agreed that Brandeis should be sworn in immediately. The Court, shy of one member for six months, was behind in its work and needed his vote to decide several cases. And La Follette felt that, symbolically, the Senate confirmation vote should be crowned now with the formal entry into the Court.

Brandeis wired the Hotel Gordon in Washington for two large, quiet, and cool rooms with a connecting bath. He and Alice took the train from Boston and reached Washington on Sunday, June 4. On the following morning Brandeis went to the Supreme Court's chambers, which were located in the Capitol. The new justice was nervous as he went to the robing room to put on his new judicial gown. All the visitor seats were filled. Hundreds of other people crowded outside the chambers in the hope of catching a glimpse of this important crusader. Finally, he entered the highly ornate chamber, with its velvet red curtains and gold braids, the high semicircular bench set slightly above the audience. While the public and his seven brethren stood in silence, Chief Justice White administered the oath. The Court marshal then escorted the new justice to his seat at the end of the bench. According to custom, each of the justices bowed as his new colleague passed by; and when he reached his seat, Justice Mahlon Pitney of New Jersey, who occupied the next chair, followed tradition and shook hands with the newest justice. Louis D. Brandeis, age fifty-nine, was now a member of the United States Supreme Court.

The Court session that began in October 1938 was Brandeis's last. By then he was nearing his eighty-second birthday and was slowing down considerably. But even in those later Court years he continued his tradition of having afternoon teas at least once a week. People of all kinds were invited. Congressmen, senators, and high government officials made appearances. But others of lesser stature were invited too. They might be people who had attracted the justice's attention because of some notable achievement, such as an invention or a new and significant book. And then there were the young people. It was, the justice thought, important to have them attend as well—clerks of the other justices or other young professionals who were becoming more common in Washington. The justice liked to use the teas to keep abreast of developments in the outside world. But he also wanted to use the opportunity to pass on advice to younger people.

Brandeis's law clerk usually assisted in the preparation of the weekly invitation lists. The justice was always open to suggestions of new people to ask to the teas. In the 1938 term the justice's clerk was Adrian Fisher, a burly football player from Tennessee known to his friends as "Butch." Fisher had a lot going for him. He had, like almost all of Brandeis's clerks, graduated from Harvard Law School with top honors. He also had a quick smile and a warm, gregarious personality. When the justice retired in early 1939, Fisher would spend hours with him, helping him on various chores and sometimes just talking about current events and life in general. In the few years left to Brandeis, Fisher would become unusually close to the old man.

But that was later. In the beginning Fisher found, like many of his predecessors, that being a clerk for Brandeis involved a formal and somewhat distant relationship. In one of those early days the two of them were discussing the next week's invitation list for the Monday tea. Fisher asked the justice if they could invite an old friend of his family's, Senator Kenneth McKellar. Fisher was a little nervous about making the suggestion. McKellar had been a populist when Tennessee first elected him to the Senate in 1916. Like many populists, however, time had taken its toll. McKellar was now known as a cantankerous conservative, an arch foe of the New Deal programs with which Brandeis was so often identified.

To Fisher's surprise, the justice was very responsive to his inquiry. Why yes, said Brandeis, he would be delighted to have Senator McKellar attend the next tea. It was, Fisher thought, a magnanimous gesture by the justice. Surely he and McKellar had nothing in common, but the justice wanted to accommodate his young clerk.

Fisher soon sensed that something else was involved. When McKellar arrived for tea the following Monday afternoon, he and the aging justice warmly embraced each other. It was, Fisher mused, a strange union. But Brandeis and McKellar had a strong bond between themselves, a bond that overcame differences in political views—and one that could not be forgotten.

There were other parts of his past that Brandeis could not forget when he became a justice of the Supreme Court. Among them were the joy and sense of accomplishment in advising presidents and shaping government policy. They were activities, however, that could not be easily pursued from his new position. He learned that almost from his first days on the Court. But he was a determined and imaginative man. If he could not do it one way, he would find another way. And eventually he did.

The Brandeis family, ca. 1855 (a year before Louis's birth). *From the left:* Amy, Frederika, Alfred, Adolph, and Fanny. *(Courtesy Charles B. Tachau)*

Real Estate and Want Ads

BOSTON, SUNDAY, JUNE 4, 1916.

Boston American

Main Sheet—Part IV.

BOSTON, SUNDAY, JUNE 4, 1916.

BOYHOOD OF BRANDEIS—AN EARLY VIEW OF THE MAN

An Unwritten Chapter in the Life of the New Justice of the U. S. Supreme Court

LOUIS D. BRANDEIS, FROM CHILDHOOD TO HIGHEST JUDICIAL HONOR IN UNITED STATES; SHOWN IN HITHERTO UNPUBLISHED SERIES OF PHOTOGRAPHS

A series of pictures of the youthful Brandeis published in the *Boston American,* June 4, 1916.

Alfred and Louis, ca. 1890.
(Courtesy Charles B. Tachau)

Alice and daughter Susan, 1893.
(Courtesy Frank B. Gilbert)

Brandeis the sought-after: a cartoon from the *Boston Post,* February 25, 1911.

Brandeis the controversial: a page from *The World Today*, January 1912.

Louis D. Brandeis, Trouble-Maker

By

Judson C. Welliver

What manner of person is Brandeis, the lawyer-business man who gives two-thirds of his time to the service of the people, who has introduced the idea, the significance, the possibilities of scientific efficiency to this country? Mr. Welliver answers this question in the excellent sketch that appears below.

"WHO is the most useful citizen of this town?" I asked about a year ago, being in Boston. Nine men answered. Six named as many different candidates; the other three named Louis D. Brandeis.

I knew Mr. Brandeis somewhat, his career a good deal, so I asked seven men, including some of the first nine:

"Who is the most troublesome man in Boston?"

Five named five different people; the other two, with notable unction and promptitude, answered:

"Louis D. Brandeis!"

I'm inclined to think that the plurality winner in both contests was accurately picked. If you wonder why the same man should win on both sides, that's easy. Louis D. Brandeis took up, organ-

Louis D. Brandeis, the apostle of scientific management

"The Blow That Almost Killed Father": from the *Boston Traveler*, January 29, 1916.

MRS. BRANDEIS SORRY TO LEAVE BOSTON FOR NEW CAPITAL HOME

MRS. LOUIS D. BRANDEIS, wife of U. S. Supreme Court Justice, who is soon to say good-bye to Boston and her many friends in this city.

Her Home Life Has Been Ideal; Has Dreaded Formal Gatherings.

When Mrs. Louis D. Brandeis closes her Dedham home to establish her family at their Summer place at South Yarmouth she will say good-bye to Boston. Mr. Brandeis' duties as Supreme Court Justice making it desirable for them to reside at Washington.

What the uprooting of associations will mean to the wife of Justice Brandeis can scarcely be appreciated.

Those who know the Brandeis family intimately say that Mrs. Brandeis especially dreads the kind of formal existence which is expected of one of her position in Washington. The calls, the afternoon teas and receptions will all be foreign to the woman who has lived for twenty-six years with her husband in absolute simplicity.

BOSTON HOME IS SIMPLE.

The Boston Brandeis home is almost severe in its freedom from bric-a-brac and cumbersome furniture. There is nothing to impede nor delay effective thinking and action.

While much has been written about Mr. Brandeis and his achievements, less is known of his wife, whom neighbors maintain is peculiarly essential to her husband in everyone of his projects.

Her early history is even more dramatic and filled with interest than is that of her famous husband.

Mrs. Brandeis' father, Adolph Goldmark, came to America a fugitive from persecutions following an uprising in Vienna in 1848. He became

Departure from Boston:
an article in the *Boston American,* July 2, 1916.

Elizabeth Glendower Evans, ca. 1910.
(Courtesy Schlesinger Library, Radcliffe College)

Alice, Louis, and Alfred with unidentified boy, 1922.
(Courtesy Charles B. Tachau)

The United States Supreme Court, 1916–1921.
From the left, top row: Brandeis, Mahlon Pitney, James C. McReynolds, John H. Clarke. *Bottom row:* William R. Day, Joseph McKenna, Edward D. White, Oliver Wendell Holmes, Willis Van Devanter.
(Courtesy Curator's Office, United States Supreme Court)

Oliver Wendell Holmes and Brandeis, ca. 1925.
(Courtesy Curator's Office,
United States Supreme Court)

The United States Supreme Court, 1925–1930.
From the left, top row: Edward T. Sanford, George Sutherland, Pierce Butler, Harlan F. Stone. *Bottom row:* James C. McReynolds, Oliver Wendell Holmes, William Howard Taft, Willis Van Devanter, Brandeis.
(Courtesy Curator's Office, United States Supreme Court)

The United States Supreme Court, 1932–1937.
From the left, top row: Owen J. Roberts, Pierce Butler, Harlan F. Stone, Benjamin N. Cardozo.
Bottom row: Brandeis, Willis Van Devanter, Charles Evans Hughes,
James C. McReynolds, George Sutherland.
*(Courtesy Curator's Office,
United States Supreme Court)*

Felix Frankfurter and Dean Acheson, 1939.
*(Courtesy Curator's Office,
United States Supreme Court)*

SEVENTEEN

The New Justice

Constitute them how you will, governments are always governments of men, and no part of any government is better than the men to whom that part is entrusted.

WOODROW WILSON

Many people at the end of the nineteenth century and the early twentieth century took a narrow view of the law. From this perspective, the law was an objective truth, one that judges—or anyone—could find if they looked hard enough. Other observers took a different view. It was absurd, said Oliver Wendell Holmes, to think that law was a "brooding omnipresence in the sky." It was nothing more than a man-made creation, something people could change at will.

In many law schools the subject was a constant point of debate. One day the question was posed to Jeremiah Smith, a Harvard law professor at the turn of the century. Do judges discover law or make it, the student asked. Smith, a former judge in New Hampshire, had no difficulty responding. "They make law," he said. "I've done it myself."[1]

The opportunity to make law, to mold political, social, and economic relationships, was an enormous power, one that could be used for good or for ill, but in either event one that enabled the judge to leave his imprint on society. And that's what made a judicial career appealing to Brandeis. He had been fighting almost his entire adult life for a vision of America, a vision that would give the individual citizen control over his life. He wanted people to have a chance to develop their talents, and that could happen, he believed, only if citizens lived and worked in an environment that was responsive to their needs and wishes. Now he was a Supreme Court justice, someone who could help the law further that goal.

He recognized that some changes in his lifestyle might be warranted. Before, as a private attorney, he had done largely as he pleased, accepting only those cases he believed in, making statements and taking whatever action would bring him closer to a chosen objective. As a Supreme Court justice, he could not have that freedom. He could not think only of himself now; he was part of an institution, one with traditions and a place in society. He revered the Court, almost with a mystical attachment. He could not, would not, say anything or do anything that cast the Court in a bad light. And that meant he could no longer appear in public as the advocate for social reform. He was a judge, someone who had to appear to be above the fray.

His colleagues from past battles recognized that, in gaining a new justice, they were losing a colleague. "Although I have done what I could in the fight for your confirmation and earnestly desired it," Amos Pinchot wrote to Brandeis, "still, now that you are actually a Supreme Court Justice, I don't know whether to be sorry or glad. So far, I think that I am sort of sorry." It all reflected the leading, and almost singular, role that the Boston attorney had played in America's life. "Taking it all together," Pinchot observed, "I don't think it is unfair to say that, for the last ten years, you have been the most vital and disturbing element in our public life. You have worked quietly, doing the unpopular things that reformers have talked or written about. . . . As long as you were in private life, it seemed to me that, if any monstrous injustice should be attempted upon helpless people, they would not lack protection." For these reasons, Pinchot said, he would "sorely" miss his compatriot.[2]

Brandeis too felt a certain sadness. It would not be the same anymore. But still he hoped he could—somehow, some way—stay in touch with matters of public policy outside the Court. And before he had even moved down to Washington, President Wilson made him feel the hope was not an idle one.

It was Mexico. For several years the United States and its neighbor to the south had been engaged in sporadic hostilities, some only verbal and others that resulted in armed combat. At times the prospect of a full-scale war seemed probable, a prospect that frightened the populations of both countries. On both sides there was now a genuine desire to ease the tension and establish friendly relations. Wilson therefore responded favorably to an overture from the Mexican government in the summer of 1916 to establish a Mexican–American commission made up of six members—three from each country—to explore the problems and recommend solutions.

Selection of the individual commissioners was obviously a matter of prime importance. They would have to be individuals who were intelligent, sensitive to the nuances of human relationships, and sufficiently imaginative to find points of agreement. And Wilson knew at least one person who fit that mold.

By the end of July rumors were circulating that the president would select Brandeis as one of the three American commissioners. Wilson's telegram confirming that rumor reached the new justice in Cape Cod on the morning of August 9, just as he and his daughter Elizabeth were about to go visit their cousins, the Wehles. Brandeis was excited about the opportunity and wanted to accept. He knew enough about Court etiquette, however, to know that he should first secure the approval of the chief justice.

Edward Douglass White of Louisiana had been appointed to the Court as an associate justice by President Grover Cleveland in 1894 at the age of forty-eight. At the time he was the much respected and very popular Democratic majority leader in the United States Senate. Taft had appointed him chief justice in 1910. Many saw an historical irony in the fact that White had served in the Confederate army during the Civil War while one of the men sitting next to him—Oliver Wendell Holmes—had fought for the Union side. Those conflicts, though, were all buried in the past. Although he was no intellectual giant, the white-haired, heavyset chief justice was an extremely likeable figure, a man who easily attracted the affections of his colleagues.

Brandeis and White had already exchanged letters on whether the new justice had to sell his numerous bonds in order to avoid conflicts of interest (White said no). And now, with the prospect of another new role, Brandeis took the train to Lake Placid in New York to confer with White at his summer home.

The two men sat on the veranda of the Whiteface Inn in the early morning of August 13. White immediately made it clear that he was opposed to Brandeis's service on the Mexican–American commission. True, as Brandeis pointed out, his predecessor, Joseph Lamar, had performed some extracurricular service for Wilson. But it had caused considerable problems for the other justices. Lamar spent literally months on the outside task. Work had to be reassigned, and even with that many matters were delayed. Since Lamar's death, White explained, the Court had been operating with only eight justices. Once again, the docket was congested, and it would be intolerable if their newest member were diverted from Court responsibilities just when they really needed him. But White added that, whatever his views, the decision was for Brandeis to make.

Brandeis left White for a while to confer with his Zionist colleague Stephen Wise, who also had a summer home on Lake Placid. Later he returned to go canoeing with White and to listen to music. And all the while White kept hammering away, expressing his opposition to any service on the commission.

Brandeis finally left Lake Placid without revealing what he would do. He wanted to take advantage of Wilson's offer. It was the kind of important task that he would have relished in the past. But he understood White's concern. It was an inappropriate way to begin a relationship with his new colleagues. The president had asked him to become a Supreme Court justice. He had accepted and, after a bitter fight, been confirmed. To do the job right would require hard work, and a lot of it. It would be unfair to himself, as well as his brethren, if his first months on the Court were devoted to non-judicial matters. He discussed it with Felix Frankfurter in New York City, and they both agreed he would have to decline. He took the train to Washington, met with the president in the afternoon of August 14, and told him that he could not serve on the commission.[3]

It was a wise decision. Although he expected to find his new job a challenge, Brandeis was not at all prepared for the amount of work and the pressure that surrounded it.

The justices decided literally hundreds of cases—some with far-reaching consequences for the entire country. Some justices did not adjust well to the demands of the job. Charles Evans Hughes was one. After he was sworn in the previous June, Brandeis followed tradition and took a carriage ride to make a courtesy call on each of the other justices. When he got to Hughes's house he learned that he had resigned from the Court to accept the Republican presidential nomination. It was a fortunate break for Hughes. The former New York governor, until recently a nervous and inveterate cigarette smoker, had been overwhelmed by the Court position. Doing all the research, preparing opinions, considering the views of his brethren—it was too much for him. It was especially difficult since there was little opportunity to talk with the other justices, exchanges that might have provided some outlet for the tension. But there was no separate Supreme Court building (and would not be until 1935). The Supreme Court's chambers and facilities were located in the Capitol, and only a couple of justices were given offices there. Most worked at home. Aside from the times when they met in open Court, the only regular meeting of the justices was the Saturday conference, when they gathered to decide cases. That was often an exhausting experience, and sometimes after a Saturday conference Hughes would go home to bed and stay there for an entire day. Brandeis even heard that at one point Hughes had undergone electric shock treatments to help him cope with the pressure.

Brandeis too was nervous about the quality of his work at first. White tried to reassure him that he would do just fine, that he would adjust to the pressures and loneliness of the job without any problem. Brandeis expected a lot from himself, though. Nothing but the highest performance would be acceptable. Still, he saw the pitfalls. He did not want to experience the pain endured by Hughes.

To help him meet the challenge, he decided to hire a recent law school graduate to assist him in the research and preparation of opinions. The Court budget allowed each of the associate justices to hire one secretary (the chief justice got two). Almost all of them, like Hughes, used the slot to employ a secretary to take dictation and write or type opinions. Few used the secretary to do substantive legal work. For Brandeis, there was almost no choice. He could write his opinions out in longhand and have drafts printed by the Court printer. But someone had to help him with the enormous amount of research he knew would be involved. It was no panacea, however. Even with the secretaries—or clerks, as they were later called—demands continued to be great, the hours of work endless.

There was, of course, no question where the clerk would come from—Harvard Law School. It was "the" law school, the one that gave Brandeis his start, the one institution besides the Court that had captured his emotions and energies. Frankfurter, now a professor there, was asked to select a top graduate to serve with the justice. The clerk could expect to put in long hours of lonely work researching cases, reviewing periodicals in the Library of Congress, or reading reports from one of the many government agencies and bureaus. There would be little time left to socialize. It was an exacting position. "Justice Brandeis' standard for our work," one clerk remembered, "was perfection as a norm, to be bettered on special occasions."[4]

The clerk would not meet with the justice before he started the job. Frankfurter would make the decision alone. The clerk's only responsibility was to report for work in September, when the current clerk was due to depart. The Court's sessions—or terms, as they are called—begin on the first Monday in October, and there was much preparation to be made for the occasion.

The clerk was never given any formal instructions by Frankfurter or Brandeis about the nature of the position. The only thing he was told concerned the confidentiality of the work. Sometimes Frankfurter, but more often the justice himself, would explain that secrecy was vital to the Court's labors, that the clerk was not to discuss his work with anyone (not even other clerks), that if anyone walked in on him he was to turn his books and papers over so that there would be no inadvertent slips, that there had never been a leak from Justice Brandeis's chambers, and that he wanted no blemishes on that record. With that warning in mind, the clerk would turn to the task ahead.

There are two principal routes by which a case reaches the Supreme Court. The first is an appeal that the law accords parties in certain cases. The second is a discretionary determination by the justices that they want to hear the case because of its significance (although they normally do not render a final decision until after another round of pleadings and an oral argument). Prior to 1925, the number of cases appealed far outnumbered discretionary grants, which are made on the basis of a party's petition for *certiorari,* or "*cert.*," in the lawyer's idiom. In that year the Congress passed a new Judiciary Act which severely limited the right of appeal and expanded the Court's discretion in taking cases. As a result, the number of *cert.* petitions increased substantially, and with the increase came a change in the work assigned to Brandeis's clerks. Brandeis would ask the clerk to review his initial judgments on whether to grant *cert.* petitions, with particular reference to the Court's jurisdiction, or authority, to hear the matter.

Prior to that time, the clerk would be asked only to help the justice prepare written opinions. The clerk was rarely asked for his view as to how a case should be decided, and those who volunteered an opinion received a short and polite response that left no doubt that there would only be one decision-maker in the chambers of Justice Brandeis. At the same time, the justice made it clear that the clerk was to act as a junior partner. Although the result could not be questioned, the justice invited—indeed, demanded—that the clerk be completely candid in assessing the merits of any argument offered by Brandeis to support the decision (or in other cases, his dissent from the decision). The justice did not want yes-men. He wanted to be challenged. The flaws of every factual proposition, every legal argument, had to be exposed before the opinion went to the printer for the final version.

Virtually all of the clerks were young men possessed of sharp minds and who were very happy to speak their piece, although some were more aggressive than others. In the early years there were vigorous discussions between Brandeis and his clerks. Usually the justice would prepare a statement of facts of the case and a preliminary legal analysis. The draft document would then be given to the clerk for his review. Every sentence, every thought, and every citation had to be checked and then checked again. There were to be no errors. The Court's prestige was on the line every time a justice issued an opinion, and there could be no mistakes. It was damaging to the Court's reputation, the justice would say, to have to grant a petition for rehearing because of a flaw in an opinion. Therefore, the clerk was to amplify the justice's points with footnotes containing the necessary factual and legal authorities. But if the clerk disagreed with any part of the opinion, he was obligated to speak up. Brandeis would listen to the clerk's explanations, then advance his own view and push the clerk to the logical limits of his argument. If persuaded by the clerk, the justice might ask him to prepare some appropriate language for inclusion in the opinion. There was little pride of authorship on the justice's part. He and his clerk were a team. And if they could not reach agreement, he would hold up the opinion for at least a couple of weeks in the hope of reaching an accommodation. If they failed after that time, they would have to agree to disagree. But through it all they had to remember that their client was the Court and no effort should be spared in serving it.

Most clerks found the whole process exhilarating. It was not a place for sensitive souls, however. The justice expected great things from his clerks. Praise was infrequent, even for the most imaginative contributions. One clerk learned the hard way. It was a patent case that concerned the technology of radios, which were fast becoming a household item. The controversy required an understanding of "frequency modulation," a scientific term that lay beyond the justice's experience. The clerk decided the best explanation was a graphic one. He set up an elaborate mechanism of wires, metal balls, and pendulums to demonstrate the meaning of frequency modulation. With carefully timed observations and examples, the clerk put on quite a show. The justice sat in a chair with his legs crossed, watching impassively. When the clerk was finished after almost an hour, he expected a smile, a handshake perhaps, but at least a pat on the back. Instead, Brandeis stood up, said thank you, and left the room. And that was that.

Sometimes even the strongest clerks felt a little uncertain about the quality of their work. On occasion Frankfurter or Alice would have to assure a clerk that he was doing well and that the justice did appreciate his efforts. Evaluations by Brandeis himself, if they were given at all, were generally designed only to point out an error by the clerk. And few of them could forget that experience. Dean Acheson, later secretary of state, recalled the time early in his tenure when he labored long and hard on a case involving Jacob Ruppert, a brewer who also owned the New York Yankees. The fruits of Acheson's efforts were found mainly in the footnotes of Brandeis's opinion, and they occupied more than half of the total words in the opinion. Acheson was proud of his accomplishment, and he decided to go down to Court to hear his justice deliver the opinion orally. As the time for delivery approached, Acheson, seated in the back, noticed that something was wrong. Brandeis kept asking the page to bring him law books. He looked troubled, and when the chief justice motioned to him to begin his opinion, Brandeis waved him on to the next case.

Fear overcame Acheson. What had gone wrong? What had *he* done? He waited for the justice back in the office. "Did you read all the cases cited in the footnotes?" Brandeis asked upon his return. Acheson replied that he had. Brandeis then put two books on his clerk's desk. "Suppose you read these two again." On further reading Acheson realized he had made a mistake. He had confused some of the cases on the many lists he used when doing research. He approached the justice and expressed his regret. It was all dismissed with a sentence. "Please remember," Brandeis told his young clerk, "that your function is to correct my errors, not to introduce errors of your own."[5]

Alice found Washington exciting at first. Shortly after their arrival she wrote to Bess Evans back in Boston that life "is a great whirl."[6] Her husband now had an official status, a stature that placed him among the most prominent of figures, and in Washington, where prominent figures abounded, that was no small accomplishment. The Supreme Court was at the center of Washington's social life, and Alice initially enjoyed the benefits of that. Tickets to attend open Court sessions on Monday mornings—when the justices read their opinions—were very much in demand. The afternoon teas were also an event. Monday was when the justices held open house. The rest of the week was divided among Cabinet members, senators, congressmen, and diplomats.

Then there were the dinner parties. In the early twentieth century, Washington was a sleepy Southern town with wide, tree-lined boulevards. There was virtually no theatre and few restaurants. Most of the evening life consisted of dinner parties. Everyone went. It was said that the only excuse for not attending was death, and then you were obligated to send your executor. People with status were in great demand, and Supreme Court justices were at or near the top of almost every list. Justice Holmes was a great favorite. And so was Justice Brandeis. He was, in addition to being a member of the Court, an engaging person, someone who could talk about anything and make almost anyone feel important. In the early days Louis and Alice went to some of the dinner parties. On occasion even the president and his wife also might be present. Through it all Alice became sensitive to her husband's position. One time after attending a party at the home of Eugene and Agnes Meyer, Alice called Agnes to remind her that only the president outranks Supreme Court justices socially and that she and her husband had not been seated properly.

Within a short time, however, Alice and her husband stopped going to dinner parties. It was primarily Louis's choice. He was now in his sixties, and he knew he could not last forever. Still, there were important things to do, ideas that had to be advanced before he left the scene. He was in good health, but he had to preserve his strength. If he wanted to achieve his goals, sacrifices would have to be made, and dinner parties were the first to go. He saw that these social events sapped the energy of aging justices. You could not do everything, and that kind of heavy socializing was a luxury he no longer needed. He and Alice decided they would not go out at all. All their entertaining would be done at home—small dinners with friends and colleagues.

Home was now a small apartment in Stoneleigh Court on Connecticut Avenue. He and Alice had always tried to live simply. Now they carried it to an extreme. The justice was a millionaire at least a couple of times over and made about $100,000 in income from his investments (at least 15 percent of which went to charity). He could have purchased a home as large as he wanted, anywhere he wanted, and furnished it with the best-quality products. But he did not want all that. It was more important than ever that his limited energies not be diverted from his work. There were already too many things to do and not enough time in which to do them. The children were now on their own. He and Alice did not need all the space they had had in their brownstone on Otis Place in Boston.

The living room was sparsely furnished with a sofa and some chairs, and the dining room had a plain wooden table on which no tablecloths were used. He and Alice each had their own bedroom, and they also had two servants—a cook and the messenger, Edward G. Poindexter, supplied by the Court.

Alice would do anything and everything she could to help conserve her husband's energies. She was strict in making sure he observed his daily schedule. He might get up at 5 or 5:30 in the morning and go to his office, which was a converted two-room apartment located two floors above his living quarters. One room was an office for his clerk, one an office for himself. There he would work until breakfast at 7 or 8, then return to the office. At 10 o'clock or so he and Alice would usually take a buggy ride with Robert Son of Battle or Sir Gareth, the Brandeis's horses, and then the justice would return to the office again. She demanded that he take frequent walks and occasional naps during the remainder of the day. If the Court was hearing oral arguments, he would leave late in the morning and return to work in the afternoon. He never worked past 5 P.M. Even if the justices were engaged in debate at a Saturday conference, that rule could not be broken. At 5 o'clock he would rise, replace his books in the green bag he had used even as an attorney in Boston, turn to White, and quietly say, "Chief Justice, your jurisdiction has now expired and Mrs. Brandeis's has begun."[7]

Alice was equally exacting in keeping her husband's appointments. If the justice wanted to see someone, Alice would either contact the person herself or have the clerk or one of the servants make the call. The justice himself almost never talked on the telephone any more. It took too much energy, and besides, as the years rolled on, he found himself becoming a little hard of hearing. If a person was told to be at the apartment at a particular time, he or she was expected to be there. Punctuality was always emphasized. And if the person was allotted five minutes, a half hour, or, on rare occasions, an hour, that was all the person got. When the time expired, Alice or the clerk would appear to announce politely that the appointment was over. The justice had other appointments, other demands on his time, and he needed his rest.

Alice was also the managing presence at the Monday teas. Everyone of course wanted to talk to the justice. And Alice made sure they all got the chance. She usually depended on the assistance of her husband's law clerk. People were ushered over to the justice, who usually sat on a black sofa in the living room, introduced to Brandeis, and left for a brief but intense conversation. The justice, as always, was interested in his guest's activities and eager to draw out the guest's views on any number of matters. After ten or fifteen minutes, Alice would bring over another guest and tactfully make the switch.

At times there were some "trying" moments. The justice was a perfect gentleman and would not sit down if he was talking to a woman who remained standing. If Alice caught a glimpse of it, she would become frantic. The assisting law clerk would feel a poke in the ribs. Why is that woman standing? Alice would demand. Doesn't she realize the justice should conserve his energy by sitting but that he won't sit down until she does? The helpless clerk would plead for patience and hope the matter would resolve itself. On one occasion a British diplomat attended the tea with his wife, whom the assisting clerk recalled as "stunning." The justice was apparently captivated and remained deep in conversation with her well beyond the allotted time. Again the clerk felt a poke in the ribs. Doesn't he realize, said Alice, that other people want to talk to him too?

No one was immune from Alice's concern. One night during the 1920s, President Wilson's widow and other guests came to dinner. Everyone was advised that the justice had to retire by 10 P.M. and that the dinner would conclude by then. As the closing hour approached, the justice was engrossed in animated conversation with Mrs. Wilson. The attending clerk felt the customary poke in the ribs. Doesn't she understand, Alice said, that it is almost 10 o'clock and that no one can leave until she does since, by etiquette, she is the ranking guest? A few mumbles from the clerk were ignored, but the crisis was averted when Mrs. Wilson rose to leave shortly before the appointed hour.

The clerks and others close to Brandeis could not help but notice the attention that Alice showered on her husband. "She brooded over the justice like a mother hen," one clerk observed. Most thought it exceeded the bounds of reasonableness. The justice, after all, looked remarkably fit, and even into his seventies he seemed quite vigorous. It seemed like too much to bear to the young law graduates. "I always thought," said one, "that the only place he could read the *New York Times* in peace was the bathroom." To some it did not matter that Alice's efforts may have contributed to the vigorous health her husband enjoyed until he was almost eighty. "It may be if you're around a woman like that," observed one insider, "you can live to a ripe old age—but it wouldn't be worth the cost to me."

For his part, Louis appreciated Alice's efforts and sacrifices. It meant all the difference in the world to him. He felt that he could not have progressed as far as he had without her, and he spoke of her to others in the most glowing terms. Unhappily, he discovered soon after coming to the Court that Alice too had her limitations.

It did not take long for Brandeis to recognize that decision-making on the Court was a political process. True, the justices generally read the briefs, listened to the oral arguments, and considered applicable law. But that was only part of it, sometimes only a small part. In most cases there were few, if any, precedents that could determine the outcome of a particular case. That in fact was why the Court often agreed to hear a matter—to have the highest court settle an important question of law. All of the justices recognized that large stakes were often involved. A president's power to take action. A legislature's right to adopt social legislation. Or the individual's right to free speech. Almost all of the justices had been appointed to the Court because of their own past involvement in politics. Each had his view of the world; each wanted to incorporate that view in the Court's decisions; and some went to great lengths to achieve that goal. In the process, fact, logic, and law sometimes took a back seat.

Brandeis was good at the game of politics. With his personality and intelligence, he could have achieved much success in bringing colleagues over to his point of view. But he rejected that approach to judicial decision-making. "I could have had my views prevail in cases of public importance if I had been willing to play politics," he told Felix Frankfurter at one point. "But I made up my mind I wouldn't—I would have had to sin against my light, and I would have hated myself. And I decided that the price was too large for the doubtful gain to the country's welfare."[8]

Instead, he decided to use the force of reason to try to persuade his colleagues. He would put great care in crafting an opinion, explaining the facts simply and marshalling the legal arguments in a cogent fashion. It was a time-consuming process because he demanded perfection and, even after all those years of advocacy as an attorney, writing remained a difficult task for him. Opinions went through dozens, sometimes scores of drafts before he pronounced himself satisfied with the product. But quality was not enough. Timing was equally important, sometimes more important. At the Saturday conferences the justices would reach a decision, and the chief justice would assign the opinions (unless he was in the minority, and in that case the senior justice in the majority would assign the opinion). Weeks, sometimes months would pass between the assignment of an opinion and the receipt of a draft for consideration. If Brandeis's views did not prevail at the conference, he might circulate a "memorandum" before the brethren had seen the draft opinion. In that way, he hoped to convince his colleagues that the wrong decision had been made.

The ploy rarely worked. In most cases the other justices had views as entrenched as Brandeis's. And he continually found that factors other than logic dominated. Year after year most of his clerks expressed amazement at the process. They had been trained in the tradition of logic and law where extraneous factors had no place. And the United States Supreme Court, they had been taught, was the citadel of reason. So exposure to the realities of judicial decision-making often produced shock. On one occasion a young clerk told the justice that he simply could not understand why there were so many dissents to an opinion that was so clearly correct. Brandeis turned in his chair. "Sonny," he said, "you know, when I first came to this Court, I thought I'd be associated with men who really cared whether they were right or wrong. But Sonny, 'tain't so."[9]

There were a few people whom Brandeis respected in those early Court years. Holmes was clearly one. Willis Van Devanter, a Republican from Wyoming, was another (even though Van Devanter was an ardent and successful practitioner of Court politics). For the rest, Brandeis thought them to be basically narrow-minded and, as he frequently told Frankfurter, "bourgeois." But these feelings he kept mostly to himself. On the surface he maintained cordial relations with all the justices. All, that is, with the exception of James McReynolds.

The former attorney general was, without doubt, one of the strangest and most complex characters ever to sit on the Court. He was a bundle of paradoxes, a man given to extremes of emotions that were inconsistent and inexplicable. Six years younger than Brandeis, McReynolds had enjoyed a general progression upward in his professional career. After graduating from Vanderbilt University and the University of Virginia Law School, he opened a law practice in Nashville, Tennessee, dabbled in politics, and eventually secured appointments in the United States Department of Justice, first as an assistant to President Roosevelt's attorney general and then assistant attorney general. He resigned in protest in 1911 when George Wickersham, Taft's attorney general, proposed a plan to implement a court order to dissolve the Tobacco Trust. McReynolds called the plan a "subterfuge" and left to practice law in New York City. Because of his well-known progressive credentials, Wilson appointed him attorney general in 1913.

Soon people began to take note of McReynolds's quirks. Colonel House, the president's principal advisor, was almost speechless when the attorney general announced his opposition to a proposed judicial nomination because the prospective nominee "had no chin." Wilson, who had difficulty maintaining personal relationships with most normal people at this time, kept his distance from

McReynolds. When a Supreme Court vacancy was created in 1914, McReynolds had the paper credentials to justify appointment, and Wilson no doubt was happy to have him out of the administration.

Throughout his twenty-seven years on the Bench, McReynolds continually exhibited the personal contradictions that mystified and often enraged his colleagues. He was in some respects a sensitive man with deep feelings. In his younger days he had established a warm relationship with a woman named Ella Pearson, and it was said that they would marry. But she died suddenly when she was only in her twenties. McReynolds remained devoted to Ella's memory, frequently visiting her grave in Louisiana and laying flowers on it. He never married.

His public relationships with other women seemed to epitomize the softness of a courtly Southern gentleman. Holmes, for one, was always impressed by the charm McReynolds showed his wife, Fanny. The former attorney general did not react to all women the same way, however. Clerks who noticed the huge poster of a naked woman over McReynolds's bed sensed that. So did women attorneys appearing before the Court. As they approached the bench, McReynolds would abruptly walk out.

There was evidence that he genuinely cared for people. He would donate substantial sums—often on a pledge of anonymity—to a children's hospital or a friend in need. But he could be unmercifully cruel with others. His clerks in particular found him to be despicable. One clerk still remembers vividly the time the justice called him in to ask a question about something the clerk had written. "What would you say about a man who had penmanship like that?" McReynolds asked the young lawyer. The clerk, bewildered by the inquiry, fumbled that it could probably stand some improvement but that at least it was legible. "No," said the justice, "I would say that that man's mother was a low woman."

McReynolds's colleagues on the Bench were not immune from this strange behavior. On one occasion a new justice lit a cigar as the justices sat down for a Saturday conference. McReynolds quickly dashed off a note and had it passed to the newcomer. "Smoking makes me sick," it said. "McReynolds." In later years Justice Benjamin Cardozo found McReynolds difficult, but they did talk on occasion. They did, at least, until the Court considered the Scottsboro matter, a case that involved the alleged rape of a white woman by nine blacks in Alabama. The defendants had been convicted by an all-white jury, and now it was being argued that the jury selection process was unconstitutional because no blacks were allowed to serve. "The damn niggers are guilty," McReynolds told the other justices in conference. "Why don't they just hang them?" Cardozo politely and quietly interjected that the question of the defendants' guilt or innocence was not before the Court, only whether their trial had been fair. McReynolds almost never talked to Cardozo after that.

McReynolds could accept criticism from others. But Cardozo was a Jew, a "Hebrew," and McReynolds did not like those people. It was no secret. After observing his reaction to Brandeis, everyone assumed that McReynolds was anti-Semitic. The justice treated the newcomer as though he did not exist. He would almost never talk to him or acknowledge his presence. One of the few times McReynolds said anything to Brandeis came at the conclusion of an oral argument. It was an admiralty case, an area in which McReynolds claimed to have special expertise. He badgered the attorney before him relentlessly with questions, repeatedly challenging the attorney's positions. As the attorney's allotment of thirty minutes neared its end, the attorney pleaded for mercy. "Your honor," he said to McReynolds, "perhaps I may not be able to convince you of the merits of my case, but I beg you to allow me in these last five minutes to try to convince your brethren." The request was granted, and afterwards, as the justices filed out of Court, McReynolds turned to Brandeis, who was right behind him, and remarked, "You know, that lawyer must have thought I was a son-of-a-bitch." He then added, "Maybe he was right."[10]

Holmes called McReynolds a "savage" who could not control or reconcile his contradictory impulses. Brandeis was more philosophical. He never gave any acknowledgment that past interactions with McReynolds—particularly the embarrassment he had caused the former attorney general during the New Haven fight—may have contributed to McReynolds's behavior. But there was never a word of anger or frustration or even hurt. Instead, Brandeis viewed it objectively, and he was able to evaluate McReynolds from a distance, as though the insults were nothing more than barbs that could not stick. ". . . McReynolds is one of the most interesting men on the present Court," he told Frankfurter at one point. ". . . I watch his face closely and at times, with his good features, he has a look of manly beauty, of intellectual beauty, and at other times he looks like a moron. . . . I have seen him struggle painfully to think and to express himself and he just can't do it coherently."[11]

Brandeis's dispassionate appraisal of McReynolds was not at all unusual. He had seen it all before in his many battles as "the people's attorney." The enemy was always there, the struggle for justice would never be finally resolved. His law clerks—young, vigorous, eager to conquer the world—could not take it in stride as easily as their boss. Once Tommy Austern, then Justice Brandeis's clerk, railed against an article on labor matters. How could the author advance a point of view that was so clearly unjust, the young lawyer demanded. "Mr. Austern," Brandeis responded, "you'll find that this world is full of sons of bitches, and they're always hard at work at it."[12]

The justice displayed a similar serenity even when his position did not prevail at the Saturday conferences. He knew what he was up against. There was no sense bemoaning losses that were sometimes inevitable, especially since nothing was ever really settled. New justices with different views could and often did later change the decisions of their predecessors. It was the way of life, even on the United States Supreme Court.

It was certainly an education for Henry Friendly when he clerked for Brandeis during the 1927 term. He remembered the case. It involved a Kentucky statute that exempted short-term mortgage loans from a recording tax. It seemed to be arbitrary and likely to be struck down by the Court as a violation of the Constitution's equal protection clause. Brandeis was not satisfied with assumptions, however. There must have been some reason why the state legislature had adopted the law, and he asked his industrious clerk to check it out. Finding legislative history for state laws was often very difficult, but Friendly was up to the challenge.

Through careful detective work he determined that the law was not arbitrary at all. Because of the manner in which they were recorded, most short-term mortgage loans were subject to a property tax; in contrast, most long-term mortgage loans escaped that property tax because they usually were made in a different form. The Kentucky legislature therefore imposed a recording tax only on the long-term mortgage loans in an effort to equalize the tax burdens.

Brandeis and his clerk prepared a memorandum explaining the discovery and citing a case to show that the state law was constitutional. The memorandum was then circulated to the other brethren. Friendly had high hopes that his diligence would be rewarded by the right decision. When Brandeis returned from the Saturday conference, Friendly was anxious. "How'd we do?" It was not favorable. "Oh," said the justice, "the usual six to three." Friendly was beside himself. How could they do that, he asked his boss. And not only was it a bad decision, he complained, it would be a terrible precedent. "Oh," Brandeis replied, "don't worry about that. Future Courts won't pay any more attention to this case than they did to the case we cited to them."[13]

Brandeis was not entirely fatalistic about these matters. He was not one to let nature take its course, and there was no reason to change now. His brethren might not always do justice, but there were other avenues outside the Court to shape public policy. The discussions concerning his possible appointment to the Mexican–American commission, however, had sensitized him to the limitations on extracurricular activities. It was not that they were completely prohibited. No, he saw that the only real restriction was that a Supreme Court justice could not do it in public. If he was to expand his reach beyond the Court, he would have to do it discreetly. And he was a master at that.

During the second Wilson administration he was virtually flooded with requests for advice by people in government and by those who wanted to influence government. Even the president needed his counsel on occasion. It was given in various ways, but usually the justice would purport to speak generally on a matter so that the listener would get the drift of how it applied to a specific question. Sometimes, however, Brandeis did not want to wait to be asked for advice. On these occasions he might get a close associate to have a particular official request a meeting with the justice. In that way there would be no appearance of Brandeis's taking the initiative to involve himself in extracurricular activities. And no one was more suited—or more eager—to assist Brandeis in these ploys than Felix Frankfurter.

By the time of Brandeis's appointment to the Bench, Frankfurter was one of his closest associates. It all happened quite naturally. Frankfurter had finished at the top of his class at Harvard Law School and shortly afterward joined Henry Stimson in the United States Attorney's office in New York City. It was a thrilling and educational experience for a young lawyer, but especially this young lawyer. Frankfurter was an immigrant from Vienna, having arrived in the United States with his parents at the age of twelve and unable to speak a word of English. Under those circumstances, success would have been difficult enough to achieve. But Frankfurter had another handicap. He was Jewish, and "Hebrews" from Eastern Europe did not always find it easy to climb the ladder to success in Protestant

America. But Felix was on his way. He had a Harvard law degree and a close association with Stimson, one of the most respected figures of the establishment.

Felix's rapid progress was not entirely due to his intelligence, although, to be sure, he had plenty of that. It was primarily his personality. It was warm, bubbling, infectious. Few could resist Felix Frankfurter's charms. "When Felix was around," one colleague later recalled, "sparks would fly." He had so many ideas, so many imaginative thoughts that one could hardly keep up with him. "Felix has more ideas per minute than any man of my acquaintance," Franklin D. Roosevelt once observed. "He has a brilliant mind but it clicks so fast it makes my head fairly spin."[14]

However overwhelming his thoughts, Felix had a way of making friends feel good about themselves. He was never at a loss for a compliment for someone else, for a gesture to invoke a sense of intimacy. In time, some people—especially scholars looking over a gulf of decades when the spirit had evaporated—attributed Felix's complimentary nature to selfish motives, to a desire to be accepted by the establishment, to ingratiate himself among powerful people who could help his career. There may of course have been some of that in Frankfurter. But his compliments were not confined to the powerful. Law students and young lawyers who had assisted him in research projects received warm, effusive letters filled with high praise. In some cases, no doubt, the flattery was feigned. But as one former student remembered, "Felix was an uninhibited person, and he would express feelings that most of us would keep to ourselves or convey only to third parties."[15]

Frankfurter did not treat everyone the same, however. Many students felt he played favorites, that he would ignore you unless you displayed some sort of brilliance, and they resented him for it. Others found that he was also capable of deep animosities. Some people, especially those who he felt had done him wrong, became the object of hatred. It was particularly apparent years later as he neared the end of his own tenure as a Supreme Court justice. He would issue venomous attacks on some of his brethren, complaining that they were treacherous fools and worse. A different kind of warmth there.

But Brandeis almost never saw that side of Frankfurter. Their first contact had been in 1905 when Brandeis delivered an address at Harvard on the ethics of law practice. Felix was in the audience, and he was very much impressed by the speech. After he joined Stimson, Felix initiated a correspondence with the Boston attorney. The contact picked up in 1911 when Frankfurter followed his boss to Washington after Stimson was appointed Taft's secretary of war. Frankfurter had great admiration for "the people's attorney." He was still something of a legend at Harvard Law School, where his academic performance remained unmatched. But Frankfurter, with all his warmth, felt that Brandeis—at least in the beginning of their relationship—was too distant, too cold. After a lunch with him in the autumn of 1911, Frankfurter confided to his diary that "Brandeis has depth and an intellectual sweep . . .; he has Lincoln's fundamental sympathies. I wish he had his patience, his magnanimity, his humor."[16]

In time, the relationship with Brandeis became an intimate one. When he was in Washington, Felix lived with some other young bachelors in a house at

1727 Nineteenth Street. At dinner time it became the meeting ground for people of all sorts—high government officials, lawyers, diplomats, and journalists. "How or why I can't recapture," Frankfurter later reminisced, "but almost everybody who was interesting in Washington sooner or later passed through that house. The magnet of the house was exciting talk, and it was exciting because talk was free and provocative, intellectually provocative."[17] Oliver Wendell Holmes, one of the frequent visitors, dubbed it the House of Truth. And it was only natural for Brandeis to stop by when he made one of his frequent trips to Washington before his Court appointment. It became a vehicle for him and Frankfurter to cement their relationship.

The two became closer when Frankfurter was considering a teaching job at Harvard Law School. Almost everyone counseled him against accepting it. Felix was so dynamic, so full of life. He would die on the vine as a teacher. Brandeis felt differently. Although he had rejected the professor's life for himself, and although he later described teachers as "largely a meek, downtrodden, unappreciated body of men," he told Felix that there was no more critical role than to shape the minds of young lawyers.[18] He was even willing to contribute money to Harvard so that they could pay Felix a decent salary. Frankfurter followed Brandeis's advice, much to his later satisfaction.

That was perhaps the first occasion on which Brandeis offered Felix financial support. It was only the start. Shortly after he began his first term as a Supreme Court justice, Brandeis sent Frankfurter a check for $250 to cover some expenses Frankfurter had incurred on some mission for the new justice. Frankfurter sent the check back, but Brandeis remained adamant. "Alice and I talked over the matter before I sent the check," he told the young law professor, "and considered it again carefully on receipt of your letter. We are clearly of opinion that you ought to take the check." It was not entirely altruistic. "I ought to feel free to make suggestions to you," Brandeis said, "although they may involve some incidental expense. And you should feel free to incur expense in the public interest. So I am returning the check."[19] And so, over the course of the next ten years or so, Brandeis would periodically give Frankfurter money, sometimes as much as $3,500 a year, with some further contributions added on occasion to cover special projects. Frankfurter even relied on Brandeis to help with family expenses in a crisis. When Felix's wife, Marion, suffered a nervous breakdown and required extensive and costly medical treatment, he applied to the justice for financial assistance. "There is little doubt," he wrote to Brandeis at the time, "that I could fill the gap through odd jobs for some of my New York lawyer friends. But I begrudge the time and thought that would take me from intrinsically more important jobs—and so I put the situation to you." Brandeis was responsive, as he always would be.[20]

Frankfurter more than justified this "investment." When Brandeis went on the Court the Harvard professor took over the cases Brandeis had been handling for the National Consumers League and other civic groups. He also accepted research suggestions from his mentor, followed up with articles of his own in *The New Republic* or other periodicals, and even did a casebook on issues of particular interest to the justice. Few, if any, of these projects reflected an idle academic interest on Brandeis's part. He wanted the articles and other ventures to be used to further some goal. Did the Court reject his views on some jurisdictional or labor issue? Perhaps Frankfurter should have the *Harvard Law Review* do an article examining the Court's decision and proposing remedial legislaton. Did developments in national politics raise questions that were receiving inadequate attention? Perhaps Frankfurter should have Herbert Croly or one of the other editors at *The New Republic* do an appropriate article. And if the magazine wanted further direction, Brandeis would be only too happy to come to New York City to dine with the editors and discuss the magazine's mission.[21]

There is no evidence that the financial assistance from Brandeis ever led Frankfurter to undertake a project inconsistent with his personal beliefs. Nor is there any evidence that the relationship with Frankfurter influenced Brandeis's votes or opinions on the Court. Quite the contrary. The relationship between the two men germinated and blossomed precisely because it was built upon a shared view of the world and measures necessary to solve its problems.

Decades later, however, a professor named Bruce Allen Murphy wrote a book claiming that the relationship with Frankfurter did have an improper influence on Brandeis's conduct in one judicial matter. It all involved Frankfurter's contributions to the defense efforts of Sacco and Vanzetti in the late 1920s. Shortly before the two Italian immigrants were executed in 1927, Frankfurter became interested in the matter and wrote some articles and a book on their case. After Frankfurter undertook this initiative—on his own—Brandeis wrote to him about the matter and specifically inquired whether he needed additional money to help cover his expenses. In August 1927, about two months later, Sacco and Vanzetti's lawyers approached Brandeis in Chatham and requested a stay of execution. Brandeis responded that he was disqualified from participating in the case and refused to consider the attorneys' request. Murphy alleged that the discussions with Frankfurter may have been a cause for Brandeis's disqualification here. Murphy concluded that "it can be said that [Brandeis] had put himself into that compromising position . . ., thereby helping to deprive convicted men of a right to a fair hearing by the Court's most liberal member."

Murphy's conclusion is unfair to Brandeis. Bess Evans had become actively and publicly involved with the Sacco-Vanzetti defense efforts long before Frankfurter. She was not only Brandeis's intimate friend; she was also staying at the Brandeis summer home in Cape Cod during much of this time. Brandeis told Frankfurter that it was her involvement—not that of the Harvard professor—that required his disqualification from the case. If Brandeis determined at an early stage that he could not participate in the Sacco-Vanzetti case because of Bess's activities, there would be no impropriety in his discussing the matter with Frankfurter or even offering to help defray his expenses. In short, there is an entirely proper explanation for Brandeis's behavior, and Murphy offered no evidence to prove otherwise. Indeed, he admitted that Bess's involvement "could have been the factor that truly did push the justice to his decision."[22]

Murphy nonetheless went on to argue that, even aside from the Sacco-Vanzetti controversy, Brandeis's relationship with Frankfurter during the Court years was unethical and that both men knew it. True, Brandeis never disclosed confidential information about pending Court cases. And there is no indication that any of Frankfurter's articles (or those of his students) strengthened Brandeis's hand at the Saturday conferences. Actually, some justices—McReynolds, for one—openly opposed the citation of law review articles in judicial opinions. But all of that ignores the basic ethical issue. The integrity of our judicial system rests upon both the reality and *appearance* of propriety. Financial support of Frankfurter's political and legal activities, it was said, may have at least appeared to be improper lobbying, and that, in turn, could have undermined confidence in the Court's integrity.

In the post-Watergate era, these points have merit. But Brandeis and Frankfurter lived in a different time. For them, the financial support did not reflect an employer–employee relationship. More than anything, it symbolized the close emotional and intellectual bond between the two men. As early as 1916 Brandeis had written Frankfurter's mother that her son had "won so large a place in our hearts and brought so much joy and interest into our lives. . . ." And in later letters Brandeis sometimes referred to the Harvard professor as "half brother, half son." From this perspective Brandeis probably viewed the payments to Frankfurter as the kind of financial help any brother or father would readily give another member of the family (a practice that Brandeis in fact followed throughout his lifetime—giving generous support to even distant members of his family).

So, contrary to Murphy's allegation, there is no basis for concluding that Brandeis recognized the impropriety of the relationship (and everything else that is known about him makes it inconceivable that he would have continued a practice he thought improper). The only evidence that Murphy can muster to show otherwise is a letter that Brandeis wrote to Judge Julian Mack in 1922, in which the justice stated that he had some "doubt" whether to give Frankfurter additional financial assistance for Zionist activities. As Brandeis explained to Mack, "You know my apprehensions of 'easier ways' and the saving grace of what many call drudgery." Brandeis's doubt here, then, obviously was based on his long-held view that people benefited from struggle and that it was not always wise to insulate people from hardship. Nothing in the letter even suggests that Brandeis had any *moral* misgivings on helping Frankfurter.

It is noteworthy here that there is no direct evidence that Brandeis or Frankfurter made any effort to keep the relationship secret. Frankfurter, for one, openly described it to many of his students. Brandeis was not one to casually discuss his private affairs, but there is no indication that he pressured Frankfurter or did anything else to keep matters confidential. Murphy, however, tried to impute sinister motives to Brandeis by citing the failure of the brethren to register any public complaint about their colleague's political activities. Surely, Murphy claimed, McReynolds would have been the first to say something if he had known of Brandeis's extra-judicial efforts. But that is not necessarily true. McReynolds himself was a generous man at times who made financial contributions to friends in need. The fact that Brandeis and his beneficiary at Harvard were involved in political affairs may have been inconsequential to McReynolds. He certainly knew that many of his brethren, most especially Chief Justice Taft, were actively involved in political matters.

Nor is there any basis for Murphy's claim that Brandeis tried to hide his extra-judicial activities from his clerks. After interviewing three of the clerks from Brandeis's later years on the Court, Murphy asserted that none of the clerks had "any inkling as to what was going on" and that they did their work "totally unaware of the stream of visitors Brandeis was receiving and counseling on a plethora of topics in the apartment below." This is simply not true. Brandeis generally did not talk on the telephone, and he may have wanted to receive visitors in the downstairs living quarters rather than disturb the clerk working in the apartment office. Moreover, the clerks' work required an extraordinary amount of time, and it is not surprising that they had little time to focus on the justice's other activities. Nevertheless, many of the clerks *were* very much aware of the stream of visitors that came through the Brandeis apartment. Thus, Harry Shulman, the clerk for the 1929 Court term, wrote to the justice after he arrived at Cape Cod for the summer vacation in June 1930, "I trust that you have settled down to a restful vacation and that you will not be unduly disturbed by Zionists and others."[23]

Despite Shulman's hope to the contrary, Brandeis could not remain aloof from Zionist matters. The cause of the Jewish homeland was now and always would remain a focus of his thoughts and activities. Indeed, one of the first issues he and Frankfurter had to resolve after his ascension to the Court was what kind of role Brandeis should play in the Zionist movement.

EIGHTEEN

The Invisible Zionist Leader

Show me a good loser, and I'll show you a loser.

JOSEPH P. KENNEDY

Louis Marshall sensed that he was losing ground. He was president of the American Jewish Committee, and he and his colleagues had done everything they could to avoid an American Jewish Congress. But by the beginning of 1916 it was clear that their hope was an empty one.

To begin with, the notion of a "congress"—a meeting of delegates chosen by democratic methods and purporting to represent the entire Jewish population in America—had enormous emotional appeal. Many Jews, but especially those who had emigrated from Eastern Europe to escape persecution, saw the congress as an embodiment of the American dream. And its importance to Jews elsewhere could not be overestimated. The outbreak of war in Europe had increased the dangers to Jewish populations in foreign lands. Without help from their brethren across the ocean, their individual rights—not to mention their very lives—were in serious danger. For these reasons alone Marshall and his followers in the AJC camp knew the popular tide was running very much against them.

Then there was the leader of the congress movement. Louis Brandeis—even before his Court appointment—had a national stature matched by few, if any, Jews. So the congress organizers were delighted when the Boston attorney yielded to pressure and agreed to address a mass rally at Carnegie Hall in New York City on January 24, 1916. It turned out to be an eloquent address, an appeal to Jews to take control of their own destiny. Like other Brandeis statements on Zionism, this one was completely devoid of any references to God or religion. Instead, Brandeis told the packed audience that the demand for democracy "rests upon the essential trust in the moral instincts of the people; potent to create their own well-being; to perfect it; and to maintain it, if an opportunity is given."[1]

Four days later Brandeis was nominated to fill a vacancy in the United States Supreme Court. It was an historic moment for American Jews. It was also an event that enhanced Brandeis's stature, and the AJC leaders began to realize that compromise was almost inevitable.

Marshall made reference to this possibility when he sent Brandeis a telegram to congratulate him on the nomination. Things were moving fast, though, and the opportunity for compromise, it seemed, would not last long. The congress supporters had already formed a Congress Organizing Committee and scheduled a preliminary conference for the end of March in Philadelphia. Marshall was not at all happy with that development. The delegate selection process ensured that the AJC and its supporters would have only minimal representation. Consequently, it was very likely that the conference, and, later, the congress, would ignore the AJC's position and embark on substantive discussions—particularly the plight of Jews overseas—that Marshall thought should be kept confidential. As the date for the conference approached, Marshall expressed his views. "The democracy of such a plan is scarcely colorable," he told a member of the organizing committee. ". . . It is obvious that the conference which you have called is to be held under such conditions as will necessarily convert it into a mass meeting, where calm discussion and consideration are quite impossible, where irreparable injury may be done to those whom we are seeking to help, by indiscreet utterances, and yet where a cut and dried program, predetermined by a small coterie constituting its managers, will be put through in accordance with the usual convention methods."[2]

Despite these objections and the absence of the AJC, the Philadelphia conference was a great success. It was attended by representatives from twenty-three states, representing more than 3,000 local, state, and national organizations. Brandeis did not attend, but his leadership was clearly evident. Among other actions, the conference elected him honorary president of the organization.

Although support for Brandeis remained undiminished by his judicial nomination, the Philadelphia conference highlighted the questions concerning his future role in the Zionist movement. After his nomination, Brandeis rejected virtually all invitations to speak in public. In part this was because his energies were focused on working with Edward McClennen and others in securing Senate confirmation. No doubt he also wanted to avoid saying anything in public that would add fuel to the controversy surrounding the nomination. Amidst this public silence, there was considerable speculation as to whether Brandeis would resign from or remain active in the movement if he were confirmed. Those who opposed Brandeis's leadership, like Jacob Schiff, hoped and expected that he would resign. Others, like Jacob deHaas, held a different view. Neither camp could know, however, how the issue would be decided. At least not until the AJC held a conference at the Astor Hotel in New York City on July 16, 1916.

The conference had been called to discuss the congress issue. In asking Brandeis and two of his colleagues to attend, Marshall gave every impression that the AJC would approach the matter with an open mind and would be most receptive to any guidance Brandeis could give them. Brandeis was now a Supreme Court justice, and he was pleased by the invitation. Zionists had enough enemies. If the AJC could be persuaded to join the congress without feeling that they had lost face, it would be immensely helpful. So the new justice went to the Astor Hotel full of hope and good will. It never dawned on him to question his willingness to retain a public position in the Zionist movement.

The meeting began in a spirit of cooperation. Brandeis and his colleagues explained the history and rationale of the anticipated congress. It would be held soon—perhaps by the autumn of 1916—and would cover a broad agenda that would extend beyond the plight of Jews in foreign lands. If the AJC disagreed with those plans, it could try to change them, but only *after* it had formally joined the congress. When their explanation was concluded, the Brandeis group offered to retire to allow the AJC members to discuss the issue among themselves. Members of the audience cried out for them to stay, and, at Marshall's specific request, Brandeis agreed. He was totally unprepared for what followed.

Members of the audience, quite agitated, stood up and began yelling at the new Supreme Court justice. The most insulting moment came when one Judah Magnes stood up, shook his finger at Brandeis, and attacked his view that, for the moment at least, the timing and scope of the congress were settled. He might be a member of the Supreme Court now, Magnes told Brandeis, but the Jewish people would ultimately repudiate his leadership.

Brandeis was completely surprised by all this, and afterwards he remained convinced that the whole meeting had been an "ambush" designed to embarrass him. An editorial in the *New York Times* a couple of days later certainly seemed to confirm Brandeis's theory. The paper was run by Adolph Ochs and his family, and they were all part of the German–Jewish community that opposed Zionism and Brandeis's leadership. And now the paper said the whole incident was uncomfortable for Brandeis personally and demeaning to the Court of which he was a member. Resignation from the Zionist movement was the only appropriate course. "It is evident," the editorial stated, "that a good deal of feeling was aroused, and altogether the general impression will be, we fear, that Justice Brandeis might with great propriety have avoided taking part in such a controversy. . . . Now that he has discharged his duty as a member of the committee appointed by the Jewish Congress Organization, we venture to express hope that he will consider he is discharged of further obligation and will in the future leave to others subjects of such [a] controversial nature."[3]

Both Marshall and Magnes wrote letters of apology to Brandeis, stating that they had not intended to embarrass him and that the vigor of the discussion reflected only the emotion inspired by the congress issue. Brandeis did not put much stock in the apologies, but none of that mattered any more. His friends and colleagues had worked hard to get him on the Court, and he did not want to do anything that would undermine public confidence in the judiciary. He really had no alternative but to resign from all public offices in Zionism. He could not afford—and he did not want the Court to risk—another fiasco like the one at the Astor Hotel. Many of his Zionist associates protested, but Brandeis ignored them. When it came to the Court's integrity, there could be no compromise.

At the same time he was not about to withdraw from the movement altogether. He would not retain any public office, he would not give public speeches, and he would, as far as the public was concerned, become invisible. But he saw no reason not to continue his activities in private. If they were done discreetly, the Court's reputation could suffer no harm. So he continued to attend (but no longer chair) the meetings of the Provisional Executive Committee; he continued to travel to New York to review the books and activities of the organization; and the people in the organization continued to defer to him as their leader. The only things he lacked, really, were a title and a public presence.

One of the first things he did was to resolve the congress issue. Ironically, Brandeis personally agreed with the AJC that the congress should concern itself only with the plight of Jews overseas. At first there was great resistance on his supporters' side to any compromise. When the Congress Organizing Committee first met in August 1916, Brandeis's proposal was rejected. Brandeis had his associates intensify their efforts, and when the issue came to another vote in September, the compromise was accepted. Under it, the congress would concern only the plight of Jews overseas and would be only a temporary body that would disband after the meeting was held.

At first blush it appeared to many people in the movement that Brandeis had compromised too much. For some it was the beginning of the end of their commitment to his leadership. But Brandeis saw the congress issue in a larger context. It was not only a question of helping protect the rights and lives of Jews in foreign lands; of even greater importance was the establishment of a permanent Zionist organization in America, one that would be disciplined, efficient, and able to breathe life into the dream of a Jewish homeland in Palestine. The compromise with the AJC was a step in that direction. And later, after America entered the war, he engineered an agreement to postpone the institution of the congress until after the war (although it never turned out to be a temporary body, as the AJC hoped—after that first meeting in 1918, the congress formally disbanded and then reorganized itself into a permanent organization).

From his first days as chairman of the Provisional Executive Committee in 1914 Brandeis had stressed the importance of fund raising. The committeee's ability to help Jews overseas would remain a mirage unless they had money, lots of money. That meant that membership had to be increased; efforts to solicit contributions had to be intensified; and discipline had to be enforced to make sure the necessary organizational tasks were performed. In letters and speeches Brandeis referred to these goals in an appropriate slogan—"Men! Money! Discipline!" No one could avoid the exhortation to do better.

Many complained about their new chairman's zeal and tenacity, but it worked. By 1919 there were more than 175,000 registered Zionists, a dramatic improvement from the 12,000 on the membership rolls when Brandeis took over. There were similar improvements in fund raising. Brandeis assumed a budget of only a few thousand dollars; within five years it approached two million. Many factors other than Brandeis's leadership helped account for these developments. But his presence represented an important influence.

There were costs for this success. Brandeis almost always saw issues in practical terms. The Zionists were, from his view, confronted with man-made problems that had to be made responsive to man-made solutions. Religious and spiritual values had little or no place in his scheme. He was therefore disturbed when his colleagues' attention was diverted from the organizational tasks to religious and cultural missions. It was all well and good to speak of the Diaspora—the dispersal of Jews away from their Biblical homeland in Palestine—but emotionalism would not advance the cause.

Many American Zionists and their organizations saw it differently. Fund raising was important, but for many people other concerns—like the perpetuation of Jewish culture and religion—assumed priority. Slowly at first, then with increasing frequency, complaints were heard that the leaders were insensitive to the real underpinnings of Zionism. None of it altered Brandeis's course. Any diffusion of goals impeded progress. Of that he was sure. Indeed, as he became more involved in Zionist affairs, he became more and more convinced of the need for a centralized organization, one that would focus energies and funds on practical matters.

By the spring of 1918 a plan had been developed. The Federation of American Zionists—a loose coalition that had existed since 1898—would be eliminated, as would all the numerous other Zionist organizations. Instead there would be one central body—the Zionist Organization of America—to which every American Zionist would belong. Moreover, the ZOA would concentrate its efforts on fund raising and the economics of developing Palestine. With one major exception—the promotion of Hebrew as the dominant language of Jews in Palestine—cultural, religious, and even political issues would receive scant attention. The Zionist organization would not be painted as the vanguard of a new country with political autonomy; instead, it would be described as a means of helping people who needed some assistance to escape persecution. This would not only be more efficient; it would also facilitate contributions from Jews who considered themselves only as American citizens and did not want to associate with a group whose first loyalties were to a national homeland somewhere else.

The plan was first endorsed by the Provisional Executive Committee and then presented to the convention of Zionist organizations in Pittsburgh in June. There was considerable debate and much dissension. Many Eastern European Jews sensed that the Zionist movement was being stripped of its emotional supports, the cultural and religious ties that fueled so many local societies. But Brandeis had faced obstacles before in his drive to effect reform. Although he made no public statements, he worked the hotel lobbies, talking to delegates, explaining the wisdom and urgency of the proposal. His lieutenants also spread the word and, in the end, the plan was adopted. In addition to the organizational change, the convention adopted a formal resolution—to be known as the Pittsburgh Platform—that committed the ZOA to protection of the rights of all peoples in Palestine, to public control of land development, to free schools, and to the use of Hebrew as the language of instruction.

Despite this apparent achievement, many delegates left Pittsburgh with a sense of disappointment. Everything was becoming a little too practical. Some people were very bitter about it. But still, no one could deny that Justice Brandeis—even as a leader behind the scenes—was a magnetic force, a man who inspired hope and dedication. At one point during the convention a delegate spotted the justice sitting alone in the gallery above the convention floor. The delegate began to wave frantically, and within a few moments all 500 delegates were standing, yelling Brandeis's name, cheering, and then breaking into song. "It was," recalled one observer, "as though a hurricane, elemental in its might, had swept through them. And it was those few moments more than anything else that occurred throughout the convention that served to create the new 'Zionist Organization of America.' "[4]

Long before the Pittsburgh Convention, Chaim Weizmann appreciated Brandeis's importance to the Zionist Movement. Unhappily for both of them, it was one of the few things they had in common.

Chaim was born in Russia in 1874. His early experiences were quite different from Brandeis's. Chaim came from a very large family—fifteen children, twelve of whom survived to adulthood. Fortunately, Chaim's father ran a lumber mill and was relatively affluent. But the dominant fact of Chaim's childhood was his religion. Unlike Brandeis, who did not witness serious anti-Semitism until his later years, Chaim saw evidence of it almost daily as a child. The schools he couldn't attend. The places he couldn't go. The identification cards he had to carry. And then there were the pogroms. After Czar Alexander II was assassinated in 1881 people began to suspect that Jews were conspirators against the state, traitors who owed allegiance to a God and a land that were not Russian. Violence became a way of life, and for many Jews, fear an everyday emotion.

All this Chaim Weizmann remembered as he grew older. It was a part of him, an indelible imprint on his memory. It shaped his approach to Zionism. Unlike Brandeis, Weizmann did not view Zionism as a social experiment, an opportunity to plan an ideal community. No, for him Zionism was a deeply felt necessity, a cause that could, literally, determine whether people lived or died. And surrounding this dream was the Biblical commitment that the Jews could return to Palestine, the Promised Land. For Weizmann, then, Zionism represented a complex of deep emotions. Brandeis could not empathize with all that.

For Weizmann there was no other way. So when Theodore Herzl, Zionism's chief founder, agreed in 1903 to accept the British offer of Uganda as the Jewish homeland, Weizmann was all sound and fury. By the turn of the century he had secured his doctorate and was on his way to becoming an accomplished chemist. But he was also a powerful speaker, and there was nothing that inspired him more than his commitment to Zionism. Weizmann could not understand Herzl's willingness to compromise on an East African colony. There was a bitter fight at the Zionist convention, a fight that Weizmann never forgot. Many delegates walked out and the issue was left unresolved.

Herzl died the following year, and slowly, almost inevitably, Weizmann began to succeed him as the foremost leader of the Zionist Movement. The offer of Uganda did not die with Herzl, however, and in 1906 Weizmann, then living in London, found himself discussing the issue with Arthur Balfour, the former prime minister and now a candidate for the House of Commons. Why couldn't the Jews accept Uganda and forget about Palestine, Balfour asked. After all, Palestine was controlled by Turkey, was inhabited by hundreds of thousands of Arabs and would pose many problems for Jewish settlement. "Mr. Balfour," Weizmann responded, "supposing I were to offer you Paris instead of London, would you take it?" Balfour looked up. "But Dr. Weizmann, we have London." "That is true," the Zionist leader responded. "But we had Jerusalem when London was a marsh."[5]

Hopes of securing Palestine as the Jewish homeland seemed dim until war broke out in 1914. Turkey had joined forces with the Central Powers against England. If the British and their allies were successful, Turkey would be ripe for dismemberment. Weizmann began to talk to government leaders in England. He knew them all well, since his agitation for aid had been continuous over the past decade. And more than that, his work as a chemist was useful to the British war effort.

Over in the United States, Brandeis was doing what he could. Soon after his appointment to the Provisional Executive Committee, he went to see President Wilson as well as the British and French ambassadors. The president was sympathetic to Zionist aims. So was the British ambassador. The French, Brandeis suspected, might be a problem.

As the tide of war began to turn in the Allies' favor, Weizmann's efforts—and prospects for success—accelerated. He pushed for a British Protectorate in Palestine, one that would explicitly recognize the area as the Jewish homeland. Urgent telegrams were being sent to Brandeis. The American government's support was critical, Weizmann said. England would not stand alone on this. Brandeis, however, was not about to be rushed. Timing was the key. In the spring of 1917 he met Balfour, then the British foreign secretary, and afterwards he went to see the president again. Wilson told the Supreme Court justice that he supported the establishment of the Jewish homeland in Palestine. But America had just entered the war, and Zionism's goals were not at the top of the president's list. Patience was counseled.

Back in London, Weizmann was operating at a feverish pace. Some of his staunchest opponents were Jewish members of government who saw Zionism as an attack upon their loyalty to England. Finally, happily, the British Cabinet tentatively approved a general declaration in September 1917 favoring the establishment of the Jewish homeland in Palestine under British auspices. The Cabinet made it clear to Weizmann, though, that it would not finalize the declaration until the United States approved. The Zionist leader immediately wired President Wilson, asking for his support. The president's response, however, was rather noncommittal, expressing sympathy but indicating that the time was not right for a public declaration.

Weizmann became frantic. If the declaration were not finalized now, he feared, there might not be another opportunity. He sent an urgent wire to Brandeis, telling him that there could be no delay in securing the president's approval. On the evening of September 23, the justice and his Zionist colleague Stephen Wise met with Colonel House in his New York City apartment. House explained to the two visitors that the president was indeed committed to Zionism and that he was prepared to make a statement that went much further than House thought advisable. But establishment of the Jewish homeland in Palestine was a delicate matter, one in which other allied governments were interested. The American government, House explained, should say as little as possible for the time being. He then prepared a response for Weizmann, and the next day Brandeis sent the cable to his counterpart in London. "From talks I have had with President and from expressions of opinion given to closest advisers," the cable advised Weizmann, "I feel I can answer you that he is [in] entire sympathy with declaration. . . . I of course heartily agree."[6]

Over the next month Weizmann and Brandeis were in frequent contact as they tried to put the finishing touches on the wording of the declaration. By the middle of October the president told House to advise the British government that the complete text had his approval. The word was passed, and on November 2, 1917, the declaration was formally released in a letter from Balfour to Lord Lionel Walter Rothschild, a Zionist benefactor. "His Majesty's Government view[s] with favour the establishment in Palestine of a national home for the Jewish people," the letter read, "and will use [its] best endeavours to facilitate the achievement of this object, it being clearly understood that nothing shall be done which may prejudice the civil and religious rights of existing non-Jewish communities in Palestine or the rights and political status enjoyed by Jews in any other country."[7]

Formulating the declaration was one thing. Implementing it was quite another. Anything could happen. In fact, the declaration itself was almost undermined shortly before its formulation. In the summer of 1917, Henry Morgenthau, a former ambassador to Turkey, believed he could persuade the Turks to renounce their alliance with the Central Powers and then sell Palestine to the Jews. It was a crazy scheme. As Weizmann later observed, Morgenthau's ambition greatly exceeded his intelligence. Because of his government contacts, however, Morgenthau convinced the State Department that the proposal was worth exploring and that he should be authorized to pursue the matter on behalf of the United States government. Zionists like Weizmann were aghast at the idea. If Turkey were separated from the central powers, there would be no spoils in Palestine to give to the Jews after the war. Weizmann traveled to Gibraltar to head Morgenthau off. For his part, Brandeis arranged to have Felix Frankfurter accompany the former ambassador and report back on developments. Within a short time Frankfurter saw the futility of the venture, and he had the State Department call Morgenthau back to Washington.

Alice was making frequent trips outside of Washington. Usually she would go to visit her mother in New York City or friends and family in Boston. Louis wrote to her almost every day she was gone. He would briefly report on his activities: a meeting with the chief justice on Court business, dinner with his old friend George Rublee, a ride in Potomac Park on his horse Robert Son of Battle. Nothing very unusual. All that changed, however, when the armistice was signed on November 11, 1918, and the world prepared for the treaty negotiations at Versailles.

For the Zionists it was the opportunity to implement the Balfour Declaration. Weizmann planned to go, and he urged that Brandeis also attend. Some Americans agreed. Stephen Wise later implored Wilson to appoint Brandeis to the American delegation. But the president wouldn't hear of it. "I named Brandeis to the Bench and you remember how difficult it was to get him confirmed," the president told Wise. ". . . If he comes here he will have to resign from the Bench. It would not be easy for me to secure Senate confirmation for another great liberal, even if I could find him. . . . Dr. Wise," Wilson concluded, "I need Brandeis everywhere, but I must leave him somewhere."[8]

Brandeis agreed with these sentiments. He did not want to appear in a public forum, especially one that would take him away from the Court's business. The chief justice's lecture on the Mexican–American commission no doubt remained fixed in his memory. Others could go instead of Brandeis, people loyal to the cause and, perhaps even more important, dedicated to him.

One of the first to go was deHaas. From Brandeis's perspective, sending deHaas to the Paris Peace Conference was eminently sensible. Jack was the one who had awakened him to Zionism, his teacher and his constant companion in Zionist struggles. No one knew more than deHaas, and no one would be more protective of Brandeis's interests. From another view, the dispatch of deHaas was clearly a mistake. It was not only his personality, which was an abrasive and dictatorial one that seemed ill suited to the sensitivity of peace negotiations; perhaps even more significant was that deHaas did not like Weizmann, and cooperation between them was probably an idle hope. His first hero was Herzl, the leader who had accepted the idea of Uganda as a Jewish homeland. Of course deHaas knew of Weizmann's opposition to and dislike of Herzl, and it was not something that would facilitate harmonious relations. Brandeis certainly knew all that, because deHaas had long ago told the justice that he did not have a high regard for Weizmann's intelligence or leadership talents.

Brandeis sent other deputies to the Peace Conference. None was more important than Frankfurter. When the Harvard law professor reached Paris in March 1919 he immediately reported back to Brandeis that, as he no doubt expected, Weizmann and deHaas were at loggerheads. Frankfurter, who maintained good relations with almost all factions, described the conflict in terms that inadvertently had a certain comical tone to them. "The deHaas that you know," Frankfurter told the justice, "is not the deHaas that Weizmann knows, for the deHaas who works with you is not the deHaas who works with Weizmann." Frankfurter was sure, however, that Brandeis and Weizmann would work together "with the happiest accord."[9] In the meantime, Frankfurter scurried about Paris, talking to President Wilson, Arab leaders, and other foreign leaders, all in an effort to unite the Zionists and to lay the foundation for a treaty provision that would recognize the establishment of a Jewish homeland in Palestine.

Frankfurter felt that he was making progress. He secured a letter from Arab Prince Feisal expressing support for a Jewish settlement in Palestine. He also obtained a letter from Wilson expressing his personal commitment to the Balfour Declaration and adding that "so far I have found no one who is seriously opposing the purpose which it embodies."[10] Indeed, the president had already appointed a commission, with the blessings of the other conferees, to review the options. Hope and excitement abounded in the Zionist camp. As the summer approached—and with it a Court recess—Frankfurter urged Brandeis to come to Paris and then visit Palestine. There he could talk to officials and inhabitants and make his own assessment.

Brandeis had not traveled abroad for many years, and, except for occasional travel to New York City and summer vacations in Massachusetts, he rarely traveled anywhere in the United States. It usually involved too much energy. But he did make exceptions for Zionist matters. And no trip seemed more exciting now, or more promising, than a trip to Palestine. In the middle of June 1919 he sailed for Europe with his daughter Susan and deHaas, who had recently returned from Paris. Alice was not up to the trip and remained behind.

It was a hectic journey, filled with appointments, inspections, and meetings. In Paris for a few days, the justice met with President Wilson and House, who was physically ill and becoming more and more isolated from Wilson. The president could no longer tolerate criticism of any kind, even from his most trusted advisor. From there Brandeis went to Egypt and then to Palestine. The first sights were a moving experience. "It is a wonderful country, a wonderful city," he wrote to Alice from Jerusalem. ". . . It is a miniature California, but a California endowed with all the interest which the history of man can contribute and the deepest emotions which can stir a people. The ages-long longing, the love is all explicable now. . . . The problems are serious and numerous," he concluded. "The way is long, the path difficult and uncertain; but the struggle is worthwhile. It is indeed a Holy Land."[11] For a man untouched by religious sentiments, it was a most unusual reaction.

By the time Brandeis returned to Paris, the pragmatic perspective was fully in place. One of the first things he did was complain to Balfour, attending the Peace Conference, about the British soldiers in Palestine. Many were clearly anti-Semitic, and they were sowing seeds of suspicion and hatred among the resident Arab populations. Some soldiers were even distributing the infamous "Protocols of the Learned Elders of Zion"—a fake document that purported to contain the Jews' scheme for attaining world power and enslaving Christians. Balfour was sympathetic to Brandeis's complaints. Within a short time many high-ranking soldiers in Palestine received transfer orders.

Dealing with Weizmann was another story. Brandeis now believed that the political maneuvering was over, that the task before Zionists was to develop Palestine, to make it a country where a people could prosper economically as well as spiritually. That was no small challenge. The land might have California's natural beauty, but there were many obstacles to its enjoyment. There were swamps, soil erosion, and, perhaps worst of all, malaria. The disease was so common that people took it for granted that they or someone they knew would get it. The flies were also plentiful, so much so that people did not even bother to flick them off their faces—they would soon enough be replaced by others. Few of the people Brandeis saw in Palestine looked healthy, and most of those that did turned out to be recent immigrants.

What was needed, Brandeis told Weizmann on his return to Paris, was a Jewish Agency, operated under the auspices of the World Zionist Organization, to devote itself single-mindedly to the elimination of these problems. Weizmann, of course, recognized the physical problems of developing Palestine. He had already spent considerable time there. But he could not accept Brandeis's conclusion that political considerations were no longer important. He knew better. And he did not like Brandeis's desire to turn the organization into a streamlined business. Like almost any politician, Weizmann wanted all the disparate groups to feel that they were a part of the action. He therefore told Brandeis that reliance should be placed on the National Councils that had been created in European countries during the war. These councils had roots in the community and could effectively involve thousands of Jews in Palestine's development.

Weizmann pushed his position vigorously. While he could be accommodating in some situations, in others he could be sarcastic, blunt, hard as nails. And that toughness produced some memorable disputes in the Zionist organization. Years later, as Felix Warburg, a Zionist activist, lay dying, his son asked if he were in much pain. The old man paused, and then whispered to his son, "This is nothing compared to some of the things I went through with Weizmann."[12]

In Brandeis, Weizmann found his match. They had met for the first time a few weeks before when Brandeis stopped off in Paris. Each was respectful but wary of the other. It was as though they sensed the personal conflicts that lay before them. Weizmann told colleagues that there was something "messianic" about the Supreme Court justice. But he soon noticed other traits as well. Brandeis, Weizmann later remembered, "was a Puritan: upright, austere, of a scrupulous honesty and implacable logic. These qualities sometimes made him hard to work with; like Wilson he was apt to evolve theories, based on the highest principles, from his inner consciousness, and then expect the facts to fit in with them. If the facts failed to oblige," Weizmann recalled, "so much the worse for the facts."[13]

The two of them argued now about the best way to build Palestine. Others participated and Brandeis, the epitome of tact, tried to gracefully steer Weizmann away from his proposal to use the National Councils. Weizmann soon confronted Brandeis and asked that personal diplomacy be put aside. What was his precise reaction to the idea? The American Zionist answered in cold, measured tones. "I am opposed to your plan both in principle and practice," he said.[14] Ultimately the Zionist group sided with Brandeis. In time it was to prove a costly victory.

By the spring of 1920 the victorious nations concluded the Treaty of San Remo and formally recognized the establishment of a Jewish homeland in Palestine under a British protectorate. To Brandeis it only confirmed his view that the time of politicking was over. The only real task was Palestine's economic development. He now had definite proposals to achieve that goal. And when he returned to London in July 1920 for the World Zionist Convention—the first since 1913—he was hopeful that his plans would meet with the convention's approval.

Brandeis was in high spirits. He loved London. It was so ordered, so efficient, so cultured, so—well, civilized. And he was very much in demand at social gatherings. Judges, government officials, law professors—all of them wanted to meet the famous Supreme Court justice. Unfortunately, Brandeis found these social gatherings much more to his liking than the convention proceedings. For all his praise of congresses and democracy, Brandeis found the Zionist meeting a little *too* democratic. People stood up and rambled on for hours on end. There were no rules, no discipline, and whenever Brandeis—who was presiding—suggested some order, he was shouted down. It was, in all, an exhausting experience. And frustrating as well.

In his opening remarks to the American delegation on the morning of July 14, 1920, Brandeis reiterated views he had expressed before. "We have come to the time," he observed, "when there are no politics that are valuable except the politics of action." One of the top priorities was to eliminate malaria. But to do that and make other improvements would require money, lots of money. A new organization had to be structured, one that would convince potential contributors that the Zionist funds were as safe as a bank's. And more than that, that a contributor could make a return on his investment. It was necessary to separate donations to the general organization from funds people gave for specific projects—funds, it was hoped, that in time could show a substantial return. To Brandeis this scheme would represent a dramatic improvement over the past. From his knowledge of the London office records, he was convinced that the World Zionist Organization—as opposed to the ZOA—had squandered much of its resources on unnecessary trips, salaries, and facilities.

To change all that, Brandeis proposed that the world organization be run by a seven-man executive committee. Weizmann and one of his colleagues would be a part of it; so would Brandeis and Bernard Flexner, a new and quite able soldier from the American side. The four of them would pick three other men with solid business credentials to join the executive committee. Although Brandeis did not identify the three businessmen to the American delegation, he and Weizmann had already decided who they would be: Lord Reading, Sir Alfred Mond, and Baron James de Rothschild. None of these men was a Zionist; like Brandeis, they viewed the development of Palestine in social terms—an opportunity to help people who suffered persecution in foreign lands. The three financiers had been told by Brandeis and Weizmann that the executive committee would not devote itself to spiritual or religious matters, only economic questions. Their acceptance had been predicated on that condition.

When the plan became known to Weizmann's colleagues, many voiced strong opposition. It would not do, they said, to have non-Zionists running the show. The World Zionist Organization could not ignore the emotional appeal of the movement. Pressure was put on Weizmann to change the plan, and he acquiesced. While Brandeis slept one night, Weizmann and some of his cohorts met with Rothschild and Mond. It was explained that the executive committee would be in charge of developing Hebrew as a national language, as well as other cultural responsibilities. The two businessmen wanted no part of that, and it was decided to create a separate committee on economic matters that would use the services of Mond, Rothschild, and Reading.

When Brandeis learned of the new plan the next morning, he was furious. In part, it reflected his conviction that the Keren Hayesod—the Europeans' proposed foundation for raising funds—was impractical because there were no procedures to assure contributors that targeted donations would be used wisely for specified purposes. Instead, the Europeans wanted to keep all moneys—including those for operating expenses—in one fund. Consequently, Brandeis feared that the funds would be used for purposes other than Palestine's development—a concern he hoped to alleviate with the new seven-man executive committee. But now it was not only a question of organization. Weizmann had betrayed him, had almost literally stolen away in the night to undo an agreement that had been reached. Never again would he trust Weizmann. Years later, when mutual friends urged a reconciliation between the two men, Brandeis remained adamant. "I can forgive," he would say, "but if you ask me to forget, you ask me to give up experience."[15]

Brandeis's reaction to Weizmann's shift was immediate and dramatic. He would have nothing to do with the World Zionist Organization leadership. In reaction, some responded that his presence was necessary to help Jews in Eastern Europe, that only he had the kind of stature to legitimize Zionism in the eyes of the gentile world—but Brandeis would not yield. He said he would accept the post of honorary president only if no American participated in the WZO executive committee. Otherwise, he said, it would appear that the Americans approved of Weizmann's plan. When two members of the American delegation objected to this condition, Brandeis decided against being honorary president. He needed—he demanded—unanimous support from his delegation.

Ironically, no American did serve on the newly created WZO executive committee. Brandeis was against their participation, and none had the courage or independence to challenge him. At least not yet. But the strains of his leadership were beginning to show. People were beginning to resent him.

To begin with, American Zionists did not like dealing with deHaas. He was unpleasant and difficult. Yet Brandeis seemed oblivious to those personality traits. Virtually everyone and everything had to be filtered through deHaas. This reflected not only Brandeis's gratitude for deHaas's early efforts to get him involved in Zionism; it also reflected Brandeis's method of operation. He was a Supreme Court justice now, with dreams to fulfill and so little time to do everything. By funneling matters through deHaas, Brandeis conserved his own energies. However efficient, the system did little to maintain high spirits.

A concerted effort was made to change all that at the London Conference. Many members of the American delegation pressured Brandeis to resign from the Court and become the full-time leader of the World Zionist Organization. Although deeply committed to the cause, Brandeis did not give serious consideration to the proposal. He still had goals for his Court work, goals that reflected a lifetime of thinking and activity. And more than that, he could not forget the people in America who had worked so hard for his appointment, people who now expected some return on their emotional investment in him. "He thought," one associate later recalled, "that his resignation from the Bench would be misunderstood by his American followers, especially his non-Jewish ones. At a point when he had reached the pinnacle, it would be difficult to explain why he was walking away from it."[16]

The decision to remain an invisible leader did not go over well with many members of the American delegation. The grumbling was becoming more vocal and more persistent. Not only did they find him too distant personally; they also felt that he was so far removed from things Jewish. He did not speak Yiddish (and often wondered why some elements of the Yiddish press in New York continually criticized his leadership). He seemed at times to have no feel for the emotions that drove people to Zionism. The Bible. Tradition. Pogroms. All these were, in a true sense, alien to his experience. One participant at the London Conference could not help but smile when he recalled in later years Brandeis's efforts to motivate his audience to join in the development of Palestine. The justice's points of reference, his vehicles of inspiration, were not great moments in Jewish history. No, he referred instead to Anglo-Saxons who had colonized and developed New England.

On the ship returning to the United States, Brandeis wrote a detailed memorandum outlining his proposals for developing Palestine. Because it was written on the S.S. *Zeeland*, the document became known as the Zeeland Memorandum, and for years afterwards it was the guiding light for Brandeis's followers. However insightful, the paper could not preserve Brandeis's status in the Zionist movement. Even he was beginning to sense that.

Albert Einstein was one of the first Jewish folk heroes in the United States. Although he was residing in Germany, Einstein's name and work were well known to the American Jew. It was his famous theory of relativity. Few knew what it meant, but everyone agreed that it was important. And Einstein, a Jew, was the one who had discovered it. He helped give Jews, even American Jews, a sense of pride, a respectability, that they needed so much.

So when Einstein accompanied Weizmann to the United States in April 1921, it was bound to bolster support for the new president of the World Zionist Organization. When the ship carrying the two men arrived in New York harbor, the thousands of people packed on the Battery became almost delirious with joy. There was shouting, singing, pandemonium. Einstein, who was not a party to any of the Zionist organizational disputes, issued a statement urging Jews to stand by Weizmann. It was the kind of endorsement that any politician would treasure.

Actually, Weizmann had been very nervous about his first trip to the United States. He was there to develop a Keren Hayesod in the United States. His trip also coincided with the ZOA convention scheduled for Cleveland in June. Weizmann knew that his followers would make an attempt to wrest control from the Brandeis faction. He was hopeful, however, that their differences could be resolved without a fight. He did not have high hopes, though. Brandeis and ZOA President Julian Mack had recruited Benjamin V. Cohen, a young lawyer, to go to London to be their eyes and ears in Zionist councils there, and Cohen reported to Mack in early 1921 that Weizmann had a "grave anxiety" that he would not be welcomed by Americans whose help he needed. It was not paranoia. As Mack well knew, Weizmann would not be received with open arms by the ZOA leaders.

In fact, the only thing Weizmann received from the American leaders on his arrival was a memorandum outlining the basis of future cooperation. The memorandum proposed a strong, centralized organization that would focus on Palestine's economic development. The Keren Hayesod would be eliminated and in its place would be substituted procedures to restrict the use of financial contributions. The memorandum was not designed as a talking paper. It was, in effect, a demand. Brandeis did not intend to compromise. He did not trust Weizmann and his colleagues. Bargaining was no longer an option. Weizmann, he told his disciples, is "incapable of keeping his word, however explicitly expressed or solemnly given. I am therefore of the opinion that no arrangement made for the future should be based as a foundation upon his having 'agreed.' "[17]

Brandeis knew that defeat was possible, if not likely. But no matter. He was prepared to walk away from the ZOA leadership and have his lieutenants resign from their positions. There were vigorous discussions on that point. Many, sensing that defeat was imminent, wanted to remain in official positions with the organization. Only in that way, they said, could they hope to influence its direction. Brandeis remained adamant. A person could not stay at the head of an organization if he disagreed with its methods of operation. It was a matter of principle, and there could be no compromise on principle. "When you get to problems where people differ," the justice explained, "you have to come to a decision. And if I come to the view that I'm 51 percent right, I have to fight for that rather than fighting with those who may differ with me only to a minor degree." So they all had to stand together.[18]

Weizmann did not appreciate all this when he read the memo that Mack gave him. He knew only that Brandeis and his group did not fully appreciate Zionism as a form of "folk renaissance." The Americans, Weizmann believed, were too preoccupied with the economics of the matter and too little concerned with the spiritual base of Zionism. For the Europeans, it was an unacceptable approach. Nonetheless, Weizmann was willing to talk with Brandeis's deputies. The meetings took place in Cleveland. Wise, Mack, and especially Frankfurter carried the ball for the Brandeis group. At one point an agreement seemed possible, but then Weizmann, pressured by his colleagues, broke off discussions on April 17. Frankfurter did not give up. A few days later he wired Brandeis in Washington that Walter Lippmann had talked to Weizmann, that he wanted to reach an agreement if "humanly possible," and that he wanted to meet with Brandeis, with Lippmann acting as an intermediary. Brandeis immediately rejected the offer. "As I see it," he told Frankfurter, "we can only weaken our position by conference.... Our strength within the organization will exist & be appreciated only if it is once understood that when we take a position—we are immovable."[19]

When the ZOA convention convened in Cleveland two months later, the expected occurred. A motion to make Mack the convention chairman was soundly defeated. The next crucial vote came on the establishment of a Keren Hayesod in the United States, one that would not distinguish between investments and donations. After hours of debate—including a four-hour speech by Frankfurter—the motion was carried by a vote of 153–71. At 1:30 in the morning, a bleary-eyed Julian Mack went to the lectern and read a letter from Louis Brandeis. It was addressed to Mack in anticipation of defeat. A hush fell over the convention floor. "With the principles and policies adopted by the National Executive Committee under your leadership," the justice wrote the ZOA president, "I am in complete agreement. Strict adherence to those principles is demanded by the high Zionist ideals.... We who believe in those principles and policies cannot properly take part in any administration of Zionist affairs which repudiates them." In the next paragraph Brandeis said he expected Mack to resign from the ZOA executive committee if the convention rejected their program. In that event he also asked that Mack present his resignation as honorary president. "Our place will then be as humble soldiers in the ranks...," the letter concluded.[20] When he was finished, Mack submitted his resignation from the executive committee along with the resignations of thirty-six men. And then they walked out of the convention.

Weizmann and his group later said that the Brandeis crowd were not good losers, that they violated an American tradition by resigning after their defeat. It was, however, to be only a temporary absence. In the meantime, Brandeis had other causes to battle. And few preoccupied him more around this time than the American citizen's freedom of speech.

NINETEEN

Protecting Speech

Necessity is the plea for every infringement of human freedom. It is the argument of tyrants; it is the creed of slaves.

WILLIAM PITT

Alger Hiss didn't know about the rule. He was sitting in a Washington restaurant on a December afternoon in 1929, enjoying the bachelor's luncheon his friends were giving him to celebrate his forthcoming marriage that weekend. Dick Field turned to Hiss. How did you do it, Alger? How did you get the justice to let you break the rule? A blank look came across Hiss's face. What rule? You know, Field responded, the rule that none of the justice's clerks can be married. At first Hiss thought that Field was kidding. When he had accepted the clerkship no one, not even the justice, had told him he could not get married. But others at the table joined in. Everyone, they said, knew that the justice did not want his clerks to be married. Fear overcame Hiss. His fiancée was at that point driving down to Washington so they could be married at his parents' home on Maryland's eastern shore. There was nothing left to do but to confess and throw himself on the mercy of the justice.

He raced over to the townhouse at 1720 Eye Street in Washington and went immediately to the justice's study. Hiss stammered that he had made a grievous error, one that really could not be changed. It was too late. It was an honest mistake, and he hoped the justice would forgive him. Oliver Wendell Holmes, dressed in his usual formal morning coat and striped trousers, looked up. What was it? Hiss confessed to his forthcoming marriage. Oh, said the justice, don't worry about that. In fact, maybe Alger should take a week off to enjoy himself. That was out of the question, the clerk responded. He would be there first thing Monday morning. Hiss left the justice's study relieved. He had been granted a reprieve.

Others were not as fortunate. Because the justice did have a rule that none of his clerks—his "boys," as he called them—could be married. He wanted a companion, someone who would be able to cater to his wants. Research was generally the least of his needs. He wanted someone to talk to, someone who would accompany him on car rides to tour the city. A wife would make other demands on the clerk, demands that might prevent him from responding to the justice.

So when Dean Acheson got married near the end of his student tenure at Harvard Law School, he learned that there was no possibility of a clerkship with Holmes. It was a great disappointment to Acheson. To him Holmes had been, always would be, the greatest Supreme Court justice. No one could match his insights into human nature and the law. And no one had his gift for expression. Holmes had a way with words that was simply extraordinary. Felix Frankfurter, who selected clerks for both Holmes and Brandeis, told Dean that there was an alternative. He could clerk for Brandeis. Hardly a compromise. And so in the autumn of 1919 Acheson, after performing some wartime service in Washington, reported for work at Stoneleigh Court.

Acheson was nervous at first, and the justice did little to ease the tension. He seemed distant and preoccupied. Polite but aloof. The justice did make it clear, however, that he expected vigorous analysis in the preparation of opinions. Acheson was to voice his views, even if they were critical of the justice's work. Acheson took Brandeis at his word, and, after several months—and many discussions—the relationship began to thaw. In fact, by the end of his two-year stint with the justice, Acheson felt a closeness toward Brandeis that he had once thought impossible. "He is a person," he wrote to Frankfurter at one point, "to whom one gets most ungodly attached, isn't he?"[1]

Acheson was especially impressed, even overwhelmed on occasion, by the justice's approach to decision-making. One case in particular stood out in his mind. The Court was considering a lower court decision, and the question was whether the lower court judge had intended to dispose of all the issues. On a first reading Acheson found the judge's opinion ambiguous and "a perfect mess." Acheson assumed that the judge was an "idiot." Brandeis saw it differently. There had to be an explanation. Through painstaking study he was able almost to recreate the judge's psychological process in writing the opinion. Brandeis determined that the second part of the opinion was written two weeks after the first part. He then proceeded to discover the law the judge had been reading during those two weeks. By the time he was finished, Brandeis had exposed the steps by which the opinion had been constructed and, with that information, was able to see that the judge had intended to dispose of all the issues. Acheson was amazed by the whole performance. The justice's perseverance was nothing short of incredible. "What I want to know," the clerk asked Frankfurter, "is what psychological process it is which keeps the Justice freshly on the trail when everyone else is sick of the subject and thoroughly convinced that the end has been reached. It isn't simply a dogged resolution to keep on looking."[2]

Acheson was not a passive observer in all this. On many matters he and the justice had vigorous debates in the preparation of opinions. And few matters took as much time as—or were more important than—the decisions concerning an individual's constitutional right to free speech.

The day before he asked Congress to declare war on Germany in 1917, President Wilson summoned Frank Cobb, editor of the *New York World,* to the White House. The president was about to take a dramatic step, and he wanted to unburden himself with someone, a person who could appreciate the consequences of what he was about to do. Once the United States entered the war, Wilson told Cobb, the world they knew would never be the same. America would be transformed by the experience. "Once lead this people into war," he told the journalist, "and they'll forget there ever was such a thing as tolerance. To fight you must be brutal and ruthless, and the spirit of ruthless brutality will enter into the very fibre of our national life, infecting Congress, the courts, the policeman on the beat, the man in the street." Free speech would be one of the first things to go. The First Amendment plainly stated that Congress shall make no law abridging speech or the right to assembly. The amendment would take on a new meaning now, Wilson said. War changed everything.[3]

Wilson knew what he was talking about. Within months after declaring war, Congress passed an Espionage Act that severely restricted speech. The law made it a crime to do or say anything designed to interfere with the recruitment of soldiers or the prosecution of the war. Dissent, as Wilson predicted, would not be tolerated. And as the president anticipated, the intolerance would outlast the war. In 1920 A. Mitchell Palmer, Wilson's new attorney general, arrested thousands of individuals suspected of being Communists. They were rounded up—on the streets, in their houses, wherever they could be found—and packed off to jail. It was an ironic and sad way to end Wilson's call eight years earlier for a New Freedom. But it reflected the popular mood. The most outrageous abuses of individual freedom were not merely excused; they were encouraged. The New York State Assembly, for example, expelled five delegates because they were Socialists. No matter that they were duly elected by the people; they held views that were un-American. "It was an American vote altogether," the *New York Times* said of the Assembly's action, "a patriotic and conservative vote. An immense majority of the American people will approve and sanction the Assembly's action."[4]

Brandeis's interest in these developments was not entirely academic. It was his daughter Susan. Her growth at law school did not entirely coincide with Louis and Alice's expectations. She seemed disheveled, unkempt, almost slovenly in her appearance. And then there was the young man to whom she had become close. He seemed to be a radical, one of the many young people who questioned the morality of America's participation in the war. It was especially troublesome to Brandeis because he knew that the Espionage Act and other wartime measures would come to the Court for decision. So when Susan informed him that she was thinking of joining a peace group, her father was not encouraging. He urged her to "refrain from talking or other activity in connection with any peace society. It might prove embarrassing," he said.[5] And when she wrote that her boyfriend was thinking of registering as a conscientous objector, her father advised against it.

Louis, and especially Alice, was disturbed by this turn of events. Susan was moving with the wrong people and in the wrong direction. In June 1917 she visited her father in Washington while her mother was vacationing in Boston. Louis had a frank talk with her about many things: Her appearance. Her lack of social graces. And this young man she wanted to marry. Things were happening too fast, Louis said. Perhaps it would be best to wait six months before making a commitment. Susan left without saying what she would do. Afterward Louis sent her a long letter. Like many parental communications, it was full of advice. But warmth and respect were also evident. "Your happiness and worldly development, dearest Susan, are my deep longing," he wrote. "Whatever I can do to advance them, you may rely upon. And yet I recognize how little there is that I can do."[6]

While Susan pondered her father's advice, Louis tried to calm Alice. He reported on his conversation with Susan and the apparent lack of progress. "[S]he really does not belong to our world," he observed. "Perhaps it is a kind of Providence leading her into another where she will fit better." It was the usual Brandeis optimism, but there was an emotional cost. Susan was, after all, his daughter, his own flesh and blood. "There are many defects in her," he wrote to Alice at a later point, "which are prominent and for which I grieve & the existence of which pain me."[7] But he would not interfere. It was her life, he told Alice. She would have to make her own decisions. In time Susan would more than justify her father's confidencc.

Other people could not bide their time. The government was vigorously enforcing the Espionage Act. Many people found that the slightest suggestion of disloyalty resulted in an arrest and a jail sentence. Not surprisingly, some said the law's restrictions on speech were unconstitutional. The United States Supreme Court, however, held otherwise. And one of the first opinions expressing that viewpoint was written by Justice Holmes. That was an important factor to Brandeis. In those first years on the Court, there was no one he respected more—or was closer to—than Holmes.

In a way, the bond between the two justices was not at all predictable. Their personalities and careers stood in sharp contrast. Oliver Wendell Holmes, Jr., was the son of Dr. Oliver Wendell Holmes, a physician in Cambridge, Massachusetts, who was widely known for his poetry. Young Wendell attended Harvard College and planned to get his law degree at Harvard as well. Before he could complete his legal studies, however, he enlisted in the army. Wendell was only twenty years old, the year was 1861, and the nation was in the throes of a civil war. Wendell was a striking young man and he made a handsome soldier. None of that helped him, though. Almost every day of his service was spent in armed combat. He was wounded a few times, once very seriously. For a young man who knew only the gentility of urban life, it was a profound experience, one that he would always remember. Years later, when corresponding with friends, he would recall the anniversaries of Antietam and other battles in which he had fought. On one of their many car rides, he would take his clerks out to Arlington Cemetery to view the graves of fallen comrades. And he would remark that World War I was not nearly as bloody as "our war."

It is not surprising, therefore, that Holmes harbored few illusions about how the real world operated. He was, almost from the beginning, cynical about law and social development. He had a low regard for the people who inhabited legislatures—"dogs," he called them. But he knew that the majority almost always had its way. It was the way of life. Not that anyone could really change things that much. Some things just happened. If you sat on it long enough, he was fond of saying, the world would hatch.

He was also fond of women, and they no doubt found him attractive. With a tall, slim build, long, dark hair, and a full handlebar mustache, he cut an impressive figure. His interest in women did not diminish when he married Fanny Dixwell or when he got older and assumed important positions. It was said, for example, that as a United States Supreme Court justice he would spend many afternoons sipping tea with a woman other than his dedicated wife. On occasion it proved embarrassing. One afternoon tea with a woman friend was interrupted by a butler carrying a note. "Wendell," it read, "I'm downstairs waiting for you in the carriage. Fanny." The justice obeyed the command.

Holmes's appeal was not confined to women. People of all kinds found him immensely attractive. He was so full of ideas, so witty. For many there was nothing more enjoyable than to spend an afternoon listening to Justice Holmes. Law professors especially sought him out, almost as a pilgrimage. One time a Brandeis clerk brought Austin Scott and Sayre MacNeil, two of his professors from Harvard, over to meet the famous Justice Holmes. The two professors gave their calling cards to the housekeeper, who then brought them up to Holmes. In due course the professors were ushered into the study. Holmes was sitting there, folding the cards back and forth. He then said, "First you shuffle and then you deal, which is Scott and which MacNeil?"[8] At other times he could be almost bawdy. "I wonder," he once observed, "if cosmically an idea is any more important than the bowels."[9]

Holmes was a tough decision maker. You did what you had to. Personal sympathy for the parties was an inappropriate basis for resolving a case. You could not keep changing rules to accommodate new situations. So he did not like it when other justices in conference deviated from established legal principles and inquired whether a particular result was just. It was "the stinking sense of justice," he would say, that undermined the proper administration of the law.[10]

Making decisions was relatively easy for Holmes. He had an uncanny ability to isolate and analyze basic issues quickly. At oral arguments he would take careful notes, and after a short while he would reach a conclusion. He would then take out paper and pen and, while the attorneys droned on, write letters to friends scattered across the country and world. Sometimes he would put his head on his arms and take a short nap (and once caused a stir when he awoke to discover the attorney still talking and muttered, audibly enough for everyone to hear, "Jesus Christ!").

If Felix Frankfurter was arguing a case, it was a different story. Frankfurter adored Holmes, viewing him almost reverentially. The admiration and affection were reciprocated. Holmes recognized Frankfurter's superior intelligence and, like Brandeis, allowed Frankfurter to select a new clerk for him every year. Holmes also found Frankfurter to be a warm, energizing personality. He enjoyed his company and, in some sense, viewed him like a son (although, when he later looked for someone to write his biography, Holmes rejected the Jewish professor as a possibility—he wanted a Yankee to do it). Once Justice McReynolds gave Frankfurter a hard time at oral argument on a law that limited women to ten hours of work. McReynolds badgered the law professor, finally snarling, "Ten hours! Ten hours! Ten! Why not four!" The law, he said, was completely arbitrary and unnecessary. Frankfurter moved toward his antagonist. "Your honor," he said, "if by chance I may make such a hypothesis, if your physician should find that you're eating too much meat, it isn't necessary for him to urge you to become a vegetarian." Holmes had been listening to the exchange intently. His reaction was immediate—and loud. "Good for you!" he shouted to Frankfurter from the bench.[11]

To almost anyone who thought about it, this delightful and brilliant justice, this giant of the law, appeared as secure as a man could be. And yet he often worried what people thought of him. Was his work good? Was he carrying his share of the Court's burden? And what did the new justice, Louis Brandeis, think of him? Holmes's clerk popped the question one day to William Sutherland, who had started clerking for Brandeis in the autumn of 1917. Why do you ask, Sutherland inquired. Because, said the Holmes clerk, my justice keeps asking me, and I want to know what I should say to him.

Within a short time, Holmes would not have to wonder. He and Brandeis would become warm and affectionate friends. They had known each other for many years, but their contact had been sporadic. Now they would spend a great deal of time together. Their relationship was a professional one, however. Although they lived only about a block from each other in those early years, they almost never saw each other socially. It may in part have been Holmes's age. He was seventy-five when Brandeis joined the Court and, like his younger colleague, wanted to preserve his limited energies. And then there was Holmes's wife. Fanny did not like Brandeis. It was not because of anything he had done or said—it was his religion. Everyone knew—or at least thought they knew—what Jews were like, and Fanny was concerned about "oriental" influences on her husband.[12]

Despite his wife's concerns, Holmes saw Brandeis regularly. They would ride back and forth to Court together, sometimes getting out of the car to walk. If an important case was being decided, or if a Court recess had prevented them from seeing each other for a long time, Brandeis would sometimes walk over to Holmes's townhouse for a talk. On many occasions their conversations would range far and wide. Shakespeare. Prohibition. Ancient Greece. The new president. But even if they discussed the law, Holmes could not always resist the temptation to be playful. The senior justice often made up new words to express his feelings and would, for example, praise Brandeis's draft opinions as "sockdological." In other instances Holmes would put the law in its proper perspective. Responding to one Brandeis draft, Holmes sent a note that read, "I drove out to the canal, where I saw two cardinals and some other birds. It was lovely there, the spring of the year again. As for your opinion, I agree."[13] Through it all, Holmes enjoyed Brandeis and found his eternal optimism particularly refreshing. "Brandeis always has left me feeling happier about the world," the older justice once confided to the British writer and teacher Harold Laski.[14]

For his part, Brandeis agreed with the consensus that Holmes was a man of uncommon intelligence and insight. And he was a wonderful conversationalist, a man who could debate almost any subject, any proposition. But Holmes had a glaring weakness as a judge. He did not appreciate the importance of knowing all the facts. Facts. Brandeis had built his career on knowing the facts. It was critical to any analysis. Holmes would whip through opinions without carefully reviewing the record and all the legal arguments. Many loopholes were left in his opinions, and they generated a fair number of petitions for rehearing. That was unacceptable, Brandeis said, and Holmes should know better.

The younger justice attributed it to Holmes's limited experience in practical affairs. Aside from a relatively short flirtation with law practice in Boston and teaching at Harvard Law School, Holmes had spent his entire professional career on the bench—first as an associate justice (and then as chief justice) on the Massachusetts Supreme Judicial Court and, starting in 1902, as an associate justice on the United States Supreme Court. For all his understanding of human nature, Brandeis would tell Frankfurter, Holmes is sometimes as innocent as a sixteen-year old girl. His perspective would be broadened if he spent some time in the real world. "Talking with Brandeis yesterday," Holmes reported to Laski one day in 1919, ". . . he drove a harpoon into my midriff by saying that it would be for the good of my soul to devote my next leisure to the study of some domain of fact—suggesting the textile industry, which, after reading many reports etc., I could make living to myself by a visit to [a textile mill] in Lawrence [Massachusetts]."[15]

It was an uphill fight for Brandeis. Holmes told other friends (but not Brandeis) that he "hated" facts—"except as pegs for generalizations."[16] Not surprisingly, he thought Brandeis's long and detailed expositions of legislative history and other factual material entirely inappropriate in a judicial opinion. It was one thing, Holmes said, to use that approach in filing briefs as a private attorney, but judges had only to issue broad pronouncements on the law. So Brandeis would keep making suggestions and sending various studies to his friend and colleague, and Holmes would just as frequently find some excuse to avoid reading them. Once Holmes was at his townhouse during a Court recess when a box containing many government reports arrived. The justice turned to his clerk. "Brandeis wants me to read all these statistics," he said. That was out of the question. "Son," he told the clerk, "you read them."[17]

For all their disagreement on the importance of facts, there was an affinity between the two men on many legal issues. Free speech was one of them. Both saw the necessity of speech in a democracy. They came at it from different perspectives, however. Brandeis understood the necessity of free speech from first-hand experience. If he had not had that right, many people could have silenced his criticism of the New Haven railroad, of the insurance industry, of a United States president. The right to speak out had given him a power, an opportunity to effect change. Holmes had no comparable experiences. His faith in the First Amendment was based largely on abstract reasoning—and, as time would show, qualified by his belief in rule by majority will.

In one of the first Espionage Act cases, Holmes penned an opinion for a unanimous Court explaining why the law was constitutional. To be sure, speech was protected by the First Amendment—but there were limitations. "The most stringent protection of free speech," Holmes wrote, "would not protect a man in falsely shouting 'fire' in a theatre and causing a panic." The same principle applied when Congress passed a wartime statute. "The question in every case," Holmes said, "is whether the words used are used in such circumstances and are of such a nature as to create a clear and present danger that they will bring about the substantive evils that Congress has a right to prevent. It is a question of proximity and degree. When a nation is at war many things that might be said in time of peace are such a hindrance to its effort that their utterance will not be endured so long as men fight. . . ."[18]

A "clear and present danger." It sounded reasonable. Brandeis quickly accepted it as a sound test to decide the limits of free speech. So when the Court decided the *Schaefer* case, he applied the "clear and present danger" test to it.

Peter Schaefer and his colleagues had been convicted under the Espionage Act for distributing reprints of press reports from Germany that questioned the wisdom of American entry into the war. The pamphlets violated Section 3 of the Espionage Act, which prohibited the distribution of "false reports" designed to undermine the war effort. The items alleged to have been falsified were clearly trivial. In one case the publication had mistakenly quoted Senator La Follette as stating that the war would create "bread riots" in the United States; he had actually referred to "breadlines." Justice Mahlon Pitney voted to let the convictions stand only because the defendants had failed to specify their objections to the alleged substantive and procedural errors. A majority of the other justices, however, overlooked that technical point and said that the convictions were proper even assuming that the defendants had preserved their right to appeal.

Brandeis felt that the majority had no reasonable basis for its decision. He and Acheson put together a dissent to explain the justice's views. "In my opinion," Brandeis said, "no jury acting in calmness could reasonably say that any of the publications set forth in the indictment was of such a character or was made under such circumstances as to create a clear and present danger either that they would obstruct recruiting or that they would promote the success of the enemies of the United States." The Court's decision was especially disturbing, he felt, because it could be used in peacetime to silence unpleasant criticism. That was no small risk. As Brandeis pointed out—and as he knew from his own battles—"an intolerant majority, swayed by passion or by fear, may be prone in the future, as it has often been in the past, to stamp as disloyal opinions with which it disagrees."[19]

A week later Brandeis expressed similar concerns in the *Pierce* case when the Court upheld convictions of Socialist Party members who had distributed pamphlets saying that Americans were fighting to protect the economic interest of financiers like J.P. Morgan. It was difficult to find this allegation false or dangerous, Brandeis observed, since many congressmen and senators had made similar complaints in debating the war resolution. It was not only a question of the right result here; Brandeis was also concerned about the broader implications of the Court's decision. "The fundamental right of free men to strive for better conditions through new legislation and new institutions will not be preserved," he concluded, "if efforts to secure it by argument to fellow citizens may be construed as criminal incitement to disobey the existing law. . . ."[20]

In both of these cases Holmes supported Brandeis's dissents. After all, the younger justice was simply applying the "clear and present danger" test formulated by Holmes. They parted company, however, when Brandeis expressed his view about its application in peacetime.

Generally Brandeis required considerable time to analyze issues, especially complex ones. Unlike Holmes, he did not, really could not, make an instant analysis of a case while listening to oral argument. In first supporting the "clear and present danger" test, Brandeis accepted it as a necessary qualification to the First Amendment, one that would restrict speech both in peace and in war. But in writing his *Schaefer* and *Pierce* dissents, he decided that restrictions during war would be entirely inappropriate during peace. It was one thing to prevent speech that might undermine the nation's defense; it was quite another to prevent speech when the nation's survival was not at stake. As he told Frankfurter, during a war "all bets are off." But not otherwise.[21]

His *Schaefer* and *Pierce* dissents tried to intimate the dangers of restricting speech during peacetime. Those cases were not directly on point, though. Both concerned violations of the Espionage Act during the war. The case of Joseph Gilbert was different.

Gilbert was a member of the Non-Partisan League who had been convicted under a Minnesota law that prohibited the teaching or advocating of pacificism. Specifically, the law prevented people from arguing that men should not enlist in the armed forces or aid in carrying out a war. The law was not a war measure; it applied even if the country were at peace with the world.

Brandeis found the law offensive. This was not a statute to protect the nation's defense. It did not relate to immediate dangers. It was simply a restriction on speech that the state found unacceptable. For Brandeis, it was the beginning of an encroachment on speech that criticized government policy and advocated reform.

There were two specific bases on which he thought the law could be overturned. One was the supremacy clause, a provision in the Constitution that enabled federal law to supersede a conflicting state law. Waging war was the business of the federal government, not of the individual states. Moreover, Congress had in fact passed the Espionage Act, an action that implicitly foreclosed state laws covering the same subject. The second possible ground for reversing Gilbert's conviction was found in the Fourteenth Amendment to the Constitution, which prohibited the states from depriving citizens of life, liberty, or property without "due process of law." It could be argued that Minnesota's statute—by being applicable in peacetime as well as in wartime—was unreasonable and therefore resulted in a deprivation of Gilbert's liberty without due process.

Acheson told Brandeis that neither argument was valid. There was no usurpation of federal authority here, he observed. The state law did not in any way interfere with the conduct of war or the implementation of the Espionage Act. Indeed, said Acheson, the Minnesota statute could be tied to legitimate state functions. The state militia was supported by state taxes, and perhaps this law was designed to prevent any obstruction with the operations of that militia. As for the Fourteenth Amendment, Acheson felt that there was no help for Gilbert there. His attorney had not clearly raised the argument, and it would be inappropriate for the Supreme Court to make it for him. Besides, said Acheson, Brandeis believed—and in his earlier opinions had stated—that the Court should not evaluate the reasonableness of state laws. As he had argued in *Muller* v. *Oregon,* the courts should overturn a state law only if there was no possible reasonable basis for it.

Brandeis apparently found Acheson's arguments on the Fourteenth Amendment persuasive. But he was not convinced on the other point. You simply could not get around the fact that the state law restricted speech, and in Brandeis's view that restriction was justified only if the federal government deemed it necessary to safeguard the conduct of war. The state law went well beyond that interest. It could even prevent parents from teaching their children to believe in pacifism.

In conference, the justices had voted to sustain Gilbert's conviction, and Justice Joseph McKenna had been assigned the opinion. He was a devout Catholic who had once considered becoming a priest. Instead he became a politician, and one could not help but suspect that his career had some divine assistance. He was not very bright, but he was personable, and in politics that can carry one a long way. He became a congressman from California and then a close friend of President William McKinley's, a friendship that led to his appointment as the United States attorney general and, in January 1898, an associate justice of the United States Supreme Court. McKenna's brethren on the Court quickly noticed that their newest member lacked brilliance. Efforts were made to be careful in the assignment of opinions to him. More than once his work was so inferior that the chief justice had to reassign it.

McKenna, then, was not a person likely to respond to a logical argument that he should ask the brethren to reverse a decision reached at conference. Nonetheless, Brandeis sent his colleague a memorandum on the *Gilbert* case, arguing that the state law should be overturned because it usurped federal functions and incidentally infringed on individuals' right to speech. Predictably, McKenna was not moved. Within a short time the senior justice returned the memorandum with thanks and a polite rejection. "You think the State has no power," McKenna wrote to Brandeis, "it being excluded by the power in Congress or superseded by the Espionage Act. I think otherwise and the conference resolved otherwise. You think there is interference with the freedom of speech: I think, first, that it is doubtful if we have any jurisdiction to so consider, and second, if we have, I do not think the statute has the breadth you attribute to it."

Brandeis could not have expected much different from McKenna. Holmes was another story. Holmes did not share McKenna's view of the Espionage Act and the First Amendment. But he accepted the state's right to adopt whatever laws it chose unless the Constitution clearly prohibited it. And he could not reach that conclusion here. He therefore told Brandeis that his proposed opinion went "too far." So when the decision was handed down, Brandeis dissented alone. As expected, he relied on the usurpation of federal functions. He also could not resist a reference to the Fourteenth Amendment. In recent cases the Court had relied on the amendment in overturning state statutes that restricted the conduct of commercial business. Such restrictions, said the Court, infringed on the individual's liberty to hold property, a right protected by the Fourteenth Amendment's due process clause. In that context, Brandeis observed, he doubted that the state could restrict what a person could teach. "I cannot believe," his dissent concluded, "that the liberty guaranteed by the Fourteenth Amendment includes only liberty to acquire and to enjoy property."[22]

Writing all these dissents was not an empty exercise for Brandeis. Perhaps they would be read by lawyers, students, government officials and others interested in public policy. "We may be able to fill the people with shame after the passion cools," he told Acheson. "The only hope is the people; you cannot educate the Court."[23]

James Landis had a gift. Most observers agreed that he was unusually intelligent, insightful, and articulate. Certainly Felix Frankfurter thought so. He asked Brandeis if Landis's clerkship with the justice could be delayed a year so that Landis could complete some research projects for the Harvard law professor. Brandeis agreed, and Landis's clerkship began in the autumn of 1925. It was, Landis later recalled, a wonderful experience, one of the best of his life. After the clerkship was over, Landis kept in regular touch with the justice. And Brandeis had much reason to be proud of this protegé. He returned to Harvard as a law professor, and, in the early 1930s he was brought back to Washington to sit on the Federal Trade Commission and then to chair the Securities and Exchange Commission. In 1937 Harvard Law School wanted him once again, this time as the dean of the school. It was quite an honor for a man of thirty-eight, and Landis was sure that Justice Brandeis would be proud of him. Landis soon reported the news. He was going to Harvard to become dean. Brandeis just looked at him. "You mean Harvard Law School?" "Yes," Landis replied. "Why do you want to take that?" the justice asked. "Well," said a surprised Landis, "it's a great promotion." Brandeis did not agree. "Anybody can be a good Dean of the Harvard Law School," he said. "Why not take some smaller school and do something with it?" It was a good thought perhaps, but the former clerk accepted Harvard's offer.[24]

Landis went on to become one of the foremost authorities on legislation and administrative law. He also developed a close friendship with Joseph P. Kennedy, and in 1960 President-elect John F. Kennedy asked Landis to examine federal agencies and propose measures to improve their efficiency. Landis did the job, as he did every job, brilliantly. But then the gift went sour. His mental health declined rapidly. He did not file income tax returns, and the Kennedy Justice Department felt compelled to prosecute him. It was an agonizing decision for the Kennedys, and the story did not have a happy ending. James Landis was found dead in his swimming pool in 1962, the victim of an apparent suicide.

It was a turn of events that no one could have predicted during those bright days of the Brandeis clerkship. Then Landis was vigorous in mind and spirit. He and the justice worked long and hard together, discussing cases, arguing about opinions. And one they debated at length involved Charles E. Ruthenberg.

Ruthenberg had been a member of the Socialist Party, and between 1909 and 1919 he ran, unsuccessfully, for various elective offices. In 1919 he joined the Communist Party. In 1922 he and fellow communists held a meeting in a desolate, wooded area of Michigan. Their secrecy was not happenstance. Ever since Attorney General Palmer's "Red Scare" in 1920, people with Ruthenberg's political views were often careful about what they said in public. Nonetheless, Ruthenberg and his colleagues were arrested and convicted of violating a Michigan law that prohibited the teaching of "criminal syndicalism"—an awkward term that referred to aberrant political philosophies like communism.

Brandeis found the state law and the whole sequence of events inexcusable. The nation was now at peace. There was no allegation that Ruthenberg's meeting threatened any immediate danger to the country or any individual. The group was of one mind politically, so there was no innocent person whose mind could be "corrupted." They had met far from civilization, and the group had not said or done anything to indicate that violence was imminent. The meeting was nothing more than an opportunity for these people to exchange views without fear of interruption by the authorities. To Brandeis their subsequent conviction was another illustration of the dangers he spoke of in the *Gilbert* case.

Unhappily, the conference concluded otherwise, and Brandeis felt obligated to issue another dissent. He prepared drafts, and Landis worked on them over the summer of 1926, exchanging frequent notes with the justice, who was then vacationing on Cape Cod. It was building into a forceful opinion, one, Landis assured Brandeis, that the next clerk, Robert Page, could help complete. Other forces were at work, however, and the dissent never made it into print. Ruthenberg died before the opinion could be completed, and the case was dismissed as moot. The work was not in vain, though. Another case was pending before the Court, one remarkably similar to Ruthenberg's.

Anita Whitney, a Wellesley College graduate, was about sixty years old. In 1919 she joined the Communist Party and attended a party convention in California. There, according to Page's memo to the justice, the convention "sang a silly song about joining the Bolshevik" and then indulged in "the usual talk about the coming struggle against capitalism. . . ." Whitney was subsequently convicted of violating California's criminal syndicalism statute, which had been adopted that year. From his research Page determined that the law was a response to criminal acts, some of them violent, that had been committed by members of the radical International Workers of the World union. Whitney was not a member of the IWW, but that didn't matter to the California courts. To them all radicals were the same. In any event, the legal issue was whether the IWW's crimes created a sufficient "clear and present danger" to justify restrictions on speech. Page could not tell from the record. He therefore suggested the possibility of sending the case back for a jury trial to evaluate the nature and immediacy of the danger.[25]

Under *Gilbert* and other cases, the "clear and present danger" test was—despite Brandeis's objection—applied to peacetime laws. But Brandeis did not entirely agree with his clerk's analysis of how that test affected Whitney's case. True, it was not apparent from the record whether the IWW's activities justified the statute. But Whitney had not challenged the factual basis of the law, and it was too late for her to do so now. When a case came from a lower federal court, the United States Supreme Court could step in and correct fundamental errors even if the parties had not raised them. But the Court did not have that power over cases coming from state courts (because, theoretically, as a federal body, the Supreme Court has a greater responsibility for the performance of federal courts than it does for state courts). Since Whitney had been convicted in a California court, the Court could not help her. (Actually a majority of the justices would not have helped her even if they had the power.)

Although Brandeis could not assist Whitney personally, he decided to use her case to convey some of the thoughts he had hoped to express in the Ruthenberg dissent. Portions of that opinion were lifted and placed in the new draft. It proved to be an extremely eloquent opinion, perhaps the most forceful of Brandeis's long tenure on the Court.

The majority opinion, written by Justice Edward Sanford, upheld Whitney's conviction. At one point Sanford suggested that the Fourteenth Amendment did not protect speech.

Brandeis concurred in the result but not the Court's reasoning. In a separate opinion, he explained initially that he did not believe it appropriate for the Court to examine the reasonableness of state laws. But in many decisions the Court had held otherwise. Therefore, the Court *could* examine the record to determine whether speech restricted by a state law did in fact pose "a clear and imminent danger." That was no easy question, because the Court—despite all its pronouncements—had never established a standard to identify dangers that were both clear and imminent. In fixing any standard, however, it was important to understand, Brandeis said, why a state cannot ordinarily restrict speech.

"Those who won our independence," he explained, "believed that the final end of the State was to make men free to develop their faculties; and that in its government the deliberative forces should prevail over the arbitrary. They valued liberty both as an end and as a means. They believed liberty to be the secret of happiness and courage to be the secret of liberty. They believed that freedom to think as you will and to speak as you think are means indispensable to the discovery and spread of political truth; that without free speech and assembly, discussion would be futile; that with them, discussion affords ordinarily adequate protection against the dissemination of noxious doctrine; that the greatest menace to freedom is an inert people; that public discussion is a political duty; and that this should be a fundamental principle of the American government." Of course, said Brandeis, there were risks in allowing free speech. Enemies of the state could recruit supporters. But the Founding Fathers, the justice observed, thought that it would be unwise "to discourage thought, hope and imagination; that fear breeds repression; that repression breeds hate; that hate menaces stable government; that the path of safety lies in the opportunity to discuss freely supposed grievances and proposed remedies; and that the fitting remedy for evil counsels is good ones."

In this context, said Brandeis, speech—even speech advocating violent measures—could not be restricted unless it amounted to incitement that would result in immediate action. "Those who won our independence by revolution," the justice observed, "were not cowards. They did not fear political change. They did not exalt order at the cost of liberty." Only the most serious dangers—risks that could not be exposed through further discussion—warranted a limitation on fundamental individual freedoms.

For all these reasons, Brandeis rejected the majority's suggestion that the

Fourteenth Amendment did not protect the rights of speech and assembly against unreasonable state action. But here there was some evidence to justify the adoption of California's criminal syndicalism statute and the belief that criminal activities were furthered by conventions like the one attended by Whitney. Whitney did not claim or show that the legislature's judgment had been unreasonable. Therefore, Brandeis concluded, her conviction must stand.[26]

Brandeis was seasoned enough to recognize that a single opinion—even a series of opinions—could not always bring about needed reforms. Certainly that was the case with respect to his *Whitney* opinion. Its call for some standard to measure "clear and imminent dangers" was plain. Yet decades later nothing had changed much. In a 1951 case, Supreme Court Justice Robert Jackson would say of Holmes' test, "All agree that it means something very important, but no two seem to agree on what it is."[27] And when President Richard Nixon tried to stop the publication of the Pentagon Papers in 1971, Court members had little to rely on except their own instincts as to what was "clear" and "imminent."

Brandeis probably could have anticipated all this ambiguity. But he was interested in concrete achievements. He was offended by state laws that restricted speech, and he thought it was equally disgraceful that the government had paid no compensation to people who had been victimized by the Palmer Raids in 1920. During the summer of 1926, when he was preparing the Ruthenberg dissent, he asked Frankfurter to consider the possibility of having someone in Congress push a bill to provide the necessary relief.

For all his charm and good intentions, Frankfurter could not satisfy this request. The times were different now. There was a new man in the White House and a new spirit in the country. Social reforms, it seemed, were at the bottom of almost everyone's list. Other concerns motivated those in and out of government. Brandeis of course knew all this, and he was not at all pleased by it. But he knew that the day of reckoning would come.

TWENTY

Striving for Normalcy

Sun and sky are gladsome today. The trees are jutting forth buds; the grass its tenderest leaves. And the birds are singing their sweetest love songs. . . . Even the impending gloom of a Republican Administration cannot dampen their ardor or suppress their joyousness.

LOUIS D. BRANDEIS TO REGINA GOLDMARK, MARCH 1, 1921

America had never seen anything like it before. The man was simply incredible. He was a large, impressive figure with a broad nose and a ready smile. And that suit he wore, the one with all those pinstripes, made him look larger still. But Babe Ruth's performance matched his physical appearance. In 1920 he hit fifty-four home runs playing for Jacob Ruppert's New York Yankees. No one had even come close to hitting that many in one season—in fact, the earlier record was Babe's own twenty-nine the previous year. Entire *teams* did not hit as many home runs in one season as Babe Ruth. And in 1921 he went even further and hit fifty-nine home runs. Americans were overwhelmed by this giant of baseball, and thousands across the country rushed to ball parks to catch a glimpse of the Big Bambino.

Babe Ruth represented more than the emergence of a sports hero. In a way, he reflected the changes that were taking place throughout the United States. The Progressive Era was over. People were no longer interested in social reform and war. Perhaps the most exciting social issue of the new decade was the Scopes trial, where, according to H.L. Mencken, "gaping primates" watched Clarence Darrow and William Jennings Bryan argue about evolution in a small, sweltering Tennessee courtroom.

President Warren G. Harding, a former Republican senator from Ohio, was inaugurated on March 4, 1921, and he promised to return the country to "normalcy." The dictionary did not define the term, but no matter. Everyone knew what he meant. Self-sacrifice was out. Self-indulgence was in. America's productivity had skyrocketed with the vast demands of maintaining the war machine. Now, in peacetime, business would reap the benefits. Consumers were inundated with new commodities and new styles. Radios. Refrigerators. Raccoon coats. Shorter hemlines (with skirts nine inches off the ground, the *New York Times* lamented that the American woman "has lifted her skirts far beyond any modest limitation"). The one thing Americans did not have—at least in lawful commerce—was liquor. Prohibition had set in, but even the law could not dampen the spirit of hedonism. People turned to speakeasies, private clubs, and bathtub gin.

It was not the country Louis Brandeis knew as an attorney in Boston. To be sure, his reform efforts had not been welcomed by everyone. But at least people listened, and many cared. However substantial his individual contributions, all of his achievements depended on the assistance of others. Now none of that seemed possible. People appeared to be more interested in acquiring material possessions than in shaping public policy. Brandeis was not entirely opposed to material comfort; he and Alice, for example, bought high-quality and expensive clothing (in fact, the justice liked his suits so much that he just kept reordering them from the same tailor in Boston). But he was continually amazed at the money other people spent and at what they spent it on. Cars were a special object of concern to him; they were so expensive and so unnecessary. It was not possible that everyone had that much money available. "I can't understand where all this (and other) money comes from," he wrote to Al in early 1923. "We are certainly not earning it as a nation. I think we must be exploiting about 80 percent of Americans for the benefit of the other 20 percent."[1]

Other social customs disturbed him as well. Tipping was "pernicious." Women who got permanents were sinful. And people who succumbed to drink were unacceptable. When one of his clerks was late to work a couple of times at the beginning of the clerkship, the justice quickly inferred the presence of liquor and moral degeneracy. "His excuses are barely plausible," Brandeis told Frankfurter. "I suspect his habits are bad—[he is] the victim of drink or worse vices. I have a sense of his being untrustworthy; and something of the sense of uncleanness about him."[2] Frankfurter was of course sympathetic, but most Americans probably would not have been. Consumption of all kinds was the rule; discipline was the exception.

Not surprisingly, people expected little from their government. Perhaps the only thing they really wanted was to be left alone. Even revelations of massive corruption could not alter the public psyche. By the middle of the decade it was learned that high officials in the Harding administration had illegally used their positions to advance private interests in oil and other natural resources. The public and the press were indeed offended—but not so much by the official wrongdoers. No, some of the harshest criticism was saved for the people who exposed the wrongdoing. The *New York Times* called them "assassins of character." The *New York Evening Post* said they were "mud-gunners."[3]

Brandeis must have remembered a similar press reaction to his initial attacks on the New Haven railroad. It was never easy to identify problems and push reform. But he had faith in people. In time, the pendulum would swing again. And he would be ready. So when former President Wilson asked if he would be interested in helping to prepare a new platform for the Democratic Party, Brandeis responded affirmatively.

There was no specific code or law that prohibited a Supreme Court justice from participating in a partisan activity. But Brandeis certainly knew that most people would have frowned on his collaboration with Wilson on a political matter. He could not have forgotten the "ambush" by the American Jewish Committee at the Astor Hotel. So he was discreet about it. There would be no speeches, no press releases. Just some correspondence and some private meetings, most of them at Wilson's house on S Street in northwest Washington.

The ex-president was not a well man. Even before he entered the White House he had suffered a number of minor strokes. The crippling blow came in Pueblo, Colorado, in 1919 while he was urging public support for the Treaty of Versailles and the League of Nations. He was immobilized, the public shut off, and his First Lady, Edith Bolling Wilson, assumed command. By the time his successor was inaugurated, Wilson had improved considerably. But he was not vigorous and never would be again. Still, he remained bitter at Senator Lodge and the others who had successfully opposed his dream of American participation in the League. He now proposed to do something about it.

Along with Brandeis he gathered together Thomas Chadbourn, a New York attorney, and Bainbridge Colby, one of his former secretaries of state. In the summer of 1921 the four men began to review and draft statements that discussed the reforms that were needed. Better conditions for the working man. More protection for small business against oppressive monopolies. And greater participation in world affairs to ensure a lasting peace.

The paper had no official status and people referred to it simply as "The Document." Wilson at one time hoped that Democratic congressional candidates would use it in the 1922 midterm elections. Bernard Baruch, the business leader and Wilson loyalist, convinced him, however, that the timing was not ripe. The Document was not in line with the country's mood. Wilson said he would wait, then, until the 1924 campaign, when the Democrats' presidential candidate could take advantage of it. It was not to be, though. Wilson died in February 1924, and the Document died with him.

Brandeis had played a principal role in editing the paper, but he did not fight for its use in the 1924 elections. He may have shared Wilson's hopes for it; but even if he did, he had other, more immediate and more personal concerns than the fate of The Document.

It was all becoming too much for Alice. Her health had never been good. She always tired easily and in Boston required the assistance of servants to meet her family's needs. At times, especially in the second decade of her marriage to Louis, she had to be hospitalized for extended periods. Despite that, she was still able to maintain an active participation in various civic activities. It might be the local art club, her daughters' schools, or a local charity. It was only natural that she try to pursue similar activities in Washington. But now almost everything was overshadowed by her husband's position. The teas, the dinners, the constant work. All of that was draining enough. But what probably made it intolerable was the isolation from a normal community life. Alice had always preferred a quiet social calendar, one that gave her time alone with Louis. But at least in Boston there were community activities she enjoyed. And she was always able to speak freely—about her family, her political views, her husband's activities. She no longer had that freedom. Her husband was a Supreme Court justice, someone whose work was a closely guarded secret, at least until opinion day. She had to be more careful about what she said and to whom she said it. She loved Louis dearly, had always been dedicated to him, had been willing to do anything for him. But everyone had their limits. Even Alice. Everything fell apart in early 1923. It got to the point where, as always, she could not stand to be away from Louis. But she could not stand to be near him either. Her whole world crumbled, and she became hysterical. On March 5, Louis reported to Susan that her mother had had a nervous breakdown. Her doctor and nurses were summoned to take care of the ailing woman.[4]

Louis could not have been entirely surprised by Alice's collapse. The previous autumn she had had a similar experience. But this time it seemed much more serious. Alice was deeply depressed, totally disoriented. There seemed to be no relief in sight. Arrangements were made to try to move her back to Massachusetts for care. Even that was questionable because the doctor was not sure the patient was able to make the trip. In the meantime Louis did the best he could, but drastic measures were clearly necessary. "Monday night was ghastly," he reported to Susan on April 11. "It is now established and we must accept the unfortunate fact that you should not come here again until after Mother has gone to Massachusetts and that you should not be near her there or communicate with her until she spontaneously asks to have you come. When she does that we shall know she has regained her health—and not before."[5] The same advice was apparently passed on to Elizabeth.

It was no doubt a disturbing experience. On many nights Louis had to sleep on the couch in his office. It was a small sacrifice. He would do what he could for his wife. He, more than anyone, knew what she had given up for him. At the same time he could not punish himself for her affliction. Some things could not be avoided. Life would have to go on. In these lonely nights in his office he longed for some diversion. Only a select few, however, could enter this very private world of his. Dean Acheson was one. The former clerk was then practicing law in Washington, and occasionally he would receive a call from Brandeis's office. Would he be interested in coming up that evening? Acheson was happy to go. And he knew that it was good for the justice. He was always interested in gossip, especially about public affairs, and when the young lawyer arrived, Brandeis would ask, almost as though they were part of a conspiracy, "Dean, what is the latest dirt?"[6]

Through it all, Brandeis retained his usual optimism. It was not because of anything the doctors had said. In fact, he had little faith in medical opinion here. No, they would do it themselves. "[B]y infinite patience and tender care," he told Susan at one point, "we shall bring Mother back to her customary health."[7] Reliance would also have to be placed on Alice's own determination to overcome her illness, and to that end Louis could think of few things better than a visit to Cape Cod.

For years now Alice and Louis had been spending almost all of their summers on the Cape. By the middle of June, after the last Court opinion had been released, the two of them—sometimes with Elizabeth or Susan, but more often without—would take the train to Boston. They would stay at the Bellevue Hotel there, meet with old friends, and once again enjoy the city that had given them so many good memories. Then, after a few days, Bess Evans or one of their daughters would arrange for a car to drive Alice and Louis out to their favorite vacation retreat in Chatham. It was a relatively large, rambling house overlooking Oyster

Pond. They liked it so much they decided to buy it in 1924—after the owner said he was prepared to sell it to someone else.

The Cape was so beautiful, the salt air so refreshing. Louis decided to take Alice back in the summer of 1923. Perhaps the change in scenery would help. Away from Washington, away from the overpowering presence of the Court. There would be nurses and servants to help. And most importantly, Bess would be there. She often stayed with Alice and Louis at the Cape, and now, more than ever, her presence was needed. Bess returned all the love and attention Louis had given her in her earlier days of grief and difficulty. She spent hours with Alice, talking to her, comforting her, while Louis took long, lonely walks by the river or on the beach.

It was a trying time for everyone. But slowly, Alice seemed to be improving. Toward the end of the summer it was decided she should spend some time at a Boston rest home. Even in her troubled state, Alice could not help but express the appreciation that Bess so richly deserved. "I can never thank you, Bessie dear, for all that you have been and done this summer," Alice wrote. "It has been a joy just to see you, but as you know more than that I have not been able to do. You I know will take me on faith & some day perhaps I shall be more myself. Life is strange & very, very difficult. Some day perhaps we shall understand what now seems very dark."[8]

The situation deteriorated when Alice returned to Washington in autumn. "Mother has several times renewed the suggestion that you should come soon, . . ." Louis wrote to Susan in October. "But Mother's condition is . . . so perplexing and she is so far below her usual level at Chatham that I think it best that you should not come at present. . . . I am spending much more time with Mother than usual," he explained, "because my presence relieves her depression. . . ." Within ten days, however, he told Susan that Mother is "surely struggling gallantly to control herself" and that perhaps they could now arrange a visit from their older daughter. But it was a delicate matter. It took almost an hour to prepare Alice for bed, and she was still subject to fitfull sleep. So Louis advised Susan to come on a Sunday morning. That way the excitement of the visit would not disrupt Alice's sleep.[9]

It remained a slow, agonizing process. Alice was beginning to regain some stability, but even by the following June, Louis was saying that "the ice is still pretty thin." Another summer at Chatham with Bess helped immeasurably, and by autumn of 1924 Alice was beginning to regain considerable strength. "Mother & I played hooky this forenoon on the Potomac," Louis told Susan in early October. "It was a grand day of sunshine after the . . . rain." A different kind of normalcy was returning, and it was most welcome.[10]

Dinners were the key. It was a way of keeping in touch—and sometimes in control. They came from all over: senators, congressmen, union men, writers, and sometimes that year's clerk. The food was not much in quality or quantity. Judge Julian Mack, a gourmet cook, used to remark that you had to eat before and after going to the Brandeis home for dinner. The clerks agreed. The traditional slice of roast beef was so thin, said one, you could almost see through it.

The conversation more than made up for the shortcomings of the food. On occasion the justice would urge one of his guests to tell a story or relate an incident. He never tired, for example, of asking Andrew Furuseth to explain to the guests why he became a seaman. Furuseth, a large Norwegian immigrant, was a self-educated man who had risen to the presidency of the International Seamen's Union. Furuseth would always be happy to oblige. In his big, booming voice, he would say, "I became a seaman because I had the insane idea, the graaaand delusion, that a seaman was a free man." And on and on it would go, with the host beaming in appreciation.

In most instances, though, Brandeis took the lead. And as America raced through the indulgent twenties, he had a lot to say. Ideas for new laws and new activities abounded. And always, in the background and at the ready, was Felix Frankfurter, eager to pursue almost any suggestion that emanated from Stoneleigh Court (or, after September 1926, from 2205 California Street—the "improvements" in Stoneleigh Court, including the new shops and stores, led the Brandeises to seek more serene quarters). Sometimes the ideas were quite far reaching. Once, shortly after Calvin Coolidge had been elected president in 1924, Brandeis reported to Frankfurter a conversation he had had with Congressman John Nelson, a progressive Republican from Wisconsin. Nelson thought—just why, it is not clear—that a coalition of progressives could be developed to control the House of Representatives. Brandeis was quick to jump on the suggestion and urged the Harvard professor "to find a group of men willing to be the politico-economic thinkers, who would, in privacy, think out what it is wise to do, why & how."[11]

Few of these suggestions resulted in concrete legislation. But, then, the justice did not expect much from Congress. In a letter to Robert Bruere, a magazine editor, Brandeis had warned that it would be unwise to "pin too much faith [on] legislation. Remedial institutions," he observed, "are apt to fall under the control of the enemy and to become instruments of oppression." Brandeis had some other advice for Bruere, and to a large extent, it reflected a lifetime of thought and experience. "Remember," said the justice, "that progress is necessarily slow; that remedies are necessarily tentative; that because of varying conditions, there must be much and constant inquiry into facts . . . and much experimentation; and that always and everywhere the intellectual, moral and spiritual development of those concerned will remain an essential—and the main factor—in real betterment." As he had in his advice to William Dunbar three decades earlier on law practice, Brandeis again focused on the individual as the source of social progress. "[O]ur objective," he told Bruere, "is the making of men and women who shall be free—self-respecting members of a democracy—and who shall be worthy of respect."

As with Dunbar, the "great developer was responsibility. Hence, no remedy can be hopeful which does not devolve upon the workers . . . responsibility for the conduct of business; and their aim should be the eventual assumption of full responsibility—as in cooperative enterprises." Through it all, however, Brandeis counseled perseverance and discipline. "It is more difficult to maintain than achieve," he observed. "It demands continuous sacrifice by the individual and more exigent obedience to the moral law than any other form of government. Success in any democratic undertaking must proceed from the individual. It is possible only where the process of perfecting the individual is pursued."[12]

It was, to say the least, advice more easily given than followed. Brandeis had long believed that the individual was "a wee thing" and that it was necessary "to adjust our institutions to the wee size of man and thus render possible his growth and development."[13] But other people had different ideas. Large corporations and corporate magnates still dominated the nation's life, and there was no indication that their growth would be or even could be curtailed. No matter. Brandeis had other alternatives, and he would take advantage of them.

Jim Rowe didn't want to go back to Montana. Although he had spent his childhood there, other environments appealed to him more as an adult. Justice Holmes, for whom he clerked during the 1934 Court term, didn't care whether Rowe returned to his home state. But Justice Brandeis did. He thought it was important for young people to develop a life in a small community, and usually there was no better place to start than the place in which one had grown up. So when Rowe attended the weekly teas—to which Holmes' clerks were regularly invited—the aging justice would ask the young lawyer, "When are you going back to Montana?" Rowe politely responded that he was not going just yet—he hadn't made up his mind. In time, after the Holmes clerkship ended, Rowe would become President Roosevelt's administrative assistant and then an influential Washington lawyer. But long before then, at one of the teas, Brandeis confronted the young man with the obvious truth. "You're not going back to Montana, are you?" No, Rowe replied, no, he wasn't. And that was the last time he was invited to a Brandeis tea.[14]

It was all very ironic—Brandeis had, like Rowe, rejected the possibility of returning to his home community, the town where his family lived, where his roots were. He had instead gone to St. Louis and then Boston in search of opportunity and excitement. As he advanced in years, however, the importance of Kentucky seemed to take hold of him. In 1924, as he neared his seventieth birthday, he and Alice discussed ways of making their own contribution to his home state, almost a gift to make up for past neglect. Eventually their thoughts settled on the University of Louisville. It was a small urban school, at best a mediocre institution with limited facilities, inadequate staff, and a low profile. It clearly needed help. And there could be few investments that would be more significant or more lasting.

He and Alice could, of course, donate money. They certainly had plenty of that—more than a couple of million dollars in investments and an after-tax income that approached $100,000. But money alone, they knew, would not do the job; good administrators and good teachers would be needed to make proper use of improved facilities and to attract quality students. As Louis explained to one of his nephews, he and Alice wanted to make the school authorities "rich in ideals and eager in the desire to attain them."[15] Therefore, he and Alice would give funds only to complete specified projects, such as the acquisition or binding of books. The justice would also donate portions of his vast library to the school and arrange for reports of Supreme Court decisions to be sent to the law school.

All of this would require careful supervision and cooperation. Louis and Alice wanted to assure themselves that promises by the school were fulfilled, that projects were completed and materials used properly. To fulfill this responsibility they looked primarily to Al's family. Each person was to be assigned a specific task. One family member had art, another sociology, Al had "Kentuckiania," and so on. And each person received repeated and detailed instructions from Uncle Louis and on occasion Aunt Alice concerning progress in a particular area.

Back in Kentucky, family members were at first enthusiastic about the idea. But Uncle Louis turned out to be a hard taskmaster. There seemed to be no end to his requests and suggestions, and there was good-natured bantering about the instructions being received almost daily from Washington. But virtually everyone was impressed with Uncle Louis's imagination and drive. There was nothing ordinary about him.

For Brandeis it was an exhilarating experience. "It is a task befitting the Adolph Brandeis family," he told Al, "which for nearly three-quarters of a century has stood in Louisville for culture and, at least in Uncle Lewis, for learning." But he was more than sentimental about it. It complemented his view that social progress depended, ultimately, on the individual and the small community. "History teaches, I believe, that the present tendency toward centralization must be arrested, if we are to attain the American ideals," he advised his brother, "and . . . for it must be substituted intense development of life through activities in the several states and localities. The problem is a very difficult one; but the local university is the most hopeful instrument for any attempt at solution."[16]

It may all have been clear in Louis's mind, but for Al it was something entirely new. He was now past seventy and did not have his brother's visions—or tenacity. And when he encountered obstacles, he became discouraged. The school administrators seemed concerned only with money and did not appear to appreciate the ideals that lay behind the generosity of the Brandeis family. The younger brother, as usual, took it all in stride. ". . . I am not in the least discouraged by any of the events or attitudes to which you refer," he told Al. ". . . Some opposition is rather to be desired as an incentive to our and others' thinking; and as a means of stirring up interest." At another point he reminded his brother that the "future has many good things in store for those who can wait and have patience and exercise good judgment." The only cautionary note concerned Al himself. Although his brother had remained relatively vigorous all these years, Louis did not want him to strain himself. The limitations of age had to be respected, and he and Alice, he said, could not achieve their goals for the university without the watchful eye of their "managing partner."[17] Sadly, it was a matter over which no one—not even Louis Brandeis—had full control.

Al died on August 8, 1928. It was a sad and mournful day. Louis spent the time reviewing many of his old letters from Al, recalling the memories, the warm feelings. Louisville. Europe. The visits in Cincinnati, Chicago, Washington, and other cities. It was hard to give up. Al had given happiness and love to others; and fortunately, much of it had been reciprocated. "The long years seem short," Louis wrote to Al's wife, Jennie, "because each brought so richly of these gifts and youth remained in body and spirit. To all of us there is comfort that to the end the beauty was unmarred, undimmed."[18] His brother's death created a void, however, that would never be filled.

TWENTY•ONE

Curbing Presidential Power

Though the President is elected by nationwide ballot, and is often said to represent all the people, he does not embody the nation's sovereignty. He is not above the law's commands.

UNITED STATES COURT OF APPEALS, DIRECTING PRESIDENT RICHARD M. NIXON TO GIVE TAPE RECORDINGS OF HIS CONVERSATIONS TO THE WATERGATE SPECIAL PROSECUTOR

Henry Friendly could not understand why the justice kept calling. It would usually happen between one and two o'clock in the afternoon when the Court was not in session. The phone would ring in the office and the voice would say, "Hello, young fella. Is your chief there?" Friendly had told Justice Holmes innumerable times that Justice Brandeis always took his lunch at that time in his downstairs apartment. So after a while Friendly felt like telling the caller that no, the justice is not in, and you know damn well he's not in. But the Brandeis law clerk did not speak his mind. Position and age were entitled to some deference. On a rare occasion, Holmes would use these phone calls to make inquiries about Court work. Once it concerned a matter involving the Interstate Commerce Commission. "Young fella," Holmes asked Friendly, "is your boss going to be prepared on the ICC case?" Friendly assured the senior justice that his boss would indeed be prepared. "Well," said Holmes, "then I guess I won't prepare. An old man's prerogative, you know."[1]

Holmes's faith in Brandeis's ICC expertise was not misplaced. Everyone on the Court—even those who abhorred his "radical" ideas—acknowledged that the man from Boston was a force to be reckoned with when it came to utility and regulatory issues. If they had any doubt on that score, it was surely erased when the Court held an extraordinary seminar in the spring of 1923 to consider a case involving the Southwestern Bell Telephone Company.

Cases involving regulation of utility rates were complex matters that escaped the mastery of most justices (and most lawyers as well). That was, in fact, one of the primary reasons why Congress created the ICC. It was hoped that the agency would develop the expertise to evaluate massive records and reach judgments that would be fair both to the consumer and the utility. Individual states no doubt relied on similar reasoning in creating public service commissions to determine local rates for railroads and other utilities.

However sound that was in theory, courts could not leave well enough alone. That was made clear when the United States Supreme Court handed down its opinion in *Smyth* v. *Ames* in 1898.[2] The principal question was the rate of return that a utility could earn on its investment. The state commission issued a judgment that it thought was reasonable. The Supreme Court thought otherwise and reversed the commission's findings. It criticized the commission because it did not adequately consider the reproduction value of the utility's property when the rates were determined. In other words, the Court said it was not enough to account for the money actually invested by the company; the commission also had to consider the amount it would cost to replace equipment and facilities. This was necessary, the Court explained, so that the utility could earn sufficient funds to allow for such replacements when they became necessary.

Brandeis had nothing but contempt for this "reproduction" theory in *Smyth* v. *Ames*. To begin with, he thought courts should be careful before trying to define property rights. He had explained his position when the Associated Press sued the International News Service for "stealing" news dispatches—a theft that usually amounted to no more than the INS's taking an item from the AP wire and including it on the INS news distribution. In 1918 the Supreme Court upheld an order prohibiting the INS from doing that. Brandeis dissented. Although he agreed that there might be some inequity in what the INS had done, he felt that the courts were "ill equipped" to determine the precise scope of the AP's property rights in news items. Though a legislature might require INS (and others) to pay AP royalties, the public interest in the news items should, Brandeis thought, deter the Court from preventing their distribution.[3]

Brandeis believed that the courts were equally unsuited to establishing rates for railroads, telephone companies, and other utilities. That was certainly evident when the Supreme Court promulgated the "reproduction" theory in *Smyth* v. *Ames*. To Brandeis, it was not only illogical; it was impractical. He of course agreed that utilities were entitled to a fair return on the money they invested—as long as it was done prudently and did not reflect extravagant expenses. But it made no sense to allow utilities to earn a return on money they had not yet contributed. Yet that could be one result under the reproduction theory. If inflation increased the value of the utility's property, then—according to the Court in *Smyth* v. *Ames*—the utility's return would also have to be increased. In other situations, the reproduction theory could be unfair to utilities. For if an economic recession meant a decrease in property values, the utility might not be able to earn a fair return on the capital it had actually paid in. Instead, a regulatory commission could point to lower reproduction costs and, as a result, lower rates as well.

All of this was so much whistling in the wind in any event. Determining reproduction values, Brandeis observed, was a "baffling" task. Utilities were not bought and sold like personal commodities in a department store. There was no ready standard to assess the value of utility service and the equipment needed to provide it. Consequently, any determination of reproduction costs by a public commission was bound to be somewhat arbitrary and subject to second-guessing by the courts. It was much better, Brandeis believed, to rely on a prudent investment theory. It would be concrete and much more conducive to review by the courts. It would also assure the utilities a fair return at all times on the money they actually spent. And if reproduction costs did rise, the utility could request an increase in rates to cover any increase in its actual investments.

Most economists agreed that the prudent investment theory was much sounder than the reproduction theory of rate making. Since none of the justices on the Court were economists, however, they did not appreciate the logic behind Brandeis's position. So when the Court was asked to decide the Southwestern Bell Telephone Company case in 1923, a majority was prepared to stand behind *Smyth* v. *Ames.* William Howard Taft was a part of that majority. The former president, who had been appointed by President Harding to be chief justice in 1921, saw no reason to disturb established precedent.

Brandeis believed otherwise. He went to the chief justice and explained his view of the case. It is doubtful that Taft fully understood what Brandeis said to him. As the former Boston attorney later explained to Felix Frankfurter, Taft didn't have the "slightest grasp" of these utility matters.[4] But Taft could readily see that his colleague disagreed with the reproduction theory in *Smyth* v. *Ames.* And the chief justice also knew that this whole question of rate making was unusually complicated and that few justices really appreciated all of the nuances. So he arranged for an entire Saturday to be set aside for a discussion of reproduction theory and its application to the *Southwestern* case. And more than that, Brandeis would lead the discussion.

This was no small gesture on Taft's part. The Court operated under the ever-present pressures of a congested docket, and Taft, as chief justice, was always anxious to move matters along expeditiously. Saturday conferences were therefore used to dispose of dozens of cases. To confine this valuable time to the discussion of one case was not only unusual; it was disruptive. Many of the justices complained to Taft that the *Southwestern* case did not deserve all this attention. Taft held firm. Brandeis had fundamental objections, this was an important area of the law, the schedule would not be altered.

No votes were changed by the session, and Brandeis remained skeptical afterwards that the brethren had been able to absorb his analysis.[5] But he greatly appreciated the chief justice's courtesy in at least giving him a chance to set forth his views. It was symptomatic of the cordial relations he established with the new chief justice. Indeed, aside from Holmes, Taft was one of the few justices with whom Brandeis enjoyed talking. He was not a brilliant man. He had, Brandeis thought, "a first-rate second-rate mind."[6] But he was a good-natured person with broad interests and an abiding interest in the law.

Taft reciprocated Brandeis's cordiality. The Ballinger–Pinchot hearings were put behind him, and he reported to his brother at the very beginning that he and Brandeis were on "excellent terms." Even their disagreements on some important cases in those early days could not disturb their friendly relations. The only time they had a heated discussion, in fact, occurred when Taft—who advised Harding on nominations to all the federal courts—asked Brandeis to let him know if he had any Democrats to recommend. Brandeis quickly replied that party labels were an inappropriate criterion when evaluating prospective judges, that the primary consideration—from his perspective, at least—was whether they took a "progressive" view of social development, and that he would not be a part of Taft's partisan calculations.

None of this affected Brandeis's evaluation of Taft's performance as chief justice; he thought it most impressive. For all his warmth and popularity, Edward White, Taft's predecessor, had not been a good chief justice. He did not prepare well for the Saturday conferences and, as a result, the discussions often rambled on endlessly. Deciding cases, especially complex ones, became a draining affair. Taft stood in sharp contrast. He prepared himself on each matter, allowed some debate as each case was called, and then moved to a vote after a decent interval. Most of the justices welcomed this new control over their deliberations. "We are very happy with the present Chief," Holmes reported to the British legal scholar Sir Frederick Pollock. "He is good-humored, laughs readily, not quite rapidly enough, but keeping things moving pleasantly."[8] Brandeis agreed, and he would wonder aloud with Frankfurter how a man who had showed almost no executive talent as president could be such a good chief justice.

For all his organization and good humor, Taft was not indifferent to how the Court came out on a particular case. He had his own views, and he was eager to have them adopted in Court decisions. But of even greater importance to him was the need for unanimity. The Supreme Court was the voice of the law in the nation. Its every word, its every action was scrutinized, analyzed, and then used for guidance by lower courts, legislatures, and private citizens. Dissension, in Taft's view, undermined the Court's prestige and authority. It fostered the impression that an issue might not be finally settled. "I don't approve of dissents generally," Taft once explained to a colleague, "for I think in many cases where I differ from the majority, it is more important to stand by the Court and give its judgment weight than merely to record my individual dissent. . . ."[9]

Brandeis understood Taft's perspective. He too was concerned with the Court's prestige. He also understood that too much dissension could be counterproductive. So he refrained from dissenting in many cases even when he disagreed with the majority decision. This was especially true in cases that involved statutory construction or other nonconstitutional matters. In those areas Brandeis, like Taft, put a high premium on making it plain that the issue was settled. And if changing circumstances required a different result, the legislature was always free to amend the law. Cases involving the Constitution were different. There, Brandeis believed, "nothing is ever settled."[10] Constitutional questions raised political issues in the highest sense of the word. The Constitution was an organic document—its principles had to accommodate changing circumstances to some extent. Unlike statutory cases, though, there was no legislature that had the freedom to alter the Constitution. Amendments to the Constitution involved instead a cumbersome and time-consuming process. Therefore, the Constitution's ability to adapt to new conditions generally depended on new interpretations by the courts. So in constitutional cases Brandeis was less reluctant to dissent. After all, his views might later be helpful to a future Supreme Court when it took a fresh look at a constitutional provision.

However sound this distinction between constitutional and nonconstitutional cases, Taft did not appreciate it. Unity was just as important, he believed—perhaps more important—when the Court decided critical constitutional issues. And so he could hardly contain his anger when Brandeis decided to dissent in a case affecting the scope of the president's power under the Constitution.

All Frank Myers wanted was $8,838.71 in back salary. The United States government resisted, however. Myers had been removed by President Wilson from his postmaster job in Portland, Oregon, in 1920, and, according to the government, he was no longer entitled to a salary. Myers disagreed and sued the government. He had been appointed postmaster in 1917, and the 1876 law that governed such appointments said he could hold the office for four years unless the president removed him "by and with the advice and consent of the Senate." In his case, said Myers, the president had not even requested—let alone secured—the consent of the Senate. Therefore, he argued that Wilson's action was unlawful and he was at least entitled to his salary for the remainder of his four-year term. To support his case, Myers pointed out that, aside from impeachment, the Constitution does not mention the removal of government officials. Consequently, he said that the president had to honor the restriction that Congress imposed on his removal power.

Eventually the case came to the United States Supreme Court. Taft was undecided about it at first. As president he had rejected the view held by Theodore Roosevelt that the nation's chief executive could do whatever he chose unless it were specifically prohibited by the Constitution or a statute. Taft held the contrary belief, that the president could not do something unless he could base it on a specific grant of power from the Constitution or a statute. "There is no undefined [residue] of power which he can exercise," Taft later said of the president, "[just] because it seems to him to be in the public interest."[11] Therefore, if Congress limited the president's power to fire government employees, the chief executive—like any other citizen—had to obey the law.

At the same time, Taft recognized the dilemma if the president had to obtain Senate approval before he could fire an employee of the executive branch who had been appointed with Senate approval. It would make it difficult to get rid of such officials, and the president might find—especially if the Senate were controlled by the opposing political party—that he had to retain public officials who were not loyal to him. Indeed, President Andrew Johnson's impeachment had been predicated on his refusal to abide by the 1867 Tenure of Office Act, a law that required the president to obtain Senate consent before he could dismiss a government official. Johnson wanted to fire Secretary of War Edward Stanton, who opposed his policy of reconciliation with the South after the Civil War. Stanton reflected the prevailing mood in the Senate, though, and Johnson knew he would not get its approval for the dismissal. Luckily for Johnson, the Senate could not muster the necessary two-thirds vote to convict him and remove him from office. But the issue of congressional control remained, and now Frank Myers was forcing the Court to resolve it.

There was vigorous debate in the conference about the *Myers* case after the first oral arguments in December 1923, but the discussions proved inconclusive. The justices asked the parties to present oral argument a second time. Afterwards,

Taft agreed that, if the president were to fulfill his executive responsibilities under the Constitution, he had to have the right to fire people as well as appoint them. Congress could not interfere with that responsibility, and so he now believed the 1876 postal law was unconstitutional. Five other justices agreed with Taft. Brandeis, Holmes, and McReynolds indicated that they took a different view.

Because of the importance of the case, Taft assigned the opinion to himself. It was tough going, however. Taft was not a facile writer, and administrative duties prevented him from giving the opinion the attention it deserved. In early November 1925, he asked the justices in the majority to have a meeting at his house to discuss the draft opinion. There it was decided that Justices Pierce Butler, Willis Van Devanter, and Harlan F. Stone would act as a committee in revising Taft's draft. Stone took the lead and, with the assistance of his clerk, virtually rewrote the rambling and disjointed document that the chief justice had produced.

None of the editorial revisions seemed to disturb Taft, and he accepted them in a spirit of cooperation. Accepting a dissent from Brandeis on this critical case was another matter. Even before he saw Brandeis's analysis, Taft was complaining about his colleague's approach. "Brandeis puts himself where he naturally belongs," the chief justice wrote his brother in late November 1925. "He is in favor evidently of the group system. He is opposed to a strong Executive. He loves the veto of the group upon effective legislation or effective administration. He loves the kicker, and is therefore in sympathy with the power of the Senate to prevent the Executive from removing obnoxious persons, because he always sympathizes with the obnoxious person. His ideals do not include effective and uniform administration unless he is the head. That, of course," Taft went on, "is the attitude of the socialist till he and his fellow socialists of small number acquire absolute power, and then he believes in a unit administration with a vengeance."[12] No doubt Taft must have mused that, if he had had his way, Brandeis would not have permitted Ballinger's dismissal of Louis Glavis fifteen years earlier.

When he was preparing a dissent, Brandeis generally did not review the majority opinion until his opinion was completed. The dissent, he believed, had to stand on its own. Of course he would read the majority opinion before finalizing the dissent. It was a way of checking the accuracy and soundness of his analysis. And if necessary, he would make further changes in the dissent to respond to points advanced in the majority opinion.

The *Myers* case, Brandeis knew, was an important decision. Although Frank Myers had not occupied a major position in government, he felt that the issues went to the heart of democratic government. Presidents could not be above the law. Unchecked presidential power—like monopoly power in the marketplace—would inevitably lead to abuse. And even if it didn't, it would only accelerate the centralization of control in the federal government and further limit the ability of communities and individual citizens to determine their own destinies.

Brandeis always tried to be careful in writing opinions, but here, especially, no stone could be left unturned. A starting point was the famous 1803 opinion of Chief Justice John Marshall in *Marbury* v. *Madison.*[13] In that case the Supreme Court said that President Thomas Jefferson could not ignore a congressional statute that, in effect, required him to honor a judicial appointment made by his arch rival, President John Adams, shortly before Adams's tenure had expired in 1801. To Brandeis that case made it clear that Congress could limit a president's power to appoint and remove government officials below the policy-making level. But Marshall's opinion was not enough, not by a long shot. Every other relevant opinion, fact, statistic, and development had to be taken into account. Warren Ege was the clerk who began the research in the spring of 1925. Constitutional cases were reviewed; political science texts were digested; congressional records were scrutinized. An effort was made to document every authoritative statement, every law, every judicial decision that recognized Congress's right to limit the president's ability to staff the executive branch. Ege prepared lists and tables that seemed endless.

In September, Jim Landis became the clerk and continued the laborious research. And it was laborious. At one point the justice told Landis that the clerk had to review every page in the Senate Journal—the record of Senate proceedings—since the adoption of the Tenure of Office Act in 1867. Brandeis did not entirely trust indexes, and he wanted to know of anything that had been said or done by the Senate on the general subject of presidential appointments and removals.

Brandeis began drafting the opinion in Chatham in the summer of 1925. It was a slow process. By October he had only a few pages completed. He would read them over, consider Landis's latest research, then mark up the draft, add handwritten passages (usually on yellow lined paper), and then forward everything to the printer so that a new draft could be prepared. By the time he got a copy of Taft's majority opinion at the end of November 1925, Brandeis was still polishing his dissent.

The chief justice's draft predictably relied on the Constitution's grant of executive power to the president, the absence of any language in the Constitution expressly limiting his power to fire government officials, and the president's need to have people of his own choosing in government. Brandeis did not doubt the wisdom of giving the president at least some control over the hiring and firing of government employees. But the scope of that control, he thought, was a policy decision to be made by Congress. It was the legislative body, after all, that made the laws the chief executive was asked to enforce. Congress also determined the tools that the president would have available in order to fulfill his responsibilities. If the president had any complaints about the arrangement, he could take them to Congress. And Brandeis could not help including in his dissent a reference to the fact that the 1876 postal law—the one that Taft found inconsistent with the Constitution—had been honored by presidents for more than forty years before Wilson ignored it in firing Frank Myers. And during those forty years, no chief executive—not even President Taft—had felt unable to fulfill his obligations.

In the end, the problem with Taft's opinion was its failure to recognize that the American constitutional system did not allow the president alone to define the scope of his powers. The American system was one in which the functions of government were divided among three principal branches—the executive, the legislature, and the judicial. Each branch had some power to check the actions of the other branches. And in some cases, the check of one branch might mean that another branch would get less than it wanted. Otherwise one of the branches might become dominant and capable of abusing the people's trust.

All of this reflected fundamentals taught in any civics class. Nonetheless, Taft's opinion did not seem to appreciate the dangers of unchecked presidential power. On December 10, Brandeis picked up the large black fountain pen he used to write opinions. As one clerk recalled, it looked like a relic from the Iron Age. The justice then took a sheet of white lined paper and drafted a new paragraph to be added to the conclusion of his dissent. "The doctrine of separation of powers," he wrote, "was adopted by the [Constitutional] Convention of 1787 not to promote efficiency but to preclude the exercise of arbitrary power. The purpose in so doing was not to avoid friction, but to save the people from tyranny. . . ." Limited power—the Brandeis philosophy. And later, with a few additional edits, this passage became the crowning declaration of Brandeis' fifty-five-page dissent.[14]

In January, Brandeis circulated his dissent to the brethren. Holmes was pleased with it. Those taking an opposite view, he said, were "cowards and dreamers."[15] Taft and the rest of the majority were not impressed, however. As Stone later told the chief justice, the Brandeis dissent incorrectly "assumed that the people speak only through legislation, forgetting for the moment that the people spoke through the Constitution and that the legislative branch, as well as other branches of the government, have only such powers as were conferred . . . by the Constitution."[16] Since the Constitution did not expressly allow Congress to limit the president's power to fire postmasters like Frank Myers, Stone concluded, it had no right to interfere.

Stone's comment overlooked one basic fact. If the congressional check on the president in every instance required an express authorization by the Constitution, there would be a severe curtailment of congressional power. Obviously, the Constitution's general provisions could not anticipate every circumstance to which they would be applied. They were statements only of general principles, fundamental concepts that could be adapted to a changing environment. Stone himself seemed to recognize that when the Court was asked to decide the *Humphrey* case nine years later.

Franklin D. Roosevelt wanted to dismiss William Humphrey. After his election to the White House in 1932, Roosevelt wanted to make every effort to end the Great Depression. One of the first priorities was to staff the government's agencies and departments with people loyal to the new president and sympathetic to his policies. Humphrey did not satisfy that test. He had been appointed to the Federal Trade Commission by President Herbert Hoover, and Roosevelt believed his philosophy to be inconsistent with the new administration's New Deal programs. The only problem was the FTC law. It said that commissioners could be removed only for inefficiency, neglect of duty, or malfeasance in office. So the president raised the question. Did he have the power to fire Humphrey without regard to the statutory limitations?

Myers clearly indicated that the answer was yes. True, the FTC was different from the Post Office. The trade commission was intended to be an independent agency responsible to Congress, not an executive department controlled by the president. Nonetheless, the language in Taft's opinion in *Myers* seemed to subject all government employees—even those in independent agencies—to the president's removal powers. At least that's what Jim Landis thought. He happened to be an FTC commissioner at the time, and he told a presidential advisor that the president could indeed fire Humphrey on the basis of the *Myers* decision.

The Supreme Court later disagreed. In a unanimous decision—supported by both Stone and Brandeis—the justices said that, although the president could remove certain executive employees at will, he had no such power with respect to members of an independent commission exercising quasi-judicial and quasi-legislative functions.[17] It was at least a partial vindication of Brandeis's dissent in *Myers*.

It was not the first time—nor the last—that Brandeis would see all or part of his earlier dissents become a majority view on the Court. Unfortunately, he did not live to witness every reversal by the Court. And of those that he missed, few would have given him more satisfaction than the 1967 Supreme Court decision on wiretapping.

TWENTY•TWO

Privacy Revisited

The quality of a nation's civilization can be largely measured by the methods it uses in the enforcement of its criminal law.

WINSTON CHURCHILL

The people at the General Electric laboratories in Schenectady, New York, could not have been happier. The experiment appeared to be a complete success. The pictures were sharp, the voices clear. It was only a matter of time now, they no doubt hoped, when every American household would have a television set. That, at least, was the hope and expectation of David Sarnoff, vice president and general manager of the Radio Corporation of America, the GE subsidiary that conducted the experiment. And he made sure that the assembled journalists and other observers appreciated the importance of what they had just witnessed. "While this is an historical event comparable to the early experiments in sound broadcasting," Sarnoff declared, "the greatest significance of the present demonstration is in the fact that the radio art has bridged the gap between the laboratory and the home."

Back in Washington, D.C., the seventy-one-year-old man saw the Associated Press dispatch. It was dated January 13, 1928. Yes, television certainly was a significant development. But it was not necessarily all to the good. Radio had provided entertainment and information to the listening public. Television might serve a similar function. But there was a difference. Television could be used for sinister purposes as well. So Justice Louis Brandeis clipped the AP report from the newspaper and put it into a file. The item could be used in an opinion he was about to write.

Thomas J. Casey was having dinner in December 1925 with his wife and daughter in their home near Seattle when federal narcotics agents arrested him. They charged him with the unlawful purchase and sale of morphine. In due course he was convicted on both grounds.

Eventually the case wound its way up to the United States Supreme Court. By then the government had dropped the sales charge against Casey. The only question was whether he had illegally purchased the morphine. Still, the government thought it had a good case. They could demonstrate that Casey had had possession of morphine. They could also show that the morphine was not contained in its original package with a tax stamp. Under the law, that omission created a presumption of illegality. Casey argued that the presumption was inequitable. In addition, he felt that the government had treated him unfairly—and Brandeis, for one, shared that view.

Casey did not fit the mold of a drug dealer. He was an established attorney in Seattle and, with silver hair and a medium build, he cut an impressive figure. Much of his law practice involved the representation of drug addicts. Because of that his face was a familiar one in the Kings County Jail. Rumor had it that he could also be a helpful friend to the "boys" behind bars. A discreet inquiry, a quick payment, and the necessary fix would be provided. The rumors were so pervasive even the jailers heard them. They also noticed that the "boys" often looked a little tipsy after a visit from Casey. So the jailers decided to find out for themselves. George Cicero, a convicted felon and drug addict, was approached by federal narcotic officers. Would he help them catch Casey? Cicero was then in jail on a forgery charge, and any cooperation from him might be beneficial when the authorities decided his fate. The narcotic agents apparently also involved the sister-in-law of Roy Nelson, another "resident" of the King County Jail. It was agreed that both Cicero and Nelson would summon Casey to the jail, give him money, and ask for morphine.

Casey soon made his appearance, talked to Cicero and Nelson, took their money, and promised satisfaction. All the transactions and conversations were observed by the federal agents, who placed themselves near the attorney "cages" where prisoners talked to counsel. Later that afternoon, Mrs. Nelson went to Casey's law office. There, in the presence of Casey and an oriental man she did not know, Mrs. Nelson was given some towels that were to be delivered to her brother-in-law. Instead, Mrs. Nelson took them to the narcotic agents, who determined upon soaking them that they contained morphine. Casey denied most of these facts at his trial, but the jury believed otherwise.

To most of the justices it was an open-and-shut case. The evidence was credible, it was substantial, and it showed beyond a reasonable doubt that Casey had been engaged in illegal drug trafficking. Holmes was asked to write the majority opinion. The assignment from Taft could not have been accidental. Brandeis was proposing to dissent, and the chief justice was pleased to see the two "liberals" on opposite sides of the fence.

As the years rolled on, Taft became more and more irritated by Brandeis's dissents. Although they were not that frequent, they usually came on important cases. And, to make matters worse, Brandeis always seemed to be able to drag Holmes along with him. The chief justice knew that the two justices rode to and from Court together, that they frequently discussed Court cases, and that Brandeis would sometimes pressure the old Yankee to join him in dissent or to write his own. The senior justice appeared to be under the spell of the former "people's attorney," and it rankled the chief justice. Holmes was "so completely under the control of Brother Brandeis," Taft observed at one point, "that it gives Brandeis two votes instead of one."[1]

So when Holmes voted with the majority in conference on the Casey matter, Taft, no doubt, was delighted. To Holmes the record clearly demonstrated that Casey was guilty as charged. Brandeis did not disagree with that conclusion, but he was troubled by the government's role in the affair. The narcotic agents had not merely stationed themselves to observe a crime that Casey committed on his own initiative; they—representatives of the United States government—had instigated the crime themselves. They had planned it, they had engineered it, and they had supervised it. To Brandeis, the government's participation was morally offensive, and he wrote a strong dissent.

The dissent was circulated to the brethren, and Brandeis surely hoped that his favorite colleague would see the light. But Holmes held firm. And he sent a memo to the justices explaining why he could not join the dissent. "I have much sympathy with my Brother Brandeis' feelings about this case," Holmes said, "but I doubt if we are warranted in going farther than to suggest a possibility that the grounds for uneasiness may perhaps be considered by another (i.e., the pardoning) power." Holmes emphasized that, when all was said and done, the narcotic agents had done nothing more than to make a "simple request" of assistance from Cicero, "the stool pigeon." "I am not persuaded," he concluded, "that the conduct of the officials was different from or worse than ordering a drink of a suspected bootlegger."[2]

Although Holmes's memo revealed no wavering on his part, Taft wanted to make sure there would be no slippage. He dashed off a note of support after receiving the memo. "I concur strongly," the chief justice told Holmes, "but I don't think you need soften your difference with B. in this case. The idea that a full-grown man and a lawyer of much practice with addicts would be led into a crime like this without being a criminal all the time is absurd."[3] And so the decision was announced by Holmes in April 1928, and Brandeis dissented, as did Justices McReynolds, Butler, and Sanford.

However much satisfaction Taft took from the split between Holmes and Brandeis, it was to be short-lived. Indeed, even while he read the opinion in *Casey,* Holmes—much to the consternation of the chief justice—was indicating his willingness to join a Brandeis dissent in another matter raising issues similar to those in *Casey*.

Spies. Their use in almost any form was inexcusable, but especially when they worked for the government. It was important, of course, to protect individual privacy from the prying eyes and ears of other citizens. Warren and Brandeis had written their *Harvard Law Review* article almost forty years earlier to explain how the law could serve this noble goal. They never addressed the issue of government spying. After all, a person had a right to expect that his government would not resort to such sordid practices. At least, that's what Brandeis thought.

Unfortunately, there were many people—including some high government officials—who believed otherwise. Domestic espionage was a tool frequently used by the government, first to uncover secret agents working for the enemy during the war, then to expose communists, socialists, and other radicals whose views seemed to un-American. And then there was Prohibition. Secret listening devices were essential—or at least some people claimed they were essential—to identifying bootleggers and tax dodgers.

Brandeis did not care if domestic espionage was effective. It was unethical, and the government had no business relying on it. In late 1920, as Attorney General Palmer's raids on suspected communists dominated the national news, he urged Felix Frankfurter to have *The New Republic* (of which he was a contributing editor) explore the whole question of spying. And if there was any doubt about the slant to take, the justice briefly outlined his views. "The fundamental objection to espionage," he told the Harvard professor, "is (1) that espionage demoralizes every human being who participates in or uses the results of espionage; (2) that it takes sweetness & confidence out of life; (3) that it takes away the special manly qualities of honor & generosity which were marked in Americans."[4] In due course a series of articles appeared in the magazine.

Brandeis found some additional satisfaction on the legislative front. He was constantly after Frankfurter to talk with Senator Burton Wheeler and other legislators about terminating the government's spy program. One means to achieve this goal was the appropriations process in Congress. It was simple. All they had to do was deny the relevant agencies the money to engage in spying. Again, determination and patience were the keys. "It may take a generation to rid our country of this pest," Brandeis wrote to Frankfurter in the summer of 1926, "but I think it probably can be done, if the effort is persistent and we are prepared for action when, in the course of time, 'the day' comes. The temper of the public at some time in conjunction with some conspicuous occurrence will afford an opportunity & we should be prepared to take advantage of it."[5] Six months later the Senate rejected a $500,000 appropriations request for "undercover" work in the enforcement of Prohibition. Brandeis passed the good news along to Frankfurter and said that *The New Republic* "should not fail to take this occasion for an attack on the spy system."[6]

Brandeis did not rely on Frankfurther alone to criticize domestic espionage. When the *Olmstead* case came along, he had his own chance.

Roy (Big Boy) Olmstead seemed to have a good thing. He and his cohorts—more than fifty of them—ran a very profitable liquor-smuggling business out of Seattle. It was no small operation. They rarely did less than $200,000 worth of business a month and probably grossed about $2 million a year. They had a ranch near Seattle, two seagoing vessels (for trips to British Columbia), an office with a central switchboard, operators, bookkeepers, delivery men, dispatchers, and even their own attorney.

They were, however, victims of their own success. The federal narcotics agents could not help but notice their activities, and once again the "undercover" men decided to step in. They placed wiretaps on the telephones of the men's offices and homes, and for five months the agents listened to every conversation—personal and otherwise—made over those phones. Their notes of the conversations occupied 775 typed pages and confirmed that Olmstead was indeed running a very successful smuggling operation. With evidence in hand, the agents arrested Olmstead and more than seventy other individuals.

In upholding Olmstead's conviction, the federal court ignored a Washington state law that prohibited wiretapping. When the Supreme Court later reviewed Olmstead's *cert.* petition, they also agreed that the state law question would not be addressed. The only issue would be a constitutional one: did the wiretapping violate the individual's right to privacy as protected by the Fourth and Fifth Amendments to the Constitution? The Fourth Amendment states that the government cannot conduct "unreasonable searches"—those not sanctioned by a search warrant or other order indicating court approval. The Fifth Amendment says that a person cannot be deprived of his liberty without "due process" or compelled to be a witness against himself in a criminal case. Since the narcotics agents wiretapped the phones without court approval, Olmstead argued that the activity violated his Fourth and Fifth Amendment rights and that, therefore, the government should not have been allowed to use any evidence it had obtained through the eavesdropping.

Brandeis recognized the significance of the case, and he began working on his opinion long before the oral argument. He was not sure whether he would be in the majority, so he styled his drafts only as a "memorandum." There was no doubt, though, where he would come out in the case.

He of course knew that the Court had decided to address only the constitutional points. But he could not ignore the fact that the narcotics agents had violated a state law when they wiretapped Olmstead's phone. To the justice, that was unpardonable and had to be condemned. It was much more important than the constitutional issues, and he hoped the Court could resolve the case without reaching those constitutional questions. On February 8, 1928, he expressed his view on a piece of yellow lined paper. "To declare that the end justifies the means would bring terrible retribution," he wrote. "Crime is contagious. In a government of laws, the Government must observe the law scrupulously. It teaches the whole people by its example. If it becomes itself a law-breaker, it destroys respect for the law. It invites every man to become a law unto himself. It invites anarchy."

Henry Friendly, the justice's clerk, reviewed the draft memorandum. Friendly recognized the force of the state law argument. But he told the justice that the constitutional point was more critical. Even the government conceded that it would lose if the Fourth and Fifth Amendments applied to wiretapping. Moreover, it would not do to rely on individual states to determine the acceptability of wiretapping. It would mean a lack of uniformity in the laws. And there could be occasions when, under proper procedures, the federal government would be justified in wiretapping but would be unable to because of state restrictions.

After listening to his clerk, Brandeis decided to rearrange the memorandum. A new section was added discussing the constitutional aspects of the case. Here Brandeis relied heavily on arguments he and Sam had made in their privacy article. Some passages were lifted from the article and, with some minor editing, inserted into the memorandum. "The makers of the Constitution," Brandeis wrote, "appreciated that to civilized man, the most valuable of rights is the right to be let alone. They did not limit its guarantees of personal security and liberty against danger to the enjoyment of things material. Happily, the law recognizes that only a part of the pain, pleasure and profit of life lies there. The law gives protection to beliefs, thoughts, emotions and sensations." This protection, furthermore, was needed even when the government was well intentioned. "Experience has taught," Brandeis continued, "that the danger of invasion by the Government of these rights of the individual is greatest where its purposes are benevolent.

Men born to freedom are alert to resent the arbitrary invasion of their liberty by evil-minded rulers. It is in the insidious encroachments by the well meaning—by those of zeal without understanding—that the greatest danger lurks."

In preparing this passage, Brandeis recognized that the literal language of the Fourth Amendment—the principal constitutional provision in question—mentions only material things. The amendment refers to the "right of the people to be secure in their persons, houses, papers, and effects, against unreasonable searches and seizures. . . ." But the Constitution's reach could not be confined to the literal language. The Court had already held on numerous occasions that constitutional provisions had to be interpreted in light of new developments. That notion was especially important in defining a person's right to privacy, because science had now produced new methods to pry into personal affairs. "Discovery and invention," Brandeis wrote in the middle of February, "have made it possible for the Government to obtain by means far more effective than stretching upon the rack disclosure of 'what is whispered in the closet.' Through television, radium and photography, ways may soon be developed by which the Government can, without removing papers from secret drawers, reproduce them in court and by which it can lay before the jury the most intimate occurrences of the home."[7]

Brandeis gave this draft, like the previous ones, to Friendly. The young lawyer scrutinized the material carefully. The reference to television troubled him. Television had no relevance to government spying. The clerk voiced his concerns to Brandeis. "Mr. Justice," said Friendly, "television really isn't appropriate here. Television doesn't work in a way so that you can take it and beam it across a street into an apartment or building and see what somebody is doing." Brandeis looked at his youthful critic. "That's exactly how it works," said the justice. Friendly persisted. The justice simply did not appreciate the mechanics of this new invention. Would the justice at least let him secure some materials from the Library of Congress so that the justice could see that he was right? "Well," said Brandeis, "you can get those materials, but you'll see you're wrong." When the opinion was printed in its final form, however, the reference to television was omitted.[8]

Meanwhile, the oral arguments were held, and in late February the justices voted to uphold Olmstead's conviction. The only issue discussed concerned the constitutional points. And on that issue, at least six justices felt comfortable upholding Olmstead's conviction.

At Friendly's suggestion, Brandeis's memorandum—which was now labeled a dissent—started off with the constitutional argument. The second part addressed the doctrine of "unclean hands"—the argument that the government could not ask the Court's assistance in convicting Olmstead when its own conduct in the case was tarnished by unlawful wiretapping. Shortly after the oral arguments, Brandeis was sufficiently satisfied with the opinion to send it to Holmes for his review. Holmes was with the majority on the first vote, and Brandeis again hoped that the logic of his dissent could persuade him otherwise.

Responding a few days later, the senior justice said that he still could not accept the constitutional argument. Holmes had great respect for Brandeis, but on occasion the junior justice seemed to forget that he was a judge and not an advocate. His long and forceful opinions sometimes revealed the drive of an attorney seeking reforms, not a judge deciding a case on the basis of existing law. Holmes saw evidence of that attitude in Brandeis's *Olmstead* dissent. "I fear," he told Brandeis, "that your early stated zeal for privacy carries you too far." He added, however, that he "wobbled" on the "unclean hands" doctrine. Brandeis saw a glimmer of light. Although Holmes had tolerated the government's entrapment of Thomas J. Casey, he might draw the line narrowly and condemn government activities that involved more than a "simple request" of a convicted felon. Perhaps some of the other justices in the *Olmstead* majority could also be persuaded that the government's unlawful wiretapping required a reversal of Olmstead's conviction. It was worth a try. After all, it might not take that much to change the result.

Toward the end of March, Brandeis circulated the portion of his opinion dealing with the "unclean hands" point. In a cover note he explained that several of the brethren had stated that they had not considered the argument and that he thought it might be useful for them to see his views on it.

Justice Stone, for one, was impressed. He agreed with Brandeis's constitutional argument. He also sensed that Brandeis was probably right on the second ground as well. "It seems to me," he told his colleague, ". . . offensive to public policy and morals for the federal government to secure convictions through sending its agents into a State who there violate the State law. . . ."[9] Despite this attitude, Stone was not yet prepared to commit himself to joining Brandeis's dissent, but he promised to think about it.

Taft was not as charitable. He was preparing the majority opinion, and he did not like these new "attacks," as he saw them, especially since the conference had originally voted to consider only the constitutional question. "Where we make a limitation we ought to stick to it," he told Justice Sanford, "and I think anyone would have done so but the lawless member of our Court."[10] But he had to admit that the entire Brandeis opinion—which was circulated in May—was powerful. "It is rather trying," the chief justice wrote his brother, "to have to be held up as immoral by one who is full of tricks all the time. . . . But he can become full of eloquent denunciation without great effort."[11]

Taft was most disturbed, however, by the opinion eventually penned by Holmes. The senior justice had finally agreed to dissent, but only because wiretapping violated state law. As in other cases, Brandeis had urged his colleague to write his own opinion and, as in other cases, Holmes succumbed to the pressure. "It is desirable that criminals should be detected, and to that end that all available evidence should be used," Holmes wrote. "It is also desirable that the Government should not itself foster and pay for other crimes, when they are the means by which the evidence is to be obtained. . . . We have to choose, and for my part I think it a less evil that some criminals should escape than that the Government should play an ignoble part." Wiretapping, the justice concluded, was "dirty business" and the courts should not "allow such iniquities to succeed."[12]

Stone—after further conversations with Brandeis—decided to support the dissent on both the constitutional and statutory grounds. Justice Butler, on the other hand, decided to dissent on only the constitutional grounds. Still, when the decision was finally announced in June 1928, there were only four dissents and Olmstead's conviction was left to stand.

Brandeis—who at first wanted to rely primarily on the statutory argument—later seemed most upset by the Court majority's narrow view of privacy in the constitutional scheme. "I suppose," he told Frankfurter, "that some reviewer of the wiretapping decision will discern that in favor of property the Constitution is liberally construed—in favor of liberty, strictly."[13]

They wanted to impeach Earl Warren. At least that's what the bumper stickers on the cars said. As the chief justice of the United States Supreme Court between 1954 and 1969, Warren engineered many decisions expanding the constitutional rights accorded to individual citizens. Many people thought that Warren and his Court went too far, that they were coddling criminals, that, as a practical matter, they were only giving wrongdoers more freedom to victimize innocent people. And one decision that fell into that category was *Katz* v. *United States,* a case in which the Court overruled *Olmstead* and held that government wiretaps had to meet the procedural requirements of the Fourth Amendment, including the need for prior judicial approval.[14] Although the decision was criticized in some quarters, Justice Brandeis no doubt would have been pleased by it, especially since this new Court majority relied heavily on his *Olmstead* dissent. There was perhaps no greater satisfaction than to be vindicated by subsequent events.

Although he missed it in *Katz,* Brandeis knew all about that kind of pleasure. He had experienced it when the Zionist Organization of America asked him to return to the fold.

TWENTY•THREE

The Resurrection of a Leader

To be seventy years young is sometimes far more cheerful and hopeful than to be forty years old.

OLIVER WENDELL HOLMES

The justice liked Paul Raushenbush. He was a tall, handsome young man. He also had a bright, gregarious personality that made him easy to like. Then there was his work. Paul used his obvious talents teaching economics at the University of Wisconsin and exploring ways to protect workers from irregularity of employment. That was certainly a subject close to the justice's heart. But even that was secondary when compared with the fact that Elizabeth and Paul were in love and seemed very happy together. To the justice, few things were as important as the welfare of his daughters. So he was quite pleased in the spring of 1925 when Elizabeth—EB, as she was called—announced her engagement to Paul. Indeed, Brandeis was fond of saying later that he was indebted to Justice George Sutherland, who wrote the opinion holding the District of Columbia minimum wage law unconstitutional; as a result of that decision, EB lost her job with the local commission enforcing the law and moved to the University of Wisconsin, where she met Paul.

The justice did not have the same confidence in Susan's choice of a husband. Susan's father had high hopes for his elder daughter. After graduation from the University of Chicago Law School, she made a courageous move to open her own practice in New York City. Success seemed to come to her easily. She became one of the first women to argue a case before the United States Supreme Court and generally won the praise of other attorneys exposed to her work. Jack Gilbert, on the other hand, was a New York attorney who did not seem to have Susan's skill or potential. So the justice thought that Susan's planned marriage to Jack in late 1925 was "unambitious." Still, he had to admit that the preceding year of their relationship had "unquestionably" been the best year in Susan's development. Maybe there was hope.[1]

Louis and Alice wanted their daughters to choose their own careers and pursue whatever interests appealed to them. At the same time, the parents hoped and expected that Susan and Elizabeth would somehow be involved in public activities of some kind. In fact, during the Depression, when many families were concerned about the next day's meal, Louis and Alice gave each of the children $10,000 in bonds that they could use for participation in public causes. They were not disappointed on that score. Elizabeth and Paul were to play critical roles in the development of model social legislation. That was a source of pleasure and pride to Louis and Alice. Susan and Jack also took up the Brandeis banner and involved themselves deeply in matters that concerned the justice. One that did in the 1920s, as it had before, was Zionism.

Jack was proud to be the son-in-law of the "Judge," as he called Brandeis, and he no doubt recognized that the justice would appreciate his interest in Zionism. Brandeis's commitment to the cause had not diminished after the Brandeis group was ousted from the leadership of the Zionist Organization of America at the 1921 Cleveland convention. Indeed, a few days after that defeat the justice met with key supporters in the law offices of Nathan Straus in New York City, and there a new program was unveiled. Brandeis reminded them that they were still members of the ZOA. They would, however, refuse to occupy any office of leadership position in the organization. They could not be a part of an administration that had repudiated their policies. They would not be idle, though. There were other alternatives for service. One option could be an economic development group to be known as the Palestine Development Council.

As Brandeis explained it, this group would collect funds from business and earmark them for specific projects. One priority, for example, would be the elimination of malaria from Palestine. And they had good reason to believe that these focused efforts would bear fruit. "To my mind," Brandeis explained at one point after the PDC had been operating for a couple of years, "the smallness of the country contributes greatly to the probability of complete success. The problems are all [surmountable]. None is so big in bulk, so complex, that wee man seems inadequate for the task. For this reason, achievement is always in sight."[2]

There were some notable accomplishments. Malaria was eradicated, and that increased Palestine's ability to absorb immigrants. But the failures overshadowed the successes. The problem, largely, was money. The PDC simply could not attract enough investments from the business world to pursue the many projects envisioned for the organization. This was not entirely a reflection of indifference on the part of American Jews; other similar demands were being made on them, and the competition proved to be too much.

Although he had said Brandeis was too occupied with practical problems and too remote from the spiritual base of Zionism, Chaim Weizmann thought that the justice did have some good ideas. And one was the creation of a fund-raising group that would concentrate on specific projects and, it was hoped, appeal to Jews who were not Zionists. By the mid-1920s Weizmann was engaged in serious discussions with Louis Marshall and other members of the American Jewish Committee to examine the possibility of a new agency, one that would allow non-Zionists to feel comfortable contributing to Palestine's development. It would take them until 1929 before they created the Jewish Agency for that purpose. But in the meantime, the affluent German–Jewish community refrained from participation in the Brandeis PDC.

During these days continual pressure was exerted for the Brandeis group to have a reconciliation with the ZOA and its new president, Louis Lipsky. But the justice was not a man given to reconciliation when basic principles were at stake. And here Weizmann's betrayal remained ever fresh in his mind. He therefore resisted any suggestions from his own supporters that they end their isolation from the ZOA leadership. "[A]s it is," he told one colleague in 1924, "I see only a probability of our being caught in traps and compromised."[3]

He did, however, maintain his interest in expanding the ZOA membership. Jack Gilbert was especially helpful there. He would spend many hours and days actively recruiting new members, would report to the justice on his progress, and would provide assurances if there was any indication of inactivity. ("Please don't think I'm letting up on getting new members," Jack wrote his father-in-law at one point.[4]) Jack was also useful when Brandeis decided to make a move to have his supporters regain control of the ZOA toward the end of the decade.

The impetus came from members of the existing administration. The ZOA was not doing well. Membership was down from a high of 176,000 at the end of World War I to less than 25,000. The budget was low, the operating deficits were high, and the tangible achievements were minimal. And if that were not bad enough, rumors of mismanagement and corruption were widespread. It was alleged that Lipsky and his colleagues had used ZOA funds to make personal loans and for other private purposes. Dissatisfaction was growing in the rank and file, and many began to wonder aloud whether it would not be better to restore Brandeis to the ZOA leadership.

Jacob deHaas raised the possibility with the justice in the spring of 1927. Brandeis immediately made it clear that he himself could not assume an active and official role in any new administration. It was not only question of judicial proprieties—age was beginning to impose other limitations. He was now seventy years old, and he did not have the stamina to undertake the responsibilities he had assumed thirteen years earlier. ". . . I have been made conscious of the great difference which five years make after 65," he told deHaas. "It would be impossible for me to do at any time anything which smacks of executive determinations, the exercise of judgment in minor matters, or participation in conferences to straighten out dissensions or controversies. . . ." Despite that, he was all for a change in the ZOA's leadership. He had nothing but contempt for Lipsky and his colleagues. He saw them not only as poor managers; they were also dishonest, and they were a major obstacle to Palestine's development. He therefore encouraged efforts for "our friends" to regain control of the ZOA. But, Brandeis declared, "there can be no compromise with Lipsky or any of his ilk. All must get out, if our friends are to go in."[5]

It became a rallying cry for the Brandeis supporters. The removal of Lipsky and his ilk. When Charles Cowen visited the justice later that year to discuss Zionist affairs, Brandeis did not hold back on Lipsky's faults. "For five minutes," he reported to deHaas, "I spoke to [Cowen] impressively and torrentially of the shame of the Jewish people which had come from [Lipsky's] self-seeking, incompetent and dishonest administration, which had prostituted a great cause; which, enjoying fat salaries in New York, let school teachers in Palestine starve with six months of salaries in arrears. . . ." Brandeis saw one option only. "Only the teachings of the prophets," he instructed Cowen; "return to truth, put an end to the lying. Turn out those who have obtained money under false pretenses and misappropriated that which they secured."[6]

Revolutions and coups take time. Although the mismanagement of funds was widely known, and although the Brandeis group had the support of Hadassah, the women's Jewish organization, Lipsky received a vote of confidence at the 1928 convention in Pittsburgh. In part, the failure to repudiate his leadership reflected the inability of the Brandeis group to advance a specific candidate to lead the opposition. Stephen Wise, Julian Mack, and others who were qualified had to bow out because of health or other commitments. Nevertheless, the Brandeis forces made a strong showing, and the Lipsky regime appeared to be in trouble. Weizmann, who supported Lipsky, was especially fearful because he recognized the leading force behind the opposition. "It is all instigated by old Brandeis," he observed, "who, hidden behind his judicial robes, is capable of the vilest intrigues and tricks worthy of the lowest type of American politician."[7] Brandeis, in contrast, was encouraged by events. "The fight was a grand one," he told Julian Mack. "And the result one in which all of us should feel much satisfaction. . . . For it discloses the depth of the degradation to which Lipsky & his ilk have carried Zionists."[8] At the time, Brandeis could not have realized that his faction would receive decisive assistance from an unexpected—and most undesirable—source.

The Jews were an inconvenience. To be sure, the British government had accepted Foreign Secretary Arthur Balfour's commitment to the development of Palestine as a Jewish homeland. But that was in 1917. The World War was raging, and who could predict the future or fully anticipate England's needs in the years to come? The plain and simple fact was that the Arabs now seemed far more important to Britain's interests than some Jewish immigrants. The Arabs, after all, controlled ports, land areas, and natural resources that could be useful to Britain's economic and military goals. What could the Jews offer? And besides, everyone knew that Jews were slippery characters, people who could not be trusted, people whose first loyalty was not to the country of their citizenship but to some Biblical homestead they hoped to restore in Palestine.

During the 1920s the British government did little to ease the tensions in Palestine. Quite the contrary. Despite Balfour's willingness—at Brandeis's urging in 1919—to remove anti-Semitic military officers, many, if not most, of the British military personnel were far more sympathetic to the Arabs than to the Jews. Although the Zionists had greatly improved Palestine for the benefit of both Jews and Arabs, the native Arab populations remained resentful of the small but steady influx of Jewish settlers. The British officials seemed to support and even encourage this resentment. At different points efforts were made to limit Jewish immigration. Similarly, throughout the 1920s the British denied Jewish settlers adequate means of self-defense. The Jews protested this policy. There had been periodic outbursts of Arab attacks, and the resident police forces did not always seem ready (or perhaps willing) to respond. And Zionists could not help but notice that the British employed far more Arabs than Jews in the police force.

Although these facts were widely known in Zionist circles, few people were prepared for the sudden and bloody explosion of violence in August 1929. Arab mobs raced through the streets, attacking Jews, their shops, their homes. When it was over more than a hundred Jews were dead, many more injured.

Zionists all over the world were incensed by the tragedy. It was not only the senseless violence. It was also the British, whose policies seemed to create an atmosphere in which Arab hostilities would be tolerated. Back in Washington, Brandeis held a meeting in his apartment to explore possible reactions to the riots. Many of those in attendance said that it was now time to have a reconciliation of Zionist factions. Their differences were small compared with their common interest in the peaceful development of Palestine as a Jewish homeland. Felix Warburg, the head of the Jewish Agency, wanted Brandeis to leave the Supreme Court and assume full-time leadership of the Zionist movement. Brandeis made it clear that that was out of the question. Warburg had an alternative. He was planning a meeting in Washington at the end of November to discuss the situation. It would be an opportunity for all Jews—Zionists and non-Zionists alike—to show unity in the face of these new developments. Would Brandeis speak at the meeting?

At first the justice was against the idea. The Astor Hotel incident thirteen years earlier was still fresh in his mind. He did not want to do or say anything in public that could become a point of controversy. But deHaas told him that this was different. It was a critical moment. The ZOA was falling apart under Lipsky. And while Weizmann was still president of the World Zionist Organization, his prestige was undermined by a close association with the British government—a government that did not seem entirely trustworthy. Only Brandeis had the stature to rally Jews at home and abroad. Only Brandeis could impress upon the British that Zionism remained a serious endeavor worthy of attention.

The justice yielded. He recognized that a few words in public might be helpful—not only in giving hope to the Zionist membership but also in convincing the British that the Balfour Declaration could not be ignored. Moreover, a few words at the Warburg meeting would probably not be embarrassing, and it would not unduly tax his limited energy. So for the first time in almost ten years, Louis Brandeis agreed to speak at a public forum.

As always, he remained the optimist. He told the audience at Warburg's meeting that the perils of the moment were indeed sad; but they also revealed the courage, the intelligence, and the persistence of the Jewish character, qualities that would, in the end, bring what they all desired in Palestine. "I have no fear," he said, "because I know in my heart, as my reason tells me from all that I have observed, not only there but elsewhere in a life that is now beginning to seem long, that those Jewish qualities are qualities that tell."[9] There was no doubt about the impact of these words. "Brandeis's reception was all one could ask for," Bernard Flexner reported to Felix Frankfurter. "He spoke extraordinarily well, was himself greatly moved and moved everyone else."[10]

Moving Jews was one thing. Moving the British was quite another. In the autumn of 1929 Brandeis had an opportunity to discuss the matter alone with Prime

Minister Ramsay MacDonald at the British Embassy in Washington. But even eloquence and logic from this aging justice were not enough to overcome British intransigence. In March 1930 the British government released a report on the Palestine situation by Sir Walter Shaw, a career civil servant. It did not carry a message of hope for Zionists. Shaw's report acknowledged the Arabs' responsibility for the August riots, but the rest of the report went to great lengths to excuse the violence. And the excuse ultimately rested on the Arabs' justified animosity toward the Jewish settlers. The Jews were, Shaw said, encroaching on land and rights that belonged to the Arabs. So Shaw recommended a reexamination of immigration policies. Lord Passfield, the British Colonial Secretary, did Shaw one better. He immediately suspended all Jewish immigration into Palestine and dispatched Sir John Hope-Simpson to conduct the additional investigations recommended by Shaw.

With despair and outrage, the Zionists saw the British turning their backs on commitments accepted in the Balfour Declaration. Meetings were held, speeches were made, and new strategies were explored by Zionist groups. Brandeis also promised to do what he could. And in June 1930 he had his chance. Sir Ronald Lindsay, the British ambassador to the United States, made a trip to Boston, and he passed word that he would be happy to see the justice, who was already in Chatham for the Court recess. On the evening of June 18, the justice went to Boston and left word at the Bellevue Hotel (where Lindsay was staying) that he would be in Room 831 and would be glad to see the ambassador at any time the following morning.

Lindsay got the message and arrived at Brandeis's room at 8:40 A.M. the next day. For almost two and a half hours Brandeis poured his heart out to the ambassador. All the hopes, fears, and criticisms of the Zionists were expressed. Brandeis began by saying that he still had confidence in the British government and the British people to honor the Balfour Declaration and properly administer the Palestinian mandate. Unlike the French, he said, they did not have a history of anti-Semitism. And they also had a sense of justice that he hoped and expected would prevail. But the British government, Brandeis continued, must not underestimate the seriousness of the present situation. The Shaw report not only represented a breach of faith on England's part; of equal, if not greater significance, he said, the report would endanger amicable relations between Great Britain and the United States.

To Brandeis, the Shaw report was very much like the congressional reports on the Ballinger affair twenty years earlier. It ignored the facts in a headlong rush to whitewash the guilty figures. Why, said Brandeis, Shaw had taken evidence from Arabs in secret sessions without any opportunity for the Jewish settlers to test the accuracy of the information. That, the justice declared, was contrary to all known principles of English and American law. And whatever the secret evidence, Brandeis went on, it could not obscure the fact that the Arabs had been the aggressors. "Jews don't murder," he declared.

Settlement in Palestine was a risky venture, he told Lindsay. Jews had to be prepared to accept hardship, even to die. Indeed, whenever people had raised the prospect of attacks by Arabs, Brandeis's response had been calm. "Oh, don't worry about that," he would assure his listener. "The Jews are good shots." All that, however, depended on the Jews' having guns to shoot. But the British, Brandeis reminded Lindsay, had confiscated arms and limited the Jews' right to possess them. If the British were prepared to protect the Jewish settlers from attacks, that policy might be acceptable. But if the local administration could not provide that protection, Brandeis told the ambassador, then the British could not deny the Jews the means to protect themselves. In closing, Brandeis acknowledged that Jewish and Arab aspirations in Palestine could not be fully reconciled. At the same time, he believed that the Balfour Declaration could be implemented in a way that would do justice to Arab interests. But it would take fair and sympathetic British policies—policies that Brandeis said he hoped to see adopted after Hope-Simpson issued his report on immigration policies.[11]

Lindsay did not debate Brandeis. He interjected questions on occasion and then left, saying only that he would take a close look at the situation. Brandeis was not satisfied with that. Even before the Hope-Simpson report was released in October, Brandeis and Frankfurter contacted Harold Laski in London. Laski was a British subject who had become friends with both Frankfurter and Brandeis when he taught at Harvard College for a few years before 1920. He had then returned to England, where he developed close relationships with his country's ruling elite. And one crucial member of that elite was Prime Minister MacDonald. Brandeis and Frankfurter said that Zionism now needed all the help it could get. Would their friend contact the prime minister and turn this thing around?

At first, Laski was more than happy to help. But the pleasure soon faded. Dealing with the Americans was not easy. Brandeis, he thought, was "intransigent and dominating, and unnecessarily prone to read evil motives into obvious actions." As for Frankfurter, Laski thought he was "like clay" in the justice's hands and seemed incapable of independent thought when Brandeis was involved. As a result, Laski found it difficult to present the Zionist cause to MacDonald and other members of his government. "All statesmanship is, after all, the power to compromise on inessentials," Laski remarked to a friend at one point. Brandeis, however, "digs himself in on what are really matters of no consequence with the passion of a tiger defending his cubs; and that makes him, in my judgment, much less effective on the big issues where he is really entitled to care." To Laski, it all reflected the Jewish mind that was full of pride and resisted assimilation.[12]

For all his intransigence, Brandeis had a good fix on the British mind as well. Shortly after he contacted Laski, the Hope-Simpson report was released. It accepted Shaw's findings and recommended that limitations be put on the purchase of land by Jews in Palestine and that immigration be suspended until Arabs were fully employed. To Brandeis this was a slap in the face of Zionism. He was not willing to compromise here; it was a matter of principle. The British had promised the Jews a national homeland in Palestine, and there could be no homeland if Jews could not emigrate there and buy land to develop. Now the British government wanted to issue only a general statement in support of Zionism. Unacceptable, said Brandeis. Only policies dealing with the specifics of the situation would be useful.

Chaim Weizmann was using his considerable contacts in the British government to support Brandeis's view, and eventually the British succumbed to the pressure. In early 1931 MacDonald issued a letter that, in "clarifying" British policy, repudiated the previous reports and opened the doors for continued Jewish settlement. It was, however, only a temporary reprieve. Within a short time the British would revive Hope-Simpson's recommendations. But by then, at least, the British would have to deal with a stronger Zionist organization, one largely under the control of the Brandeis group.

The Arab riots in August 1929 had underscored the impotence of the Lipsky regime. Not only was the ZOA riddled with mismanagement; it was equally clear that the leadership was something less than magnetic. For all his faults Lipsky was dedicated to Zionism, but neither he nor any of his colleagues had the prestige of Brandeis. They did not even have the support of the justice. And in moments of crisis—like the one in the summer of 1929—there was no one in the ZOA whose words could command respect and inspire action. So the pressure intensified for the Brandeis group to take up the reins of leadership once again.

In May 1930 Brandeis and his lieutenants responded to these overtures with a letter to the ZOA leaders outlining the conditions under which they would return. In essence, they wanted the organization to be turned over to a select group of administrators who would, for the immediate future at least, have absolute power. To ensure fairness, none of the administrators were to have ties to either the Lipsky or Brandeis groups. After financial and managerial matters were put back into shape, a new leadership would be elected by the membership.

To the existing ZOA leadership, the most notable feature of the proposal was the exclusion of Lipsky and his colleagues from any further managerial role in the organization. The ZOA wanted Brandeis and his group back, but did they have to repudiate Lipsky? Questions were raised about ambiguities in the Brandeis letter and whether there was room for compromise. The justice remained adamant and told his followers that they were not even to discuss the meaning of the letter. "The thing that ZOA members must do," he told Julian Mack, "is to find themselves. That involves thinking. And perhaps they would come nearer to doing that if left to the consideration of our statement unaided by our interpretation."[13]

Still, the pressure for compromise continued to build. And some of Brandeis's supporters, such as Mack, wanted to accommodate the Lipsky group to some extent. To be sure, new leadership was needed, but they did not have to completely alienate existing members. And besides, some of them could be helpful in rebuilding the organization. In the early summer of 1930 there were several meetings at the Brandeis home in Chatham. In the course of the discussions the justice dictated a letter to the delegates at the forthcoming ZOA convention. The Jewish press had carried editorials urging Brandeis himself to assume the presidency, and large segments of the rank and file echoed this plea. Brandeis therefore had to explain why he could not accept the assignment. "I appreciate the generous suggestion which many of you have made that I again assume the official responsibility of leadership in the ZOA," the letter read. ". . . Added years make it impossible for me to assume now the official responsibilities of leadership as I did prior to 1921, but I am ready now as then to serve the cause. Necessarily the service to be rendered must be limited in scope to advising from time to time when requested on questions of major policy."[14]

At the convention there were many speeches. Stephen Wise, Brandeis's disciple, said that the present leadership was morally bankrupt and that there could be no progress until the justice and his group were back in control. The speech upset almost everyone, even the Brandeis supporters—at that very moment they were in a hotel room with the Lipsky group trying to resolve the leadership problem with a minimum of hostility. After many hours of uncertainty, Bob Szold, a member of the Brandeis group, approached the lectern to read the justice's letter to the delegates. He then added that he had talked to Brandeis and that the justice was now prepared to accept *any* new ZOA administration elected by the membership—even if it rejected the conditions that Brandeis had advanced in May. For a moment there was only stunned silence. Brandeis, it now appeared, was willing to compromise. Then the speakers outlined the face-saving deal that they had reached: a new administration of eighteen members, twelve to be selected by the Brandeis group, six to be selected by the Lipsky group. After the details of the proposed compromise had been explained, Louis Lipsky stepped forward, grabbed the hand of Jacob deHaas, Brandeis's chief advisor on Zionism, and held it high in a show of unity. Overcome by emotion, the huge gathering sprang to its feet cheering and singing "Hatikvah" ("The Hope"), the Zionist anthem. Szold was elected to the chairmanship of the executive committee, and a new era, it seemed, was about to open, one full of hope and excitement.

Over the next couple of years Szold and his group began the slow process of rebuilding the Zionist organization. Although the work was often tedious and demanding, there was a conviction, shared by Brandeis, that they were at least moving in the right direction and that success was within their grasp. But Hitler changed everything.

The evidence was there for anyone not blinded by false hopes. Hitler's rise to high position in the German government was an ominous sign for that country's Jews. Brandeis himself received a steady stream of reports from Jewish agencies in London about the widespread anti-Semitic activities in Germany. It was distressing—and it looked as though things would get a lot worse before they got better.

Shortly after Hitler's appointment as chancellor in January 1933, Stephen Wise came to see the justice. Wise had seen many of the letters and cables received by Brandeis. What could be done? Wise asked. Brandeis was a fighter by nature, but you could not ignore reality. To him there was only one alternative. "The Jews must leave Germany," he told his visitor. "There is no other way."[15]

It was advice easy to give, difficult to follow; Wise knew that. So he planned a large protest meeting at Madison Square Garden in New York City to dramatize the persecution of Jews in Germany. Publicity, he thought, might discourage the anti-Semitic activities. The German Embassy and the United States State Department felt otherwise and urged the Zionist leader to call off the meeting. Assurances were given that, despite a few isolated and unauthorized attacks, the Jews in

Germany would be protected from persecution. Any protest meeting, these government officials said, would only further antagonize the anti-Semitic elements in Germany. For a moment Wise was in doubt as to the right course. He went to see Brandeis and explained the facts. What should I do? he asked. Again the justice was succinct and to the point. "Make the great protest meeting as good as you can," he told Wise.[16] The advice was heeded. More than 20,000 people attended the rally in March 1933, with another 50,000 jammed outside.

Brandeis, meanwhile, was not content to advise Zionists. A new president was inaugurated in March 1933, and the justice hoped that Franklin D. Roosevelt's administration would be responsive to this new Jewish problem in Europe. Felix Frankfurter told Raymond Moley, a State Department official, that the new secretary of state, Cordell Hull, should see Justice Brandeis and get a "dispassionate" view of the German situation. Within a short time Hull came to the California Street apartment to meet with Brandeis. The justice told him about the cables and letters. Germany's Jews, Brandeis warned, were in trouble, and the United States had to help. And at that point—when there was no state of war between Germany and the United States—the most effective weapon was an American boycott of German goods. Boycotts had worked for the American Revolutionaries against the British; perhaps they would work now. But the government had to lead the way.

Hull was impressed by the Brandeis lecture. But other, less sympathetic forces were in control. The boycott proposal never got far—although Brandeis would invoke the suggestion for years to come whenever the discussion concerned the possibilities of an American response to anti-Semitism in Germany.[17] He of course continued to believe that individuals should shape their own destinies. But there were some things people could not do for themselves.

Brandeis did not confine his recommendations for government assistance to instances of Jewish persecution. Even in the United States—where social problems rarely approached the danger then found in Germany—there were occasions when a helping hand was needed. And in deciding judicial cases, Brandeis did all he could to preserve that option for state governments.

TWENTY • FOUR

The Review of Social Legislation

Laws are like sausages. They're okay as long as you don't see how they're made.

MARK TWAIN

If there was anyone who looked like a chief justice of the United States Supreme Court, it was Charles Evans Hughes. Tall, well built, with a finely chiseled face and a full, well-shaped beard, Hughes looked like the embodiment of Zeus himself. His demeanor added to the aura of his presence. He was courtly but firm, and his every statement seemed to reflect a storehouse of knowledge. Although a bundle of nerves inside, to the casual observer Hughes appeared to be nothing but self-controlled and self-confident.

Anyone familiar with Hughes's career would expect no less. It was truly remarkable. He had achieved fame at the turn of the century as the attorney who assisted the New York legislature in exposing corruption in the insurance industry. After that, it was almost an easy step to the governor's mansion in Albany. His skills as a politician and a lawyer were widely known, and in 1910 President Taft appointed him to the United States Supreme Court as an associate justice. Hughes was not entirely comfortable on the Court and was quite happy to leave in 1916 to accept the Republican presidential nomination. After losing a close election to President Wilson, he took up residence at a prestigious Wall Street law firm. He represented both the mighty corporations and struggling unions, and, in the course of one of his several arguments before the Supreme Court, he impressed Justice Brandeis as the best oral advocate to come before that Bench.

Hughes's prestige was unequaled in certain circles—especially Republican ones—and in 1921 President Harding named him secretary of state in his new Cabinet. After a few years, however, Hughes tired of public life and left to return to law practice—this time, he hoped, for good. But it was not to be. William Howard Taft, the current chief justice, was very ill and getting worse. He had had a heart attack in 1924, and now all the years of hard work were taking their toll. He did not sit with the Court after January 1930, and in early February he resigned.

Although President Hoover had many candidates to replace Taft, he settled on Hughes, and within a month of Taft's resignation the former justice was in place as the new chief. Sadly, one of his first responsibilities was to travel to Tennessee to attend the funeral of Justice Sanford, who died suddenly in early

March. And then Taft passed away. It was in all the newspapers. Still, the clerk of the United States Senate informed Reynolds Robertson, Hughes's clerk, that the Senate had to receive an official notification of Taft's death from the chief justice. Since Hughes was out of town, Robertson went over to Eye Street to secure the documentation from the acting chief.

Oliver Wendell Holmes enjoyed being the temporary chief justice—it injected a little variety into his life. So he was quite happy to give the senators the document they wanted. He took out his pen and then turned to Robertson. To whom do I address this letter? The president of thc Senate, the clerk responded. Holmes began to write and then stopped. Who's the president of the Senate, he asked Robertson. The vice president of the United States, came the reply. Holmes began to write and then stopped again. Who's the vice president now? Robertson provided the name of Charles Curtis and Holmes, now satisfied, drafted the note and then looked up at Robertson. "I'm like Sherlock Holmes," said the senior justice. "I don't keep inconsequential facts in my head."[1]

For all his playfulness, Holmes too was slowing down, and it was a matter of grave concern to Brandeis. The first critical blow came in April 1929 when Holmes's wife, Fanny, died. They had been a devoted couple, and the old justice was overcome with grief. Every day he would drive to Arlington and place a red rose on Fanny's grave. "A companionship of sixty years is more than one can bargain for," he wrote to Harold Laski, "a companionship that has made life poetry. If I can work on for a year or two more, it is well enough—and if not, I have lived my life."[2]

Brandeis appreciated his friend's deep loss, and he tried to comfort him. And for Brandeis, there was no better medicine than concentrated work; it could divert the mind for at least a few hours or days. So he told Holmes about the *Schwimmer* case, a controversy that raised serious constitutional issues about the freedom of speech. The case concerned the right of Quakers to retain their conscientious objection to war. A majority of the Court had upheld a congressional law that, in effect, prevented Quakers from becoming naturalized citizens unless they renounced their beliefs and took an oath to bear arms in defense of the country. Holmes looked at the case and agreed with Brandeis that a strong dissent was required. It was his last—and perhaps most powerful—opinion on free speech. (There is, he wrote, nothing more important in our Constitution than "the principle of free thought—not free thought for those who agree with us but freedom for the thought we hate."[3])

It was only a temporary reprieve for Holmes. He was, after all, approaching his ninetieth birthday, and there were now many things he could not do. Fanny Holmes had tried to anticipate her husband's needs if he should be left alone. When she first became sick, she brought in Mary Donnellan, a young Irish girl, and trained her to take care of Wendell. Mary was devoted to the justice, and she diligently attended to him. But all the help in the world could not stave off the inevitable. His stamina began to wane, and his figure became a little more stooped. ("The jack-knife won't open" he would say.) He had never had much store for facts and research, and now he told his clerks, his "boys," that they need not spend any time reading cases to prepare opinions. He was interested only in his favorite author—himself—and they could just use his old opinions, which were readily available at the townhouse.

The clerks were not the only ones to notice the change in Holmes. The brethren were also aware of it. His output diminished, and the naps, even during oral argument, became more frequent and of longer duration. The head would droop, almost touching the note cards in front of him, and then, after a while, he would wake with a start. It was embarrassing, and some of the justices approached Hughes. Someone had to tell the old Yankee that the time for retirement had arrived. The chief justice went to Brandeis. He had promised Holmes long before that he would tell the senior justice if he was no longer useful to the Court and should step down. But Brandeis could not keep the promise. He agreed that Holmes should leave the Court, but he thought the word should first come from the chief.

On a January morning in 1932, Chief Justice Hughes arrived at Holmes's townhouse and was ushered upstairs to the justice's study. After a short while they sent word to Chappie Rose, Holmes's clerk, to get a specific volume of the United States Code. They didn't tell Rose why they needed that particular volume, but he knew it contained the law relating to resignations by Supreme Court justices. After about an hour Hughes, tears streaming down his cheeks, walked down the stairs and quietly left. Although nothing had been said, Rose knew what had happened. He rushed upstairs to Holmes's study. The justice, dressed as usual in formal wear, was sitting passively in the overstuffed chair. And there was Mary Donnellan, her head on Holmes's knees, sobbing uncontrollably. After a little while there was a knock at the front door, and Justice Brandeis was led upstairs to spend some time alone with the ex-justice.

It was not an entirely sad occasion for Holmes. After almost fifty years as a jurist—thirty of them on the United States Supreme Court—he had tired of the routine with its many pressures and demands. He could now read what he wanted, nap when he wanted, take rides in the country when he wanted. "It was," Chappie Rose later recalled, "like school was out."[4] And then there were the visitors. Learned Hand, the eminent federal judge in New York City, would take the train down every two weeks or so, spend about an hour trading dirty jokes with Holmes, and then take the train back to New York. Members of the Court brethren would also periodically call on Holmes. But no one appeared as often as Justice Brandeis. Twice a week, almost like clockwork, he would come to the townhouse. Mary Donnellan would advise Holmes that Justice Brandeis was on his way. The old man's eyes would light up and a smile would envelop his face. When Brandeis arrived, Mary would take him upstairs to the study. Holmes would lift himself, slowly but steadily, out of the chair and embrace Brandeis, saying, "My dear friend, my dear friend." Then Mary would leave them to talk about Shakespeare, the spring flowers, Greek literature—almost anything but Court business. And in those long talks, Brandeis began to appreciate that Holmes—for all his lack of practical experience—understood people far better than most. When Hitler came to power, for example, Holmes warned Brandeis that it was an ominous sign and might well lead to barbaric policies. Afterwards—when Hitler's atrocities became well known—Brandeis recalled Holmes's observation in a conversation with Felix Frankfurter. "We used to think that he was naïve," Brandeis remarked, "but he saw deeper into the nature of man than any of us."[5]

There were other changes besides those in the Court membership. The nation's economy, for one. For so many years things had seemed so good. Commerce flourished; stock prices soared; material comforts abounded. And there seemed no end in sight. After all, it was now part of the national creed. "The business of America," President Calvin Coolidge had said, "is business." And then in October 1929, with another president at the helm, something happened. "There has been a little distress selling on the Stock Exchange," said Thomas Lamont of the prestigious Morgan banking house. ". . . We have found that there are no houses in difficulty, and reports from brokers indicate that margins are being maintained satisfactorily." There was, he added, no fundamental problem that should cause any concern.[6]

It was, of course, one of the greatest understatements of all time. The insignificant problem was nothing more than the onslaught of a nationwide depression from which the country would not recover until World War II.

To Brandeis, the stock market crash reflected poor leadership. The people in control were simply not paying attention. He saw it even in the Hoover administration. Brandeis knew Herbert Hoover very well. The Hoovers had dined on several occasions at the Brandeis apartment during the second Wilson administration. Brandeis had been very impressed with the young engineer, and the justice was instrumental in having Wilson appoint him as the Food Administrator to supervise relief efforts for war-torn Europe. The position catapulted Hoover into the national spotlight, and Harding later named him secretary of commerce. Brandeis's initial pleasure in the appointment soon evaporated. Slowly he began to lose confidence in Hoover. The justice watched economic developments like a hawk, and he was not sure that Hoover fully understood what was happening. You can't trust his figures, Brandeis would repeatedly say of the commerce secretary. And the basic problems remained intact. Business was still producing too much. Even people concerned with material comforts could not consume all the goods and services being offered. "This wild stock speculation far exceeds in height and endurance the limits which seemed to me possible," Brandeis wrote to his son-in-law Jack Gilbert in October 1928. ". . . I still think the day of sorrow is not remote."[7] To Brandeis, then, the economy was a house of cards that would have to fall sooner or later, and, for him, the sooner the better.

So he was not upset by the stock market crash. Perhaps now people would appreciate their own limits as well as their country's. Perhaps now, he told Bess Evans, there would be "purgation and sanity in living." Yes, he told her, there was reason to believe the country had "emerged from the black night of the Harding–Coolidge regime—and may rejoice again." And later, when asked if he thought the worst was over, he would reply, almost cheerfully, "Oh yes, the worst took place in the prosperous days before 1929."[8]

The Depression had other incidental benefits. Of primary importance to Brandeis, it underscored the need for—and wisdom of—communities' being able to control their own affairs. If corporations got too large and standards too loose, the community could not protect itself from corruption or economic manipulation. And if one needed proof, it was now evident in the hardships that people had to endure—hardships that arose, in Brandeis's eyes, because there had been no limit to what business could do in the blissful days before the crash. He was an optimist, though. Faced with these problems, the state and local governments would devise adequate remedies, solutions that would protect the competitive spirit and yet prevent the indiscriminate production of goods and services. But above all, citizens and their local representatives would have to make the choices. The courts could not—indeed, should not—make the choices for them.

All of this was consistent with views that Brandeis had expressed for many years. In his very first opinions as a Supreme Court justice the former "people's attorney" had asserted that state legislatures should be accorded the freedom to adopt laws responsive to local conditions and that courts should not interfere if there were facts to indicate that the legislature's judgment was reasonable. In no other way, said the new justice, could we "have a system of living law."[9] "Unless we know the facts on which the legislators may have acted," he observed at one point, "we cannot properly decide whether they were (or whether their measures are) unreasonable, arbitrary, or capricious. Knowledge is essential to understanding; and understanding should precede judging." And the courts should not stand in the way if the facts called for novel approaches. "Sometimes," he concluded, "if we would guide by the light of reason, we must let our minds be bold."[10]

Even judicial precedent should not impede local control. To be sure, court decisions deserved respect. And more than that, prior decisions could be guideposts to settle later controversies. To the legal profession, this reflected the doctrine of *stare decisis*—the notion that past decisions governed future ones. It was a firm tradition, one that the justices invoked often in deciding the fate of legislation. Brandeis too accepted the principle in most situations. "But the doctrine of *stare decisis*," he told his brethren in one 1927 case, "does not command that we err again when we pass upon a different statute. In the search for truth through the slow process of inclusion and exclusion, involving trial and error, it behooves us to reject as guides the decisions upon such questions which prove to have been mistaken. . . . The logic of words should yield to the logic of realities."[11] So if the legislature had reason to believe that a previous law was inadequate, the courts should not oppose change—whatever the thrust of the earlier law.

Brandeis expressed these beliefs in dissenting opinions. Time and time again a majority of the Court struck down almost any form of social legislation—whether it be restrictions on employment agencies, the weights of loaves of bread, minimum wages for workers, or the compensation a state could provide to injured employees. And in almost every case the majority relied on the Fourteenth Amendment, and especially its "due process" clause. Laws that restricted the conduct of business, the majority invariably said, deprived the individual of property without due process of law (although the same Court majority would have no pause if the state legislation restricted the citizen's freedom of speech). It was disheartening to Brandeis. On numerous occasions he told Felix Frankfurter that there was no answer to the problem except to repeal the Fourteenth Amendment (and in due course the Harvard professor wrote an article for *The New Republic* recommending just that).

The elevation of Hughes to the Court, Brandeis thought, offered some hope that the future might be different. And if there was any doubt about the reasonableness of that hope, it evaporated—at least for a time—when the Court decided the *O'Gorman & Young* case in 1931. At issue was a New Jersey statute that required uniformity in the payment of insurance commissions to company agents. The law stated, in effect, that an insurance company could not employ one agent at a rate different from another agent's. Four members of the Court argued that the law was unreasonable. After all, they said, it was common knowledge that different agents might, because of differences in competence, be entitled to a different commission. On this basis, these justices said that the New Jersey law stripped individuals of their constitutional right to make contracts. Speaking for the other five members of the Court, Justice Brandeis said it was not necessary to know the actual facts. The legislature's judgment "must prevail" unless the law's opponents could demonstrate that the measure was utterly arbitrary, and, Brandeis concluded, no such demonstration had been made here.[12]

Brandeis's delight with the *O'Gorman* opinion was short-lived. Within about a year the Court took a step backwards. The case concerned an Oklahoma statute that required parties to obtain a government certificate of necessity before they could enter the ice business. A majority of the Court said the law was plainly unreasonable. The government could regulate entry into only those businesses that were affected with a public interest, and they could see no basis for placing the ice business in that category.

Brandeis was not one to downplay the importance of competition, and he too had grave doubts about the utility of the Oklahoma statute. But he was not a legislator, and he could not say that there were no facts to justify the law. Perhaps it was cut-throat competition. Or maybe it was price gouging by dominant firms. And in a state like Oklahoma—where refrigerators were still a luxury owned by only a few—how could a group of men sitting hundreds of miles away in Washington, D.C., say that the ice business was not vital to the public interest there?

The Court majority's decision was especially disturbing to Brandeis because it limited the states' right to respond to the Depression. "The people of the United States," he wrote in dissent, "are now confronted with an emergency more serious than war." Many people, he observed, thought the root of the country's economic ills was "unbridled competition." Others had different views. But one thing was clear. "All agree," the justice said, "that irregularity in employment—the greatest of our evils—cannot be overcome unless production and consumption are more nearly balanced." For Oklahoma legislators, that balance required—in the ice business at least—a government certificate before someone could enter the competition. The state apparently believed that that was the best way to take control of the situation.

"Whether that view is sound," Brandeis remarked in his dissent, "nobody knows. The objections to the proposal are obvious and grave. The remedy might bring evils worse than the present disease. The obstacles to success seem insuperable. The economic and social sciences are largely uncharted seas. . . . Man is weak and his judgment is at best fallible." But the seemingly impossible could happen. It had happened before. Earlier generations had thought the idea of flying far-fetched, and now it was a reality. The answer, then, was readily apparent. "There must be power in the States and the Nation to remould, through experimentation, our economic practices and institutions to meet changing social and economic needs. I cannot believe," he added, "that the framers of the Fourteenth Amendment, or the States which ratified it, intended to deprive us of the power to correct the evils of technological unemployment and excess productive capacity. . . ." Rather, they probably saw great benefits in a state's controlling its own affairs. "It is one of the happy incidents of the federal system," Brandeis continued, "that a single courageous State may, if its citizens choose, serve as a laboratory; and try novel social and economic experiments without risk to the rest of the country." Brandeis recognized that the Court could invoke some constitutional phrase to prevent the experiment. "But in the exercise of this high power," he warned, "we must be ever on our guard, lest we erect our prejudices into legal principles." He then borrowed a sentence from an earlier dissent: "If we would guide by the light of reason, we must let our minds be bold."[13]

It was a powerful dissent that received front-page attention in newspapers across the country. But still, Brandeis was not entirely satisfied with it—because he really did not like the Oklahoma law. He wanted an opportunity to speak to his brethren, to the legal profession, to the country, in defense of a law he supported, one that would attack the true cause of the nation's problems—big corporations. He did not have long to wait.

Paul Freund did not want to accept the offer from Northwestern Law School. It was not that he was opposed to the idea of teaching as a career; in fact, in time he would join the faculty of Harvard Law School and become one of the nation's preeminent constitutional scholars. But as his clerkship with Justice Brandeis neared its end in the spring of 1933, Freund decided instead to remain in Washington, D.C., and accept a position with the Treasury Department.

The clerk knew that his boss would be disappointed with the choice. Brandeis now saw great virtues in the teaching profession. He specifically told Frankfurter that, all things being equal, he would prefer as a clerk someone who was interested in teaching as a career. And if the clerk had the skills and temperament, Brandeis would urge him to consider joining a law school faculty. Freund certainly had the qualifications. His keen intelligence was obvious, and Brandeis apparently recognized that it could be put to good use in a classroom. Freund was aware of Brandeis's feelings, so as he prepared to make his move, he wrote the justice a long letter, an "apologia" to explain why he was not going to leave Washington after all.[14]

Freund's decision did not seem to have any adverse effects on his relationship with the justice. No doubt that reflected, in part at least, the considerable contributions Freund had made to the justice's opinions. And one opinion that had required much work—and was very important to Brandeis—was the opinion they crafted in the *Liggett* case.

The Louis K. Liggett Company operated 549 department stores—a chain—throughout the country, and many of the stores were located in Florida. There, as in most states, the Liggett Company had to pay taxes for the privilege of doing business. There was nothing wrong with that. The courts had long held that such taxes were valid. The Florida law, however, did have one unusual feature that disturbed the company. If the company operated stores in more than one county, it paid a higher tax than if all its stores were located in the same county. Many people assumed that the law was expressly designed to discourage the growth of chain stores like Liggett's. Whatever the motivation, the Liggett Company thought that it was unfair discrimination and that the law deprived it of "the equal protection of the laws" to which it was entitled under the Fourteenth Amendment. So Liggett and twelve other large corporate chains filed a lawsuit on behalf of themselves and other similarly situated corporations, arguing that the Florida statute was unconstitutional.

For a long time Brandeis had been on the lookout for a case through which he could expound upon his views concerning corporations. In 1928 he had written a relatively short dissent to a Court decision that struck down a Pennsylvania law imposing a higher tax on corporations operating taxis than on partnerships operating taxis. The Court said that the discrimination was arbitrary and therefore a violation of the equal protection clause. Brandeis disagreed. To him the distinction between corporations and partnerships was entirely reasonable. "[T]here are still intelligent, informed, just-minded and civilized persons," he observed, "who believe that the rapidly growing aggregation of capital through corporations constitutes an insidious menace to the liberty of the citizen. . . ."[15]

Although he still subscribed to those views, the taxi dissent did not contain a full examination of the reasons why corporations were such a menace to liberty. Now, in 1933, there was a real need for that kind of exposition. The nation was in the throes of a severe depression, and Brandeis wanted to demonstrate that much of the problem reflected the uncontrolled growth of corporations. In the *Liggett* case he would lay it all out. Any reader of his opinion would not only know why the Florida law was reasonable; the reader would also understand why laws like Florida's were essential to the survival of industrial democracy.

Even before the justices met at conference to consider the case, Brandeis directed Freund to begin the collection of supporting materials that could be used in the footnotes. Among other things, Brandeis instructed Freund to get the files in the 1930 *Stratton* case.[16] Brandeis had prepared an opinion there that he had never used, and, because that case raised issues similar to those in the *Liggett* case, the files would contain useful sources. But that was only a start. Freund was to leave no stone unturned in his quest for relevant statistics, studies, and commentary. The clerk responded dutifully. Bibliographies covering corporate taxes, economic development, mergers, and other subjects were obtained. Major texts were consulted. And so were obscure pamphlets that had not been copyrighted in the Library of Congress. Freund even had the librarian at the Bureau of Standards (who was Italian) translate some Italian literature.

In early February 1933 the justices voted to overturn the Florida statute. The majority agreed—at least in principle—that state laws were presumed valid unless shown to be arbitrary. But here the law was unfair on its face, and, in their view, there were no facts to rescue it. Brandeis, Harlan F. Stone, and Benjamin Cardozo—the former chief judge of New York's highest court who had replaced Holmes—disagreed and voted to dissent.

Back in the California Street office, Brandeis and Freund continued to digest material. The opinion itself was going through literally dozens of drafts. In a way, it reflected almost a lifetime of experience and thought, and Brandeis obviously wanted it to be clear, thorough, and persuasive. By the end of February he was ready to circulate it to his colleagues.

Initially, the opinion cited the *O'Gorman & Young* case and stated that the Florida law was presumed valid unless there were facts to show otherwise. To Brandeis there were no such facts in the record, and therefore the law should be sustained. But apart from that argument—which required only a few pages—the opinion stated that there was another, separate ground on which the law should be upheld. All of the parties challenging the law were corporations. They contended that the law, *as applied to them,* was unfair. It might be, Brandeis said, that different considerations would be involved if the parties were individual citizens. But in the case of corporations, Florida might have valid reasons for distinguishing between companies that operated in one county as opposed to those who operated in several counties. It was a way of discouraging corporate growth, and that, in Brandeis's view, was a worthy goal. The opinion then unleashed a long and abundant recitation of statistics and studies to show that corporations posed a danger to the community and the individual. Virtually none of the materials discussed in this part of the opinion were part of the record in the case; and there was nothing in the opinion to indicate that the Florida legislature had in fact considered them. Indeed, the opinion did not contain any reference at all to the legislative history. But years ago—beginning with the *Muller* case—Brandeis had accepted the validity of using materials outside the record to support legislative judgments. And if there was a possibility that the Florida legislators had considered those materials, that was, to him, enough to sustain the law.

The import of the material collected by Freund was clear. Originally states had adopted laws to allow corporations because they were thought to be an efficient mechanism to conduct business. But recent data indicated that the growth of corporations was having unintended—and undesirable—effects. The facts show, the opinion declared, "that size alone gives to giant corporations a social significance not attached ordinarily to smaller units of private enterprise. Through size, corporations, once merely an efficient tool employed by individuals in the conduct of private business, have become an institution—an institution which has brought such concentration of economic power that so-called private corporations are sometimes able to dominate the State." To support this view, the opinion cited statistics showing that 200 corporations, run by only a few hundred people, controlled about one-fourth of the nation's wealth. "Such is the Frankenstein which States have created by their corporation laws," Brandeis said.

The opinion ended with an eloquent appeal to recognize how this affected the current plight of the country. "There is a widespread belief that the existing unemployment is the result, in large part, of the gross inequality in the distribution of wealth and income which giant corporations have fostered," the opinion said; "that by the control which the few have exerted through giant corporations, individual initiative and effort are being paralyzed, creative power [is being] impaired and human happiness [is being] lessened; that the true prosperity of our past came not from big business, but through the courage, the energy and the resourcefulness of small men; that only by releasing from corporate control the faculties of the unknown many, only by reopening to them the opportunities for leadership can confidence in our future be restored and the existing misery be overcome; and that only through the participation by the many in the responsibilities and determinations of business can Americans secure the moral and intellectual development which is essential to the maintenance of liberty." If the citizens of Florida held those views, Brandeis said, there was nothing in the Constitution to prevent the adoption of laws to implement them. "To that extent," the opinion concluded, "the citizens of each State are still the masters of their destiny."[17]

Among the brethren there were several—particularly conservative members who opposed Brandeis's social views—who were disturbed by his use of materials that were not a formal part of the case. Where is that in the record? they would ask rhetorically. Or, when was that subject to cross-examination by the parties? To them it was unthinkable that a Court decision should rely on material that none of the parties had considered, let alone discussed. So Brandeis could not have held out much hope that his long dissent would impress the justices in the *Liggett* majority. But he had to feel at least a little disappointed when Cardozo and Stone also refused to join his dissent. But neither of them could understand why the dissent had such a long discussion on corporations and their danger to the community. "I agree with your use of the presumption of constitutionality, and with your conclusion," Stone wrote to Brandeis on March 1, 1933. "I do not say I disagree with the rest of it, but it goes further than I am inclined to go, because I do not think it necessary to go that far in order to deal with this case. . . . I think you are too much an advocate of this particular legislation." In Stone's view, the dissent had to say only that Florida could increase the tax on companies that did more business and that, although perhaps imperfect, it was reasonable for the legislature to base the tax to some extent on the number of counties in which a company had stores. Cardozo, he said, was preparing an opinion along those lines. When Brandeis finally got the Cardozo dissent, he was philosophical about it. "Well," he told Freund, "it's probably better this way. I can speak for myself." No compromises would have to be made to accommodate the views of a colleague.[18]

Freund did not usually go to Court to hear the justices deliver opinions. But this was different. *Liggett* had involved so much work, and it was so important to the justice. So Freund made the trip down to the Capitol, and he was filled with excitement when the time came for Brandeis to speak. The justice began by stating, "I think the judgment of the Legislature of Florida should be affirmed for three reasons." Freund was taken aback. That was not how the opinion began. And that was not the only surprise. Freund had worked on the opinion for months, and, in that moment, he was not sure what the three reasons were. The opinion seemed to rely on only two. Freund quickly realized that the justice had adapted the opinion for oral delivery. And as he sat there listening to his justice, he began to appreciate what a powerful advocate Brandeis must have been as an attorney in Boston. Freund knew him only as a gentle man in his late seventies—a deep thinker, scholarly in his approach to opinions, almost passive in his reaction to personal disputes, and, in general, so much like, well, like a *judge.* It was hard for Freund to imagine him as a practicing attorney. But now Brandeis was clearly energized. He leaned over the bench, looked directly at his audience, and spoke in an almost colloquial manner. "You know," he declared in a strong voice, and then, after a pause, "we all know, why States pass these laws." And if there was any doubt among his listeners, he gave them the facts.[19]

Brandeis was proud of the *Liggett* opinion, and he distributed more than a hundred copies to friends, editors, and members of the legal profession. From many sources there was much praise. Frankfurter called it "one of his enduring monuments." Norman Hapgood was equally impressed by the opinion, but he could not resist his "editorial impulses" and told Brandeis that the reference to "Frankenstein" in describing corporate giants was not quite right. Frankenstein, after all was the name of the scientist. Brandeis, Hapgood said, obviously meant to refer to "the Frankenstein monster." The justice agreed, and, when the opinion was printed, the change was made.[20]

Brandeis was not as responsive when Henry Friendly made his observation about the *Liggett* case shortly after the opinion was delivered. The former clerk had worked on the 1928 taxi case, so he was familiar with Brandeis's concern with corporations. Friendly had just come from Tallahassee, Florida, though, where he had had a chance to see the Florida legislators in action. And he could not help but notice the considerable power of the drug-store industry—a group that had lobbied hard for the anti–chain-store tax law. Friendly saw an amusing contrast between the logic of Brandeis's opinion and the realities of legislative behavior. "You know," he told his former boss on a short stopover in Washington, "I was down watching the Florida Legislature, and I don't think they had any of those social benefits in mind that you discussed. I think they were just influenced by the drug lobby." Brandeis did not smile or respond in any way. He just moved on to a new subject.[21]

It was not just another birthday. When Justice Louis D. Brandeis turned seventy-five in 1931 it was cause for national celebration. He had been on the Court for fifteen years and his prestige could not have been greater. The congratulations, thousands of them, poured in from almost every corner of the country—from former colleagues, from people he did not know, from lawyers, from union leaders, and from people who had heard that "the people's attorney" tried to defend the individual citizen when issuing opinions. Law reviews published long articles examining his opinions, and Felix Frankfurter had several collected in a book with a foreword by Oliver Wendell Holmes. There were also tributes from family members. Elizabeth's birthday note included a discussion of her and Paul's efforts in Wisconsin to push for unemployment compensation legislation, a measure that coincided with her father's concern with regularity of employment. "It does seem . . .," she wrote, "that a very small group can accomplish a good deal if they stick together and stick to the job (provided the times are reasonably ripe for the fight). We submit these startling discoveries for your consideration. Somehow," she dryly added, "they have a familiar ring! As teachers, in short, we salute our wisest and most effective colleague." But perhaps no birthday tribute was more unusual than the one that came from Louis's old friend Herbert White. "Under separate cover," White told his companion of several decades, "I am having mailed to you a Schick razor which I hope you will have enough mechanical ability to understand and use."[22]

No doubt Brandeis had the ability and energy to handle the razor. But other activities were being eliminated from his schedule. During the 1920s he and Alice had gone to Fletcher's Boathouse in Washington, D.C., and taken many canoe rides—or "paddles," as he called them—down the Chesapeake & Ohio Canal. But as he moved closer to his eightieth birthday that was no longer possible. His work habits were also affected. In earlier years he had spent most of his days (when he was not in Court) in the rented apartment that he had converted into an office for himself and his clerk. But by the autumn of 1933 all that began to change. He now spent most of his working hours at the desk in his bedroom-study in the apartment one floor below in which he and Alice lived. He might spend a few hours before breakfast in the office, but by the time the clerk got there around 9 o'clock, the justice was gone.

The clerks now saw very little of their boss. They might confer with him first thing in the morning and sometimes in the evening, but aside from these short visits, most communication between justice and clerk was by notes. The long discussions that had characterized the early clerkships were now a thing of the past. And while Brandeis had previously taken control of every opinion, he now began to experiment by allowing the clerk to draft an entire opinion by himself. The clerks were not entirely happy with the new arrangement. They felt very isolated, almost as if they were working for an institution rather than a man, and some of them resented it—although they were still proud to have the honor of being a Brandeis clerk.

Despite all the shortcomings, Nathaniel L. Nathanson found the clerkship to be an instructive experience. Unlike the other clerks, he had gone to Yale Law School. In the year following his graduation he worked as Felix Frankfurter's research assistant at Harvard, and after that he accepted a clerkship with Julian Mack, who was a judge on the United States Court of Appeals in New York City. One day Frankfurter called him to ask if he would like to clerk for Brandeis, and so in the autumn of 1934 Nathanson found himself in Washington.

One of the things that Nathanson noticed about the justice was his economy of expression. In the little time they spent together Brandeis rarely engaged in idle talk. Even when discussing Court business, he seemed to pack a lot of meaning into a few words. And then there was his sense of humor. The justice never joked about any subject, but on occasion Nathanson glimpsed a small smile and a twinkle in the eye that revealed a wry wit. It happened one time when they were discussing a memo that Nathanson had prepared to urge Brandeis to join an opinion by Cardozo. The case concerned a New Deal law that Brandeis opposed, and he had indicated earlier that he did not share his colleague's views. In a meeting afterwards, Nathanson argued vigorously that Cardozo's analysis was correct. After his clerk had finished, Brandeis looked at Nathanson and, with a small grin, said, "I don't think you're right on the law, but even if you were I would still be resolute." On another occasion the Court was about to issue an opinion upholding a decision that Nathanson had worked on when he had clerked for Judge Mack. The Court's opinion, however, was going to rely on an argument that Nathanson had researched and had rejected as not valid. He went to the justice with his complaint. Brandeis smiled again. "I will not say you are wrong," he said. And that was it.[23]

None of these interactions, however, surprised Nathanson as much as the opinion the justice planned to write in the case involving the Nashville, Chattanooga and St. Louis Railway. The controversy revolved around a Tennessee law that required railroads to pay one-half the cost of grade crossings that the state highway commission determined to be necessary for safety purposes. In this particular instance the highway commission decided that an underpass was needed in the small town of Lexington and that, under the law, the railroad company had to bear half the cost. The railroad sued in state court, arguing that the law, as applied here, was arbitrary and therefore a violation of the Fourteenth Amendment's due process clause. The underpass, they said, was not intended to correct any problems created by the railroad; it was needed only to facilitate the construction of a new highway. The Tennessee Supreme Court ultimately rejected the railroad's argument, and the company appealed to the United States Supreme Court.

Nathanson was shocked when he learned that the conference had voted to reverse the Tennessee court. And he was even more disturbed when he found out that his boss was going to write the Court's opinion. Nathanson knew all about the decision in *O'Gorman & Young,* and he knew that for almost twenty years Brandeis had argued that the Court should not use the due process clause in a "substantive" manner to second-guess state legislatures. After all, they were the ones most familiar with local conditions and needs; if they enacted a law, Brandeis had declared repeatedly, it should be overturned only if there were no facts to justify it. A law could not be set aside merely because it did not anticipate every situation or result in perfect justice.

These were not just abstract principles any more. Nathanson had researched the particular area of law involving grade crossings. On numerous occasions the Court had rejected the claims of a railroad that it was being asked to pay an unduly large share of the costs for a grade crossing. The Tennessee case did have some unusual features, including the fact that the highway here was part of the national road system subsidized by the federal government. But none of these distinctions—in Nathanson's mind, at least—was enough to overcome those earlier decisions.

Nathanson shared his views and research with the justice. For Brandeis, however, other forces were at work. To begin with, he did not like cars. He felt that they were part of the extravagant living that had characterized the 1920s and had helped plunge the nation into the Depression. He had also been telling people for years that he opposed the establishment of a national road system because, among other reasons, he thought it was a costly venture that the government would be unable to maintain. And if the funds were available, it would only mean that other, more worthwhile activities would suffer. His concern on this score was later confirmed when Nathanson uncovered a chart showing that Tennessee spent more on highways than it did on education. Brandeis was appalled, and even after the Tennessee case was closed he kept the chart in his apartment, presumably to show visitors the depths to which the country had slipped. So when Nathanson argued that there was no substantive due process violation here, the justice merely smiled. "Well, you know Justice Holmes' test for a substantive due process violation," he remarked. " 'Does it make you puke?' " And the Tennessee law, at least as applied here, flunked the test.[24]

So Brandeis was prepared to send the case back to the Tennessee courts to review the facts. It might be, he wrote, that the state law could be valid in one set of circumstances and not valid in another. After all, the underpass here did not appear to be necessary to protect people from the railroad. Rather, it was needed only so that cars and trucks—vehicles that deprived the railroad of business—could travel on the national road at high speeds. Nathanson was particularly amazed at the ease with which Brandeis then distinguished Court decisions that pointed to a different result. In one footnote the justice cavalierly dismissed ten cases by stating that none of those cases involved "a record embodying facts similar to those presented [here]."[25] And in distinguishing other cases, Brandeis identified differences in facts without explaining why they might warrant a different result. For example, he did not feel obligated to follow some earlier decisions requiring railroads to pay for grade crossings because in those cases, Brandeis observed, "the new highway was an incident of the growth of development of the municipality in which it was located"—not part of a national highway system.[26] But nowhere did he say why that was a relevant distinction.

Ironically, Stone and Cardozo dissented from the decision with language that, in another case, might have been written by Brandeis. "[T]here is nothing in the evidence or in the special facts relied on by the [railroad]," they said, "to sustain a finding of arbitrary action by the State of Tennessee or its official representatives; that on the contrary the separation of grades is conceded to be necessary to give protection to travelers against perils created by the railroad. . . ." Since there was at least one reasonable basis for the state's action, Stone and Cardozo said the railroad could not win—even if it could show that there were some flaws in the state's reasoning.[27]

As for Nathanson, he could not help but question the legitimacy of the whole process. "It may be shocking to mention them in the same breath," he wrote to Frankfurter, "but I sometimes wonder whether the Justice or McReynolds votes more in accordance with his prejudices. . . ."[28] Frankfurter could not have been completely surprised by this reluctant observation. He knew Brandeis intimately. The justice was not a passive decision-maker who remained aloof from controversy until it reached the courthouse steps. Indeed, while Nathanson was conveying doubts to Frankfurter, the Harvard professor was working with Brandeis to help promote shifts in President Roosevelt's New Deal programs.

TWENTY • FIVE

Old Ideas in New Hands

I pledge you, I pledge myself, to a new deal for the American people.

FRANKLIN D. ROOSEVELT, ACCEPTING THE 1932 DEMOCRATIC PRESIDENTIAL NOMINATION

Brandeis was proud of Alice Grady. She had come a long way since she first reported for work at the firm of Warren & Brandeis in 1894. It was not only her superb skills at organizing the office and satisfying the many demands of her boss. Grady had other virtues as well. And one of them was her dedication to the Savings Bank Life Insurance program, or SBLI, which Brandeis had initiated in the first decade of the twentieth century to provide wage earners with low-cost life insurance. Perhaps it was her background. She had not grown up in affluence, and she apparently understood the importance of SBLI to wage earners who had difficulty obtaining security for their families. Even before Brandeis was appointed to the Supreme Court, Grady became involved in the implementation of the program. She talked to state administrators, savings bank officials, and even the mayor of Boston. She also expended considerable effort to publicize the program. One of her more notable achievements on that front was a movie that featured Brandeis himself explaining the benefits of SBLI. Grady had the movie distributed to savings banks and civic groups in the hopes that they too would see the benefits of the program.

Brandeis watched all this with much satisfaction. After all, there could be few activities more rewarding to the community—and the individual—than savings bank insurance. So when he readied for the move to Washington in the summer of 1916, he informed his long-time secretary that she would not be going with him. The Court allowed each justice to hire only one secretary, and Brandeis had decided to fill the position with a recent law graduate to help him with research. And besides, there were more important things for Grady to do in Boston.

Grady accepted the decision, and shortly after Brandeis left, the governor appointed her deputy commissioner of SBLI in Massachusetts. Her relationship with Brandeis then moved on to a new level. There was frequent communication between them on the progress of the program. Brandeis not only gave Grady advice from his small apartment in Washington; he also provided money—for salaries, for Christmas parties for administrators, and for specific projects designed to advance the program. And he was pleased, very pleased, with the results. After the Depression struck, he never tired of showing visitors the charts he kept at the ready. The statistics were indeed impressive. At a time when banks were collapsing and other insurance companies were going bankrupt, the savings bank program moved right along. The number of participating banks steadily increased, as did the number of policies issued under the program. And less than 1 percent of the policies lapsed because of the wage earner's default.

The entire lesson of savings bank insurance could not be learned from statistics alone. There was also something to be learned from those who administered it. And no one provided a better example than Grady. "Now look at Miss Grady and how she lives her life," Brandeis would tell visitors in Washington. "She chose a vocation, a small one if you will, seemingly small, but she gave her life to it, and slowly it has grown and grown. If there were an Alice Grady in every community, our country would flourish with civic virtues and people would not be so tempted to look to Washington for help in tasks neglected at home."[1]

No doubt these thoughts on Grady and savings bank insurance remained uppermost in Brandeis's mind when he considered measures to lift the country out of the Depression. New problems required imaginative solutions. And perhaps now—as in the case of SBLI—it was time to use respected institutions to perform additional services. Here Brandeis focused on the United States Postal Department. Almost everyone was familiar with the town post office. It was a part of community life, a place that people recognized and trusted. Why not use it, then, to counter the power of big banks? It was not an idle suggestion. Big banks were, in Brandeis's mind, a principal cause of the Depression—they had used other people's money to invest in new business, and there was no end to the schemes they had devised and plants they had built. That went a long way to explain why the country had been overcapitalized and producing too much. So Brandeis thought it would be wise to give the Postal Department the power to open checking and savings accounts. He would also designate the Postal Department as the agency responsible for the issuance of securities. At the same time he would prohibit banks from doing more than one service. No longer would banks be allowed to invest in new ventures for themselves with the deposits of their customers. It was time for the law to recognize that no man—or bank—could serve two masters.

There were other elements to the Brandeis recovery plan. Reducing both corporate and individual wealth was of course essential. He favored taxes to limit the size of corporations. He also endorsed tax laws to limit the amount of money a person could inherit (since inherited wealth represented the product of someone else's labors and did little except to create a privileged class).

Limiting corporate and individual assets, however, would not be enough. Brandeis understood that most people in these hard times did not have to worry about excess wealth. And to him, there was no mystery to the poverty that enveloped the country. The ever-present breadlines and apple pushcarts on the streets underscored once again the need for regularity of employment. People needed jobs, steady jobs that would provide both money and dignity. There too Brandeis had an answer. He admired the British economist John Maynard Keynes, agreeing with Keynes that the only solution now was a massive public works program. It would take millions of public dollars, but there really was no other course. And it would not be so bad—the government could concentrate on tasks that the private sector was likely to ignore, such as afforestation, irrigation, adult education, recreational parks.

There was one last feature to the Brandeis recovery program: unemployment compensation. For more than two decades he had argued that the worker had to have some protection against economic uncertainty. He therefore supported a program that would require employer contributions to a fund that could support workers if they found themselves without a job. And more than that, the program had to be administered by the individual states. He did not want relief measures to result in an oversized federal government. "You must remember," he told Harry Shulman, one of his law clerks, "that it is the littleness of man that limits the size of things we can undertake. Too much bigness may break the federal government as it has broken business."[2]

The justice was happy to describe his recovery plan to any visitor who expressed an interest. And many were very interested. After all, the Brandeis name was famous as a social activist and thinker. Some were impressed with the originality of the justice's thinking. Others thought he was trying to turn the clock back. This was certainly the view of Raymond Moley, a member of the "brains trust" that advised Franklin D. Roosevelt during the 1932 campaign. It was absurd, said Moley, to pursue "the traditional Wilson–Brandeis philosophy that if America could once more become a nation of small proprietors, of corner grocers and smithies under spreading chestnut trees, we should have solved the problems of American life."[3] To Moley and other skeptics, the drift toward "bigness" was inevitable. Large corporations and large governments were needed to handle the demands of a large country. The answer, then, was not to destroy large aggregations of finance and power but to harness them for the public good.

Brandeis rejected out of hand the view that the growth of corporations and governments was inevitable. Man made those institutions. Man could control them—if he wanted. It required only will power and discipline. He knew from experience that those were effective tools. So the justice was spirited in response to those who expressed doubts about his recovery plan. Why shouldn't we turn the clock back? he would say. The country had turned the clock back on Prohibition. It could be done in other areas as well. Besides, there was no need to compromise at the planning stage. Now the nation's leaders should focus on what was needed. If circumstances later dictated adjustments, there would be plenty of time to compromise. And so Brandeis watched with interest—and hope—as the nation prepared to inaugurate a new president on March 4, 1933. He had promised the electorate a "new deal," and Brandeis had reason to believe that it would turn things around.

Oliver Wendell Holmes continued to adore Felix Frankfurter like a son. The Harvard professor remained a never-ending source of ideas and conversation. There was also no question about the love that he showered on the former justice. In Frankfurter's eyes the old man was the embodiment of perfection. Frankfurter's friends and colleagues could not recall any occasion on which he criticized Holmes for anything. Holmes too took delight in Frankfurter's activities and achievements. And there were many of them. He has, Holmes once told Harold Laski, "an unimaginable gift of wiggling in wherever he wants to. . . ."[4] So it was hardly surprising that Frankfurter had established a warm relationship with Franklin D. Roosevelt.

They had actually known each other for some time—since 1906, when a mutual friend had introduced them. They had also seen each other frequently during the Wilson years when Frankfurter held an assortment of positions and Roosevelt was an assistant secretary of the navy. Afterwards Roosevelt was struck by polio and retired as a cripple to his family's estate at Hyde Park, New York. Their contact was sporadic until Roosevelt—much to his family's surprise and displeasure—decided to return to public life. After Roosevelt's election as governor of New York in 1928, the contact between politician and professor became more frequent, and Frankfurter spent many hours on the phone and in visits to Hyde Park talking to Roosevelt about matters of public policy.

Frankfurter, however, hoped that Alfred E. Smith—Roosevelt's predecessor as New York governor, who had lost a presidential bid to Hoover in 1928—would get the Democratic nomination in 1932. Smith was an accomplished and dedicated leader, Frankfurter told friends. Roosevelt, in contrast, did not have Smith's political sophistication or courage. Roosevelt had, for example, chosen to accommodate rather than purge the political bosses in Tammany Hall. No, if Roosevelt won the Democratic nomination, Frankfurter observed, "it will certainly prove there is no limit to the amount of fumbling one can do and still win a game."[5]

Roosevelt knew nothing of Frankfurter's true feelings, so Frankfurter was able to retain a close relationship with the New York governor after he won the nomination and defeated Hoover in the 1932 election. They discussed a variety of people and policies, but few things dominated Frankfurter's conversations as much as his references to Louis D. Brandeis. The Harvard professor had for many years passed on advice to Roosevelt from Brandeis. Shortly after the election Roosevelt expressed a desire to see the justice, and Frankfurter arranged a meeting at Washington's Mayflower Hotel. Their talk was brief, but Brandeis was impressed. "My short talk with Franklin Roosevelt was encouraging," he reported to Bess Evans. "He has learned much; and realizes, I think, the difficulties of the task."[6]

In managing the affairs of state, few decisions were as important as Cabinet appointments. And so Brandeis later asked Frankfurter to arrange another meeting with the president-elect, and the Harvard professor scheduled it at the Mayflower in January 1933.

Alice Brandeis was concerned about the meeting. She did not oppose her husband's contacts with public officials, but Louis was very susceptible to colds. She would, of course, take care that he was properly dressed for the cold weather when he left for the meeting. But precautions had to be taken to make sure that there were no open windows and unexpected drafts once he got to the hotel. So Paul Freund, the justice's clerk, was dispatched to the Mayflower Hotel the day before the meeting to make sure that there were no dangers in Brandeis's visit. At the Roosevelt suite a secretary assured Freund that there would be no problems since the president-elect did not like drafts either.

The next day Brandeis and Freund were driven to the Mayflower in the justice's rented car. Brandeis was ushered in to see Roosevelt. Brandeis's purpose was to recommend that Frances Perkins be appointed to the Cabinet as labor secretary. It was not a casual recommendation. Perkins was a person who would probably be sympathetic to the Brandeis recovery program. She had been born in Boston, had grown up in Worcester, and had received her college degree from Mount Holyoke College. She was bright, articulate, energetic, and, perhaps most importantly, dedicated to social reform. She had spent her early years working with Jane Addams in Chicago's Hull House and then moved to New York to work with Florence Kelley in the National Consumers League. Her talents and hard work were eventually rewarded with government jobs—most recently as Governor Roosevelt's industrial commissioner.

The Brandeis endorsement could not have hurt Perkins, because later Roosevelt did indeed ask her to head the Labor Department, thus making her the first female Cabinet officer in the nation's history. Although Brandeis was happy about the Perkins appointment and would use his influence to place other people in key government posts, there was one person he did not want to "lose" to the new administration: Felix Frankfurter. A few days after his inauguration, Roosevelt summoned Frankfurter to the White House and offered him the position of solicitor general of the United States, a position that would give him control over the government's cases before the Supreme Court. To almost any lawyer it would have been an exciting opportunity, but Frankfurter hesitated. If he had to manage the government's cases before the Supreme Court, he would not have time to advise the president on social policy. Roosevelt pushed, though, saying he ultimately wanted to put Frankfurter on the Supreme Court and it would be easier to do that politically once Frankfurter had served as solicitor general. Although he appreciated Roosevelt's sentiments, Frankfurter said he would first like to consult some friends, including Justice Brandeis. Most of these friends urged Frankfurter to take the position. But not Brandeis. He said it would be "absurd." There was much to be said for a teacher's career. And besides, Brandeis knew that Frankfurter would have much more impact on the development of law as an unofficial advisor to the president than as solicitor general. So Frankfurter turned the offer down.[7]

From Brandeis's perspective it was clearly the right decision. Things were happening in Washington. New people were coming to town to take important jobs. New ideas were being bandied about. And new laws were being drafted. As he told one of his sons-in-law, "FDR seems to have enough business to employ the 13,250,000 [who are] idle."[8]

As a Supreme Court justice, however, Brandeis could not become directly involved in all these political activities. He had to be discreet. When people came to see him on political matters—as they often did—he would speak in general terms, often relying on parables to make his point. If the writer or visitor requested advice on a specific piece of legislation or policy, the justice would usually say that he was "precluded" from responding. Frankfurter was an exception. Theirs was an intimate relationship, one of complete trust and confidence. So Brandeis always felt free to speak frankly about any subject, except, of course, pending Court cases. And if the justice wanted policymakers to consider his views, he relied on Frankfurter to make sure the message was received.

The justice could not have had a better emissary of his ideas and proposals. And so the two of them spoke and corresponded often about developments in the new administration, such as people who had been or should be appointed to vacant positions. (Frankfurter's efforts in this area were so successful that people in Washington—in some cases with resentment—referred to the new herd of young and idealistic government lawyers as Frankfurter's "Happy Hot Dogs.") But neither Frankfurter nor Brandeis was content to see friends and colleagues receive administration appointments. They were interested in results. And so they monitored the progress of new policies. What proposals were being debated in administration halls? What pressure groups were holding sway in Congress? And, perhaps most importantly, what was the president thinking?

Others around the president recognized the close relationship between Roosevelt and Frankfurter, and many of them did not like it. Frankfurter, they said, was Brandeis's agent, and there would be nothing more disastrous for the country, they believed, than to see Brandeis's ideas adopted as national policy. The competition for the president's ear took on a conspiratorial air. Raymond Moley, who was the administration's principal clearinghouse for relief proposals, told colleagues that Brandeis was a dangerous influence, that he had been President Wilson's "dark angel," and that he was "hovering again in our neighborhood, only he was a Justice now, and he had to have his deputies." Rexford G. Tugwell, another member of Roosevelt's "brains trust" and now an assistant secretary of agriculture, agreed. He spoke of Brandeis as "the old man in the shadows" who had "mysterious channels" to the White House. (It was ironic that, when Tugwell prepared to leave government a few years later, Henry Wallace, the secretary of agriculture and Tugwell's nominal boss, sent Brandeis an invitation to a stag dinner they were holding in Tugwell's honor.[9])

For all the sinister characterization of their activities, Brandeis and Frankfurter really had little influence on policy in the early days of the Roosevelt administration. The president had great respect for the justice and, with a mixture of reverence and affection, called him Isaiah, after the Biblical prophet. The president had a similar respect for Frankfurter and the proposals he continually offered. But Roosevelt had other plans. He was, above all else, a politician. He was not interested in social creeds. He was interested only in proposals that might provide some relief against the Depression. And on that score Roosevelt tended to side with Moley, Tugwell, and others who accepted the presence of big business and urged a system that would rely on cooperation with corporate giants. After all, big business had played and would presumably continue to play a major role in national life. If reforms could be instituted without antagonizing them, that was far better politically than the collision course advocated by Brandeis and Frankfurter.

There were, nonetheless, some measures in the early days of the New Deal that pleased Brandeis. Frankfurter and his lieutenants were the principal draftsmen of a new securities law that would make more information available to the public and help prevent the kinds of abuses that had contributed to the stock market crash. And the Banking Act, signed into law on June 16, 1933, separated commercial banks from their investment affiliates and generally made it more difficult for them to speculate with other people's money. But for the most part, the early New Deal legislation and activity reflected the Moley–Tugwell view.

Despite the few bright spots, Brandeis was largely disappointed with what he saw. It was not what he had expected or hoped. "Of course," he told one of his sisters-in-law, "life in Washington now is stirring, intellectually, far more so than I have ever known it."[10] But many of the ideas were going in the wrong direction. The Agricultural Adjustment Act was a clear example. The law was designed to revive sagging farm prices by paying farmers to limit crop production. The scheme was to be financed, in part at least, by a new tax on food processors, the middle men who were accused of retaining what little profit was left in farming. Even before the law was enacted, Brandeis was "worried as thunder" about it, and he openly expressed his concerns to Gardner Jackson, who was working with the administration in framing the bill. The justice felt that the law would not help the tenant farmer who had the greatest need. Rather, the bill would only accelerate the growth of corporate farm operations that would buy land and then accept payments from the government to let it lie fallow. Brandeis continued to meet regularly with members of the Agricultural Adjustment Administration after the bill became law, and he repeatedly warned his visitors that they were going down the wrong path (although later he would put his personal feelings aside and vote to uphold the constitutionality of the AAA when the Court rendered its decision in 1936).[11]

Then there were the gold policies. Before Roosevelt's inauguration the value of the dollar was based on the international gold standard. It involved a complex set of procedures and formulas, but, in essence, it limited the United States government's discretion in assigning a new international value to the dollar. The new president was troubled by that limitation. Economists told him that recovery required inflationary actions that would increase prices and stimulate the flow of money in commerce. That course was blocked, however, as long as the United States remained on the gold standard. The answer, Roosevelt was advised by some, required that the government buy gold on the international market at inflated prices. The more Roosevelt paid for an ounce of gold, the less value the dollar would have in relation to gold; and the ultimate result would be an increase in the prices of commodities.

To Roosevelt it all made sense. The only question was whether he had the legal authority to purchase gold at inflated prices. Imaginative lawyers in the Treasury and Justice Departments told him that he did. He could take gold in exchange for bonds of the Reconstruction Finance Corporation, which would be priced to give gold a higher value. There was one dissenting voice to this plan: Dean Acheson. The former Brandeis clerk had prospered since his days at the Court. He had become a partner in the prestigious Washington law firm of Covington & Burling. He was now an impressive figure. Tall, urbane, with a full mustache and a quick intelligence. Not surprisingly, he had established many important relationships in Washington, and in 1933 Roosevelt had appointed him undersecretary of the treasury.

To Acheson it was really quite simple. The law expressly stated that gold could not be purchased for more than $20.67 an ounce. No amount of imaginative interpretation could get around that. Or at least so he thought. The president was willing to believe otherwise, and Acheson found himself in fundamental disagreement with the new administration's policy. Perhaps he was wrong. He went to see his mentor. Attorney General Homer S. Cummings supported the president, he told Brandeis. Should I back off? To Acheson, the response seemed like words from the Delphic oracle, but the message was clear. "Dean," the justice said, "if I wanted a legal opinion, I would prefer to get it from you than from Homer Cummings."[12] By the autumn of 1933 Acheson had resigned.

That did not end Brandeis's involvement with the administration's gold policies. Among other measures, the government repudiated its contractual obligation to pay government bonds with gold. It would be too costly after the revaluation of gold, and it would therefore interfere with the administration's inflationary monetary policies. So people were told that the government, *their* government, would no longer honor the gold-clause provisions of bond contracts. Instead, people would be paid in dollars.

As Brandeis later explained to Frankfurter, he was "out of sympathy" with the government's action.[13] It was not right for the government to break its promise to the people. The government, after all, instructed people by its own example. But when the bondholders took their case to the Supreme Court in 1935, Brandeis put aside his personal feelings and supported the majority decision that left the government's policy intact. Chief Justice Hughes, writing the majority opinion, acknowledged that the repudiation of the gold clauses was unlawful, but then—in a very clever move—rejected the bondholders' claims because they had failed to show that the government's action damaged them. The individual citizen could not obtain gold on the open market, and, since there had been only modest changes in price levels, the bondholder could not be harmed if he were paid in dollars; indeed, he would receive a windfall if he were paid in gold.

Brandeis watched with great interest when it came time for Justice McReynolds to speak on behalf of the four dissenters. It was a stinging, passionate statement. "It is impossible almost to overestimate the results of what has been done here this day," McReynolds exclaimed. "The Constitution as many of us have understood it, the Constitution that has meant so much to us, is gone. The guarantees that men and women have supposed protected them against arbitrary action have been swept away." Brandeis later reported to Frankfurter that McReynolds's speech "was really impressive; better than anything I have ever heard from him."[14] It was only a matter of time before they were on the same side.

Despite the numerous visitors and the press of Court business, the Brandeis household was rather quiet. Alice was nearing seventy, Louis was approaching eighty, and they were content to spend many hours alone with each other. But it was not an entirely passive existence. Brandeis continued to observe and talk with visitors about Roosevelt's New Deal program—now with mounting agitation. And one thing that especially disturbed him was the National Industrial Recovery Act.

When Roosevelt signed the recovery measure into law on June 16, 1933, he called it "the most important and far-reaching legislation ever enacted by the American Congress."[15] Many people shared that view. The law was certainly an innovative—if not daring—attempt to put the country back on its economic feet. In essence, it empowered the president to approve codes that would govern the conduct of business in specific industries. The law was very clear that the president's approval gave the codes the force of law, and anyone in the particular industry who violated the code could be fined and even jailed. Almost everything else about the law was vague. There was no direction as to who exactly was authorized to develop these industrial codes. Nor was there much guidance as to the kinds of provisions the codes had to include to make them acceptable to the president. Section 7 did recognize labor's right to engage in collective bargaining and did require all codes to contain provisions relating to maximum hours, minimum wages, and appropriate working conditions; but no one was quite sure exactly what that (or anything else) meant when it came to specifics.

The vagueness of the law reflected the ambivalent feelings of the legislators who adopted it. Many congressmen and senators were convinced, like Roosevelt, that price increases were a necessary ingredient to any recovery. So there had to be some way to allow members of an industry to prevent the kind of cut-throat competition that had driven prices downward. At the same time, many populist leaders recognized that price fixing was one of the most potent tools of monopoly, and virtually no one wanted to foster the growth of monopolies. Congress was not sure how to resolve the dilemma, so it didn't. On the one hand, the law said that industry members would be immunized from the antitrust law if they met together to draft codes and fix prices. On the other hand, the law expressly prohibited monopolies and monopolistic practices.

Even before the bill was enacted, Roosevelt, confident of success, asked Army General Hugh Johnson to head the National Recovery Administration, which would become the new agency to oversee the development and implementation of the industry codes. It was a natural choice. Johnson had had experience with the War Industries Board in World War I. He had also spent countless hours with other administration officials in hammering out a bill that the president could present to Congress. When the group finally reached agreement in the middle of May 1933, Johnson was hopeful that the proposal would have dramatic results after it was enacted. He certainly had many thoughts on how they could be achieved. But he also knew he could benefit by the advice of more experienced hands. So when Lewis Strauss, the investor and sometime government official, told him he was going to see Justice Brandeis toward the end of May, Johnson asked if he could go along.

Brandeis was of course happy to pass on advice. It was most important, he told Johnson, that you not try to do too much. Man had his limitations, and if

Johnson and the NRA did not recognize them, their venture was doomed to failure. Johnson heard Brandeis, but he was not really listening. There was so much they *could* do with the NRA, so much they *had* to do.

And so Johnson undertook a frenetic pace after the NRA came into being. He raced around the country talking to business and labor groups, urging, cajoling, pleading for cooperation and action. In time, the most important industries drafted codes, the president approved them, and the blue NRA eagle became a common sight in the stores and offices of American's business establishments.

It was, however, a house of cards. The groups drafting the codes had few labor and consumer representatives. To almost no one's surprise, the labor provisions required by Section 7 were weak. Labor leaders complained bitterly that the NRA was a fraud, and they began to refer to it as the "National Run Around." The public also felt cheated. The codes fixed prices at levels that gave higher profits to business but virtually nothing to the consumer. And despite the law's prohibition of monopolistic practices, there were pervasive complaints that large corporations were using the codes to squeeze out small business.

All of this was confirmed in May 1934 with the release of a report by a special investigative board headed by the noted lawyer Clarence Darrow. The slide downward was rapid after that. Many business, labor, and consumer groups began to boycott the NRA and the codes. In times of economic crisis, they said, it was not fair to ask obedience to laws that only aggravated the situation. The criticism of Johnson intensified; his driving and often abrasive personality, it was said, was a major irritant in the whole affair. He turned to drink, but that solved nothing. Pressure for his resignation grew.

In the middle of September 1934, Johnson decided to give a radio address to respond to his critics. It was a rambling, defensive speech. That was no surprise. His reference to a Supreme Court justice was. "During this whole tense experience," Johnson said, "I have been in constant touch with that old counselor, Judge Louis Brandeis."[16] Although rumors of Brandeis's influence were widespread in Washington, this was the first public declaration that the justice was a part of the government's policy-making apparatus.

It certainly was dramatic, and it prompted a spate of newspaper articles discussing the proprieties of a Supreme Court justice's advising a president. Although Johnson's claim sounded intriguing, there was actually little truth to it. Aside from that one visit in May 1933, Brandeis had actually talked to Johnson only a few times—the last occasion being when the NRA administrator came to say that he had not followed Brandeis's advice and regretted it very much. Unfortunately, no one knew that Johnson's claim on radio was a gross exaggeration.

Paul Freund was sitting in his office in the Reconstruction Finance Corporation when the call came. Justice Brandeis wanted to see him at the apartment immediately. When the former clerk arrived at California Street, Brandeis told him he was expecting a telephone call and he wanted Freund to take it. In due course the phone rang and Freund answered it. Judge Julian Mack, who was close to many administration officials, wanted some guidance. The language was guarded, almost conspiratorial, but it all revolved around the president's forthcoming press conference. "The Skipper will be asked at his press conference about the offender," Mack told Freund. "The offender is contrite and is willing to say anything. Ask Justice Brandeis what the offender should say." Freund told Mack to hold on while he relayed the message. "Tell him," Brandeis said, "the thing for the General to say is nothing." When Freund reported back, Mack exploded. "Did you tell him what I said?" When Freund replied that he had, Mack demanded that he ask Brandeis again. The answer remained the same. "Tell the General to say nothing," Brandeis said, "and I'll explain the facts to the Chief Justice." After Mack hung up, Brandeis told Freund the facts. Johnson had done the "manly" thing in coming to him to express his error, the justice explained, and there was really nothing that Johnson could truthfully say about the radio address except that he was drunk. "And I wouldn't want him to have to say that," Brandeis told Freund. Several months later—after much agonizing—Johnson wrote Brandeis a letter, apologizing profusely for his "stupid inadvertence" and telling the justice that he was "on a kind of pedestal" in Johnson's heart and "almost the last man" he "would think of hurting."[17]

In time the controversy over the Johnson speech died down. The agitation over the NRA did not. Although Johnson was soon replaced by Donald Richberg, the administration he headed encountered a new obstacle: the United States Supreme Court.

The first major test came in 1935 and involved the interstate transport of "hot oil"—oil that was produced in violation of state codes that limited production levels. The codes were an effort to control supply and push prices upward. The National Industrial Recovery Act authorized the president to ban the shipment of "hot oil" in interstate commerce, and Roosevelt had done just that. Now an oil shipper complained to the Court that the law involved an unconstitutional delegation of authority to the chief executive. The Congress was supposed to make the laws; the president was supposed to enforce them. But here, it was argued, the president alone, without meaningful standards, decided whether to ban the shipment of "hot oil." Not only that, his order could result in fines and jail for anyone who disobeyed it. The president, in other words, did not merely execute the laws here; he also made them.

Brandeis agreed with all that. But he was even more appalled by the way the president enforced his orders. It was almost impossible for anyone outside of Washington to know about them, let alone what they entailed. Brandeis had already talked to Tommy Austern, a former law clerk now at Covington & Burling, as well as Justice Department officials, about the need for a reporting service that would periodically publish executive orders (an idea that would later lead to creation of the *Federal Register*). If there was any doubt about the need for a federal reporting service, it washed away when the shipper's attorney explained to the Supreme Court that his client knew nothing about the president's order until the government attorney visited him in Texas and took it out of his hip pocket.

Not surprisingly, the Court, with Brandeis's support, invalidated the particular provision of the NRA that delegated all this power to the president. The justice then passed the word that the Roosevelt administration was facing disaster. He had earlier conveyed the impression to some friends in government that he was prepared to hold some measures (like those involved in the "hot oil" case) unconstitutional. Now he again made it clear that Roosevelt faced serious dangers if he persisted in his present course. "It can't go on like this much longer," he remarked to one of Frankfurter's protegés in government.[18]

And indeed it didn't. The day of reckoning came on May 27, 1935—"Black Monday," it was later called. It was the last opinion day of the Court term, and one that President Roosevelt would long remember. In unanimous decisions, the Court struck a major blow at the president's recovery efforts. Justice Sutherland gave the opinion reversing Roosevelt's effort to fire FTC Commissioner William Humphrey; Chief Justice Hughes wrote the opinion that invalidated the entire NIRA; and Justice Brandeis issued the decision that held the Frazier–Lemke Act unconstitutional. Hughes apparently wanted all three opinions handed down before the Court left for the summer recess, and he was grateful that Brandeis had been able to complete his opinion on time.

Brandeis was actually sympathetic with the goals of the Frazier–Lemke Act, which was designed to provide relief to farmers who could not meet their mortgage payments. In essence, the law established a complicated procedure that allowed the farmer to stay on the land and pay off the debt later. However wise the law was from a social point of view, Brandeis could not get around the fact that it simply cut off the rights of the person holding the mortgage. It was one thing for the government to give a helping hand; it was quite another to pay for it by almost literally taking money out of someone else's pocket. Brandeis felt that the law deprived people of their property without due process and therefore violated the Fifth Amendment.[19]

That last opinion day, however, was more, much more, than three decisions that affected specific Roosevelt administration actions. To Brandeis the three decisions signaled a halt to the growth of the federal government. And Brandeis wanted to make sure that the president got the message. He sent for Thomas G. Corcoran and Benjamin V. Cohen.

Tommy "The Cork" Corcoran had clerked for Holmes during the 1926 Court term. After a brief stint at law practice, Corcoran was persuaded by Brandeis and Frankfurter to come to Washington in the last days of the Hoover administration to work in the Reconstruction Finance Corporation, a governmental relief organization. When Roosevelt came to town, Corcoran found the adjustment easy. He was one of Frankfurter's star pupils, and for good reason. Few people were as quick and as smart as Corcoran. There was also the Corcoran personality. Always a joke, a warm smile, perhaps even one of the many Irish ballads he knew. He had been one of Holmes's favorite clerks, and after he joined the White House staff on Frankfurter's recommendation, he became one of Roosevelt's favorite assistants.

Long before he reached the White House, Corcoran had collaborated with Cohen in drafting numerous pieces of New Deal legislation. It was, at first glance, an unlikely match. In contrast to Corcoran's ever-present ebullience, Cohen was quiet, shy, almost retiring. His career was also very different from Corcoran's. Cohen had clerked for Judge Julian Mack after getting law degrees from the University of Chicago and Harvard. He had thought about practicing law, but Mack and Brandeis persuaded him in 1919 to go to London to be their representative in Zionist councils. Cohen worked hard for the cause, and in time almost everyone—Brandeis included—came to appreciate his intelligence and political sensitivity. Frankfurter agreed with this assessment, and Cohen received high-level appointments in Roosevelt's Interior Department. Formal bureaucratic lines were almost meaningless, though. Cohen was a principal draftsman of the Securities Act of 1933 and other New Deal measures that had nothing to do with Interior business.

Cohen and Corcoran seemed to do everything together. They even lived together in a Georgetown townhouse. People called them "the gold dust twins." And one of the most important things they did together—religiously—was keep in touch with Frankfurter. They sent him long letters and memos describing developments in government and seeking his advice. They also reported to Frankfurter about their regular visits with Justice Brandeis—what he believed, what he recommended. The communications with Brandeis, however, were confined to generalities (often consisting of points Brandeis had been advocating for decades). Cohen and Corcoran were careful never to discuss specific legislative provisions or strategies with the justice. "He was such a conscientious bastard," Corcoran later recalled, "that he would have disqualified himself from a case involving a law if he thought he were involved."[20] And one of the last things Cohen and Corcoran wanted was to lose a supporting voice on the Court.

Brandeis, of course, knew that Cohen and Corcoran kept in constant touch with Frankfurter. So it was only natural for him to summon them to explain the significance of the Court's three New Deal decisions on May 27, 1935. The three of them met in the justices' robing room shortly after the opinions were delivered. Brandeis was excited, almost agitated. "You have heard our three decisions," he gasped. "They change everything." Cohen and Corcoran, Brandeis said, must get Frankfurter to come down from Cambridge immediately so he could explain it all to the president. "You must also explain it to the men Felix brought into the government," Brandeis demanded. Corcoran suggested that the three decisions might undercut Congress's consideration of legislation that Brandeis favored. The justice was not interested. "The President has been living in a fool's paradise," he told the young lawyers. "The Court unanimously has held that these broad powers cannot be exercised over matters within the States. All the powers of the States cannot be centralized in the Federal Government." Brandeis also had a message for the new lawyers who now populated the government bureaucracy. "As for your young men," he told his visitors, ". . . tell them to go home, back to the States. That is where they must do their work."[21]

All in all, then, Brandeis was pleased with this new turn of events. The Court decisions would, he felt, awaken people to the dangers of the course set by the Roosevelt administration. The news was trumpeted in headlines across the nation the following day. "I think," Brandeis told Julian Mack, "that our Court did much good for the country yesterday."[22]

The president took a different view. He was dumbfounded by the Court's decisions. He had already lost some cases, so the Court's hostility to the New Deal was not entirely surprising. But now the Court had reversed three major actions in one day. And the opinions were unanimous. That really galled Roosevelt.

"Well, where was Ben Cardozo?" he asked his advisors. "And what about old Isaiah?"[23] In a press conference the president expressed his bitterness. Although he had privately told Frances Perkins that the NRA was "an awful headache," and although the law was facing major revision in Congress, he told the assembled reporters that the NRA decision was the most upsetting because it relegated the country "to the horse-and-buggy definition of interstate commerce."[24]

Back in Chatham, however, Brandeis, now on his summer vacation, remained pleased with the Court's work. In a confidential interview with two reporters he explained why. In the *Humphrey* case, he said, the president had wanted to replace a commissioner on the Federal Trade Commission—an independent agency—because he disagreed with the president's political views. "If men on the Federal Trade Commission and similar government agencies are not allowed to exercise their independent judgment," he observed, "we should have in effect a dictatorship or a totalitarian state." What would happen, he rhetorically asked, if Huey Long—the populist demagogue from Louisiana—"were President and such a doctrine prevailed?" As for the NRA, Brandeis said, it was impossible to believe that a few individuals could supervise hundreds of codes governing business across the United States. And from a purely legal perspective, he had already told intimates that he did not see how any good lawyer could have thought the NRA was constitutional.[25]

So Brandeis looked to the future with optimism. And it reflected far more than the decisions handed down on Black Monday. Indeed, the irony was that the tide had already turned in the Roosevelt administration. While the Court was rejecting the actions of the First New Deal, Frankfurter and Brandeis were gaining the upper hand in shaping the legislative program for the Second New Deal.

TWENTY • SIX

The Born-Again Administration

If only Business could become still more articulate in its true feelings toward F.D.R. that even his genial habits would see the futility of hoping anything from Business in '36. . . .

FELIX FRANKFURTER TO LOUIS D. BRANDEIS, MAY 6, 1935

The president did not like the jokes. They were full of hostility, and he could not understand that. He had tried to revive the economy, and the business world could only profit from that. And yet businessmen never seemed to be satisfied. They complained if everything did not go their way. First there was the Securities Act of 1933, and then the Securities Act of 1934. Together these measures empowered a new Securities and Exchange Commission to regulate stock transactions. Businessmen did not like that at all. Wall Street was their private domain. It did not matter to them that stock abuses had contributed to the crash. And then there was the National Recovery Administration. Businessmen were very slow to share rising profits with the consumer or the unions. Still, they resented the president's pressure for them to be more giving.

The business animosity was reflected in the cartoons that appeared in trade periodicals. One had a little girl complaining to her mother that Little Johnny had written a dirty word in some wet cement: *Roosevelt.* "I get more and more convinced," the president privately said of business leaders, "that most of them can't see farther than the next dividend."[1] In the summer of 1935 *Business Week* reported that relations between business and the administration had reached the divorce courts.

It was not entirely personal pique on the president's part. The political winds were shifting, and he wanted to take advantage of them. Populist demagogues seemed to be gaining a stranglehold on public opinion. Father Charles Coughlin was giving radio broadcasts in which he railed against the greedy politicians and corporate magnates who made national policy. The broadcasts struck a responsive chord in the listening public, and Coughlin had a large following across the nation. But no one seemed more persuasive—or more dangerous—than Huey Long. He had established a firm political base among the people in his native Louisiana. He talked their language, understood their problems, and, above all, promised to protect their interests. Before he was forty they had elected him governor and then to the United States Senate. Washington gave him a national base, and he used it with great effect. As the 1936 presidential election approached, Roosevelt began to sense that the most serious threat to his political future was not the conservative corporate world but Huey Long. So Roosevelt tried to steal some of Huey's thunder by proposing measures that would mark him as the people's president.

All of this coincided with the rise of influence wielded by Brandeis and Frankfurter. Roosevelt had always had a certain sympathy for their proposals, and now the politics of the situation made it easier to incorporate them into national policy. As the summer of 1935 began, Frankfurter found himself living at the White House. His wife was staying in California, and Roosevelt said he needed the companionship and advice of the Harvard professor more than ever. As before, Frankfurter kept Brandeis informed of developments—the president's plans, his hopes, his doubts, and his frustrations. And as before, Brandeis felt free to make his views known to the president—through Frankfurter and, on other occasions, through Norman Hapgood, Tommy Corcoran, and other visitors who had the president's ear.

Nothing was of greater concern to Brandeis now than the unemployment compensation legislation that was nearing the final stages of enactment in Congress. Though it was not everything Brandeis had wanted, he still had much reason to feel satisfied with the law that was emerging.

Much of the credit belonged to his daughter Elizabeth and her husband, Paul. Long before Roosevelt reached Washington they had been working hard in Wisconsin to mold a state law that would provide unemployment compensation. They were victorious in 1932, and the measure included many elements that Brandeis himself had proposed more than twenty years earlier. Every employer was required to put a certain amount of money in a fund that would be used to compensate its workers during periods of unemployment. The amount of funds depended on the employer's "experience rating." Those who maintained regular employment had to deposit less than employers whose business operations involved frequent layoffs. The experience rating, then, became an incentive for business firms to provide regular employment.

The law had its shortcomings. At a time when business was struggling to make ends meet, it was not easy to put aside money for any purpose, no matter how laudable. Reliance on the experience rating also meant that businesses hit hardest by the Depression would have to contribute the most to the unemployment compensation fund—even though they might be the ones least able to afford it. This pitfall was partially offset by the fact that the maximum contribution an employer would have to make was 2 percent of its total payroll.

However imperfect, the Wisconsin law marked the first effort by a state to establish an unemployment compensation fund. Elizabeth and Paul felt that the law could set an example for other states, and they were anxious to have the support of the federal government in achieving that goal. Fortunately, they had an enthusiastic colleague who shared their hope—and was in a position to do something about it.

Brandeis was delighted with the enactment of the Wisconsin plan, and he agreed that it should be a model for other states. In the summer of 1932 he invited numerous local government and business leaders out to Chatham to talk with Elizabeth and Paul, who were enjoying a vacation at the Cape with Elizabeth's parents. During the meeting the justice spoke, confidentially, of his own interest in the Wisconsin law, urging those in attendance to develop a similar law for Massachusetts.

There was not much movement over the next year. Business was very resistant to providing unemployment compensation funds that came out of their pockets. Under the new president, though, Brandeis hoped, almost expected, that that opposition could be overcome. In the summer of 1933, Elizabeth and Paul were again vacationing at Chatham and again discussing the different kinds of federal law that might be useful. Finally the justice broke in with a pointed question. "Have you considered the case of *Florida* v. *Mellon*?" he asked the two reformers.[2] Elizabeth and Paul slowly grasped his meaning. In that case the United States Supreme Court had upheld a federal law that enabled people to use state inheritance taxes as a credit against federal inheritance taxes. The analogy to unemployment compensation was clear. Federal law could establish a federal tax on employers to establish an unemployment compensation fund; the employer's tax, however, could be reduced by any taxes or contributions it made to a state unemployment compensation plan. Since states would probably prefer to increase their tax revenues rather than the federal government's, the law would encourage individual states to adopt unemployment compensation laws.

The plan was perfected over the fall, and in early January 1934 Brandeis arranged for a meeting at the home of Catherine Filene Shouse, the daughter of his good friend Lincoln Filene. Elizabeth, visiting her parents for the Christmas vacation, attended. Filene was also there. But the most important guests were Frances Perkins, who was still Roosevelt's labor secretary, and Senator Robert Wagner of New York, an established political figure who had already introduced legislation to help the unemployed worker. Brandeis did not attend, but his presence was evident. Filene led the discussion, making discreet references to the views of "our learned friend." Perkins and Wagner were persuaded that the plan had great merit. Wagner said that he would introduce such legislation in the Senate, and they also expressed confidence that Congressman David Lewis of Maryland would agree to introduce a similar measure in the House of Representatives.

Drafting the bill was relatively easy. Even before the meeting had adjourned Elizabeth called Paul in Wisconsin and told him that his services had been volunteered for the task. Paul immediately came to Washington and, with the assistance of Paul Freund and Labor Department officials, he produced a bill along the lines discussed at the meeting.

Getting the bill through Congress was quite another matter. Many of Roosevelt's advisors, including Rexford Tugwell, opposed the modified Wisconsin plan in the Wagner–Lewis bill. The introduction of individual state laws, these advisors said, would produce a crazy-quilt pattern of standards that might or might not provide needed relief. Those opposed to the Wisconsin plan also thought it would be more efficient and more effective if the federal government collected the contributions and then supervised their distribution to the states. In short, these advisors wanted to develop national standards and centralize the law's administration in Washington.

Elizabeth appreciated that these views might hold sway in the White House. But she had an ally who had resources of his own. So she continually wrote to her father from Wisconsin, expressing her frustrations and making suggestions as to how the Wagner–Lewis proposal could be advanced. It was primarily a matter of using contacts. One in particular involved Harry Hopkins, who headed the Civil Works Administration. Hopkins, a gaunt, chain-smoking man, combined a zest for action with a heartfelt sympathy for the unemployed. (When someone brought him a program proposal that would "work out in the long run," Hopkins's reaction was quick. "People don't eat in the long run," he snapped. "They eat every day."[3]) As Elizabeth surmised, Hopkins's considerable energies and achievements had earned him the president's respect. "The enclosed suggests another little job for you!" she wrote her father in early February 1934. "I suppose Tom Corcoran can arrange to bring Hopkins in to see you. We gathered that Hopkins is ace high with the President and hence very important."[4]

Unfortunately, Hopkins, at least initially, tended to agree with Tugwell that a centralized federal unemployment compensation program was needed. But all was not lost. Brandeis was just as eager as Elizabeth—perhaps even more eager—to see the Wagner–Lewis proposal succeed. He monitored the situation closely and used his influence. By April 1934 he reported to Elizabeth that Perkins and Wagner were "working on the President to come out for the bill" and that passage seemed likely before Congress adjourned.[5]

The optimism was premature. The president was being pushed in the opposite direction, and by spring he was prepared to recommend a centralized federal program. Once again, however, Brandeis was not willing to accept defeat. The president was surely a man who would listen to reason, and Brandeis was good at reasoning with people.

Ray Moley and Corcoran arranged for Roosevelt to see the justice before he left for his summer vacation in Chatham. At 4:30 in the afternoon on June 7, 1934, Brandeis entered the Oval Office to have tea with the president. Roosevelt had a copy of a message he had just delivered to Congress on a broad range of social insurance issues, and he said he wanted to read it to the justice. When he reached the part about unemployment compensation, Brandeis stopped him, and for the next forty-five minutes told the president why the Wagner–Lewis proposal was preferable. It would not foster a large centralized federal government. Initiative and administration would remain in the hands of the individual states. Roosevelt responded that he was not committed to the means of implementation, and he was willing to consider the Wagner–Lewis approach.

Brandeis left the White House with some hope, and the next day he wrote Elizabeth not to be discouraged by press reports of the president's congressional message. He then related his conversation with Roosevelt and closed by reminding her that he had "left some efficient friends in Washington who are to work for the true faith during the summer."[6]

Brandeis, however, was not one to leave everything in the hands of friends, no matter how efficient they were. He had Felix Frankfurter come to Chatham as soon as the Harvard professor returned from Oxford, England, where he had been teaching for the 1933–34 academic year. In early July, Brandeis briefed Frankfurter on developments with respect to the unemployment compensation proposals and urged him to point the president in the right direction.

Frankfurter, the master "insider," played his hand deftly. He no doubt sensed that people like Tugwell—who favored the national plan—had the upper hand with Roosevelt for the moment. So he proceeded cautiously. In numerous conversations and letters, Frankfurter talked to Roosevelt and his chief advisors about the need for careful study before making a commitment. At opportune moments, though, he gave a nudge in Brandeis's direction, saying that a national system of unemployment compensation did not require a national administration. At the same time, Wagner, Lewis, and others were surely informing the president that there was little support in Congress for the national plan. The idea of a large, centralized bureaucracy in Washington was still unacceptable to many, and the Wisconsin plan offered the chance for an effective system of unemployment compensation without the burdens of an enlarged federal government.

Meanwhile, Roosevelt had established a Committee on Economic Security, to be chaired by Perkins. The committee was directed to study the questions of unemployment and old-age insurance and make some recommendations by December 1934. Lobbying was intense, but ultimately the committee voted to endorse the Wagner–Lewis bill. Part of the pressure came from Roosevelt himself, who gave a speech in November to express his support for the Wisconsin plan. That support, in turn, no doubt reflected Roosevelt's concern with what the fate of the law would be in the courts. Challenges were continually being made to his New Deal legislation, and some of them were successful. If Brandeis favored the plan, there was at least one vote for it, and perhaps it would be more palatable to the other justices as well. So when the president made his legislative recommendations on social insurance in January 1935, they included a modified version of the Wagner–Lewis bill. And, after much maneuvering and haggling, the bill was finally signed into law by Roosevelt in August 1935.

Brandeis had much reason to be satisifed. Although the new law included some modifications he did not favor, it did embody the heart of his porposal—experience ratings for individual employers and administration by the individual states. He also had to take pleasure from the reaction to the new law. Within two years of the law's passage, every state adopted some form of unemployment compensation. Now at last there was some basic protection against irregularity in employment.

Life was now much more suited to Holmes's interests and energies. As a retired justice, he spent much of his time listening to a clerk—whom the Court still provided—read books of various sorts. Literature. Greek history. Shakespeare. Almost anything but law. But when Osmond K. Fraenkel, a New York lawyer, collected some of Brandeis's early articles and statements in a book, Holmes felt obligated to take a look. So Jim Rowe, the clerk for the 1934 Court term, began to read it to the retired justice. Holmes began to groan. It was all so dry, he said. Railroad management. Industrial insurance. Economic regulation. Rowe, young, polite, eager to please, said they didn't have to finish it. They could put the book aside and find another. "No, no," said Holmes. "Brandeis is going to ask me what I think of it." So Rowe continued to read and Holmes continued to groan.[7]

Whatever Holmes's reservations, many other people were showing a renewed interest in Brandeis's writings. His views on monopolies and competition seemed to have a new relevance in the wake of the stock market crash. A new edition of *Business—A Profession* was issued. And Sherman Mittell, the young publisher with the National Home Library Foundation, brought out an inexpensive reprint of *Other People's Money*.

Brandeis thought that the reprint, as well as the Foundation in general, was a worthy enterprise. Reform required public education, and Mittell's operation would make it easier for people to learn about important issues. Mittell also seemed to be the right person for the job—vibrant, dedicated, anxious to please the justice. Brandeis thus maintained regular communication with Mittell, meeting him in Washington, corresponding with him, and generally advising him on the Foundation's affairs. Books it should publish. Radio programs it should air. Vacations that Mittell should take to relieve the constant strain of running a low-cost press. And if money was needed, Brandeis was only too happy to lend a helping hand.

Educating the public was, in some respects, secondary to educating the president. Much of Roosevelt's early legislative program reflected a belief that government and business could cooperate in an effort to revive the economy. That was a misguided hope, Brandeis told visitors. The conflict between business and government was "irrepressible," and Roosevelt could not succeed until he recognized that.

So Brandeis was quite happy when the president urged Congress in early 1935 to adopt a bill that would regulate utility holding companies—organizations that were built like pyramids on top of innumerable corporate subsidiaries. Brandeis felt that utility holding companies represented some of the worst features of corporate bigness. There were too many operations to be controlled by single individuals, he thought. And, of course, there were the conflicts of priorities and interests that undermined efficient and fair management. Most of this would have been unacceptable in any industry. But utilities provided essential services to the public. It was especially important that their operations be streamlined and scrupulous. In June 1935 Brandeis wrote to Norman Hapgood that, if Roosevelt's holding company bill succeeded, "we shall achieve considerable [progress] toward curbing Bigness. . . ."[8]

Brandeis himself discussed the issues generally with Corcoran and Cohen, who were the principal architects of the holding company bill. And while he did nothing specific to advance the cause in Congress, he must have been pleased when a stiff regulatory law was later adopted.

However great his interest in the holding company bill, Brandeis remained far more concerned about the president's tax policies. To his mind, there was no substitute for a dramatic increase in taxes on giant corporations; it was the only way to limit corporate growth and provide the revenues for a massive public works program. And as time went on, it seemed that Roosevelt was beginning to appreciate that. In December 1934 Frankfurter told Brandeis that the president "meant business as to tax matters" and that plans were already in the works for some major proposals.[9]

Roosevelt was not about to be rushed, however, and by spring nothing had happened. Brandeis was not the only one who was disappointed. Many congressmen and senators were also becoming disenchanted with the president because of his failure to move against corporate conglomerates. Brandeis had already alerted Frankfurter to the fact that Roosevelt's relations with progressive senators "will need much revising."[10] Frankfurter was apparently one of those who urged the president to correct the problem, and a conference was arranged in May 1935 between Roosevelt and six leading progressives in the Senate, including Burton Wheeler and Bob La Follette, Jr. It was, from all accounts, an open and frank meeting about the discord that had developed between the administration and the progressive forces in Congress. Specific mention was made of the president's tax policy—or, rather, the lack of it.

Roosevelt seemed moved by the meeting. Business was clearly on the other side. Economically and politically there could be nothing better than higher taxes on large corporations. The president wanted the word passed to Brandeis that he was ready to act. Frankfurter reported back to Roosevelt with the predictable reaction. "I wish you could have seen Brandeis's face light up," said the Harvard professor, "when I gave him your message about your tax policy and the forthcoming message about it. His eyes became glowing coals of fire and shone with warm satisfaction."[11]

The tax message was sent to Congress on June 19, 1935. Among other things it proposed a graduated tax on corporate incomes (replacing the existing tax of 13.75 percent with a tax ranging from 10.75 to 16.75 percent), a tax on intercorporate dividends, a federal inheritance tax, and a study to determine how the taxing power could be used to limit undistributed corporate surpluses. The business community was, to say the least, enraged by the president's tax package, and the rumors were widespread that Justice Brandeis and his disciples were the motivating force. "I have read all of Justice Brandeis's writings on the subject," Robert Wood of Sears, Roebuck and Company told the president, "and . . . I am sure no greater fallacy was ever enunciated."[12] Many elements in Congress agreed with Wood, and when the bill finally passed at the end of August of that year it included amendments that restricted the reach of the president's proposals.

Brandeis was pleased nonetheless. The new law might not be everything he wanted, but at least it was a start, perhaps, maybe an opening wedge. Even before the bill was passed, the justice told Hapgood that Roosevelt was "making a gallant fight and seems to appreciate fully the evils of bigness." And when the president signed the measure into law Brandeis wrote to Frankfurter that Roosevelt had "rendered a great service" and "comes out on top."[13]

The slide downward was not long in coming. Many people both in and out of the administration regarded the new law as counterproductive. The economy could not be revived, they said, if the government was stripping business of money needed to expand operations. The criticism mounted after Congress adopted the Revenue Act of 1936 shortly before the presidential nominating conventions. Although the law added only a small tax on undistributed corporate surpluses, it fueled agitation in the business community and elsewhere that the president was continuing to move in the wrong direction. Joseph Eastman, Brandeis's colleague from Boston days and later an ICC commissioner, believed that the taxes were unnecessarily hurting the railroads. Harry Hopkins, Bernard Baruch, and Joseph Kennedy—all close advisors of the president—told him that a recession was inevitable unless the new business taxes were eliminated.

By 1938 Congress yielded to the pressure and repealed or weakened all of the new taxes. Although Roosevelt did propose several public works programs that involved the expenditure of billions of dollars, they never reached the magnitude advocated by Brandeis. In part, that was not really possible because the taxes on corporate wealth—even those included in the revenue laws of 1935 and 1936—were never large enough to support the massive spending envisioned by the justice. He was hardly in a position to complain, though. His actions in early 1937 had contributed to Roosevelt's most serious political setback—one that later made it difficult for the president to command the large congressional majorities that he had secured at the beginning of his presidential tenure.

TWENTY • SEVEN

Packing the Court

We have a legislative body, called the House of Representatives, of over four hundred men. We have another legislative body, called the Senate, of less than a hundred men. We have, in reality, another legislative body, called the Supreme Court, of nine men; and they are more powerful than all the others put together.

SENATOR GEORGE W. NORRIS, 1930 CONGRESSIONAL DEBATE

George Anderson did not like it. The United States Supreme Court was blocking recovery. Anderson could appreciate the need to satisfy appropriate legal standards. He was, after all, a lawyer himself and now a judge on the United States Court of Appeals in Boston. Still, law was ultimately a social instrument, and any way you looked at it, the Court was not doing its job. It was striking down New Deal legislation and making it difficult, if not impossible, for the president and the Congress to pull the country out of the Depression. Black Monday—that day in 1935 when the Court unanimously reversed three major government actions—was not even the worst of it. The Court had taken other actions which were contrary to established legal principles.

There was, for example, the decision on the Guffey–Snyder Act. The law was a response to the sad plight of the mining industry. Intense competition and abundant supplies had driven prices downward. Many mines could not survive, and most of those that did operated at bare subsistence levels. Mine workers were among the hardest hit. They had no right to engage in collective bargaining and little leverage to assure themselves of steady jobs and safe working conditions. The Guffey–Snyder Act was designed to correct all this. It gave the miners the right to engage in collective bargaining and guaranteed them minimum job standards. Mine operators were protected by other provisions that limited production levels and guaranteed minimum prices. Most people thought that the law was a reasonable approach, but the Supreme Court held otherwise. A majority of five said that the labor provisions were unconstitutional and, since they were intertwined with the law's other provisions, the entire Act was invalid. The majority ignored a statement in the law that said it would remain in force even if some provisions were declared unlawful; in that event, the unlawful provisions would simply be discarded. That kind of "severability clause" had been accepted by the Court in other cases, and many wondered why the Court refused to honor it here.[1]

Then there was the Railroad Retirement Act case. The law established a pension system for railroad workers. Because railroads operated in interstate commerce, the Supreme Court had held on numerous occasions that Congress could regulate railroad financing, mergers, operating conditions, and accident liability. This was hardly surprising, since the commerce clause in the Constitution specifically empowered Congress to regulate interstate commerce. Somehow, though, the same majority of the Court that overruled the Guffey–Snyder Act also found the railroad pension system to be unconstitutional. Chief Justice Hughes said in dissent that the decision was "a departure from sound principles" and "an unwarranted limitation upon the Commerce Clause of the Constitution."[2]

These and other Court decisions created confusion, bitterness, and frustration. It was wrong, some said, for the Court to demand perfection in an imperfect world. The president and the Congress were confronted with an economic problem of unimaginable dimensions, one that had no precedent in the nation's history. To be sure, there was some groping in the dark and some mistakes. But whatever their technical defects, the Guffey–Snyder Act, the Railroad Retirement Act, and other social measures represented a good-faith effort to rescue the country from economic strangulation. The Court could not stand in the way forever. The Constitution was not worth saving if it meant the destruction of the country. "The way out will be found shortly," one newspaper commented, "because it must be found."[3]

Anderson shared the frustration and bitterness, especially with the four justices who continually voted against almost anything Roosevelt did. "The Four Horsemen" they were called. To Anderson they were too conservative and too willing to reject innovative social measures because of outdated legal views. The only thing they seemed to have in common—aside from their political beliefs—was age. Pierce Butler, a Harding appointee, was seventy; James McReynolds, a Wilson appointee, was seventy-four; George Sutherland, another Harding appointee, was also seventy-four; and Willis Van Devanter, a Taft appointee, was seventy-seven. Perhaps they could be replaced soon.

George had always been blunt with his friend Louis Brandeis. There was no reason to change now. "[Y]our Court," the judge wrote to Brandeis in January 1937, "by its usurpation of unconstitutional legislative functions, is our present greatest menace to the successful ongoing of a wholesome national life. The present problem is whether there are likely to be such deaths or resignations as will enable the . . . President . . . to reconstitute the Court as to bring it back to its appropriate functions. We may hope for that result," Anderson concluded. "But judges and other pensioners rarely die seasonably."[4]

Ironically, at eighty, Brandeis was the oldest sitting justice. But he could certainly understand Anderson's complaint. Years before he had told Felix Frankfurter that there "can't be too much apprehension about [the] evil effects of old age." Many justices, he remarked, including John Marshall—perhaps the greatest chief justice in history—had served long after their utility had ended. It was not that old age had made them senile. No, said Brandeis, the problem was a failure to grow with the times, to adapt settled principles to new circumstances.[5] And, like Anderson, Brandeis thought the Court's recent actions provided some evidence of that.

Brandeis was not entirely in sympathy with Roosevelt's New Deal. There were too many inexperienced people in too much of a hurry. Too little thought was given to complex problems in drafting major economic and social legislation. Still, there was no question that a majority of the Court—and especially the Four Horsemen—had gone too far. Some leeway had to be given to the people's representatives in Congress. To those he could trust, Brandeis privately complained about the divided Court and the harm its decisions were causing the country. So he was probably prepared to see some new initiatives from the White House to deal with the Court. But the president surprised even him.

Franklin D. Roosevelt, Oliver Wendell Holmes once said, had only a second-class intellect. He added, however, that Roosevelt had a first-class temperament. Roosevelt's other attributes included good looks, charm, and an unusual magnetism. It was a winning combination. After graduation from Harvard College and Columbia Law School at the turn of the century, he won fame as a crusading state senator in New York. Broader frontiers soon beckoned. With his love of ships and his respect for cousin Theodore—who had preceded Taft in the White House—it was only natural that Roosevelt seek the position of assistant secretary of the navy in Woodrow Wilson's administration. After all, cousin Theodore had also occupied that position in his climb to the presidency. To some it probably seemed like a minor post. But Roosevelt parlayed the job into a major policy-making position, one that gave him national attention and ultimately the Democractic vice presidential nomination on the losing ticket with James M. Cox in 1920.

Throughout these years—as well as his tenure as governor of New York and even president of the United States—Roosevelt refused to adopt any specific political philosophy. "I'm a Christian and a Democrat—that's all," he would tell inquiring reporters.[6] He was a man of the moment, sensitive to his political environment and willing to adjust to it.

Making decisions, even tough ones, came naturally to Roosevelt. Perhaps it was the ready confidence he exuded. Or perhaps the bout with polio put everything in perspective. ("If you had spent two years in a bed trying to wiggle your big toe," he commented in later years, "after that anything else would seem easy."[7]) Whatever. If the situation demanded action, he was almost always up to the task. And as the 1936 presidential election approached, a situation that demanded attention—and action—was the United States Supreme Court.

Roosevelt was frustrated and angry as he watched the Supreme Court dismantle his legislative programs. Something had to be done. Something would be done. Timing was important, however. In private conversation the president railed against the Court and asserted the need for some response. But nothing would be done, he said, until after the election. He hoped that the people would return him to the White House by a wide electoral margin. With that popular mandate, he would have the opportunity—and political strength—to do the job. So he bided his time, telling his supporters that there would be no short-cuts and that any corrective action would satisfy the letter and spirit of the Constitution. But never once during the campaign did Roosevelt indicate what he had in mind—probably because he wasn't sure what he *could* do, let alone what he would do.

After his overwhelming victory over Alfred M. Landon, the president sent for Homer S. Cummings, the attorney general. The time for action had arrived, and Roosevelt needed some ideas. Secrecy was important, however. No one was to know of their deliberations. Surprise was essential to their strategy. Cummings understood at once and told the president that he would use only two top aides from the Justice Department. Excited by the stealth and magnitude of the project, Cummings returned to his office to find the solution.

It came from a most unlikely source: James McReynolds. During his tenure as Wilson's attorney general, McReynolds had directed a study of the federal judicial system. Because federal judges held their positions for life, there was no way to force a retirement. The study found that there were many senior judges who were too old to cope with the rigorous physical and mental demands of the position. McReynolds therefore recommended a procedure to side-step senior federal judges who could retire but wouldn't. The president could appoint a new, younger judge to sit with the older judge, and the new judge could be given an edge in decision-making power.

Cummings saw his opening. The plan was simple. The president would appoint a new justice to the Supreme Court for every sitting justice who did not resign at the age of seventy. The limit of sitting justices would be raised from nine to fifteen. It was all constitutional. In fact, the first Supreme Court had had only six members, and at one point during the Civil War the number of authorized justices had been ten. So there was nothing magical about the number nine. The political benefits of Cummings's proposal were clear. If adopted by Congress, it would enable Roosevelt to "pack" the Court immediately with five new justices—men who would presumably be sympathetic to the New Deal. That would shift the balance of power in favor of the president's programs.

Cummings was exhilarated by his discovery, and he wrote to the president, saying that he was "bursting" with ideas and that he wanted to talk with him soon.[8] Roosevelt was indeed delighted with the plan, and he directed Cummings to begin the preparation of a bill and a message that could accompany its delivery to the Congress. One thing would have to be sacrificed, however. Honesty. The president did not want a blunt attack on the Court. People might resent that. So Cummings prepared an elaborate bill ostensibly designed to deal with the efficiency of the entire federal judiciary. The Court-packing proposal was only a small part of it. As for the presidential message, that too would have to be camouflaged. Nothing would be said of the president's real purpose for proposing the legislation—instead, he would base it on the need to make the Court more efficient. They could argue that the Court could do more work with more justices.

As matters neared completion, a few more select advisors were drafted into the conspiracy to help. One of them was Tommy Corcoran, and he was appalled when he learned of the president's proposal.

Corcoran was no babe in the woods. Nor was he a moral purist. An effective leader did not have the time or energy to explain the wisdom of everything he had to do. Sometimes deception and lying were necessary. "A great man," Corcoran later observed, "cannot be a good man."[9] But the president's plan was doomed to failure. He knew because he had proposed one like it the year before.

When criticism of the Court was running at a high pitch, Benjamin Cohen and Corcoran prepared a speech for Senator Burton Wheeler that suggested an increase in the Court's membership. Wheeler had never used the speech, and later, after conversations with people in Congress, Corcoran became convinced that the proposal would not have succeeded anyway. However much they disagreed with the Court's decisions, most congressmen and senators seemed to oppose any presidential tampering with the Court. Everyone understood the constitutional separation of powers, and it remained an inviolable principle of government. But the president was in no mood to be turned aside. Corcoran, the loyal advisor, suppressed his doubts and offered to do what he could. And among other things, he asked the president if they could at least warn Brandeis. The old justice would not be pleased, Corcoran knew, and he wanted to soften the blow.

With Roosevelt's blessing, Corcoran rushed to the Court and found Brandeis in the justices' robing room. As the justices walked down the corridor to hear oral arguments, Corcoran hurriedly told the justice about the president's proposal. Brandeis was not happy. Whatever its sins, the Court was a separate and equal branch of government. It was not a stepchild of the president's to be scolded and reshaped. The anger was evident in the blue eyes and in the crisp reaction. "Tell the President," Brandeis said, "that he's gone too far this time and that he's making a great mistake."[10]

Roosevelt was annoyed by the advice. Perhaps Brandeis did not fully appreciate the dilemmas confronting the chief executive. Roosevelt had become increasingly disappointed with Brandeis. True, he had voted to uphold most of the New Deal legislation. But some of his votes—especially on Black Monday—were inexplicable to the president, and to mutual friends he remarked that the justice was "not always consistent."[11] So Roosevelt was not likely to abandon the Court-packing plan because of Brandeis's opposition—or because of anyone else, for that matter, not even the congressmen and senators whose support was of obvious importance. On the morning of February 5, 1937, the congressional leaders were assembled in the Cabinet Room of the White House, and in a summary fashion Roosevelt told them that he had just sent a bill and message to Capitol Hill to deal with the Court problem. No comments were solicited; none was given. A few days later, however, the congressional leaders came back to tell the president that they had doubts, serious doubts. Would he reconsider? Out of the question, said Roosevelt. "The people are with me. I know it."[12] For once he was about to become a victim of his own self-confidence.

Louis was losing his friends. Bess Evans was perhaps of greatest concern to him. She was extremely ill in Boston. She was so weak that she could not even write letters. Her secretary, Anna, was devoted, but nothing could hold back the inevitable. In late October 1936 Bess dictated a letter to Louis. "Anna says you will want to know how I am—which is 'fair to middlin',' " the letter said. "What a queer business this is of dying. It goes very slowly."[13] Within a year she was gone.

Then there was Jack deHaas. He was now an outcast in Zionist circles, without money or friends—except for Brandeis. In early 1937 he was hospitalized with leukemia. The justice was troubled. He sent word that he stood ready to help his "teacher in Zionism" with financial assistance for hospital bills. It did not matter. Within a couple of weeks he was gone too. But Brandeis did not expect to lose Norman Hapgood so soon. The aging editor wrote his friend in April 1937 that he was going into the hospital for a prostate operation. "I am told," Norman advised him, "that my constitution is in such good shape that there is no appreciable danger, but the time has come when this thing has no proper place in my anatomy."[14] It was, unfortunately, unfounded optimism. Hapgood died shortly after the operation.

Brandeis himself was beginning to show signs of advanced age. His frame was still slim and erect, although there was now a slight stoop in his walk. The eyes retained their sparkle, but they seemed more deep-set than before. And his hair, once well groomed and dark, was now tousled and white, with a slight tinge of purple. He was an imposing figure, and many people—especially those from a younger generation—said he looked like a Biblical prophet, more of an institution than an ordinary mortal.

One person who held that view was Marquis Childs, a thirty-four-year-old reporter for the *St. Louis Post-Dispatch.* Brandeis liked reporters. He had dealt with them regularly since his crusading days in Boston, thought they played a critical role in public affairs, and had a certain curiosity about their profession and the political gossip they acquired in their travels. He was particularly fond of reporters from the St. Louis papers. Perhaps it was because St. Louis was where he had made his first start in law. More likely he appreciated their abiding interest in the Supreme Court and developments in the law. Irving Dilliard, Charles Ross (later President Harry Truman's press secretary), and others in the St. Louis crowd were writing thoughtful pieces about the Court's work in the early 1930s when most other papers concentrated on the activities of the president and the Congress. They became regular guests at the teas and often visited with the justice at his California Street apartment when the Court was in recess. So it was only natural for them to bring Childs with them to one of the teas, especially since the young reporter had just completed a book about social democracy in Sweden, a book that attracted Brandeis's attention. He was convinced that the Swedes had conquered the problem of bigness and had reached the proper balance between individual freedom and government intervention.

Childs was taken by the old man—his keen intellect, his insights into human nature and social developments, his love of political affairs. Years later Childs was asked if he liked Brandeis. "You liked him like you like the Washington Monument," he remarked. "He was a monumental figure. A vital figure of his times. It was exciting just to know him."[15] So Childs was very happy when he and the justice began to meet regularly. Brandeis never discussed personalities, only issues. And in early 1937 Childs was anxious to know what the justice thought about the president's Court-packing plan.

It was not an idle inquiry on Childs's part. Senator Wheeler, who was also friendly with Childs, asked the reporter to find out what "his friend Brandeis" thought about Roosevelt's proposal. Although a progressive Democrat from Montana, Wheeler was leading the opposition to the proposal, and he probably thought that his cause would receive a substantial boost if Brandeis—the great liberal, Democratic justice—supported the opposition. Wheeler was not disappointed by Brandeis's reaction. The justice told Childs in confidence that Roosevelt's proposal was "a very destructive blow" and that "it impugned the integrity of the Court."[16]

No doubt Brandeis's response emboldened Wheeler and his group to approach the chief justice. In his message Roosevelt had said that the Court was far behind in its work and that additional justices were needed to help the Court handle its expanding caseload. As an example, the message said that, in the last fiscal year, the Court denied 717 of the 867 *cert.* petitions presented to it, and, if government cases were excluded, the Court granted only 108 of the 803 *cert.* petitions presented by private parties. The Senate opponents hoped to secure testimony from Hughes that the Court was fully abreast of its work and that the large percentage of *cert.* denials reflected only the lack of merit in the dismissed petitions. And it would be most helpful, the Wheeler group reasoned, if the chief justice could be the lead-off witness when the Senate Judiciary Committee hearings commenced on Monday, March 22, 1937.

On March 18, Wheeler and two other senators from the Judiciary Committee called on Hughes at his home. Would he testify that the Court was functioning efficiently and that the president's stated basis for the Court-packing plan was a fraud? The chief did not like the proposal and expressed his willingness to appear before the Senate committee. He did not see any impropriety. After all, he, Van Devanter, and Brandeis had testified a couple of years earlier on a bill relating to judicial procedures. He told the senators that he would get back to them after consulting Brandeis.

Both Brandeis and Van Devanter were opposed to any testifying by any member of the Court. It was unseemly, they said, for the Court to involve itself publicly in political controversies. The dignity of the Court could not be compromised. Brandeis agreed with Hughes, however, that there would be no impropriety if the chief, in response to a request from the committee, wrote a letter giving the facts.

Meanwhile, Alice Brandeis had paid a visit to Wheeler's daughter, with whom she was friendly. As Alice was leaving the apartment, she told her host, "You tell your obstinate father we think he is making a courageous fight."[17] It could not have been coincidental. Armed with that information and Childs's report, Wheeler called on Brandeis at his California Street apartment. The senator needed a statement from the Court. Only the justices could speak authoritatively about the level of their workload. Testimony was out of the question, Brandeis said. But he reminded Wheeler of Hughes's offer to write a letter and urged the senator to call the chief and make the request. The justice led Wheeler to the telephone and waited while the senator talked to Hughes. The chief was willing, but it would take some time. That would not do, Wheeler said. The letter had to be ready on Monday when the hearings opened. Hughes yielded and began at once to prepare the letter.[18]

On Sunday, March 21, Wheeler returned to Hughes's house for the letter. It was just what the senator needed. In clear, dispassionate tones it stated that the Court was abreast of its work, that the president's message created an erroneous impression, and that more justices would not help even if there were a problem. "An increase in the number of Justices of the Supreme Court," Hughes said, ". . . would not promote the efficiency of the Court. . . . There would be more judges to hear, more judges to confer, more judges to discuss, more judges to be convinced and to decide."[19] Hughes advised Wheeler that he had consulted only Brandeis and Van Devanter but that their concurrence was sufficient. "[T]hey are the Court," he told the senator.[20] With a broad smile the chief then handed the letter to Wheeler. "The baby is born," he said.[21]

The letter had its intended impact. The president's duplicity was exposed, and it seemed that the Court-packing plan would face a rocky road in the legislative chambers.

Roosevelt was angered by the letter. But he was especially troubled by Brandeis's concurrence. The justice had been, in effect, a senior counselor to the president. Roosevelt had solicited his views and on occasion had followed his advice. Despite the Black Monday votes, Roosevelt wanted to think of Brandeis as an ally. And although he knew that the justice opposed his plan, he never expected Brandeis to say so publicly. At first it was astonishment. "I never thought old Isaiah would do that to me," the president told Corcoran. It then turned to bitterness. You simply did not turn on your friends—even if you opposed something they did. It was not "cricket."[22]

In time Roosevelt's anger subsided. Corcoran's did not. He had been a regular visitor to the Brandeis home. He was one of the justice's "little soldiers" in the war against monopoly and special interest. But no more. He paid a courtesy call on the justice in June 1937 when the Court term ended, but he would not go again. Ben Cohen now went alone, and when the justice asked for Tom, Cohen made up an excuse. When Cohen reported Brandeis's inquiry, Corcoran remained adamant. "He did not shoot straight with us last year," he said, "and it is best not to renew the relationship."[23]

Frankfurter was similarly upset by Brandeis's support of the Hughes letter. The Harvard professor now adored the president. Holmes had died in 1935 and Roosevelt had become the central figure in his life. Years later, when he lay dying, Frankfurter implored an associate to tell the whole story. "Let people see how much I loved Roosevelt," he said, "how much I loved my country, and let them see how great a man Roosevelt really was."[24] Frankfurter had serious doubts about the Court-packing proposal too, but he would not express them in public. Perhaps he did not want to discourage Roosevelt from appointing him to the Supreme Court. More likely it reflected the professor's genuine affection for the president.

Frankfurter's feelings toward Hughes were quite different. He thought him pompous, conniving, duplicitous. "Charles the Baptist," he sarcastically called him. And if one needed proof of the chief's evil nature, it was evident in his ability to secure Brandeis's support for the Senate letter. Frankfurter did not like to criticize anything Brandeis did, but he could not help pouring his heart out in a letter intended for Brandeis.

Of course, Frankfurter wrote, Roosevelt had "dished up phony arguments" to support the Court-packing plan. Frankfurter did not "relish some aspects of the president's proposal." At the same time, he added, "no student of the Court can be blind to its long course of misbehavior." And, perhaps worst of all, there was no excuse for Hughes's public intervention in a political matter—especially when he claimed only to be a neutral conveyer of fact. Frankfurter saw through that posture, and it made Brandeis's involvement that much more troublesome. "I resent the C.J.'s putting you in the front line," the letter said, "even with your approval."[25]

Frankfurter never sent the letter. Perhaps it was too blunt. No matter. He would get his chance later to express his feelings to Brandeis. The Court made sure of that.

Justice Owen Roberts would not go along with the other three brethren. The case involved a New York state law establishing a minimum wage. Elizabeth and Paul had helped Benjamin Cohen draft the measure, so Brandeis did not participate in the deliberations. The Four Horsemen thought the law was unconstitutional because it interfered with the individual's "liberty of contract" under the Constitution. To support their argument they pointed to the *Adkins* case, which was decided in 1923 and which struck down a Washington, D.C., minimum wage law. The other three justices—Hughes, Stone, and Cardozo—wanted to overrule *Adkins*, but none of the parties had asked the Court to do that. Still, Hughes, Stone, and Cardozo thought that the New York case could be distinguished from *Adkins* because there were more facts in the record to justify the law. Roberts rejected that approach. He would consider overruling *Adkins* as a bad decision, but he would not try to run around it with artificial distinctions. That would be "disingenuous." So the Court invalidated the New York law by a vote of 5–3.[26] Unfortunately, Roberts did not write an opinion to explain his views.

The decision was handed down in March 1936, and it fueled the fears of the Roosevelt administration that the Court would never approve social legislation. Brandeis, of course, knew otherwise. Although he did not participate in the decision, he had to have been aware of the feelings Roberts expressed at conference. In the right case, with both Brandeis and Roberts participating, the decision would go the other way.

Later, when Roosevelt stalwarts learned the truth of Roberts's views, they were greatly disturbed. Brandeis, they said, should have passed the word to the administration. It might have eliminated the need for a Court-packing plan. As it was, Roberts's view of *Adkins* became publicly known on March 29, 1937—one week after the Hughes letter was read at the committee hearings. The Court had been asked to overrule *Adkins* and approve a Washington state minimum wage law. With both Brandeis and Roberts participating, the Court upheld it by a vote of 5–4.[27] Roberts did not issue any opinion to explain why he was now willing to overrule *Adkins* when only a year earlier he had voted with the majority to reaffirm *Adkins.*

To public observers it appeared that Roberts's switch was a direct response to Roosevelt's Court-packing plan. This approval of social legislation undercut the president's real motivation (which was widely recognized in Congress and elsewhere), and people began to joke that "a switch in time saves nine." In truth, of course, it was not so. Roberts had indicated his willingness to overrule *Adkins* in the New York case, and the vote on the Washington law—with Roberts voting approval—had been taken before Roosevelt had unveiled the Court-packing proposal. The announcement of the decision was delayed only because Stone was absent, and, until he voted, there was a 4–4 deadlock.

The Washington decision did indeed signal a reversal in the Court's attitude toward social legislation. Within a couple of weeks the Court approved the National Labor Relations Act, a major New Deal law governing management–labor relations. The crisis was over. No longer did the president need to pack the Court. As one senator observed, "Why run for a train after you've caught it?"[28]

Meanwhile, Brandeis wrote Frankfurter that he must have been pleased by the decision to overrule *Adkins*, since Frankfurter had been the losing attorney in that case. The Harvard professor, unaware of the truth, took the occasion to criticize Roberts's switch as "a shameless, political response" and to tell Brandeis that he opposed Hughes's intervention in "a political fight." Brandeis quickly responded that he reserved comment "until there is chance for a talk, saying only that you are laboring under some misapprehensions." In April the two men openly discussed the issues. Frankfurter expressed his feelings plainly, and, after they cleared the air, he departed with the friendship intact.[29]

It did not entirely remove the resentment that other Roosevelt advisors felt toward Brandeis, especially when they learned that he had urged Van Devanter not to retire. By the mid-1930s the justice from Wyoming had developed paralysis of the pen. Although dedicated to the Court and conscientious about his work, he could not produce more than a few opinions a year. Arthritis had set in and writing was physically painful to him. In addition, he wanted to be careful in his opinions. After all, his strength, his major contribution to Court deliberations, was his grasp of technical procedures and his ability to be exacting. Any opinion of his had to meet the high standards he set for himself.

Court watchers took note of Van Devanter's shortcomings. They hoped, almost expected, that he would resign and give Roosevelt a chance to make a judicial appointment, one that could perhaps shift the balance of power and avoid the crisis that eventually produced the Court-packing proposal. Unbeknownst to these hopeful watchers, Brandeis—the justice on whose support the administration wanted to depend—was telling Van Devanter that he should not resign, that his comments at the Saturday conferences were indispensable, and that the Court could not function without him.

Although they were flattering, it is doubtful that Brandeis's urgings delayed Van Devanter's departure. He knew he was not carrying his share of opinions. But he feared the impact that resignation would have on his personal financial situation. Unlike other federal judges, Supreme Court justices could not retire. They had to resign. That was a significant distinction, because the Constitution prohibited Congress from reducing a judge's income, and a retired judge—although inactive—retained his constitutional protection against income reduction by Congress. A justice who resigned lost his status and that protection. So justices who resigned not only had to pay tax on their pension income (which they did not pay on their salary); they also had to worry that their pension income could be reduced (a possibility that was very real since, in an economy measure, the Congress had cut Holmes's pension in half for one year after he resigned). Congress recognized the problem and rectified it in early 1937. Van Devanter told Brandeis he would now retire. Brandeis in turn had Childs pass the word to Wheeler, and it was engineered so that Van Devanter's intention to retire was announced on May 18, 1937—the same day the Senate Judiciary committee voted to reject the president's Court-packing proposal. By summer the proposal was dead. There would be no expansion of the Court's membership.

Brandeis must have taken some satisfaction from the outcome. His beloved Court remained untarnished. Other matters were giving him pleasure as well. And one of substantial significance was the vindication of his views on picketing.

TWENTY • EIGHT

The Triumph of Labor

The "closed shop" seems to me opposed to our ideas of liberty as presenting a monopoly of labor which might become as objectionable a monopoly as that of capital.

LOUIS D. BRANDEIS, MARCH 31, 1913

The relationship was not what it appeared to be. On the surface it seemed that Brandeis was close to Benjamin Cardozo. A former New York State judge, Cardozo had been appointed to the Court by President Hoover to take Holmes's seat. It had not been an easy decision. True, Cardozo's credentials as a thoughtful and conscientious judge were impeccable. But he presented two "problems." First, he was known as a liberal, a "bleeding heart" who sometimes seemed more concerned with the plight of oppressed individuals than with the fortunes of giant corporations. The second problem compounded the first. Cardozo was Jewish. It would not do, people told the president, to appoint a second Jew to the Court, especially one from New York who did not "understand" business affairs. Cardozo had his supporters, though. Perhaps the most influential was Justice Harlan F. Stone. He was a close friend of Hoover's who played medicine ball and then had breakfast with him almost every morning at the White House. And Stone told Hoover that the Court needed Cardozo, so much so that Stone was willing to resign himself in the event Hoover wanted to balance the Cardozo appointment with the simultaneous appointment of a conservative from the South or West. The president yielded at last, without forcing Stone's resignation, and Cardozo was nominated in February 1932.

Brandeis knew Cardozo, at least by name. He had read his opinions, some of which reached the United States Supreme Court. Cardozo had also become involved in some of the extracurricular activities discussed by Frankfurter and Brandeis. From this exposure Brandeis had great respect for Cardozo's intelligence, and he was pleased with the appointment.

Once on the Court, Cardozo often found himself agreeing with Justice Brandeis. On those few occasions when they parted company, Cardozo would write an almost apologetic note to his senior colleague, saying that he regretted the disagreement, that he did it with some trepidation because Brandeis was right so often, but that it was something he felt compelled to do. During the summers the two justices exchanged warm, chatty letters describing their activities away from the Court. And after the Court-packing plan was announced, Cardozo, Stone, and Brandeis began meeting at Brandeis's apartment on Friday evenings to discuss strategy for the Saturday conferences. For many years the Four Horsemen had met together—sometimes during drives to and from Court—to exchange views on pending cases. As the Court crisis took center stage on the national scene, the other three justices apparently felt that a counterbalancing strategy was needed.

For all their seeming personal and professional affinity, Cardozo and Brandeis were quite different. Cardozo had grown up in the rough-and-tumble world of New York politics. It was not entirely filled with pleasant memories. Three years after his birth in 1870 his father had been forced to resign as a New York Supreme Court judge because of numerous allegations that he had misused his office. Everyone assumed that the elder Cardozo was guilty, and the family afterwards kept the window shutters closed, as though the darkness would protect them from the evil thoughts of their neighbors.

Matters went from bad to worse for young Benjamin. By the time he was fifteen, both his parents were dead and he was raised by his older sister Ellen. It was a most unusual relationship, one that grew in intensity with the years. The two of them spent considerable time together, and to close friends Cardozo confessed that he could never marry and leave Ellen alone.

A diminutive man with a soft, delicate face and silken white hair, Cardozo had an appearance well suited to his temperament. Quiet, shy, self-effacing, deferential. It was difficult to understand how he could have ascended the ranks of the New York judiciary, where lower court judges are elected, and appointments to the Court of Appeals—the state's highest court—are often dictated by political considerations. But Cardozo had a keen intellect and an ambition that was well disguised.

In Washington, Cardozo took a large, sumptuous apartment. He had a live-in maid who took care of all household chores, including the cleaning of the plain black suits that he always wore and that were hung daily in the bathroom. Cardozo did not like Washington or life on the United States Supreme Court. In contrast to the constant bustle of New York City, the nation's capital seemed like a sleepy Southern town with almost no city life. And unlike the camaraderie that he had enjoyed at the New York Court of Appeals, Cardozo found the life of a Supreme Court justice to be very isolated and very lonely. Until the new Court building was opened in 1935, the justices rarely saw one another outside the Saturday conferences and open Court sessions, and even after 1935 some justices, like Brandeis, continued to work at home instead of at the new offices now available to them. Not that it would have made much of a difference. With the possible exception of Stone, Cardozo did not really care that much for the other brethren. Not even Brandeis.

Despite his respect for Brandeis's intelligence, Cardozo could not identify with Brandeis's lifestyle. It was so austere, so devoid of the material comforts that Cardozo appreciated. After the Friday evening meetings Cardozo would return to his apartment to discuss the cases with his clerk. And on occasion he would poke fun at Brandeis's "peculiar" ways. The shabby furniture. The sparse food. The small quarters.

Brandeis had his own criticisms of Cardozo, but they did not relate to lifestyle. They concerned the art of judging. Brandeis found Cardozo too timid, too sentimental in approaching decisions, especially difficult ones. Brandeis often required considerable time to think a problem out, but once he reached a conclusion, he did not rethink it and wonder whether he was really right. Few decisions were entirely free from doubt, and Brandeis believed, and was fond of saying, it was sufficient if you're 51 percent right. So the senior justice did not worry about the personal impact of his decisions if he thought the result was legally correct. It might be a widow seeking insurance proceeds on her husband's death. Or a young child demanding financial support from her divorced parents. It did not matter. Brandeis could reject such claims if he thought the law pointed in the other direction.

Brandeis tried to explain all this to Cardozo, that he should not agonize over decisions, that it was enough to be 51 percent right. To which Cardozo responded, but how can I be sure I'm 51 percent right and not 49 percent right?[1]

Cardozo was not the only one to recognize the ease with which Brandeis made decisions. Willard Hurst noticed it shortly after he began his clerkship with the justice in the autumn of 1936. Like other clerks in these later years, Hurst saw Brandeis infrequently, usually once in the morning for a half hour and then again in the evening before dinner. There were no long debates between clerk and justice. Like other clerks in these later years, Hurst also observed that Brandeis was a man of few words.

There was, for example, the case of the alien who had been mistreated by the United States Immigration Service. It was a gross miscarriage of justice, Hurst told his boss, one that should move the United States Supreme Court to grant review and correct. No, said Brandeis, it was not the Court's function to make sure that justice was done in every case. He felt sympathy for the alien, but there was nothing unusual about the case that would warrant the Court's attention. If a lower court had made an error, somebody else would have to correct it.

Then there was the case involving the Public Works Administration. Brandeis supported the PWA's use of public funds to create jobs for the unemployed. When the PWA law was challenged, Brandeis was designated to write an opinion for the majority saying that the Court did not have jurisdiction to consider the case. Cardozo, for one, was shocked by the result. To him the jurisdictional base was clear, and he was very curious to see how Brandeis would explain the Court's decision. Since his clerk, Joseph L. Rauh Jr., was friendly with Hurst, Cardozo periodically would inquire when the Brandeis opinion was going to be circulated. Over at California Street, Hurst had to convey the unhappy news to the justice that, after a week of research, he could not find anything to justify the Court's decision. Brandeis did his own investigation, which only confirmed Hurst's conclusion. "Well," Brandeis told his clerk, "we'll turn it back to the Chief. He's very adept at finding ways to decide these things." The opinion was then reassigned to Hughes, and, within a short time, he issued an unsigned opinion for the Court sending the case back to the lower court because of certain procedural "irregularities." Neither Cardozo nor his clerk was impressed. "The biggest pack of bullshit you want to see," Rauh later recalled.[2]

Brandeis did not want the Court to avoid all matters of public policy, however. That became evident to Hurst when the Court agreed to hear a case involving the improper use of inside information in bank closings. To Hurst it was an open-and-shut case, one clearly settled by established law. During the Depression people had frequently tried to take unfair advantage of inside bank information, and the courts had uniformly condemned the practice. So Hurst could not understand why the United States Supreme Court would waste its valuable time deciding a case that raised no new questions of law. The clerk raised the matter with Brandeis. There was a gleam in his eye and a small smile on his lips. "Well," said the justice, "we thought there was too much of this thing going on and that we should say something about it."[3]

It was similar to the attitude Brandeis had when the *Senn* case came to the Court. It raised familiar questions of labor law, and there were many grounds on which the Court could have refused to hear the matter. But Brandeis saw a chance to use the case to announce a new principle of law, and one did not casually turn aside opportunities like that.

Paul Senn thought the union was being unreasonable. Like other businesses, tile laying was hit hard by the Depression. Senn had been a tile layer for many years, working out of his home in Milwaukee and responding to calls from individual customers. But business had slowed down considerably, and in 1935 he made only $1,500, half of which came from his own labor. The other half represented his profit after paying others whose help he sometimes needed.

Senn did not belong to the Tile Layers Union, which had only forty-one members in the Milwaukee area. Nor did his helpers receive wages as high as the union asked. But he told the union representatives that he would sign an agreement to make his operation, such as it was, a closed union shop. He would use only union men to help him and he would pay the higher wages the union demanded. There was only one qualification. He would not, really could not, give up the tile work he did for himself. Senn said he would be happy to join the union, but that was not possible since the union charter required members to have a three-year apprenticeship, and it was too late for Senn to begin a training program. He did tell the union representatives, however, that he would refrain from working himself as soon as he acquired enough business. But right now he and his family could not survive financially if he had to hire union men to do all his work.

The union rejected Senn's offer. It was all or nothing, they said. No exceptions. So Senn said it was nothing, and he refused to sign the union agreement.

The union did not accept defeat graciously. Two men began to picket in front of Senn's house, carrying signs that said Senn was "unfair." The union also sent letters to architects and contractors, warning them that, if they hired a tile layer who was not on the "approved" list, the union would picket the job site. Senn was not on the list, and the union made good on its promise. When Senn left to go on a job, union men followed him in a car so that they could picket in front of the building or construction site where he was working.

The pressure was too much, and Senn went to court. He argued that he had a right to work with his own hands and that the union pressure was improper. The union apparently agreed that there was some merit to Senn's argument. The union's attorney said that his clients would no longer follow Senn in an automobile, send letters to architects and contractors, or picket Senn's working locations. But the union insisted that it had a right to picket in front of Senn's house. To support this argument the union pointed to a Wisconsin state law that allowed picketing if it were peaceful. The state courts agreed with the union, and Senn ultimately brought his complaint to the United States Supreme Court.

The conference voted 5–4 to reject Senn's claim, and the opinion was assigned to Justice Brandeis. It could not have been a casual assignment. Hughes was very careful in the distribution of opinions, and he must have realized that the *Senn* case bore a remarkable similarity to the 1921 *Truax* case.[4] The only major difference was the result. In *Truax* the court invalidated a state law very much like Wisconsin's. Brandeis had issued a vigorous dissent in *Truax*. Now he could transform the dissent into a majority decision.

The issue was a fundamental one. Could labor engage in collective action—whether it be a strike, a boycott, or a picket—to make its views known and force a resolution of a labor dispute? For decades courts had answered the question in the negative. At the slightest hint of a strike an employer would rush to court and secure an injunction to prevent disruption by disgruntled employees. The practice became so widespread that it was referred to as "government by injunction." Even the passage of a federal law could not produce a different result. Section 20 of the 1914 Clayton Act expressly stated that "no restraining order or injunction" could be issued against a union unless it was "necessary to prevent irreparable injury." The law also said that a court could not prohibit anyone "from ceasing to perform work," from recommending that others not work, or from engaging in peaceful picketing. Despite this clear statutory language, a majority of the Supreme Court concluded in 1927 that a stonecutters union could not refuse to work on material cut by non-union workers. Brandeis protested, asserting that the Court's decision, in effect, forced people to do work they did not want to do—a result, he said, that "reminds of involuntary servitude."[5]

Not surprisingly, in *Truax* the Court majority also took a dim view of an Arizona statute similar to Section 20. The opportunity to conduct business, the majority said, is a property right protected by the due process and equal protection clauses of the Fourteenth Amendment. Therefore, the state could not pass a law that, under the facts of the case, allowed unhappy employees to picket in front of a restaurant and pressure people not to patronize their employer's business.

Time had intensified the debate. The Depression had generated many labor disputes. Employees began to feel more than ever that unions were their only salvation. In 1932 Congress passed the Norris–LaGuardia Anti-Injunction Act, which again tried to sanction the kinds of union activities approved in the Clayton Act. None of it seemed to matter. Labor disputes continued to erupt in violence, and as Brandeis was preparing to write the *Senn* opinion in 1937, none seemed more bloody than those involving the United Auto Workers in Detroit.

Brandeis no doubt hoped that a Court opinion in *Senn* could help strengthen the union movement and restore balance to management–labor relationships. It was not entirely clear, however, that the Court had jurisdiction to consider the case. In memos to the justice, Hurst pointed out that Senn's complaint had relied exclusively on state law except for a brief reference to the Fourteenth Amendment. The trial court completely ignored the federal question, as had the Wisconsin Supreme Court in its first decision. In its second opinion, the Wisconsin court denied a motion by Senn that invoked his constitutional right under the Fourteenth Amendment.

In other circumstances, Brandeis was very receptive to any reasonable argument that the Court had no jurisdiction to consider a case. He generally believed that the Court should not decide questions it did not have to. But *Senn* was different, and Brandeis and his clerk developed language that gave a plausible basis for jurisdiction.

That did not resolve all their problems. When the justice gave Hurst his draft opinion, it included a flat statement that the union's picketing was permissible because "freedom of speech is guaranteed by the Federal Constitution." In contrast to many of Brandeis's earlier opinions, there was no historical or legal analysis to support this basic proposition that picketing was a constitutionally protected activity. Hurst, however, was asked to find some support for the bald statement. After a week he reported back that he could not find any decisions to justify Brandeis's assertion. "Well," said the justice, "we'll let it stand anyway."[6] As for *Truax,* the opinion said that that case was not applicable because picketing employees there had used language that was not protected speech, including "libelous attacks and abusive epithets against the employer and his friends."[7]

In time *Senn* received the recognition that Brandeis desired. Later Court decisions accepted a union's constitutional right to picket and defined the limited circumstances in which it could be controlled. It was a clear endorsement of views Brandeis had been expressing on the Court for twenty years. No doubt he was pleased with the result. But it did not compare with the satisfaction he felt on being vindicated in *Erie.*

TWENTY • NINE

The Passing of "Old Swifty"

A foolish consistency is the hobgoblin of little minds. . . .

RALPH WALDO EMERSON

It was not the best way to begin a clerkship. But David Riesman was not one to keep thoughts bottled up inside. He had established an outstanding record at Harvard College and Harvard Law School by speaking his piece. And so he told the justice at the outset what he thought of Zionism. Brandeis inquired in the autumn of 1935 whether Riesman might be interested in attending one of the group's regular meetings. But the young lawyer would have none of it. Zionism, he told Brandeis, was nothing more than Jewish fascism—an attempt by one set of people to impose their views and take control of land that belonged to another people. The subject was never discussed again.

Riesman's first major collaboration with the justice on an opinion did little to improve relations between them. It was the "berry box" case. Oregon had passed a law that authorized the establishment of standards for boxes that would contain fruits or vegetables to be sold in the state. A California company challenged the standards for raspberries and strawberries. The company said that it would be too costly for it to change its machinery to meet the new standards. This was especially unfair, the company asserted, since there was no reasonable basis for the standards and that, in fact, they had been adopted in order to limit competition from box manufacturers outside of Oregon. It was for these reasons that the California company argued, among other things, that the law and the berry box regulations represented an unconstitutional interference with interstate commerce. Brandeis asked Riesman to find out whether there was any merit to the California company's argument. Riesman, enterprising as well as bright, was able to locate the man responsible for the law, and he confirmed that Oregon had in fact taken the action in order to restrict competition from other states. Riesman returned to Brandeis, eager to share the fruits of his diligence and to help write an opinion that Oregon's conduct was indeed unconstitutional. To Riesman's great disappointment, the justice showed little interest in his findings. Brandeis apparently did not care what the motivations were. He could conceive of facts to justify Oregon's behavior, and that was enough. For example, uniformity in berry containers might reduce the amount of public deception in the sale of berries. So, relying on the reasoning used in *O'Gorman & Young,* Brandeis drafted an opinion for the Court upholding the law.[1]

To Riesman it seemed that the justice was bent on legitimizing state legislation at almost any cost. In part, Riesman's frustration reflected his failure to appreciate the very limited role that Brandeis envisioned for federal courts. As the justice once explained to Felix Frankfurter, he felt that "in no case practically should the appellate federal courts have to pass on the construction of state statutes." Rather, he believed that state courts should be the ones to interpret their respective state laws (although the federal courts would remain available under Brandeis's view to determine whether state laws conflicted with the federal Constitution). Brandeis's position here flowed from his general dedication to local control—a dedication that also led him continually to urge Frankfurter, as well as the senators and congressmen who dined with him, to consider legislation that would restrict federal court jurisdiction.[2]

Riesman knew none of this. So he did not hesitate—at least initially—to make his views known to the justice. "We have had several good scraps," he reported to Frankfurter after the berry box case was decided, "but remembering your warning, I don't push him when I see his mind is made up—as it generally is." The young lawyer could not help wondering, however, whether the justice really needed him. Years later, recalling his experience with Brandeis, Riesman still had serious doubts that he had made a useful contribution.[3]

For all their disagreements, Riesman and Brandeis were of one mind on at least one matter: the resolution of the TVA case. The Tennessee Valley Authority, created by an act of Congress in 1933, was designed to use energy created by federal dams in the Tennessee Valley to provide low-cost electricity for the resident population. Brandeis viewed it as an exciting and imaginative experiment. When the bill was signed by Roosevelt, the justice jokingly told his family, "Mr. President, I like the sample and will take a dozen." And later he advised Frankfurter that Arthur Morgan and David Lilienthal, two TVA administrators, had "the most alluring jobs" in government.[4]

Not surprisingly, a challenge to the TVA soon reached the United States Supreme Court. The controversy arose out of a contract between the TVA and the Alabama Power Company. The company had agreed to sell the TVA some facilities. They also had agreed to limit the areas in which they would offer services—a move designed to avoid competition that could be economically harmful to both parties. All of the common stock of the Alabama Power Company was owned by a holding company, and, on the surface at least, it was satisfied with the TVA contract. Not so some preferred stockholders. They thought that the contract gave away too much. And they were also unhappy because the TVA, in their view, was an unconstitutional entity. The government, they claimed, could not go into the energy business—or any other business, for that matter. Government was not a commercial enterprise but a civic one. Therefore, they said it was improper for the power company to make a contract, any contract, with the TVA concerning power.

The first issue was whether the preferred stockholders had the right to bring the lawsuit against the TVA. If they did not have "standing" to sue, then the Court could dismiss the case without deciding the constitutionality of the TVA. The question, then, was whether preferred stockholders—who had no voting power in the company—had a sufficient interest in the matter to acquire standing.

Five of the justices, led by Hughes, concluded that the preferred stockholders could bring the legal action. These stockholders believed the contract would hurt the company, they had a financial interest in the company, and they had complied with the applicable court rule that required them to ask the company itself to institute the lawsuit before taking action themselves. Although there was no prior case dealing with preferred stockholders, the Supreme Court had allowed common stockholders to bring lawsuits even if the stockholders' interest was small. Hughes and the other four justices thought that those cases were applicable here. "A close examination of these decisions," the Hughes opinion observed, "leads inevitably to the conclusion that they should either be followed or frankly overruled. We think," the opinion for the five justices said, "that they should be followed, and that the opportunity . . . to prevent illegal transactions . . . should not be curtailed because of reluctance to decide constitutional questions."[5] The Hughes opinion then went on to say that the power company had acted reasonably and that there was nothing unconstitutional about the TVA—at least in this transaction. Congress has a constitutional right to dispose of government property, and, Hughes remarked, the TVA was merely a means of selling energy that was an incidental product of a federal dam serving legitimate navigation and flood control functions.

Brandeis did not disagree with Hughes's constitutional analysis. But he felt that the case should have been dismissed without deciding the constitutional issue because, in his view, the preferred stockholders did not have a right to bring the lawsuit. In a concurring opinion supported by three other justices, Brandeis argued that the preferred stockholders had only a relatively small financial interest in the power company, that there was no "showing" that company officials had acted unlawfully or under improper pressure, that there was no "showing" how the preferred stockholders would be injured by the TVA contract, and that, in these circumstances, compliance with court rules could not justify the lawsuit. Brandeis acknowledged that some prior Court decisions could be cited to allow the action; but he urged that those cases "now be disapproved" as unwise.[6]

Brandeis recognized that it might be convenient to allow the lawsuit and have a Court decision on whether the TVA was constitutional. But convenience was not the governing consideration. The Court should not decide a constitutional issue " 'unless absolutely necessary to a decision.' " Even if a constitutional issue was properly presented in the record, the Court should avoid it "if there is also present some other ground upon which the case may be disposed of."[7]

Many legal scholars were impressed with Brandeis's concurring opinion. Frankfurter told a friend that it represented "one of the high water marks of Supreme Court jurisdiction in constitutional controversy."[8] The euphoria did not last. Within a couple of years even Frankfurter would wonder how the same man who wrote that concurring opinion could write the opinion in *Erie*.

Harry Tompkins never knew what hit him. He was walking down the path parallel to the railroad tracks in the small village of Hughestown, Pennsylvania, in the early morning hours of Friday, July 27, 1934. He heard the whistle and saw the light of the oncoming train. He kept on walking. He had traveled that path hundreds of times before, and trains had passed him without incident. This time it was different. A door or some other part of a train car had swung loose, and it caught Harry with terrific force. When he regained consciousness in the hospital, his right arm was gone.

Things could not have been worse for the twenty-seven-year-old Tompkins. He had already lost his job in the local factory, and now, with only one arm, it would be difficult, maybe impossible, for him to support his young wife and infant daughter. His only hope was to sue the Erie Railroad Company, whose train had hit him. So when he heard that Bernard Nemeroff, a man his own age, was trying to build a law practice in New York City, Harry decided to give him the case. After all, Erie was a New York corporation, and maybe it would be best to have a New York lawyer.

Nemeroff and his associates no doubt thought that Tompkins had a sympathetic case. True, Tompkins had been trespassing when the accident occurred, since the footpath was located on railroad property. But there could be no question that the railroad had acted negligently in allowing the door or other object to swing loose. With the right jury and a little luck, they would all do well.

The only possible wrench in these plans was the law. In Pennsylvania a railroad did not owe any duty of care to a trespasser until it discovered him. Since it was dark when Tompkins was hit, the railroad would probably have little difficulty in winning the case if Pennsylvania law applied. In most other states, including New York, a different rule governed. If the railroad knew that a footpath along its tracks was commonly used by the public, then the railroad had the usual duty to avoid any negligent actions that could harm those walking on the footpath. And, most importantly for Tompkins, under New York law the railroad had that duty even though it did not know that a specific person was using the path at a specific point in time.

The question, then, was whether the courts would apply New York or Pennsylvania law. It was no simple matter. In situations like these, courts generally applied the law of the state in which the accident occurred. Furthermore, Section 34 of the Judiciary Act of 1789 said that federal courts had to honor the laws of the states (unless they were inconsistent with the United States Constitution, treaties, or federal laws). But in an 1842 Supreme Court decision—*Swift* v. *Tyson*—Justice Joseph Story said that the section applied only to written laws.[9] Federal courts were free to ignore state court decisions and apply "general law" if the state law had not been reduced to legislation. The theory, and hope, of *Swift* was that every judge, federal and state, would find the same answer to a legal question since the law was an objective truth capable of being discovered by anyone.

These expectations were soon dashed by reality. Different judges came to different conclusions, and soon people began to "shop around" for the most favorable forum in which to bring a lawsuit. The inequity of the situation reached new heights in the *Black and White Taxicab* case in 1928.[10] A Kentucky railroad company wanted to give a local taxi company an exclusive license to service its railroad station. Unfortunately, Kentucky court decisions prohibited exclusive licenses for taxi companies. Applying "general law," however, federal courts had held otherwise. So the local cab company created a new corporation in Tennessee. If any other Kentucky cab company challenged the exclusive license, the law suit would involve citizens from different states (Tennessee and Kentucky), and that diversity of citizenship, plus the great amount of money in controversy, would enable a federal court to take jurisdiction of the case. The plan worked like a charm. A competing company did attack the exclusive license, the matter went to federal court, and the federal judge, relying on *Swift,* ignored the Kentucky decisions and applied the "general law" that allowed exclusive taxi licenses.

Brandeis was outraged by this result. It not only reflected an unfair discrimination in the implementation of the law; it also meant that the state could not control its own affairs. It confirmed his view that the jurisdiction of federal courts had to be reduced. So he joined Holmes's vigorous dissent to the Court decision approving the grant of the exclusive license to the Tennessee taxi company. And he responded enthusiastically when Frankfurter suggested the possibility of drafting legislation to limit diversity of citizenship jurisdiction for federal courts and thus prevent a recurrence of the inequity in the taxi case. In fact, Brandeis told Frankfurter to whom the draft should go—Senator Tom Walsh, the progressive Democrat who sat on the committee that had considered Brandeis's Court nomination. Frankfurter followed up on the suggestion and Walsh did indeed introduce the bill, but nothing came of it. Still, Brandeis was hopeful that the Court would have another opportunity to repudiate *Swift.* And, perhaps with a different membership, the Court would take advantage of the opportunity.

The case of *Erie Railroad Company* v. *Tompkins* gave the Court its chance. Federal District Court Judge Samuel Mandelbaum, sitting in New York, had rejected the railroad's argument that he must apply Pennsylvania law. The jury was told that, under general law, Tompkins had only to show that the railroad was negligent. They accordingly found in Tompkins's favor and awarded him $30,000. The award was upheld in the United States Court of Appeals.

By the time the case reached the Supreme Court, no one—not even the railroad—had mentioned *Swift,* let alone argued that it was unconstitutional or based on an erroneous interpretation of Section 34 of the 1789 Judiciary Act. Instead, Erie simply argued that the law in Pennsylvania was so clear and so well established that federal courts were bound to honor it. They made the same argument in the United States Supreme Court—only now they had a more sympathetic audience.

The retirement of Willis Van Devanter and, shortly afterwards, George Sutherland had enabled Roosevelt to appoint two new justices to the court—former Senator Hugo Black of Alabama and former Solicitor General Stanley Reed. Those were significant changes, since both Van Devanter and Sutherland had been with the majority in the 1928 taxi case. Indications were that Black and Reed would vote differently if the issue came up again.

There was another notable change in the Court's membership. Taft had been chief justice in 1928, and he too was a part of the taxi case majority. If there was any doubt about how the new chief felt, it was dispelled when he opened the Saturday conference discussion on *Erie.* "If we wish to overrule *Swift* v. *Tyson*," Hughes said, "here is our opportunity."[11] Only eight justices participated in the discussion. Cardozo was absent because of the heart ailment that would kill him before the year was out. Everyone voting agreed that the judgment in favor of Tompkins had to be reversed. The opinion was assigned to Brandeis.

The aging justice wanted to bury *Swift* and leave no possibility of its resurrection. A 1923 article by Charles Beard in the *Harvard Law Review* suggested that *Swift* was based on an erroneous interpretation of Section 34 and that federal courts were obligated to apply state court decisions even if the principle of law was not included in a specific statute. There were two problems with the use of that article, however. First, it had been available to the Court when it decided the 1928 taxi case, and, second, a new statutory construction of Section 34 could, in any event, be changed again by a later Congress with different views. So Brandeis's draft stated that *Swift* not only reflected an erroneous interpretation of congressional intent; of greater significance, Brandeis asserted that *Swift* was inconsistent with the Constitution. On this latter point, the draft opinion argued that Congress has only the powers specified in the Constitution and that no provision entitled Congress to use federal courts to create a new substantive law different from applicable state law. There is, said the draft, no "federal general common law." If this constitutional argument were accepted by the Court, it would be extremely difficult to revive *Swift* in years to come.

It was a tough row to hoe. Justices Pierce Butler and James McReynolds were shocked by Brandeis's opinion. He had always maintained that the Court should not decide issues that were not before it. He had also said that constitutional issues should be avoided altogether if another ground was available to justify a result. Here, neither the railroad nor Tompkins had argued that *Swift* was wrong in any respect, let alone that it was unconstitutional. Moreover, it was unnecessary to reach the constitutional issue. Butler and McReynolds believed that Tompkins had acted carelessly by staying on the footpath when he saw the train coming, and, under Pennsylvania as well as New York law, Tompkins could not recover damages if he had been negligent.

If Brandeis nonetheless insisted on making the constitutional argument, then Butler had another concern. A 1937 congressional statute—an outgrowth of the Court-packing crisis—stated that the Court had to request the views of the attorney general if it was about to declare a federal law unconstitutional. If Brandeis persisted, Butler said, then the Court had to reset the case for oral argument and take the views of the government, as well as of the parties, on the constitutional issue.

Justices Reed and Harlan F. Stone had a slightly different view. They were prepared to say that *Swift* was wrong because it relied on an erroneous interpretation of Section 34. After all, why shouldn't federal courts recognize the decisions of state courts? But like Butler and McReynolds, Reed and Stone saw no reason to reach the constitutional issue. Brandeis himself had explained in his TVA opinion that the Court should not resolve a constitutional issue unless it was necessary, and here there was a clear alternative.

Brandeis no doubt was troubled. As things stood, only three justices (besides himself) stood behind his opinion. The remaining four justices in the case were against his constitutional claim. He needed at least one more justice to have a majority for his position. Perhaps further discussion could secure the needed fifth vote. He had no luck with Reed. In response to a note from the new justice, Brandeis proposed to include in his opinion some obscure language to indicate that the result of *Swift*—but not Section 34 itself—was unconstitutional. Reed found the proposal unsatisfactory and told his senior colleague that he would prepare a concurring opinion to set forth his views.

Stone was more promising. On the afternoon of March 24 he came to visit Brandeis at the California Street apartment. They discussed the case. Brandeis surely called upon all his powers of logic and persuasion. Stone was impressed and left Brandeis saying that he would "abide by the opinion" unless he advised Brandeis otherwise. The next day Stone suggested that the senior justice add some language to the opinion to strengthen the constitutional point. The Court ordinarily would not abandon a case like *Swift* that had been accepted for almost a century, Stone's language said; however, "the unconstitutionality of the course pursued has now been made clear and compels us to do so." Brandeis accepted Stone's suggested change, and when the opinion was announced on April 25, 1938, five justices agreed that *Swift* was unconstitutional. It was, said Hughes, an "excellent burial service!"[12]

Brandeis too was pleased with the opinion. "Yes," he told Willard Hurst, who had written to congratulate him, "the Tompkins case gives satisfaction. It has already relieved our Court . . .; should relieve federal courts; and, which is most important, tend to develop the morale of State courts and the quality of their work."[13] Whether the decision did in fact improve state courts is open to question. But the opinion has not been reversed by any subsequent Court. It has, however, been a constant topic of discussion. Indeed, Brandeis no doubt would have been happy to know that the decision has been one of the most frequently cited by federal courts—between 1938 and 1978, a total of 3,467 times, or an average of about one and one-half times per week during that period.[14] Few law students graduate without knowing the sad tale of Harry Tompkins and the Erie Railroad.

Sometime before his death in 1946, Judge Mandelbaum took down from his bookshelf the volume of the United States Reports that includes the *Erie* decision. Scholarship was not Mandelbaum's strong suit, and he was not very articulate. Politics had been the only basis for his court appointment. But Mandelbaum wanted to express his views on the outcome of the case that he had heard as a trial judge. No one had told him about *Swift* v. *Tyson.* And surely he never expected this case, *his* case, to be the subject of a Supreme Court opinion by Justice Brandeis, one that people would examine and debate for years to come. In his own inimitable style, Mandelbaum laid it all out in the margin of the *Erie* opinion page that referred to the trial judge. "Because the Swift Tyson case," he wrote, "although before this case I never knew of its existence to be truthful and for the confusion this decision brought about, it might have been better to leave it alone and stand by good old Swifty."[15]

THIRTY

Final Touches

They did not yet see, and thousands of young men . . ., now crowding to the barriers of their careers, could not see that if a single man plant himself on his convictions and then abide, the huge world will come round to him.

RALPH WALDO EMERSON

It was not a good omen for the Jews. Arab hostility toward the Jewish settlers in Palestine had always bubbled near the surface, and in April 1936 it erupted into a new wave of violence. Once again Arab mobs conducted a rampage that left many Jews dead, others injured, and all deeply affected. Once again the British resorted to a commission to study the problem and make recommendations. In Zionist circles there was little doubt of the conclusions the commission would reach. Even before the investigation began, Prime Minister Stanley Baldwin proposed to suspend all Jewish immigration into Palestine.

The Jews were beside themselves. It was not merely a question of the British commitment to the Balfour Declaration. For Germany's Jews it was literally a matter of life and death. Stephen Wise, the American Zionist leader, was especially disturbed by the turn of events. He had just completed a visit to Europe. He had talked to people. He had seen evidence. German Jews were in great danger, and for most the only hope was emigration to Palestine. On his return Wise asked to see Roosevelt himself, and after a short conference at the White House, the president sent word to the British that the United States would regard a suspension of immigration as a "breach" of the Balfour Declaration. Baldwin yielded, and the suspension order was lifted. Nothing would be done, His Majesty's Government said, until the commission issued its report.

Brandeis watched all these developments closely. He continued to believe that German Jews had to leave their country. When a visiting Berlin lawyer told him that the danger was greatly exaggerated, the justice disagreed vigorously and bluntly told his visitor that it was "folly" for Jews to stay in Germany and that "there is no hope for anyone who does not emigrate." So when Wise advised him of Roosevelt's communication to Baldwin, Brandeis was elated. Wise, he said, had "performed a marvelous feat," adding that "nothing more important for us has happened" since the international acceptance of the Balfour Declaration.[1]

The euphoria was short-lived. In July 1937 the British commission chaired by Viscount Peel released its report. To the surprise of the Zionists—and perhaps the British government as well—the report contained an objective and very critical analysis of British policies in Palestine. The main problem, the commission observed, was that for almost two decades the British had been promising the Jews one thing and simultaneously promising the Arabs something else. If England had simply established boundaries for the Jewish homeland at the end of the World War, the problem would probably be behind them. But simple solutions were no longer possible. The aspirations of the Jews and Arabs were irreconcilable. The commission therefore recommended that Palestine be partitioned into three separate parts: a Jewish state that would occupy about 1,550 square miles with a western boundary on the Mediterranean Sea; an Arab state in the larger and more eastern part of Palestine; and a neutral zone that would include Jerusalem and Bethlehem and be supervised by the British.

Virtually no one liked the Peel proposal. The Arabs quickly convened a summit meeting and condemned it. Jews—Zionist and non-Zionist alike—also argued against the proposal's adoption. It was inconceivable, they said, to accept a Jewish homeland that did not include Jerusalem. The Jews were also disappointed because the Peel proposal would include the Negev Desert and Judea—two areas of prime importance in Jewish history—in the Arab state.

Brandeis's criticism was not governed by an emotional tie to a Biblical past. It was practical. If the Jews were to develop Palestine economically, they had to have an adequate supply of land. And besides, he did not look kindly upon a government, even a foreign one, breaking its promises. The British could not escape their commitment to the Jews. So he eventually instructed his disciples to "stand firm against partition." In his mind it was a "stupid, ignoble action."[2]

Not every Zionist shared Brandeis's view. Chaim Weizmann, for one, saw partition as the only possible alternative. It might not be the best solution for the Jews, but it was at least a solution. And right now, whatever their aspirations, Jews were not in the driver's seat. Brandeis probably expected nothing different from Weizmann. The justice still saw the World Zionist leader as a slippery and untrustworthy character too willing to accommodate his friends in the British government. But David Ben-Gurion was different. The small, bushy-haired Ben-Gurion, age fifty-one, was a fiery, almost militant leader. A Russian by birth, Ben-Gurion had emigrated to Palestine in 1906 and had became the founding force of the Jewish Labor Party. Brandeis respected Ben-Gurion. Like the former "people's attorney," he was a fighter, a man unafraid to pursue his dreams. The justice began meeting with Ben-Gurion in the early 1930s to discuss various social and economic projects for Palestine. At one point Brandeis offered Ben-Gurion a $20,000 donation to help develop a port on the Gulf of Akaba so that the Jews could have an outlet to the Red Sea. The justice's confidence in Ben-Gurion grew with time, and by 1936 he was making thousands of dollars available to him to use as he saw fit. And when the British remained unable to protect Jewish settlers, Brandeis gave Ben-Gurion $40,000 so that the Haganah, the Jewish defense organization, could arm itself.

Because of this close relationship, Brandeis and his group felt disappointed—almost betrayed—when they learned that Ben-Gurion supported the Peel proposal to partition Palestine. The Jewish leader was no doubt anxious to explain his position, and in early September 1937 he journeyed to Chatham to discuss the situation at the justice's summer retreat. For one hour Ben-Gurion spoke without interruption. True, he said, Jews had a moral right to a real Jewish homeland, one with larger boundaries that included Jerusalem. But they could not ignore reality. Even a smaller Jewish state would be better than the present British administration of Palestine. Moreover, said Ben-Gurion, there was considerable pressure from some Jewish elements, especially the Eastern European groups, to accept partition. So, although the plan was far from perfect, Ben-Gurion thought it best to empower the World Zionist executive committee to begin negotiations with the British. Perhaps discussion could lead to a larger area.

Brandeis then spoke for an hour without interruption. To him, the pressures and probabilities described by Ben-Gurion were similar to those that had induced Theodore Herzl to favor the British offer of Uganda as a Jewish homeland. Ben-Gurion's judgment, Brandeis said, was misguided in the same way that Herzl's was. The justice recognized that it was difficult to demand full satisfaction from the British. He added that he also did not like to question the views of a man who had to live with the problems of Palestine on a daily basis. But, said Brandeis, his distance from the "battlefield" gave him a more objective perspective, one that took the long view. When Brandeis finished, the two men spoke for an additional ten minutes. Although he respected Brandeis, Ben-Gurion told him frankly that his position remained unchanged.[3]

Ben-Gurion did not have to negotiate with Brandeis, because a few weeks earlier the World Zionist Congress had already voted to explore the partition proposal with the British. Nothing came of it, however. The British appointed yet another commission to examine the matter. By the end of 1938 the British concluded that the partition proposal was politically and financially unworkable, and it was heard of no more.

None of this helped the Jews. The British were not going to turn against the Arabs, and the Arabs refused to recognize that the Jews had any right to be in Palestine. In early 1939 rumors spread that the British, frustrated with the Palestinian problem and eager to concentrate on their own defenses against Germany, were planning to prohibit all Jewish emigration to Palestine. Zionists became frantic. On February 26, 1939, Brandeis sent a personal plea to British Prime Minister Neville Chamberlain. "I cannot believe," he told the British leader, "that your Government has fully considered how gravely shattered would be the faith of the people of this troubled world in the solemn undertakings of even democratic governments if Great Britain so drastically departed from her declared policy in reference to the Jewish National Home. I urge you," Brandeis implored Chamberlain, "to consider the cruel plight of the Jews in the world today and not to crush their most cherished and sanctified hopes."[4] Within eight days Ambassador Ronald Lindsay responded for Chamberlain, saying only that Brandeis's views would be given careful consideration and that he should reserve final judgment until the British government reached a definitive conclusion.

Brandeis was not satisfied with that. In the late afternoon of March 9 he was driven to the White House and ushered into the Oval Office. Despite the split on the Court-packing plan, Roosevelt gave no appearance of any rift with Brandeis. In talks with Zionist colleagues, the president always spoke warmly of the justice.

"Isaiah is a grand old man," he told Wise at one point in 1938.[5] And, most importantly, he displayed considerable sympathy in private meetings whenever Zionists spoke of Palestine or the plight of Germany's Jews. But, he would repeatedly say, there was a limit to what he could do. Max Warburg, a German banker, told Roosevelt that nothing could be done, and the president repeatedly invoked that comment whenever Zionists urged some kind of action by the American government. In any event, the president was at least willing to listen, and he saw no harm in hearing Brandeis out this March afternoon.

Brandeis briefly described the situation, showed Lindsay's response to Roosevelt, and urged that he advise the British that the United States would not look favorably upon any prohibition of Jewish emigration to Palestine. Within a week Brandeis wrote to Roosevelt that he now had confidential information concerning England's intended course of action: the creation of a single independent state in Palestine that would confine Jews to minority status; restriction of immigration to 10,000 a year until 1944, and immigration after that only with the consent of the Arabs; and severe restrictions on the right of Jews to buy land. It was, for all practical purposes, a complete reversal of the Balfour Declaration. Roosevelt nonetheless advised Brandeis that, despite his best efforts, he probably could do no more than have the announcement of the policy postponed for a short while.

The ax fell on May 17, 1939, when the Chamberlain government issued its White Paper on Palestine. The only major variation from the policy anticipated by Brandeis was the number of immigrants to be allowed. Instead of permitting 50,000 over the next five years, the British would allow 75,000. In all other respects the final policy was the same.

The phone kept ringing at the Brandeis apartment. Zionists from all over the country wanted the views and advice of their most esteemed leader. Adrian Fisher, who began his association with Brandeis as a clerk in September 1938, was summoned to the apartment. He was asked to answer the telephone, give messages to Brandeis, and relay responses to the caller. To intimates Brandeis said, almost plaintively, "Where will a poor Jew go now?" The same sentiment was included in a public statement Brandeis gave to Solomon Goldman, the new president of the ZOA. "What does the world propose to do," he asked, "with the Jews for whom exile is enforced?" The answer would be received in due course, and it would not be pleasant.[6]

By the time the Chamberlain government crushed the hopes of Jews, Brandeis had retired from the Court. The limitations of age made it difficult for him to keep up with the demands of judging. His energy was more limited than ever, he often needed a magnifying glass to read, and his hearing was becoming impaired. "I am as usual," he wrote to one of his daughters at one point, "but the auto men are right. Old machines are unreliable and the maintenance cost [is] high."[7] When the 1936 Court term finished in June 1937, he went to Hughes and offered to retire to make room for a younger man. The chief justice turned aside any suggestion of retirement, saying that the Court needed Brandeis.

Other Court watchers felt differently. Acheson, a devoted friend and disciple of the justice, told friends that Brandeis had become "institutionalized" and that it was time for him to step down. Corcoran had similar feelings. The Court needed an injection of new blood, and if Brandeis retired, Roosevelt would have an opportunity to appoint Frankfurter.

The objective evidence suggested that Acheson and Corcoran had the better view. In the 1937 and 1938 terms Brandeis produced relatively few opinions, and none of them entailed the kind of effort he had made in earlier years. Illness also sapped his strength to a greater degree than before. In the spring of 1938 he became seriously ill. Some doctors thought it might be evidence of a weak heart. He was advised not to exert himself in the slightest. Guests at the teas now noticed that the justice never stood but remained seated on the black mohair sofa. Those who came to dinner were told that the justice had to retire by nine o'clock.

Alice was more conscious than ever of her husband's limitations—if that was possible—and it could, ironically, produce some comic moments. It was the autumn of 1938, and Adrian Fisher received a call from Mrs. Brandeis. Plainly agitated, she explained that the justice was on his way back from Court, that the elevator wasn't working, that of course the justice could not climb five floors of stairs, and what was the clerk going to do about it? Butch Fisher did not lack imagination. He hustled down to the foyer of the building and secured a straight-backed wooden chair and the assistance of the janitor, a large black man who Fisher thought should have been a professional football player. When the justice arrived the two young men explained that the elevator was not working and directed him to sit on the chair. Brandeis, dressed in an overcoat and a brown derby, did as he was told without saying a word, and, while he sat quietly on the chair, the two men carried him upstairs. For Fisher it was one of the most memorable moments of his clerkship. "I'll never forget that," he said years later. "Brandeis in his overcoat and derby, serene as could be, taking it all in stride as though there was not the slightest problem, looking straight ahead."[8] The delivery of Brandeis to his doorstep did not complete their labors, however. In her excitement Alice had rushed downstairs to supervise everything. Since she too had a weak heart, Fisher and the janitor had to return to the foyer and then carry her back to the apartment as well.

It could not go on like this for long. And it didn't. In January 1939 Fisher received a call from Graham Claytor, his predecessor, who informed him that the justice had become ill while sitting on the bench, that they were bringing him home, and that Fisher should arrange for a doctor to be there. It was the grippe, and then he had a heart attack. It required him to be absent from work for a month. He returned to the Court in early February, but he knew it was no use. He summoned Frankfurter to his apartment. Ironically, Frankfurter was just about to complete his first week as a Supreme Court justice. Roosevelt had nominated him to replace Cardozo, who had succumbed to heart disease in July 1938. And so, after those many years of collaboration, he would have a chance to sit side by side with Brandeis.

When Frankfurter reached the California Street apartment, Brandeis informed him that he was planning to retire. Frankfurter responded as only Frankfurter could. He was full of eloquence and warm sentiment over the sad occasion, and he expressed his feelings at great length The ever-patient Brandeis listened without interruption. When Frankfurter finished, Brandeis made it clear that other things were on his mind. "Well," he told the former professor, "that's not why I called you here. What are we going to do with Adrian?" Frankfurter quickly offered to use the Brandeis clerk himself, and so, while Fisher continued to assist Brandeis on non-judicial chores, he finished the term with a different justice.[9]

On February 13, 1939, Brandeis wrote the necessary letter to Roosevelt. "Dear Mr. President," it said. "Pursuant to the Act of March 1, 1937, I retire this day from regular active service on the bench." Roosevelt responded the same day. "One must perforce accept the inevitable," he said. But he added that the "country has needed you through all these years, and I hope you will realize, as all your friends do, how unanimous the nation has been in its gratitude to you." Well, maybe not unanimous. A few days later the brethren sent Brandeis a warm letter on his retirement. Everyone signed it—everyone, that is, except McReynolds. Whatever his other faults, he was not a hypocrite.[10]

Although he was off the Court, Brandeis was not indifferent to its future course. His most immediate concern was his replacement, and of course he had a suggestion on that score. He had long viewed William O. Douglas as a bright and energetic lawyer. Perhaps more important was that Douglas shared Brandeis's dim view of large corporations and, in Brandeis's view, was willing to do something about it when he left his teaching post at Yale Law School to assume the chairmanship of the Securities and Exchange Commission. Douglas would make periodic visits to California Street, and the two of them would discuss the evils of big business. When Douglas left, Brandeis would turn to his clerk with a smile and say, "He's quite a fellah."[11]

No doubt Brandeis hoped and expected that a man like Douglas would continue to fight "the curse of bigness." So when he met with Roosevelt on March 9, 1939, to discuss Jewish affairs, he recommended that Douglas be nominated to fill his seat. Ten days later the nomination was sent to the United States Senate. Other forces were also at work, to be sure; but the endorsement from Brandeis could not have hurt.[12] Although at the time he was unaware of Brandeis's role, Douglas was deeply touched by his elevation to the Court. "I am overwhelmed and filled with a deep sense of humility," he wrote to Brandeis the day after the nomination was announced. "These feelings are due in part to my realization of the magnitude of the task. But in main they are due to my recognition of the great responsibility of one who is asked to wear your robe. . . . If the Senate confirms, I pray God may give me power to maintain your high standards and to serve the sense of liberalism in accordance with your noble traditions."[13] Brandeis, for one, was confident that Douglas was up to the challenge.

Louis and Alice had always loved the house at Chatham. Now it became one of the best places at which to enjoy Louis's retirement. No more *cert.* petitions to review for the next Court term. No more communication with law clerks about the progress of elaborate opinions. Instead, the summers were completely devoted to talking to people and taking advantage of summer activities. Canoeing was still a favorite pastime. Since Alice and Louis could no longer paddle themselves, the children had to assist. Elizabeth and Paul, as they had before, continued to spend summers in the Chatham house. Susan and Jack had their own house nearby. Because it was difficult to get to the beach from the Brandeis home, everyone went over to Susan and Jack's house. There, Alice and Louis were helped into the middle of the canoe so that they could face each other, and then Elizabeth and Paul would literally assume the laboring oars.

Much time was spent with the grandchildren. Susan and Jack had three children. Louis, the oldest, was in his early teens, followed closely behind by Alice and Frank. Elizabeth and Paul had only one child, Walter, since Elizabeth had had a difficult birth and had been advised by doctors not to have any more. Brandeis was very interested in the grandchildren, would ask about them when they were away from him, and made sure that each made an appointment with him during the summer so that he could talk to each alone. "It was," his granddaughter Alice recalled years later, "a caring thing, because we felt he wanted to sit down with each one of us and find out about the courses we were taking, the things we were doing, and things like that."[14]

Dinners at Chatham were also an event for the children as well as everyone else. The main course generally was duck, since there was a duck farm nearby. While Alice sliced the bird, Louis would lead an animated conversation among family and guests about a wide range of subjects. Current events dominated the talk at the dinner table and on other occasions as well. Germany had invaded Poland on September 1, 1939, and the discussion almost inevitably led back to the causes of conflict and its future course. Many people thought that the Versailles Treaty, which had officially terminated the First World War, lay at the root of the problem. The treaty had exacted heavy reparations from the defeated German nation, made economic recovery difficult, imposed severe restrictions on the country's ability to arm itself, and generally crushed the dignity of a people known for their pride in the Fatherland. Brandeis did not share this prevalent view. He agreed that the treaty might include some unfair provisions, but he felt that the hostilities reflected the aggressive nature of the German people themselves. "What can be done with such people?" he rhetorically asked his guests at one point. "Even if the treaty were the best that the wisdom of man and virtue of man can devise, what can be done with the German people? If it were [up to] the Germans . . ., they would kill every one."[15] The German aggression was especially disturbing because of its implications for European Jews. In that regard Brandeis lumped the Germans together with the British, whose indifference to Jewish persecution was almost as offensive. Indeed, a few years before the invasion of Poland, Brandeis shocked a couple of visitors by saying with great fervor that he wished the British and Germans would kill each other off.[16]

In these and other matters Brandeis was not always confined to being a passive observer. He would periodically visit or write the president at the White House about Jewish affairs, and always Roosevelt was warm, sympathetic, and seemingly eager to do what he could. The nation appeared greatly resistant to becoming involved in the European conflict, and that factor would almost always be invoked as a limitation on the administration's response to any perceived injustice to the Jews in Palestine or Europe.

Brandeis had a little more control over the situation when public discussion was renewed on the Ballinger–Pinchot controversy that had brought him national fame in 1910. The controversy was resurrected when the *Saturday Evening Post* published an article in May 1940 by Harold Ickes, Roosevelt's secretary of the interior. Ickes said that a recent biography of former President Taft had inspired him to investigate Ballinger's role in the affair, that the true facts were at variance with the public perception of Ballinger as a villain, that Ballinger had displayed honesty and dedication in handling the infamous Cunningham coal claims, and that "the American people owe both contrition and atonement to the maligned memory of a fine and devoted public servant." Although the article focused on the alleged misdeeds of Glavis and Pinchot, Brandeis too was criticized. The "astute" Boston attorney, said Ickes, had made "a mountain out of this mole hill" and thus had misled the public into believing that there was a "conspiracy" to cover up official wrongdoing when, in truth—according to Ickes—Ballinger had acted properly in the disposition of the Cunningham claims.[17]

Brandeis attributed Ickes's article to a desire to get back at Pinchot, who was still a force in national politics and who had recently used his influence to prevent Ickes from expanding the reach of his department's powers. It was, the ex-justice told a friend, "a crazy and crazing lust for power, and hate of those who have frustrated his efforts for dominion."[18] Brandeis was still a fighter, though, and he had a vehicle for bringing his viewpoint to public attention: Alpheus T. Mason, a Princeton University professor of political science.

Brandeis's relationship with Mason went back almost ten years. Mason wrote a detailed law review article analyzing Brandeis's pre-Court career, and the work impressed Brandeis. This respect increased a couple of years later with the publication of a book by Mason examining Brandeis's Court opinions. The two men began to correspond and also to meet periodically in Washington and Chatham. The bond between them intensified when Mason wrote another book called *The Brandeis Way,* an historical account of Brandeis's efforts to establish low-cost savings bank life insurance in Massachusetts. The book was published in 1938 and coincided with the enactment of a similar law in New York. Brandeis worked closely with Mason on the book, and his hope was that its publication would help educate other states on the benefits of savings bank life insurance.

By this time, Mason was preparing a full biography of Brandeis. Obviously, some of the material would concern the Ballinger–Pinchot controversy. So Brandeis made clear his hope that Mason would convert that material into an article that could offset the furor triggered by the Ickes article. Mason went one better. He had the material issued as a small book entitled *Bureaucracy Convicts Itself.* It was a scholarly review of the record, and, according to *The New Republic* reviewer at least, Mason "won the battle" and subjected Ickes to "the novelty of defeat."[19]

All of this probably made Brandeis feel comfortable with his decision to help Mason on the biography. On the one hand, the former justice did not want to authorize any biography of himself. When people asked him in earlier years if he planned to write his memoirs, he would say, with obvious reference to his judicial opinions, "I think you will find my memoirs have been written."[20] Still, he wanted to cooperate with Mason. The Princeton professor was clearly a sympathetic scholar. With access to his recollections and private papers, Brandeis no doubt believed that the story of his life would be told in the right way.

Frankfurter opposed Brandeis's decision. The new Supreme Court justice did not share Brandeis's respect for Mason's work, and he urged his mentor to await another, more qualified biographer. Brandeis refused to yield. He began to meet with Mason on a more regular basis to discuss past events, and he instructed his old law firm to allow Mason access to files concerning his public activities. Frankfurter did not suffer a total defeat, however. Brandeis entrusted his Court papers to the former Harvard professor and gave clear instructions that Mason was not to see these, even after his death. Brandeis obviously wanted to protect the confidentiality of communication with fellow justices and others who would survive him. But Frankfurter took the instructions literally. Years later, when Frankfurter was the only one of Brandeis's former brethren still on the Court, and when Frankfurter was making the Brandeis Court papers available to others to write about Brandeis, he would continue to deny Mason access, invoking Brandeis's instructions that Mason should not see his Court papers.

The disagreement over the Mason biography did not appear to alter Frankfurter's relationship with Brandeis in those last years. He continued to rely on Brandeis in advising Roosevelt on matters of policy, he continued to send Brandeis drafts of his Court opinions, and he continued regular visits with the ex-justice. Others, especially in Zionist circles, also continued to visit Brandeis, but the old man knew that it was no longer the same. He was too far from the center of action, too remote from the decisions being made on a daily basis. "All I can do now," he told his niece Fanny, "is to let people talk to me and imagine I help them. I don't—but. . . ." His voice trailed off, and, after a pause, he changed the subject.[21] He was no longer an integral part of the struggle, no longer a power to be reckoned with. The end was near.

Death came suddenly. When he and Alice returned from Chatham in September 1941, Washington was hit by an unusual spell of hot weather. Louis had always liked the heat, but now he could no longer handle it. A bout with pneumonia the previous summer had greatly weakened his body, and this new hot spell incapacitated him for days. "Your uncle has felt the terrific heat we have been having ever since our return," Alice wrote to their nephew Louis Wehle on September 27, ". . . he is going it slowly but serene as ever. It knocked me pretty much flat," she added, "but I think we are over the worst of it."[22] A week later Frankfurter came for one of his visits, and as usual the conversation ranged far and wide. Brandeis spoke highly of Roosevelt, saying he was a "noble figure" who equaled Jefferson and approached Lincoln in greatness. The former justice also reminded Frankfurter that "the greatest mistakes men make derive from two weaknesses"—"the inability to say no" and "the unwillingness to take a vacation when they should and therefore going on in the making of important decisions when their judgment [is] fatigued and not well poised."[23] When Frankfurter left the California Street apartment, he could not know that he would never see Brandeis again.

It happened the next day while he and Alice were taking a morning drive in Washington's Rock Creek Park. He was rushed to a hospital, where it was diagnosed as another heart attack. He slipped into a coma, and in the early evening of Sunday, October 5, 1941, Louis Brandeis, five weeks shy of his eighty-fifth birthday, passed away.

It was, by any reasonable standard, an extraordinary life. Brandeis's many activities reflected not only the work of a man with keen intelligence and an unusual talent to organize others; those activities also revealed an individual with an incredible drive to succeed, to make people understand, to shape the world according to basic principles that he cherished. These activities were complemented by his optimism. It was eternal, unshakeable. He always approached a problem with faith that an answer would be found—although he realized that some answers required patience, and he had a good deal of that as well. And then there was the magnetic quality of his personality. It was difficult to define with precision. Perhaps the charm, the melodious voice, those penetrating eyes. You could quarrel over its source, but you could not doubt that his presence in any endeavor added a sense of purpose that many found irresistible. It was evident in his early fights in Boston. It was there when he assumed a leadership role in the Zionist movement. And it threaded his many labors on the Supreme Court. Even adversaries recognized his ability to understand and then master almost any situation—and all with an eye on some chosen goal. "My, how I detest that man's ideas," Justice George Sutherland once said of Brandeis. "But he is one of the greatest technical lawyers I know." Others, like Charles Mellen, Richard A. Ballinger, and Chaim Weizmann, might have used different words to express their views, but the judgment would have been the same.[24]

However considerable his talents and achievements—and they were indeed remarkable—Brandeis did have faults. The drive that propelled him to success often reflected a moral code that was, in many respects, truly his own. He could, as in the case of the Equitable Assurance Society, sidestep conflicts of interest that would have given others pause. He could, as in the case of the gas fight, discard professional obligations that stood in the way of some higher goal. And, as evidenced in the *Erie* and *Chattanooga Railway* cases, he could ignore his own judicial pronouncements to achieve a result that, to him at least, was more important.

None of this was done for personal gain. One can search in vain through Brandeis's most private letters and communications for even a hint that any activity, any position, any opinion, or any statement was undertaken for financial or professional achievement. Still, even his most ardent supporters sometimes found him to be an enigma, a man who operated on a different wavelength from other people. As one Boston attorney rightly explained to the Senate subcommittee considering his judicial nomination in 1916, Brandeis was "intensely centered in carrying out his own ideas and his own ideals, which . . . are pure, which are high minded," but that led him on occasion to "do things of a startling character."[25]

Brandeis's death, like his life, attracted worldwide attention. Not all of it was favorable. He was a man who jealously guarded his privacy. Few were allowed into the intimacy of his world. For those who remained outside he could appear aloof, indifferent to the ordinary emotions that drive people. This was especially true in his later years. There were so many things to accomplish, so little time in which to do them. He was, one associate recalled, a man with a dream in a hurry. More than one colleague in those later years remarked that he seemed to hoard his time as though it were a valuable trust.

Primarily for these reasons he was careful not to squander time on unnecessary matters. Appointments were held to a minimum. Letters were written quickly, in longhand, and they were so crisp, so much to the point that they almost seemed abrupt, imperious. Ben Cohen felt that way at first. Quiet, shy, sensitive, Cohen confessed to Julian Mack in the 1920s that Brandeis seemed cold and unappreciative of Cohen's many labors and sacrifices for the Zionist cause. Of course it was not so. There were few people Brandeis respected more than Ben Cohen in terms of intelligence and dedication. After being told of the situation by Mack, Brandeis corrected Cohen's erroneous impression. But not everyone could be approached in this way, and it showed. "[T]here certainly was never anyone with a greater impersonal passion than LDB . . .," one Zionist leader wrote to Frankfurter shortly after Brandeis's death. ". . . I suspect that few if any people were ever fond of him in a cozy comfortable sort of way and that he mattered personally only to those few who knew how to reach [him] through veneration and respect."[26]

Those who did reach him found an affection and loyalty that were quite unusual. Acheson was one. After clerking for Brandeis, he maintained regular contact with him to talk about the Court, current events, and personal affairs. Acheson spoke of these memories at a small gathering of family and friends at the California Street apartment on October 7. Brandeis was to be cremated and his ashes placed in an urn underneath the University of Louisville—the school whose affairs had attracted considerable money and attention from Louis and Alice over the preceding fifteen years. Since there would be no funeral, this small gathering was the only opportunity to eulogize the former justice. Acheson made the most of it.

He focused on the clerks who had served with Brandeis. "Throughout these years we have brought him all our problems and troubles," Acheson remarked, "and he had time for all of us. In talk with him the problems answered themselves. A question, a comment . . . and we wondered why the matter had ever seemed difficult." It all reflected Brandeis's attachment to the clerks. "I have talked, over the past twenty years, with the Justice about these men," Acheson said. "I have heard him speak of some achievement of one of us with all the pride and of some sorrow or disappointment of another with all the tenderness of a father speaking of his sons. He entered so deeply into our lives because he took us so deeply into his."[27]

Of course, that was not entirely true. Many of the clerks felt very removed from the justice. But whatever their view of his personality, few could doubt that he was a powerful influence. You could challenge the wisdom of his view that individual development was the key to social progress. You could disagree with his crusade against "the curse of bigness." And you could question his objectivity in deciding cases. But you could not ignore the intellectual and moral energy generated by his presence. He made you wary of assumptions. He made you think. And he gave you faith in the future.

It was ironic in a way. As a young man Louis Brandeis had rejected teaching as a career. Now, in retrospect, his most significant achievements seemed to be as a teacher. His statements and opinions became guideposts for future students and future decision-makers. In many quarters his views were accorded a reverence reserved for only a very few figures. Louis D. Brandeis, a man who had shunned idols, had become one himself.

ACKNOWLEDGMENTS

A work of history like this is rarely, if ever, the product of a single individual's labors. My book is no exception. Over the past few years I have received help from numerous people throughout the country. To them I owe much, and I would like to use this opportunity to express my appreciation.

Some of the most important assistance came from libraries that house the various manuscript collections that provided the primary source of information for the book. In every instance the library staffs were friendly and cooperative. The particular libraries I used are identified in the bibliographical notes and sources section that follows. Five libraries deserve special mention, however.

Janet Hodgson and Tom Owen at the University of Louisville extended themselves well beyond the call of duty in responding to my many inquiries and requests. Since Louisville holds the bulk of Brandeis's non-judicial papers, this assistance was invaluable.

Erika Chadbourn at Harvard Law School was equally responsive to my research needs. This too proved to be critical, as Harvard contains virtually all of Brandeis's Court papers. Thanks also go to Paul A. Freund, who granted me access to those papers.

A third significant source of materials is found at Brandeis University. Under the auspices of a special advisory commission, the University produced an annotated microfilm collection of the justice's pre-Court papers. Since much of this writing was buried in obscure journals and dusty alcoves, the commission's compilation was most useful in charting Brandeis's views on public issues. William Goldsmith, the project director (and now a professor at the University), attended to all my requests for copies and other information with rare enthusiasm. He was also helpful in arranging my review of the papers of Susan Brandeis Gilbert, the justice's daughter, shortly after they were first opened to the public in the fall of 1981. The review of those papers was also made possible by the cooperation of Frank Gilbert, the justice's grandson, and Victor Berch, who is in charge of Special Collections at Brandeis University.

Thanks likewise go to James O. McReynolds for granting me access to the restricted papers of his uncle, Justice James C. McReynolds, at the University of Virginia. Mr. McReynolds also helped by responding to my many questions and in suggesting other sources of information.

I am equally appreciative of the efforts made on my behalf by the staff of the Montgomery County Library in Rockville, Maryland. Whenever I needed a book or microfilm on loan from another library, they were always anxious to help.

Libraries were not the only source of information. Numerous individuals generously shared their recollections and historical records with me. Charles Tachau, a Brandeis relative, made available materials in his private collection, including family photographs and letters that date as far back as 1865; Paul and Gisela Stanton were then kind enough to translate the letters that were in German. Michael Bohnen, an attorney with Brandeis's former law firm in Boston (now called Nutter, McClennen & Fish), gave me a privately published history of the firm as well as access to the surviving case files from Brandeis's private law practice (which became available in 1978 and are now housed with the other pre-Court papers at the University of Louisville).

The book also profited immeasurably from the interviews I conducted with people who knew Brandeis. These individuals reached back into their memories to relive incidents and recall observations that in some cases went back more than sixty years. I am especially grateful for the patience shown by those who received requests for second and third interviews or for written clarification of specific points. The individuals who were interviewed include the following: David C. Acheson (the son of Dean Acheson, a Brandeis clerk), Alice Acheson (Dean Acheson's widow), H. Thomas Austern (Brandeis clerk), Barry Bingham (Louisville journalist), Marquis Childs (Washington journalist), W. Graham Claytor (Brandeis clerk), Benjamin V. Cohen (Brandeis colleague in Zionist and political matters), Thomas G. Corcoran (Holmes clerk and Brandeis colleague in political matters), Irving Dilliard (Washington journalist), Mary Donnellan (Holmes housekeeper), Adrian S. Fisher (Brandeis clerk), Paul A. Freund (Brandeis clerk), Henry J. Friendly (Brandeis clerk), Frank Gilbert (Brandeis grandson), Alger Hiss (Holmes clerk), Donald Hiss (Holmes clerk), J. Willard Hurst (Brandeis clerk), Louis L. Jaffe (Brandeis clerk), Francis Kirkham (Hughes clerk), John Knox (McReynolds clerk), Ward E. Lattin (McReynolds clerk), Max Lerner (writer and journalist), John E. Lockwood (Holmes clerk), Samuel Maslon (Brandeis clerk), Nathaniel L. Nathanson (Brandeis clerk), Alice Gilbert Popkin (Brandeis granddaughter), Edward F. Prichard, Jr. (Frankfurter clerk), Joseph L. Rauh, Jr. (Cardozo and Frankfurter clerk), Elizabeth Brandeis Raushenbush (Brandeis daughter), Walter Raushenbush (Brandeis grandson), David Riesman (Brandeis clerk), H. Chapman Rose (Holmes clerk), Catherine Filene Shouse (daughter of Brandeis friend Lincoln Filene), William Sutherland (Brandeis clerk), Charles Tachau (Brandeis relative), Eric Tachau (Brandeis relative), and Howard Westwood (Stone clerk).

Numerous other individuals took time from busy schedules to review all or part of the manuscript. Their comments and suggestions helped sharpen the book's focus and correct inaccuracies (although any remaining errors and all judgments remain my responsibility alone). These readers include Raymond S. Calamaro, Nelson L. Dawson, Paul A. Freund, William Goldsmith, Janet Hodgson, Cornell Jaray, Renee Licht, Tom Owen, Ira Shapiro, Melvin I. Urofsky, and David Wigdor. Special thanks on this score go to Douglas Katz. He not only gave the manuscript a close reading; he also managed to endure seemingly endless discussions about every aspect of the book without losing his interest or insight.

Joyce Penn, a law student at the time, provided able research assistance at an early stage of the project.

Allene Comiez typed the bulk of the manuscript with unusual skill and dedication. Debbie Brown and Karen Potter helped with the typing at other points.

I also benefited from the generous support of the American Philosophical Society and the Philip M. Stern Foundation.

My literary agent, Oliver Swan, and my editor, John Kirk, were instrumental in the inauguration and completion of the project. I owe them a great debt. I am also grateful to Eric Newman, who was masterful in guiding the book through the production process.

Words are plainly inadequate, though, to express my appreciation to my wife, Jan. She gave the manuscript a critical reading and never seemed to tire of discussing the book's development. And more than that, she and our daughter, Lindsay, were constant reminders that, however immersed I became in the past, there was still much more to enjoy in the present.

And finally my parents. They did not conduct any research or write any part of the book, but their imprint is there nonetheless.

Potomac, Maryland L.J.P.

NOTES AND SOURCES

There is a massive amount of published literature available by and about Louis Brandeis, about the people with whom he worked, and about the times in which he lived. The notes that follow this narrative provide a fair indication of the broad range of secondary sources that were used in the preparation of this biography. Although they have several shortcomings, the collective writings by Alpheus T. Mason remain a significant starting point for any study of Brandeis, but especially of his pre-Court career. On the Court years, the most important published works are Dean Acheson's *Morning and Noon* (1965), Alexander M. Bickel's *The Unpublished Opinions of Mr. Justice Brandeis* (1957), and numerous articles by Paul A. Freund.

Despite the breadth of published material, I relied principally on primary source materials. These sources included interviews with people who knew Brandeis personally, published letters, and unpublished manuscript collections.

Quotations derived from interviews are indicated in the footnotes. In some other instances, especially relating to controversial areas, I have also identified any reliance on interviews. Collectively, the interviews provided the most revealing glimpses of Brandeis. I was particularly fortunate to have had the opportunity to talk with his surviving daughter, Elizabeth Brandeis Raushenbush, all of the eleven surviving Brandeis law clerks, and some other individuals who worked closely with Brandeis in non-judicial matters. In a few instances people gave me information with the understanding that the source of the information would not be identified. I have honored these requests for confidentiality.

The published letters I used are also identified in the footnotes. A special word should be said, however, about the five-volume set of *The Letters of Louis D. Brandeis* (1971–1978) edited by Melvin I. Urofsky and David W. Levy. That collection is by no means comprehensive. For example, it does not include literally thousands of Brandeis letters contained in the papers of Susan Brandeis Gilbert (which, unfortunately, did not become available until after their work was completed). Nonetheless, Urofsky and Levy have provided an invaluable service to all Brandeis scholars by gathering his letters from numerous and widely scattered locations, by deciphering a handwriting that is not always legible, and by adding useful notes to explain and amplify references in the letters. Without their efforts my work would have been much more tedious and time consuming. The *Letters* are identified in the footnotes as "Letters," with additional notations to indicate the volume number. References to Brandeis in the letters (and elsewhere in the footnotes) are identified by his initials, "LDB." For ease of reading, I have corrected spelling and grammatical errors in the letters (and other documents). In no event did I change any words or substance.

The principal manuscript collections I used are identified in the following list. Because most of them are cited frequently as the source for quotations and other statements, I have used in the footnotes the shorthand descriptions given in italics. The descriptions immediately below each identify the full name and location of the particular manuscript collection. The most useful collections were the voluminous Brandeis files at the University of Louisville, the Brandeis Supreme Court papers at Harvard Law School, the Frankfurter Papers, the Gilbert Papers, and the papers of Brandeis's former law firm in Boston, now called Nutter, McClennen & Fish.

Manuscript Collections

Baker Papers
Papers of
Ray Stannard Baker
Library of Congress
Washington, D. C.

Columbia Papers
Columbia University Oral History Project
Columbia University
New York, New York

Evans Papers
Papers of
Elizabeth Glendower Evans
Radcliffe College
Cambridge, Massachusetts

Frankfurter Papers
Papers of
Felix Frankfurter
Library of Congress
Washington, D.C.

Gilbert Papers
Papers of
Susan Brandeis Gilbert
Brandeis University
Waltham, Massachusetts

Harvard Papers
Papers of
Louis D. Brandeis
Harvard Law School
Cambridge, Massachusetts

Holmes Papers
Papers of
Oliver Wendell Holmes
Harvard Law School
Cambridge, Massachusetts

House Papers
Papers of
Edward House
Yale University
New Haven, Connecticut

La Follette Papers
Papers of
Robert M. La Follette
Library of Congress
Washington, D.C.

Louisville Papers
Papers of
Louis D. Brandeis
University of Louisville
Louisville, Kentucky

McReynolds Papers
Papers of
James C. McReynolds
University of Virginia
Charlottesville, Virginia

NMF Papers
Papers of
Nutter, McClennen & Fish
University of Louisville
Louisville, Kentucky

Pinchot Papers
Papers of
Gifford Pinchot
Library of Congress
Washington, D.C.

Roosevelt Papers
Papers of
Franklin D. Roosevelt
Roosevelt Library
Hyde Park, New York

Tachau Papers
Papers of
Charles B. Tachau
Louisville, Kentucky
(private collection)

Taft Papers
Papers of
William Howard Taft
Library of Congress
Washington, D.C.

Tugwell Papers
Papers of
Rexford G. Tugwell
Roosevelt Library
Hyde Park, New York

Wehle Papers
Papers of
Louis B. Wehle
Roosevelt Library
Hyde Park, New York

Wilson Papers
Papers of
Woodrow Wilson
Library of Congress
Washington, D.C.

BEGINNINGS AND ENDINGS

1. Interview with Mrs. Dean Acheson, April 30, 1981; interview with Graham Claytor, October 15, 1980; interview with David Riesman, May 5, 1981.

Interviews with Benjamin V. Cohen, August 13, 1979, February 26, 1981; interview with Thomas Corcoran, November 21, 1979.

"Anti-Jewish Riots Sweep Reich to Avenge Diplomat's Killing; Greatest Terror Orgy Since '33," *Washington Star,* November 10, 1938, p. 1.

Interviews with Adrian Fisher, August 11, 1980, September 17, 1980.

Letter from Benjamin V. Cohen to Felix Frankfurter, November 21, 1938, Frankfurter Papers. The times for Brandeis's meeting with Roosevelt are taken from the Ushers' Diary in the Roosevelt Papers. The president's statement on British immigration policy is reported in S. Rosenman (ed.), *The Public Papers and Addresses of Franklin D. Roosevelt, 1938 Volume: The Struggle for Liberalism Continues* 609 (1941). *See* LDB to Robert Szold, November 24, 1938, *Letters,* Vol. V, p. 605, wherein Brandeis expresses his satisfaction with Roosevelt's statement.

For Brandeis's relationship with the Haganah and David Ben-Gurion, *see* Melvin I. Urofsky, *American Zionism from Herzl to the Holocaust* 379–380 (1976); LDB to Robert Szold, May 23, 1939, *Letters,* Vol. V, p. 619; Files Z/P 61–2, 62–3, 63–1, 66–2, 67–1, 70–1, Louisville Papers.

Chapter One
THE EARLY YEARS

1. George H. Yater, *Two Hundred Years at the Falls of the Ohio: A History of Louisville and Jefferson County* 59 (1979).
2. Quoted in *id.*, p. 55.
3. *Reminiscences of Frederika Dembitz Brandeis* 34 (1944) (privately published); Diary of John Lyle Kind 3 (entry of June 28, 1849), Wehle Papers.
4. *Reminiscences of Frederika Dembitz Brandeis*, p. 31.
5. Quoted in Josephine Goldmark, *Pilgrims of '48: One Man's Part in the Austrian Revolution of 1848 and a Family Migration to America* 202 (1930).
6. Quoted in *id.*, pp. 204–5.
7. Quoted in *id.*, p. 207.
8. A good summary of the forces leading to Kentucky's decision against secession is found in E. Merton Coulter, *The Civil War and Readjustment in Kentucky* 18–56 (Peter Smith ed. 1966). *See also* Yater, *Two Hundred Years at the Falls of the Ohio*, pp. 80–85.
9. Coulter, *Civil War and Readjustment in Kentucky*, p. 53.
10. Ernest Poole, "Introduction," Louis D. Brandeis, *Business—A Profession* xi (1933 ed.). *See* Yater, *Two Hundred Years at the Falls of the Ohio*, p. 88; Coulter, *Civil War and Readjustment in Kentucky*, p. 166.
11. Copies of these letters are in the Tachau Papers.
12. *Letters*, Vol. I, p. 1.
13. *Reminiscences of Frederika Dembitz Brandeis*, p. 20.
14. Quoted in Bert Ford, "Boyhood of Brandeis: An Early View of the Man," *Boston American*, June 4, 1916.
15. Quoted in Edgar Clifton Ross, "An Analysis of Louis D. Brandeis," *Eastern and Western Review*, August 1916.
16. Quoted in Alpheus T. Mason, *Brandeis: A Free Man's Life* 31 (1946).
17. Felix Frankfurter, "Mr. Justice Brandeis," 55 *Harvard Law Review* 181, 183 (1942).

18. Ernest Poole, "Introduction," *Business—A Profession*, p. xi.
19. LDB to Stella and Emily Dembitz, April 22, 1926, *Letters*, Vol. V, p. 219.
20. *See* Robert Shackleton, *The Book of Boston* 230–31 (1923).
21. *See* Arthur E. Sutherland, *The Law at Harvard: A History of Ideas and Men 1817–1967* 49 (1967).
22. Quoted in Edward F. McClennen, "Louis D. Brandeis as a Lawyer," 33 *Massachusetts Law Quarterly* 1, 5 (1948); Bert Ford, "Boyhood of Brandeis: An Early View of the Man."
23. LDB to Otto Wehle, March 12, 1876, *Letters*, Vol. I, p. 6; LDB to Amy Brandeis Wehle, January 20, 1877, *id.*, p. 14. *See also* Louis D. Brandeis, "The Harvard Law School," *The Green Bag*, January 1889, p. 10.
24. LDB to Amy Brandeis Wehle, April 5, 1877, and December 2, 1877, *Letters*, Vol. I, pp. 16–17, 19–20.
25. Quoted in Mason, *Brandeis: A Free Man's Life*, p. 44 (emphasis in original).
26. LDB to Walter Bond Douglas, January 31, 1878, *Letters*, Vol. I, p. 21.
27. In Brandeis's day a 90 or so on a test score was required to receive an "A." By the twentieth century, however, the system was changed so that a person with a test score of about 75 would receive an "A." Also, the law curriculum is now a three-year period instead of a two-year one. *See* James Landis, "Mr. Justice Brandeis and the Harvard Law School," 55 *Harvard Law Review* 184 (1942).
28. Quoted in Poole, "Introduction," *Business—A Profession*, p. xii.
29. Quoted in Mason, *Brandeis: A Free Man's Life*, p. 45; *Reminiscences of Frederika Dembitz Brandeis*, p. 29.
30. Louis B. Wehle to Alpheus T. Mason, June 16, 1943, Wehle Papers.
31. LDB to Frederika Dembitz Brandeis, August 2, 1878, *Letters*, Vol. I, p. 26.
32. *Reminiscences of Frederika Dembitz Brandeis*, p. 22; Mason, *Brandeis: A Free Man's Life*, p. 51.
33. LDB to Jennie Brandeis, September 9, 1928, File 18066, NMF Papers.
34. LDB to Otto Wehle, April 1, 1879, *Letters*, Vol. I, p. 34 (emphasis in original). A good summary of LDB's stay in St. Louis is contained in Burton C. Bernard, "Brandeis in St. Louis," 11 *St. Louis Bar Journal* 54 (1964).
35. Louis D. Brandeis, "Liability of Trust-Estates on Contracts Made for Their Benefit," 15 *American Law Review* 449 (1881), reprinted in Osmond K. Fraenkel, *The Curse of Bigness: Miscellaneous Papers of Louis D. Brandeis* 275 (1934). *See* LDB to Otto Wehle, April 1, 1879, *Letters*, Vol. I, p. 33; Oliver Wendell Holmes, Jr., to LDB, July 7, 1881, Holmes Papers.
36. LDB to Amy Brandeis Wehle, January 1879, *Letters*, Vol. I, pp. 28–29; LDB to Amy Brandeis Wehle, February 1, 1879, *id.*, p. 30.

Chapter Two
THE BOSTON PRACTICE

1. Quoted in M. Bradley, *Samuel Dennis Warren* 2 (1956).
2. Quoted in *Nutter, McClennen & Fish: The First Century, 1879–1979* 2 (1979) (privately published).
3. Quoted in *id.*, pp. 2–3.
4. LDB to Samuel D. Warren, Jr., May 30, 1879, *Letters*, Vol. I, p. 35.
5. Quoted in Alpheus T. Mason, *Brandeis: A Free Man's Life* 57 (1946). It should be noted that Brandeis and other family members sometimes referred to his sister as "Fanny" and at other times as "Fannie."
6. LDB to Charles Nagel, July 12, 1879, *Letters*, Vol. I, p. 37.
7. *Id.*, p. 39.
8. *Id.*, pp. 41–42.
9. LDB to Alfred Brandeis, July 31, 1879, *id.*, p. 44.
10. Quoted in Mason, *Brandeis: A Free Man's Life*, p. 61. The Rhode Island case was *Allen* v. *Woonsocket*, 13 R.I. 146 (1880).

11. Quoted in Mason, *Brandeis: A Free Man's Life*, p. 61.
12. Felix Frankfurter to Alexander M. Bickel, November 13, 1956, Frankfurter Papers (Frankfurter was quoting and agreeing with a comment by one of Brandeis's law clerks); LDB to Charles Nagel, July 12, 1879, *Letters*, Vol. I, p. 40; LDB to Amy Brandeis Wehle, January 2, 1881, *id.*, p. 62.
13. Oliver Wendell Holmes, Jr., to LDB, September 4, 1902, File M17–1, Louisville Papers.
14. Quoted in Mason, *Brandeis: A Free Man's Life*, p. 66.
15. Quoted in Alfred Lief, *Brandeis: The Personal History of an American Ideal* 27 (1936); LDB to Adolph Brandeis, May 30, 1883, *Letters*, Vol. I, p. 65.
16. Quoted in Mason, *Brandeis: A Free Man's Life*, p. 69; LDB to Alfred Brandeis, March 21, 1887, *Letters*, Vol. I, p. 73.
17. *See* James M. Landis, "Memorandum Detailing Conversation with LDB at a Dinner at the Hotel Bellevue," June 2, 1932, Frankfurter Papers.
18. Quoted in S.S. Miller, "Notes on Certain Influences in the Life of Mrs. Glendower Evans," August 19, 1938, Evans Papers; "Memoirs of Elizabeth Glendower Evans" 5 (undated), *id.*
19. "Memoirs of Elizabeth Glendower Evans," p. 5.
20. *Id.*; Elizabeth Glendower Evans to LDB, December 1, 1908, Evans Papers.
21. LDB to Elizabeth Glendower Evans, August 7, 1887, *Letters*, Vol. I, pp. 73–74.
22. Elizabeth Glendower Evans to LDB, September 7, 1935, File SC 15–3, Louisville Papers.

Chapter Three
THE PUBLIC ADVOCATE EMERGES

1. LDB to Frederika Dembitz Brandeis, November 12, 1888, *Letters*, Vol. I, p. 75.
2. LDB to Alfred Brandeis, September 11, 1880, *id.*, p. 57. For a good summary of Mugwump politics in Boston, *see* G. Blodgett, *The Gentle Reformers: Massachusetts Democrats in the Cleveland Era* (1966).
3. Quoted in "Memoirs of Elizabeth Glendower Evans," 3 (undated), Evans Papers. *See also* Alfred Lief, *Brandeis: The Personal History of an American Ideal* 32–33 (1936).
4. *See* Letter to Alumni of Harvard Law School, August 9, 1886, *Letters*, Vol. I, p. 69; James Landis, "Mr. Justice Brandeis and the Harvard Law School," 55 *Harvard Law Review* 184 (1942).
5. S. Warren and L. Brandeis, "The Watuppa Pond Cases," 2 *Harvard Law Review* 195 (1888); S. Warren and L. Brandeis, "The Law of the Ponds," 3 *Harvard Law Review* 1 (1889).
6. LDB to Joseph Beale, March 19, 1912, File 22663, NMF Papers. *See* File 23778, NMF Papers.
7. 4 Harvard Law Review 193, 195–196, 205 (1890).
8. *Id.*, p. 213 (footnote omitted).
9. *See* James H. Barron, "Warren and Brandeis, *The Right to Privacy*, 4 Harvard Law Review 193 (1890): Demystifying a Landmark Citation," 13 *Suffolk University Law Review* 875, 880–81, 895–97 (1979), and sources cited there.
10. Roscoe Pound to Senator William Chilton, February 8, 1916, Frankfurter Papers.
11. William Prosser, "Privacy," 48 *California Law Review* 383 (1960).
12. P. Dionisopoulos and C. Ducat, *The Right to Privacy* 20 (1976).
13. Alpheus T. Mason, *Brandeis: A Free Man's Life* 70 (1946).
14. For example, Harry Kalven, "Privacy in Tort Law—Were Warren and Brandeis Wrong?" 31 *Law & Contemporary Problems* 326, 329, n. 22 (1966).
15. Prosser, 48 *California Law Review* at 423 (footnote omitted).
16. *Boston Herald*, January 1, 1890, reprinted in *Saturday Evening Gazette*, January 11, 1890, p. 2; *Boston Post*, January 5, 1890, reprinted in *Saturday Evening Gazette*, January 11, 1890, p. 2.
17. *Saturday Evening Gazette*, September 20, 1890, p. 1; *Saturday Evening Gazette*, January 22, 1888, p. 2; *Saturday Evening Gazette*, June 7, 1890, p. 3. *See generally* Barron 13

Suffolk University Law Review at 891–907. Barron summarized much of the literature on the Warren and Brandeis article; he also did a considerable amount of original research into press coverage at the time the privacy article was published.
18. *See* LDB to Samuel D. Warren, Jr., April 8, 1905, *Letters*, Vol. I, p. 302. One biographer has suggested that the cause of Warren's concern was some photographs of his daughter taken by a newspaperman. *See* Lief, *Brandeis: The Personal History of an American Ideal*, p. 51. I could not find anything to substantiate that view.
19. *Saturday Evening Gazette*, February 9, 1889, p. 2.
20. Allon Gal, *Brandeis of Boston* 36 (1980).
21. Interview with Thomas G. Corcoran, October 17, 1980; Interview with Learned Hand, p. 81, Columbia Papers; Felix Frankfurter to Alexander M. Bickel, November 13, 1956, Frankfurter Papers.
22. LDB to Alice Goldmark, December 28, 1890, *Letters*, Vol. I, p. 97; LDB to Alice Goldmark, November 29, 1890, *id.*, p. 95; LDB to Alice Goldmark, February 26, 1891, *id.*, p. 100.
23. Freedom of Information Act, 5 U.S.C. § 552; Sunshine in Government Act, 5 U.S.C. § 552b.
24. Quoted in Mason, *Brandeis: A Free Man's Life*, p. 89. *See* LDB to George W. Anderson, March 6, 1916, *Letters*, Vol. IV, p. 104.
25. Argument of Louis D. Brandeis before the Joint Committee on Liquor Laws of the Massachusetts Legislature (February 27, 1890), pp. 7, 17–18, Scrapbook I, Louisville Papers.
26. LDB Notes for MIT Lectures, p. 175, File A4–3, Louisville Papers.
27. *Id.*, pp. 179–80.
28. *Id.*, p. 15. *Compare* Louis D. Brandeis, *Other People's Money and How the Bankers Use It* 91–109 (Harper Torchbook edition 1967).
29. Livy S. Richard, "Up from Aristocracy," *The Independent*, July 27, 1914.
30. Hearings before the Committee of the Whole Board of Aldermen, *Care and Management of the Public Institutions*, Vol. III, 3629–30 (1894).
31. *Id.*, p. 3632.
32. Quoted in Mason, *Brandeis: A Free Man's Life*, p. 92; *Boston Herald*, January 12, 1897.

Chapter Four
THE PRIVATE LIFE

1. Quoted in Dean Acheson, *Morning and Noon* 48 (1965).
2. *Reminiscences of Frederika Dembitz Brandeis* 16 (1943) (privately published).
3. Interview with Charles B. Tachau, September 16, 1980. *See* LDB to Adolph Brandeis, December 16, 1889, *Letters*, Vol. I, p. 84.
4. LDB to Alice Goldmark, October 2, 1890, Gilbert Papers; Alpheus T. Mason, *Brandeis: A Free Man's Life* 73 (1946); Elizabeth Glendower Evans, "Justice Brandeis in the Intimacy of His Home," *The Jewish Advocate*, November 14, 1931.
5. Alice Goldmark to LDB, December 11, 1890, Gilbert Papers; LDB to Alice Goldmark, December 4, 1890, and March 15, 1891, *Letters*, Vol. I, pp. 95, 101.
6. LDB to Alice Goldmark, October 1, 1890, *Letters*, Vol. I, p. 92; LDB to Alice Goldmark, January 7, 1891, *id.*, p. 99.
7. Alice Brandeis to Elizabeth Glendower Evans, March 27, 1891, Evans Papers.
8. LDB to Elizabeth Glendower Evans, March 31, 1893, *Letters*, Vol. I, p. 110; Alice Brandeis to Elizabeth Glendower Evans, May 3, 1893, Evans Papers.
9. Interview with Elizabeth Brandeis Raushenbush, May 31, 1980; Evans, "Justice Brandeis in the Intimacy of His Home."
10. *Id.*
11. *See*, for example, grocery lists in Files 17732, 18334, NMF Papers.
12. Jean B. Tachau to Allon Gal, October 10, 1973, Tachau Papers.
13. Interview with H. Thomas Austern, January 12, 1981.

14. Interview with Elizabeth Brandeis Raushenbush.
15. LDB to William H. Dunbar, February 2, 1893, *Letters*, Vol. I, p. 109.
16. Quoted in Mason, *Brandeis: A Free Man's Life*, p. 78.
17. Allon Gal asserts that Brandeis was ostracized from social life in Dedham because he was Jewish and a social reformer. Gal, *Brandeis of Boston* 171–73 (1980). Although Gal is probably right to some extent, it is also true that Brandeis's restricted social life was due in great part to Alice's poor health. *See* Felix Frankfurter to Alexander M. Bickel, November 13, 1956, Frankfurter Papers.
18. Alice Brandeis to LDB, March 10, 1896, Gilbert Papers; LDB to Elizabeth Brandeis, December 29, 1900, *id.*
19. A. Cabot, "Sketch of Samuel Dennis Warren," reprinted in M. Bradley, *Samuel Dennis Warren* 11 (1956); *Nutter, McClennen & Fish: The First Century, 1879–1979* 5–6 (1979) (privately published).
20. *Wisconsin R.R.* v. *Price County*, 133 U.S. 496 (1889); LDB to Alfred Brandeis, March 20, 1889, *Letters*, Vol. I, p. 78.
21. *See*, for example, *S.D. Warren Estate* v. *Para Rubber Co.*, File 6479, NMF Papers. An excellent summary of Brandeis's legal practice is found in E. McClennen, "Louis D. Brandeis as a Lawyer," 33 *Massachusetts Law Quarterly* 1 (1948).
22. LDB to Amy Brandeis Wehle, February 1, 1895, *Letters*, Vol. I, p. 120.
23. Edward A. Filene to LDB, November 11, 1936, File M9–16, Louisville Papers.
24. *See* correspondence in Files 4223, 18337, NMF Papers.
25. *See* Mason, *Brandeis: A Free Man's Life*, pp. 80–82.
26. LDB to William H. Dunbar, February 2, 1893, *Letters*, Vol. I, pp. 106–9.
27. Quoted in Mason, *Brandeis: A Free Man's Life*, pp. 80–82.
28. Quoted in *Nutter, McClennen & Fish*, p. 7.
29. LDB to William H. Dunbar, August 19, 1896, *Letters*, Vol. I, p. 124.
30. LDB to William H. Dunbar, November 2, 1896, reprinted in *Nutter, McClennen & Fish*, pp. 11–12; McClennen, "Louis D. Brandeis as a Lawyer," 33 *Massachusetts Law Quarterly* at 23–24.
31. *See*, for example, Alice H. Grady to LDB, December 18, 1909, File 18337, NMF Papers; Alice H. Grady to LDB, January 5, 1915, File Z/P 2–5, Louisville Papers.
32. Alice H. Grady to LDB, December 28, 1906, File M 17–1, Louisville Papers. Much of the discussion here concerning Grady is based on an interview with Elizabeth Brandeis Raushenbush and numerous files in the NMF Papers.
33. *See* LDB to Alfred Brandeis, July 28, 1904, *Letters*, Vol. I, p. 262.
34. *Nutter, McClennen & Fish*, pp. 14–15. Professor Mason has stated that Brandeis was making almost $50,000 by 1890. *See* Mason, *Brandeis: A Free Man's Life*, p. 640. Although it is possible that Brandeis was making that much then, I could not substantiate it. It may be overstated somewhat, though. Figures for 1894 indicate that, in that year at least, Brandeis earned only $6,800 from the firm. File 7263, NMF Papers.
35. Quoted in Alfred Lief, *The Brandeis Guide to the Modern World* 38 (1941); Edward A. Filene, "Louis D. Brandeis as We Know Him," *Boston Post*, March 4, 1916.

Chapter Five
THE TRANSIT FIGHTS AND THEIR AFTERMATH

1. LDB to Alfred Brandeis, March 20, 1886, *Letters*, Vol. I, p. 68.
2. Much of the material for this discussion, as well as the remaining parts of Chapter Five, relies on a summary of the transit controversies that was apparently prepared by Filene and can be found in File NMF 1–5a, Louisville Papers. *See* Richard Abrams, *Conservatism in a Progressive Era* 53–79 (1964).
3. LDB to editor of the *Boston Evening Transcript*, April 30, 1897, *Letters*, Vol. I, p. 128.
4. Urofsky and Levy state that Brandeis made these arguments before he sent the letter to the *Transcript*. LDB to William Ames Bancroft, May 21, 1897, n. 1, *id.*, p. 132. The Filene

summary referred to in note 2 above, however, states that the Municipal League made its presentation on May 12, 1897, after Brandeis sent the letter. Since Urofsky and Levy do not cite any source for their claim, I have relied on the Filene summary.

5. LDB to Albert E. Pillsbury, May 20, 1897, *id.*, p. 131.

6. *Hearings before the Subcommittee of the Senate Committee on the Judiciary on the Nomination of Louis D. Brandeis to be an Associate Justice of the Supreme Court of the United States, Part I* (hereafter *Nomination Hearings*), 64th Cong., 1st Sess. 654 (1916).

7. *See* LDB to Board of Railroad Commissioners, October 21, 1897, *Letters*, Vol. I, p. 133; Abrams, *Conservatism in a Progressive Era*, pp. 64–65.

8. Quoted in Abrams, *Conservatism in a Progressive Era*, p. 65.

9. Robert A. Boit to LDB, March 21, 1900, File NMF 4–2, Louisville Papers.

10. LDB's statement is found in File NMF 1–5, Louisville Papers.

11. *See* Abrams, *Conservatism in a Progressive Era*, p. 62; LDB to Edward H. Clement, April 18, 1900, *Letters*, Vol. I, p. 142.

12. LDB to Edward McClennen, February 28, 1916, *Letters*, Vol. IV, pp. 93–94.

13. *Boston Evening Transcript*, June 19, 1901.

14. Quoted in *Nomination Hearings*, pp. 658–59.

15. Albert E. Pillsbury to LDB, April 30, 1902, *Letters*, Vol. I, p. 191.

16. Elizabeth Glendower Evans, "People I Have Known: Alice Goldmark Brandeis," *The Progressive*, July 26, 1930; LDB to Alice Brandeis, September 15, 1900, Gilbert Papers.

17. LDB to Alice Brandeis, August 21, 1901, Gilbert Papers.

18. LDB to Edward A. Filene, June 1, 1901, *Letters*, Vol. I, p. 170; LDB to William H. McElwain, June 18, 1902, *id.*, pp. 204–5. *See* LDB to Benjamin F. Keith, November 5, 1901, *id.*, p. 176.

19. Osmond K. Fraenkel, *The Curse of Bigness: Miscellaneous Papers of Louis D. Brandeis* 263–65 (1934).

20. Benjamin Wells to LDB, April 4, 1903, File NMF 6–5, Louisville Papers.

21. LDB to George V. Crocker, March 20, 1903, *Letters*, Vol. I, p. 227.

22. From a history of the Good Government Association prepared by George Nutter, a Brandeis law partner, quoted in Abrams, *Conservatism in a Progressive Era*, p. 144.

23. LDB to Elizabeth Glendower Evans, August 6, 1896, *Letters*, Vol. I, p. 124.

24. Quoted in Elizabeth Glendower Evans, "Mr. Justice Brandeis: The People's Tribune," *The Survey*, October 29, 1931.

25. Quoted in Edward A. Filene, "Louis D. Brandeis as We Know Him," *Boston Post*, March 4, 1916.

26. Henry Cabot Lodge to Theodore Roosevelt, September 22, 1902, Elting E. Morison (ed.), *The Letters of Theodore Roosevelt*, Vol. I, pp. 528–29 (1951).

27. LDB to Clarence Darrow, December 12, 1902, *Letters*, Vol. I, p. 213. *See* LDB to Henry Demarest Lloyd, December 20, 1902, *id.*, p. 219.

28. Louis D. Brandeis, "The Employer and Trade Union," in *Business—A Profession* 17 (1933 ed.).

29. Quoted in *La Follette's Weekly Magazine*, May 24, 1913, p. 5.

30. This account of the debate is taken from the *Boston Herald*, December 5, 1902.

31. Quoted in Felix Frankfurter and Nathan Greene, *The Labor Injunction* 143 (1930).

32. *Duplex Co.* v. *Deering*, 254 U.S. 443, 488 (1921) (dissent). *See* Files 5–9, 5–10, Harvard Papers.

33. *United Mine Workers* v. *Coronado Coal Co.*, 259 U.S. 344 (1922).

34. Brandeis–Frankfurter Conversations, File 114, Harvard Papers. The typed version in the Frankfurter Papers quotes Brandeis as stating ". . . they will take [it] from Taft but wouldn't from us." Since the Harvard Papers include Frankfurter's original handwritten notes, I have chosen to rely on them here. *See* Alexander M. Bickel, *The Unpublished Opinions of Mr. Justice Brandeis: The Supreme Court at Work* 97 (1957).

Chapter Six
THE GAS FIGHT

1. Edward Warren to LDB, April 30, 1904, NMF File 10–1, Louisville Papers.
2. LDB to Edward Warren, May 2, 1904, *Letters*, Vol. I, p. 252.
3. LDB to Edward Warren, May 9, 1904, *id.*, p. 254.
4. Statement of LDB before the Joint Legislative Committee on Public Lighting, March 9, 1905, pp. 1–2, 6, 8–9, 11, Clipping I, Scrapbook Box 233, Louisville Papers.
5. Quoted in the *Boston Globe*, March 9, 1905.
6. Quoted in Alpheus T. Mason, *Brandeis: A Free Man's Life* 132 (1946).
7. Edward Warren to LDB, March 10, 1905; LDB to Edward Warren, March 13, 1905, *Letters*, Vol. I, pp. 292–93.
8. *Hearings before the Subcommittee on the Committee on the Judiciary on the Nomination of Louis D. Brandeis to be an Associate Justice of the Supreme Court of the United States, Part I*, 64th Cong., 1st Sess. 1309, 1312 (1916).
9. *Id.*, p. 1312.
10. Quoted in Alfred Lief, *Brandeis: The Personal History of an American Ideal* 79 (1936).
11. *See* Alice H. Grady to LDB, March 31, 1905, File NMF 10–1, Louisville Papers. Grady advised Brandeis that Sprague had canvassed the gas commissioners and found them unanimously opposed to the sliding scale system. Within a short time after the meeting with Richards, Brandeis was advised by Babson that the possibility of its adoption by the legislature was remote. Thomas M. Babson to LDB, May 4, 1905, *id.*
12. *See* LDB to Floyd E. Chamberlain, May 10, 1905, *Letters*, Vol. I, p. 323.
13. George W. Anderson to LDB, May 6, 1905, File NMF 10–1, Louisville Papers.
14. *See*, for example, *Letters*, Vol. I, pp. 334–40, 352, 358–59.
15. Edmund Billings to LDB, November 21, 1905, File NMF 8–2, Louisville Papers.
16. LDB to Charles P. Hall, January 25, 1906, *Letters*, Vol. I, p. 399.
17. *See*, for example, LDB to Edwin A. Grozier, May 5, 1906, *id.*, p. 431.
18. LDB to Alfred Brandeis, May 20, 1906, *id.*, p. 436.
19. LDB to Alfred Brandeis, May 27, 1906, *id.*, p. 438.
20. For Brandeis's overall view of the gas legislation, *see* his article "How Boston Solved the Gas Problem" in *Business—A Profession* 99 (1933 ed.).

Chapter Seven
THE STRUGGLE FOR SAVINGS BANK LIFE INSURANCE

1. Quoted in Alpheus T. Mason, *The Brandeis Way: A Case Study in the Workings of Democracy* 87 (1938).
2. *See id.*, pp. 91–92.
3. LDB to Edward F. McClennen, February 11, 1916, *Letters*, Vol. IV, p. 51.
4. LDB to Policy Holders of Equitable Life Assurance Society, July 22, 1905, *id.*, Vol. I, pp. 341–45.
5. LDB to Adolph Brandeis, July 27, 1905, *id.*, p. 351.
6. Louis D. Brandeis, "Life Insurance: The Abuses and the Remedies," in *Business—A Profession* 125 (1933 ed).
7. *Id.*, p. 142.
8. *Id.*, pp. 153–54.
9. *Id.*, pp. 158–59.
10. LDB to Alice Brandeis, July 7, 1905, Gilbert Papers.
11. LDB to Alice Brandeis, September 15, 1906; LDB to Alice Brandeis, November 21, 1906; LDB to Alice Brandeis, November 25, 1906; LDB to "Our Girls," August 7, 1907, Gilbert Papers.

12. LDB to John E. Pembar, February 4, 1908, *Letters*, Vol. II, p. 74. *See* LDB to Gertrude B. Beeks, April 21, 1908, *id.*, p. 129; LDB to Eben S. Draper, June 5, 1908, *id.*, p. 176.
13. LDB to Walter Channing Wright, November 24, 1905, *id.*, Vol. I, p. 381.
14. LDB to Charles P. Hall, June 12, 1906, *id.*, p. 446.
15. LDB to Norman Hapgood, June 25, 1906, *id.*, p. 448.
16. LDB to Edward F. McClennen, February 11, 1916, *id.*, Vol. IV, p. 52.
17. *See* John P. Frank, "The Legal Ethics of Louis D. Brandeis," 17 *Stanford Law Review* 683, 690–92 (1965).
18. Louis D. Brandeis, "Wage-Earners' Life Insurance," *Collier's* magazine, September 15, 1906, reprinted in *Business—A Profession*, pp. 160–87, and in Mason, *The Brandeis Way*, pp. 311–25.
19. Quoted in Mason, *The Brandeis Way*, pp. 134–35.
20. LDB to Norman White, August 1, 1906, *Letters*, Vol. I, p. 464.
21. Quoted in *Mason, The Brandeis Way*, p. 175.
22. Quoted in the *Boston Post*, November 14, 1906.
23. LDB to Henry Morgenthau, Sr., November 20, 1906, *Letters*, Vol. I, p. 483.
24. W.H. Scott to LDB, December 5, 1906, quoted in Mason, *The Brandeis Way*, p. 197.
25. LDB to W.H. Scott, December 6, 1906, *Letters*, Vol. I, p. 508.
26. William L. Douglas to Massachusetts Savings Insurance League, January 14, 1906, quoted in Mason, *The Brandeis Way*, p. 161.
27. LDB to Alfred Brandeis, January 3, 1907, *Letters*, Vol. I, p. 514.
28. LDB to Alfred Brandeis, March 21, 1907, *id.*, p. 530.
29. Quoted in Mason, *The Brandeis Way*, p. 183.
30. Warren A. Reed to LDB, March 23, 1907, quoted in *id.*, pp. 184–85.
31. LDB to William S. Kyle, April 29, 1907, *Letters*, Vol. I, p. 559.
32. Quoted in Mason, *The Brandeis Way*, p. 217.
33. LBD to Alfred Brandeis, June 13, 1907, *Letters;* Vol. I, p. 584.
34. Alfred Lief, *Brandeis: The Personal History of an American Ideal* 105 (1936).

Chapter Eight
THE RISE AND FALL OF THE NEW HAVEN RAILROAD

1. Theodore Roosevelt, *Presidential Addresses and State Papers*, Vol. IV, 419–20 (1910). *See generally* Jerold S. Auerbach, *Unequal Justice: Lawyers and Social Change in Modern America* 14–39 (1976); David W. Levy, "The Lawyer as Judge: Brandeis' View of the Legal Profession," 22 *Oklahoma Law Review* 374, 376–80 (1969).
2. Louis D. Brandeis, "Opportunity in the Law," in *Business—A Profession* 329, 337, 339, 340, 342 (1933 ed.).
3. Quoted in Matthew Josephson, *The Robber Barons: The Great American Capitalists, 1861–1901* 299 (1962 ed.).
4. *See* Richard Abrams, *Conservatism in a Progressive Era* 194–97 (1964).
5. Testimony of Louis D. Brandeis before the Joint Special Committee on Railroads and Street Railway Laws, July 11, 1905, p. 20, File NMF 1B–1, Louisville Papers.
6. *Boston Globe*, June 23, 1906.
7. LDB to William H. Dunbar, June 12, 1907, *Letters*, Vol. I, p. 583; LDB to Edward A. Filene, June 29, 1907, *id.*, p. 592; LDB to Alfred Brandeis, June 19, 1907, *id.*, p. 585.
8. Testimony of Louis D. Brandeis before the Legislative Committee on Railroads, June 10, 1907, pp. 3, 18, 20, File NMF 1B–1, Louisville Papers.
9. *Id.*, pp. 198, 211.
10. LDB to Massachusetts Board of Railroad Commissioners, October 19, 1907, *Letters*, Vol. II, p. 30. Brandeis's identification of the New England Security & Investment Company was incorrect in that he switched two of the words.
11. LDB to Alfred Brandeis, October 19, 1907, *id.*, p. 31.
12. Testimony of Louis D. Brandeis before the Commission on Commerce & Industry, November 22, 1907, p. 7, File NMF IC–4, Louisville Papers.

13. LDB to E. Louise Malloch, November 4, 1907, *Letters*, Vol. II, p. 44.
14. Louis D. Brandeis, *Financial Conditions of the New York, New Haven and Hartford Railroad Company and of the Boston and Maine Railroad* 13, 41 (1907) (privately published).
15. Quoted in Henry Lee Staples and Alpheus T. Mason, *The Fall of a Railroad Empire: Brandeis and the New Haven Merger Battle* 35–36 (1947).
16. LDB to Alfred Brandeis, January 2, 1908, *Letters*, Vol. II, p. 61; LDB to Alfred Brandeis, October 19, 1907, *id.*, p. 31.
17. Staples and Mason, *The Fall of a Railroad Empire*, p. 183. *See* Abrahams (ed.), "Brandeis and Lamont on Finance Capitalism," 47 *Business History Review* 72 (1973).
18. Louis D. Brandeis, "The New England Transportation Monopoly," in *Business—a Profession*, pp. 262, 275, 276, 278.
19. LDB to Alfred Brandeis, February 10, 1908, *Letters*, Vol. II, p. 77.
20. LDB to Alfred Brandeis, March 27, 1908, *id.*, p. 111.
21. Transcript of Debate Between Louis D. Brandeis and Timothy Byrnes before the Cambridge Citizens Trade Association, March 25, 1908, pp. 12, 15, 40, File NMF IT–1, Louisville Papers; *See Letters*, Vol. II, p. 137.
22. LDB to Joseph Walker, May 19, 1908, *id.*, p. 157.
23. *See* LDB to Alfred Brandeis, February 2, 1908, *id.*, p. 68; LDB to Theodore Roosevelt, April 21, 1908, *id.*, p. 130; Staples and Mason, *The Fall of an Empire*, p. 62.
24. LDB to Alfred Brandeis, May 18, 1908, *Letters*, Vol. II, p. 156. *See* LDB to Alfred Brandeis, May 18, 1908, *Letters*, Vol. II, p. 155. Edwin Grozier had earlier asked Brandeis to take over the *Post*'s editorial pages. Brandeis declined, but he did maintain a close relationship with Grozier. E.A. Grozier to LDB, August 29, 1907; LDB to E.A. Grozier, September 3, 1907, File 16598, NMF Papers.
25. LDB to Alfred Brandeis, June 14, 1908, *Letters*, Vol. II, p. 185.
26. Transcript of LDB Interview with the *Boston Herald*, July 10, 1908, File 17720, NMF Papers; LDB to Alfred Brandeis, July 13, 1908, *Letters*, Vol. II, p. 198.
27. LDB to Edward A. Filene, May 24, 1909, *Letters*, Vol. II, p. 262; *see id.*, pp. 260–61.
28. Louis D. Brandeis, "Arguments before the Committee on Railroads," May 19, 1909, pp. 2, 15–16, File 17720, NMF Papers.
29. LDB to Alfred Brandeis, May 22, 1909, *Letters*, Vol. II, p. 259.
30. LDB to Alfred Brandeis, June 6, 1909, *id.*, p. 279; LDB to Alfred Brandeis, June 15, 1909, *id.*, p. 282.
31. LDB to Alfred Brandeis, June 18, 1907, *id.,* Vol. I, p. 584. *See,* for example, *Fall River News,* May 28, 1908; *Boston Globe,* March 7, 1913.
32. LDB to Norman Hapgood, September 25, 1911, *Letters*, Vol. II, pp. 500–501.
33. LDB to Eugene Foss, April 15, 1912, *id.*, p. 584.
34. Memorandum of LDB meeting with Governor Foss, September 9, 1912, File NMF IK–2, Louisville Papers.
35. The *Boston Post*, December 1, 1912.
36. *Letters*, Vol. II, p. 729.
37. *Id.*, Vol. III, p. 72.
38. Quoted in Staples and Mason, *The Fall of an Empire*, pp. 134–35.
39. *See* memoranda and correspondence in File NMF IM–2, Louisville Papers.
40. *See* memoranda and correspondence in Files NMF IN–1, IN–3, Louisville Papers; Diaries of Edward House, Book III, pp. 324, 330, House Papers; Alfred Lief, *Brandeis: The Personal History of an American Ideal* 293–96 (1936). I have no direct evidence that McReynolds expressed resentment toward Brandeis on this matter. However, given Brandeis's prominent role in the affair, the public attacks it generated against McReynolds, and the attorney general's thin skin, there seems little doubt that he did resent Brandeis. It is also noteworthy here that McReynolds always seemed "tired" to Brandeis whenever they met on New Haven matters; more likely, it was McReynolds's distaste at having to meet with the Boston attorney. However, McReynolds could not say anything directly to Brandeis because of Brandeis's well-known intimacy with both Wilson and House. *See* LDB to Alice

Brandeis, December 18, 1913; LDB to Alice Brandeis, February 27, 1914, *Letters*, Vol. III, pp. 224, 259; LDB to Alice Brandeis, November 24, 1913, LDB to Alice Brandeis, "Mother's Birthday," 1914, Gilbert Papers.
41. George R. Conroy, "Schiff and Brandeis," *Truth*, April 18, 1914; LDB to Alfred Brandeis, April 9, 1913, *Letters*, Vol. III, p. 58.
42. ICC Report No. 6569, In re *Financial Transactions of the New York, New Haven & Hartford Railroad Co.*, Doc. No. 543, United States Senate, 63rd Cong., 2d Sess. 2, 6, 16–17, 35 (1914).
43. Louis D. Brandeis, "Monopoly A Failure," *Business America*, August 1913, pp. 120–121.
44. Quoted in Lief, *Brandeis*, p. 266.

Chapter Nine
THE BALLINGER–PINCHOT CONTROVERSY AND ITS AFTERMATH

1. William Howard Taft to Richard A. Ballinger, September 13, 1909, Taft Papers.
2. Louis Glavis to William Howard Taft, September 20, 1909, *id.*
3. William Howard Taft to Gifford Pinchot, January 7, 1910, reprinted in *Investigation of the Department of the Interior and the Bureau of Forestry*, Senate Doc. 719, 61st Cong., 3rd Sess. 1289–90 (1910) (hereafter *Hearings*).
4. *See* LDB to Norman Hapgood, March 14, 1916, *Letters*, Vol. IV, p. 118.
5. *Hearings*, p. 4046. *See id.*, p. 5010.
6. *Id.*, pp. 4017–31.
7. *See id.*, pp. 952–53, 1248.
8. *Id.*, p. 330.
9. *Id.*, pp. 60–61, 853–55.
10. *See id.*, p. 4909.
11. *Id.*, pp. 3980–81.
12. *Id.*, pp. 949–55.
13. Quoted in Norman Hapgood, *The Changing Years* 186–87 (1930).
14. *Hearings*, p. 4074.
15. *Id.*, p. 4918.
16. *Id.*, pp. 4129–30. Portions of the transcript here have been deleted to facilitate reading.
17. Quoted in James Penick, Jr., *Progressive Politics and Conservation: The Ballinger–Pinchot Affair* 43 (1968).
18. Quoted in Harold Ickes, "Not Guilty: An Official Inquiry into the Charges Made by Glavis and Pinchot Against Richard A. Ballinger, Secretary of the Interior, 1909–1911," 18 (GPO 1940).
19. *Hearings*, pp. 4918–4919.
20. *See* Ickes, "Not Guilty," pp. 26–27.
21. Quoted in James David Barber, *Presidential Performance: Predicting Performance in the White House* 176 (1972).
22. Archibald Butt, *Taft and Roosevelt: The Intimate Papers of Archie Butt*, Vol. I, 294 (1930).
23. William Howard Taft to Horace Taft, June 6, 1909, quoted in Gifford Pinchot, *Breaking New Ground* 431 (1947).
24. *Hearings*, pp. 3858–59. Portions of the transcript here have been deleted to facilitate reading.
25. *Id.*, p. 3805.
26. William Howard Taft to Richard A. Ballinger, September 13, 1909, Taft Papers.
27. LDB to Alfred Brandeis, November 4, 1908, *Letters*, Vol. II, p. 213.
28. Quoted in Ickes, "Not Guilty," p. 47, n. 18.
29. LDB to Regina Wehle Goldmark, March 2, 1910, *Letters*, Vol. II, p. 325. *See* LDB to Alfred Brandeis, February 28, 1910, *id.*, p. 324.
30. *Hearings*, p. 4492.
31. *Id.*, pp. 4070–71; *Providence Journal*, May 11, 1910.

32. *Hearings*, p. 3868.
33. *Id.*, p. 3881.
34. Alice H. Grady to Alfred Brandeis, May 13, 1910, File NMF 33–2, Louisville Papers.
35. LDB to Alfred Brandeis, May 1, 1910, *Letters*, Vol. II, pp. 332–33.
36. LDB to Alice Brandeis, April 23, 1910, Gilbert Papers.
37. *See* Frederick M. Kerby, "A Washington Plot That Failed" (1924), an unpublished manuscript in the Pinchot Papers.
38. *Hearings*, pp. 3865–67. Portions of the transcript here have been deleted to facilitate reading.
39. LDB to Alice Brandeis, May 13, 1910, Gilbert Papers.
40. Quoted in Hapgood, *The Changing Years*, p. 190.
41. *Hearings*, pp. 4922–23.
42. Interview with David Acheson, January 8, 1981.
43. Interview with Gardner Jackson, pp. 493–94, Columbia Papers.
44. LDB to Alfred Brandeis, June 14, 1910, *Letters*, Vol. II, p. 348.
45. *See*, for example, LDB to Robert M. La Follette, July 29, 1911, *id.*, p. 467.
46. The *Washington Times*, April 20, 1911.
47. Quoted in Alpheus T. Mason, *Brandeis: A Free Man's Life* 283 (1946).
48. Interview with William A. Sutherland, November 7, 1980.

Chapter Ten
A NEW LABOR–MANAGEMENT PARTNERSHIP

1. A. Lincoln Filene to Edward A. Filene, July 18, 1910, Filene Papers, quoted in *Letters*, Vol. II, p. 365, n. 2.
2. Louis D. Brandeis, *Business—A Profession* 21–22 (1933 ed.).
3. Osmond K. Fraenkel, *The Curse of Bigness: Miscellaneous Papers of Louis D. Brandeis* 36 (1934).
4. LDB Speech to Buyers' Conference, March 15, 1913, File NMF 57–3, Louisville Papers.
5. LDB to Julius H. Cohen, July 24, 1910, *Letters*, Vol. II, p. 366.
6. *Minutes of Joint Conference Between the Delegates of the Joint Board of the Cloak, Suit & Skirt Makers' Unions, and the Delegates of the Cloak, Suit & Skirt Manufacturers' Protective Association* (hereafter *Minutes*) 2 (1910), File NMF A5–3, Louisville Papers.
7. *Id.*, pp. 4, 8, 9.
8. Quoted in Jacob deHaas, *Louis D. Brandeis: A Biographical Sketch* 51 (1929); Milton R. Konvitz, "Louis D. Brandeis," in Simon Noveck (ed.), *Great Jewish Personalities in Modern Times* 300 (1960).
9. *Minutes*, p. 293.
10. *Id.*, pp. 294–98.
11. *Id.*, p. 338; LDB to Alice Brandeis, July 31, 1910, Gilbert Papers.
12. LDB Speech to Buyers' Conference.
13. "Text of the Protocol Agreement," Dept. of Commerce & Labor, Bulletin No. 98 of the Bureau of Labor 211–13 (1912).
14. Quoted in *Letters*, Vol. II, p. 485.
15. "Brandeis Union Shop Plan Makes for Peace," *Boston American*, November 12, 1911.
16. "The 'Preferential Shop,' " *Boston Transcript*, April 6, 1912.
17. Isaac Hourwich to LDB, May 27, 1913, *Letters*, Vol. III, p. 105, n.2.
18. LDB to Henry Moskowitz, May 28, 1913, *id.*, p. 105.
19. Proceedings of the Meeting of the Board of Arbitration, Vol. II, pp. A22–A23 (August 1913), File NMF 42–3, Louisville Papers.
20. Quoted in Alpheus T. Mason, *Brandeis: A Free Man's Life* 309 (1946).
21. Proceedings of the Meeting of the Board of Arbitration, 13 (January 1914), File NMF 42–3, Louisville Papers.
22. LDB to John A. Dyche, February 11, 1915, *Letters*, Vol. III, p. 428.
23. LDB to Leo Mannheimer, February 11, 1915, *id.*, p. 429.

24. Quoted in Mason, *Brandeis: A Free Man's Life*, p. 313.
25. LDB to George W. Kirchwey, July 30, 1915, *Letters*, Vol. III, p. 562.
26. Brandeis, *Businesss—A Profession*, pp. 71–72.
27. *Id.*, pp. 59, 61.
28. *Id.*, p. 76.
29. LDB to A. Lincoln Filene, June 1911, *Letters*, Vol. II, p. 444. The same letter is located in File 22660, NMF Papers, and dated June 5, 1912. There is insufficient evidence to determine which date is correct.

Chapter Eleven
GRAPPLING WITH THE RAILROADS

1. Interview with Alger Hiss, August 4, 1981.
2. *See* Albro Martin, *Enterprise Denied: Origins of the Decline of American Railroads, 1897–1917* 221, 248 (1971).
3. These new laws overturned Supreme Court decisions that limited the ICC's power to review rates. *See ICC* v. *Alabama Midland Ry.*, 168 U.S. 144 (1897); *Cincinnati, N.O. & Texas Pacific Ry.* v. *ICC*, 162 U.S. 184 (1896).
4. *In the Matter of Proposed Advances in Freight Rates by Carriers*, Senate Doc. 725, 61st Cong., 3rd Sess. 1145–47 (1911) (hereafter *Rate Hearings*). Portions of the transcript have been deleted here to facilitate reading.
5. *Id.*, pp. 1174–79. Portions of the transcript have been deleted here to facilitate reading.
6. *Id.*, pp. 2024–25.
7. *Id.*, p. 1972.
8. *Id.*, pp. 5255–56.
9. *Id.*, p. 5262.
10. *Id.*, pp. 2400–01.
11. *See* LDB to Horace B. Drury, January 31, 1914, *Letters*, Vol. III, p. 240.
12. *Rate Hearings*, pp. 2617, 4800, 5263.
13. LDB to O.L. Dickinson, November 29, 1910, *Letters*, Vol. II, p. 388.
14. "Railway Rates and Railway Efficiency," *Railway Gazette*, December 2, 1910, p. 1035.
15. *See* Martin, *Enterprise Denied*, pp. 218–22.
16. Quoted in William J. Cunningham, "Scientific Management in the Operation of Railroads," 25 *Quarterly Journal of Economics* 555 (May 1911).
17. Louis D. Brandeis, *Business—A Profession* 53 (1933 ed.).
18. *Eastern Advance Rate Case,* 20 ICC 243, 279 (1911).
19. Louis D. Brandeis, "A Victory for Conservatism," *Moody's Magazine*, March 1911, pp. 164–65.
20. Osmond K. Fraenkel (ed.), *The Curse of Bigness: The Miscellaneous Papers of Louis D. Brandeis* 191 (1934).
21. LDB to May C. Nerney, September 18, 1914, Letters, Vol. III, p. 298.
22. LDB to Livy S. Richard, May 1, 1913, *id.*, p. 79.
23. LDB to Alfred Brandeis, May 12, 1913, *id.*, p. 85.
24. James S. Harlan to LDB, August 15, 1913, File NMF 57–1a, Louisville Papers.
25. Clifford Thorne to LDB, October 24, 1913, *id.*
26. LDB to Alice Brandeis, November 26, 1913, Gilbert Papers.
27. *Hearings on the 5% Rate Case*, Senate Document 466, 63rd Cong., 2nd Sess. 5259 (1914) (hereafter *5% Rate Case*).
28. *Id.*, p. 103.
29. *Id.*, pp. 5244–45.
30. *Id.*, p. 5260.
31. *Hearings before the Subcommittee of the Committee of the Judiciary on the Nomination of Louis D. Brandeis to be an Associate Justice of the Supreme Court of the United States, Part I*, 64th Cong., 1st Sess. 9 (1916).
32. *Id.*, p. 19.

33. *Id.*, p. 21.
34. *Rate Hearings*, pp. 5260–62.
35. *5% Rate Case*, 31 ICC 351, 360 (1914).
36. Alfred Brandeis to LDB, October 31, 1914, File NMF 65–1, Louisville Papers.
37. LDB to Alfred Brandeis, November 4, 1914, *Letters*, Vol. III, p. 345.
38. *New York Times*, October 21, 1914, p. 10.
39. LDB to Alfred Brandeis, October 24, 1914, *Letters*, Vol. III, p. 339.
40. Quoted in Alpheus T. Mason, *Brandeis: A Free Man's Life* 522 (1946).

Chapter Twelve
A NEW WINDOW ON SOCIAL LEGISLATION

1. Alice H. Grady to LDB, January 19, 1912, File NMF 37–3, Louisville Papers.
2. *Boston Sunday American,* October 13, 1911, p. 1.
3. Interview with William Sutherland, November 7, 1980. Sutherland learned of this story in a conversation with the little boy after he had grown to adulthood.
4. *Holden* v. *Hardy*, 169 U.S. 366, 395 (1898).
5. *Lochner* v. *New York*, 198 U.S. 45, 57 (1905).
6. Josephine Goldmark, *Impatient Crusader: The Life of Florence Kelley* 149–50 (1953).
7. Quoted in *id.*, p. 154.
8. Quoted in *id.*, p. 143.
9. Brief for the State of Oregon, *Muller* v. *Oregon*, December 1907, pp. 18, 45, 58, 113.
10. Quoted in Alpheus T. Mason, *Brandeis: A Free Man's Life* 250 (1946).
11. *Muller* v. *Oregon*, 208 U.S. 412, 419–21 (1908).
12. Felix Frankfurter, "Hours of Labor and Realism in Constitutional Law" (1916), reprinted in 2 *Selected Essays on Constitutional Law* 699, 709 (1938). The original "Brandeis brief" was used to show that a state had a reasonable basis for its action. Decades later, reform lawyers successfully used the Brandeis brief to demonstrate in cases of racial discrimination that the state had no reasonable basis for its action. For example, *see Brown* v. *Board of Education*, 347 U.S. 483 (1954). The divergent uses of the brief are not necessarily inconsistent. In both situations the brief relied on facts to support a legal presumption on behalf of an oppressed group—in one case state legislation for women who worked too many hours; in the other case judicial enforcement of a constitutional right for blacks who encountered arbitrary discrimination by the state. *See* Paul A. Freund, *The United States Supreme Court: Its Business, Purposes and Performance* 150–54 (1961).
13. Dean Acheson to Felix Frankfurter, November 16, 1920, Frankfurter Papers.

Chapter Thirteen
FINDING A NEW PRESIDENT

1. Belle La Follette to LDB, June 15, 1910, File SC 1–2, Louisville Papers.
2. Robert M. La Follette to LDB, June 23, 1912, *id.*
3. Quoted in Matthew Josephson, *The Robber Barons: The Great American Capitalists 1861–1901* 280 (1934).
4. Quoted in Gabriel Kolko, *The Triumph of Conservatism: A Reinterpretation of American History, 1900–1916* 61–62 (1963).
5. *Standard Oil Co. of New Jersey* v. *United States*, 221 U.S. 1 (1911).
6. *Hearings before the Committee on Interstate Commerce, United States Senate, on Control of Corporations, Persons and Firms Engaged in Interstate Commerce*, 62nd Cong., 2d Sess, 1146, 1154–55, 1166, 1167, 1174, 1225–26 (1911); *Boston Globe,* December 16, 1911.
7. LDB to Alice Brandeis, December 16, 1911, Gilbert Papers.
8. *Hearings before the Committee on the Judiciary, House of Representatives, on H.R. 11380, H.R. 11381, H.R. 15926, and H.R. 19959*, 62nd Cong., 2d Sess. 23 (1912).
9. LDB to Alfred Brandeis, February 7, 1912, *Letters*, Vol. II, p. 542, n. 1.
10. *Boston Journal,* September 22, 1911.

11. LDB to Scott Bonham, January 16, 1912, *Letters*, Vol. II, p. 539.
12. *Boston Journal,* September 23, 1911.
13. LDB to Alfred Brandeis, July 28, 1912, *Letters*, Vol. II, p. 653.
14. LDB to Belle La Follette, February 7, 1912, *id.*, p. 542.
15. Amos Pinchot to LDB, February 9, 1912, File NMF 34–1, Louisville Papers.
16. LDB to Amos Pinchot, February 13, 1912, *Letters*, Vol. II, p. 546.
17. LDB to George Rublee, March 16, 1912, *id.*, pp. 568–69.
18. LDB to Alfred Brandeis, April 30, 1912, *id.*, p. 611.
19. LDB to Norman Hapgood, July 3, 1912, *id.*, p. 633.
20. *Id.*, p. 643.
21. LDB to Woodrow Wilson, August 1, 1912, *id.*, p. 658.
22. Woodrow Wilson to LDB, August 7, 1912, *id.*, p. 659.
23. Interview with LDB, March 23, 1929, Baker Papers; LDB to Robert M. La Follette, May 26, 1911, *Letters*, Vol. II, p. 443.
24. *Boston Post*, August 29, 1912.
25. LDB to Alfred Brandeis, August 29, 1912, *Letters*, Vol. II, p. 661.
26. *Cleveland Press*, October 11, 1912.
27. LDB to Alfred Brandeis, September 15, 1912, *Letters*, Vol. II, p. 673.
28. Woodrow Wilson to LDB, September 28, 1912, *id.*, p. 685.
29. LDB to Woodrow Wilson, September 30, 1912, *id.*, p. 687.
30. *See* memoranda in File NMF 53–1, Louisville Papers.
31. LDB to Alice G. Brandeis, October 11, 1912, *Letters*, Vol. II, p. 702.
32. Robert J. Collier to LDB, October 30, 1912, File NMF 52–1, Louisville Papers.
33. LDB to Robert J. Collier, November 9, 1912, *Letters*, Vol. II, p. 711.
34. Wilson to LDB, November 19, 1912, *id.*, p. 709, n. 2.
35. Henry L. Higginson to Woodrow Wilson, October 11, 1912, Higginson Papers.
36. Diary of Edward House, Book I, p. 21 (November 16, 1912), House Papers.
37. *Id.*, p. 23 (November 21, 1912).
38. James Ford Rhodes to Woodrow Wilson, December 19, 1912, quoted in Alpheus T. Mason, *Brandeis: A Free Man's Life* 386 (1946); Edward R. Warren to Woodrow Wilson, November 18, 1912, quoted in *id*; George Anderson to Woodrow Wilson, December 24, 1912, Wilson Papers; *Truth*, November 30, 1912.
39. Norman Hapgood to Woodrow Wilson, January 30, 1913, Wilson Papers. *See* Stephen S. Wise, *Challenging Years* 170–71 (1949).
40. LDB to Alfred Brandeis, March 2, 1913, *Letters*, Vol. III, p. 37; LDB to Alice Brandeis, March 8, 1913, Gilbert Papers.
41. LDB to Robert M. La Follette, July 9, 1913, *id.*, p. 130.
42. Arthur S. Link, *Wilson: The Road to the White House* 489 (1947).

Chapter Fourteen
THE NATION'S ADVISOR

1. Louis D. Brandeis, "Business—A Profession," in *Business—A Profession* 2, 3, 12 (1933 ed.).
2. Quoted in Gabriel Kolko, *The Triumph of Conservatism: A Reinterpretation of American History 1900–1916* 150, 157 (1963).
3. Quoted in *id.*, p. 222. *See* Melvin I. Urofsky, *A Mind of One Piece: Brandeis and American Reform* 80–84 (1971).
4. Quoted in Kolko, *Triumph of Conservatism*, p. 141.
5. LDB to Woodrow Wilson, June 14, 1913, *Letters*, Vol. III, pp. 114, 115. At the president's request, Brandeis sent this letter to Wilson to summarize the views he had given to him orally at their meeting of June 11, 1913.
6. Quoted in Alpheus T. Mason, *Brandeis: A Free Man's Life* 398 (1946).
7. LDB to Norman Hapgood, February 27, 1911, *Letters*, Vol. II, pp. 412–13.

8. LDB to Alfred Brandeis, September 2, 1913, *id.*, Vol. III, p. 165.
9. LDB to Norman Hapgood, September 30, 1913, *id.*, p. 182.
10. Louis D. Brandeis, *Other People's Money and How the Bankers Use It* 12–13 (1967 Harper Torchbook ed.).
11. *Id.*, pp. 35–37.
12. The articles were criticized by the banking industry as unfair. *See* Lawrence Chamberlain, "Mr. Brandeis and Investment Banking," *Harper's Weekly*, January 17, 1914.
13. Brandeis, *Other People's Money*, p. 32.
14. *See*, for example, Note, "Mr. Justice Brandeis, Competition, and Smallness: A Dilemma Re-Examined," 66 *Yale Law Journal* 69, 72, 77 (1956); Urofsky, *A Mind of One Piece*, pp. 65–66.
15. LDB to Alice G. Brandeis, February 27, 1914, *Letters*, Vol. III, p. 259.
16. Alice Grady to Joseph Eastman, February 25, 1914, File NMF 63–5, Louisville Papers.
17. LDB to Alfred Brandeis, February 22, 1913, *Letters*, Vol. III, p. 246.
18. Woodrow Wilson to James McReynolds, December 19, 1913, Wilson Papers.
19. Woodrow Wilson, *Messages and Papers of the Presidents* 7914 (1921).
20. LDB to Alfred Brandeis, January 23, 1914, *Letters*, Vol. III, pp. 236–37.
21. *Hearings on Trust Legislation before the Committee on the Judiciary, House of Representatives*, 63rd Cong., 2d Sess. 675, 690 (1914).
22. LDB to Alice Brandeis, "Mother's Birthday," 1914, Gilbert Papers. *See* LDB to Alice Brandeis, March 7, 1914; LDB to Alice Brandeis, March 18, 1914, *id.*
23. Quoted in interview with George Rublee, Columbia Papers, pp. 109, 114. In this interview Rublee states that the meeting with Wilson occurred on June 10, 1914. Brandeis's contemporaneous letters to Alice, however, state that the first meeting occurred on May 21, 1914, and that they made another "descent upon the President" on June 10, 1914, when they encountered difficulties in Congress. LDB to Alice Brandeis, May 21, 1914; LDB to Alice Brandeis, June 10, 1914, Gilbert Papers. Because Rublee's interview occurred decades after the event, I have chosen to rely on Brandeis's contemporaneous account.
24. *Federal Trade Commission* v. *Gratz*, 253 U.S. 421, 427 (1920).
25. *Id.*, p. 437.
26. Interview with LDB, March 23, 1929, Baker Papers.
27. *Dr. Miles Medical Company* v. *Park & Sons Company*, 220 U.S. 373 (1911).
28. LDB to Treadwell Cleveland, Jr., June 18, 1913, *Letters*, Vol. III, pp. 120–21.
29. Brandeis, "Competition That Kills," in *Business—A Profession*, p. 251.
30. *Id.*, pp. 257, 261.
31. *Hearings on Resale Price Maintenance before the Committee on Interstate and Foreign Commerce, House of Representatives*, 64th Cong., 1st Sess. 8–9, 28 (1915).
32. Quoted in *American Column Co.* v. *United States*, 257 U.S. 377, 393 (1921).
33. Undated memorandum by LDB, File 9–2, Harvard Papers.
34. *See Maple Floor Mftrs. Assoc.* v. *United States* 268 U.S. 563 (1925). One authority concluded that the Miller–Tydings Act "tended to restrict production, prevent change, hold up prices and bilk the consumer." Ellis W. Hawley, *The New Deal and the Problem of Monopoly* 268 (1966).
35. "Mr. Brandeis on the Cost of Living," *New York Herald Tribune*, March 3, 1912.
36. Louis D. Brandeis, "True Americanism," in *Business—A Profession*, pp. 365, 368, 373–74.

Chapter Fifteen
THE EMERGENCE OF A ZIONIST LEADER

1. *Reminiscences of Frederika Dembitz Brandeis* 32–33 (1943) (privately published).
2. LDB to Lehman Pickert, December 17, 1907, File 16598, NMF Papers.
3. LDB, "What Loyalty Demands," File 14539, *id.*
4. Solomon Goldman (ed.), *The Words of Justice Brandeis* 87 (1953).

5. *Id.*, p. 156.
6. Jacob Schiff to Max Mitchell, February 17, 1913, quoted in Yonathan Shapiro, *Leadership of the American Zionist Organization 1897–1930* 64 (1971).
7. Jacob deHaas, *Louis D. Brandeis: A Biographical Sketch* 151 (1929).
8. LDB to Bernard G. Richards, February 2, 1911, *Letters*, Vol. II, p. 402. There is contradictory evidence as to when deHaas and Brandeis talked about Lewis Dembitz. deHaas's 1929 book states that it was in December 1910. deHaas, *Louis D. Brandeis*, pp. 51–52. In 1940 Brandeis told Professor Mason it was in August 1912. Alpheus T. Mason, *Brandeis: A Free Man's Life* 443 (1946). On balance, it appears that deHaas is probably right. In 1926, deHaas wrote a letter to Brandeis referring to the 1910 interview and how Brandeis had made deHaas repeat the story to his daughter Susan when he visited Brandeis in August 1912. *See* deHaas to LDB, November 1, 1926, File Z/P 33–1, Louisville Papers. Brandeis may have had this second telling of the interview in mind when he described it to Mason. Since Brandeis was eighty-three when he talked to Mason, and since everyone's memory—at whatever age—is capable of tricks, deHaas's version of events is more likely to be accurate.
9. Quoted in Melvin I. Urofsky, *American Zionism from Herzl to the Holocaust* 8 (1976).
10. *Id.*, pp. 86–91.
11. LDB to Alfred Brandeis, January 7, 1912, *Letters*, Vol. II, p. 537.
12. Quoted in deHaas, *Louis D. Brandeis*, p. 157.
13. Quoted in *id.*, pp. 161–62.
14. Quoted in *id.*, pp. 182, 185–86, 190.
15. *American Israelite*, July 1, 1915.
16. LDB to Alfred Brandeis, February 14, 1915, *Letters*, Vol. III, p. 443.
17. Cyrus Adler to LDB, July 21, 1915, File Z/P 11–1, Louisville Papers.
18. LDB to Cyrus Adler, July 28, 1915, *Letters*, Vol. III, pp. 552–54.
19. Cyrus Adler to LDB, August 3, 1915, File Z/P 11–1, Louisville Papers.
20. LDB to Cyrus Adler, August 10, 1915, *Letters*, Vol. III, p. 567.

Chapter Sixteen
FIGHTING FOR CONFIRMATION

1. Osmond K. Fraenkel (ed.), *The Curse of Bigness: Miscellaneous Papers of Louis D. Brandeis* 55, 68–69 (1934).
2. Quoted in Josephine Goldmark, *Impatient Crusader: The Life of Florence Kelley* 168 (1953).
3. *Stettler* v. *O'Hara*, 243 U.S. 629 (1917).
4. Louis D. Brandeis, *Business—A Profession* 349–50 (1933 ed.).
5. Diary of Edward House, Book V, p. 226 (November 14, 1914), House Papers.
6. William Kent to Woodrow Wilson, January 27, 1916, Wilson Papers.
7. *New York Times*, January 3, 1916; *Washington Herald*, January 12, 1916.
8. Quoted in A.L. Todd, *Justice on Trial: The Case of Louis D. Brandeis* 28 (1964).
9. Quoted in *id.*, p. 77.
10. *New York Sun*, January 29, 1916; January 31, 1916.
11. Alice G. Brandeis to Alfred Brandeis, January 31, 1916, *Letters*, Vol. IV, p. 54, n. 2.
12. Quoted in Todd, *Justice on Trial*, p. 86.
13. Quoted in *id.*, p. 80.
14. Charles Russell to LDB, January 30, 1916; LDB to Charles Russell, February 10, 1916, *Letters*, Vol. IV, pp. 41–42.
15. *Hearings on the Nomination of Louis D. Brandeis to be an Associate Justice of the Supreme Court of the United States, before the Subcommittee of the Committee on the Judiciary, United States Senate* (hereafter *Hearings*), 64th Cong., 1st Sess., Part I, 8 (1916).
16. *Id.*, p. 46.
17. *Id.*, p. 45.
18. Quoted in Todd, *Justice on Trial*, p. 101; Edward McClennen to Brandeis, Dunbar & Nutter, February 9, 1916, File NMF 76–1, Louisville Papers.

19. *Hearings*, p. 117.
20. *Id.*, p. 119.
21. George Nutter to Edward McClennen, February 9, 1916, File NMF 76–1, Louisville Papers.
22. LDB to Alfred Brandeis, February 12, 1916, *Letters*, Vol. IV, p. 54; *The New Republic*, March 11, 1916, p. 6. *See* Walter Lippmann to LDB, February 18, 1916, File NMF 77–2, Louisville Papers.
23. *Hearings*, p. 149.
24. *Id.*, p. 476.
25. *Id.*, p. 284.
26. Cornelia Warren to LDB, February 16, 1916; LDB to Cornelia Warren, February 17, 1916, *Letters*, Vol. IV, pp. 71–72.
27. Quoted in *Hearings*, p. 942.
28. *Id.*, p. 727.
29. LDB to Robert M. La Follette, May 5, 1911, *Letters*, Vol. II, p. 431.
30. *Hearings*, p. 250.
31. Quoted in *id.*, p. 937.
32. *Id.*, p. 160. Under present ethical standards, an attorney should not accept employment against a former client if the new matter is substantially related to the substance of the former representation. *International Electronic Corp.* v. *Flanzer*, 527 F. 2d 1288, 1291 (2d Cir. 1975). Thus, a lawyer should not represent a client to attack a contract or other document he prepared for an earlier client. That is almost precisely what Brandeis did, however; although the 1911 United lease was not the same in all respects with the 1906 lease, the basic issue—the use of tying claauses—was the same. (On Brandeis's behalf, it should be noted that the law on ethics is more clearly articulated today than it was in his time.) *See* John P. Frank, "The Legal Ethics of Louis D. Brandeis," 17 *Stanford Law Review* 683, 703–706 (1965).
33. *Hearings*, pp. 787–89.
34. *Id.*, p. 790.
35. *Id.*, p. 1078.
36. *Id.*, pp. 287, 299.
37. LDB to Edward McClennen, March 9, 1916, *Letters*, Vol. IV, pp. 110–11.
38. *Hearings*, p. 338.
39. *Id.*, p. 301.
40. *Id.*, pp. 654–55, 659–61. Portions of the transcript have been deleted here to facilitate reading.
41. *Id.*, p. 615.
42. *Id.*, pp. 619–20.
43. *Id.*, p. 770.
44. Quoted in Todd, *Justice on Trial*, pp. 133, 157; Edward F. McClennen to George Nutter, March 4, 1916, File NMF 76–1, Louisville Papers.
45. LDB to Edward F. McClennen, March 9, 1916; Edward F. McClennen to LDB, March 10, 1916, *Letters*, Vol. IV, pp. 114–15.
46. Quoted in Todd, *Justice on Trial*, p. 163; *Hearings*, pp. 1226–27.
47. LDB to Norman Hapgood, March 14, 1916, *Letters*, Vol. IV, pp. 118–19. *See* LDB to Felix Frankfurter, March 18, 1916, *id.*, p. 129.
48. *Hearings*, p. 1226.
49. *Id.*, pp. 1239, 1251.
50. *Id.*, p. 1316.
51. Edward F. McClennen to LDB, March 15, 1916, *Letters*, Vol. IV, p. 125.
52. Quoted in Stephen Wise to LDB, May 10, 1916, File NMF 77–2, Louisville Papers.
53. Quoted in Todd, *Justice on Trial*, p. 136.
54. George Anderson to LDB, March 25, 1916, File NMF 77–1, Louisville Papers.
55. *Hearings, Part II*, pp. 234, 374.
56. Quoted in Todd, *Justice on Trial*, p. 205.

57. Edward F. McClennen to LDB, May 4, 1916, File NMF 76–2, Louisville Papers.
58. Woodrow Wilson to Charles Culberson, May 8, 1916, Wilson Papers.
59. George Nutter to Edward F. McClennen, May 9, 1916, File NMF 76–2, Louisville Papers.
60. *Letters*, Vol. IV, p. 192.
61. Edward F. McClennen to Office Committee, April 10, 1916, File NMF 76–1, Louisville Papers.
62. *See* Alfred Brandeis to LDB, May 9, 1916, File 22629, NMF Papers.

Chapter Seventeen
THE NEW JUSTICE

1. Quoted in Arthur E. Sutherland, *The Law at Harvard: A History of Ideas and Men 1817–1967* viii (1967).
2. Amos Pinchot to LDB, June 6, 1916, *Letters*, Vol. IV, pp. 239–40.
3. This account is based on Brandeis's handwritten summary of events in File G1–1, Louisville Papers.
4. Dean Acheson, *Morning and Noon* 78 (1965).
5. *Id.*, pp. 79–80.
6. Alice G. Brandeis to Elizabeth Glendower Evans, April 1917, Evans Papers.
7. Quoted in Acheson, *Morning and Noon*, p. 80.
8. Brandeis–Frankfurter Conversations, p. 17, Frankfurter Papers.
9. Interview with James Landis, p. 73, Columbia Papers.
10. *Id.*, p. 87.
11. Brandeis–Frankfurter Conversations, pp. 12–13.
12. Interview with H. Thomas Austern, January 12, 1981.
13. Interview with Henry Friendly, December 27, 1980. *See* Henry Friendly to LDB, November 12, 1936, File M9–1, Louisville Papers; *Louisville Gas and Electric Co.*v. *Coleman*, 277 U.S. 32 (1928).
14. Quoted in Joseph P. Lash (ed.), *From the Diaries of Felix Frankfurter* 46 (1975). For a variety of views on Frankfurter, *see* Liva Baker, *Felix Frankfurter* (1969); H.N. Hirsch, *The Enigma of Felix Frankfurter* (1981); Michael E. Parrish, *Felix Frankfurter and His Times* (1982).
15. Interview with Paul Freund, February 11, 1981.
16. Lash, *From the Diaries of Felix Frankfurter*, p. 104.
17. Harlan B. Phillips (ed.), *Felix Frankfurter Reminisces* 106 (1960).
18. *See* LDB to Frederick Wehle, November 19, 1927, *Letters*, Vol. V, p. 153.
19. LDB to Felix Frankfurter, November 25, 1916, *Letters*, Vol. IV, pp. 266–67. A fuller discussion of the Brandeis–Frankfurter relationship is found in Nelson L. Dawson, *Louis D. Brandeis, Felix Frankfurter and the New Deal* (1980), and Bruce Allen Murphy, *The Brandeis/Frankfurter Connection: The Secret Political Activities of Two Supreme Court Justices* (1982).
20. Felix Frankfurter to LDB, September 29, 1924, Frankfurter Papers.
21. On LDB's close relationship with *The New Republic, see* his correspondence with Herbert Croly and others in Files SC 2–1, SC 4–2 and WW 8–3, Louisville Papers.
22. Murphy, *The Brandeis/Frankfurter Connection,* p. 82; Phillips, *Felix Frankfurter Reminisces,* p. 210.
23. LDB to Emma Frankfurter, November 14, 1916, *Letters*, Vol. IV, p. 265; LDB to Felix Frankfurter, September 24, 1925, *id.,* Vol. V, p. 187; Murphy, *The Brandeis/Frankfurter Connection*, pp. 44–45; Harry Shulman to LDB, June 7, 1930, File M4–2, Louisville Papers; interview with Adrian Fisher, August 11, 1980, interview with J. Willard Hurst, May 31, 1980; interview with David Riesman, May 5, 1981; Lewis H. Weinsteir "Letter to the Editor," *Harvard Law Record*, April 16, 1982, p. 11.

Chapter Eighteen
THE INVISIBLE ZIONIST LEADER

1. Quoted in Jacob deHaas, *Louis D. Brandeis: A Biographical Sketch* 222 (1929).
2. Louis Marshall to Bernard G. Richards, undated, File Z/P 15–1, Louisville Papers.
3. *New York Times*, July 18, 1916.
4. Emanuel Newman, "Two of the 'High Spots' at the Pittsburgh Convention," *Maccabean*, August 1918.
5. Chaim Weizmann, *Trial and Error* 110–11 (1949).
6. LDB to Chaim Weizmann, September 24, 1917, *Letters*, Vol. IV, p. 310. *See* Diary of Edward House, Book XI, pp. 290–91 (September 23, 1917), House Papers.
7. Quoted in *Letters*, Vol. IV, p. 321.
8. Stephen Wise, *Challenging Years* 178–79 (1949).
9. Felix Frankfurter to LDB, March 3, 1919, File Z/P 26–2, Louisville Papers.
10. Woodrow Wilson to Felix Frankfurter, May 16, 1919, Frankfurter Papers.
11. LDB to Alice G. Brandeis, July 10, 1919, *Letters*, Vol. IV, pp. 417–18.
12. Quoted in Melvin I. Urofsky, *American Zionism from Herzl to the Holocaust* 243–44 (1976).
13. Weizmann, *Trial and Error*, p. 248.
14. Quoted in deHaas, *Louis D. Brandeis*, p. 120.
15. Quoted in Harlan Phillips (ed.), *Felix Frankfurter Reminisces* 181 (1960).
16. Interview with Benjamin V. Cohen, October 8, 1980.
17. LDB to Julian Mack et al., February 18, 1921, *Letters*, Vol. IV, p. 534.
18. Interview with Benjamin V. Cohen, December 24, 1980.
19. Felix Frankfurter to LDB, April 25, 1921, File Z/P 28–1, Louisville Papers; LDB to Felix Frankfurter, April 26, 1921, *Letters*, Vol. IV, p. 553.
20. LDB to Julian Mack, June 2, 1921, *Letters*, Vol. IV, pp. 562–63. A few weeks later Brandeis sent a letter to the World Zionist Organization resigning as honorary president of that body. That is anomalous since overwhelming evidence indicates that he had refused to accept that post. *Compare* LDB to Executive Council of the World Zionist Organization, June 19, 1921, *Letters*, Vol. IV, p. 567, *with* "Review of the London Conference," reprinted in deHaas, *Louis D. Brandeis*, pp. 235–41. For a review of Brandeis's activities during these first phases of his Zionist career, *see* Ezekiel Rabinowitz, *Justice Louis D. Brandeis: The Zionist Chapter of His Life* (1968).

Chapter Nineteen
PROTECTING SPEECH

1. Dean Acheson to Felix Frankfurter, March 2, 1921, Frankfurter Papers.
2. Dean Acheson to Felix Frankfurter, March 15, 1920, *id.*
3. Quoted in Arthur Link, *Woodrow Wilson and the Progressive Era 1910–1917* 277 (1954).
4. Quoted in Frederick Lewis Allen, *Only Yesterday: An Informal History of the Nineteen Twenties* 58 (Perennial Library ed., 1964).
5. LDB to Susan Brandeis, April 11, 1917, Gilbert Papers.
6. Quoted in LDB to Alice Brandeis, July 9, 1917, *id.*
7. *Id.*
8. Interview with James Landis, p. 83, Columbia Papers.
9. Oliver Wendell Holmes to Frederick Pollock, Mark deWolfe Howe (ed.), *Holmes–Pollock Letters*, Vol. II, 22 (1961).
10. Quoted in D. Danelski & J. Tulchin (eds.), *The Autobiographical Notes of Charles Evans Hughes* 176 (1973).
11. Harlan Phillips (ed.), *Felix Frankfurter Reminisces* 102 (1960).

12. Interview with Thomas Corcoran, November 21, 1979; Interview with Alger Hiss, August 4, 1981.
13. Quoted in Interview with James Landis, p. 73.
14. Oliver Wendell Holmes to Harold Laski, May 8, 1918, Mark deWolfe Howe (ed.), *Holmes–Laski Letters*, Vol. I, 153 (1951).
15. Oliver Wendell Holmes to Harold Laski, May 18, 1919, *id.*, p. 204.
16. Oliver Wendell Holmes to Harold Laski, December 27, 1925, *id.*, p. 810.
17. Interview with Thomas Corcoran.
18. *Schenk* v. *United States*, 249 U.S. 47, 52 (1919). For a good discussion of Holmes's and Brandeis's legal philosophies on free speech and other issues, *see* Samuel J. Konefsky, *The Legacy of Holmes and Brandeis: A Study in the Influence of Ideas* (1956).
19. *Schaefer* v. *United States*, 251 U.S. 466, 483, 495 (1920) (dissenting opinion).
20. *Pierce* v. *United States*, 252 U.S. 239, 253, 273 (1920) (dissenting opinion).
21. Brandeis–Frankfurter conversations, p. 23, Frankfurter Papers.
22. *Gilbert* v. *Minnesota*, 254 U.S. 325, 334, 343 (1920) (dissenting opinion). *See* Files 5–12, 5–13, Harvard Papers; Dean Acheson to Felix Frankfurter, January 17, 1921, Frankfurter Papers.
23. Dean Acheson, *Morning and Noon* 94 (1965).
24. Interview with James Landis, p. 68.
25. Robert Page to LDB, October 27, 1926, File 44–9, Harvard Papers.
26. *Whitney* v. *California*, 274 U.S. 357, 372, 373, 375, 377 (1927) (concurring opinion).
27. *Dennis* v. *United States*, 341 U.S. 494, 567, n. 9 (1951) (Jackson, J., concurring).

Chapter Twenty
STRIVING FOR NORMALCY

1. LDB to Alfred Brandeis, January 3, 1923, *Letters*, Vol. V, p. 82.
2. LDB to Felix Frankfurter, October 7, 1928, *id.*, p. 359. The clerk, Irving Goldsmith, later proved to be satisfactory to Brandeis.
3. Quoted in Frederick Lewis Allen, *Only Yesterday: An Informal History of the Nineteen Twenties* 128 (Perennial Library ed. 1964).
4. LDB to Susan Brandeis, March 5, 1923, Gilbert Papers. This description is also based in part on an interview with Adrian Fisher, August 11, 1980. Fisher had been told about Mrs. Brandeis's breakdown by Dean Acheson, who was very close to Brandeis at this time.
5. LDB to Susan Brandeis, April 11, 1923, Gilbert Papers. The details of Alice's earlier problems are not known. However, in reporting her nervous collapse to Susan on March 5, 1923, Brandeis said she was put "to bed again under Dr. Parker's care." It is also clear that her earlier illness required her to be absent from home for an extended period. *See* LDB to Susan Brandeis, November 14, 1922, *id.*; LDB to Susan Goldmark, November 14, 1922, *Letters*, Vol. V, p. 76. Brandeis did not fully identify Dr. Parker, but he apparently is referring to Henry Pickering Parker, a graduate of Johns Hopkins Medical School who had offices at 1728 Connecticut Avenue NW, which was down the street from the Brandeis apartment. Efforts to confirm Brandeis's use of this Dr. Parker—by speaking with descendants or obtaining medical records—proved unsuccessful.
6. Dean Acheson, *Morning and Noon* 47, (1965). Portions of this paragraph are based on an interview with Alice G. Popkin, July 19, 1980.
7. LDB to Susan Brandeis, October 14, 1923, Gilbert Papers. *See* LDB to Susan Brandeis, November 23, 1923, *id.*
8. Alice G. Brandeis to Elizabeth Glendower Evans, September 1923, Evans Papers. The year on the letter is not entirely legible, but, given the other known facts, it must be 1923.
9. LDB to Susan Brandeis, October 4, 1923; LDB to Susan Brandeis, October 14, 1923, Gilbert Papers.
10. LDB to Susan Brandeis, June 3, 1924; LDB to Susan Brandeis, October 1, 1924, *id.*
11. LDB to Felix Frankfurter, January 1, 1925, *Letters*, Vol. V, p. 156.
12. LDB to Robert W. Bruere, February 25, 1922, *id.*, pp. 45–46.

13. LDB to Harold Laski, September 20, 1921, *id.*, p. 17.
14. Interview with James Rowe, October 17, 1980.
15. LDB to Frederick Wehle, November 19, 1924, *Letters*, Vol. V, p. 153. *See* Bernard Flexner, *Mr. Justice Brandeis and the University of Louisville* (1938) (privately published).
16. LDB to Alfred Brandeis, February 18, 1925, *id.*, p. 163.
17. LDB to Alfred Brandeis, January 15, 1927; LDB to Alfred Brandeis, January 16, 1927; LDB to Alfred Brandeis, May 26, 1927; LDB to Alfred Brandeis, November 29, 1927, *id.*, pp. 261, 289, 315.
18. LDB to Jennie Brandeis, August 8, 1928, *id.*, p. 349.

Chapter Twenty-One *CURBING PRESIDENTIAL POWER*

1. Interview with Henry Friendly, December 27, 1980.
2. 169 U.S. 466 (1898).
3. *International News Service* v. *Associated Press*, 248 U.S. 215, 248, 267 (1918) (dissenting opinion).
4. Brandeis–Frankfurter Conversations, p. 7, Frankfurter Papers.
5. *See Southwestern Bell Telephone Co.* v. *Public Service Commission*, 262 U.S. 276, 289 (1923) (concurring opinion). Brandeis wrote several other opinions challenging *Smyth* v. *Ames* and the Supreme Court's willingness to substitute its view for the considered findings of a government agency. *See*, for example, *St. Louis & O'Fallon Ry. Co.* v. *United States*, 279 U.S. 461, 488 (1929) (dissenting opinion); *Crowell* v. *Benson*, 285 U.S. 22, 65 (1932) (dissenting opinion); *St. Joseph Stock Yards Co.* v. *United States*, 298 U.S. 38, 73 (1936) (concurring opinion). After Brandeis left the Court, it finally accepted the analysis of his concurring opinion in *Southwestern Bell* and held that regulatory agencies no longer had to use reproduction values in setting utility rates. *Federal Power Commission* v. *Hope Natural Gas Co.*, 320 U.S. 591 (1944).
6. Brandeis–Frankfurter Conversations, p. 6.
7. William Howard Taft to H.D. Taft, July 6, 1921, Taft Papers.
8. Oliver Wendell Holmes to Frederick Pollock, May 21, 1922, Mark deWolfe Howe (ed.), *Holmes–Pollock Letters*, Vol. II, p. 96 (1941).
9. Quoted in Alpheus T. Mason, *William Howard Taft: Chief Justice* 223 (1965).
10. Brandeis–Frankfurter Conversations, p. 16. *See Burnet* v. *Coronado Gas & Oil Co.*, 285 U.S. 393, 406–8 (1932) (dissenting opinion).
11. William Howard Taft, *Our Chief Magistrate and His Powers* 139–40 (1915).
12. William Howard Taft to H.D. Taft, November 23, 1925, Taft Papers.
13. 1 Cranch 137 (1803).
14. This discussion is based primarily on Files 39–8 to 39–11, 40–1 to 40–9, 41–1 to 41–10, Harvard Papers; Interview with James M. Landis, pp. 38–39, Columbia Papers. *See Myers* v. *United States*, 272 U.S. 52 (1926).
15. Oliver Wendell Holmes to LDB, February 18, 1926, File 41–3, Harvard Papers.
16. Quoted in Alpheus T. Mason, *Harlan F. Stone: Pillar of the Law* 230 (1956).
17. *Humphrey's Executor v. United States,* 295 U.S. 602 (1935).

Chapter Twenty-Two *PRIVACY REVISITED*

1. Quoted in Henry Pringle, *The Life and Times of William Howard Taft*, Vol. II, 969–70 (1939).
2. Memorandum from Oliver Wendell Holmes, undated, File 45–6, Harvard Papers.
3. William Howard Taft to Oliver Wendell Holmes, undated, Holmes Papers.
4. LDB to Felix Frankfurter, November 26, 1920, *Letters*, Vol. IV, p. 510.

5. LDB to Felix Frankfurter, June 23, 1926, *id.*, Vol. V, p. 224.
6. LDB to Felix Frankfurter, December 26, 1926, Frankfurter Papers.
7. These and other quotations are taken from drafts and notes in Files 48–3 to 48–7, Harvard Papers.
8. Interview with Henry Friendly, December 27, 1980.
9. Harlan F. Stone to LDB, March 23, 1928. File 48–5, Harvard Papers.
10. William Howard Taft to Edward T. Sanford, May 31, 1928, Taft Papers.
11. William Howard Taft to H.D. Taft, June 8, 1928, *id. See Olmstead* v. *United States*, 277 U.S. 438, 471 (1928) (dissenting opinion).
12. *Olmstead* v. *United States*, 277 U.S. at 470 (dissenting opinion).
13. LDB to Felix Frankfurter, June 15, 1928, *Letters*, Vol. V, p. 345.
14. 389 U.S. 347 (1967).

Chapter Twenty-Three
THE RESURRECTION OF A LEADER

1. LDB to Felix Frankfurter, December 11, 1925, *Letters*, Vol. V, p. 197.
2. Quoted in Jacob deHaas, *Louis D. Brandeis: A Biographical Sketch* 282 (1929).
3. LDB to Harry Friedenwald, February 3, 1924, *Letters*, Vol. V, p. 113.
4. Jack Gilbert to LDB, February 2, 1931, File Z/P 49–3, Louisville Papers.
5. LDB to Jacob deHaas, June 5, 1927, *Letters*, Vol. V, p. 291.
6. LDB to Jacob deHaas, December 24, 1927, quoted in Melvin I. Urofsky, *American Zionism from Herzl to the Holocaust* 325 (1975).
7. Quoted in Urofsky, *American Zionism*, p. 331.
8. LDB to Julian W. Mack, July 5, 1928, *Letters*, Vol. V, p. 347.
9. Osmond K. Fraenkel (ed.), *The Curse of Bigness: Miscellaneous Papers of Louis D. Brandeis* 256 (1934).
10. Bernard Flexner to Felix Frankfurter, November 26, 1929, File Z/P 35–5, Louisville Papers.
11. LDB Memorandum of Conversation with Sir Ronald Lindsay, undated, File Z/P 43–3, Louisville Papers. *See* LDB to Julian Mack, June 19, 1930, *Letters*, Vol. V, p. 428. This discussion is also based in part on interviews with H. Thomas Austern, January 12, 1981, and with Paul A. Freund, February 12, 1981.
12. Harold Laski to Oliver Wendell Holmes, September 30, 1930; Harold Laski to Oliver Wendell Holmes, December 27, 1930, Mark deWolfe Howe (ed.), *Holmes–Laski Letters*, Vol. II, 1298–99, 1301–2 (1951).
13. LDB to Julian Mack, June 12, 1930. *Letters*, Vol. V, p. 427.
14. LDB to ZOA Delegates, June 28, 1930, *id.*, pp. 429–30. For Lipsky's view of the figures involved here, *see* his book *A Gallery of Zionist Profiles* (1956).
15. Stephen Wise to LDB, September 19, 1933, Carl Hermann Voss (ed.), *Stephen S. Wise: Servant of the People* 194 (1969); Stephen Wise, *Challenging Years* 237–50 (1949).
16. *Id.*
17. *See* correspondence in File Z/P 56–2, Louisville Papers; Paul A. Freund, "Justice Brandeis: A Law Clerk's Remembrance," 68 *American Jewish History* 7, 16–17 (1978).

Chapter Twenty-Four
THE REVIEW OF SOCIAL LEGISLATION

1. Interview with Francis Kirkham, April 27, 1981. Robertson related this incident to Kirkham, who succeeded Robertson as Hughes's clerk.
2. Oliver Wendell Holmes to Harold Laski, May 23, 1929, Mark deWolfe Howe (ed.), *Holmes–Laski Letters*, Vol. II, 1152 (1951).
3. *United States* v. *Schwimmer*, 279 U.S. 644, 653, 655 (1929) (dissenting opinion). Part of this discussion relies on an interview with John E. Lockwood, April 1, 1981.

4. Interview with H. Chapman Rose, April 20, 1981.
5. Quoted in Felix Frankfurter to Mark deWolfe Howe, December 28, 1956, Frankfurter Papers. This discussion also relies on interviews with Mary Donnellan, December 6, 1980; Donald Hiss, March 30, 1981; and James Rowe, October 17, 1980.
6. Quoted in Frederick Lewis Allen, *Only Yesterday: An Informal History of the Nineteen Twenties* 274 (Perennial Library ed. 1964).
7. LDB to Jack Gilbert, October 11, 1928, Gilbert Papers.
8. LDB to Elizabeth Glendower Evans, October 30, 1929, Evans Papers; quoted in Paul A. Freund, "Mr. Justice Brandeis: A Centennial Memoir," 70 *Harvard Law Review* 769, 781 (1956).
9. *Adams* v. *Tanner*, 244 U.S. 590, 597, 600 (1917) (dissenting opinion).
10. *Burns Baking Co.* v. *Bryan*, 264 U.S. 504, 517, 520 (1924) (dissenting opinion).
11. *DiSanto* v. *Pennsylvania*, 273 U.S. 34, 37, 42 (1927) (dissenting opinion).
12. *O'Gorman & Young* v. *Hartford Insurance Co.*, 282 U.S. 251, 258 (1931).
13. *New State Ice Co.* v. *Liebmann*, 285 U.S. 262, 280, 306–11 (1932) (dissenting opinion).
14. Paul A. Freund to LDB, June 17, 1933, Frankfurter Papers.
15. *Quaker City Cab Co.* v. *Pennsylvania*, 277 U.S. 389, 403, 410 (1928) (dissenting opinion).
16. *Stratton* v. *St. Louis Southwestern Ry.*, 282 U.S. 10 (1930). *See* Alexander M. Bickel, *The Unpublished Opinions of Mr. Justice Brandeis: The Supreme Court at Work* 119–63 (1957).
17. The discussion of the *Liggett* opinion to this point relies primarily on the material in Files 81–1 to 82–14, Harvard Papers, and an interview with Paul A. Freund, February 11, 1981. *See Liggett Co.* v. *Lee*, 288 U.S. 517, 541, 565–67, 580 (1933) (dissenting opinion).
18. Harlan F. Stone to LDB, March 1, 1933, File 82–13, Harvard Papers; interview with Paul A. Freund, February 11, 1981.
19. Interview with Paul A. Freund, February 11, 1981.
20. Felix Frankfurter to Harlan F. Stone, March 23, 1933, Frankfurter Papers; Norman Hapgood to LDB, March 14, 1933, File 82–14, Harvard Papers.
21. Interview with Henry Friendly, December 27, 1980.
22. Elizabeth Brandeis Raushenbush to LDB, November 12, 1931, File M4–2, Louisville Papers; Herbert White to LDB, November 12, 1931, File M6–1, *id.*
23. Interview with Nathaniel L. Nathanson, December 17, 1980.
24. *Id.* This discussion is also based on interviews with H. Thomas Austern, January 12, 1981; David Riesman, May 5, 1981; Catherine Filene Shouse, May 21, 1981; Files 93–9 to 93–16, 94–1 to 94–9, Harvard Papers; Nathaniel L. Nathanson, "Mr. Justice Brandeis: A Law Clerk's Recollections of the October Term 1934," 15 *American Jewish Archives* 6 (1963).
25. *Nashville, Chattanooga & St. Louis Ry.* v. *Walters*, 294 U.S. 405, 431, n. 40 (1935).
26. *Id.*, 294 U.S. at 430.
27. *Id.*, 294 U.S. at 434.
28. Nathaniel L. Nathanson to Felix Frankfurter, March 4, 1935, Frankfurter Papers.

Chapter Twenty-Five *OLD IDEAS IN NEW HANDS*

1. Quoted in Elizabeth Glendower Evans, "Interesting People I Have Known: Alice Grady, Brandeis's Aide," *Springfield Republican*, June 3, 1934.
2. Harry Shulman, "Memorandum of Talk with L.D.B.—December 8, 1933," Frankfurter Papers. *See* LDB to Elizabeth Brandeis Raushenbush, April 22, 1933; November 19, 1933, *Letters*, Vol. V, pp. 514–15, 527–28; Nelson L. Dawson, *Louis D. Brandeis, Felix Frankfurter and the New Deal* 29–35 (1980).
3. Raymond Moley, *After Seven Years* 24 (1939). *See* Raymond Moley, *The First New Deal* 275 (1966).
4. Oliver Wendell Holmes to Harold Laski, July 30, 1920, Mark deWolfe Howe (ed.), *Holmes–Laski Letters*, Vol. I, 272 (1951).

5. Felix Frankfurter to Charles Burlingham, quoted in Joseph P. Lash, *From the Diaries of Felix Frankfurter* 42 (1975). *See* Nelson L. Dawson, "Louis D. Brandeis, Felix Frankfurter and Franklin D. Roosevelt: The Origins of a New Deal Relationship," 68 *American Jewish History* 32 (1978).
6. LDB to Elizabeth Glendower Evans, November 27, 1932, Evans Papers.
7. Max Freedman (ed.), *Roosevelt & Frankfurter: Their Correspondence, 1928–1945* 110–14 (1967); the discussion of the Roosevelt meeting in January 1933 is based on an interview with Paul A. Freund, February 12, 1981.
8. LDB to Jack Gilbert, May 18, 1933, Gilbert Papers.
9. Quoted in Rexford G. Tugwell, *The Brains Trust* 60 (1968). *See* "Notes for a New Deal Diary," p. 13, Tugwell Papers; Henry Wallace to LDB, undated, File SC 19–1, Louisville Papers.
10. LDB to Alice P. Goldmark, January 11, 1934, *Letters*, Vol. V, p. 531.
11. Interview with Gardner Jackson, pp. 417–20, Columbia Papers.
12. Quoted in Dean Acheson, *Morning and Noon* 180–81 (1965).
13. Brandeis–Frankfurter Conversations, p. 29, Frankfurter Papers.
14. Quoted in 79 *Congressional Record* 2717 (1935); LDB to Felix Frankfurter, February 24, 1935, Frankfurter Papers. The gold clause cases begin with *Norman* v. *B & O Railroad Co.*, 294 U.S. 240 (1935). In an earlier case, Brandeis had taken a more stringent view of the government's impairment of contract rights. *Lynch* v. *United States*, 292 U.S. 577 (1934) (the government cannot reduce the benefits of war-risk insurance contracts in order to reduce government expenditures).
15. Quoted in *New York Times*, June 17, 1933.
16. Quoted in Frank Kent, "The Great Game of Politics," *Baltimore Sun*, September 15, 1934.
17. Interview with Paul Freund, February 12, 1981; Hugh Johnson to LDB, June 1, 1935, File M17–16, Louisville Papers. *See* LDB to Felix Frankfurter, September 22, 1934, Frankfurter Papers; Paul Freund to LDB, May 19, 1933, File SC 10–1, Louisville Papers. Professor Murphy, allegedly relying on an interview with Professor Freund, quotes Judge Mack as asking Freund, "What does Louis want the President to say—some response must soon be made." Bruce Allen Murphy, *The Brandeis/Frankfurter Connection: The Secret Political Activities of Two Supreme Court Justices* 149 (1982). This quotation is inconsistent with what Professor Freund later told me, and he subsequently approved the accuracy of my transcription here of the telephone conversations between him and Judge Mack.
18. Interview with Benjamin V. Cohen, February 26, 1981 (relating a comment to Thomas G. Corcoran, with whom Cohen lived and worked). *See* Adolph Berle, Jr., to Franklin D. Roosevelt, April 23, 1934, Roosevelt Papers; Rexford Tugwell, "Diaries," 75 (April 26, 1934), Tugwell Papers. In his diary entry, Tugwell states that "Brandeis sent word, in effect, that he was declaring war" on the New Deal. Tugwell's characterization of Brandeis's message probably should not be taken at face value. To begin with, it was not a direct quotation of something Brandeis said to Tugwell but rather Tugwell's interpretation of a comment passed on to him by someone else. As indicated earlier in this chapter, however, Tugwell was very suspicious of Brandeis (as well as of Frankfurter) and was likely to impart the most sinister meaning to anything the justice said. Murphy quotes the Tugwell diary entry without question but does not cite any other material to show that Brandeis actually said he was "declaring war" or something similar. Murphy, *The Brandeis/Frankfurter Connection*, p. 140.
19. *Louisville Joint Stock Land Bank* v. *Radford*, 295 U.S. 495 (1935).
20. Interview with Thomas G. Corcoran, November 21, 1979. Murphy states that Brandeis actively supervised the drafting of specific provisions of the Securities Act of 1934. Murphy, *The Brandeis/Frankfurter Connection*, p. 136. This is inconsistent with Corcoran's (and Benjamin V. Cohen's) statements to me that Brandeis never got involved in the specifics of this or other legislation. None of the other materials cited by Professor Murphy shows otherwise. *See* Robert Cover, "The Framing of Justice Brandeis," *The New Republic*, May 5, 1982, p. 17.

21. Memorandum by Benjamin V. Cohen, undated, Frankfurter Papers; Harry Hopkins, "Statement to Me by Thomas Corcoran Giving His Recollection of the Genesis of the Supreme Court Fight," April 3, 1939, Hopkins Papers.
22. LDB to Julian Mack, May 29, 1935, File Z/P 61–1, Louisville Papers.
23. Quoted in Eugene Gerhard, *America's Advocate: Robert H. Jackson* 99 (1958).
24. Frances Perkins, *The Roosevelt I Knew* 252 (1946); President Roosevelt's Press Conference, May 31, 1935, Roosevelt Papers.
25. Quoted in Alpheus T. Mason, *Brandeis: A Free Man's Life* 619–620 (1946).

Chapter Twenty-Six
THE BORN-AGAIN ADMINISTRATION

1. Quoted in Eric F. Goldman, *Rendezvous with Destiny: A History of Modern American Reform* 281 (Revised ed., 1955).
2. Quoted in Paul A. Raushenbush and Elizabeth B. Raushenbush, *Our "U.C." Story: 1930–1967* 38 (1979) (privately published). ("U.C." refers to unemployment compensation legislation.)
3. Quoted in Goldman, *Rendezvous with Destiny*, p. 257.
4. Elizabeth B. Raushenbush to LDB, February 5, 1934, File G7–1, Louisville Papers.
5. LDB to Elizabeth B. Raushenbush, April 20, 1934; April 22, 1934, *Letters*, Vol. V, pp. 536–37.
6. LDB to Elizabeth B. Raushenbush, June 8, 1934, *id.*, pp. 539–40.
7. Interview with James Rowe, October 17, 1980.
8. LDB to Norman Hapgood, June 15, 1935, *Letters*, Vol. V, p. 555.
9. Felix Frankfurter to LDB, December 20, 1934, File G9–2, Louisville Papers.
10. LDB to Felix Frankfurter, March 12, 1935, Frankfurter Papers.
11. Felix Frankfurter to Franklin D. Roosevelt, May 16, 1935, Max Freedman (ed.), *Roosevelt & Frankfurter: Their Correspondence, 1928–1945* 271 (1967).
12. Robert E. Wood to Franklin D. Roosevelt, July 18, 1935, Roosevelt Papers.
13. LDB to Norman Hapgood, August 2, 1935, *Letters*, Vol. V, p. 556; LDB to Felix Frankfurter, August 30, 1935, Frankfurter Papers.

Chapter Twenty-Seven
PACKING THE COURT

1. *Carter* v. *Carter Coal Co.*, 298 U.S. 238 (1936). *See* Paul A. Freund, "Charles Evans Hughes as Chief Justice," 81 *Harvard Law Review* 4, 13, n. 45 (1967).
2. *Railroad Retirement Board* v. *Alton R. Co.*, 295 U.S. 330, 375 (1935) (Hughes, C.J., dissenting). *See* Freund, 81 *Harvard Law Review* at 13, n. 45.
3. *St. Louis Star-Times*, June 4, 1936.
4. George W. Anderson to LDB, January 3, 1937, File SC 19–1, Louisville Papers.
5. Brandeis–Frankfurter Conversations, p. 2, Frankfurter Papers.
6. Quoted in Frances Perkins, *The Roosevelt I Knew* 330 (1946).
7. Quoted in Arthur M. Schlesinger, Jr., *The Crisis of the Old Order* 406 (1957).
8. Homer S. Cummings to Franklin D. Roosevelt, December 1936, Roosevelt Papers.
9. Quoted in Arthur M. Schlesinger, Jr., *The Coming of the New Deal* 584 (1959).
10. Interview with Thomas G. Corcoran, November 21, 1979.
11. Franklin D. Roosevelt to Norman Hapgood, July 10, 1935, Roosevelt Papers.
12. Quoted in Joseph Alsop & Turner Catledge, *The 168 Days* 79 (1938).
13. Elizabeth Glendower Evans to LDB, October 27, 1936, File SC 17–1, Louisville Papers.
14. Norman Hapgood to LDB, April 9, 1937, File G12–2, Louisville Papers.
15. Interview with Marquis Childs, July 3, 1979.
16. *Id.*
17. Quoted in Alpheus T. Mason, *Brandeis: A Free Man's Life* 626 (1946).

18. There are some minor discrepancies among the various accounts of Wheeler's telephone call to Hughes. Relying on an interview with Wheeler seven years after the incident, Mason says that Brandeis suggested the letter and urged Wheeler to call despite the senator's protest that he did not know Hughes. This account is consistent with the description in Alsop & Catledge's *The 168 Days*, pp. 125–26, which presumably is also based on an interview with Wheeler. Both accounts, however, are inconsistent with Hughes's autobiographical notes, which in turn are based, in part at least, on contemporaneous notes he made of his conversations with Wheeler. According to Hughes, it was he who suggested the idea of the letter to Brandeis and he passed the word to Wheeler that he would be prepared to write a letter giving the facts. D. Danelski & J. Tulchin (eds.), *The Autobiographical Notes of Charles Evans Hughes* 305 (1973). Because it is based on Hughes's contemporaneous notes, I have chosen to rely on his account, but the matter is not free from doubt. *See* Freund, 81 *Harvard Law Review* at 27.
19. *Senate Report No. 711*, 75th Cong., 1st Sess. 38–39 (1937).
20. Quoted in Freund, 81 *Harvard Law Review* at 27.
21. Quoted in Merlo Pusey, *Charles Evans Hughes*, Vol. II, 755 (1951).
22. Interview with Thomas G. Corcoran.
23. Quoted in Benjamin V. Cohen to Felix Frankfurter, October 11, 1937, Frankfurter Papers.
24. Max Freedman (ed.), *Roosevelt & Frankfurter: Their Correspondence, 1928–1945* 744 (1967).
25. Felix Frankfurter to LDB, March 26, 1937, Frankfurter Papers.
26. *Morehead* v. *Tipaldo*, 298 U.S. 587 (1936). *See* Freedman, *The Correspondence of Roosevelt & Frankfurter*, pp. 392–95.
27. *West Coast Hotel Company* v. *Parrish*, 300 U.S. 379 (1937).
28. Quoted in Alsop & Catledge, *The 168 Days*, p. 152.
29. Felix Frankfurter to LDB, March 31, 1937, Frankfurter Papers; LDB to Felix Frankfurter, April 5, 1937, *id.* Professor Murphy states that their differing views of the Court-packing plan "brought an end to [Brandeis's] special relationship with Felix Frankfurter" and "seems to have caused a permanent strain on their friendship." Bruce Allen Murphy, *The Brandeis/Frankfurter Connection: The Secret Political Activities of Two Supreme Court Justices* 180–81 (1982). Murphy cites two sources for this conclusion: the subsequent decrease in frequency and intimacy of correspondence between the two men, and an interview with Edward F. Prichard, Jr., who clerked for Frankfurter after the latter joined the Supreme Court. Neither source, however, justifies Murphy's conclusion, and, in fact, the evidence shows clearly that Brandeis and Frankfurter remained close. To begin with, Brandeis's age severely limited his activities, and he was ill for substantial periods between 1938 and 1941. As a result, there was less for the two men to discuss, and Brandeis in any event did not have the energy to maintain lengthy correspondence. Still, the two men saw each other regularly, and Frankfurter continued to seek Brandeis's views on public affairs. *See* Chapter 30. As for Prichard, he told me in an interview (after Murphy's book was published) that Frankfurter remained close to Brandeis and never criticized him, even when speaking of the Court-packing plan (which he often did). Prichard also attributed the decrease in correspondence to Brandeis's decreased energies and activities. Interview with Edward F. Prichard, Jr., June 14, 1982.

Chapter Twenty-Eight
THE TRIUMPH OF LABOR

1. *See* Joseph L. Rauh, Jr., et al., "A Personal View of Justice Benjamin N. Cardozo: Recollections of Four Cardozo Law Clerks," 1 *Cardozo Law Review* 1 (1979). The two Brandeis opinions referred to in this discussion are *John Hancock Mutual Life Ins. Co.* v. *Yates*, 299 U.S. 178 (1936) and *Yarborough* v. *Yarborough*, 290 U.S. 202 (1933). *See* Paul A. Freund, *The Supreme Court of the United States: Its Business, Purposes and Performance* 130–32 (1961).

2. Interviews with J. Willard Hurst, May 31, 1980; Joseph L. Rauh, Jr., January 26, 1981. *See Duke Power Co.* v. *Greenwood County*, 299 U.S. 259 (1936).
3. Interview with J. Willard Hurst.
4. *Truax* v. *Corrigan*, 257 U.S. 312 (1921).
5. *Bedford Co.* v. *Stone Cutters Association*, 274 U.S. 37, 56, 65 (1927) (dissenting opinion).
6. Interview with J. Willard Hurst. *See Senn* v. *Tile Lawyers Union*, 301 U.S. 468, 478 (1937).
7. 301 U.S. at 479–80.

Chapter Twenty-Nine
THE PASSING OF "OLD SWIFTY"

1. Interview with David Riesman, May 5, 1981. *See Pacific States Box and Basket Company* v. *White*, 296 U.S. 176 (1935).
2. LDB to Felix Frankfurter, February 16, 1936, Frankfurter Papers. *See* LDB to Felix Frankfurter, January 31, 1925; February 3, 1925; April 2, 1925; February 11, 1928; March 4, 1928, *Letters*, Vol. V, pp. 159, 170, 322, 326.
3. David Riesman to Felix Frankfurter, November 21, 1935, Frankfurter Papers; interview with David Riesman.
4. Fanny Brandeis to LDB, October 30, 1937, File M5–1, Louisville Papers; LDB to Felix Frankfurter, June 13, 1933, Frankfurter Papers.
5. *Ashwander* v. *Tennessee Valley Authority*, 297 U.S. 288, 321 (1936).
6. 297 U.S. at 341, 352 (concurring opinion).
7. 297 U.S. at 346–47 (citations omitted).
8. Felix Frankfurter to Charles E. Clark, February 18, 1936, Frankfurter Papers.
9. 41 U.S. (16 Pet.) 1 (1842).
10. *Black and White Taxicab and Transfer Co.* v. *Brown and Yellow Taxicab and Transfer Co.*, 276 U.S. 518 (1928).
11. Quoted in Merlo Pusey, *Charles Evans Hughes*, Vol. II, 710 (1951).
12. LDB handwritten note on letter from Harlan F. Stone to LDB, March 23, 1938, File 107–7, Harvard Papers; Harlan F. Stone to LDB, March 25, 1938, *id*; Charles Evans Hughes to LDB, slip opinion return, undated, File 107–9, *id*. *See Erie Railroad Company* v. *Tompkins*, 304 U.S. 64 (1938).
13. LDB to J. Willard Hurst, May 22, 1938, File 114–20, Harvard Papers.
14. Irving Younger, "What Happened in *Erie*," 56 *Texas Law Review* 1011, 1012 (1978).
15. Quoted in Younger, 56 *Texas Law Review* at 1030.

Chapter Thirty
FINAL TOUCHES

1. LDB to Stephen S. Wise, November 21, 1935, *Letters*, Vol. V, p. 562; LDB to Stephen S. Wise, September 4, 1936, *id.*, p. 576.
2. LDB to Robert Szold, January 2, 1938, *id.*, p. 593; LDB to Bernard Flexner, October 12, 1938, *id.*, p. 602.
3. LDB to Julian W. Mack et al., September 1937, File Z/P 67–1a, Louisville Papers. *See* correspondence in Files Z/P 66–2, Z/P 70–1, *id.*
4. LDB to Neville Chamberlain, February 26, 1939, *Letters*, Vol. V, p. 612.
5. Quoted in Stephen S. Wise to LDB, January 22, 1938, File Z/P 69–1, Louisville Papers.
6. Melvin I. Urofsky, *American Zionism from Herzl to the Holocaust* 389 (1976); Zionist Organization of America, *Brandeis on Zionism* 155 (1942); interview with Adrian Fisher, August 11, 1980.
7. Quoted in Melvin I. Urofsky, *Louis D. Brandeis and the Progressive Tradition* 170 (1981).

8. Interview with Adrian Fisher.
9. *Id.*
10. LDB to Franklin D. Roosevelt, February 13, 1939; Franklin D. Roosevelt to LDB, February 13, 1939, *Letters*, Vol. V, p. 610.
11. Nathaniel L. Nathanson, "The Philosophy of Mr. Justice Brandeis and Civil Liberties Today," 1979 *Illinois University Law Forum* 261, 266 (1979).
12. I have no direct evidence that Brandeis made the recommendation at this particular meeting. However, the circumstantial evidence clearly supports that conclusion. To begin with, there is no question that he did make the recommendation. Interview with Adrian Fisher. *See* William O. Douglas, *Go East, Young Man* 449 (1974). It is extremely doubtful that Brandeis would have made the recommendation over the telephone, since he almost never used the telephone and, in any event, it is the kind of proposal that Brandeis would have preferred to make in person (where logic might be aided by his presence). Between the day of his retirement and the day the Douglas nomination was submitted, Brandeis met with Roosevelt only once, on March 9, 1939. According to the Usher's Logs in the Roosevelt Papers, the meeting lasted from 5:09 P.M. to 6:22 P.M., certainly enough time for Brandeis to discuss Jewish affairs and the Douglas nomination. It is extremely doubtful that Brandeis would have discussed his replacement prior to his retirement since, until his heart attack in January 1939, he was not sure exactly when he would retire. *See* Paul A. Freund, "Charles Evans Hughes as Chief Justice," 81 *Harvard Law Review* 4, 29 (1967).
13. William O. Douglas to LDB, March 20, 1939, File 114–11, Harvard Papers.
14. Interview with Alice G. Popkin, July 19, 1980.
15. Fannie Brandeis, "Memorandum of Conversation with Uncle Louis and Redvers Opie," September 15, 1939, File M2–5, Louisville Papers.
16. Interview with David Riesman, May 5, 1981.
17. Harold Ickes, "Guilty! Richard A. Ballinger—An American Dreyfus," *Saturday Evening Post*, May 25, 1940, pp. 9, 126, 128.
18. LDB to Bernard Flexner, May 23, 1930, *Letters*, Vol. V, p. 641.
19. *The New Republic*, June 23, 1931, p. 104. The writings of Mason referred to in this discussion are "Mr. Justice Brandeis and the Constitution," 80 *University of Pennsylvania Law Review* 799 (1932), *Brandeis: Lawyer and Judge in the Modern State* (1933), *The Brandeis Way* (1938), and *Bureaucracy Convicts Itself* (1941).
20. Quoted in Paul A. Freund, "Justice Brandeis: A Law Clerk's Remembrance," 68 *American Jewish History* 7, 16 (1978).
21. Fannie Brandeis, "Conversation with LDB," May 19, 1940, File M2–5, Louisville Papers.
22. Alice G. Brandeis to Louis B. Wehle, September 27, 1941, Wehle Papers.
23. Max Freedman (ed.), *Roosevelt & Frankfurter: Their Correspondence, 1928–1945* 618 (1967); Joseph P. Lash (ed.), *From the Diaries of Felix Frankfurter* 271 (1975).
24. Quoted in Samuel J. Konefsky, *The Legacy of Holmes and Brandeis: A Study in the Influence of Ideas* 305 n.54 (1956).
25. *Hearings before the Subcommittee of the Committee on the Judiciary, United States Senate, on the Nomination of Louis D. Brandeis to be an Associate Justice of the Supreme Court of the United States, Part I*, 64th Cong., 1st Sess., 300 (1916) (testimony of Sherman Whipple).
26. Jonas Friedenwald to Felix Frankfurter, October 8, 1941, Frankfurter Papers.
27. Dean Acheson, "Mr. Justice Brandeis," 55 *Harvard Law Review* 191 (1942).

INDEX